Memory and Remembering

To my memories of my father and mother

By
John A.
Groeger

Memory and Remembering

Everyday memory in context

LONGMAN

Addison Wesley Longman Limited,
Edinburgh Gate, Harlow,
Essex CM20 2JE, England
and Associated Companies throughout the world.

Published in the United States of America
by Addison Wesley Longman Inc., New York

First published 1997

ISBN 0 582 29220 4 PPR

British Library Cataloguing-in-Publication Data
A catalogue record for this book is
available from the British Library

Library of Congress Cataloging-in-Publication Data

Groeger, John A., 1959-
    Memory and remembering: everyday memory in context/John A. Groeger.
        p. cm.
    Includes bibliographical references and index.
    ISBN 0–582–29220–4 (pbk.)
    1. Memory.   2. Recollection (Psychology)   3. Memory–Age factors.
4. Memory disorders.   I. Title.
BF371.G74 1997
153.1′2–dc21   96–51084
                                                            CIP

Set in 11 1/4 / 12 pt Perpetua by 32
Produced by Longman Asia Limited, Hong Kong
PPLC/01

Contents

Acknowledgements

I embarked upon writing this book with considerable excitement and some trepidation. When I teach I rarely encourage the sense of enthusiasm that some of my teachers, especially Susan Aylwin at Cork and Billy Brown in Belfast, evoked in me. I would like to think that the discipline of writing this book, and especially the fascinating ideas and research it gave me the opportunity to dwell upon, has made me a better teacher and a more challenging colleague.

For reasons that are explored over the next few hundred pages, I am unable to remember all those whose support and forbearance have made the writing of this book possible. I gained inestimably, both academically and personally, from the years I spent at the Applied Psychology Unit in Cambridge. In what were halcyon days under Alan Baddeley, I was able to chat to and marvel at many, many outstanding cognitive psychologists. The Unit's then commitment to outstanding theoretical, and theoretically driven, applications of cognitive psychology to everyday tasks has had an enormous influence on me, and on what I write. I am especially in the debt of Debra Bekerian, a former colleague and friend at the APU, for her resilience in coping with my impassioned questioning and extensive discussions about memory. To these, and other colleagues, if it is any reassurance, when writing this book I frequently felt that I might have listened more closely!

My arrival at Surrey with the intention of writing a book in the first year of my Professorial appointment was greeted with alacrity by my Head of Department, Ian Davies. His support, and that of those colleagues working with me on my various research contracts, Sarah Greening, David Field and James Whalen, ensured that the time I needed to write this book was always available. My other colleagues and students here and at Leeds were unwitting but essential sounding boards for the ideas I have attempted to explore.

From the initial proposal to its final production, Sarah Caro of Addison Wesley Longman has been invaluable. Her commitment and belief in the project helped to sustain it at its lowest and least productive ebb. At its final stages, Margaret Lawler and Lynette Miller took painstaking care to be certain that what I wrote would be less obscure and complete with respect to figures, references and tables. Perhaps all too typically, my final thanks go to Rosie Dickson, for unselfishly feeling that what was important to me was important to her.

John A. Groeger
University of Surrey

Chapter 1

Memory, remembering and basic events

> **Chapter outline:** This first chapter introduces the major themes in the book. It rehearses some fundamental issues about the nature of the world we experience, how well, or badly, these are stored in memory, and what we remember of the basic attributes of our world.

Key topics

- Background
- Major issues in memory and remembering
- Events: Segments of everyday experience
- Remembering the sensory characteristics of basic events
- Summary: Events, everyday memory and laboratory studies
- Further reading

Background

From the first moment I saw his wonderfully expressive face turn to camera, and heard Richard Burton in his lyrical Welsh accent intone the following monologue from Peter Shaffer's *Equus* (1977), I have been haunted by the issues it raises. Burton, playing a tortured psychiatrist, Dysart, is thinking about a young male patient of his who has brutally mutilated some horses he had previously adoringly tended in their stable.

Dysart: With one particular horse, called Nugget, he embraces. He showed me how he stands with it afterwards in the night, one hand on its chest, one on its neck, like a frozen tango dancer, inhaling its cold sweet breath. 'Have you noticed' he said, 'about horses: how they'll stand one hoof on its end, like those girls in the ballet?'

Now he's gone off to rest, leaving me alone with Equus. I can hear the creature's voice. It's calling me out of the black cave of the Psyche. I shove in my dim little torch, and there he stands – waiting for me. He raises his matted head. He opens his great square teeth, and says – *[Mocking]* 'Why? ... Why Me?...Why – ultimately – Me? ... Do you really imagine you can account for Me? Totally, infallibly, inevitably account for Me? ... Poor Doctor Dysart!

Of course I've stared at such images before. Or been stared at by them, whichever way you look at it. And weirdly often now with the feeling that *they* are staring at *us* – that in some quite palpable way they precede us. Meaningless, but unsettling ... In either case, this one is the most alarming yet. It asked questions I've avoided all my professional life. *[Pause]*. A child is born into a world of phenomena all equal in their power to enslave. It sniffs – it sucks – it strokes its eyes over the whole uncomfortable range. Suddenly one strikes. Why? Moments snap together like magnets, forging a chain of shackles. Why? I can trace them. I can even, with time, pull them apart again. But why at the start were they ever magnetised at all – just those particular moments of experience and no others – I don't know. *And nor does anyone else ...*

... 'Account for me', says staring Equus. 'First account for Me ...'

(Shaffer, 1973, pp. 75–76)

Major issues in memory and remembering

How is it we remember some things and apparently not others? Why is it that we do so? Herman Ebbinghaus, over one hundred years ago, addressed these same issues, albeit more prosaically: 'Mental states of every kind – sensations, feelings, ideas – which were at one time present in consciousness and then have disappeared from it, have not with their disappearance absolutely ceased to exist. Although the inwardly-turned look may no longer be able to find them, nevertheless they have not been utterly destroyed and annulled, but in a certain manner they continue to exist, stored up, so to speak, in the memory' (Ebbinghaus, 1885, 1964, p. 1). The answers he provides show Ebbinghaus in a rather more exciting and modern light than he is sometimes cast, as the originator of the *nonsense syllable*: 'In a first group of cases we can call back into consciousness by an exertion of the will directed to this purpose the seemingly lost states ... that is, we can produce them voluntarily ... the will, so to speak, has only discovered it and brought it to us again' (Ebbinghaus, 1885, 1964, p. 1). He distinguishes another group of mental states which 'once present in consciousness return to it with apparent spontaneity and without any act of the will; that is, they are reproduced involuntarily ... as more exact observation teaches us, the occurrence of these involuntary reproductions is not an entirely random and accidental one. On the contrary they are brought about through the instrumentality of other, immediately present mental images (Ebbinghaus, 1885, 1964, p. 2). And finally there is:

---

a third and large group to be reckoned with here. The vanished mental states give indubitable proof of their continuing existence even if they themselves do not return to consciousness at all, or at least not exactly at the given time ... this effect results from the frequent conscious occurrence of any condition or process, and consists in facilitating the occurrence and progress of similar processes ... most of these experiences remain concealed from consciousness and yet produce an effect which is significant and which authenticates their previous existence.

(Ebbinghaus, 1885, 1964, p. 2)

These quotes encapsulate the major issues which will be addressed and readdressed throughout this book: Which aspects of experience are remembered, and under what conditions? What does this tell us about the nature of our memory? To what extent must we ourselves be involved in the act of learning or retrieving the information we ultimately store? Does this tell us anything about ourselves and the people we are?

■ Events: Segments of everyday experience

Experience is segmented such that we are able to distinguish one event from another. Actually defining what constitutes an event is rather difficult. We might think back to something which happened, such as England's victory over Australia in the quarter-final of the Rugby Union World Cup in 1995, but doing so probably evokes something else which happened at the same time: Rob Andrew's last minute winning drop goal. This too is clearly an event, albeit subsumed within the event which is the match itself, and it too can be broken down into other events, the moment he kicked the ball, the ball sailing high over the bar between the posts, the exhausted elation of the players, and perhaps the cheers of others watching around us.

One way of resolving the difficulty of defining an event is to try to identify at what point people think that 'something different' has happened, even if it is related to the preceding event. A number of studies reviewed by Hirsh and Sherrick (1961), some decades ago, help to address this issue. These sought to identify the minimum gap (i.e. '*asynchrony*') required between the occurrence of presentations in order for people reliably to notice two events rather than one (i.e. successive versus simultaneous). The answers depend on whether the events are visual or auditory, and also whether the same visual or auditory receptors are stimulated, or whether different receptors are involved. If the same presentation is made to both ears (i.e. *binaurally*), then a time gap of more than 2 milliseconds is required if people are to notice two rather than just one stimulus. However, if the presentations are made dichotically (i.e. the first to one ear, the second to the other ear), then two events will be detected even where the stimuli are offset by just 1 ms (Hirsh and Sherrick, 1961). This difference in sensitivity between our ability to determine whether auditory events are simultaneous or successive helps us to localise sound sources. If a sound arrives at both ears at the same time, then it is likely to be directly ahead or behind us; a sound that reaches one ear before the other is almost certainly located to one side of us.

If two static stimuli are presented to each eye separately (i.e. *dichoptically*), with a time gap of less than 40 ms, they are seen as one unchanging stimulus. With a larger gap they are seen as separate stimuli. If, however, the same presentation is made to the same area of the retina, and the asynchrony is above 40 ms, people tend to report a flickering of the stimulus, thus indicating that they have detected some discontinuity of the stimuli. Where the stimulus is presented to one retinal area, and then to an adjacent area about 10 ms later, people tend to report seeing one stimulus, but that it has moved. Where the asynchrony is above 20 ms, and presentations are made to adjacent retinal areas, this 'apparent movement' illusion disappears, and people will tend to report noticing two static, rather than one moving, stimulus. (The effectiveness of these asynchronies depends on the duration of the stimuli; see Westheimer and McKee, 1977.) Thus, if we hear or see something, we should know that it is a repeated experience, rather than the same experience, as long as there is at least a relatively small gap between the two. These are, of course, separate events, although we normally tend to think of events as being much longer.

Thus, when remembering particular experiences, it feels more appropriate to think of an event being a speech, rather than a word within it; a walk, rather than an individual footstep.

■ Remembering the sensory characteristics of basic events

Size

Memory for size has been investigated in a number of ways. Robinson and Standing (1990) have shown that when differently sized pictures and words were presented during encoding, subjects reliably determined whether they had or had not previously seen each picture or word. However, when required to determine whether each picture or word encountered during recognition was presented at its original size (i.e. size recognition), size alteration impaired recognition memory for the size of both word and picture stimuli. This effect is asymmetric with pictorial stimuli, with (originally) larger stimuli being mistaken for smaller versions of those stimuli at recognition. Earlier, Kosslyn and Alper (1977) required subjects to build pairs of images of standard objects. Some objects which were similar in size were imaged as such, while others were imaged as smaller than the item with which they were paired. Results showed that objects imaged as relatively smaller were recalled less well. Interestingly, it emerges from a recent study by Legault and Standing (1992) that photographs are drawn smaller from memory than from sight, while line drawings are not. It is therefore possible that the asymmetry in size recognition of pictures is due to subjects remembering pictorial stimuli as smaller than actual size, thus leading them to erroneously choose smaller versions of the stimuli in size recognition tasks.

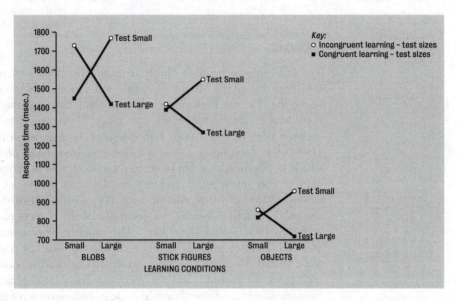

Fig 1.1 Mean recognition times for blobs, stick figures and objects learned small and large and tested under same-size or different-size conditions (after Jolicoeur, 1987).

Jolicoeur (1987) found strong size-congruency effects in recognition memory (Fig 1.1). Large and small versions of objects were encountered during the learning phase. Subjects were later required to identify those sized-objects they had previously encountered from among a set composed of equal numbers of original and new items. Objects tested at the same size as shown in the learning phase were recognised more quickly and more accurately than shapes tested at a different size. In a subsequent study discussed in the same paper this size-congruency effect was found for line drawings of natural objects and for unfamiliar shapes. The magnitude of the size-congruency effect depended on the degree of discrepancy between the learning size and the test size. More recently, Jolicoeur has clarified aspects of this size-congruency effect (Milliken and Jolicoeur, 1992). By independently varying viewing distance and image size, the retinal and 'perceived' size of images were dissociated, the results showing clearly that retinal size was less important than the perceived size of images in determining recognition-memory performance. Milliken and Jolicoeur (1992, p. 95) conclude that 'the size-congruency effect in memory for visual shape may occur as a result of changes in the perceived size of shapes between the encoding and the testing phases, with little or no contribution of retinal size per se'.

These studies show that size is not necessarily well remembered, at least with relatively unfamiliar experimental stimuli. A similar conclusion emerges from studies which have investigated remembered size of far more frequently encountered objects. For example, Kirkland and Flanagan (1979) investigated whether, some 10 years after coins were withdrawn from circulation, people were able to reliably determine which of 32 brass discs were identical in size. They found that the higher-valued coin of three was erroneously matched with discs larger than its actual size, whereas lower-value coins were remembered as smaller than the originals. Thus, once again size is poorly remembered, and is subject to a semantic or, perhaps linguistic, bias (i.e. the value of the coin).

Location

The reliability of people's ability to remember where objects were located has also been explored. Moore, Richards and Hood (1984), in a large-scale study using the Tactual Performance Test, found that memory for location varied considerably across the adult age range. This age dependence on location memory performance brings into question the suggestion by Hasher and Zacks (1984) that location is one of a number of basic types of stimulus information which is effortlessly or automatically encoded. Crook, Youngjohn and Larrabee (1990) also investigated memory for location across a sample of over 500 adults. Using a virtual environment (i.e. touch sensitive screen in 12-room computer-simulated house), subjects placed 20 objects in particular locations, and then had to find these later. The number of objects located on the first and second attempts was strongly correlated with age and Wechsler Memory Scale Paired Associate Learning. Additional significant relationships were found with gender, education, and the Wechsler Adult Intelligence Scale (WAIS) Digit Symbol sub-test. This shows that age and several of the sub-tests which comprise standard measures of intelligence predict individual ability to retrieve location information detail. This is clearly contrary to the suppositions of Hasher and Zacks with regard to the automatic encoding of location information.

In an earlier study, using undergraduates, Mandler and Parker (1976) report results which also seem at variance with the Hasher and Zacks hypothesis that location information is automatically encoded. The Mandler and Parker study involved retrieval of several different kinds of information in complex pictures, line drawings of real-world scenes, or of unorganised collections of objects. The level of organisation of the pictures had little effect on memory for size, orientation, or physical appearance of objects in the pictures. There was relatively little loss of these types of descriptive information when subjects were tested a week later. However, organisation of the pictures had a major effect on memory for location of objects represented in the pictures: recognition of object locations declined at different rates depending on where in the scene objects were originally located. Object-location recognition on the horizontal dimension declined markedly for both organised and unorganised pictures over the course of a week. In contrast, performance remained high on the vertical dimension for organised pictures, but systematic distortion occurred on this dimension for unorganised pictures. On the basis of these results, we might expect that with real world scenes, which are inherently organised, memory for where objects are located will be less accurate for some locations than for others. We will return to this issue later when we consider attention focusing and eyewitness testimony. The automatic encoding of other basic information will be addressed more fully in later chapters.

BOX 1.1: Remembering locations

Hirtle and Kallman (1988) examined whether clustering would occur in the memories of 39 undergraduates for an area in which (1) locations were designated by pictures and (2) the entire area was available for study. Subjects memorised the location of 10 pictures situated within a map. These were urban scenes of a school, police station, restaurant and post office and rural scenes of a forest, barn, cornfield and pasture. Between these clusters two other scenes were depicted: a picture of the roadside and of a fire station. Two groups of subjects took part, one for whom the urban cluster was located towards the top left of the map, with the rural scene represented towards the bottom right, with this being reversed for the other group. Immediately, or two days later, subjects were tested for their memory of the locations, using comparative judgement and distance estimation tasks. Subjects clustered information on the basis of pictorial similarity, with similar pictures misremembered as having been located closer together than they actually were (a finding Hirtle and Kallman refer to as a 'constriction effect'). This constriction was greater with the largest actual distances between objects. Subjects were also asked to judge the proximity of the two other locations (roadside and fire station) to the urban and rural scenes. As the figure below shows, subjects judged the within-cluster (i.e. fire station with urban, roadside with rural) pairs as closer than what were in fact equidistant between-cluster pairs.

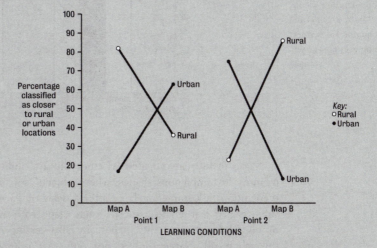

Changes in remembered location as a function of map context (after Hirtle and Kaliman, 1988)

Hirtle and Kallman's (1988) results suggest that clustering of spatial landmarks is the critical element in the way we form a mental representation of space.

Shape

Recent research by Farah, Rochlin and Klein (1994) strongly suggests that previously encountered shapes can be recognised, irrespective of whether or not the viewing angle at which they are encountered at test phase is similar to the angle at which the shapes were previously viewed. These findings contrast with previous research in this area in which this orientation invariance effect was not found with wire forms. Using stimuli which convey surface and/or volume information (which wire forms generally cannot), Farah and colleagues showed that shape recognition is orientation invariant even after relatively long periods of time (Fig 1.2). This suggests that relatively basic shape primitives, such as those invoked by Shepard and Metzler (1971), may be routinely represented and used by the visual system. These results strengthen the traditional view that the object property 'shape' is well recognised, although the apparent accuracy of shape-recall may be obscured by difficulties in the way retrieval is demonstrated. Two aspects of these findings are worth considering in the light of the way in which other issues about shape retrieval have been addressed – the role of linguistic labels and intermodal transfer of shape information (see section on touch, p. 12).

Fig 1.2 Percentage correct decisions for same shapes at the same orientation and same shapes at a different orientation, for contour and surface versions of shapes (after Farah, Rochlin and Klein, 1994). *Note*: Diff-Diff responses are correct rejections of non-target stimuli

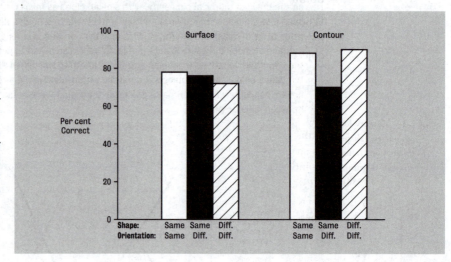

Nagae (1980) investigated whether the availability of verbal labels influenced memory for ambiguous shapes, when subjects were required to perform a shape-recognition task immediately or after a delay of 15 minutes or one week. Earlier, subjects had learned to associate each shape with an irrelevant or relevant label, or else did not label the shapes. By also testing memory for the labels used, through recall, Nagae showed not only that relevant verbal labels considerably improved memory for shape, but also that the verbal labels with which the ambiguous shapes were associated served to help subjects to discriminate, or uniquely identify, the shapes during encoding. This, as we might expect, benefited recognition of shapes, but this advantage only held for 'relevant' shape-labels, that is, those which could be used to refer to certain aspects of the shapes.

Contrasting performance in the two delayed recognition conditions showed that the labels were later used as a basis for categorising the shapes, and thus that shape recognition and recall of discriminating stimulus labels are interdependent. Earlier, Santa (1975) took advantage of people's ability to recognise degraded versions of previously encountered stimuli (i.e. *redintegrative memory*), in order to assess whether the benefits of labelling shapes were attentional or memorial in origin. Santa showed that redintegrative memory was substantially better when subjects trained under shape-naming conditions, rather than under control conditions, where shape-naming was not required. This training-with-labels effect was even more apparent when the use of labels was also permitted in the transfer test conditions. This result supports the view that the benefit of labelling shapes is not merely due to greater attention being paid to relevant details during encoding. These benefits were greater for meaningful, rather than meaningless labels. Taken together, the studies reported by Nagae and Santa show that access to verbal codes strongly influences performance on tasks that require the integration and retrieval of visual information.

Colour

While the colours of objects seem among their most readily apparent attributes, there is abundant evidence that colour is but one of many separable attributes an object may possess. This is one of the main claims of feature-integration theory. There is clear support for this theory in important studies by Stefurak and Boynton (1986). Subjects saw coloured objects, but were prevented from naming them by carrying out a concurrent mental arithmetic task. Afterwards, subjects had to indicate whether test items were different in colour or shape from the items originally encountered (Fig 1.3). Where both the colour of a test item and its shape were thought to have been encountered previously, the subject then had to indicate whether this particular colour–shape conjunction had been previously

Fig 1.3 Memory for colour and shape conjunctions (after Stefurak and Boynton, 1986).

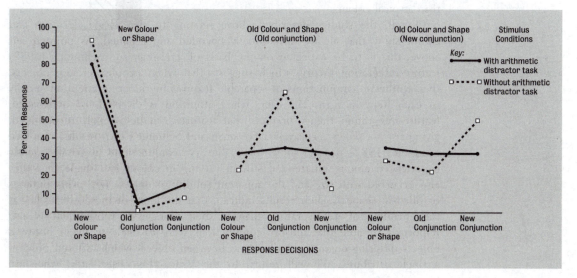

encountered. Results showed that retrieval of colour–shape conjunctions was very inaccurate. In the second study, subjects' attention was directed to either colour or shape during encoding, and they were asked later whether test items were 'new' or 'old'. Once again, the independence of colour and form was observed, and, importantly, 'neither facilitation nor inhibition was observed as the non-attended dimension was varied' (Stefurak and Boynton, 1986, p. 174). Similarly, Styles and Allport (1986) showed that even at very brief exposures, the category of item to which an object belongs can be reliably discriminated, but this category-based information is not bound to information about relative position or colour.

Much earlier, Sinson and Wetherick (1973, 1976) showed a dissociation between colour and shape processing in Down's syndrome children. Both the Down's syndrome and normal children could do simultaneous matching of items on the basis of their colour or shape, while the normal group were also able to successively match and point to named shapes. However, while the Down's syndrome group made many errors in successively matching colours and in pointing to named colours, they experienced no difficulty in successively matching and naming shapes. Thus, while equally capable of identifying colours and shapes, remembering colour, even over very brief periods, proved difficult – indicating the separateness of the retention of colour and form information. Park and Puglisi (1985) have shown that the colour of pictures was generally better remembered than the colour in which words were presented under incidental memory conditions. This raises an important issue. Many of the studies reported above made use of random shapes to which colours were arbitrarily assigned; where colour and an object are intrinsically linked (e.g. red–blood) or commonly encountered (e.g. red–apple or green–apple), memory for colour–shape conjunctions is considerably better. In a similar vein, Ratner and McCarthy (1990) contrasted the effectiveness of the physical characteristics of colour and the influence of the socio-cultural context of colour, i.e. the typicality of object–colour associations. The objects used, all of which were ecologically or culturally relevant, were better remembered where they were encountered in typical rather than atypical colours.

Overall, the studies described above relating to size, shape, location and colour show that all are differentially encoded and retained. As pointed out above, this is to be expected on the basis of Treisman and Schmidt's (1982) feature-integration theory, which suggests that when people perceive objects, they synthesise conjunctions of separable features by directing attention serially to each item in turn. However, when attention is diverted, or overloaded, feature-integration theory predicts that features can be wrongly recombined, giving rise to *illusory conjunctions*. Treisman and Schmidt's own results, reported in their 1982 paper, show that illusory conjunctions were frequently experienced among unattended stimuli varying in colour and shape, but they also occurred with size and the apparent solidity of objects (i.e. using outlines or filled-in shapes). Their results indicate that the locus of these effects lies at the encoding of items, rather than at their storage or retrieval. It is also important to note that illusory conjunctions were as likely to occur between objects differing on many attributes as between objects which differed only on a single attribute. We will return to the issues this raises later, when we consider further Hasher and Zack's view that fundamental information about objects is encoded automatically, and also when we discuss the sources of error in eyewitness testimony.

Smell

The advantage that naming gives in memorising shape and colour is much less marked with information about smell. Indeed, perhaps because of technological difficulties in presenting and measuring memory for smell, there is a relative paucity of studies of olfactory memory in humans (see Engen, 1987). An exception to this is work reported by Barker and Weaver (1983), who found that when asked to match either a 1.33- or a 5.0-ppm pyridine olfactory stimulus, undergraduate subjects consistently picked a concentration weaker than the standard. As we shall see below, this tendency to remember smells as being less intense than they actually were is mirrored by results emerging from studies of taste.

Rather surprisingly, perhaps, studies of memory for smell are rather more prevalent in clinically oriented investigations. Luria (1968), for example, discusses the fact that S, a patient who shows the classical dissociation of short- and long-term memory systems, as the result of lesions following an aneurysm with haemorrhaging in the limbic areas of the brain, experienced losses that included a primary lesion of his sense of smell and a suppression of tendon reflexes. After the aneurysm sac was removed, S's confusion began to disappear, but it became apparent that while his long-term memory was unaffected, his ability to imprint, store, and recall immediate experience, including those of smell, was impaired.

Odour discrimination deficits have also been reported in schizophrenia (e.g. Wu, Buchsbaum, Moy and Denlea, 1993; Malaspina, Wray, Friedman and Amador, 1994). Schizophrenics did poorly on both a Smell Identification Test (SIT) and an olfactory match-to-sample memory test relative to matched controls. Wu and colleagues report that the deficit in performance on the olfactory match-to-sample test was present even when the shared performance between it and the SIT was controlled for. Interestingly, this was supported by positron emission tomography (PET) scan studies, suggesting that schizophrenics may have dysfunctional limbic systems. The findings that schizophrenics also have deficits in olfactory identification and olfactory memory are consistent with the notion, pointed to by Luria, that the limbic system is closely involved in olfactory memory.

Other clinical populations also show olfactory deficits. Kesslak, Cotman, Chui and Vanden-Noort (1988) also show olfactory deficits in Parkinsonian patients, particularly with regard to identifying common odours, where Parkinsonian patients scored at an anosmic level. This capacity is reduced in Alzheimer's disease patients, but these were severely impaired in their ability to use novel odours in a match-to-sample task. Kesslak and colleagues report that multiple sclerosis sufferers do not exhibit detectable differences in olfactory functioning. In the final chapter of this book we will look at these dysfunctions in considerably more detail.

Touch

Information about the shape of objects can be encoded from touch (i.e. haptic information) as well as from vision. Lawrence, Cobb and Beard (1978) show that active exploration or manipulation of objects at both encoding and test yielded substantially better object recognition performance than when manipulation was permitted at inspection only, or at test only. The latter conditions also differed, with object recognition benefiting more from manipulation at inspection than at test.

Earlier, Abravenel (1973) contrasted the recognition performance of a large number of undergraduates for shapes that were encountered visually or haptically (i.e. by touch), using a matching paradigm. Significantly better shape-matching performance was found for those subjects who saw, rather than touched, the objects at encoding, but the level of recognition performance in both cases was similar across retention intervals of 5, 15 and 30 seconds (Fig 1.4). Kiphart, Auday and Cross (1988) also show that haptic memory changes little over the course of 24 hours, even where motor and non-motor tasks were interposed between acquisition and the retention test. Differential performance for haptically rather than visually encoded objects has also been reported by Davidson, Cambardella, Stenerson and Carney (1974). Three-dimensional shapes were explored through vision or touch. Retention of information was assessed through matching with original objects and lures (i.e. distractors). Older children (11 years) performed better than younger children (8 years) with all matching tasks, and both groups also showed decrements with increasing memory demand (number of stimuli).

Fig 1.4 Recognition of touched and seen objects as a function of retention interval and test conditions (after Abravenel, 1973).

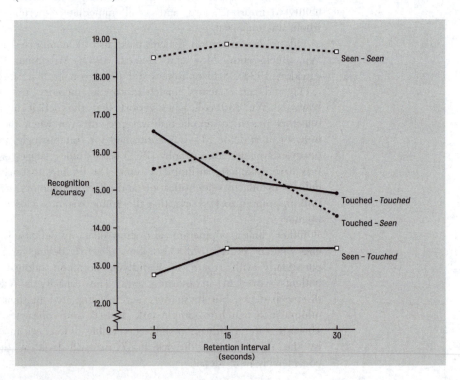

Effects of memory demand were greater in all touch conditions, indicating that retention of haptic information was more difficult. Davidson and colleagues interpreted these results as evidence for relatively poorer encoding, transformation, and storage of tactual information.

Abravenel (1973) also explored people's ability to visually recognise objects they had touched, and haptically recognise objects they had seen. In both cases substantial intramodal transfer of knowledge was apparent, although retention was superior where acquisition occurred under visual conditions. The reverse asymmetry, improved retention where initial encoding was tactile, was reported by Juurmaa and Lehtinen (1988), in which children drew the shapes they encountered, but only with complex objects. Although Newnham and McKenzie (1993) have recently suggested that such an asymmetry may underlie the difficulties experienced by, and the poorer performance of, 'clumsy' children, it seems unlikely that these results reflect real intramodal asymmetries, but rather that they stem from individual differences and perhaps asymmetrical retention conditions. It seems rather more likely that differences in intramodal transfer reflect modality differences in retention condition tests, and a differential efficiency in sighted subjects in building equally detailed representations from haptic exploration as they might do on the basis of visual exploration of objects.

Parallels have been drawn between the ways in which visual or tactile learning occurs and the ways in which vision and touch are integrated in behaviour (Klatzky, Lederman and Matula, 1993), but these are outside the scope of the present review. The very important work by Saywitz, Goodman, Nicholas and Moan (1991) and Leippe, Romanczyk and Manion (1991), which addresses memory for being touched, rather than touching, is discussed in a later chapter, where the remembering of personally significant events is considered.

Taste

Investigations of memory for taste have been conducted largely within the framework of consumer research. Barker and Weaver (1983), for example, had over 300 undergraduates taste 10 ml of 15 per cent sucrose and asked them to remember the strength of the solution. They were retested with different sucrose concentrations (i.e. 5, 10, 15, or 20 per cent sucrose) at one of four delay intervals (1, 5, or 15 minutes or 72 hours). Subjects reliably reported that 5 per cent sucrose was less sweet and that 20 per cent sucrose was sweeter than the original. However, when the original 15 per cent concentration was re-presented, almost two-thirds of subjects considered it to be sweeter than the original, regardless of the delay interval between the two stimuli. This tendency to remember the original stimulus as being less sweet was also reflected in the finding that two-thirds of those tasting 10 per cent sucrose reported that it was as sweet as or sweeter than the original 15 per cent standard. These findings were confirmed in a further study which used a magnitude estimation procedure. Thus, olfactory and gustatory stimuli are remembered as being substantially weaker as soon as the memory for these stimuli can be tested, but then remains relatively unchanged, at least for several days.

Several studies show that memory for tastes is subject to various enduring and transitory influences. Stevenson and Prescott (1994) showed that previous experience of tasting chilli affected the judgements that subjects made of the 'burn' intensity of capsaicin. Mood also exerts an influence on hedonic flavour judgements. Pliner and Steverango (1994) induced positive, negative or neutral moods in subjects, who then tasted four pleasant and four unpleasant flavours. Following a delay, subjects were tested on their recognition memory for the flavours. The findings show very marked mood congruence effects. Subjects who had undergone negative mood induction correctly identified more of the unpalatable flavours, while those who had experienced a positive mood induction correctly identified more of the pleasant flavours (Fig 1.5).

Fig 1.5 Taste recognition accuracy as a function of stimulus valence and mood induction (after Pliner and Steverango, 1994).

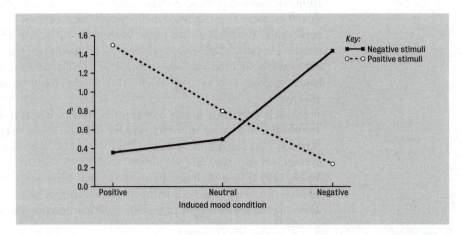

Fehm, Reutter, Zenz and Born (1993) showed that taste detection acuity and free recall of tastes vary with time of day. In placebo conditions, taste detection and recall performance were shown to be better in the morning than in the evening. Other conditions investigated by Fehm and colleagues showed that hydrocortisone treatment suppressed this circadian variation.

Sound

Memory research is dominated by the study of the encoding and retrieval of verbal materials. Much of this research has used verbal stimuli which is heard rather than read and, as we shall see, there is substantial evidence that verbal material which is read is re-encoded phonologically. A number of highly important standard findings have effectively mapped out the structures and processes involved in the encoding, storage and retrieval of verbal information. Among these important effects are the word-length effect, which indexes the limits of auditory short-term memory; the word-superiority effect, which notes the facility with which humans process meaningful rather than meaningless information; and the enhanced retrieval of stimuli which are encoded meaningfully, whether that meaningfulness is determined by the similarity between the circumstances of encoding and retrieval, or through the processing of semantic or personal associations. These findings will be addressed in much more detail later, and here, therefore, we consider some other relationships between memory and sound.

Sound is an important contributor to determination of where objects are located. Rhodes (1987) investigated the spatial properties of auditory memory and attention. As expected on the basis of previous work (e.g. Shelton and Searle, 1980), she found that the time for attention shifts was a linearly increasing function of the angular distance moved for distances up to 90 degrees. That is, as is well known, localisation of sound becomes increasingly difficult as the object to be located is angularly displaced from the ears. What Rhodes showed, however, is that localisation proved more difficult if subjects were also concurrently performing a memory task. Rhodes interprets these results as indicating that 'auditory spatial information, like visual spatial information, was represented analogically and that this structure constrained the way that attention was moved within the representation' (Rhodes, 1987, p. 1). As we shall see in Chapter 3, where we consider the working memory hypothesis, concurrent memory tasks can seriously disrupt attention allocation. Another parallel has also been made between basic memory phenomena and sound localisation. When a brief sound is heard in a normal sound-reverberating room, it is immediately followed by numerous echoes, which result from the original sound bouncing back from objects in the room, its ceiling, floor and walls. Tzeng (1976), summarising other research, points out that only the first sound to arrive at the ears appears to be used in its localisation (i.e. the *precedence effect*), but goes on to suggest that the processing of verbal information can be seen as a reverberating system and rehearsal as analogous to the occurrence of echoes. Tzeng demonstrates, in support of this analogy, that the first exposure of a verbal stimulus also has special properties.

As Bower and Holyoak (1973) point out, recognition of natural sounds depends greatly on the similarity of the interpretations made of those sounds when they are heard during encoding, and the interpretations made of sounds during a later retention or recognition test. Undergraduate subjects listened to a number of ambiguous sounds, and attempted to say which of the sounds in a later recognition test had been heard earlier. Some subjects were given labels for sounds encountered at study and during the test phase, while other subjects generated their own labels for those sounds. Bower and Holyoak showed that recognition memory was far better where sounds encountered during encoding were accompanied by the same labels at retrieval, even where new labels generated during the retrieval phase were highly plausible. Unusually in the context of many other memory findings, it did not appear to matter whether the labels were self-generated or experimenter-generated. Bower and Holyoak also point out that false alarms to new sounds were partly determined by their tendency to generate the labels of old stimuli.

BOX 1.2: Memorising environmental sounds

Bartlett (1977) replicated (Experiment 1) and extended (Experiment 2) the Bower and Holyoak (1973) findings, by showing that labelling is not the only effective technique for memorising environmental sounds. His second study shows that recognition after presentation of sounds was qualitatively different from recognition after presentation of sounds accompanied verbal labels, and from recognition after presentation of verbal labels alone. Sixteen subjects heard 32 environmental sounds, 16 heard the labels for these sounds, and 16 heard both. Immediately after presentation of the sounds they were asked to free recall the sounds and/or labels they had heard. They then underwent a recognition task in which previously heard and new labels and/or sounds were presented, and finally all subjects took a cued recall test, in which they had to say which sound was paired with which label (whether this was one provided by the experimenter, as in the sound plus label or label alone condition, or one they had thought up themselves, i.e. in the sound-only procedure free recall phase). As the figure shows, compared with those which were not remembered in the initial recall test, those sounds which subjects had recalled in the free recall test, and were later able to remember in the cued recall test were better recognised when accompanied by labels at encoding, and, to a lesser extent when only their labels were given at encoding. This pattern reversed for those which subjects failed to remember in the cued recall task. However, compare this with the performance in the sound-alone condition. Here, sounds which were not recalled during the free recall procedure, were actually better recognised that those which were. On the basis of these findings, Bartlett makes a convincing case that encoding physical information about sounds is of greater importance for sound recognition than for verbal free recall, and that verbalisation is of greater importance for free recall than for recognition.

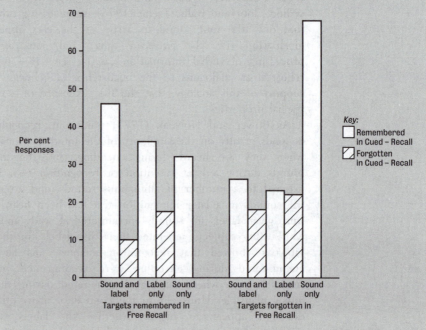

Recognition of previously remembered and forgotten sounds as a function of labelling (after Bartlett, 1977).

Much later, using a very different type of task, Thompson and Pavio (1994) showed, in a study where a distractor task prevented rehearsal and sub-vocalisation, that recall was best for the items which combined both sound and vision, but the benefits of visual and phonological information were additive relative to pictures or sounds alone.

Summary: Events, everyday memory and laboratory studies

This chapter began by asking some rather large questions, and yet much of the chapter has been concerned with how we remember relatively small events. Not only that, but the title of this book explicitly suggests that our concern is with 'everyday' events and memories. Anybody who approaches this book expecting example after example of applied or real world memory investigation will be, I regret to say, disappointed. There are such examples, and my fascination with the complexity of the driving task, and how it can be used to explore cognitive processes, is much in evidence. However, just as in the preceding sections, my overall concern is with findings which are drawn from carefully controlled investigations, especially those which have theoretical points to make. But why then choose the title I have? The answer to this is complex, but I hope it is convincing.

Some time ago, Neisser (1978) inflamed some of the more traditional memory researchers by claiming that 'If X is an important or interesting feature of human behaviour, then X has rarely been studied by psychologists'. Perhaps in order to redress the balance of insults, Banaji and Crowder (1989), in a much cited paper, write of the 'bankruptcy of everyday memory'. I think that there is much to be said, indeed much has been said, in support of these positions. On the one hand, albeit to a lesser extent in recent years, memory researchers have always appeared to be rather more concerned with laboratory-based findings, rather than with their real world applications. In contrast, much early work on 'everyday memory' seemed very much divorced from the theoretical concerns of earlier work, and appeared to offer little promise of theoretical advance on its own. I believe that adequate measurement and control, a hallmark of rather hard-bitten empiricism, is essential if we are to understand phenomena. At the same time, I feel that purging situations of any everyday relevance is not only unwise when it comes to applying for research funding, but it is at least arguable that even the best controlled studies need to capitalise to some extent on just that everyday relevance, if we are to have any reasonable chance of the subjects we test carrying out the task we would actually wish to (or actually think we have) set them.

There is another reason for not being overly concerned about the gap between laboratory-based memory research and that carried out in everyday settings. Recently, John R. Anderson (1991; Anderson and Milson, 1989), has argued that human memory is adaptive, that is, its functionality has been moulded by the world in which we have made use of our memory capacities. In an argument that is at the least very challenging, he suggests that human memory can be understood as an optimal solution to the information-retrieval task that human memory faces. According to Anderson, memory uses statistics derived from past experience to predict what memories are currently relevant and thus, those which might need to be retrieved. This does not imply any actual logical deduction in choosing optimal behaviour, but merely postulates that behaviour will be optimised given the tasks we ordinarily face. Whether or not we agree with this postulate, and it has been a matter of extensive debate (see Anderson, 1991), it argues strongly for ensuring that the tasks we perform on subjects should be as relevant as possible, but in turn that even in the highly abstracted constraints of the laboratory, such optimised memory operations will be much in evidence.

This struggle between the 'real' world and experimental control has raged as long as memory research has been carried out. Many decades ago now, Sir Fredric Bartlett (1932), who arguably pioneered the study of everyday memory, was very caustic indeed about the emptiness of Ebbinghaus's approach to the scientific study of memory. I would not expect to convince some others of this, but my own feeling is that if some laboratory work were never to lead to a real world application, or to a deeper understanding which could ultimately be applied, then there would be little merit in pursuing it. If a piece of applied work merely involved the unquestioning application of some facts derived from another context, without at least the prospect that these ideas might be tested or further refined, then it is hard to see where the science in the whole enterprise lies. For me, the 'real world' and the laboratory act as joint constraints, both of which need to be satisfied, and ideally would be all the time.

■ Further reading

Anderson, J. R. (1991). Is human cognition adaptive? *Behavioral and Brain Sciences, 14*, 3, 471–517.

Anderson, J. R. and Milson, R. (1989). Human memory: An adaptive perspective. *Psychological Review, 96,* 4, 703–19.

Banaji, M. R. and Crowder, R. C. (1989). The bankruptcy of everyday memory. *American Psychologist, 44,* 1185–93.

Bartlett, F. C. (1932). *Remembering.* Cambridge: Cambridge University Press.

Ebbinghaus, H. (1885, 1964). *Memory: A contribution to experimental psychology.* New York: Dover Publications. (Originally published in 1885.)

Neisser, U. (1978). Memory: What are the important questions? In M. M. Gruneberg, P. E. Morris, and R. N. Sykes (eds), *Practical aspects of memory.* London: Academic Press.

Discussion points
- What do you think memory is?
- How similar are our memories of experiences derived from different senses?
- Should laboratory and everyday memory research relate to each other? How?
- Is memory adaptive?

Chapter 2

Demise of the modal model

> **Chapter outline:** Following the models of human memory presented by Broadbent (1958), Waugh and Norman (1965) and especially that proposed by Atkinson and Shiffrin (1968) it has become traditional to distinguish between a number of stages of remembering or storing information. The generality of this position has meant that it is frequently referred to as the *modal model*. Although this view has been subject to massive revision, it is nevertheless a useful context in which to consider more recent developments. This chapter considers the modal model, the evidence on which it was based, and that which ultimately brought about its demise.

Key topics

- The multi-store modal model
- Sensory information storage
- Short-term storage
- Forgetting
- Summary: Importance of the modal model
- Further reading

■ The multi-store modal model

Fig 2.1   The multi-store modal model (after Atkinson and Shiffrin, 1968).

Atkinson and Shriffin's (1968) *multi-store model* of memory incorporates three separate storage stages: a sensory information store or sensory information register; a short-term and a long-term store. These are depicted in Figure 2.1.

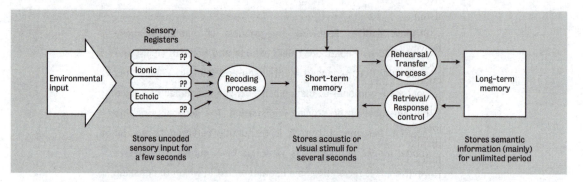

When a perceptual system detects information, a perceptual record of this information is formed and maintained briefly in the *sensory information stores.* These records are of the sensory characteristics of the information which has been encoded, and survive in that form for less than a few seconds, although the persistence of the perceptual record varies with the sensory modality activated (see Crowder, 1976). Because these perceptual records persist for such a short time, the capacity of the sensory information stores has proved difficult to establish. However, sensory information stores were generally thought to be capacity-free (see Atkinson and Shiffrin, 1968).

Categorisation mechanisms attempt to identify the perceptual records residing in the sensory information stores and, when categorised, representations of these categorised records enter a *short-term store*. The short-term store holds about five category representations at a time, for a few seconds. If these records persist for long enough they enter the *long-term store*, which is said to be unlimited in capacity and duration. Thus, information passes from its initial, capacity free, registration phase, through a temporary capacity-limited short-term store, to a long-term store which is immeasurably large and of substantial duration. Information passes through the initial stage because it lasts for long enough to gain access to any vacant slots in short-term memory. These slots become free either because information is lost, or because it is transferred to the longer term store. The likelihood of successful transfer from short- to long-term memory depended, within the Atkinson and Shiffrin framework, on rehearsal, that is, intentional repetition of the information encoded in the short-term store. In this chapter we will be primarily concerned with the first two stores, where retention is relatively brief. Necessarily, however, in order to make clear how these stores were considered to operate we will more later consider enduring memories, and how these fail to be retrieved and are altered by experience.

Sensory information storage

Iconic memory: Capacity, duration and coding

Look briefly at the letters presented in Figure 2.2. The chances are that if you looked at it for less than one second you would remember no more than four or five letters. In studies in which the exposure time is carefully controlled (e.g. using a *tachistoscope*), subjects perform at about the same level, even when exposure is limited to about 50 milliseconds. What Sperling (1960) found, however, was that if people were asked to report one line, 'top', 'middle' or 'bottom', they could recall, on average, more than three of the four in any line cued. This *partial report technique* showed that even with very brief visual presentations, subjects have many more items available for report than is evident when subjects are asked to report all that they remember from the display (i.e. *whole report*). On the basis of this, Sperling argued that for some time after the display has been removed, all of the information is available for report, but this fades rapidly. Neisser (1967) introduced the term icon (hence *iconic memory*) to refer to this fast-fading image.

Fig 2.2 Sample materials for Sperling task.

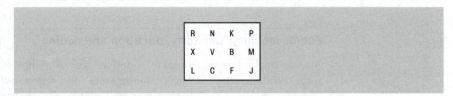

Sperling (1960) studied the persistence of this advantage of partial report over whole report by presenting similar arrays of letters but delaying the instruction as to which row should be reported. He was able to show that the advantage of partial over whole report lasts for about half of one second, where the luminance of the displays used was constant throughout. When luminance levels were adjusted, by altering the relative brightness of the image of the visual array by darkening what subjects see before and after the 'flash' which illuminates the array of letters, Sperling showed that increases in relative brightness of the array increased the length of time for which partial report is 'better' than whole report, up to some four or five seconds after initial presentation.

This reflects another property of the visual sensory information store: preceding or subsequent presentations which are of a similar energy (or brightness) level to the information to be remembered will serve to wipe or wash out the record of the registered information, or prevent its being registered in the first place. This is known as *energy masking*. Masking also occurs where preceding or subsequent presentations are visually similar to the information to be remembered, especially where the interval between the pattern mask and the target presentation is relatively brief. This is known as *pattern masking*. These two types of masking were shown to have rather different effects on the storage of briefly presented visual information: energy masking occurs at a retinal level (i.e. presentations of target and mask must be to the same eye for interference to occur), while pattern masking can interfere with the processing of information even when masks and targets are presented to different eyes (see Turvey, 1973). This shows that the interference caused by pattern masking lies deeper in the visual system, whereas that of energy masking, which Sperling showed influenced the partial–whole report advantage, lies earlier in the system, at a retinal level.

The simple ploy of cueing subjects to report part of what they see, rather than the whole of what they see, has been used by others neatly to demonstrate some other characteristics of what Neisser (1967) called iconic memory. Cueing by vertical, rather than horizontal spatial position helps to show that something approximating the whole display is temporarily available (see Sperling, 1960). Use of differently coloured letters, with instructions to report those of one colour, or size or shape (e.g. upper or lower case letters) has shown that perceptual records reflect the surface characteristics of the stimuli seen (e.g. Turvey and Kravetz, 1970; von Wright, 1968, 1970). However, combining digits and letters, with instructions to report the members from one or other category does not yield a partial report–whole report difference (e.g. Sperling, 1960; Turvey and Kravetz, 1970). Taken together these studies show that iconic memory lasts briefly, is perceptually based, is prior to categorisation of the stimuli registered and is located early in the visual system.

Echoic memory: Capacity, duration and coding

As one might imagine, because sound is generally encountered in a sequential form, manipulating acoustic information in order to search for similar phenomena in the auditory domain has been rather more of a challenge. However, we are probably all familiar with a phenomenon which helps to show the persistence of relatively raw auditory codes. How often have you had the following experience? You are only half listening to a conversation and do not quite hear what has been said, you ask the speaker to repeat it but, by the time the speaker begins to repeat it, you have a very strong feeling that you know what the speaker is going to say. One explanation of this is that even for unattended sounds we are capable of quickly retrieving recently heard material from some rather raw unprocessed auditory store.

This supposition is supported by a range of empirical studies which have attempted to set the boundaries of such raw auditory images. Howell and Darwin (1977) have shown that when asked whether two sounds were in fact the same phoneme, subjects were faster for acoustically similar sounds, but only when the delay between the two presentations was less than 750 milliseconds. Earlier, Plomp (1964) cleverly sought to describe the fading trace of a burst of noise by presenting one 200 ms burst of noise followed by another. The subject's task was to indicate when the second noise-burst began. By covarying the delay between the offset of one sound and the onset of the other, and by varying the loudness of the second sound, Plomp was able to show the fading intensity of the first sound. Where the offset–onset interval was in the region of 80 ms even a very quiet noise burst (circa 15 dB, i.e. about a quarter of a normal speaking volume) was reliably detected. Where the interval was less, the second sound needed to be considerably louder in order to be detected as reliably (Fig 2.3). In other words, the persistence, or *echoic image*, of the first sound became confused with the onset of the second sound, until it was rendered less confusable by augmenting the volume or waiting for the echoic image to fade. Later, in another particularly clever study, Efron (1970a, 1970b, 1970c) asked subjects to make a light come on just as a tone finished. The tone actually lasted for between 30 and 100 ms. Irrespective of the tone's actual duration, subjects set the onset of the light about 130 ms after the tone had actually ended. This is more or less the absolute length of the echoic image determined with the Plomp procedure.

Fig 2.3 Minimum detectable interval between noises as a function of loudness (after Plomp, 1964).

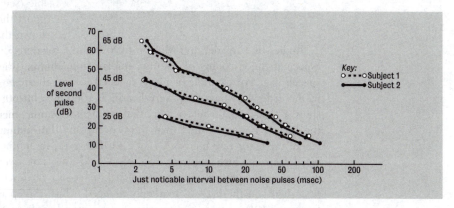

In a finding analogous to those reported by Turvey (1973) with regard to visual stimuli, Deatherage and Evans (1969) showed that a masking sound presented after, but to the same ear as a brief target stimulus, seriously interfered with detection performance, but did not do so to the same extent where the target and mask were presented to different ears.

In an attempt to mimic Sperling's earlier research in the visual domain, Darwin, Turvey and Crowder (1972) presented sounds from three different locations (e.g. right, left, ahead) and contrasted performance under whole-report and partial-report (i.e. location) instructions. They found a substantial advantage for partial report, but this advantage declined as the cue identifying the location to be recalled was delayed by at least four seconds. This boundary was confirmed by a study reported by Glucksberg and Cowan (1970), which took advantage of the fact that separate information presented to both ears can be processed independently, at least to some rudimentary level. They presented separate streams of prose to both ears. The subject's task was to attend to and repeat the continuous prose presented to one ear, while ignoring the prose, in which digits were embedded, presented to the other. Occasionally, a light would appear, which was the signal for subjects to say whether a digit had just been presented in the unattended speech stream. Where the light preceded the 'unattended' digit by more than about four seconds, performance declined markedly. Other studies have shown that unattended traces survive for rather longer than five seconds, where the unattended materials are followed by silence, rather than speech or other potentially masking sounds (Cowan, Lichti and Grove, 1988; Groeger, 1986, 1988).

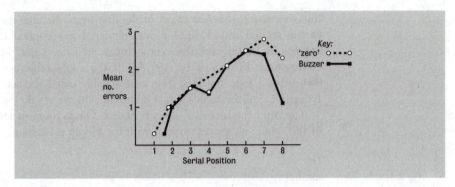

Fig 2.4 Increased error as a function of similarity between final and other stimuli (the Suffix Effect) (after Crowder, 1971).

Studies by Crowder and Morton (1969) and Crowder (1971) explored another aspect of the encoding of auditory information, that is, the extent to which it is speech-like. For example, subjects listened to and attempted to recall eight digits in the order in which they were heard, as soon as a buzzer sounded. The results show a classic *serial position curve*, that is, digits towards the beginning and end of the list are better recalled than those occupying the middle positions in the list, where the error rate increases (Fig 2.4). However, in another condition using the word 'zero', which subjects had been told was not a legitimate digit to be remembered but was simply the signal to recall, retrieval performance on the final digits on the list was markedly reduced. Thus, the speech-like nature of the final sound heard gave rise to what has become known as the *suffix effect*, that is, categorical similarity between the penultimate and final sounds heard interferes with memory performance. That this reflects categorical, rather than precategorical acoustic storage, as was originally thought, emerges clearly from a study by Ayres, Jonides, Reitman, Egan and Howard (1979). Ayres and colleagues contrasted the degree of impact on memory for the final items of a sequence of seven single-syllable words, when speech syllables or musical sounds were used as suffixes. Both influenced performance, but speech suffixes had a substantially greater effect. The study included a critical condition in which one sound ('wa') was used as both a musical and a speech sound suffix. It interfered with performance much more when it was interpreted as a speech sound than when it was thought of as a musical sound. This demonstrates very clearly that the relationship between the list items and the suffix is the crucial determinant of the suffix effect.

In summary, there is abundant evidence that very short-term sensory stores exist, at least for auditory and visual information, and probably for other modalities also. As long as the intensity or duration of the stimulus is sufficient to allow its detection, these echoic and iconic stores serve to prolong brief stimuli, such that they are available for long enough to permit further analysis (see Coltheart, 1983). These differences between visual and auditory sensory stores, not least the duration for which they are held in precategorical form, is probably determined by the temporal characteristics of the information they evolved to deal with as well as physiological limitations in our ability to deal with fast-fading auditory and visual information. Nevertheless, Atkinson and Shiffrin (1968) correctly recognised the importance of sensory registers as the gateway to more lasting memories, but the account they offer is not sufficiently sophisticated to cope with what seem to be layers of sensory storage, which at their most basic merely register information, but which then appear to be subject to different levels of precategorical analysis and different sites and types of masking. When it becomes clear to which category of item the registered information belongs, it is then subjected to rather more sophisticated memorial processes.

■ Short-term storage

The views of the short-term store which the Atkinson and Shiffrin (1968) model summarised assume that it is of limited capacity, and that it performs various control activities, including coding, decision and retrieval strategies and especially the control of rehearsal. As mentioned above, rehearsal was thought to be the basis on which all information passes into the permanent or long-term store. Much of the evidence for the distinction between short-term and long-term stores, which the modal model set out to account for, came from the serial position curve, storage capacity and duration, coding differences and neurological findings. These served both to establish the modal model as the dominant view, but also, as we shall see, to undermine and eventually overthrow it.

Serial position curves and rehearsal

The serial position curve arises when a list of stimuli is heard or read, at a fixed rate (e.g. 1 per second) and recalled. The typical pattern which emerges is of a u-shaped curve, with subjects being far more likely to recall the first items they encountered (i.e. the *primacy effect*) and also the last few items they encountered (i.e. the *recency effect*), than any of the items in the middle portion of the list. This occurs across a range of list lengths and types (see suffix effect studies above with 8 digits; and 10, 20, 30 word lists used by Postman and Phillips, 1965 and Glanzer and Cunitz, 1966 (see Fig 2.5)). A small alteration to this method, incorporating a brief delay (e.g. 15 seconds) between the last item in the list and recall, had important consequences (see Fig 2.5). During this interval the subject is occupied with some other task, such as counting backwards in threes from some large number. Under these *delayed recall* conditions, Postman and Phillips (1965) found that the recency effect was abolished. The modal model provided a very straightforward explanation of these findings. The items making up the primacy effect were recalled from the long-term store, while the items comprising the recency effect were recalled directly from those currently available in the short-term store. When recall was delayed, the short-term store is busily engaged with the additional task and as a result of this, rehearsal is prevented. As a result, the primacy effect remains unaffected, but the recency effect is destroyed. When recall is delayed, but this interval is unfilled, the recency effect is once again very evident (see Baddeley and Hitch, 1977). Obviously, in such circumstances, rehearsal of the items in the short-term store is no longer prevented, and the recency effect should and does, emerge. Many researchers have noted that subjects, under free recall conditions, tend to produce more recent items first and only then produce items they encountered earlier. It has

been suggested that this reflects a naturally developed strategy to prevent older items overwriting the more recent and less well rehearsed items in the short-term store (Tulving and Arbuckle, 1963). The same authors show that the recency effect is very much reduced if subjects are made to recall list items in the order in which they were heard (i.e. *serial recall*).

Fig 2.5 Recall as function of serial position and delay (the Serial Position Curve) (after Glanzer and Cunitz, 1966).

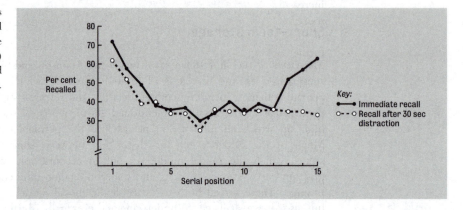

Glanzer (1972) demonstrated that a range of variables (e.g. presentation rate, the familiarity of the words, etc.) had little or no effect on the recency portion of the curve, but did influence what was thought to be the long-term component. The rehearsal-based explanation of how items were transferred into the long-term store gained further support from a study by Rundus (1971) (Fig 2.6), in

Fig 2.6 Per cent recall as a function of input position and number of rehearsals (after Rundus, 1971).

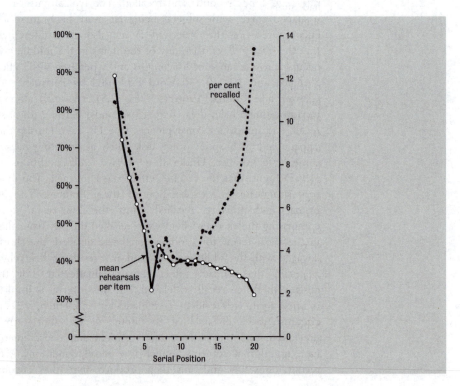

which subjects were encouraged to rehearse aloud, thus allowing the actual number of rehearsals to be counted. This revealed that the initial items were rehearsed most often with the rate of rehearsal per item reducing rapidly, and remaining flat over the remainder of the list. When subjects recalled these subsequently, the standard serial position curve was again evident. The fact that increasing the interitem spacing from three to nine seconds, thus allowing for more rehearsal between items, enhances recall of the initial and middle portions of the list, but has no effect on the later items (see Glanzer and Cunitz, 1966), further encourages the view that rehearsal serves to increase the likelihood that items will reach some more enduring memory.

This account is embarrassed by a number of more recent findings. Tzeng (1973) had subjects participate in a free recall task in which they were presented with unrelated words, followed by a 20-second filled delay. As one might expect, this eliminated the recency effect. Other subjects were encouraged to count backwards for 20 seconds between items. Remarkably, both primacy and recency effects were observed despite what has become known as the *continuous distraction* procedure. Studies by Bjork and Whitten (1974) and Hitch, Rejman and Turner (1980) have replicated and considerably extended these findings. According to the modal model explanation, the continuous distraction prevents rehearsal of all items, and also serves to replace items to be learned in the short-term store. This should produce a flat trace, rather than the serial position curve which actually emerges.

The claim that sheer amount of rehearsal leads to better remembering is also undermined by a number of other studies. Glenberg, Smith and Green (1977) had subjects study a four-digit number for two seconds, and then rehearse a single word for 2, 6 or 18 seconds, after which they were required to recall the four-digit number. In all, subjects participated in 64 trials, after which, to their surprise, their retrieval of the interpolated words was tested. The amount of rehearsal was only weakly related to subjects' ability to identify words they had rehearsed from among others presented in a recognition test. Their level of recall performance was only 11, 7 and 12 per cent respectively for words in the 2, 6 and 18 second rehearsal intervals. Craik and Watkins (1973) report a very clever study in which subjects were told to try to remember the last word in a list which began with a particular target letter (e.g. f). The lists were composed of words such as: house, fire, dog, money, full, car, garden, lorry, fox, bees, deer, store, heart, mouse, fool, football, glass, boot, dress, horse. As subjects heard each f-word they were not sure whether it would be the last, so each f-word would be rehearsed until the next one was encountered, when rehearsal of the new f-word would begin. By constructing the lists carefully, Craik and Watkins were able to vary the amounts of rehearsal each item would receive. After studying 27 lists of this sort, subjects were given a surprise recall test, but no relationship was found between the amount of rehearsal each item received and the frequency with which it was recalled.

Although some are sceptical that they are actually the same effect (e.g. Schwartz and Reisberg, 1991), long-term recency effects have also been reported by a number of authors. Baddeley and Hitch (1977) showed that rugby players, when attempting to recall the teams they had played against earlier in the season, showed clear evidence of a recency effect, with the number of interpolated games, rather than time, being the critical factor. Roediger and Crowder (1976) asked subjects to recall, in any order, as many American presidents as they could remember. When the frequency with which presidents were mentioned was plotted against the period in which they had been in office, Roediger and Crowder found, in addition to irregularities due to certain presidents being well remembered, very clear primacy and recency effects. It is very likely that such long-term recency effects have a different origin and explanation to those on which the modal model is based, as Schwartz and Reisberg (1991) have argued, but the similarities between these long-term recency effects and those which emerge from the continuous distractor paradigm are rather striking. We will return to recency effects in the next chapter, but for the moment, even if these are set aside, the evidence for the role of rehearsal and the serial position curve effects which emerged from more recent studies is rather damaging.

Storage capacity and duration

Another reason why the modal memory account was favoured over the view that memory was simply unitary, was that the short-term store appeared to have a far lower capacity than the long-term store. The standard estimate for the capacity of the short-term store is traditionally given as 'the magical number seven, plus or minus two' (Miller, 1956). Most investigators have since concluded that this estimate is rather high and that the maximum number is closer to five items or less (see Baddeley, 1990). However, even accepting this lower estimate, it should be remembered that this refers to 'chunks', which may be individual items in some contexts (e.g. daffodil) or combinations or related items (e.g. daffodil, tulip, rose, daisy, etc.) in the context of other lists. Similarly, strings that are well beyond the short-term store's capacity (e.g. 1-7-8-9-1-4-9-2-2-0-0-1-1-0-6-6), are not so if these are encoded as dates of the French Revolution, Columbus, space travel and the battle of Hastings.

Even if the lower estimate of the short-term store's capacity is accepted, it should presumably reflect the size of the recency effect, which is purportedly a read out of the contents of the short-term store. Glanzer and Razell (1974) in a meta-analysis of over 20 studies showed that the average size of the recency effect is 2.2 words. However, in studies they report in the same paper, the size of the recency effect for proverbs (e.g. 'too many cooks spoil the broth') was also 2.2, and 1.5 for unfamiliar sentences.

Wickens (1972) described another now well-established phenomenon. Given exemplars from one category (e.g. daffodil, tulip, rose, daisy, pansy, lily), subjects will immediately recall these reliably. Repeating this with different exemplars of the same category, the number subjects recall will gradually reduce. Surely, if the short-term store reflects an autonomous store, with a fixed number of slots, its capacity should remain constant. This gradual reduction in the capacity of the short-term store is not due to fatigue, since if the next list is drawn from a different category, the number recalled returns almost to its original level. These phenomena are known as *proactive interference* (i.e. old information interferes with the acquisition of related new information) and *release from proactive interference* (i.e. a category shift revitalises acquisition; see Wickens, Born and Allen, 1963; Loess,

1968). A further example of interference is reflected in the fact that letters are lost more quickly from the short-term store if, in the interval between the last item and recall, subjects are required to say the alphabet backwards than if they count backwards. The more similar the distractor task is to the materials to be remembered, the shorter is the duration that information can be held in the short-term store (see Wickelgren, 1965).

In passing it is worth noting that some authors (e.g. Glenberg, Bradley and Stevenson, 1980; Parkin, 1993) have suggested that the recency effects obtained under immediate free recall, delayed free recall and free recall under continuous distractor conditions, can all be well accounted for by a single relatively simple rule. This rule, called the *constant ratio rule*, states that the probability of recall of any item is the ratio of the interitem interval divided by the delay between item presentation time and the start of recall. While this undoubtedly fits some of the data rather well, it clearly cannot fit data from very similar paradigms, such as where (a) the interval between the last item and recall is unfilled, but of the same duration as a filled interval (e.g. Baddeley and Hitch, 1977), and (b) the interpolated task is similar to the materials to be remembered (e.g. Corman and Wickens, 1968; Wickelgren, 1965).

The modal model cannot easily account for results of this sort, since as we shall see later its primary recourse in explaining the loss of information from the short-term store is displacement by other items. There is an explanation, but it is in terms of interference, a primary source of forgetting envisaged in the modal model's description of the long-term store. Whatever the explanation, it seems as if related information in long-term memory interferes with the information in the short-term store, but this seriously undermines the case for the short-term store being regarded as autonomous. Clearly the capacity of the short-term store is a rather slippery notion. Although it is obviously less than what we might consider to be our long-term memory, the interdependencies between the short- and long-term stores which can serve to reduce or increase the capacity of the short-term store, pose still more difficulties for the modal model.

Coding differences

In the postwar years the Post Office funded a substantial amount of research at the Applied Psychology Unit (APU) in Cambridge. In the course of this research one of the senior researchers, Ruben Conrad, noted that many of the errors people made in recalling telephone codes, which at the time included both letters and numbers, were similar in sound to the correct letter. Thus, P was more likely to be misrecalled as the acoustically similar V, rather than the visually similar R. In the traditions of much of the finest APU research Conrad (1964) noted that under laboratory conditions, similar error patterns emerged when subjects tried to discriminate between letters presented in background noise. Baddeley (1966a), who worked for a time as Conrad's research assistant, extended this research beyond individual letters to words, showing that sequences of acoustically similar words (e.g. man, map, can, cap, mad) were much more difficult to recall immediately than sequences of words similar in meaning (e.g. big, huge, broad, tall, long). In contrast, in a similar study, this time incorporating a delay which included an interpolated task and repeated testing, Baddeley (1966b) showed that over longer periods of time a *semantic similarity effect* rather a *phonological similarity effect* was evident. This offered a rather neat discrimination between the coding typical of the short-term and long-term stores. The suggestion that the two stores differed in terms of encoding was supported by further work by Kintsch and Buschke (1969) and Sachs (1967).

However, once again more recent studies have muddied these rather clear waters. Bower and Springston (1970) showed increased memory span for meaningful trigrams (e.g. IBM, FBI, USA) over meaningless trigrams, thus showing that semantic coding could be used to advantage in short-term storage. Similarly, Potter and Lombardi (1990) showed that subjects were unable to reliably determine which of two versions of a sentence they had originally heard (i.e. 'The knight rounded the palace searching for a place to enter' or 'The knight rounded the castle searching for a place to enter'), if in the interim they had heard a list containing the word castle. Conrad (1972), returning to the fray, using a version of the *Brown–Peterson task*, showed that deaf children made errors which suggested visual rather than acoustic or other types of confusion. (The Brown–Peterson task requires subjects to memorise a trigram, e.g. TRW, whilst counting backwards from a three-digit number presented immediately after the trigram.) Baddeley (1986) reviews a number of other studies which show semantic and lexical processing effects in short-term memory tasks.

Retrieval

Sternberg (1966, 1969, 1975) developed a method for studying access to memorised information. The *Sternberg paradigm* requires subjects to hold a number of items in memory (e.g. 4 1 6 3 9) and then to decide, as quickly as possible, whether a 'probe' item (e.g. 7) is a member of the memorised set. Sternberg found a strong linear relationship between the time taken to make the decision and the size of the set to be searched (Fig 2.7), with the decision taking about 38 ms longer for each additional item in the search set. With the exception of a memory set of one item, where positive decisions (item is contained in memory set) are about 50 ms faster than negative decisions (item is not contained in memory set), positive and negative decisions take equivalent amounts of time. The Sternberg paradigm gave rise to what virtually became a cottage industry in demonstrating the effects held for different types of materials and, less successfully, for different memory set sizes (see Glass, 1984 for review). The results of these and the original studies have a number of implications.

It is inconceivable that when attempting to search for someone's name, or the word appropriate for a particular purpose, we do this by searching every name or word we have ever encountered. After all, for an adult with a reasonably average vocabulary of at least 50,000 words (see Aitchison, 1994), it should take about five minutes to select every word he or she might wish to use. Such considerations gave rise to the view that short- and long-term memory must be searched in different ways. Sternberg's results were originally thought to reflect an *exhaustive serial search* with every item in the memory set being considered in turn. Thus, even when a match was found early in the list between a probe item and an item in the search set, the search and comparison operation continued until the end of the list. Sternberg argued that, at least for set sizes which are less than or equal to the number of items that can be perfectly recalled, *exhaustive serial search* is more efficient than a search process which terminates part of the way through the list and then needs to be checked for accuracy. In contrast, memory search for more enduring memories was thought to be parallel, with, as it were, different places being searched simultaneously.

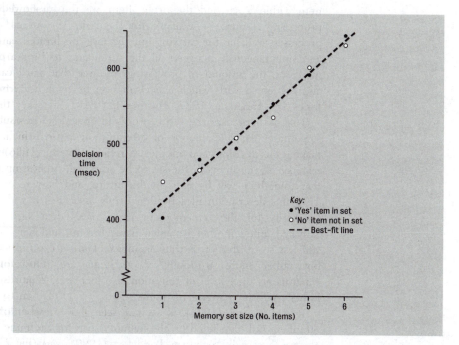

Fig 2.7 Time taken to decide that an item was or was not in a memory set, as a function of memory set size (after Sternberg, 1969).

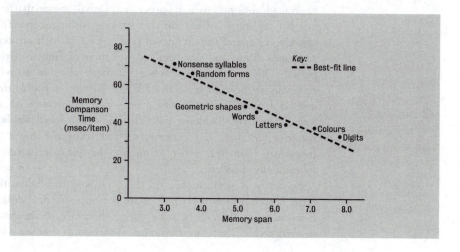

Fig 2.8 Relationship between memory span and performance on Sternberg task with different materials (after Cavanagh, 1972).

Cavanagh (1972) has shown that there is a linear relationship between decision time on a Sternberg task and the memory span for different types of materials. Memory comparison time is longer for those types of material for which memory span is lowest (e.g. nonsense syllables and random forms), while memory comparison time is lowest for those materials for which memory span is larger (e.g. digits) (Fig 2.8). Because it is not simply the number of items searched which predicts performance in the Sternberg task, but also the types of items, we need some way other than exhaustive search to explain Cavanagh's results, even from short-term tasks. Such alternatives are available in terms of *limited capacity parallel retrieval models*. These are based on two proposals. First, the speed with which a decision can be made (i.e. that an item within a set and the probe item are the same) depends on how much processing resource is available for the task. The second proposal is that the processes available for carrying out the task are limited, and are divided equally and simultaneously between all the candidates to be searched. As the set size increases, the amount of processing resource that any one item has is reduced and the speed with which a decision can be made is reduced accordingly (see Jones and Anderson, 1987; Townsend, 1990).

This account uses the term 'processing resource' in two ways, one to reflect something like the amount of attention or effort which can be allocated to making the decision, and another to reflect something like the level of activity or *activation* of the items in the set to be searched. Activation reflects the likelihood that something will be used in the future, and how recently it has been used. Thus this description of activation firmly associates it with an item's utility and familiarity for the rememberer. Thus, one's own surname would be highly activated, one's mother's maiden name less so, and her mother's maiden name still less so. Activation is thus an index of one's exposure to an item. Similarly, but rather more artificially, when items are rehearsed during a memory experiment, their level of activation also increases. This allows us to explain two rather confusing patterns of results.

First, Cavanagh (1972), as we have seen above, found that performance on the Sternberg task depended on the memory span for the materials used. In the next chapter we will see that Baddeley (1990) suggests that the size of the phonological loop (which processes verbal materials) is determined by the number of items which can be spoken within about 1.5 to 2 seconds. The speaking rate, and thus rehearsal rate, for items such as nonsense syllables, words and digits differ, and as a result so will their likelihood of rehearsal within a given period. Digits will thus be rehearsed more often in a given period. As a result each will be more highly activated, and the time taken to decide whether a probe item is a member of the rehearsed set or not will be shorter, just as Cavanagh found. Similarly, Baddeley and Ecob (1973) showed that if an item occurs twice within a Sternberg task memory set task, thus allowing it to be rehearsed more frequently than the other items in the set, decisions about that item are substantially speeded.

Secondly, if performance on the Sternberg task really reflected an exhaustive serial search which was appropriate for short-term memory, but not for long-term memory, then the set size effects described above should not be found with delayed recall. There are numerous demonstrations that when words are learned, but rehearsal of them is subsequently prevented, similar set-size effects emerge as for retrieval of items from short-term memory (e.g. Anderson, 1983; Gillund and Shiffrin, 1984). Thus, for recently activated, but also for less active, more weakly established, knowledge, Sternberg set size effects emerge.

Once again, with respect to retrieval processes, the argument for a separation between short- and long-term memory is not as clear as it was once thought to be. As we shall see from the next section, a similar picture emerges when we consider neurological evidence.

Neurological evidence

In research that has become a classic of its genre, Milner (1966) and Shallice and Warrington (1970; Warrington and Shallice, 1969) describe two amnesic patients, referred to as H.M. and K.F. respectively, who performed very differently on standard memory tests. H.M. at the time of original testing had digit span performance well within the normal range (Milner, 1966) and continued to have long afterwards (Ogden and Corkin, 1991), but very poor memory for longer term events (Milner, 1966; Ogden and Corkin, 1991). H.M.'s deficits arose following an operative procedure which removed substantial tissue from his *temporal lobes* and *hippocampus* on both sides of his brain, which was successful in 'treating' his severe epilepsy. In contrast, K.F. had remarkably poor digit span, less than two items, and a recency effect of just one item (Shallice and Warrington, 1970), but very good performance on tasks which were thought to reflect an intact long-term store. K.F. had suffered damage to his left parieto-occipital region following a motor-cycle accident. This resulted in speech difficulties, in his case very poor repetition, which is characteristic of conduction aphasia. Conduction aphasics also generally have good comprehension, but their spontaneous speech frequently includes phonemic errors.

K.F.'s deficits were originally thought to reflect the reverse of those of H.M., neatly completing the circle. However, subsequent analysis of K.F. has revealed very substantial long-term learning abilities, for example, he was able to learn a ten-word sequence in fewer trials than normal controls, and still retained seven of the ten words two months later (see Parkin, 1993, p. 121), in addition, rather more significantly perhaps, to living a relatively normal life (see also patients reported by Basso, Spinnler, Vallar and Zanobio, 1982). This is at variance with what might be expected from a simple modal model account, where very poor functioning of the short-term store should be associated with profound difficulties in everyday performance. Furthermore, the steady passage of rehearsed information from the short-term store to the long-term store should also be impeded by very poor memory span.

The Atkinson and Shiffrin (1968) multi-store model still offers a reasonable account of the phenomena it was designed to explain. However, as investigation became more detailed, the limitations of the modal model as an explanatory framework became increasingly clear. In a sense, the concrete ways in which the properties of stores and their operations were described, not only set a research agenda, but also proved its downfall. Originally set up to make the case for separating different memory functions, the modal model has succeeded in doing so. Since it began to decline, two opposing views have emerged about how the difficulties should be resolved. On the one hand researchers, largely based in America, have sought to conceive of accounts of the phenomena described above which treat short-term memory as a particularly well-activated portion of long-term memory. The other view, developed by Alan Baddeley and colleagues, is essentially a much revised multi-store view, albeit painstakingly ground out empirically over 25 or so years. Both will be considered in the next chapter. Before doing so, let us consider a number of explanations of forgetting.

Forgetting

Displacement, decay and interference

When the modal model was in its prime, it was thought that loss of information from the short-term store was primarily due to *displacement*, or perhaps *trace decay,* while failure to retrieve information from the longer-term store was due to interference from what had already been learned (i.e. *proactive interference*) or interference from new learning on what had previously been learned (i.e. *retroactive interference*).

Displacement occurred because short-term stores were of limited capacity: when new material was to be learned, it simply displaced older items from the short-term store. Waugh and Norman (1965), for example, showed that memory for a piece of information was best predicted by the number of items encoded after that item, rather than by the duration for which the test item had been stored. Baddeley (1986), on the other hand, favours a duration-based (i.e. *trace decay*) explanation of loss of information from the short-term store. The argument behind Baddeley's assertion is that since, as we have seen, the rate of rehearsal determines forgetting, decay obviously does play a key role in forgetting of recently learned items, and thus displacement alone cannot provide a complete explanation of how information is lost from the short-term store. Forgetting due to displacement or trace decay can be prevented by rehearsal, either because rehearsal reactivates fading traces or because it displaces 'old' items with 'new' versions of the same items.

It has been clear since earlier this century that activity between learning and retrieval can dramatically influence retrieval. In their classic study, Jenkins and Dallenbach (1924) had two subjects learn *nonsense syllables*, retrieval of which was tested after intervals of one, two, four, or eight hours, with subjects sometimes sleeping between learning and retrieval. In both cases, over the first few hours, retrieval success reduced as time proceeded. Critically, however, retrieval success no longer decreased when the subject slept between learning and test (see also Hockey, Davies and Gray, 1972). Another early study shows that the nature of the activity interpolated between learning and test has a considerable effect on retrieval. McGeogh and McDonald (1931) systematically investigated this by altering the relationship between the lists of adjectives to be remembered, which had been learned until they could be perfectly recalled serially, and the activity carried out for the ten minutes between learning and test. McGeogh and McDonald used two criteria to assess the amount of forgetting: the number of adjectives correctly recalled, and the number of trials required to regain the perfect serial recall criterion. Figure 2.9 shows their results, clearly reflecting the disturbance caused by the degree of similarity between the items to be learned and the interpolated activity. The widely established effect whereby newly processed information reduces our ability to remember previously acquired information reflects *retroactive interference*. This arises when more recently learned information causes the forgetting of material learned earlier.

Fig 2.9 Effects of interpolated learning on serial recall and re-learning of a list of adjectives (after McGeogh and McDonald, 1931).

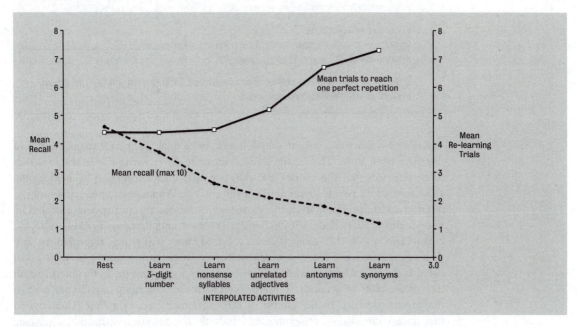

Two other phenomena form the basis of interference effects. *Proactive interference* arises when material already learned makes the learning of newer material more difficult or impossible. Suppose you have to learn successive lists, each made up of different items of the same type (e.g. names of cars). On the basis of previous findings the chances are that you will remember fewer items from each list than you did for the list before. This demonstrates how proactive interference operates. However, if you now try to learn a list of the same size, but composed of items from a different category (e.g. flower names), you will remember almost as many items as you did from the first list of cars (see Wickens, Born and Allen, 1963; Loess, 1968). This is known as *release from proactive interference*. Most processing changes result in some release, but semantic shifts are most robust (see Wickens, 1970). The traditional procedures for establishing interference effects are shown in Box 2.1.

BOX 2.1: Establishing interference effects

Imagine you have to learn two lists of words. By alternating periods of learning and inactivity and by changing which list you are asked to recall, the two major interference phenomena can be easily demonstrated.

List 1: north, hear, door, market, early, left, role, keep, father, valley, centre, corner
List 2: meat, barn, voice, coal, mile, person, about, hill, music, paper, neck, wall

Retroactive Interference

Control:	Learn list 1	Do nothing	Recall List 1
Experimental:	Learn list 1	Learn list 2	Recall List 1

If the Experimental group remembers fewer List 1 items than the Control group, retroactive interference has occurred.

Proactive Interference

Control:	Do nothing	Learn list 2	Recall List 2
Experimental:	Learn list 1	Learn list 2	Recall List 2

If the Experimental group remembers fewer List 2 items than the Control group, proactive interference has occurred.

Earlier we saw some ways in which interference might influence the operation of the short-term store. That is, the more similar the distractor task is to the materials to be remembered, the shorter the duration that information can be held in the short-term store (see Corman and Wickens, 1968; Wickelgren, 1965). The role of interference in forgetting from the short-term store was also neatly demonstrated by Keppel and Underwood (1962). Earlier, Peterson and Peterson (1959) using the *Brown–Peterson task* (i.e. subjects learn a list of three items, e.g. three letters, and then engage in some interpolated activity, e.g. backward counting, until a recall signal is given) found that while without delay subjects were perfectly able to recall the trigram after 18 seconds of interpolated backward counting, only 20 per cent of the trigrams learned in the course of the experiment were recalled. They argued that since counting and remembering letters do not interfere with each other (see McGeogh and McDonald 1931, above), these results could not be due to retroactive interference, and so must be due to trace decay (or displacement). However, detailed exploration of data from the Brown–Peterson task by Keppel and Underwood (1962) showed that forgetting did not occur for the first trigram in the study, but gradually increased throughout the study. This was, quite reasonably, interpreted by Keppel and Underwood (1962) as reflecting a detrimental influence of prior learning, namely proactive interference. These studies undermine the view that short- and long-term memory can be discriminated on the basis of how information is lost from these stores.

Interference and retrieval failure

It has generally been found that *retroactive interference* is greatest when there is a great deal of material interpolated between learning and test (e.g. Melton and Irwin, 1940), while *proactive interference* is greatest when a large amount of material has preceded learning (e.g. Underwood, 1957). *Release from proactive interference* was neatly demonstrated by Gardiner, Craik and Birtwisle (1972). Using a Brown–Peterson procedure, subjects learned sequences of flower names. As the study proceeded the clusters of flower names changed subtly from those of cultivated flowers to wild flowers. Subjects did not notice this change but their memory performance showed increasing effects of proactive interference (Fig 2.10). Another group of subjects, who had been warned of the change showed an improvement in memory for the different category items, which is characteristic of release from proactive interference. The third group used, however, were told of the category shift only after the items had been presented, but before they were required to recall them. This group also showed substantial release from proactive interference (see Fig 2.10), demonstrating that given appropriate search cues the effects of interference can be overcome.

Fig 2.10 Release from proactive interference as a presentation of retrieval cues at learning and test. (after Gardiner, Craik and Birtwisle, 1972).

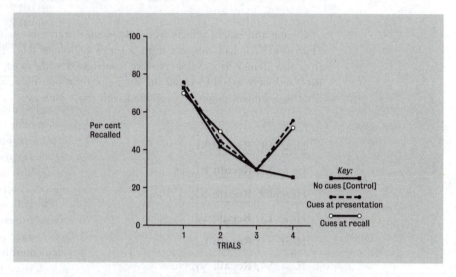

Two other studies demonstrate the capacity of cueing to overcome interference effects. Tulving and Psotka (1971) showed that memory cueing eliminates retroactive interference. Subjects learned a number of lists, each composed of 24 items. Each list was itself organised into six quite different categories of four items each. Subjects learned each 24-word list and were tested immediately afterwards. At the end of the study, subjects attempted to recall as many items as they could from the whole study. The results obtained revealed the classic interference effect: recall from lists deteriorates as a function of the number of items between learning and test (Fig 2.11). Note that this occurred even with lists which had some inherent organisation, even though this might in principle allow the possibility for release from proactive interference, had subjects noted the shift in categories. However, when subjects were tested with cued recall, that is when they were given the label for each of the smaller four-item categories, recall was dramatically different, showing very little effect of the number of items between learning and test.

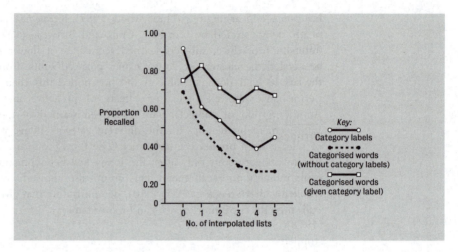

Fig 2.11 Category label cues reduce retroactive interference in categorised word lists (after Tulving and Psotka, 1971).

Key:
Category labels
Categorised words (without category labels)
Categorised words (given category label)

Cueing and search effects were also demonstrated in another important study. Shiffrin (1970) had subjects learn a series of longer (e.g. 20 items) and shorter (e.g. five items) lists. Subjects were confronted with shorter (S) and longer (L) lists, and were asked to recall the list before the one they had just heard or seen. That is, a subject might be presented with trials such as:

Hear: S1;

Hear: L1; **Recall:** S1;

Hear: S2; **Recall:** L1;

Hear: L2; **Recall:** S2;

Hear: L3; **Recall:** L2;

Hear: S3; **Recall:** L3;

Hear: S4; **Recall:** S3; etc.

According to an interference view, the size of the list just learned should substantially affect the level of recall from the list preceding it. Thus, recall of S1 would be better if S2 has just been heard than if L2 had just been heard; recall of L1 should be better when S2 has just been heard than when L3 has just been heard. A search explanation, on the other hand, would suggest that longer lists should be recalled worse than shorter lists, but should not be influenced by the size of the interpolated list. This is precisely the pattern of results Shiffrin found. Items from shorter lists are easier to remember because they are intrinsically more memorable, not because a certain number of items are learned before or after them.

Although the empirical basis of interference theory is very strong, proponents have failed to propose and support adequate theories for determining the basis on which interference should occur, and have neglected crucial issues such as the nature of the representations used in short- or long-term stores. While it is widely accepted that interference effects can indeed be reliably demonstrated, interference as an account of forgetting is now regarded as unfashionable, in part because of the intricacies which must be resorted to in order to provide accounts of more complex phenomena. At first sight it thus seems that interference is difficult to relate to everyday situations. However, similar types of forgetting can be seen in phenomena which surround post-event information and research on the reliability of the courtroom testimony of eye witnesses.

Witness accounts and post-event information

Just as with traditional interference effects, laboratory-based studies which have explored the reliability of witness accounts have also shown that subjects' recollection of events as experienced can be altered by subsequent experience.

Typical of the procedures used is a study reported by Loftus, Miller and Burns (1978). Subjects watched a series of slides in which a red Datsun approached and stopped at an intersection, turned the corner and then hit a pedestrian. Half of the subjects saw a slide in which there was a Stop sign at the intersection, half saw a slide where there was a Yield (i.e. Give Way) sign at the intersection. Later, some 20 minutes or a week later depending on the condition, subjects were asked a number of questions about the events they had seen. Some of these questions contained information consistent with the slides they had seen (e.g. 'Did another car pass the red Datsun while it was stopped at the Stop sign?'); for some subjects the information embedded in the questions was inconsistent with what they had seen (e.g. 'Did another car pass the red Datsun while it was stopped at the Yield sign?'); while for others the sentences to be answered were neutral with respect to the manipulation (i.e. 'Did another car pass the red Datsun while it was stopped?'). In the final part of the study subjects were shown pairs of slides and were asked to identify those which they had already seen. In this case the critical comparison is what subjects decided when confronted with a slide showing the red Datsun stopped at a Stop sign, and a slide showing the red Datsun stopped at a Yield sign. Where subjects had answered questions which contained consistent information, just 20 minutes after seeing the slides, 75 per cent of subjects correctly chose the 'old' slide. Where the information encountered during the second phase of the study was inconsistent with what they had seen earlier, the correct slide was chosen by only 41 per cent of the subjects. Fifty-nine per cent of those subjects who encountered neutral information identified the critical slide correctly. The effects were even more dramatic when the misleading information was encountered one week after the slides had originally been seen.

An earlier study by Loftus and Palmer (1974) had subjects look at a series of slides in which two cars collided. Soon afterwards subjects were asked to estimate the speeds of the vehicles, with half of the subjects being asked to say how fast the cars had been travelling when they 'hit' each other, and half of the subjects being asked to say how fast the cars had been travelling when the cars 'smashed into' each other. The estimated speeds were 34 mph and 41 mph respectively. More crucially, asked a week later to say whether or not they had seen broken glass on the road (there was none), 14 per cent of subjects who were asked the question where the word 'hit' was used said they had seen glass, while 32 per cent of subjects in the 'smashed into' condition falsely claimed to have seen glass on the road. Loftus (1974) has also shown that *leading questions* which use the definite article rather than the indefinite article are more likely to give rise to this *misinformation effect*, as do questions made up of embedded clauses rather than direct questions (see Loftus and Greene, 1980). Studies which have incorporated rewards for correct answers and second guesses in the event of incorrect identifications have shown that demand characteristics, or differences in confidence, do not lie at the heart of these effects (see Loftus, Miller and Burns 1978).

The interpretation of these results has proved somewhat controversial. Two related explanations, both suggested by Beth Loftus, imply that either the 'old' information was not encoded to begin with (the vacant slot hypothesis, Loftus and Loftus, 1980), or that the new, perhaps misleading, information overwrites the 'old' information. Both accounts assume that whether because of a failure of encoding, or because of this process of *updating* of the memory record, the old information is lost (see Loftus, 1979). That this is not inevitably the case was neatly demonstrated by Bekerian and Bowers (1983). By showing that the misleading information was much less effective when the slide sequence was watched in the order in which it was originally seen, rather than in the random order originally used by Loftus and colleagues, Bekerian and Bowers were able to show that both forms of information coexisted in memory (the *coexistence hypothesis*). In other words, the strength of the original narrative structure, once reinstated by watching the material in its original order, was sufficient to make the 'old' information more available than the misleading information. This was sufficient to overcome our bias towards recollecting our most recent involvement with some particular information rather than our original encounter with it (see Hintzman, 1990; Morton, 1994; see also 'headed records' Chapter 4, p. 85, for further discussion of this precedence of recent records). Thus, the Bekerian view, which is also evident in her discussions of recovered memories (see Bekerian and Goodrich, 1995), is that the old information is not lost or overwritten, but simply rendered less accessible than other types of information.

Although McCloskey and Zaragoza (1985) failed in their attempts to replicate the Bekerian and Bowers finding, results from studies using a different methodology suggest that the original information is not destroyed. Subjects saw a picture of, for example, a workman picking up a hammer. They are later given misinformation that the workman picked up a wrench, suggesting that studies which, after the presentation of misleading information, go on to force a choice between the original and the misleading information tell us little about whether updating occurs. Instead they suggest that if the misleading information actually updates or otherwise interferes with the original information, then misled subjects who have to choose between old information and completely new information (e.g. 'Did the workman pick up a hammer or a saw?'), should choose the old information less often than subjects who have not been misled. Using such procedures, McCloskey and Zaragoza (1985) consistently failed to find a misinformation effect, thus indicating that at least in these circumstances, updating does not occur. Instead they suggest that two factors govern the misinformation effect. First, original information may not be encoded in the first place, or may be forgotten through interference. In either case, the memory record is incomplete, and these gaps in the record are filled by later information.

Secondly, McCloskey and Zaragoza suggest misinformation reflects some confusion as to whether the original or misleading information is appropriate. The merits of this forgetting and response bias account of the misinformation effect has been actively debated (see Belli, 1989; Zaragoza and McCloskey, 1989), but more recent results, by Dodson and Reisberg (1991) strongly suggest that the original information is rendered inaccessible rather than updated or lost, since they found evidence of a misinformation effect using an indirect, implicit memory, technique. Although the debate is far from resolved, it seems more likely than not that both the original and misleading information have been encoded and are available, although the more recently encountered information is considerably more likely to be retrieved. In interference terms, previously learned information can be rendered inaccessible by information encountered subsequently. What the post-event information literature seems to show is that the information is neither over-written nor necessarily permanently lost. Importantly, however, it shows how what seemed rather dry issues can be addressed in everyday memory contexts which may dramatically affect individuals' lives. These issues will be addressed again in later chapters, where recovered memories and the cognitive interview, which enhances the recall accuracy of witnesses, will be discussed.

Summary: Importance of the modal model

The research just described, which attempts to understand the processes which may give rise to inaccurate remembering, follows directly from the concerns earlier memory theorists also shared. However, the contrasts between this and earlier work is quite stark. It seems, at once, relevant and vibrant in comparison with work which appears not just more painstaking but also less relevant to everyday concerns. I believe such starkness is misleading. Without the increasing maturity of empirical approaches to the study of memory, as reflected in the continual clarification of the modal model, the flexibility and, perhaps, more lax empiricism typical of eyewitness testimony research would have been less acceptable to the scientific community than it has proved to be. But the rise and fall of the modal model represents more than just a cutting of empirical and conceptual teeth. It teaches us some very important lessons about the enterprise we are engaged in when we study memory: it is crucial to strive for precision so that statements about the functioning of some hypothetical store or process can be empirically tested; the structural characteristics (e.g. capacity, duration, etc.) and representational characteristics (e.g. coding, association, etc) of memory, together with the processes which combine with structure and representation to allow tasks to be performed, are central to any description of how memory operates; brain functioning, at least as we understand it thus far, and the memory tasks people perform, or are required to perform, in their ordinary lives, serve both to inform and constrain the way we conceptualise memory.

It is hard to escape the conclusion that the modal model has ultimately failed to provide a coherent account of memory and its operation. It has proved impossible firmly to separate notional short- and long-term stores on the basis of different coding, retrieval, forgetting and neurology. Issues such as the control of processing, the capacity and duration of the short-term store, unsatisfactory accounts of the serial position curve and the role of rehearsal, have all undermined the modal model. However, it has served us well in identifying key issues which future theories must address, and stimulated the building of a solid empirical basis on which these developments can be founded. In the next chapter, we will encounter two very different accounts of transitory memory which arose out of the ashes of the modal model.

■ Further reading

Anderson, J. R. (1995). *Learning and memory: An integrated approach*. New York: Wiley.

Baddeley, A. D. (1990). *Human Memory: Theory and Practice*. Hove: Lawrence Erlbaum Associates.

Cohen, G. (1989). *Memory in the real world*. Hove: Lawrence Erlbaum Associates.

Parkin, A. J. (1993). *Memory: Phenomena, experiment and theory*. Oxford: Blackwell.

Searleman, A. and Herrmann, D. (1994). *Memory from a broader perspective*. New York: McGraw-Hill.

Schwartz, B. and Reisberg, D. (1991). *Learning and memory*. New York: Norton.

Discussion points

- Is sensory memory actually memory? Is it sensory?
- Is information we encode ever lost? Why?
- Discuss the strengths and weaknesses of the case for the modal model.
- How would interference theory account for effects of post-event information?

Chapter 3

Transitory memories

Chapter outline: The findings which initially supported and ultimately undermined the modal model, which were considered at length in the previous chapter, nevertheless reflect many fundamental properties of memory. In this chapter two quite different advances on the modal model will be considered. The first sought to shift the debate away from the structural properties of putative memory stores to the processes which operate at encoding and retrieval. The second sought to address the shortcomings of the modal model through a rigorous and determined grinding out of empirical results – these serve to isolate the functional properties of short-term memory which are required to allow us to engage in a wide variety of tasks.

Key topics
- Transitory memories
- Levels of processing
- Working memory
- Summary: From short-term to working memory
- Further reading

■ Transitory memories

While the type of short-term memory envisaged in the modal model is difficult to sustain, this does not undermine the case for separating, as memory theorists from James (1890) to Baddeley (1990) have done, a primary or temporary store and one in which memories reside more permanently, generally referred to as secondary or long-term memory. As we shall see below, two quite different approaches to what is usually referred to as short-term memory have emerged in response to problems with the modal model. Later in this book (Chapters 11 and 12) we will consider another, which views temporary memory not as something separate from long-term memory, but as a subset of more enduring memories which are temporarily more highly activated, that is, more available. These issues will be returned to throughout this book, but for the moment, in order to preserve a theoretically neutral stance, I will refer to the contents of what has been called primary or short-term memory as transitory memories. This deliberately avoids isolating special functional characteristics, and concentrates instead on the phenomenal aspects of what is remembered briefly in the course of performing some task and the ways in which such memories are manipulated. As such, although one should be cautious about the parallel, transitory memory shares much with attention and consciousness (see also Baddeley, 1993). Transitory memory is contrasted with more enduring memory, which will be discussed in the next chapter.

■ Levels of processing

Rehearsal

In the previous chapter we saw that advocates of the Atkinson and Shiffrin (1968) version of the modal model stressed the importance of rehearsal in the transfer of material from transitory to more enduring storage. However, studies which actually manipulated the amount of repetition items received showed that this did not necessarily lead to more enduring memories. Craik and Lockhart (1972) distinguished between *maintenance rehearsal*, in which an item might simply be repeatedly said or thought about, and *elaborative rehearsal*, where the item to be remembered is thought about from different points of view (e.g. a work colleague's phone number is remembered as 41, his age when I got to know him, 59, my year of birth; and 85, the year I came to work there). Maintenance rehearsal, Craik and Lockhart argued, would not lead to more enduring memories, but elaborative rehearsal would. There are telephone numbers I have dialled more recently, and perhaps more often, but few that I remember as clearly. The core of Craik and Lockhart's proposal was that stimuli can be processed in different ways: some ways of processing stimuli (e.g. repetition) are relatively shallow, while others are deeper (i.e. allow or require greater elaboration). They argued that the retrieval of a stimulus improves as a function of the depth to which it is processed at learning – their original proposal suggesting that depth of processing was a continuum rather than a number of discrete levels.

Self-relevance and the generation effect

Just as a technique (i.e. use of dual tasks) was particularly important to the development of Baddeley's ideas of working memory, exploration of Craik and Lockhart's 'levels of processing' framework was also greatly aided by a particular type of experiment. Typically subjects perform some analysis of stimuli (i.e. the *orienting task*) and their ability to remember these stimuli is then tested. Three studies help to illustrate important aspects of the levels of processing framework.

Rogers, Kuiper and Kirker (1977) asked subjects to make various decisions (structural appearance, acoustic properties, meaning or personal-relevance) about 40 adjectives. The results of an unexpected recall test are presented in Figure 3.1. More adjectives were recalled as the analysis required of them became more complicated, with – as is typical of such studies – orthographic processing leading to less successful recall than phonological processing, which is in turn worse than semantic processing. The fact that having to decide whether or not material is personally relevant leads to better recall has been widely demonstrated (e.g. Klein and Kihlstrom, 1986; Klein, Loftus and Burton, 1989), and has been referred to as the *self-relevance effect*. In fact, the effect extends to situations where subjects are asked to make decisions about whether particular terms apply to other people the subject knows well (see Matlin, 1989).

Fig 3.1 Word recall as a function of orienting task (after Rogers, Kuiper and Kirker, 1977).

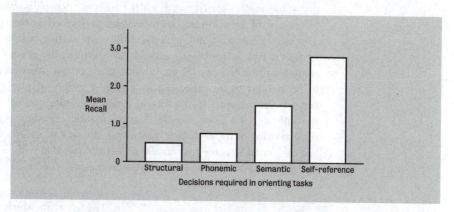

A related phenomenon is the *generation effect*, first reported by Slamecka and Graf (1978). Subjects who provide their own associations for words perform better than subjects who learn associations provided by others. For example, subjects might be asked to generate a word which rhymed with 'sow' which begins with the letter 'b' (i.e. bow). Other subjects might be asked to try to remember word pairs taken from these associated pairs (e.g. sow – bow). Both groups might then be tested by having to provide the word they learned to associate with 'sow'. Generally, subjects who generate the associate, rather than simply learn the associate, perform better. The generation effect has been demonstrated in tasks involving free recall, cued-recall and recognition. The orienting task, or rule to be followed in generating the associate, has also been extensively investigated, as has the type of material to be learned. In general, the generation effect has been successfully replicated in a wide range of circumstances, except those in which the items to be learned are meaningless, where the relationships generated by subjects have not been thought about sufficiently, or where the non-generated items undergo deep processing (e.g. Nairne, Pusen and Widner, 1985; Payne, Neely and Burns, 1986). Hirshman and Bjork (1988) have suggested that self-generation not only enhances the attention to the materials to be learned during encoding, but also leads the subject to attend to the relationship which specifically links the two items more than if the subject simply reads or hears the items to be remembered. This allows more effective retrieval routes to be formed, resulting in increased remembering.

Intentional versus incidental learning

For the most part, subjects in these studies were not expecting to have their ability to remember the materials processed in the orienting task tested, that is, the studies involved *incidental learning* rather than *intentional learning*. Various studies have addressed the issue of how important is the intention to remember. Hyde and Jenkins (1973) report a study in which subjects performed various orientation tasks, which varied in terms of the meaningfulness of the processing required of them. Half of their subjects were prewarned of an upcoming memory test, while others were not. Those expecting a test performed no better than those who were not forewarned of the upcoming test (see Fig 3.2). Similarly, Mandler (1967) has shown that subjects who sorted words on the basis of their pleasantness, but who were not prewarned of an upcoming memory test, performed as well (68 per cent) as those who were prewarned and performed the same sorting task (69 per cent). Generally, where the type of processing carried out is similar, the effect of an intention to learn is minimal (see Nelson, 1976). Intentionality, on the other hand, allows the materials to be learned to be processed in a greater variety of ways. With an explicit, but general, instruction to memorise materials, subjects will often encode them semantically (see Craik, 1977). Since semantic encoding generally yields superior remembering of more shallow processing, the lack of difference between intentional and incidental learning may simply reflect the fact that with or without the intention to learn materials for some later test, information is encoded semantically.

Fig 3.2   Per cent recall as a function of orienting task and intentions to learn (after Hyde and Jenkins, 1973).

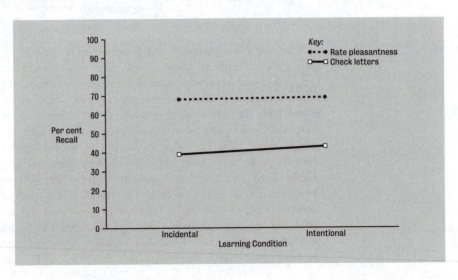

The coordinality assumption, minimal core encoding and congruence

Craik and Lockhart (1972) suggested that a limited-capacity but flexible processor was responsible for determining the processing carried out during an orienting task. Thus, if subjects are checking words for the presence of certain letters, this central processor ensured that the stimulus was processed orthographically. As part of this proposal they suggested that no processing other than that required to perform the orienting task was performed on the stimulus (i.e. the *coordinality assumption*). This proposal had the advantage that 'levels' of processing, although a continuum, were effectively insulated from one another. However, in its strictest sense it could not be true, otherwise Stroop (1935) tasks (i.e. naming the colour of ink in which colour words are written) would not show the pattern of interference they do (i.e. the word RED takes longer to read if it is written in green ink, than if it is written in red ink). This and other difficulties, such as the notion that depth of processing was a continuum, caused the theory to be revised by Craik and Tulving (1975).

Craik and Tulving (1975) abandoned the coordinality assumption, suggesting instead that every stimulus undergoes what they called *minimal core encoding*. This minimal core encoding involves structural analysis and some degree of semantic analysis. Following minimal core encoding, the stimulus was then subjected to further analysis as (consciously) determined by subject's construal of the task demands. The notion of a continuum of depth was also abandoned in favour of well-encapsulated, distinct, levels of processing. The revised account also made more explicit aspects of the earlier proposal. Specifically while depth of processing was said to determine the likely success of retrieval, within the semantic domain elaboration also contributed to memorability. Thus, determining that 'robin' is a bird requires less elaborate processing than to deciding whether 'robin' successfully completes a sentence such as 'The _____ sat on the window ledge', which in turn requires less rich encoding than determining whether you prefer robins to crows.

Elaborateness and distinctiveness and transfer appropriate processing

Elaboration also serves to account for another frequently observed phenomenon. Where the subject makes a positive decision about a stimulus encountered during an orienting task (e.g. is a yacht a ship?), that stimulus is generally better remembered than when a negative decision is made (e.g. is a robin a ship?), see Figure 3.3. This effect, known as the *congruency effect*, is usually explained in terms of retrieval cues, for example, 'ship' may help to retrieve 'yacht' from memory rather more than it helps the retrieval of 'robin'. However, it is also possible that while the proposition that a robin is a ship is easily rejected, the proposition that a robin sits on a window ledge might require more elaborate processing in order to reach positive conclusion.

Fig 3.3 Remembering as a function of decision congruity and orienting task (after Craik and Tulving, 1975).

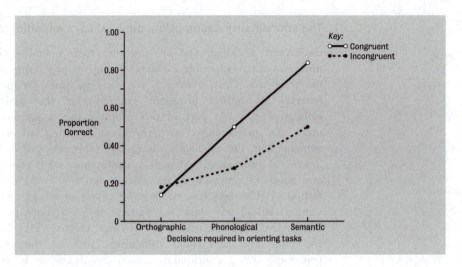

Elaborateness and *distinctiveness* (Anderson and Reder, 1979; Craik and Lockhart, 1986) have both been used to account for the remembering advantage that deeply processed items appear to have. The elaboration hypothesis suggests that deep processing leads to a more rich, complex encoding, which allows a broader range of retrieval routes, and consequently, less likelihood of retrieval failure. The distinctiveness explanation suggests that the deeper the level of processing, the more distinctive the representation of that item is in memory, which confers on it a ready advantage when it is to be retrieved. While at face value the levels of processing account has considerable appeal, the notions of minimal core encoding, elaboration, congruency and, especially whether depth is measurable independently of retrieval success, have all caused severe difficulties for the theory.

Studies of the priming obtained by detectable but not identifiable words show no evidence of semantic processing (e.g. Groeger, 1986, 1988), while elaboration, congruence and depth all have an unsatisfactory circularity to the way in which they are defined. More serious still, however, was the obvious but important point demonstrated by Morris, Bransford and Franks (1977). They showed that deep (i.e. semantic) processing does not inevitably lead to better memory. For example, subjects carrying out a rhyme judgement orienting task performed much better on a later recognition test which required them to identify words which rhymed with those they had studied, than subjects who learned the same words while carrying out a semantic orienting task. Deeper processing is only advantageous where the memory test assesses deep processing. Some tests require shallow processing. One method of measuring remembering (e.g. recognition of rhyming associates) may reveal that a particular learning strategy (e.g. rhyme judgements against some standard) has been effective while a different measure of remembering (e.g. recognition of semantic associates) may suggest that learning has not taken place. This raises important issues which are addressed in the next section, its implications for the levels of processing view of memory are serious. *Transfer-appropriate processing,* as Morris, Bransford and Franks (1977) refer to it, challenges the idea that depth is always best, and that elaborateness or distinctiveness inevitably lead to increased levels of remembering.

In summary, the levels of processing framework, and the research it stimulated, helped to highlight the operations performed during learning and the flexibility with which information could be encoded. However, while more detailed exploration has exposed its weaknesses as a theory of memory, its heuristic value and stress on the different forms of rehearsal and encoding which stimuli may receive maintains its place in the literature. In subsequent sections we consider rather more closely how what is learned may be represented, stored and manipulated in the course of task performance.

Working memory

Working memory (Baddeley, 1986, 1990, and originally Baddeley and Hitch, 1974) is essentially a range of ways of carrying out different tasks. It currently comprises three main elements: an attention and control system (i.e. the central executive) together with two slave systems, one system for dealing with acoustic information (i.e. the phonological loop) and one system for dealing with visual or spatial information (i.e. the visuo-spatial sketch pad). For reasons we will address below, the two slave systems are composed of two components, a passive store, together with an active process which allows information of a specific type to be manipulated. In the case of acoustic information, the phonological loop is broken down into an active articulatory loop and a phonological store, while the visuo-spatial sketch pad has both a visuo-spatial store and a visuo-spatial control process. The working memory framework is depicted in Figure 3.4.

Fig 3.4 The working memory model (after Baddeley, 1990).

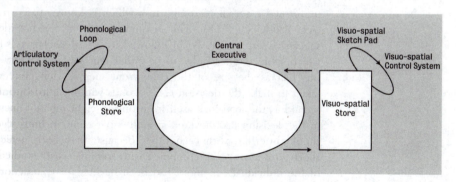

Dual-task methodology

As suggested above, the working memory model developed over the course of many years, moving from an initially simple store plus control process architecture to the complex system we have today, with changes being made only after the steady accumulation of empirical data which not only warranted a change to the system, but which also help to specify the nature of the changes which should be made. Although the undercurrent of neuropsychological evidence on which the model is based has swelled considerably in recent years, the model has also depended greatly on the use of the secondary or *dual-task methodology*. Basically, this involves getting the subject to do two things at once. The logic is that if the two tasks are similar to each other, needing access to the same information, processes or stores, then performance on one or other task, or both tasks, will suffer. Without a performance decrement, the two tasks or activities are assumed to be independent of one another. This methodology has proved invaluable in exploring a structure which is hypothetically composed of systems which may interact, or which may be separate.

Before describing each of the components in detail, let us first consider some studies which demonstrate features of the methodology, and which are rather difficult to incorporate within a unitary conception of the short-term store. Baddeley (1986) describes a study in which the free recall of lists of unrelated words was investigated, reasoning that if digit span reflects the maximum capacity of the short-term store, ability to remember the lists of unrelated words should suffer if the two tasks were combined. When the free recall task was performed without a secondary task, the familiar serial position curve was very evident. When subjects rehearsed aloud three digits, while performing the free recall task, the pattern of results was virtually identical. Even while rehearsing aloud six digits, a very strong serial position curve still emerged. In this condition, the primacy effect was slightly weaker than in the other conditions, but the recency component was unchanged. Thus, while a memory load equivalent to or above the capacity of the short-term store reduced slightly the longer term component of the serial position curve, the same load seemed to be carried without cost to the capacity of short-term memory.

A second study, also summarised in Baddeley (1986), shows that concurrently rehearsing digits to be remembered had no effect on how accurately subjects performed a verbal reasoning task which is known to correlate with intelligence (see Baddeley, 1968). The reasoning task involved the presentation of two successive letters (e.g. B, A) followed by a sentence (e.g. B is not followed by A) which subjects must judge to be either true or false. What did happen, however, was that as the size of the concurrent memory load increased so did the time taken to make the decision (2.2 seconds without a load), but only by about half a second as the load increased from one to eight digits. Throughout, the error rate in the decision task hovered around 5 per cent. In both studies, two tasks which should interfere with each other because they both notionally depend on the short-term store were combined with minimal cost. It was as if some other part of the individual's memory had been devoted to the secondary task. This led to considerable exploration of a hypothetical phonological slave system, which will be described in the next section.

The phonological loop

As mentioned above, the phonological loop is composed of two sub-systems, a phonological store which passively holds speech-based information, for one and a half to two seconds before it decays, and an articulatory control process which allows (a) sub-vocal rehearsal of the contents of the passive store, thus preventing decay, and (b) intake of written material and its conversion into a phonological code (i.e. representing it as a sound), thus registering it in the passive phonological store. The effects of the articulatory control process are normally observed through the imposition of *articulatory suppression*, that is, when the subject, in addition to performing the immediate memory task, is prevented from using articulatory mechanisms by having to repeat sounds, whether these are meaningful or meaningless (e.g. the-the-the- etc. or bla-bla-bla-bla- etc.).

Let us consider three sources of evidence for the speech-based nature of the phonological store and the role of the active rehearsal process. The first is the *phonological similarity effect*, which shows that subjects find it more difficult to remember strings such as PGTVCD than RHXKWY (Conrad and Hull, 1964; Baddeley, 1966a, 1966b). Baddeley (1990) suggests that the effect arises because such stimuli are confusable within the phonological store, leading to poorer recall. Articulatory suppression removes the phonological similarity effect when the items to be remembered are presented visually. Thus PGTVCD and RHXKWY would be equally memorable, because articulatory suppression prevents the visual code being converted into a phonological code, the subject being forced to rely on the visual properties of the consonant strings. When consonant strings are heard rather than seen, no visual to acoustic recoding is required, and thus where the elements of strings are highly confusable, articulatory suppression does not remove the phonological similarity effect. That is, subjects find it more difficult to remember strings such as PGTVCD than RHXKWY. It is presumed that this is because auditory material has direct access to the phonological store (Baddeley, Lewis and Vallar, 1984). Note that we would not expect articulatory suppression to make performance worse with auditory presentation unless the items used for suppression and the information to be remembered are phonologically similar.

A second effect, which testifies to the speech-like nature of the phonological store is the *unattended speech effect*. Originally described by Colle and Welsh (1976), but rediscovered by Salame and Baddeley (1987), the effect shows that immediate recall of visually presented words or digits is impaired if the visual presentation is accompanied by irrelevant spoken material. Salame and Baddeley (1987) showed that this disruption was caused even when subjects were told that the spoken material was irrelevant. More importantly, they also showed that a similar level of disruption occurred irrespective of whether the spoken materials were words or nonsense syllables. A subsequent study showed that 'unattended' digits, and sounds which sounded like digits, interfered to a similar extent when digits were presented visually. This was taken to indicate that phonological storage is not at the level of words, and was originally taken to suggest that phonemes, or perhaps the articulatory commands required to produce these sounds, reflected the type of storage in the phonological store. The intensity at which the sounds are presented does not appear to matter, given that they are audible but not ear-splittingly loud (Salame and Baddeley, 1987). It is worth noting that noise, given a speech-like rhythm by adding or omitting pulses, does not give rise to the unattended speech effect, but that music with voices does, as does instrumental music, irrespective of whether it was classical or modern (Salame and Baddeley, 1989).

Although the disruption is much less than occurs with speech-like materials, this raises doubts about whether the unattended speech effect really indicates speech-like encoding in the phonological store. If articulatory suppression prevents the subject from translating the visually presented items to be remembered into a phonological code, some other type of memory store must be used to support performance. Assuming that this other store is not in itself intrinsically less effective, then the unattended speech effect, which corrupts the phonological store, should not affect performance. Salame and Baddeley (1982) have shown that this is the case. However, if the items to be remembered are heard rather than seen, then the direct access to the phonological store which this affords should be disrupted under unattended speech conditions. This has also been found to be the case (Hanley and Broadbent, 1987).

The third effect of note is the *word-length effect*. Baddeley, Thomson and Buchanan (1975) show that the time taken to read words aloud and the successful immediate recall of words are closely related. A subsequent study in the same paper indicates that memory span represents the number of items that can be uttered in about two seconds. More recent research has gone on to demonstrate the importance of this effect. Naveh-Benjamin and Ayres (1986), for example, measured relations between reading time and memory span in English, Spanish, Hebrew, and Arabic. Reading rate was measured either in speeded reading of digits or in normal-pace reading of stories. Faster speeded and normal-pace reading rates for a language were associated with larger memory span for speakers of that language. Closer to home, Ellis and Hennelly (1980) show that the additional length of digits spoken in Welsh largely explains the consistently lower digit span performance of Welsh-speaking children on the Wechsler Intelligence Test. This is confirmed by recent work by Hoosain and Salili (1987) who showed that among undergraduates who spoke both English and Chinese, pronunciation speed and sound duration for numbers in Chinese are faster than those in English. Digit spans in Chinese were also larger than in English, and Hoosain and Salili also showed that there is a correlation between a subject's pronunciation speed for numbers and their digit span in that language. Similar results have recently been shown by Chincotta and Underwood (1996) with respect to Finnish and Swedish. It is worth noting, that since digit span is generally regarded as an index of the capacity of the short-term store, these results indicate that the same individual might have different short-term store capacities for each of the structurally different languages in which they are fluent. This forces us to radically reconsider what we believe the short-term span actually reflects.

Returning to the word-length effect, the evidence again appears to suggest that a speech-like encoding of items to be remembered is retrieved during recall. Baddeley, Lewis and Vallar (1984) show that when articulation is suppressed during encoding and retrieval, the word-length effect is effectively abolished. As we have seen above, the speech-like nature of the encoding is rather questionable. For example, it was mentioned above that the finding that instrumental music created a similar effect to that caused by unattended speech, suggested that storage in the phonological store was not precisely speech-like. A recent study confirms this. Bishop and Robson (1989) present evidence that some more abstract phonological or acoustic code is used, rather than one based on articulation. They compared the performance of individuals who are congenitally speechless (anarthric) or speech-impaired (dysarthric) with that of age- and sex-matched ordinary controls, who articulated during the memory tests. There was no impairment of memory span in speech-impaired subjects, all subjects showing normal phonological similarity and word-length effects in short-term memory.

Although the proposal as to the speech-like nature of encoding in the phonological store is somewhat unconvincing, the evidence for a passive, fast-fading store together with an active, rehearsal-like process which also serves to convert text to sound appears solid. Let us now turn to the other slave system envisaged by Baddeley.

Visuo-spatial sketch pad

Research on the visuo-spatial sketch pad has traditionally lagged behind that on the phonological loop, although the increased availability of multi-media platforms may well do much to redress this. Another source of reasons as to why research on the visuo-spatial sketch pad has been rather slower to get off the ground has been the traditional hesitancy psychologists have had in accepting imagery as a valid phenomenon. Over the last two decades, however, excellent research by Roger Shepard and Steve Kosslyn has done much to legitimise its study. This research has recently been very thoughtfully reviewed (see Kosslyn, 1991). Two lines of research are considered here, both of which show that visual images are manipulated, presumably in some relatively short-term visual or spatial memory.

Shepard and Metzler (1971) showed that people can accurately manipulate images of complex shapes. Subjects were shown line-drawn pictures of complex shapes, which look like contorted, three-dimensional question marks, and were asked to judge whether a subsequent picture was the same or of a different object. The shapes shown were either identical to each other, the same shape rotated by up to 180 degrees, or different shapes. The amount of rotation, or angular disparity, dramatically influenced the time subjects took to make the correct decision, with one increasing linearly as a function of the other. With each additional 60 degree difference in orientation, response time increased by one second. Shepard and Metzler interpreted these results as indicating that subjects rotate a visual representation of the target shape continuously until it lines up with the new shape; the more rotation is required, the more time it takes to do so. Kosslyn (1975) asked subjects to imagine pairs of objects in different settings (e.g. a cat next to an elephant, a flea next to an elephant). The rationale for doing so was that in some cases the cat would be imagined as larger (e.g. with flea) than in others (e.g. with elephant), and that in such cases, subjects should be able to make judgements about the cat (e.g. has ears) faster. This is exactly what was found.

More recently, Kerr (1983) has shown that subjects who are congenitally blind perform visual imagery tasks in much the same way as sighted subjects. Thus, when they manipulate an imagined shape, decision time is once again a linear function of the reorientation required, and verification time decreases with the imagined size of the object they are making decisions about. Farah (1988) reports results which support this view, but importantly shows that where subjects are sighted, they use visual and spatial properties simultaneously. Thus, it appears that for most of us both visual and spatial codes are available, although most of the time they are combined in allowing us to perform various tasks. As a result, it has been rather difficult to separate them empirically.

In spite of these issues, it now seems, on the basis of a range of research, that memory performance with visuo-spatial information depends on both a passive store which holds visuo-spatial information, and a visuo-spatial control process which can (a) rehearse the contents of the passive store, thus preventing decay; and (b) take in written material and convert it into a visuo-spatial code (i.e. represent it as an image), thus registering it in the passive visuo-spatial store. Rather more of the justification for these points is by analogy rather than through direct empirical observation than was the case with the phonological loop. This is partly because of the lack of a concurrent task which is as robust as articulatory suppression is in the case of the phonological loop. Two tasks have been most widely used, a pursuit rotor task which requires that subjects track the circular movement of a point of light and tasks developed by Brooks (1967, 1968).

BOX 3.1: Visuo-spatial memory tasks

Brooks (1967, 1968) devised a number of tasks which have been used extensively to explore the basis of transitory visuo-spatial memory. Two tasks will be described here. The first required subjects to imagine tracing their way around the angles comprising a block capital letter, and to decide whether each angle was either on the outside (signalled by a Yes response) or on the inside (signalled by a No response) of the figure. Thus, starting at the bottom right hand corner of the letter H (see Figure below) and tracing anti-clockwise, the correct responses would be 'Yes, Yes, Yes, No, No, Yes, Yes, Yes, Yes, No, No, Yes'. Brooks included conditions in which the subject spoke the answers aloud, or pointed to them on a sheet of paper which had the words Yes and No printed in random locations.

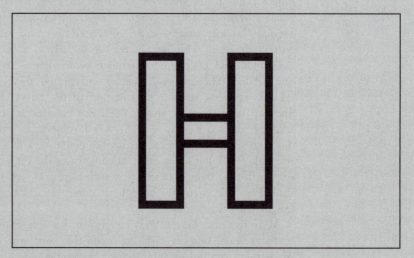

The Brooks letter tracing task

As might be expected, Brooks (1968) found that combining visual imagery and a manual response proved more difficult than imagining the letter and speaking the response, while with a comparable verbal task (deciding whether or not words in familiar phrases were nouns (e.g. 'Too many cooks spoil the broth' would be 'No, No, Yes, No, No, Yes') he showed that performance deteriorated when subjects spoke rather than pointed to their responses.

The more widely used, and much adapted, Brooks task required subjects to imagine placing numbers in the squares of a four-by-four matrix, according to instructions but always starting with the square two in from the left and two down from the top of the matrix. The following figure shows one such correctly completed matrix, together with the standard directional instructions and those for a nonsense version of the task. Having encoded the sentences using the matrix (standard version) or without the aid of the imagined matrix (nonsense version) subjects were required to recall the instruction sentences verbatim.

	1	8	
	2	7	6
	3	4	5

The Brooks matrix task

Standard version:	Nonsense version:
In the first square put a 1	In the first square put a 1
In the next square *down* put a 2	In the next square *slow* put a 2
In the next square *down* put a 3	In the next square *slow* put a 3
In the next square *right* put a 4	In the next square *bad* put a 4
In the next square *right* put a 5	In the next square *bad* put a 5
In the next square *up* put a 6	In the next square *fast* put a 6
In the next square *left* put a 7	In the next square *good* put a 7
In the next square *up* put an 8	In the next square *fast* put an 8

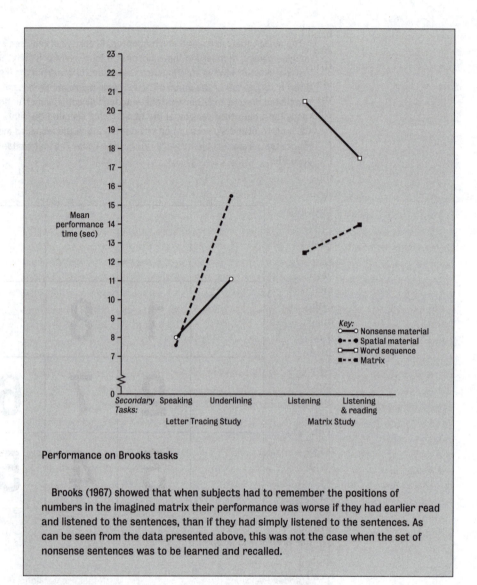

Performance on Brooks tasks

Brooks (1967) showed that when subjects had to remember the positions of numbers in the imagined matrix their performance was worse if they had earlier read and listened to the sentences, than if they had simply listened to the sentences. As can be seen from the data presented above, this was not the case when the set of nonsense sentences was to be learned and recalled.

Much other evidence to show that combining visuo-spatial tasks is difficult has recently been reviewed by Logie (1995). Baddeley, Grant, Wight and Thomson (1975) had subjects learn a list of 10 words by rote, or by using a mnemonic, which required them to associate each word with a particular location on their university campus. As we will see in later sections of this book, better recall is to be expected from those who use more elaborate encoding and retrieval strategies. Subjects were tested while carrying out a pursuit rotor tracking task, or without any secondary task. It would be expected that subjects learning the words by rote would make use of the phonological loop, and thus requiring the performance of a concurrent visual-spatial task during retrieval should not affect performance. Subjects who learn the words using the imagery-based mnemonic, on the other hand, will necessarily engage in some visuo-spatial processing during encoding and retrieval. This ought to be disrupted by requiring subjects to also perform a visual tracking task during retrieval. This is precisely the pattern that was observed. Those who learned the words by rote were unaffected by retrieving the words while performing a spatially demanding task, but the performance of those who used the imagery strategy was much reduced when also using the pursuit rotor.

In the same paper, Baddeley and colleagues report a study in which memory for concrete (and thus highly imageable) words is better than for abstract (and thus non-imageable) words. However, while memory for both types of words is significantly reduced when performing a tracking task while learning the paired associates, no interaction is evident between word-imagability and retrieval conditions. These results require closer examination. Imageable words are intrinsically more memorable, even for people who cannot use their visual properties. Thus, for example, Zimler and Keenan (1983) compared the abilities of sighted and congenitally blind subjects to remember paired-associates, which included words whose referents were high in either visual or auditory imagery. Congenitally blind subjects, like sighted subjects, recalled more high-visual-imagery pairs than any others. The second experiment Zimler and Keenan report used a free-recall task for words grouped according to modality-specific attributes, such as colour and sound. Blind subjects performed as well as sighted subjects on words grouped by colour. In fact, the only consistent deficit in both experiments occurred for sighted subjects in recall of words whose referents are primarily auditory. It is possible therefore that in the study reported by Baddeley, Grant, Wight and Thomson (1975) subjects remembered the paired associates without using a visuo-spatial route. If that were the case, then the decrement in recall produced by the tracking task in both conditions may simply reflect a simple effect of having subjects learn words and track a target simultaneously. A second issue is whether it is important to ensure that the concurrent spatial tracking task is carried out at both encoding and retrieval or simply at retrieval alone. A similar problem emerged in earlier studies in relation to the effects of articulatory suppression on the word-length effect. This is in contrast to earlier studies which showed that, for auditory stimuli, the word-length effect is not abolished with articulatory suppression when it occurs at presentation but not at recall (e.g. Baddeley, Thomson and Buchanan, 1975).

Taken together, studies by Baddeley and Lieberman (1980) and Baddeley, Grant, Wight and Thomson appear to show that the visuo-spatial sketch pad is primarily spatial, rather than visual. As we have seen in our discussion of the phonological loop, conflicting views over the nature of the encoding employed in passive stores is not new. Rereading the studies in preparation for writing this book, I am struck by the ingenuity, but also the Heath-Robinson character of the earlier studies, especially when compared with more recent methodologies, which incidentally redress some of the visual rather than spatial imbalance.

Bob Logie (1986) reported a series of four studies which involve an unattended pictures effect, which is analogous to the unattended speech effect described above. Subjects learned lists of auditorially presented concrete words using an imagery strategy or by rote, with irrelevant speech or irrelevant line drawings being presented at the same time. Logie found that irrelevant speech

Fig 3.5 Effects of presenting irrelevant pictures or irrelevant speech when learning words using rote rehearsal or imagery (after Logie, 1986).

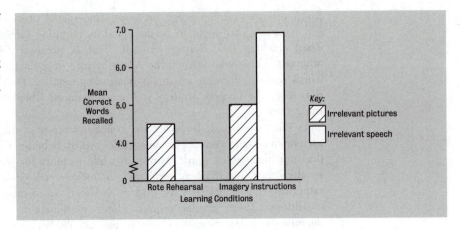

had no effect on retrieval when words were learned using the imagery strategy, but irrelevant pictures reduced the number of concrete words very substantially. In contrast, irrelevant speech and irrelevant pictures had very similar effects when the words were learned using the rote rehearsal strategy (Fig 3.5). Note that since the words to be learned were heard rather than seen on presentation, irrelevant speech would not have been expected to impair performance. Similar effects emerged from studies in which colour patches, rather than line drawings, were used, and from studies using continuously changing dot patterns as the irrelevant stimuli (see Quinn and McConnell, 1994; Logie, 1995).

More recently Smyth and Scholey (1994) have investigated whether the time taken to move between targets in an array is related to what they term 'spatial rehearsal', thus attempting to examine whether *movement-time effect* might provide a visuo-spatial counterpart to the word-length effect. Subjects were shown a random arrangement of squares on a touch-sensitive computer screen. Each square changed from white to black in order to signal the order in which positions should be remembered. Spatial memory span was assessed by changing the number of squares displayed and then by having subjects touch those squares which had changed colour in the order in which they did so. By changing the size of the squares displayed it was possible to disaggregate movement time from spatial memory span. Unfortunately, despite the ingenuity of this procedure, the results seem equivocal, in that at least for nine-square displays, the time taken to move between targets does not relate to level of performance on immediate or delayed recall contrast performance, although the movement-time effect does emerge with larger displays. Nevertheless, the work of Smyth and her colleagues is very important since it attempts to link the visuo-spatial sketch pad more directly with the control of human movement.

Thus, although less well developed than research on the phonological loop and given the intrinsically different properties of the visual and auditory systems, research on the visuo-spatial sketch pad has provided evidence for the involvement both of a passive visuo-spatial store, and an active, imagery-based rehearsal process.

Central executive

The difficulties in researching the slave systems are increased still further when attempting to study the final component of the system, the central executive. This has lead Baddeley (1986, 1990) to admit that it is the least well documented aspect of the system. Nevertheless, a body of evidence suggests that the central executive is involved in combining information from the slave systems and scheduling their operating, extracting information from longer term memories, selection and implementation of strategies, attention, planning, decision making, and even consciousness. Because of this variety of roles played by the central executive, most of the demonstrations of its operations relate to rather complex, often non-laboratory-based tasks.

Thus, for example, a former colleague of mine carried out a study of drivers' decisions to accept, and ability to drive through, various gaps presented to them. Brown, Tickner and Simmonds (1969) showed that while performing Baddeley's (1968) verbal reasoning task (i.e. two letters presented, BA, and subjects have to decide whether the sentence 'A is not preceded by B' is correct), subjects were well able to drive through gaps before them, but the concurrent reasoning task did affect their judgements of which gaps were too wide or too narrow to drive through. Note the selective nature of this interference; occupying the central executive with a reasoning task does not necessarily affect each aspect of a very well practised routine behaviour. It is often in relation to the timing and initiation of activity that its effects are most frequently observed. Duncan, Williams and Brown (1991), again studying the actual driving behaviour of subjects, showed that even with this highly practised activity, interference from a secondary task (i.e. random generation – having to generate, at say one per second, sequences of letters or digits which have no linking pattern) was restricted to decision-making components (e.g. gap accepted when overtaking) but did not influence more routine elements (e.g. time taken to change gear). We will have rather more to say about these data in Chapter 12 on skilled behaviour, but for the moment the point to be made is that tasks which involve reasoning or interference with, or guarding against the use of, well-practised sequences of activity, cause considerable difficulties with the performance of other complex activities.

As reviewed above, a number of studies, carried out under laboratory conditions, have shown that memory loads alone (e.g. having to remember increasing numbers of digits) do not influence central executive performance (e.g. performing a verbal reasoning task; see Baddeley, 1986). This shows that memory capacity and reasoning ability are relatively independent. A fascinating demonstration of this, and the different contribution of the slave systems and the central executive comes from a study cited in Baddeley (1990, p. 134), carried out in conjunction with Bradley, Hudson and Robbins. As has been shown in a number of different domains (e.g. go, chess and bridge), expert players can recall much more from brief glimpses of card or board positions than non-experts. This difference reduces markedly if the cards or positions are random or otherwise not legitimate (see Ericsson and Kintsch, 1995; Chapters 11 and 12 this volume). What Baddeley and colleagues did was to show positions taken from actual expert chess games, and ask subjects with different levels of skill in chess to reproduce these. They used a rather neat measure of performance, namely the net number of positions correct (that is, the number of correctly placed pieces minus the number of pieces placed in the wrong locations). Subjects were tested under a number of different conditions: when not performing a secondary task (control), under articulatory suppression, visuo-spatial interference (by having subjects press a preordained sequence of keys on a hidden calculator), or central executive interference (through random generation). Three effects are worthy of particular note: (a) weak players performed less well than strong players, irrespective of the secondary task used during retrieval, (b) central executive interference made performance worse than visuo-spatial interference, but both were associated with worse performance than in the other two conditions; and (c) interference with visuo-spatial processing and interference with central executive processing appears to reduce the difference between stronger and weaker players (see Fig 3.6).

Further examples of the role of the central executive come from patients, particularly those who have sustained damage to their frontal lobes. Shallice (1982) argues that frontal lobes are involved in retrieving and combining action plans, as well as in organising and controlling action. Patients of this type experience difficulties associated with a breakdown in what he (and Don Norman) had earlier described as the supervisory attentional system (SAS; see Norman and Shallice, 1980, 1986). The SAS is in turn often equated with the central executive. Lhermitte (1983) describes a patient with 'utilisation behaviour', who seemed to be able to retrieve easily the use particular to a whole range of objects, but who found it very difficult actually to perform these actions.

Fig 3.6 Effects of secondary tasks on strong and weak chess players: Articulatory suppression, and visuo-spatial and central executive interference and chess (after Baddeley, 1990).

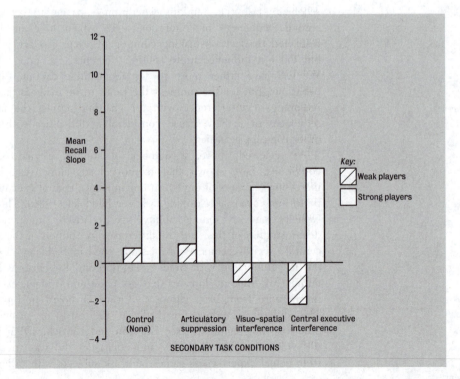

In what might seem a contradictory finding, frontal patients have difficulty in switching from one rule to another (thus exhibiting extensive *perseveration*), and also with tasks requiring *fluency* (e.g. name as many football teams as quickly as possible without repeating any). Where errors are not made, frontal patients, albeit correctly, are typically painfully slow at performing the task. Baddeley and Wilson (1986) describe a patient who found it very difficult to generate exemplars of a particular category (e.g. animals), but who when given multiple retrieval cues (e.g. animal beginning with the letter C), was able to retrieve the correct category member. Baddeley interprets this as showing that, since there is no well-learned rule for performing fluency tasks, the person must build and run a retrieval strategy to do so, whilst also monitoring the candidates generated for errors. He supports this view by citing other evidence which shows that category generation is among the few retrieval tasks which are substantially interfered with by attention-demanding secondary tasks (Baddeley, Lewis, Eldridge and Thomson, 1984). Parkin (1993) reports a patient (C.B.) with what has become known as dysexecutive syndrome, who not only experiences considerable difficulty in recall tasks, but also recognition tasks in which some more strategic (in this case context-based) rather than familiarity-based retrieval is required (see also Chapters 6 and 7, and especially Chapter 14 this volume).

■ Summary: From short-term to working memory

The working memory framework grew, in part, from the problems the modal model had in accounting for the serial position curve, different duration and capacity estimates for short-term memory, a dependence on phonological coding, and patients with patterns of deficits which ran counter to what would be expected from the modal model. To a greater or lesser extent, each of these difficulties are solved or circumvented by the working memory framework. These solutions partly depend on its inherent complexity. The different estimates of capacity and duration, which appeared to conflict, are seen as reflecting the capacities and durations of different aspects of working memory, and especially of different components of the systems operating in concert. Serial position effects arise in part as an interaction between the sequential encoding facilitated by the phonological loop, but also as the result of more general retrieval strategies controlled by the central executive. Coding differences are easily supported by the range of components within working memory. Also it not only serves better to describe the range of difficulties which patients like H.M. and K.F. (the amnesic patients described in Chapter 2) experienced, but also a wide range of other combinations of deficit.

Thus, for example, amnesic patients with hippocampal formation damage were shown, in extensive tests of their transitory memory abilities, to have normal short-term memory functioning despite having severely impaired long-term memory abilities (Cave and Squire, 1992). This supports the conclusions suggested above that transitory acquisition and retrieval is independent of the formation and retrieval of more enduring memories. However, this relationship is not transitive. Evidence from K.F. was originally thought to show that because he was capable of longer term learning, in spite of the fact that his digit span was severely limited, longer term learning must be possible without access to short-term memory. Because of the reconceptualisation of short-term memory in terms of multiple stores, such as in Baddeley's working memory framework, there is no need for impaired digit span to lead to a complete absence of long-term learning. This was neatly demonstrated by work with a patient (P.V.) who had suffered a cardiovascular accident involving the left perisylvian region (Baddeley, Papagno and Vallar, 1988). Just like K.F., this patient had a very poor digit span (2 items), but it was also clear that she was quite capable of longer term learning. However, when tests were devised which required her to use phonological coding of the material, rather than some other route, this capacity for long-term learning disappeared.

Approaching this issue from a different point of view, Gathercole and Baddeley (1990) investigated the language learning of children, aged between four and six years, who differed in the speed with which they could repeat single non-words. They found that children with slower repetition rates had more difficulty in learning and retaining arbitrary, unfamiliar names for toys. Clearly, if we assume that learning such new names for important objects in their environment is equivalent to vocabulary acquisition, then non-word repetition rate demonstrates the role of the articulatory loop in language learning. This is confirmed by work with adults whose task was to learn Russian vocabulary. This showed that while articulatory suppression did not impair paired associate learning in the subject's native language, it did impair learning of the new Russian terms.

Taken together, these studies show that actual or simulated damage to the individual's short-term phonological memory substantially reduces the person's ability to form more enduring phonologically-based memories. What, at present, we do not know to the same extent is whether actual or simulated damage to transitory visuo-spatial storage similarly affects long-term learning and retention of visuo-spatial information (but see Logie, 1995). However, at least with respect to sound-based memories, it would seem clear that the formation and retrieval of more enduring memories requires intact transitory capacities.

Not only is working memory supported by a coherent methodological approach, but it has also been extensively applied to the performance of a wide range of everyday tasks. We have considered some of these above, such as driving and chess playing, as well as a range of visual, spatial and verbal tasks. In recent years however, people have employed the working memory framework to investigate the acquisition and development of mathematical skills, comprehension, reading, vocabulary and second language skills. Gathercole and Baddeley (1993) and Hulme and MacKenzie (1992) provide excellent accounts of these more specialist applications.

In addition to the difficulties in resolving issues with respect to the actual nature of the encoding operating in the two slave systems, the main difficulties with regard to the working memory framework lie in the under specification of the central executive. Given the range of operations of different types in which the central executive is involved, it seems very unlikely that it will prove to be a single unitary structure. Phil Barnard, a former colleague of Alan Baddeley's at the Applied Psychology Unit, has already gone some way towards unpacking the operations involved (see Teasdale and Barnard, 1993), within his interacting cognitive sub-systems. At this stage, however, given the empirical grinding out of new components which is typical of how research on working memory proceeds, we are left with a central executive which serves to organise and control action, is engaged in the retrieval of categories, procedures, and so on from longer term memory, and allows the slave systems to communicate with each other, whilst also acting as a general decision, planning and scheduling mechanism. These issues will be addressed again throughout this book.

Further reading

Baddeley, A. D. (1986). *Working memory*. Oxford: Oxford University Press.

Baddeley, A. D. (1990). *Human memory: Theory and practice*. Hove, U.K: Lawrence Erlbaum Associates Ltd.

Kosslyn, S. M. (1994). *Image and brain: The resolution of the imagery debate*. Cambridge, MA: MIT Press.

Logie, R. H. (1995). *Visuo-spatial working memory*. Hove, U.K: Lawrence Erlbaum Associates Ltd.

Parkin, A. J. (1993). *Memory: Phenomena, experiment and theory*. Oxford: Blackwell.

Schwartz, B. and Reisberg, D. (1991). *Learning and memory*. New York: Norton.

Discussion points

- Levels of processing is a good idea but a bad theory. Discuss.
- Which everyday tasks might we have difficulty in combining? Why?
- Does working memory solve the problems with the modal model?
- Is transitory memory any more than attention?

Chapter 4

Enduring memories

Chapter outline: The conception of short-term memory offered by the modal model is unable to deal with the range of empirical findings which Baddeley's working memory copes with comfortably. Although working memory helps us to understand how information may occasionally survive the ravages of ongoing activity, Baddeley's framework really offers very little insight into why events long since completed are often successfully remembered. Craik and Lockhart's levels-of-processing framework, on the other hand, demonstrates that the overlap between the way in which information is encoded and the way in which retrieval of that information is assessed is crucial to successful remembering. The elaborateness and distinctiveness of encoding influence the amount of overlap required between encoded and retrieval cues, and thus both the success and durability of remembering. The concepts of elaborateness and distinctiveness imply the existence of a well-structured coherent body of enduring experiences. This chapter will consider theories which have sought to describe both the structure and content of this enduring body of experience, traditionally referred to as long-term memory. Before doing this we need to look again at issues raised in the first chapter of this book concerning the need to be clear about how different ways of assessing remembering relate to putatively different types of memory.

Key topics
- Indices of remembering
- Types of memory
- Organisation and structure
- Schemata and scripts
- Headed records
- Summary: Enduring memories
- Further reading

■ Indices of remembering

Transfer-appropriate processing, which operationalises the need for overlap between learning and tests of that learning, not only serves to qualify the levels-of-processing view, but it also makes a more fundamental point about how learning and memory should be measured. One way of stating this is that the relationship between task requirements operating during learning, and the task requirements operating during the assessment of that learning, needs to be carefully considered when we evaluate performance. At face value this makes the same sort of point that psychometricians refer to as validity, that is, we must be sure that what we are measuring is actually what we want to know about, and not just some loosely associated surrogate of it. If we wish to measure what phonological information people can retrieve from an earlier learning episode, whatever the learning strategy used, then we need to use indices that reflect phonological awareness (e.g. rhyme judgements). Merely using a semantic recognition task, cued-recall, or even an open-ended recall procedure may show no evidence of phonological learning, even though we know that the learning strategy used is sufficient for learning to have taken place. We must be careful not to assume that learning has not taken place at all. Only when we know what a particular index of remembering assesses, and use it appropriately, can we conclude that certain types of information or details about a stimulus have not been retrieved.

Direct and indirect measures of remembering

Richardson-Klavehn and Bjork (1988) contrasted what they term *direct measures* and *indirect measures* of memory. *Direct measures* are defined as 'those tasks in which the instructions at the time of the memory test make reference to a target event (or target events) in the personal history of the subject' (e.g. by mentioning the spatiotemporal context – time of day, date, environment – in which the event occurred). The subject is deemed successful in such tasks when she/he gives behavioural evidence of knowledge concerning that event' (Richardson-Klavehn and Bjork, 1988, p. 477). *Indirect measures* are defined as those tasks 'requiring the subject to engage in some motor or cognitive activity, when the instructions refer only to the task at hand, and do not make reference to prior events. The measures of interest reflect a change (typically a facilitation) in task performance observed by comparing performance with relevant prior experience to performance without such experience (a control condition)' (Richardson-Klavehn and Bjork, 1988, p. 478). Thus a direct measure of remembering might require subjects to decide which of two words they have just read, while an indirect test might assess remembering by comparing how much more quickly subjects can decide that a stimulus they have seen before is a word than a stimulus they have not seen before. Note that the latter may show facilitation because of *repetition priming* (i.e. determining that 'nurse' is a word is easier if the subject has just read the word 'nurse', see Cofer, 1967), *associative or semantic priming* (i.e. determining that 'nurse' is a word is easier if the subject has just read the word 'doctor', see Meyer and Schvaneveldt, 1971), *graphemic priming* (e.g. 'blow' preceded by 'blot', see Groeger, 1986) or *phonological/morphological priming* (e.g. 'blow' preceded by 'dough', see Groeger, 1988). Some indirect measures of memory are more familiar in an everyday context. Evaluative judgements, skilled performance and conceptual, factual or perceptual knowledge may all be used to assess learning without requiring the subject to retrieve a specific instance, or without reference to the circumstances in which the information or knowledge was originally acquired.

Implicit and explicit memory

Richardson-Klavehn and Bjork (1988) contrast direct and indirect ways of measuring memory with different types of memory experience, or what has become known as the distinction between *implicit memory* and *explicit memory*. According to Schacter, 'implicit memory is revealed on tasks that do not require reference to a specific episode' (Schacter, 1985, p. 353) or 'when performance on a task is facilitated in the absence of conscious recollection' (Graf and Schacter, 1985, p. 501). Explicit memory, on the other hand, requires conscious recollection of prior experiences (Graf and Schacter, 1985) and even 'awareness of the learning episode' (Roediger and Blaxton, 1987, p. 351). The distinction is therefore based, in part, on the phenomenal experience of the rememberer. By definition, retrieval of information from implicit memory cannot be under conscious control. On the other hand, as discussed in the first chapter, researchers since Ebbinghaus (1885, 1964) have pointed out that explicit remembering may occur voluntarily (i.e. trying to remember) or spontaneously (i.e. being reminded of something, or having intrusive thoughts as the result of, for example, *post-traumatic stress disorder*). Spontaneous remembering does not appear to require obvious linkages between the current situation and the information retrieved, thus providing a limiting case for the need for figural overlap between encoding and retrieval as envisaged by Craik and Lockhart.

BOX 4.1: Direct and indirect measures of remembering

In recent years, there have been many demonstrations of a dissociation between implicit and explicit memory. Verfaellie, Bauer and Bowers (1991) investigated the list learning ability of an amnesic patient T.R., and that of normal control subjects. Thirty minutes after learning, all subjects were given a recognition test for previously learned items. During this test the subjects' accuracy and *electrodermal activity* (a generic term including the measure formerly known as *galvanic skin response*, i.e. an increase in skin conductance caused, for example, by increased sweating because of stress) were measured. Obviously, recognition accuracy served as a direct measure of remembering (i.e. identifying those items learned previously) while Verfaellie and colleagues proposed that a difference in electrodermal activity for 'old' and 'new' items might also reveal recognition of original items. As might be expected of an amnesic, T.R. performed substantially worse in the overt recognition task than normal controls. Thus, on an direct measure of explicit memory, there was little evidence of learning. On the other hand, the electrodermal activity of normal subjects and T.R. showed a large discrepancy for 'old' and 'new' items. Thus, still employing a direct measure methodology, but by augmenting this with an indirect index of performance, it was clear that at some level which was not sufficient to sustain conscious recognition of the items, old and new items were discriminated. However, this result may be accounted for by positing separable memory systems (e.g. explicit and implicit memory) or by suggesting that the results merely reflect the operation of a single system in which non-recognised targets were simply less highly active or less discriminable than overtly recognised targets. This would suggest that the electrodermal activity brought about by 'hits' and 'misses' should differ. Since the recognition accuracy of normal subjects was very high, Verfaellie and colleagues addressed this issue by examining T.R.'s data. This revealed no correlation between overt recognition accuracy and the level of electrodermal activity, thus supporting the idea of separable explicit and implicit systems. Importantly, the study also serves to demonstrate that implicit memory can potentially influence explicit memory performance.

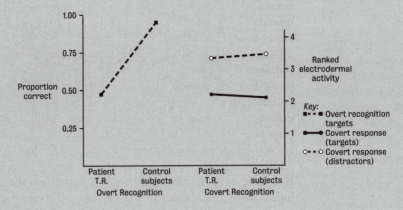

Overt and covert recognition of previously seen items by an amnesic patient T. R. (after Verfaillie, Bauer and Bowers, 1991)

Earlier, Tulving, Schacter and Stark (1982) contrasted word learning performance using a direct measure of memory (i.e. an old–new recognition test of words) and an indirect measure called *fragment completion* (i.e. where the subject is presented with an incomplete picture or word, and is asked to complete it, with no reference to any previous learning episode). After an hour, Tulving and colleagues found that about half of the completions generated were words encountered in the earlier learning phase. Recognition performance was at a slightly higher level. These results are easily accounted for in terms of repetition priming. After one week, however, while the level of fragment completions using target words declined very little, recognition performance declined markedly. Tulving and colleagues considered that these results reflected the operation of separable memory systems by showing that the probability of correct fragment completion was no greater for correctly recognised targets than for those which were not correctly recognised. Furthermore, the longevity of explicit and implicit memory appear markedly different. For example, Sloman, Hayman, Ohta, Law and Tulving (1988) have shown that repetition priming effects can be observed up to some 16 months later, while Tulving, Hayman and MacDonald (1991) have shown evidence of repetition priming in amnesic patients some 12 months after the original learning episode. (As we will see in Chapter 11, such priming may depend considerably on the extent to which the same actions are required for responding; see also Fendrich, Gesi, Healy and Bourne, 1995.)

There are many other demonstrations that learning can process in the absence of a capacity to report upon it or interrogate this learning. In an important series of studies, Berry and Broadbent (1984) investigated subjects' ability to perform complex control tasks (e.g. output of a PC-based sugar production factory, or passenger-bus allocation). While subjects performed as if they had learned the contingencies between numbers of workers and sugar production or passengers and allocation of buses to different routes, they were quite unable to give any insight into the principles which governed their performance. They interpreted these results as evidence for implicit learning of the operating principles of each system, although there are many difficulties with the measures used of the subjects' awareness of the contingencies operation. It may not be reasonable, for example, to expect subjects to verbalise this sort of knowledge. The same difficulties do not apply to other studies of quite complex learning. Nissen and Bullemer (1987) and later Howard and Howard (1992) had subjects learn to press the computed keys directly under one of four screen positions in which an asterisk appeared. The order in which the asterisk appeared in a position was not random but followed a complex pattern which repeated after 12 or 16 presentations. The speed with which subjects responded showed a clear increase after substantial practice (see Fig 4.1). From these results we do not know whether subjects are or are not aware that they are learning the sequence. However, when the task was subtly changed (i.e. subjects had to press the key under the position in which the asterisk will appear next), it was clear that when required explicitly to use the sequence learning which the previous condition had clearly shown had taken place, performance was more or less at chance.

Fig 4.1 Median response time to random and sequential trials (after Howard and Howard, 1992).

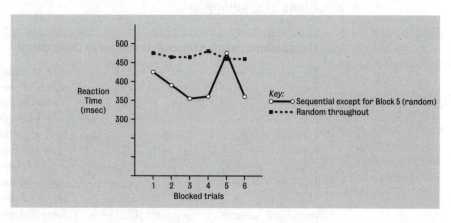

These and other studies led to an intense interest in trying to identify the properties of these memory tasks and memory systems (see Richardson-Klavehn and Bjork, 1988; Hintzman, 1990; Schacter, Chiu and Ochsner, 1993). An excellent overview of the neurological evidence for such distinctions has also been provided. Summarising the current state of the evidence, Squire, Knowlton and Musen (1993) suggest that 'The major distinction is between conscious memory for facts and events and various forms of non-conscious memory, including skill and habit learning, simple classical conditioning, the phenomenon of priming and other instances where memory is expressed through performance rather than by recollection' (1993, p. 457). Squire and colleagues point out that even though a range of different terms have been used to reflect this distinction, the separation is essentially between memory which is dependent upon the integrity of the *hippocampus* and anatomically related structures in the diencephalon and the medial temporal lobe (see Zola-Morgan and Squire, 1993), and memory abilities which depend on dissociable systems other than the diencephalon and the medial temporal lobe. Studies of both amnesic patients, whose ability as measured by conventional indices of memory functioning is weak, but whose ability to perform a wide variety of other tasks is normal, and Alzheimer, Parkinsonian and Huntingdon patients, attest to this sort of distinction (e.g. see Heindel, Salmon and Butters, 1991 for distinctions between Alzheimer, Parkinsonian and Huntingdon patients; and also Chapter 14).

There are parallels between the effects of intentionality on learning and on remembering. Just as learning is possible with or without the intention to do so, remembering is also possible with or without the intention to do so. Just as intention does confer an advantage on learning, since it allows encoding to come under strategic control, intention can also facilitate remembering through the use of retrieval plans and strategies, or the interrogation of the memory record for particular information (see Williams and Hollan, 1981). However, while incidental learning may not ordinarily allow certain types of detailed information to be ·encoded, unintentional retrieval (whether from implicit memory or involuntary explicit memory) is almost, by definition, limited in flexibility.

Types of memory

The episodic, semantic and procedural distinction

The previous section sought to portray one way of thinking about differences in memory systems. This depended on the requirements of various tasks in terms of access to a particular learning episode, and on a subjective or phenomenal feeling that one is remembering something from one's past, rather than somehow knowing it otherwise. Another type of distinction that has become popular is between what philosophers such as Gilbert Ryle (1949) would have referred to as *declarative knowledge* (i.e. factual knowledge about something) and *procedural knowledge* (i.e. knowledge which supports performance of various tasks). Following Tulving (e.g. 1972, 1983, 1989) distinctions are now made between enduring memories which are episodic (i.e. what Tulving originally described as an individual's autobiographical record of past experience), semantic (i.e. our knowledge of language, facts, concepts, etc.) and procedural knowledge (i.e. that which supports skilled performance). Tulving's notion of an autobiographical past was originally intended to identify those memories which arise out of the individual's involvement with particular knowledge, and relates directly to being able to access the experience one has of acquiring the information. The distinction between conceptual or factual knowledge and procedural knowledge will be considered in greater detail below, and especially in Chapters 10, 12 and 14. For the moment however, let us consider the distinction between episodic and semantic information, and episodic and procedural knowledge.

As we will also see in later chapters, memories of our own personal past which are regarded as self-defining are worth distinguishing from episodic memories, such as knowing that a few minutes ago I made myself a cup of expresso coffee. Nevertheless, as is clear from our earlier discussion of implicit and explicit memory, what unifies both forms of episodic memories is that they give rise to a particular state of phenomenal awareness which reflects explicit memory – what most of us would agree is the state of remembering something. While retrieval from semantic or procedural memory may demonstrate that something has been learned, the circumstances in which it was learned may no longer be available for retrieval. Thus, making my expresso using my new coffee maker, without the aid of instruction booklets or any awareness of using rules or procedures, reflects retrieval from procedural memory. The knowledge that the coffee is made by Lavazza from Arabica beans reflects retrieval from semantic memory. I can recall, vaguely, looking at the coffee pack, and times when I read the leaflet accompanying the coffee maker, but 'remembering' these episodic memories seems quite independent of the act of making the coffee or of knowing that the coffee is pure Arabica.

Memory awareness: Knowing and remembering

Tulving (1985, 1989) discusses a distinction between 'remembering' and 'knowing', or as he terms them *autonoetic* and *noetic* awareness. Gardiner (1988) reports a number of very neat studies which show how this distinction can be demonstrated empirically. Two of these studies are particularly worthy of note.

Fig 4.2 The know–remember distinction as a function of associative or phonological encoding (after Gardiner, 1988).

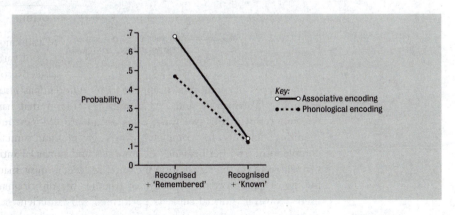

In the first study, Gardiner manipulated the processing which was carried out on words during a learning episode (Fig 4.2). Following Craik and Tulving

(1975), Gardiner had subjects pay attention to the meaning of words presented to them, by requiring them to make associative judgements, or to their phonology, by making rhyme judgements. Subjects later performed a standard old–new recognition task, but were then required to judge whether they *remember* that the 'old' word occurred on the list, that is, consciously recollect reading it, or simply *know* that the 'old' word was on the list, but cannot consciously recollect actually reading it. As would be predicted from a levels-of-processing framework, words associatively encoded were better recognised than those phonologically encoded. However, the more important result is that although many fewer correct recognitions were based on knowing, rather than remembering, the orienting task manipulation was effective only for remembered judgements (see Fig 4.2).

The second study uses results reported by Slamecka and Graf (1978), who showed that subjects remember items they generate better than those which are simply listened to or read (i.e. the *generation effect*). Gardiner replicated this effect, but showed once again that recognised and remembered judgements of old items were more likely than recognised and known. However, the generate–read manipulation only had a significant effect with recognised and remembered judgements. Importantly, when tested one week later, the generation advantage enjoyed by remembered items faded over the course of week (Fig 4.3). Neither the generate–read manipulation nor the interval affected the percentage of words correctly recognised but not consciously remembered.

Fig 4.3 The know–remember distinction as a function of retention interval and encoding instructions (after Gardiner, 1988).

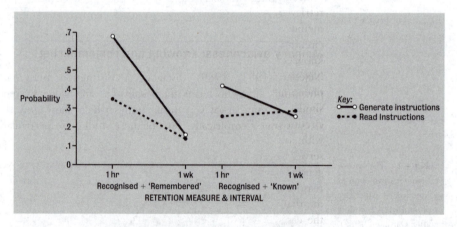

Such types of memory also appear to be differentially affected by amnesia. For example, Warrington and Weiskrantz (1974) tested memory for recently encountered words in two ways, using a standard old–new recognition task and by requiring subjects to complete words given their initial letters (i.e. stem-completion). The performance of amnesics and normal controls was, as expected, very different on the recognition measure. Indeed, amnesics showed similar memory for the original words irrespective of whether the direct or indirect test had been used. However, normal subjects performed substantially better on the direct than on the indirect measure. What is important, however, is that memory performance was the same for normal subjects and amnesics on the indirect test. That is, it would seem that something like implicit memory is intact in amnesic patients.

Problems of *source amnesia* also attest to the distinction between episodic memories and those lacking information regarding the learning episode. This is typically assessed by encouraging subjects to learn new facts in a particular setting, and later testing this by requesting the factual information together with some circumstances which identify when, where, and so on it might have been learned. Even when steps are taken to equate the performance of semantic memory (i.e. level of factual recall) by, for example, amnesic and normal subjects, substantial differences still emerge in what might be regarded as episodic memory. Schacter, Harbluk and McLachlan (1984) and Shimamura and Squire (1987), for example, show that amnesics show less source awareness than normal subjects, while McDaniel (1984) and McAndrews, Glisky and Schacter (1987) show similar results for older but not for younger subjects.

There is also good evidence that procedural knowledge can be both acquired and retrieved despite a relative absence of episodic memory. The patient H.M., although having no conscious recollection of any of the learning episodes which lasted over several weeks, or even of having performed the tasks before, showed good evidence of procedural learning on tasks such as the pursuit rotor and mirror drawing task (see Parkin, 1993). Parkin (1993) and Parkin and Leng (1993) report a number of case studies which show that in spite of dense amnesia, residual capacity for procedural learning and retrieval of previously learned procedures are preserved even where the patients' episodic memory performance is minimal.

Studies show that semantic and procedural knowledge can both be acquired and retrieved with no more than a minimal episodic capacity. However, where episodic memory is intact there is abundant evidence that awareness of learning and its circumstances are precursors to performance that relies on semantic or procedural knowledge. Neisser (1981) for example, in describing the memory of John Dean, a Nixon aide during the Watergate scandal (see Chapter 10), identified a phenomenon which he termed *re-episodic blurring*. This occurs where separate, but similar, episodes which are repeatedly encountered are merged. Under such circumstances, the details of single episodes may become detached and associated with, or replace, details from another similar episode. This re-episodic blurring serves to allow information from different episodes to be combined into a single generic memory, a sort of summary case which serves to identify what might reasonably be expected in such circumstances in the future. It seems plausible to me that this process might underlie the formation of both semantic knowledge, in the case of concepts and facts, and procedural knowledge, in the cases of actions and procedures (see Schwartz and Reisberg, 1991). In the next sections, we consider the sorts of structures which are thought to underlie knowledge which endures in memory for long periods of time, if not permanently.

■ Organisation and structure

Category membership

Imagine for a moment that you can see a cat. It may have long hair or be smooth, may have a tail or not, be any one of a range of colours, may be silent or purring, be a playful kitten or a streetwise tom. There seems no difficulty in deciding that it is a cat, and the variety of ways in which cats vary cause us little surprise, except perhaps in the more extreme cases. We seem to understand what cats are, some would say that we have a concept of what cats are, just as we have for dogs, books, cars, activities and so forth. However, as Wittgenstein (1953) pointed out, the characteristics of members of what we call a category are probably shared by some but not all members of that category. Defining what might be the necessary attributes (i.e. shared by all category members) and sufficient attributes (i.e. only possessed by category members) has proved impossible, and an empirically irresolvable issue (see Smith and Medin, 1981). Most particularly, as we shall see below, there is no empirical support for the implications that: (a) because of the notion of necessary and sufficient attributes, categories have fixed boundaries (i.e. something either is, or is not, a cat); and (b) all the category members sharing such characteristics are equally representative of that category. The result is that although a convenient way of thinking about categories or concepts, this so-called *classical view of category membership* has been all but abandoned. Instead another aspect of what Wittgenstein proposed has gained some measure of acceptance. He suggested that instead of there being defining attributes for category membership, what category members share is a kind of family resemblance. Many attempts have been made to turn this philosophical notion into a psychological theory, but the most influential of these has been the work of Eleanor Rosch (Rosch 1973, 1978; Rosch and Mervis, 1975).

The classical view and family resemblance

The classical view of category membership carries with it the notion that categories are hierarchically organised, thus, dogs and cats, while different from each other are also members of the same superordinate category – animals. As we shall see below, when network theories are discussed, use of defining attribute approaches to the hierarchical organisation of categories has also proved unsuccessful. Based on ideas popular in anthropology, Rosch proposed that categories were indeed hierarchically organised, into what she called basic-level categories (i.e. the level at which we interact with objects and category members in our everyday life, e.g. cars, books, chairs, computers), and a level of category organisation more specific than this, which was called the subordinate level (e.g. cars: Alfa Romeo Boxer, Golf, Passat, Escort; computers: p.c., Apple Macs, Psions). Above basic level categories are superordinate categories which combine basic level categories into more generic categories such as vehicles, furniture, and so on.

This approach to the issue of hierarchical organisation is exemplified by Rosch, Mervis, Gray, Johnson and Boyes-Braem (1976), who had subjects list all attributes of items carefully chosen to reflect these different levels of categories (e.g. vehicles, cars, types of car). They found that very few attributes were listed for superordinate categories, while far more attributes were listed for both basic and subordinate categories. At the subordinate level, many of the attributes listed were repeated across different category members, while at the basic level, the attributes tended to be those which distinguished between category members (e.g. cars, buses, bicycles). There is therefore considerable redundancy in the information available about subordinate category members, with considerably more informativeness (or discrimination power) in the attributes listed for categories at the basic level. Rosch and colleagues suggest that basic level categories are the first acquired by children, are the level at which adults normally name objects, and are the most general level at which similar motor movements are used for interacting with objects. Intrinsic to the proposal is also the notion that particular experience within a domain may alter the nature of what is represented at this basic level; thus we might expect expert car mechanics to have a different basic level category with respect to cars than I would have, and the child with a detailed knowledge of dinosaurs (see Chi and Koeske, 1983), to have a more sophisticated basic level for the category of dinosaurs than either me or the motor mechanic. This relationship between domain experience and changes in what constitutes basic level information may thus help to shed some light on the process of category learning. What it also implies, however, is that at different levels of the hierarchy, categorical representations are nested within each other, or at least organised economically, so that, for example, aggregate information, rather than details about particular instances, serve our conceptual processing.

The prototype view and graded structure

The *prototype theory* does not attempt to identify the boundary conditions for category membership, that is, the defining attributes, but instead uses the concept of an average category member (or prototype), which is based upon the experience one has had with category members. In essence, what is proposed is that people develop good examples of different things, and use the degree of similarity between these averaged stimuli and any new stimulus to determine its category membership. Obviously one might begin by averaging stimuli of all sorts, thus leaving the young child with a very undifferentiated conceptual understanding of the world. With feedback, experience and learning by example, this undifferentiated mass becomes more specialised for the individual child's environment and the tasks the child performs. An extreme example of this is the amazingly detailed knowledge of dinosaurs possessed by the child described by Chi and Koeske (1983). Two aspects of prototype theory are particularly important. First, under prototype theory categories have *fuzzy boundaries*, that is, there is no fixed point at which something ceases to be a member of one category and becomes a member of another. The second is the related notion that categories have *graded structure*, that is, some category members are further away from the prototype than others, or are less typical than others (see Barsalou, 1992).

Thus, as Malt and Smith (1984) have shown, an apple is a more typical, or better, example of a fruit than an olive, and a robin is a better example of a bird than a penguin. Rather remarkably, even categories which are well understood and have definable boundaries (e.g. odd and even numbers) show graded structure. For example, Armstrong, Gleitman and Gleitman (1983) showed that when asked to rate, on a 0 to 7 scale, the extent to which numbers were good examples of odd or even numbers, subjects considered 4 and 8 very good examples of even numbers, but 34 and 106 poor examples of even numbers, and 3 and 7 good examples of odd numbers, but 447 and 501 much less good examples of odd numbers (Fig 4.4). We will return to this issue in Chapter 6 which deals with the relationship between membership and frequency, but it is worth noting in passing that some numbers being better examples than others can lead to problems when people are asked to estimate the frequency of events (e.g. drinks or pills they have taken, numbers of accidents, etc.).

Fig 4.4 Typicality of odd and even numbers (after Armstrong, Gleitman and Gleitman, 1983).

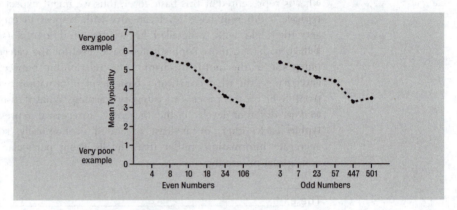

Schwartz and Reisberg (1991) identify a number of converging lines of evidence which support prototype theory. These include:

1. Sentence verification: The time taken to decide that a sentence (e.g. 'a robin is a dog') is correct depends in part on whether it is true or false, the familiarity of the subject with the terms and domain, but also how close the exemplars referred to in the sentence are to the putative prototype for that category. Thus, subjects will be quicker to decide that a 'robin is a bird' than to decide that a 'penguin is a bird'.

2. Production: Subjects asked to list category members are more likely to list exemplars close to the prototype, and are more likely to mention these early in their listing. The suggestion is that the search begins with the prototype and works outwards from it (see Barsalou, 1983).

3. Picture identification: Subjects determine that pictures are or are not objects from a particular category more quickly when the pictures are prototypical of exemplars close to the prototype (e.g. Smith, Balzano and Walker, 1978).

4. Explicit judgements of category membership: Judgements of the typicality of various category exemplars tend to reflect the distance of these exemplars from the prototype (e.g. Armstrong, Gleitman and Gleitman, 1983; Malt and Smith, 1984).

5. Induction: Subjects seem more willing to apply a new fact learned about a typical category member (e.g. robin) to all category members, including less typical category members (e.g. penguin), but are less likely to make inferences from the atypical to the category as a whole or to more typical members (see Rips, 1975).

While each of these relies to a greater or lesser extent on the notion of a prototype, thus leading to a certain circularity in argument, the range of techniques available for identifying exemplars which are prototypical allows for these to be identified with one procedure, and tested using another. A fascinating line of research by Barsalou (1988) distinguished between what we called goal-derived categories (e.g. things to bring on a journey) and ad hoc categories (i.e. categories which we build in order to respond to an unfamiliar request, e.g. list the things you would need for a picnic on the moon). What Barsalou (1988) shows is that both the more usual goal-derived categories and ad hoc categories show graded structure: some exemplars are seen as more typical than others, and these are verified faster. Category structure can also vary depending on the perspective subjects are asked to take. Thus, as Barsalou and Sewell (1984) have shown, subjects asked to take an American perspective when judging the typicality of various birds yield a different graded category structure than when those same students are asked to adopt the perspective of a Chinese student. In the first case robins and eagles are seen as typical birds, in the second case swans and peacocks are rated as more typical.

The exemplar-based approach

The above discussion reveals an important property of semantic or conceptual knowledge; it has sufficient stability to allow for performance to be consistent, but is sufficiently adaptable to allow performance to be flexible with regard to its circumstances of use. This flexibility poses some problems for prototype theory. A second problem lies in the fact that the assumptions about how prototypes operate assume a knowledge of the category structure beyond what would be available from the prototype, if it simply reflected averaged or typical values for certain attributes. Specifically, in some cases we draw on knowledge about category members rather than on information which might easily be retrieved from a prototype. This is the essential aspect of what has become known as *exemplar theory*. When we categorise something we retrieve a specific remembered instance, and use this rather than some averaged prototype as the basis for comparison. Importantly, while prototype theory suggests that in making categorical judgements about, say, dogs, the individual always relies on comparisons with the same prototype, the exemplar-based approach suggests instead that different specific remembered instances may be used. This allows performance to vary depending on the test circumstances, allows for the construction of ad hoc categories, but also allows a stable graded category structure to emerge. Since it is more likely that more typical exemplars will be selected as the basis for comparison than less typical, exemplar theory can account for both categorical stability, instability and graded structure (see Schwartz and Reisberg, 1991; Brooks, 1987; Hintzman, 1986). It is worth bearing in mind that this notion of an exemplar, or a specific remembered instance, does not seem very different to what we described above as an episodic memory.

Where a precise match between a previous instance and some new stimulus is not found, analogical processes can be used to determine some relationship between some new and some old event. Thus, on encountering a complex roundabout for the first time as a learner driver, I may retrieve instances of other roundabouts, of other complex junctions, or even memories of driving on curved roads. This identifies one of the problems with exemplar-based theories. The 'retrieve an instance and draw some analogy' technique is satisfactory in constrained situations, and determining which instance will be retrieved can be predicted on the basis of the maximal featural overlap between the new and old stimulus (see Barsalou, 1992). However, in less constrained everyday circumstances, there seems to be no satisfactory explanation of which features it is important to match and which can be ignored (e.g. maybe curves are irrelevant, and the possibility of traffic from the left is what is important, as with other junctions), neither is there any satisfactory explanation of which analogy might be drawn (e.g. when driving ahead at a roundabout I should signal left before I make my exit, unlike with most other junctions).

The problem is that even though we may satisfactorily retrieve an exemplar from the past, we need to use more than just the information from that exemplar to make our decision as to whether the retrieved exemplar really is sufficiently relevant (i.e. is the degree of overlap good enough?) and which aspects of it should form the basis of the analogy. These are also issues which pose difficulties for prototype theory. Nevertheless, both prototype and exemplar-based theories account for a broad range of empirical findings. Indeed, it may be that some of the difficulties these accounts run into are in part due to the tendency to study their operation in isolation, that is, when only one prototype holds sway or when only one type of instance is retrieved. Perhaps under normal circumstances, relationships between different concepts and categories serve to identify which information is important, and the basis on which analogies should be drawn.

Early network theories: Collins and Quillian

Earlier we briefly considered what were called classical views of concepts and categories. These suggested that category members had certain characteristics, and that categories had some degree of hierarchical organisation. One of the earliest computational forays into this area was the propositional network theory proposed by Collins and Quillian (1969), see Fig 4.5. Each concept in the network is represented by a node (e.g. fish), and certain properties are associated with this node (e.g. has gills, can swim). Some nodes (e.g. fish) are subordinate to others (e.g. animal), but superordinate to others (e.g. mackerel). It is therefore hierarchical, and assumes that concepts have defining attributes. This hierarchical assumption also had other implications within the Collins and Quillian framework, namely, subordinate nodes inherited the attributes linked to superordinate nodes. Thus we know that a mackerel is striped, lives in sea-water, but also that it has fins, has gills, can swim (i.e. attributes linked with fish), and also that it breathes, eats, and has skin (i.e. inherited from animal).

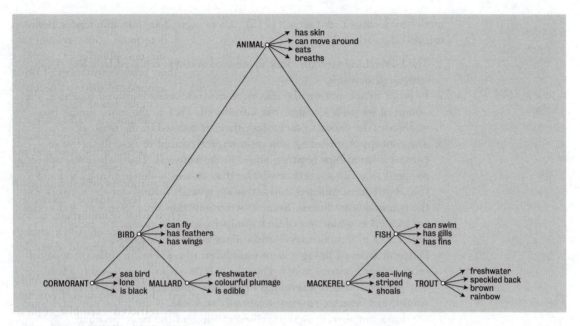

Fig 4.5 Hypothetical memory structure (after Collins and Quillian, 1969).

Together the notion of hierarchical structure and inheritance of attributes form the principle known as *cognitive economy*. The central predictions are that in order to answer a question such as 'is a fish an animal?', the subject must traverse this hierarchical structure, with more time taken when different levels of the hierarchy must be searched for the attributes which help to resolve the question. Thus, it should take longer to verify that 'a mackerel is an animal' than to decide that 'a mackerel is a fish', and 'a mackerel is sea-dwelling' should be verified more quickly than 'a mackerel breathes'.

While these relatively straightforward predictions were initially supported, many other empirical findings led to the abandonment of the specifics of the Collins and Quillian framework. Thus, for example, the findings we considered earlier that sentences involving more or less typical exemplars of a concept were verified more or less quickly are difficult to explain within this model. Similarly, as Conrad (1972) pointed out, the differences in verification times across the putative levels of the hierarchy seemed to be due to the frequency with which different attributes were associated with 'nodes'; and thus, semantic relatedness, rather than a hierarchical structure with inheritance, might just as easily account for the findings. Also, as Rips, Shoben and Smith (1973) pointed out, locating nodes at different levels in the hierarchy is a rather arbitrary process since, for example, a sentence such as 'a dog is an animal' is verified more quickly than 'a dog is a mammal', even though mammal is a subordinate category of animal, rather than vice versa.

Spreading activation and semantic memory

These results, together with the logical and philosophical difficulties of the defining attribute account of category structure led to the proposal of a network model by Collins and Loftus (1975). There were four key differences between this and the earlier theory:

1. The hierarchical structure was abandoned and was replaced by a less rigidly structured network.
2. In order to account for the effects of semantic relatedness and typicality, the notion of semantic distance was introduced. That is, the more similar two nodes are, the closer to each other they are located in the network.
3. The concept of spreading activation was introduced to describe active or current relationships between nodes in the network. Thus, when the subject is required to verify a sentence which refers to two nodes (e.g. mackerel and fish), both are stimulated, and activation spreads throughout the network until the two nodes are linked. Because activation takes time to spread, and nodes are located as a function of their similarity to other nodes, the earlier differences in sentence verification times could be explained.
4. Different types of linkages were introduced to account for different types of relationships between nodes. Thus, 'is a' links (as in 'a mackerel is a fish'), 'has' links (as in 'a mackerel has fins'), 'can' links (as in 'a mackerel can swim'), can depict a range of relationships, while 'is not', 'has not', and 'can not' links can also be used to represent some of the more peculiar relationships, for example, a whale is not a fish.

Given that this new network theory was derived in order to account for the existing empirical findings, it is hardly surprising that it did so effectively. On the way, however, it also provided a reasonable account of other phenomena (such as semantic priming, i.e. because activation will spread throughout the network when 'bread' and 'butter' are stimulated, the naming of the word 'jam' will also take less time). Unfortunately, the range and complexity of the assumptions made in order to do so served to reduce the credibility of this type of network account of conceptual processing (e.g. see critiques by Johnson-Laird, Herrmann, and Chaffin, 1984; Morton, Hammersley and Bekerian, 1985). We will return to more specific proposals of how network theories are involved in memory many times in this book; an excellent overview of current computational models is available in Churchland and Sejnowski (1992).

Schemata and scripts

Origins and generality of schema theory

Although popularised in the work of Sir Fredric Bartlett (1932), in fact the notion of a schema goes back to Head (1920), a Cambridge colleague of Bartlett's, and even earlier to the eighteenth-century German philosopher Kant (1963). According to Searleman and Herrmann (1994, p. 124) a *schema* is 'a mental model or representation, built up through experience, about a person, an object, a situation, or an event'. Essentially, a schema is simply an organised body of general information or beliefs. The generality of application of the notion of a schema can be readily seen in the following quote from Morton and Bekerian

(1986): 'The schema framework has been used to describe how people go about interpreting sensory data, retrieving information from memory, organising actions, determining goals or behaviour, allocating processing resources and, generally, directing overall processing in attentional, perceptual and memorial systems' (p. 64).

A script is a specific type of schema which is an amalgamation of knowledge of particular types of frequently encountered events that people can abstract from, and use when similar events are encountered in the future (Abelson, 1981; Mandler, 1984). Thus, for example, I have a script for what to expect and do when giving an academic talk. Extending the script analogy, it has been found useful to divide the script into scenes, that is, events that form one part of the script. Thus, the academic talk is comprised of various scenes, such as being introduced, thanking the introducer, outlining the subject matter of the talk, giving the body of the talk, summarising and concluding, taking questions, being thanked. Two ways of coordinating scripts have been proposed. These discriminate between MOPs and TOPs. Memory organisation packets (MOPs), combine scenes from different scripts. Thus, being introduced when giving an academic talk, and being introduced to important visitors, share some features, but are different. Nevertheless, the commonalities which MOPs represent can help me to know what to expect when being introduced at, for example, a meeting of a committee I have not attended before. Thematic organisation points (TOPs) are higher order organisations of scripts which do not rely on the similarity of the scenes which comprise scripts, but which link scripts on the basis of more abstract themes. Thus, I have a script for watching cricket with friends, for listening to election results alone late at night, relaxing with drinks after a hearty dinner, and for driving fast. For me these are all 'activities I enjoy', which hardly have overlapping scenes but are nevertheless strongly linked, thematically.

Properties of schemata

Schemata are discrete, abstract knowledge structures which represent past actions or experiences. They are not abstract rules, but are derived from (repeated) experience. Schemata can represent knowledge of all kinds, from procedural knowledge of driving, to our understanding of what to expect at a psychology conference, to the knowledge of typography we might use to decipher the letters on the programme of that conference. They incorporate both generalisations from the experience we have had as well as the facts we have been taught. The recurrent elements of an experience are represented as 'slots' in a schema which has been abstracted for events of that particular type. This may involve a fixed core of information, together with variables. For example, in driving at a roundabout (Fig 4.6), we probably have expectations that we will encounter the traffic typical of an urban or town setting (default values). However, roundabouts are also encountered near motorway junctions (optional value), which in turn influences what we may have to do by way of monitoring the external scenes (i.e. motorway roundabouts are very much larger, have more complex entry and exit regimes, such as traffic lights, and thus different requirements in terms of visual scanning, etc.), or reacting to traffic (i.e. the car is likely to be travelling more quickly and out steering paths/turning circle will be different). Finally, we may have expectations that traffic will be encountered, and perhaps even the type of traffic (e.g. heavy trucks are more likely at motorway roundabouts than town roundabouts), but certainly not of its individual characteristics (e.g. red articulated truck, etc.).

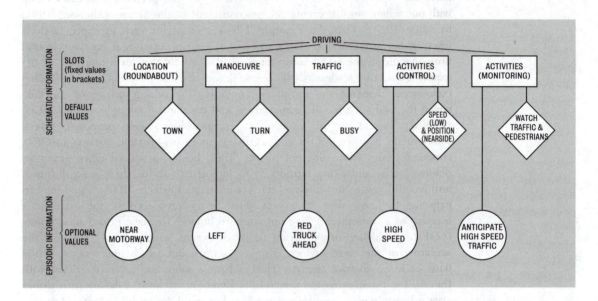

Fig 4.6 A schematic view of driving at a roundabout.

Schemata are organised at different levels of abstraction, and hence embed within each other to form packets of knowledge which are specific to certain tasks, themes or situations, or which are general across many circumstances and situations. Examples of how this occurs have already been considered in relation to MOPs and TOPs above.

Any experienced event will evoke the general structure available from memory which offers the best match to the information being processed. This will be instantiated, that is, the empty slots of the schema are filled with perceptual or schema-derived information. The instantiation of one schema inhibits other schemata at the same level, but not those embedded within it. When particular aspects of an event are sufficiently irregular or unexpected, in terms of the schema which has been activated, to have consequences for the organisation or contents of the schema itself, episodic traces of the relevant deviations are formed. Thus, at the most concrete level of a schema there are fragments of episodic memories, or specific instances. These are labelled with pointers which serve to identify each with the schema with which the deviations are associated (Schank, 1980; see also Graesser and Nakamura, 1982). Schemata are modified, or new schemata are formed, as a consequence of new experience. This may incorporate both generalisations from the experience we have actually had as well as the facts we have been taught or otherwise encountered.

Effects of schemata

The concept of a schema is widely invoked to describe a range of perceptual, attentional, construal and retrieval effects. It is generally thought that schemata guide the selection and encoding of information. Since information is encoded within pre-existing schemata, they also exert substantial influence on storage. In doing so, schemata help to integrate information we are currently experiencing with our long-term past in a single representation. In supplying default values and by influencing what we experience and store, schemata greatly aid our interpretation and understanding of situations. The effect of this is also to normalise experience, that is, to make events more consistent with prior experience than they might otherwise be. Finally, schemata also exert considerable influence on retrieval, in that events tend to be recalled in a way which is consistent with schema-driven prior expectations.

Schema theory has not been without its critics (see Alba and Hasher, 1983; Morton, Hammersley and Bekerian, 1985). These criticisms have largely been concerned with the difficulty of defining what a schema actually is, and in determining what information comprises any particular schema in a way which avoids a circularity of definition. Schema theory, because it serves to aggregate experiences rather than preserve episodic information, can also have difficulty in accounting for retrieval which is highly detailed and accurate but situation specific. Nelson (1986) has also addressed the problem of how schemata are acquired in the first place, where the infant, presumably, has no prior experience with which to drive expectations or experience which can be specialised to allow the formation of other schemata. Finally, schema theories have also been criticised for glossing over the procedures involved in the selection or retrieval of the most appropriate schema for a particular situation. Schematic influences are more fully explored in Chapter 5, where their impact on remembering is considered, Chapter 10, where the concept of a self-schema is addressed, and Chapter 12, where procedural knowledge is discussed.

BOX 4.2: Enduring memories

Harry Bahrick has done much to encourage the view that where information is learned to a high level, often through distributed practice over substantial periods of time, this information can be remembered even after decades of disuse. The findings, which first suggested that some form of permastore existed, were published by Bahrick, Bahrick and Wittlinger (1975). This study showed that given lists of names and class photographs from their graduation year, people were reliably able to identify 90 per cent of individuals in the class photograph, even after 25 years, which was the same level of performance achieved by people who had graduated just three months before. Even after nearly 50 years, correct recognition and identification performance was still in excess of 75 per cent. When subjects were simply given photographs, and asked to generate the names for the photographed individuals, performance was, as to be expected, rather worse. However, name recall given a picture cue was 70 per cent some three months after graduation, and about 50 per cent after 25 years. Remarkably, almost 50 years after graduation, name recall was still in excess of 15 per cent.

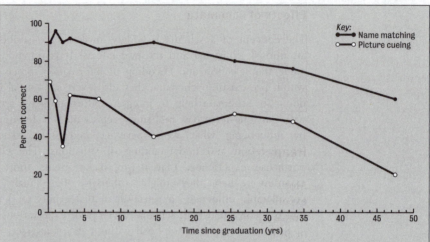

Memory for faces of classmates in the very long term (after Bahrick, Bahrick and Wittlinger, 1975).

Bahrick (1984) has also studied the long-term retention of Spanish learned at college, but practised relatively little since then. He controlled for each individual's original level of learning by referencing each subject's score to the subject's original score in a class test. Recognition performance, where subjects given Spanish vocabulary had to choose the correct English equivalent, or vice versa, was superior to recall of vocabulary, irrespective of whether the correct answer was a Spanish or an English word. The superiority of recognition over recall remains throughout the 50 year span studied. In both cases, the first three years or so after this test show the greatest decline in level of performance. Afterwards, performance, about 40 per cent in the case of recall and 70 per cent in the case of recognition, remains more or less stable. Reading comprehension paralleled recognition performance, diverging only where subjects had studied Spanish some 50 years before.

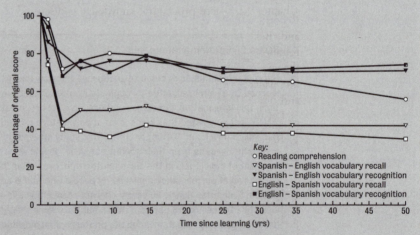

Retention curves for Spanish over 50 years (after Bahrick, 1984).

Finally, the role of further training once learning has been consolidated has also recently been demonstrated by Bahrick and Hall (1991). They showed that quite high levels of retention of high school algebra were achieved by people despite 50 years of not using it, but only by those who, having learned algebra at high school, later went on to take further courses in mathematics. Together these studies make a strong case for the preservation of overlearned knowledge in the very long term, even where its use is, at best, occasional. We will return to this topic in later chapters where exceptional remembering and the relationship between memory and skill is discussed.

Headed records

Most of the theories we have discussed thus far suggest that individual experiences are either aggregated into larger similar experiences, or, at least, that similar experiences are organised such that those which are similar are 'close to' or prime each other. In the late 1970s and early 1980s, John Morton and Debra Bekerian outlined a very different conceptualisation of long-term memory, which they called headed records (see Morton, Hammersley and Bekerian, 1985; Morton and Bekerian, (1986; Morton, 1994). The following is an example of a headed record for my professional interview at the University of Surrey.

Heading: Waiting for interview at Surrey; Saturday 17 December 1994.

Record: I get to the interview a little later than I wanted, because my taxi from the hotel is late in arriving. I am nervous as it pulls up outside Senate House and when taking the lift to the interview room. I wait outside, trying to keep calm, thinking of what questions I may be asked. The secretary to the interview committee emerges from the interview room, and ushers me inside.

Records of experience

Records are the unit of recallable information in memory (Morton, Hammersley and Bekerian, 1985). They are what our 'memory' returns to us when we remember something. Each record has a heading, which is different in content to the information contained in the records. Experience is encoded within records, but when memory is searched, the remember only has access to the headings, and not directly to the contents of a record.

Let us first consider the properties of records:

1. Records are discrete, that is, independent of one another. No connections link records which may be similar to each other.
2. Access to records is all or none. When a record is retrieved, access is available to all its contents.
3. Records are not restricted in the amount or format of information they contain. Instead, within the headed records framework, capacity limitations and so on are determined by demand at storage and/or conditions pertaining at retrieval.
4. Information can be duplicated across records. This is counter to the 'avoidance of redundancy' requirement which permeates so many theories.
5. Records are not subject to alteration either by modification or addition of new information.

Each record has a heading, and it is these, rather than memory records that are searched. The properties of headings are:

1. The format of information contained in headings is different from that of records.
2. The heading need bear no propositional relationship to the content of its record.
3. The information in the heading will determine the discriminability of its related record when access is required to it.
4. Headings are not subject to change.
5. The contents of a heading are inaccessible and can never be recalled.
6. Headings comprise literal representations of an event, including environmental features and internal state; together with some information about registers automatically updated reflecting mood and physiological state, location (i.e. where we are, e.g. which country, city, general locale); temporal detail (e.g. what day it is, time of day, etc.); and source information (e.g. who one is talking to).

The headed records retrieval process

Given the task of remembering something, search proceeds in parallel and is controlled by a retrieval description (i.e. some specification of what is being searched for) and a task description (i.e. the goals and reasons behind the search). Search terminates when some match is found between the information specified in the retrieval description and that in the heading of a record. The nature and extent of the match required between the retrieval description and the heading will be a function of the type of information in both (e.g. if a word is searched for then the match must at least be at a lexical level). Although headings are searched in parallel, only one record is retrieved or consulted/evaluated at a time. According to the theory, the most recent matching heading is more likely to be retrieved.

Since the search process does not have access to the contents of a record, the information required by the rememberer may not be contained within the retrieved record. When this happens, the rememberer is left somewhat confused, wondering what to do with the retrieved information, and perhaps why it has been retrieved. A subsequent search will then ensue, with, perhaps, an amended retrieval description to prevent repeated retrieval of the same, inappropriate record. Failure to update the retrieval description could lead to the repetitive thought patterns characteristic of depression (see Chapter 9). As Morton and colleagues make clear, 'the processes responsible for forming descriptions and headings must be closely related to those responsible for creating headings. At least they must both have access to the same guiding principles'. With some perspicacity, they continue 'We merely note, as an interesting developmental problem, that these principles will have to be learned by the child and that if the principles change then the retrieval of records laid down before the change would be very problematical' (Morton, Hammersley and Bekerian, 1985, p. 10).

The headed records theory has neither been particularly influential, or been the subject of much empirical research. It is included here because it offers an economical and, perhaps deceptively, simple account of long-term memory. Its primary strength, I would suggest, lies in its concentration on episodic knowledge, and its avoidance of the aggregating of individual experiences which is typical of so many accounts of how knowledge is stored in a more established form. It shares this episodic quality with Logan's (1988) instance theory (see Chapter 12), with which it shares interesting parallels. Headed records also avoids a range of problems inherent in other theories, and can offer insightful accounts of empirical findings which have received attention subsequent to the publication of the theory (e.g. the *mis-information effect*, *infantile amnesia*, context reinstatement, multiple personality disorder and *recovered memory*; see Chapters 2, 9, 10 and 13).

Summary: Enduring memories

The foregoing sections sought to distinguish between the different types of knowledge which endure over long periods of time — episodic, semantic and procedural — and the ways in which the retrievability of this knowledge can be manifested. Such retrieval may be reflected in the individual feeling that he or she is remembering having made some effort to do so, acting in a way which demonstrates that something has previously been learned, and in spontaneously thinking about events from the past (even without the deliberate attempt to retrieve such information). Each of the theories of how such knowledge is organised and structured has advantages and disadvantages. Prototype and network theories seem economical in terms of the efficiency of representation and storage, but they also seem too inflexible to account for the diversity of performance observed in studies which show that graded structure is evident in formal and ad hoc categories. Network theories, especially those relying on spreading activation, offer a better insight into retrieval processes, but then so too do accounts which make no appeal to activation or the interrelationship of information (e.g. headed records). Schemata and scripts offer intuitively plausible accounts of how the representation of repeated events can be understood, but the difficulties in determining the obligatory and incidental contents, and also in dealing with schema-consistent and schema-inconsistent episodic detail are profound. These issues will be addressed in greater detail in the next chapter.

Further reading

Barsalou, L. W. (1992). *Cognitive psychology: An overview for cognitive scientists*. Hillsdale, NJ: Lawrence Erlbaum Associates.

Churchland, P. S. and Sejnowski, T. J. (1992). *The computational brain*. Cambridge, MA: MIT Press.

Estes, W. K. (1994). *Classification and cognition*. Oxford: Oxford University Press.

Kosslyn, S. M. and Koenig, O. (1992). *Wet mind: The new cognitive neuroscience*. New York: Free Press.

Morton, J., Hammersley, R. H. and Bekerian, D. A. (1985). Headed records: A model for memory and its failures. *Cognition, 20*, 1–23.

Richardson-Klavehn, A. and Bjork, R. A. (1988). Measures of memory. *Annual Review of Psychology, 39,* 475–543.

Schank, R. C. and Abelson, R. (1977). *Scripts, plans, goals and understanding.* Hillsdale, NJ: Lawrence Erlbaum Associates.

Squire, L. R., Knowlton, B. and Musen, G. (1993). The structure and organisation of memory. *Annual Review of Psychology, 44,* 453–95.

Discussion points	

- How do the different measures of remembering map on to the types of knowledge we possess?
- What are the distinguishing features of exemplar, prototype and network accounts of categorisation?
- Try to develop a schema for one everyday event you regularly perform.
- Think of an experience you can remember well and one you remember badly. Compare how the information in each might be described within the headed records framework.

Chapter 5

Remembering complex events

Chapter outline: This chapter overviews the standard effects observed when people try to remember complex events. Each section focuses in detail on the factors which influence our memory of complex everyday events such as pictures, faces and stories. The nature of what is retrieved, and what is forgotten, as the result of a wide range of different manipulations across these different types of event, indicates the existence of underlying organisational tendencies, such as schemata or prototypes. These serve to structure our attention to, interpretation, and remembering of, complex events; are a function of experience, and both facilitate and inhibit remembering.

Key topics
- Pictures
- Faces
- Stories
- Summary: Commonalities in remembering complex events
- Further reading

■ Pictures

Proverbially at least, pictures are worth a thousand words. There is abundant evidence that they are remembered better than words, and indeed that they are remembered differently to words.

Pictures versus words

A range of research has shown that recall and recognition of pictorial information is better than purely verbal information, and also that non-verbal memory storage is more stable than verbal memory storage over intervals of hours to days. Let us look at this *picture superiority effect* in a little more detail.

Gillund and Shiffrin (1981) showed that complex pictures were recalled better than abstract words. The proportion of items recalled decreased when the list length was increased, whether the increase was accomplished by adding items of the same type (words to words or pictures to pictures) or the other type (words to pictures or pictures to words). These list length effects were obtained regardless of blocking or mixing at presentation or test. Purdy and Luepnitz (1982) showed that regardless of whether the recall test was immediate or delayed (by up to 48 hours), subjects who saw pictures showed significantly greater recall than subjects who saw words. With regard to recognition, Haber and Myers (1982) showed, using a signal detection analysis, that recognition accuracy was greatest for the pictograms and poorest for words. This was so whether or not subjects were required to respond 'old' when the item itself, irrespective of its form, had previously been encountered, or whether subjects were required to respond 'old' only when the form in which the item appeared in the recognition test was identical to its form during the study phase. Subjects were most accurate when probed with the same form as presented. Hart and O'Shanick (1993) contrasted forgetting rates for words, pictures, and designs, which had been learned to an equivalent criterion. Forgetting rates were similar across an initial 10-minute retention interval, but there was a more rapid loss of words than pictures and designs from 10 minutes to two hours. Memory for words and pictures steadily declined between 10 minutes and 48 hours, but there was no further loss for designs after two hours (Fig 5.1). Thus, not only is recall and recognition of pictorial information better than purely verbal information, the work of Hart and O'Shanick also suggests that non-verbal memory storage is more stable than verbal memory storage over relatively long intervals.

It might be thought that pictures are more memorable than words because pictures access superior sensory or physical encoding, rather than because of enhanced semantic or conceptual encoding. The results of Snodgrass and Asiaghi (1977) challenge this explanation. They showed, just as Haber and Myers (1982) did later (see above), that changing the rule for identifying old and new items had no effect on recognition memory, nor did providing an opportunity for differential encoding by prior instructions. By dissociating stimulus-form from stimulus-memory in this way, Snodgrass and Asiaghi (1977) were able to show that the picture superiority effect relies jointly on enhanced semantic and sensory properties of the stimulus.

Fig 5.1 Recognition of words, pictures and designs after different retention intervals (after Hart and O'Shanick, 1993).

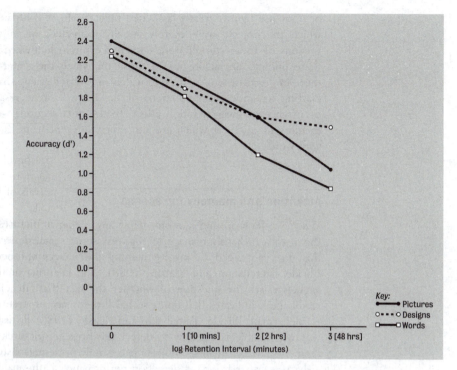

Weldon, Roediger and Challis (1989) showed that words were remembered better than pictures on word-fragment and word-stem completion tasks, under implicit and explicit retrieval conditions. This relative difference between words and pictures under implicit data-driven conditions seems to reflect the procedures used. For example, the importance of enhanced conceptual or semantic processing of word and picture stimuli is also shown by the final study reported by Weldon, Roediger and Challis (1989). Here, when extra-list semantic cues were combined with the word fragments used in explicit retrieval conditions, pictures and words were recalled equally well. A recent study by Dewhurst and Conway (1994) suggests that recollective experience, that is, awareness that one is actually remembering a specific event, may also be a prerequisite for the picture-superiority effect to occur. This suggestion echoes earlier findings reported by Weldon and Roediger (1987), who contrasted the success with which pictures and words were remembered where implicit or explicit retrieval tests were employed. The first study reported by Dewhurst and Conway replicates the picture superiority effect in free recall. They go on to show that words produced greater priming on a word fragment completion task. However, their final study demonstrated that greater priming is obtained with words in word fragment completion tasks, but greater priming was obtained with pictures on picture identification tests. It would seem therefore as if when appropriate implicit measures are taken, both pictures and words show priming effects.

There are also parallels and differences, between words and pictures in terms of another standard memory finding – the generation effect. Peynircioglu (1989) reports a number of studies in which drawing objects to be remembered, scenes or nonsense figures greatly facilitated their recall, as compared with conditions in which the objects were merely visually inspected, or in which already drawn versions of these stimuli were copied. Peynircioglu makes the point that while these findings are analogous to those on which the generation effect is based, they are inconsistent with the widely advocated view that activation of pre-existing semantic representations of the items is a necessary condition for the occurrence of the generation effect. In the next sections we consider aspects of memory for pictures which are altogether different from those readily observable with words.

Attention and memory for scenes

When we look around a room, or at any scene, or the objects which comprise them, we can hardly manage to suppress some semantic interpretation, although this does not need to involve naming the images we derive (see Biederman, Blickle, Teitelbaum and Klatsky, 1988). The near inevitability of this semantic analysis raises the question of whether the fact that such interpretations are so readily built indicates that doing so has little or no resource implications.

Biederman, Blickle, Teitelbaum and Klatsky (1988) present results which show that when subjects attempt to detect the presence of a target object among an array of spatially organised objects in a briefly presented display (100 ms), there is a sharp decrease in object detection performance as the numbers of other objects in the display increases. This indicates that object detection, at least in these circumstances, is an attention-demanding process. Interestingly, no benefit was observed for targets that were likely to co-occur with the distractors, although this might have emerged had the numbers of relevant trials been increased considerably.

Recently, Antes and Kristjanson (1993) investigated effects of cognitive-resource demands on picture-viewing patterns. The eye fixations of undergraduates were recorded as they watched pictures and concurrently performed one of a number of listening tasks. Half of the subjects were asked to remember certain objects from the pictures and half had no memory instructions. Concurrent auditory monitoring increased interfixation distances and the frequency of fixations on regions of high informativeness, and decreased the area of the pictures explored and the memory for objects in the scenes.

Memory load also influences aspects of the ways in which scenes are remembered. Intraub and Hoffman (1992) showed, under conditions of high memory load (60 pictures and 50 paragraphs), that subjects frequently reported memory for photographs that they had actually never seen, but had read about. The tendency to do so was unaffected by whether the retrieval test occurred immediately after encoding, or after one week. Having subjects rate the imagery value of the passages they read substantially reduced these source-confusion errors.

Insight into the ways in which attention is allocated during encoding and retrieval is provided by a number of studies reported by Helene Intraub. In a fascinating study, Intraub and Richardson (1989) show that during recall and recognition of photographed scenes, subjects include objects which were outside the camera's field of view. They also show that this is not merely a production effect, since, in a second study, subjects rated target pictures as being closer up than before, and frequently mistook extended-boundary distractors as targets. Intraub, Bender and Mangels (1992) later addressed three alternative explanations of these effects: object completion, distortion toward a perceptual schema, and normalisation toward a prototypic view. In separate studies, undergraduates viewed 16 close-up, prototypic, or wide-angle views of objects for 15 seconds each. Immediately, or 48 hours later, they rated test pictures on a five-point scale as 'same', 'closer up', or 'farther away' (Fig 5.2). Results ruled out object completion because boundary extension occurred when the picture contained no incomplete objects. Immediate tests supported the perceptual schema hypothesis because all unidirectional distortions involved boundary extension. Delayed tests were more suggestive of a memory schema effect because wide-angle pictures yielded boundary restriction.

Fig 5.2 How beliefs about what we saw change with time: Usual perspectives are likely to seem closer, but unusual perspectives seem further away (after Intraub, Bender and Mangels, 1992).

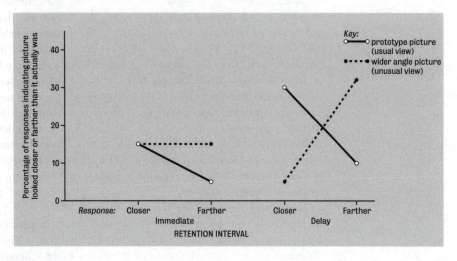

Static scenes: Organisation, priming and durability

Mandler and Ritchey (1977) showed that where complex pictures are internally coherent, certain types of information remain virtually intact over a four-month period, while other types of information were lost almost immediately. The internal coherence of the scene, or that imposed on it by subjects, appears to give rise to these schema-like effects on memory for scenes. Frieske and Park (1993) have recently examined the effects of organisation and working memory on younger and older adults' scene memory. Subjects discriminated transformed pictures from unchanged study items in organised or unorganised scenes. Memory for two types of scene transformations were investigated: relocation and substitutions. Organisation had similar effects on young and older adults, improving memory for relocation but not substitutions. Working memory performance significantly predicted scene memory, except for relocation in organised scenes.

If some schematic organisation is indeed a property of the ways in which scenes are interpreted and remembered, then such structures should exhibit priming effects, or be invoked by preceding pictures with schema-related cues. Reinitz, Wright and Loftus (1989) showed that when scenes were preceded by object names (e.g. cat) or category names (e.g. supermarket) both immediate and delayed recognition performance was facilitated. While this may seem a rather artificial procedure, it has recently been shown that the expectations subjects have about what they are about to see has considerable effects on both the time they allocate to different aspects of the scene, and also on their memory for elements of that scene (see Hanna and Loftus, 1992).

Pezdek, Maki, Valencia-Laver and Whetstone (1988) show that although people are able to distinguish large sets of old pictures from new distractor pictures, their ability to detect missing elaborative visual details is more limited. When people are presented with simple and complex pictures and then tested in a same–changed recognition test with a simple or complex form of each, a measure of accuracy (d') is greater for the simple than the complex picture, giving rise to what has become known as the *asymmetric confusability effect* (Pezdek and Chen, 1982). Pezdek and colleagues suggest that pictures are schematically encoded such that the memory representation of both simple and complex pictures is similar to the simple form of each, although they concede that some of the non-schematic elaborative information in complex pictures is stored in memory. The fact that a sentence, which described the central schema in the picture presented immediately afterwards, exaggerated the asymmetric confusability effect, strongly indicates that schematic processing underlies the effect. Other research by Pezdek (1987) indicates that subjects were less accurate at detecting deletions from changed complex pictures than at detecting additions to changed simple pictures.

Homa and Viera (1988) report a study in which undergraduates' recognition of previously seen pictures was investigated under conditions which incorporated highly similar picture-foils and long retention intervals. Recognition performance deteriorated over time. However, a confusion analysis indicated that recognition-errors were based on physical similarity, even after nearly three months. Interpreting these results, Homa and Viera (1988) state that they 'refute the hypothesis that the memorial representations for pictorial variations converge to a common, thematic code after lengthy delays; instead, non-thematic, analogue information is encoded and preserved for lengthy time periods' (p. 411). Intraub and Nicklos (1985) show that questions which encourage attention to physical aspects of an object, rather than semantically oriented questions, lead to better free recall of pictured objects. Mitchell and Brown (1988) also found that episodic recognition of pictures deteriorated over time, but also report repetition priming, that is, a naming advantage for previously named pictures, lasting for at least six weeks. This naming advantage lasted irrespective of whether subjects were able to make accurate new–old recognition memory decisions about individual stimuli. These results also indicate a dissociation between explicit and implicit memory with pictorial stimuli (see Chapter 4), although as we have seen above this may depend on the use of appropriate procedures.

MacLeod (1988) also reports important results which show the longevity or durability of picture memory, but from a rather different paradigm. A number of experiments were carried out which explored individuals' ability to remember words, simple line-drawing pictures, and complex photographic pictures after retention intervals which ranged from two to ten weeks. These studies showed that items of each type, which could neither be recalled nor recognised, were relearned quicker than unrelated control items were learned (thus indicating a 'saving' and hence some residual memory for the item) (Table 5.1). However, this advantage was apparent only where learning was assessed using a recall procedure; recognition tests of relearning consistently failed to detect this same relearning advantage for apparently forgotten items. The fact that effects of savings were demonstrated under recall, but not under recognition conditions, suggests that the classic argument that relearning serves a trace-strengthening function is incorrect, and that savings effects in relearning are better understood as assisting the retrieval of information rather than augmenting its internal representation.

Table 5.1 Proportions of correctly recalled and recognised new, remembered and forgotten line drawings, photographs and words following relearning.

	Line drawings		Photographs		Words	
Recognised						
Recall	.66	.24	.61	.19	.48	.11
Recognition	.85	.72	.85	.69	.81	.66
Not recognised						
Recall	.44	.29	.33	.18	.32	.12
Recognised	.83	.75[a]	.72	.65[a]	.61	.62[a]
	Old	New	Old	New	Old	New

Note: [a] = not significant
After MacLeod, 1988

Rapidly changing scenes

Potter (1976) explored the hypothesis that pictures presented in a rapid sequence at rates comparable to eye fixations are understood and then quickly forgotten. Subjects were given an immediate test of recognition memory for the pictures, and in other groups they searched for a target picture. When the target had only been specified by a category label, detection of a target was strikingly superior to recognition memory. Detection was slightly, but significantly better for pictured than named targets. In a subsequent study, pictures were presented very briefly (50 to 120 ms), and then followed by a masking stimulus. At presentation rates of 120 ms recognition memory was as accurate as detection had been in the previous study. Potter interprets these results as indicating that on average a scene is understood and so becomes immune to ordinary visual masking within about 100 msec but requires about 300 msec of further processing before the memory representation is resistant to conceptual masking from a following picture. These issues were explored further by Loftus and Ginn (1984). They showed that immediate picture-memory performance was disrupted by an energy mask, whereas delayed picture-memory was disrupted by an attention-demanding mask, but not by luminance, when the memory task followed 300 ms after the offset of the picture (Fig 5.3). This difference between the effects of central and peripheral masking shows that delayed picture-memory tasks are consistent with the view that picture-memory is not resource free, and also testifies to the existence of fast-fading iconic storage (see Chapter 2).

Fig 5.3 Differences in recall from pictures as a function of retention interval and masking (after Loftus and Ginn, 1984).

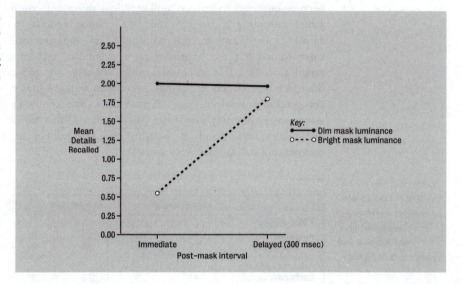

The effects of an attention-demanding mask on delayed recall are analogous to results reported by Intraub (1984), who tested the *conceptual-masking hypothesis*. This holds that a visual event will automatically disrupt processing of a previously glimpsed picture if that visual event is new and meaningful. The results showed that a blank field, repeating the same picture, and new nonsense picture did not disrupt memory as much as a new meaningful picture, thus providing support for the conceptual-masking hypothesis. Earlier, Intraub (1981) showed that when a sequence of pictures is rapidly presented, viewers can reliably detect a verbally specified target-picture. Targets were specified by name, by a superordinate category label, or a negative category (e.g. 'something that is not edible'); pictures were presented at 114, 172 or 258 ms per picture. In each of the target specification conditions, detection of targets was worse than immediate recognition of targets in a control condition – indicating that rapidly presented pictures may be momentarily understood at the time of viewing and then quickly forgotten.

These effects of conceptual masking share similarities with results reported recently by Marks (1991) from studies of more slowly presented static images. Marks showed that manipulations of orienting task used during encoding influences how well the names of pictured items and the visual details of the pictured items are remembered. As an orientation task, although not expecting to have to remember the pictures (of examples of clothing, furniture, tools, toys, etc.), subjects made judgements about whether the pictures contained three specified colours, whether the picture generally faced a particular direction, or whether a particular object would usually belong in such a scene. The results indicate that the nature of the memory test influences the effectiveness of different encoding conditions (Table 5.2). Recall and recognition of pictures' names were best after subjects judged scene encodings, next best after they judged orientation, and poorest after they judged colour.

However, the results for the recognition of pictures' visual details were quite different. Subjects were shown original pictures and similar pictures which had been changed in certain ways. Of these distractors, one-third were items from the same category as the original but which had not appeared in the set encountered earlier, and were the same colour as the original, one-third were from the same category and had the same name and colours as the originals, but were different versions or exemplars of that category, while one-third were identical to the original except that the colours and orientations of the original items were changed. Analyses of accuracy (d') suggested that type of encoding task had no effect on memory for visual details, whereas analysis of net hit rate (i.e. hit-rate minus false-alarm rate) suggested that memory for visual details was impaired by conceptual encoding (judging the appropriateness of a picture in a scene).

Table 5.2 Increasing percentages of false recognition following changes in object characteristics and orienting tasks.

| | Orientation task: | | |
Visual details:	Colour	Orientation	Scene
Different name/different object/same colour	10	12	07
Same name/different object/same colour	21	24	29
Same name/same object/diff. colour and orientation	33	53	59

After Marks, 1991

The patterns of hits and false alarms reported by Marks are also quite striking. Irrespective of the orientation task, where people encountered an object from the appropriate category in the correct colour, around 10 per cent of the time they incorrectly believed this to have been seen earlier. This false alarm rate increased to about 25 per cent when the object name and colour are correct, even though the object itself had never been seen before. Finally, and very strikingly, even when they were explicitly attending to the colour of the object, the fact that it was the same object even though its colour and orientation had changed, seemed enough to encourage people to believe they had seen it before (33 per cent). This explicit attention to colour was of some benefit, but explicit attention to orientation is not: even with the colour and orientation altered, a false alarm rate of over 50 per cent was found whether or not orientation or more general aspects of the scene were being attended to.

Dynamic versus static images

Goldstein, Chance, Hoisington and Buescher (1982) compared recognition performance for static and moving images. In one condition, eight-second film segments, derived from a 10-minute study film, and from other sections of the same film, were used as targets and foils. In a second condition, freeze frames from the film segment and from other portions of the film were presented as targets and foils. Control subjects saw still pictures and were tested on still targets and foils, all derived from the films. The results showed that recognition memory for dynamically presented material was significantly better than memory for the same information presented in a static form (Table 5.3).

Table 5.3 Recognition accuracy of dynamic and statically presented film clips.

Learn	Test	Recognition accuracy (d′)
Dynamic images	Dynamic images	2.61
Static images	Static images	2.22
Dynamic images	Static images	2.08

After Goldstein, Chance, Hoisington and Buescher, 1982

Both memory and attention can be influenced by a range of cinematic effects. Boltz, Schulkind and Kantra (1991) manipulated the relative placement of music, such that music either accompanied a film scene's outcome, and thereby accentuated its affective meaning, or foreshadowed the scene, and thereby created expectancies about the future course of events. Background music was either congruent or incongruent with the affect of an episode's outcome. When subjects later recalled the series of filmed episodes, results show that expectancy violations arising from mood-incongruent relations led to better memory in the foreshadowing condition, while mood-congruent relations led to better performance in the accompanying condition. Results from a recognition task revealed that scenes unavailable for recall were recognised when cued by background music (see also Chapter 9).

Kraft, Cantor and Gottdiener (1991) examined memory for visual narratives as a function of cinematic structure. Four visual narratives were constructed, with each narrative taking place within a single location and presenting an interaction between two main characters. Narratives began with or without an 'establishing shot', and preserved or violated directional continuity. Kraft and colleagues showed strong influences of 'establishing shots' and directional continuity on subjects' memory for the depicted events. Their findings indicate that directional continuity is used to determine and preserve the flow of action, while establishing shots also serve as a basis for enhancing subjects' ability to remember depicted activities in the appropriate sequence. There is a clear parallel here between the priming and cueing effects of verbal labels and themes on the subsequent interpretation of, and memory for, static images.

Boltz (1992) examined the effects of temporal accent structure on the remembering of filmed narratives, by varying the placement and number of commercial breaks. Commercials either highlighted a story's underlying organisation by occurring between major episode boundaries (i.e. at breakpoint locations), or obscured this structural arrangement by occurring within episodes (i.e. at non-breakpoints). Relative to the accentuation of non-breakpoints, results indicated that the attentional highlighting of episode boundaries yielded higher recall and recognition performance, and better memory for temporal order information and details from the story's plot. Selective recall and recognition of breakpoint scenes was significantly higher than that of non-breakpoints, suggesting that people use episode boundaries as referents for attending and remembering. These findings illustrate certain structural invariants across environmental events and ways in which event structure can be used in remembering. We will return to these themes on many occasions throughout this book.

■ Faces

Facial features and prototypical faces

Individual features of faces contribute much to successful face recognition, but so too does the relationship between these features. McKelvie (1976) demonstrated that masking eyes and mouths has different effects on face recognition performance. Subjects were just as confident and just as quick to respond, but made more errors when the eyes were masked than when the mouths were. These results suggest that, in general, eyes are more important than the mouth in facilitating face recognition. This increased importance of the upper portion of the face in recognition judgements has been confirmed in rather more elegant research, recently reported by Reynolds and Pezdek (1992). Two studies explored the relative memory for five facial features (hair, eyes, chin, nose, and mouth) among subjects who first viewed slides of faces, and later performed a recognition task with identical or changed versions of each face. Both experiments showed that the upper-face features (i.e. hair and eyes) were recognised better than the lower-face features (i.e. nose, mouth, and chin). Other studies have sought to address the relationship between facial features.

Haig (1986) reports a small but important study in which four target faces were image processed and separated into 162 contiguous squares. These could be displayed in their correct positions in any combination of 24 or fewer squares. Subjects were required to judge which of the four target faces were displayed during each one-second presentation. The results, which show the proportion of correct responses for each of the 162 squares, were taken by Haig to 'support the proposition that memory, as applied to facial recognition, involves the "hard-wired" storage of a bland prototypical face upon which may be superimposed the deviant or anomalous features that help distinguish one familiar face from another' (p. 386). Later, Bruce, Doyle, Dench and Burton (1991) reported a series of eight studies which clearly show that subjects can distinguish between configurations of facial features they had previously been exposed to, and new configurations of features which are very subtly different. They also interpret their findings as evidence for the formation of a 'prototypical' configuration of facial features, which is tuned to the particular qualities of particular exemplars. Much earlier, Goldstein and Chance (1980) proposed a 'schema' theory to explain the comparative efficiency of own-race face recognition with other-race recognition, correlation between own-race and other-race recognition performance measures, and inverted face recognition. These issues will be addressed below.

Recognition of own- and other-race faces

Shepherd, Deregowski and Ellis (1974) showed that European subjects were better able to recognise European faces than African faces, while African subjects were superior at recognising African faces compared with European faces. Chance, Turner and Goldstein (1982), report a rather tantalising result which suggests that own-race superiority for facial recognition emerges relatively late in development. While subjects less than 12 years of age recognised Caucasian and Oriental faces equally well, adults were much more accurate at identifying own-race as opposed to Oriental faces. This suggests that some learned distinction underlies the own-race effect. Shepherd and colleagues interpreted their results as reflecting better recognition for faces of members of their own groups as the result of frequent experience with them.

Table 5.4 Accuracy (d′) of own- and other-race face recognition.

Observers:	Faces Caucasian	Japanese
Caucasian	1.36	0.77
Japanese	0.84	1.53

After O'Toole, Deffenbacher, Valentin and Abdi, 1994

This suggestion gains some support from the findings of Goldstein and Chance (1985) who showed that subjects trained on Japanese face-digit pairs were significantly better at recognising unstudied Japanese faces, even up to some five months after training. More recently, O'Toole, Deffenbacher, Valentin and Abdi (1994) were able to show the other-race effect with Caucasian and Japanese stimuli for both Caucasian and Japanese observers (Table 5.4). Fascinatingly, in a second study, Caucasian observers rated the faces used in the recognition task in terms of a number of variables including typicality, familiarity, attractiveness and memorability. Just as in previous research (cited by O'Toole et al., 1994, p. 208), for Caucasian faces, typicality is composed of two orthogonal components, one in which typicality is independently related to attractiveness and familiarity ratings, while the other component involves an independent relationship between typicality and memorability ratings. However, for Japanese faces, typicality was related only to memorability, that is, attractiveness and familiarity were not related to typicality. It is tempting to suppose that the reciprocal result would also emerge were ratings to be made by younger and older non-Caucasian observers. If it did, it might indicate that own–other race differentiation, which Chance and colleagues found emerged in early adolescence, might depend on attractiveness and constitution of peer-groups.

Facial orientation

Partly for practical and partly for theoretical reasons, a number of studies have considered the fact that faces in different orientations are not all equally well remembered. Powerful effects of encoding and retrieval context have also been reported in connection with face-recognition, especially in relation to eye-witness testimony. These are discussed in later chapters. Here we consider findings which do not relate explicitly to context.

Walker-Smith (1980) studied recognition for facial identity, expression, and orientation in a successive face comparison task. Subjects made same–different judgements about pairs of face photographs that could differ in any one of these respects. Changes in identity were noticed more readily than changes in expression and orientation. Recognition tests after a one second retention interval yielded similar performance to the no-delay condition. However, after just a 20 second delay, some expression and orientation information had been lost, although accuracy for identity judgements remained unchanged. In general, identity judgements have been found to be robust over much longer retention intervals. For example, Chance and Goldstein (1987) show that number of correct recognitions of faces (i.e. hits) did not decline over a period of seven days, although the number of faces thought to have been seen, but which had not actually been seen (i.e. false alarms), increased with delay between encoding and test. Response times, for both hits and false alarms, increased with retention interval.

A number of studies have shown asymmetries in face-perception and recognition, showing preferences for left-half-face views over right-half-face views (see Rhodes, 1985). Rhodes's own studies have shown perceptual asymmetries favouring the half-face on the observer's left for both unfamiliar faces and famous faces, under free-viewing but not when fixations were controlled. However, these different scanning or attentional strategies, which favour the half-face normally seen on the observer's left, are not retained in memory. Bruce, Valentine and Baddeley (1987) contrasted the recognition memory performance of subjects for three-quarter, full-face, and profile views of familiar and unfamiliar faces. When the decision to be made was whether the face presented was of a highly familiar colleague, three-quarter and full-face were recognised as readily as each other, with profiles being less well recognised. In a sequential matching task, in which subjects had to decide whether successive photographs were of the same individual with whom subjects were familiar, there was no particular advantage for the three-quarter view, although profiles again produced decrements in performance. When the same faces were shown to subjects who were unfamiliar with the individuals shown, decisions about three-quarter views were made more quickly, and profiles again proved difficult. These studies show that the nature of the retrieval task is once again important: matching different views of an individual is more difficult than deciding whether the individual shown is familiar.

Rather more attention has been devoted to people's processing of inverted faces. McKelvie (1985) asked undergraduates to categorise photographs of faces on the basis of their gender or attractiveness, and later to recognise those they had encountered. When faces were presented in their normal orientation, the accuracy and confidence of subjects' recognition judgements were greater for faces for which attractiveness rather than gender judgements had been made. However, inverted faces were recognised much less well, irrespective of whether they were initially encoded during liking or sex judgement orienting tasks. Valentine and Bruce (cited in Valentine, 1988, p. 474) showed that less familiar stimuli show a greater *inversion effect*, that is, recognition of other-race faces was more disrupted by inversion than recognising own-race faces. Echoing McKelvie's findings, they found that making personality judgements or naming distinctive facial features had no effect on ability to recognise inverted faces. The fact that orientation towards distinctive features gave no advantage in the inversion recognition phase suggests that the difficulties encountered with inverted faces are not perceptually based. Results reported by Diamond and Carey (1986) also indicate that the effect of orientation on memory for faces does not depend on inability to identify single features of these stimuli upside down. Reviewing the results on face-inversions and recognition, Valentine (1988) concluded that the inversion effect does not constitute evidence for a unique process in face recognition, and that the effect is best interpreted in terms of expertise in face processing and the homogeneous nature of faces as a stimulus class. His recent series of studies which combine the effects of distinctiveness, inversion, and race confirm this view (see Valentine, 1991) and offer a more general and integrated account of face recognition.

Typicality, familiarity and distinctiveness

It has been widely reported that familiar faces are better recognised than unfamiliar faces. Klatzky and Forrest (1984) sought to assess the contribution of orientation-specific information, facial features and verbalisable, personal-category information to this so-called famous-face advantage in recognition. They concluded that none of these variables were in themselves sufficient to account for the recognition advantage enjoyed by familiar faces over unfamiliar ones, and instead they suggest that face recognition relies on some form of abstract non-verbal memory representation. Bartlett, Hurry and Thorley (1984) report results from a series of studies which they interpreted as indicating that the effect of distinctiveness in recognition memory for previously unfamiliar faces can be accounted for in terms of the differential perceived familiarity of distinctive and typical faces. According to this view, typical faces are likely to be thought to be familiar, but unusual faces, once encountered, are still more likely to be thought familiar. Valentine and Bruce (cited in Valentine, 1988) challenged the view of Bartlett and colleagues. In their study, postgraduates and staff from their own and other psychology departments rated the distinctiveness and familiarity photographs of male members of staff from their own department. They found that in fact the effects of distinctiveness and familiarity in the recognition of highly familiar faces are independent, and better understood in terms of facial prototypes.

Courtois and Mueller (1981) demonstrated that face recognition was better when either the target or distractor faces were distinctive with respect to the other faces encountered – the effect lasting up to 28 days after original encoding. More recently, attempts to determine what actually constitutes facial distinctiveness per se have proved rather less successful, with derived measures of distinctiveness showing only small correlations with memorability (see Bruce, Burton and Dench, 1994).

One approach to studying the role of distinctiveness has involved contrasts between recognition memory for photographs, line drawings and caricatures. It is reasoned that since caricatures distil the essence of a face, they provide representations which are closer to some underlying schematic face-representation. Tversky and Baratz (1985) showed that subjects performed better with photographs on name recall, face recognition, and name-face verification reaction time, than with line-drawn caricatures. Rhodes and Moody (1990) found that veridically drawn faces were recognised more rapidly than caricatures. In contrast, in their first study, Mauro and Kubovy (1992) showed that caricatures were recognised better than faces, and that true caricatures of previously seen faces were recognised better than the faces from which the caricatures had been developed. They report involved sequential tachistoscopic presentation of faces and their caricatures, with subjects having to decide whether the two stimuli were the same or different. Because subjects took longer to distinguish between the stimuli when a somewhat blurred face preceded its caricatures, Mauro and Kubovy concluded that caricatures are more similar to the encoded representation of a face than are stimuli in which the distinctive features are de-emphasised. However, if this were the case, one might expect the representation of the real face to prime identification of the following caricature, thus leading to faster rather than slower decisions, if not errors. There is no evidence that this occurs. It is, in any case, a rather peculiar argument. Caricatures do indeed yield very distinctive representations of faces, drawing attention as they do to some features more than others. However, this does not mean that such features map on to any typicality–distinctiveness dimensions unconsciously used to represent faces. Furthermore, determining to what extent the internal caricature has been distorted so that an actual face can later be remembered is a far from trivial problem.

Labelling faces

We frequently need to associate faces with verbal information of some sort, whether it is a name or some other personal detail, such as an individual's occupation. Although this is probably among the most frequently performed paired-associate task in everyday life, the difficulties associated with remembering someone's name are well known. These difficulties have been explored in a number of studies. McWeeny, Young, Hay and Ellis (1987) found that names are more difficult to associate with unfamiliar faces than are occupations. Earlier, Klatzky, Martin and Kane (1982) had shown that faces could be related to occupational categories, but that there was a cost in doing so. When faces which had been associated with a particular category were presented, they were recognised more frequently and more quickly. However, when the same labels were presented with previously unseen faces, recognition errors occurred. In a forced-choice recognition test, in which distractors were highly similar to originally seen faces, congruent occupational labelling failed to increase recognition of previously seen faces. Thus, these results show that interpreting faces with respect to some categorical information must have altered some semantic properties attributed to the face, rather than emphasising the distinctiveness of some of its physical properties. Had it been so, old items would have been better recognised in the forced choice study. Considering the McWeeny results, it seems likely that forming semantic associations to an individual's name is rather more difficult than to the person's occupation, leaving rather more potentially successful retrieval routes available when direct face–name retrieval fails. Since occupations are intrinsically more imageable than given or surnames, this would not be surprising in a wider memory context (see section on exceptional remembering, Chapter 11).

A number of studies suggest that some faces are attended to more closely than others. In their study, Klatzky et al. (1982) report that faces which were rated as more stereotypical were also more recognisable, regardless of any accompanying labels. Earlier, McKelvie (1976) distinguished between faces that proved difficult to label and those for which labelling was relatively easy. When recognition memory for faces was tested later, hard-to-label faces benefited more from having labels available than did easy-to-label faces. However, when subjects were instructed to attend to all of the face's features during encoding, even the recognition of easy-to-label faces was enhanced. Thus, where faces are typical in some way, they are probably attended to less. Attaching a verbal label to a face makes that face more distinctive, in that it serves to direct attention to specific facial features during viewing. However, these features may or may not be of assistance in any later recognition test, since the features attended to may be common to both target and distracter faces. In a very different context, Chapman and Groeger (1995) report that recognition of risk-related films of traffic scenes are disrupted in a similar fashion (see Chapter 9).

These studies show that learned labels may misdirect attention. However, it is also important to realise that names, while they may have special properties, are essentially still verbal stimuli, and as a result may also be subject to the ways in which verbal stimuli vary. Thus, surnames may be more or less 'concrete', which may cause difficulty in using surnames as labels which orient attention to specific facial features. Similarly, since high-frequency words are generally better recalled (see next chapter), high-frequency surnames may be less prone to forgetting. Valentine, Bredart, Lawson and Ward (1991) have shown that in tasks that require access to memory for specific individuals, the effect of surname frequency is analogous to the effect of distinctiveness in face recognition (Fig 5.4).

Fig 5.4 Classification of faces as 'British' as a function of frequency and familiarity of surname (after Valentine, Bredart, Lawson and Ward, 1991).

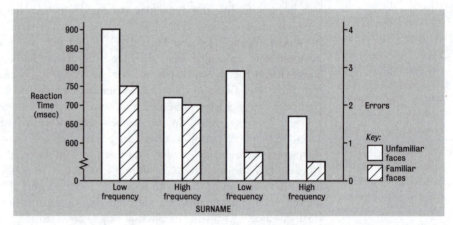

It has been assumed that while names may be relatively special verbal labels, they are separate from the faces and person representations to which they refer. As a result of processing failures, names may be retrieved without faces and vice versa. The model of face recognition proposed by Bruce and Young (1986) explicitly predicts dissociations of this sort, as it does the existence of brain-injured patients who may remain able to decide whether a face is familiar or not, but who cannot access person information such as occupation. Such patients have recently been reported (e.g. de Haan, Young and Newcombe, 1991).

Are faces special?

From the studies reviewed earlier, it seems likely that some fundamental organisation of facial properties form the basis of an abstract schematic or prototypical representation, which in turn guides much of our processing of faces. Given the many ways in which the human face is important to us, it would not be surprising if its processing, and especially our ability to recognise it, were not 'special' in some ways. However, it seems clear from a number of studies (e.g. Myles-Worsley, Johnston and Simons, 1988), that complex visual stimuli from other domains in which we may be expert are remembered equally well.

BOX 5.1: Expertise in X-ray interpretation and remembering

Miles-Worsley and colleagues examined the performance of observers with different levels of radiological experience on recognition memory tasks. The stimuli used were slides of faces and equal numbers of clinically normal and clinically abnormal chest X-ray films. Recognition memory for faces was uniformly high across all levels of radiological experience. X-ray films with clinical abnormalities were better recognised as a function of degree of radiological experience and, for the most experienced radiologists, was equivalent to memory for faces. However, recognition memory for normal films actually decreased with radiological experience from above chance to a chance level. Thus, radiological expertise allows clinically relevant stimuli to be better detected and remembered, but highly similar stimuli, which may not be relevant to clinical diagnosis, seem to be forgotten. Arguably, for the expert radiographer, stimuli without clinical abnormalities form, and later reinforce, notions of what schema-inconsistencies are not associated with clinical abnormality. In the less experienced radiographer, who may possess less differentiated schema, many more clinically normal and abnormal X-rays will be schema-inconsistent, and thus are more likely to be remembered.

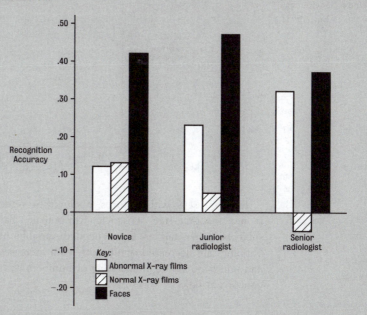

Recognition accuracy for faces, abnormal X-ray films, and normal X-ray films as a function of radiology experience (after Myles-Worsley, Johnston and Simons, 1988).

Work by Diamond and Carey (1986) also challenges the view that faces are special. In two studies reported in that paper, they report that people whose knowledge of dogs was sufficient to allow them reliably to discriminate between different dogs of the same breed, showed as large inversion effects with upside-down photographs of dogs as did their memory for inverted faces. It seems possible, from more recent work, that domain experience rather than domain expertise is sufficient for differential remembering to emerge. McKelvie, Standing, St.-Jean and Law (1993) contrasted male and female differences in memory for everyday complex visual stimuli line drawings (Exp. 1) and photographs (Exp. 2) of faces and cars (Fig 5.5). Recognition memory for faces was better than for cars in both studies. The second study they report reveals an intriguing sex-difference, in that photographs of cars were better recognised by men than by women (Fig 5.5), while recognition memory for photographs of children was better for women than for men. That such differences did not emerge from the earlier study, in which line drawings were used, is consistent with the findings of other studies which have contrasted performance with photographs and line-dawn facial caricatures. Nevertheless, McKelvie and colleagues' second study demonstrates clearly the influence of what might now be regarded as traditional stereotypical sex-role related influences on recognition memory for complex pictorial stimuli.

Fig 5.5 Recognition of cars, own-sex and other-sex faces as a function of gender (after McKelvie, Standing, St.-Jean and Law, 1993).

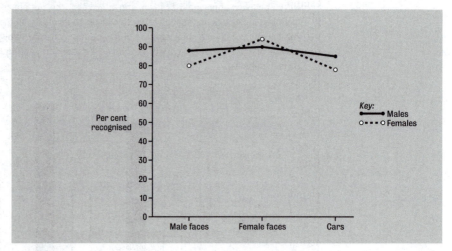

Finally, just as with pictures, it should be remembered that of processing faces is not resource-free. Hiscock, Kinsbourne, Samuels and Krause (1987) had subjects finger tap as they encoded variable numbers of numbers and faces. Tapping rate decreased significantly with increases in memory load, for both faces and numbers, although encoding of numbers was the more demanding of the two concurrent tasks.

Stories

Stories generally include participants, and the goals they are attempting to attain; details of their thoughts, actions and interactions with each other as well as animate and inanimate objects; information which supports some interpretation, and perhaps some information which offers some resolution or explanation of the events depicted. Each of these features have been studied to a greater or lesser extent in research on memory for text or story-like materials. Just as with faces, as noted above, the interplay between these basic elements, and how this interplay is organised and represented in memory have been the focus of research.

Actions, consequences and causes

Goals, actions and their effects, real and inferred, provide an organisational structure for many different types of story, and concern most of what we might see as the plot of a story. Reiser, Black and Lehnert (1985) showed that subjects, when asked to sort stories into groups which had the same kind of plot, did so according to thematic patterns instead of specific story content. Thus, to cite the example Reiser and colleagues use, subjects distinguished between stories involving competition and retaliation and those involving competition and change of mind. When asked to write stories with the same kind of plot as a set of exemplar stories, subjects wrote stories with essentially the same configuration of plot units as the exemplars. Subjects considered the actions undertaken by the protagonist to resolve a problem to be more central components of the thematic representation than the problem situation motivating those actions.

Sometimes elements of the plot are not explicitly stated, but are inferred by the reader or listener. Baggett (1975), for example, explored the nature of the memory representation of two types of information in picture stories: surface information, arising directly from pictures which occur in the stories; and conceptual information, easily inferable when integrating the pictures into a connected story, but arising potentially also from pictures not in the stories. Baggett's results indicate that, while viewing, the observer made inferences necessary to form a coherent story, rejecting improbable pictures. Such plot elements constrain what we expect to occur next. At other stages, background knowledge exerts a considerable influence on what is encoded and remembered.

Owens, Bower and Black (1979) showed that when subjects learned a series of actions of a character, their memory was strongly influenced by beliefs about that character's motives. Motives allowed subjects to decide the meaning of the actions, their importance, and their interconnections. Recall and recognition showed that subjects distorted many of the colourless events to be motive relevant. Thus, although motives helped to connect the disparate actions represented in the stories, and thus aided comprehension and memory, they also interfered with accurate recording and recall of the details. The importance of motives and consequences varies with age. Surber (1982) carried out a study in which the effects of the order of presentation of motive and consequence information on the moral judgements of children were contrasted. The positions of motives and consequences were varied factorially. In each case the most recently encountered piece of information was most influential. Results also showed a developmental shift in the weights of motives and consequences. For older children, motives counted for more than did consequences, while for younger children, the weight of consequences was larger than the weight of motives. This is the pattern of findings we might well expect given more recent findings which suggest that an understanding of others' motives and thoughts (i.e. theory of mind) develops as children age (see Chapter 13).

Goals identified in the story also serve to determine which elements are seen as relevant and irrelevant. This also has consequences for memory. In a study reported by Hudson (1988), children listened to stories about familiar events (a trip to McDonald's and grocery shopping). These stories contained actions which might be expected in those situations (i.e. script-actions), irrelevancies that did not affect the goal of an event, and disruptions that did disrupt the accomplishment of event goal. They then participated in a recall or recognition test, either immediately or after a day's delay. Only recall performance showed an effect of delay on remembering. Disruptions were recalled better than irrelevancies, and this effect was more pronounced in delayed recall. Both types of atypical actions were recognised as well. Script actions were least well recalled and, as emerged from the recognition studies, script actions were confused with other typical actions not included in the stories (i.e. false alarms). These results (Fig 5.6) are consistent with those which emerge from studies of adult story memory, and strongly suggest that some underlying structural principles support our encoding and remembering of stories.

Fig 5.6 Children's recall and recognition of script-based, script-irrelevant and script-disruptions (after Hudson, 1988).

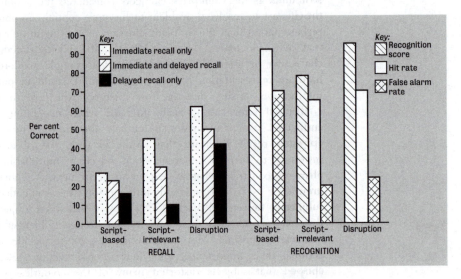

There is abundant evidence that the causal structure of a story is important for its comprehension and memory. Gee and Grosjean (1984), for example, found that in the retelling of a learned story, spontaneous pause durations at sentence breaks were highly correlated with the importance of these points as predicted from a plot unit model of the text. Only low correlations were obtained, however, when reading pause durations were correlated with the model. Trabasso and Van-den-Broek (1985) demonstrate that causal representations of the narrative events used in a number of experimental studies, account for substantial proportions of common and unique variance in immediate and delayed recall, summarisation, and judged importance of events. Precisely how these causal representations are to be realised has been a matter of some debate.

Scripts, story-grammars and schema-based accounts

Bower (1976) discusses the processes individuals use to understand and remember simple stories. According to his analysis, simple stories or folk tales have a definite abstract structure (grammar rules). From experiencing hundreds of such stories over their lifetime, people acquire this abstract framework about simple stories and use it to reconstruct stories which they have heard. If a text violates some of the critical rules, then it seems less coherent, is harder to learn, and is forgotten more readily. Propositions within a story are ordered hierarchically; elements at higher levels in this hierarchy are most likely to be remembered and to be included in summaries. The plot structure of a study can be distinguished from its content, and transfer learning effects can be examined across successive passages. About the same time Thorndyke (1977) offered a similar account, proposing a hierarchical organisational framework of stories in memory, determined by a story-grammar, representing the abstract structural components of the plot. Empirical results were reported in support of these ideas, showing that comprehensibility and recall were a function of the amount of inherent plot structure in the story. Thorndyke also reports, as would be predicted from the Bower framework, that subjects tended to recall facts corresponding to high-level organisational story elements rather than lower-level details, and that story summaries from memory tended to emphasise general structural characteristics rather than specific content. Caccamise and Kintsch (1978) have also shown that superordinate propositions and macro-propositions of a text are more likely to be recalled.

Black and Bower (1979) showed that story statements cluster into episodes, and that memory representations of statements also cluster into separate episode chunks in memory. Their first study showed that the recall of episode actions depends on the length of that episode, but not on the lengths of other episodes. Adding more actions to an episode increased recall of the original actions but did not affect recall of other episodes. Furthermore, subjects rated the original actions as more important than the added actions, thus suggesting that unimportant actions increased the recall of important actions in that episode. A second study showed that the more subordinate actions an episode contains, the more likely a statement summarising that episode is to be recalled. Glenn (1978) examined the role of length and of episodic structure in childrens' recall of simple stories, showing remarkably similar results to those reported by Black and Bower. The episodic nature of story encoding and recall provides a clear account of results recently reported by Boltz (1992), and discussed above. Boltz, it will be recalled, found that commercials either highlighted a story's underlying organisation by occurring between major episode boundaries (i.e., at breakpoint locations) or obscured this structural arrangement by occurring within episodes (i.e., at non-breakpoints). Compared to non-breakpoints, results indicated that the attentional highlighting of episode boundaries yielded higher recall and recognition performance, and better memory for temporal order information and details from the story's plot (Fig 5.7). This is just as would be expected from the role of episode boundaries, as shown by Black and Bower.

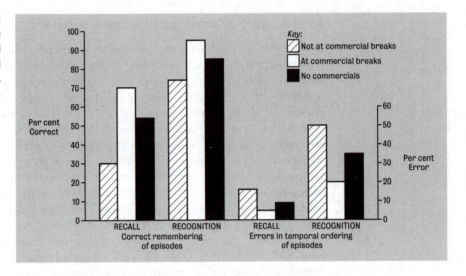

Fig 5.7 Commercial breaks enhance episodic remembering and retrieval of temporal structure (after Boltz, 1992).

Kintsch and Kintsch (1978), on the other hand, discuss the role of schemata in comprehending stories (showing that schemata are culture-specific), and their role in guiding the comprehension process. Children were shown picture stories consisting of several pictures without text. The stories were well-structured and contained two or more causally and temporally related episodes. The children were asked to describe each picture and, after seeing all the pictures, to recall the story without the pictures. The pictures were either presented in their normal or in their scrambled order. A comparison between responses in the normal condition, when subjects were telling a story, and in the scrambled condition, when they were merely responding to the pictures, demonstrated that even the four-year-old children were guided by what Kintsch suggests is some schematic organisation of the story. Those parts of their descriptions that were best integrated into a story were recalled best, while non-integrated descriptions tended to be forgotten. Similar findings are reported by Poulsen, Kintsch, Kintsch and Premack (1979).

As can be seen from the brief description above of Thorndyke's approach to story comprehension and memory, the story-grammar account focuses on the hierarchical structure of events and the centrality of certain plot elements. Schema-based accounts, or at least strong versions of the schema account, predict the construction of a canonically ordered representation during processing of prose comprehension. Weaker versions of the schema account are virtually indistinguishable from a goal-oriented, episodic, story-grammar account. A further account can be found in Schank and Abelson's (1977) script theory, which emphasises structure and the temporal sequence of events. Nelson and Gruendel (1986) distinguish five properties of scripts: (1) scripts are organised sequentially; (2) they are organised around a central event; (3) they are generalised and include slots for variable elements; (4) they are similar across individuals who share the same experience; (5) they are consistent across repeated experience. This listing makes clear that although a range of nomenclature has been developed in relation to scripts, schema and story-grammar-based accounts of story memory, the structures proposed overlap greatly in functional terms, if indeed they are not interchangeable in most instances.

A number of studies have claimed to test the differences between these accounts. Baker (1978), for example, examined the effect of input sequence on memory for simple stories. After reading stories written in either chronological or flashback sequence, subjects made a decision about the underlying order of occurrence of two events. Decisions about input order were faster and more accurate than decisions about underlying order when the stories contained flashbacks, indicating that subjects based their responses on a memory representation that preserved the input sequence of events. Decisions were easier when the events in the story had a logical progression rather than an arbitrary ordering, thus demonstrating an influence of prior knowledge and, one might think, schema-like processing. Baker, however, suggests that the flashback results conflict with a strong schema-based approach to story memory, and presumably also with accounts based on causal structure and scripts. The latter, it will be remembered, predicts construction of a canonically ordered representation during processing. Yussen, Huang, Mathews and Evans (1988) reported that story schemata served to organise recall of scrambled versions of stories, strongly influenced recall of details and gist, and demonstrated that the schema's influence on the organisation of memory holds over time and serves to buttress the more abstract and general elements of the narrative. Whether story schemata do so more than would story-grammars, or scripts was not explored, but it seems unlikely that they would do so.

In a study reported by Gibbs and Tenney (1980), undergraduates listened to a series of stories based on everyday activities, such as taking a shower, which, in Schank and Abelson's (1977) terminology, have familiar scripts. Script implications, like getting undressed, were either made explicit in the story or were left implicit. Unpredictable script variables, such as the temperature of the water, were specified. On an immediate sentence recognition test, subjects detected changes in script variables more accurately than changes in the explicitness of the script implications. After a delay, test sentences with added or deleted script implications were falsely recognised and were judged to be as familiar as test sentences with no changes. These results support the hypothesis that the memory representation for stories includes relevant script knowledge, or at least reflects some higher order structure within which story-like material is interpreted and remembered. Galambos and Rips (1982) contrasted predictions about the organisation in memory of routine events derived from Schank and Abelson's (1977) script theory, which emphasises the temporal sequence of events, and story grammars, which focus on events' hierarchical structure or centrality. Subjects ranked both the sequence and centrality of routine events. Centrality, but not sequence, influenced time to decide whether an episode belonged to a routine, while sequence alone affected decisions about which of two episodes occurred earlier, but this sequence effect was opposite to that predicted by script theory. Findings suggest that sequence and centrality information, while very important in comprehension and memory, may be computed as needed, rather than precompiled. This is contrary to the tenets of some versions of script theory.

One might imagine that if we did indeed possess structures for interpreting goal-related material in story-like materials, those which shared similar goals might be confusable, or might influence one another. Seifert, McKoon, Abelson and Ratcliff (1986) found that cross-episode influences (i.e., when two episodes with a shared theme are connected through a thematic structure) on comprehension and memory were rather weak. The first two studies reported in their paper showed that verification time for a test sentence from one story was reduced when an immediately preceding test sentence came from a thematically similar story. However, this only arose when subjects were given explicit instructions to rate the similarities of the two stories concerned. Other studies they report also show some facilitation for sentence comprehension and memory, but again only where the preceding stories had been extensively studied beforehand. Seifert and colleagues conclude that during reading of an episode, thematic information may be encoded to lead to activation of similar episodes and formation of connections in memory between episodes, but such encoding is effortful, strategy dependent and greatly influenced by task difficulty.

Finally, Iran-Nejad (1986) draws attention to another important way of evaluating these accounts, in a discussion of how the various theories cope with stories which prove to have surprise endings. Comprehension of a story is said to occur when the sequence of events in the story matches the sequence of events in an underlying script or structure. Comprehension of surprise endings, on the other hand, while accounted for in the same way by story-grammar theories, are handled differently by a more schema-based, constructive approach, which holds that surprise-ending stories invoke and maintain two incompatible global schemata. In a compelling argument, Iran-Nejad concludes that only the latter type of theory can provide a coherent picture of what is involved in the comprehension of surprise-ending stories.

Although evidence appears to favour schema-based accounts, it is difficult to anticipate how the debate over which theory best accounts for our story memory will finally be resolved. None of the accounts offered have gone unchallenged, or have not been somewhat embarrassed by empirical evidence. At the same time, as has been known since the time of Bartlett (1932), it is clear that organisational tendencies influence our interpretation and reproduction of story-like information, and that the principles involved extend across a range of materials. It seems most likely that recurrent themes and causal sequences play a strong role in these organisational tendencies (see Van-den-Broek and Lorch, 1993).

Themes and different perspectives

The foregoing sections make clear that, when reading or hearing texts, people, perhaps unintentionally, adopt particular ways of interpreting the incoming information. A number of studies show quite dramatically that people can also be encouraged to do so by external instruction, and can invoke something akin to the schema-like structures they might spontaneously employ in other circumstances.

In an important study Bransford and Johnson (1972) found that providing a title prior to learning a prose passage reliably increased the number of ideas which could be recalled from it. There was comparatively little benefit from providing such titles once the passage had been read, which suggests that, as the passage was being read, impressions as to its central themes were being formed. This is confirmed by the reports of subjects who took part – 'Ss in the present experiments who were not provided with the context or topic prior to hearing the passage reported that they actively searched for a situation that the passage might be about; generally they were unable to find one suitable for understanding the entire passage, although they could make parts of it make sense' (Bransford and Johnson, 1972, p. 715). Predebon (1984) and Groeger and Bekerian (1995) provide replications of these findings, albeit in a rather different context. These studies will be considered in greater detail later when the relationships between memory and time are addressed (Chapter 7).

Anderson and Pichert (1978) report two fascinating studies in which subjects read a story about two boys 'playing hooky' from school, from the perspective of either a burglar or a person interested in buying a home. After recalling the story once, subjects were directed to shift perspectives and then recall the story again. The results of both experiments show that, on their second recall, subjects recalled significantly more information important to the second perspective that had been unimportant to the first one. They also recalled less information unimportant to the second perspective that had been important to the first one. In addition to demonstrating that people can be encouraged to adopt particular, schema-like, orientations towards both the encoding and retrieval of information, they also demonstrate that information which was thought not to be recallable can become so, given the appropriate retrieval conditions. In a further study, Anderson, Pichert and Shirey (1983) showed that the schema operative during reading appeared to influence not only the likelihood that certain text elements would be learned but also their longevity in memory. Schmidt and Schmidt (1986) report findings that adults may be able to switch story perspectives more easily than children. This may be a reflection of the differential ability of adults and children to think about situations from the perspectives of others (see Chapter 13).

BOX 5.2: Schema effects in text processing

Research by McDaniel, in a similar vein, extends these findings significantly. McDaniel (1984) examined recall for a story in which letters were deleted from words contained in one-third of the idea units. Results show that recall was significantly better for those ideas with letters deleted than for those with letters intact (see figure), and, following Anderson and Pichert, that recall was enhanced when subjects were encouraged to adopt the perspective of either a home buyer or burglar, or, as in the final study, when the subject adopted the perspective of either a shipwrecked person or a florist while reading a story about seagulls. Taken together, the findings show that recall of idea units was an additive function of (1) an idea's importance to the perspective adopted and (2) the letter-deletion manipulation. McDaniel and Kerwin (1987) replicated these findings, and also found that recall tests one week later showed that both the encoding perspective, and the deletion task, contributed independently to performance. Recognition was enhanced by the letter deletion task, but there were no differences as a function of idea unit importance. These results suggest that both proposition-specific and schema-related processing are important for long-term retention of narrative prose, and that any successful model of story memory should incorporate both elaborative-processing and schema-based mechanisms.

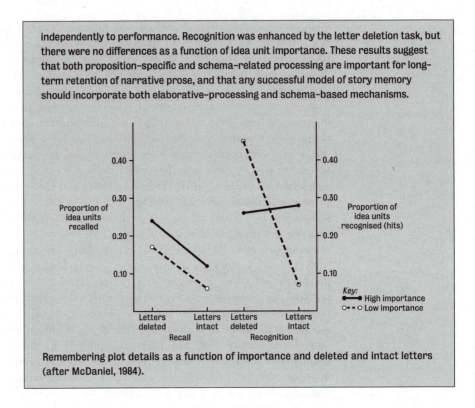

Remembering plot details as a function of importance and deleted and intact letters (after McDaniel, 1984).

Inconsistent information

Whatever the precise nature of the structures underlying comprehension and recall, there is much evidence to show that they have substantial effects on the remembering of relatively transitory details, such as the surface structure of the story, and information incompatible with the subject's interpretation of the story.

Gernsbacher (1985) in a series of six experiments, shows that shortly after a sentence has been comprehended, information about its exact surface form (e.g. its word order) becomes less available, and provides results which suggest why this is so. Most of the studies made use of picture stories. In the first study, Gernsbacher showed that significantly more surface (left–right orientation) information was lost after comprehending several picture stories than was lost when just one was presented. The second study explored this effect further, finding that more surface information was lost after comprehending an entire picture story than was lost after half of one story was presented. In the third and fourth studies reported, subjects segmented the picture stories into their constituent phases; where phase boundaries were not crossed subjects retained much more surface form information than they did where these boundaries were crossed. Gernsbacher outlines a number of ways in which these results can be interpreted, which variously suggest that surface information loss is the result of performing grammatical transformations (the linguistic hypothesis), exceeding short-term memory limitations (the memory-limitations hypothesis), integrating information into gist (the integration hypothesis), but each of these provides an unsatisfactory account of the data. Instead, he hypothesised and provided support for a fourth explanation of surface information loss – that it occurs because of shifting from building one substructure to initiating another (the processing shift hypothesis). In an earlier study, Caccamise and Kintsch (1978) showed that when subjects' immediate recognition of stories they read was tested by either a verbatim or paraphrase test form, much of the surface level information was well preserved. However, when recognition was tested after a week's delay, only the surface details of the more important information in a story was still well recognised. This selective presentation of details about central events rather than details of peripheral events, or even peripheral events themselves, is something we will re-encounter later in respect of threat-related memories. (see Chapter 9).

Similar findings emerged from a study of children's memory for incongruous story details. Ceci, Caves and Howe (1981) showed that when familiar TV characters were described as having attributes that were incongruous with those that the subjects thought them to have, these incongruous details influenced immediate recall (Fig 5.8). However, subjects who retrieved information about the central characters three weeks later were shown to be systematically distorted by prior information, the incongruous information being lost. Long-term memory for unfamiliar characters in a parallel version of the story showed no such shift, indicating that memory distortion for incongruous information was influenced by children's prior knowledge, and was not the result of random forgetting. Davidson and Hoe (1993) also explored children's recall and recognition memory for typical and atypical actions in script-based stories. Atypical actions varied in plausibility, from entirely plausible to plausible within the sentence but implausible within the story, to implausible. On the recall task, children reported more atypical than typical script actions, and the less plausible, atypical actions were better recalled than the more plausible, atypical actions. On the recognition task, however, each type of atypical action was equally well recognised. Children also had difficulty distinguishing between typical script actions present in the stories and script actions not present in the stories but equally typical.

Fig 5.8 Preschoolers' recall and recognition of typical and atypical actions (after Ceci, Caves and Howe, 1981).

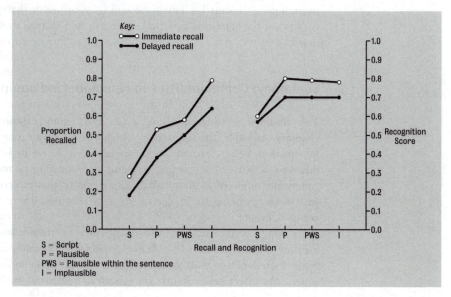

Schmidt, Schmidt and Tomalis (1984) investigated children's memory for stories containing a non-specific premise sentence open to multiple interpretations. The ambiguous idea was followed by two sentences which cued one interpretation of the premise (consistent cues). In some stories, these cues were preceded by or followed by a third sentence which cued an alternative meaning of the ambiguous idea (inconsistent cues). The results showed developmental differences in comprehension and memory as a result of the presentation and positioning of the contradictory information. Story interpretation was facilitated when only consistent cues were encountered. When inconsistent information was encountered between the ambiguous idea and the two consistent cue sentences, kindergarten children had more difficulty understanding the text than when the two consistent cues followed the ambiguous idea immediately. In this case, the inconsistent information was simply discounted. Older children included the discordant information, but did not change the organisation of the story, while even older children showed intra-story integration with reorganisation of schemas when sufficient inconsistent information was presented.

Finally, in this brief overview of the effects of incongruous material, the findings of O'Sullivan and Durso (1984) deserve particular mention. They report a study in which subjects listened to descriptions of stereotypical characters, followed by additional information varying in level of relevance to, and congruence with, the initial information. It was found that the introduction of information that was highly incongruent with the schema made schematic information more memorable, under both immediate- and delayed-recall conditions. This effect may be one means by which inappropriate schemata persevere in the face of counter evidence. However, the data help to make a wider point. Even though schema, story-grammar and script-based theories account for many of the findings discussed above, phenomenally at least, events which are surprising, and particularly those elements of situations which conflict with our expectancies are not only generally noticed, but also appear to act as psychological landmarks. This issue will be returned to later in Chapter 7, where we discuss the temporal ordering of events, and discuss event memory in greater detail.

■ Summary: Commonalities in remembering complex events

The findings considered above echo and extend those reported in earlier chapters. Arguably, the differences which emerge relate more to the nature of the information being learned or remembered (e.g. reading prose is obviously a different activity to inspecting a picture or watching a movie), rather than to generically different memory which is specific to that material. Here I summarise what I see as being the major overlaps in remembering these different types of complex events.

As long as the way in which memory is tested is consonant with the learning mode, pictures of events, especially moving pictures of events, are remembered better than verbal versions of the same information. This picture superiority effect relies jointly on enhanced semantic and sensory properties of the stimulus, but it also seems that realising that one is remembering a scene is also important.

A number of effects are observed across materials. These include the generation effect, transfer-appropriate processing, implicit and explicit memory, and extra-list cueing. What these commonalities do is to demonstrate that these are general properties of how memory operates, although they also serve to qualify some of the interpretations which have previously been made of these effects. For example, that fact that pictorial material also yields a generation effect (i.e. copying aids learning), is inconsistent with the assumption that the effect arises through reactivation of pre-existing semantic representations. Instead, it would seem that the activity involved in making a copy (whether through speaking, drawing, gesturing, etc), serves to increase or enhance the retrieval routes available to the rememberer. Importantly, this explanation extends the generation effect beyond familiar knowledge. Similarly, observing a re-learning effect in recall, but not in recognition, suggests that the classic argument that relearning serves a trace-strengthening function is incorrect, and that savings effects in relearning are better understood as assisting the retrieval of information rather than in terms of some augmenting of its internal representation.

Although discriminating between script-based, schema-based and story-grammar-based accounts of text memory has proved difficult, the regularity with which findings demonstrate the influence of underlying organisational tendencies adds to one's conviction that such structures exist. Here, evidence from memory for faces and their caricatures, and that which shows that people remember unseen aspects of scenes, contributes considerably. Specifically, such evidence may serve to limit ideas of how abstracted these underlying representations are (i.e. it seems likely that more or less veridical features are encoded), and perhaps even the level at which contents are represented (i.e. object-oriented) and the properties which are and are not preserved within these contents (e.g. eyes, but not orientation). Furthermore, the importance of episodic contents and structure emerges from each of the complex events we have considered, as does the feeling that taking advantage of these organisational tendencies is not cost-free in resource terms. For example, during reading of an episode, thematic information may be encoded to lead to activation of similar episodes and formation of connections in memory between episodes, but such encoding is effortful, strategy-dependent and greatly influenced by task difficulty. Similarly, looking at and remembering moving or static pictures is also not resource-free.

This overview of memory and complex events also uncovers connections between these findings and other issues which will be addressed later in this book. For example, research which shows how the use of music and intermissions in movies and commercials can serve to change the interpretation and memorability of complex everyday events is obviously important. So too are the findings described above, which show that the own-race effect can be undermined through extensive practice, leading to a specialisation which is not only visual, but which also alters conceptual and preference-based judgements. These findings not only demonstrate the acquisition of everyday expertise (Chapter 12), but go beyond this to show linkages between cognition and affect (Chapters 9 and 10).

■ Further reading

Abelson, R. P. (1981). Psychological status of the script concept. *American Psychologist, 36,* 715–29.

Bartlett, F. C. (1932). *Remembering.* Cambridge: Cambridge University Press.

Davidson, D. and Hoe, S. (1993). Children's recall and recognition memory for typical and atypical actions in script-based stories. *Journal of Experimental Child Psychology, 55,* 104–26.

Intraub, H., Bender, R. S. and Mangels, J. A. (1992). Looking at pictures but remembering scenes. *Journal of Experimental Psychology: Learning, Memory and Cognition, 18,* 180–91.

Schank, R. C. (1982). *Dynamic memory: A theory of reminding and learning in computers and people.* New York: Cambridge University Press.

Schank, R. C. and Abelson, R. (1977). *Scripts, plans, goals and understanding.* Hillsdale, NJ: Lawrence Erlbaum Associates.

Valentine, T. (1995). *The cognitive and computational aspects of face recognition.* London: Routledge.

Discussion points

- Is a picture memory really worth a thousand words?
- Why do we forget some people's names?
- Compare and contrast different accounts of story recall and recognition.
- How well do theories of transitory and more enduring memory account for memories of more complex events?

Chapter 6

Frequency and repetition

Chapter outline: In previous chapters we have considered a number of findings which show that events which are repeated are treated differently in accounts of both transient and enduring memory. Traditionally these effects are described as effects of exposure, rehearsal and familiarity. In this chapter we take a closer look at the notion of frequency, its effects across a range of tasks, the explanations which have been offered of these effects, and how frequency and repetition impact on tasks we perform in everyday life.

Key topics
- Practice
- Retention of repeated items
- Frequency estimation
- Frequency of generated and encountered experience
- Episodic recognition
- Summary: Frequency and its implications
- Further reading

■ Practice

Massed vs. distributed practice: Acquisition

Since the early work of Ebbinghaus (1885, 1964), researchers have repeatedly shown that massed and distributed practice have different effects on both learning and retention. *Massed practice* refers to situations in which an activity or highly similar activities, and no others, are encountered repeatedly within learning episodes which are close to each other in time. Typically massed practice leads to faster learning than *distributed practice*, during which similar and dissimilar activities are mixed within the same episode, and where learning episodes may be temporally more disparate. A study by Baddeley and Longman (1978) shows the effects of massed and distributed practice among post office workers who were being trained to type postcodes (i.e. zip codes) as part of the early stages of introducing 'automated' letter sorting in the British Post Office. This showed that even after post office workers had learned the position of keys on the keyboard, the practice regime was a significant factor influencing their rate of learning and retention, as assessed by the percentage of correctly pressed keys per minute (Fig 6.1). Those who had one hour of practice per day (not shown in figure) learned faster than those who had two one hour sessions per day, and those who had one two-hour session per day. The additional time spent training did help the latter groups to achieve a higher level of performance overall, but as a caution to this it is worth noting the performance of a further group who endured a practice regime which involved two two-hour sessions per day.

Fig 6.1 Acquisition and retention of typing skill as a function of practice (after Baddeley and Longman, 1978).

This difference between the effectiveness of massed and distributed practice holds across a range of different types of stimuli and modalities, as long as the criterion of success that we use for learning is based on the immediate results of learning. This might involve measures of learning such as the number of attempts

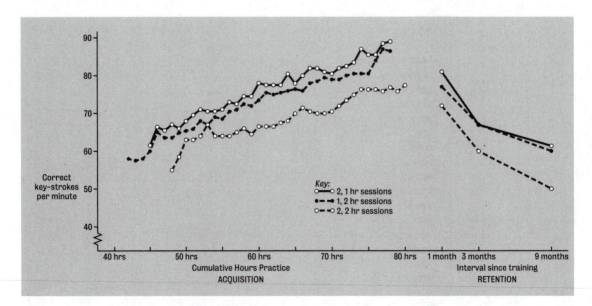

Key:
○—○ 2, 1 hr sessions
●--● 1, 2 hr sessions
○--○ 2, 2 hr sessions

Correct key-strokes per minute

40 hrs   50 hrs   60 hrs   70 hrs   80 hrs   1 month 3 months   9 months
Cumulative Hours Practice   Interval since training
ACQUISITION   RETENTION

required, the time taken in training or the effort involved in reaching a particular level of accuracy, for example 100 per cent recall of a list of digits, or a paired-associate task, such as learning who did what experiment when. The difference is actually due to the effectiveness of learning under massed circumstances. Obviously, in most cases distributed practice will be spread out over a longer period of time than massed practice, which is by definition more concentrated, but even when the amount of time actually spent in training is equated, as in the Baddeley and Longman (1978) study, the advantage of massed practice is still very evident. Although fatigue and boredom can reduce the effectiveness of massed practice, the quickest and most cost-effective way of training to a criterion is through temporally concentrated periods of repeated consistent practice.

Massed vs. distributed practice: Retention and generalisation

However, it is rather questionable whether the level of performance we achieve immediately after a training session is the most appropriate criterion for successful learning in everyday life. Even those brimming with crammed information before an exam may sleep the night before they take their test, walk to the examination hall, chat to other people, find their desk and read the examination paper. As soon as there is a delay between the learning episode and when performance level is assessed, and especially where the conditions under which we learn are different to those in which we are tested, how well we used to be able to perform is much less important than how well we can do in the new situation. When it is how well we retain what we have learned which is important, all other things being equal, those who learned under a distributed practice regime perform better (Hagman, 1983). However, there are important caveats to this general principle.

BOX 6.1: Acquisition, retention and generalisation

Shea and Morgan (1979) report a study in which people learned to touch blocks in one of three sequences – the sequences being shown to subjects in diagrammatic form before each trial began. During each session, subjects performed 18 trials of each sequence. These trials were either blocked, so that the 18 trials for one sequence were performed before trials with the next sequence were begun, or mixed, so that trials with each sequence were randomised across the session. The figure shows that subjects performed the task more quickly where the sequences were blocked, although by the sixth session, both groups were performing equally well. Later, subjects were tested by having to perform the same sequences, either in blocked trials with the same sequences, or intermixed trials of the same sequences. Those who learned with blocked trials of the same sequence performed better when tested with blocked trials, than when they were confronted with mixed trials at test. Those who learned in mixed conditions performed well when tested in mixed conditions, just as we might expect on the basis of the transfer-appropriate processing principle. However, those who learned under mixed trial conditions also performed very well when tested under blocked conditions, suggesting that these subjects were better able to generalise what they learned to new test situations. As the figure also makes clear, in general, retention deteriorates as the time between learning and testing increases. Once again, however, there is an exception to this general rule; those who learn under blocked-trial conditions, are initially tested under blocked trial conditions, and are then tested again, 10 days later, under blocked conditions, appear to improve. It may be that what is happening here is that people actually become better at being tested, given practice, where the tests used are consistent, but not where trials are randomised. It would be intriguing to re-run this study, but this time varying and controlling the order of blocks between learning and testing in order to see how robust the effect of being retested actually is; and also to extend testing for those who learned under mixed conditions to still more demanding test circumstances (e.g. using novel but similar stimuli) in order to assess the limits of the increased generalisability of knowledge acquired through distributed practice.

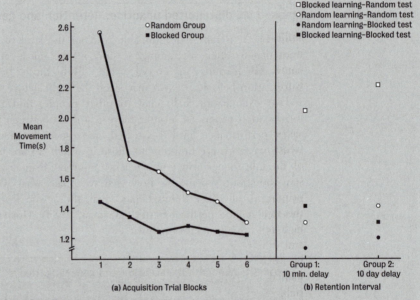

Acquisition and retention of skill as a function of mixed and unmixed learning and testing (after Shea and Morgan, 1979)

Thus, learning something under varied conditions, over a longer period of time, requires more training if we are to reach a particular level of performance, but what we learn is retained for longer after the training and practice has ceased. This depends, of course, on the similarity between learning and testing conditions, although it does appear that learning under distributed practice conditions facilitates transfer of learning, at least to more simple testing conditions. We will return to the application of these principles in later chapters, where we discuss skill development and ways of enhancing our ability to remember. The contrast between massed and distributed or spaced practice has also been addressed, but considerably clarified, in more recent debates on the effects of repetition and spacing on retrieval.

◼ Retention of repeated items

Repetition priming

As we have seen above, there are substantial benefits of re-encountering something we have already processed. Generally we find it easier, and quicker, to make the same decisions about something than to make decisions about it that we have not already made. Thus, reading aloud a word for the first time is far more ponderous and much slower than when we reread that word later. We may, of course, remember when we last encountered the word, the efforts we made to pronounce it, the criticism or correction we received. However, it appears that realising we are remembering such episodic details is not necessary for our performance to change. For the most part the studies reviewed in this section will consider tasks in which the subject is not explicitly asked to remember, but where the effect of repeating an item is gauged by the extent to which it facilitates or hinders the subject's ability to perform some task other than intentionally trying to recollect the item or its attributes. Often, these indirect tasks have required subjects to name, pronounce or determine whether or not some item is a word or non-word.

Forster and Davis (1984), for example, show that lexical decisions are faster for items which have already been encountered. They also show that this *repetition priming effect* is stronger for low-frequency words than for high-frequency words, and hypothesise that this *frequency attenuation effect* is the result of the greater availability of 'episodic traces' of high frequency words (we shall see why this might be so in the section below on spacing effects). When the priming stimulus was rendered undetectable (through masking), thus minimising the influence of episodic traces from the prime, constant repetition effects for high- and low-frequency words were obtained. A distinction between episodic and other aspects of repetition priming is also reflected in the studies reported by Mitchell and Brown (1988), who found that previously named pictures were named faster than new pictures. The magnitude of this naming facilitation was stable over the six-week period studied. Mitchell and Brown go on in further studies to show that, while this repetition priming effect remained stable over time, performance on a recognition task, namely determining whether items seen were 'new' or 'old', declined substantially over that period. Moscovitch and Bentin (1993) also show that when repetition effects, as measured by lexical decision, were not significantly above baseline for words seen only once, recognition was also at chance level. Incidentally, the Mitchell and Brown (1988) study also echoes other aspects of the findings reported by Forster and Davis, in that they point out that naming facilitation for repeated pictures occurred regardless of whether those particular pictures were consciously recognised.

For repetition priming to occur, it is important that the repetitions are not consecutive. Marohn and Hochaus (1988a) and Park and Kanwisher (1994) demonstrate that consecutive repetition priming causes a phenomenon termed the *repetition blindness effect*, in which literal repetition of an item severely diminishes the processing of the second presentation of that item. In the earlier of these studies, it was demonstrated that, compared to unrelated targets, semantically related targets had longer apparent durations and were identified with greater accuracy. Repeated items, in contrast, had shorter apparent durations and poorer identification accuracy than did unrelated control targets. Semantic priming, therefore, affected the fluency with which target words were perceived, and increased their apparent duration. In a follow-up study, Marohn and Hochaus (1988b) show that the increased difficulty in identifying consecutive items was not eased when the second presentation was presented in different letter case format, thus demonstrating that effects of consecutive priming are not the consequence of the physical similarity between the priming and target words, and that what they term 'cognitive refractoriness' goes beyond the physical features of the letters to the word as a whole unit. Park and Kanwisher (1994) report seven studies which address these issues systematically. In their final study subjects watched a screen on which letters were presented in rapid succession and merely had to say whether one or two vowels had been presented in sequences which ranged from 6–17 letters, and state their confidence in their decision. Each string contained one vowel, two identical vowels or two different vowels; the positions at which these occurred in each trial varied, as did the number of consonants which intervened between each vowel. Figure 6.2 shows the mean sensitivity for detecting the second vowel when it was the same as or different from the first. What Park and Kanwisher show very clearly is that the repetition blindness effect depends on the lag between the two presentations of the identical stimulus. They interpret these results as indicating that repetition blindness arises through a failure to interpret the second token as a new token of a particular type.

Fig 6.2 Repetition blindness as a function of the number of consonants intervening between two targets (after Park and Kanwisher, 1994).

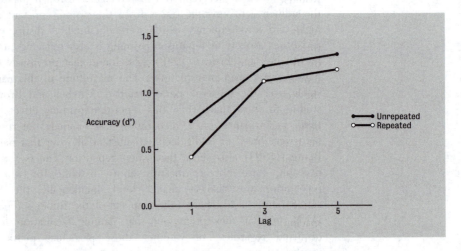

The suggestion that meanings rather than physical features are crucial is strengthened by studies which have sought to explore what effect changes in context have on repetition priming. Bainbridge, Lewandowsky and Kirsner (1993) show that repetition priming is either eliminated or significantly reduced if a change in context also alters the perceived sense of a non-homographic target word. If perceived sense is not altered, a change in context is inconsequential. This is confirmed by studies of event-related potentials (ERPs) and repetition effects (see Besson and Kutas, 1993).

Taken together, the findings considered above point strongly to the role played by contextually meaningful episodic traces in facilitating, or inhibiting, later processing of what would normally be regarded as similar items. It seems clear also that these unintentional processing 'fluencies' underlie, but can also be distinguished from, phenomenological feelings of actually remembering. Let us now turn to more direct tests of retrieval, in which people are actually required to learn various items they encounter, either because they are told to, or because it would be impossible to perform some later task without doing so.

Retention when repeated items do not follow each other immediately

One way of conceiving of what is happening within a learning episode is that various aspects of each event encountered are processed, with or without an intention to later use those aspects which are processed in some task. A concrete example of this would be where subjects are confronted with a succession of words which they are told they will later be asked to remember. Let us assume for the moment that all the words are different from each other, but equally familiar to the subject, and are not associated with each other, whether through their meaning, sound or orthography. Under such circumstances, as we found in the studies discussed in previous chapters, we would expect those in the initial portions of the list to be well recalled relative to those which were presented in the middle of the list, while those at the end of the list will be best remembered of all. If the study were rerun enough times such that each word occurred an equal number of times in each position on the presentation list, we would expect to find that all words would be remembered equally often. What will happen, however, if we allow some of the words to be repeated in the list?

A range of studies show that those which are repeated, even once, will be better remembered than those which only occur once on the list (Fritzen, 1975; Hastie, 1975). However, what we might not expect is that the words will be remembered better if they are relatively far away from each other, an effect which is usually referred to as the *spacing effect*. Thus, as Greene (1989) found, subjects told beforehand that they will be asked to recall words (i.e. intentional condition) show that memory for repeated items on a list improves as a function of the spacing between repetitions. The same effects were also observed where subjects were not told that they would have to recall the items presented (i.e. incidental condition) (Fig 6.3). Intentions to remember are clearly important to the spacing effect, under certain retrieval conditions, since Greene also showed that spacing effects are eliminated under incidental conditions where recognition, or frequency-estimation or frequency-discrimination, rather than recall of the words is required.

This is similar to the result noted by Hastie (1975), who found that free recall

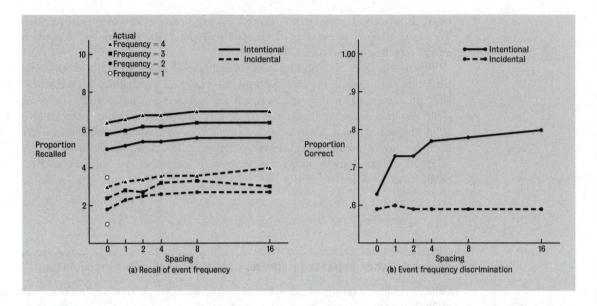

Fig 6.3 Effect of retention on recall and discrimination of event frequency (after Greene, 1989).

of once-presented words accompanied by twice-presented words was inhibited only when the subject was instructed, before list presentation, to distinguish between once- and twice-presented words during free recall. In contrast to free-recall performance, recognition memory for once-presented words occurring in lists containing twice-presented words was not impaired. It is likely that, left to their own devices, subjects determine that repeated items are likely to prove more important in whatever task follows. By requiring them to make non-semantic kinds of judgements about the words as they encounter them (e.g. graphemic judgements), the spacing effect in recall tasks is much reduced (see Challis, 1993).

Other findings also demonstrate that the meaning of the stimuli encoded is an important aspect of the spacing effect. Kahana and Greene (1993), for example, showed that no spacing effect was found in free recall of lists containing items which were highly semantically similar. However, in retrieval conditions which required greater differentiation of the meanings of the individual words, such as recognition or frequency-discrimination tests, reliable spacing effects were demonstrated, when subjects were anticipating a later test (see Greene, 1989 above). Procedures which require less meaningful aspects of words to be addressed (e.g. perceptual clarification, relative frequency discrimination, absolute frequency estimation), consistently show no effects of spacing (Greene, 1989; Perruchet, 1989). It was suggested above, following Forster and Davis (1984), that the frequency attenuation effect (i.e. the fact that low-frequency words show greater repetition priming effects than do high-frequency words) means that items more frequently encountered were more likely to generate episodic traces. This gains some support from these studies, given that they show that reencountered items, about which decisions are made (see Forster and Davis, 1984), are themselves more memorable.

Retention when repeated items follow each other immediately

So far, we have considered studies which have in the main prevented identical words from following each other immediately. Ranschburg found that recall of repeated items which are presented in short sequences is poor. This appears to indicate that massed practice of items actually leads to poorer memory for massed items than for equivalent items, when they do not immediately follow one another. Limitations of this so-called *Ranschburg effect* were noted by Mewaldt and Hinrichs (1977), who found that recall improved considerably when these clusters of identical items were repeated frequently throughout longer lists. This is due, in large part, to the fact that repeated items are more likely to be retrieved than those which are not repeated. As Challis and Sidhu (1993) show, in a study in which subjects saw or heard words presented once, or repeated four or sixteen times in massed fashion, massed repetition did enhance performance on various explicit tests (free recall, recognition, question-cued recall, and word-fragment-cued recall). Interestingly, in the light of what we discussed above in relation to repetition priming, massed repetition did not increase priming on word-fragment completion (an implicit test of retention) beyond that obtained from a single presentation. Thus, while massed repeated items are better remembered than those which are not repeated, it also appears generally true that immediate repetitions of items are less successful than spaced repetitions of items at promoting remembering.

Fig 6.4 Percentage word recall as a function of retention interval, massed or distributed presentation and presentation frequency (after Shaughnessy, 1977).

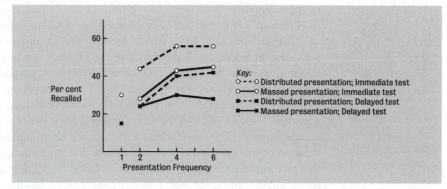

Bray and Robbins (1976) studied the effects of delay on the spacing effect on recalled items, using a continuous paired-associate task, varying the retention interval after one or two presentations of a pair of words. The lag between presentations was also varied. Half of the items were tested immediately, and all of the items were tested after a delay. Subjects were instructed to recall the response and to indicate the presentation frequency for each item. Results showed a spacing effect only for items correctly judged as repetitions at the time of test, on both immediate and delayed tests. Overall responding was generally greater for items given an immediate test, in contrast to those only given the delayed test. A similar interplay of sensitivity to the frequency of repetitions, delay and the spacing effect was also found by Shaughnessy (1977). Here, students were presented with a long list of words in which items were repeated a varying number of times, according to either an immediate repetition schedule or a spaced presentation schedule.

Following list presentation, subjects were given either a frequency-judgement test (Exp. I) or a free-recall test (Exp. II). In both experiments, the retention test was given either immediately after or 24 hours after list presentation. As we might expect from the Ranschburg effect, on the immediate test, immediately repeated items were recalled worse than spaced items. They were also judged to have occurred less frequently. This is consistent with the idea that immediately repeated items are more poorly registered in memory. What is surprising, however, is that although on the delayed frequency judgement test immediately repeated items were again judged to have been less frequent, there was no difference in the recall of twice-presented massed practice and distributed practice items (Fig 6.4). This apparent contradiction will be addressed later.

Explaining the spacing effect

Various explanations have been offered for the spacing effect, involving rehearsal, attention allocation and the existence of multiple traces in memory. Greene (1989) originally speculated that the massed versus distributed effects found with the spacing of items might be due to a rehearsal strategy that allots fewer rehearsals to items repeated in massed fashion. Studies which have sought explicitly to control or manipulate the amount of rehearsal given to items suggest that this is not an adequate explanation. An earlier study demonstrates this, and other, important effects.

Hintzman and Rogers (1973) capitalised on an earlier finding (cited in Hintzman and Rogers, 1973, p. 430) which showed that complex visual scenes are not rehearsed, in testing the hypothesis that the effect of spacing on memory is due to rehearsal. In their first experiment, vacation slides were presented, in which both the number of repetitions and the spacing of repetitions were varied. Subsequent frequency judgements showed an effect of spacing similar to that found using verbal materials. Their second and third studies investigated the effects of filled and unfilled spacing intervals. They conclude that 'the spacing effect is primarily a function of the duration of the spacing interval', and further that 'no evidence supported the notion that pictures are rehearsed' (Hintzman and Rogers, 1973, p. 430). Thus, rehearsal seems unlikely to be the sole factor in a general explanation of the spacing effect. More recently, Greene has suggested that 'several distinct processes underlie the spacing effect' (Kahana and Greene, 1993, p. 159); these include attention distribution, habituation-recovery and time allocation during learning.

A related, but different, account of the spacing effect, depends on the attention allocated to items which are massed in presentation. Using a paired-associate task Wenger (1979) had subjects recall lists containing critical pairs, that were repeated twice at lags of 0, 3, and 8 intervening events. Different groups of subjects were visually presented with these at either a slower or faster rate of presentation. Wenger found a clear massed practice-distributed practice effect at the slow presentation rate, which was eliminated at the faster presentation rate. He suggests that the reason for this is that massed presentation results in less attention being devoted to repeated items. Thus, when people are forced to attend fully to both occurrences during massed repetition in a sufficiently attention-demanding task, the differences between massed and spaced distribution of items should, and does, disappear. Without the requirement to attend closely, people 'habituate' to immediately repeated presentations. This suggestion gains further support from an earlier study by Hintzman and colleagues.

Hintzman, Block and Summers (1973) carried out two studies in which a combined frequency- and modality-judgement task was used to investigate incidental memory for input modalities of repeated words. In each experiment, words were presented in which frequency of occurrence (0, 1, or 2 times) was orthogonally combined with the modality of each presentation, such that the modalities of repeated words were switched or remained the same. In the second experiment, the spacing of repetitions was varied. The findings showed that frequency judgements increased, and then decreased slightly, as a function of spacing. Neither the absolute level of judged frequency, nor the magnitude of the spacing effect, depended on whether the two presentations occurred in the same modality. In both modalities repeated words were remembered accurately, except at short spacing (which we might expect from the Ranschburg effect). These results were interpreted as showing that the spacing effect is due to a failure to encode (or later retrieve) subsequent occurrences of a word when they closely follow the first occurrence. In a subsequent study, Hintzman, Summers and Block (1975) show that subjects do not seem to amalgamate these repeated experiences of items into a single occurrence of particularly long duration, but instead forget repeated items. Tantalisingly, they suggest that interrupted stimuli are recognised better than those which are not interrupted. The interruption adds to the distinctiveness of the repeated stimuli, and hence to the attention allocated to it. This supports the habituation-recovery account of the spacing effect. Such an account has obvious similarities to that offered by Park and Kanwisher (1994) with regard to repetition blindness.

The time devoted to processing repeated items was more directly investigated by Rose (1984). Earlier, Cuddy and Jacoby (1982) suggested that spacing aids memory for a repeated item to the extent that the subject reconstructs the processing previously carried out on the repeated item. Rose investigated whether the spacing effect is due to forgetting of the item's prior presentation. In his study, subjects were presented with sequences of words, each of which was accompanied by a short question that required a yes or no answer. Most words were repeated, and several levels of spacing were used. For some subjects, the words were repeated with the same question; for other subjects, different questions accompanied each repetition. Subjects were then asked to judge how often each word occurred within the question task. Memory was measured in terms of probability of a recognition hit, and by a recall test that preceded the frequency judgement. The results were largely as anticipated in Cuddy and Jacoby's (1982) hypothesis. A large decline in reaction time occurred when an item was repeated in the same-question condition, even after a spacing of 40 intervening items. This shows that less processing time is devoted to repeated items.

Overall, Rose's study obviously supports the view that memory for a prior presentation can influence a later presentation of that item, and that spacing of items leads to multiple representation in memory. As we saw above, Hintzman argues that repeating items with minimal spacing does not lead to the formation of single experiences of apparently longer durations. With increased spacing, however, it seems very likely that different traces are formed (see Macey and

Zechmeister, 1975; Hintzman and Block, 1973). Such traces seem to be formed as items are encoded, even if the purpose of their encoding differs from time to time. For example, Whitten and Bjork (1977) showed, in a complex study, that increased delay of the re-presentation of a word, and increased delay before being tested for recall of its first presentation both lead to increased recall of that item. In another condition, they show that if the second presentation requires simple rehearsal of the item (rather than recall or its simply being re-presented), no spacing effect is obtained. This latter result strengthens the view that rehearsal, in and of itself, does not explain the spacing effect, but also shows that a variety of different ways of encoding the same item may lead to increased recall of that item, if it is repeatedly encountered under spaced presentation conditions.

In summary, although repeated presentation of information enhances its likelihood of retrieval, the circumstances of these repetitions strongly influence the effects observed. Where repetitions are spaced, the benefits of repetition on retention increase, perhaps for up to as many as 40 intervening events. It seems likely that where items are massed in presentation, later repeated items in the cluster will be attended to less, and, as a result, be processed less elaborately. In contrast, where the repetition occurs in the context of different, rather than repeated words, or where different aspects of the word are considered, more elaborate processing is likely, and, as a result, so too is improved retention. This, however, depends on the way in which retention is assessed, the ways in which the items are encoded, and whether or not the subject is expecting a later retention test. It also depends, it would seem, on the subject's noticing that the events processed differ in frequency. In the next section we consider frequency estimation in a wider context.

Frequency estimation

Determining whether or not an event happened is considerably easier, and considerably more accurate, than knowing how many times an event which did take place actually occurred. While this may seem obvious, understanding why it is so, and the conditions under which it is so, poses considerable challenges. It raises important issues about the nature of the information which we encode and retrieve. Frequency estimation is subject to a range of heuristics and biases (see Tversky and Kahneman, 1977). These allow rapid, efficient and consistent judgements to be made, but may cause such judgements to be inherently inaccurate. This is particularly so where there is little control over the properties of events, the attention devoted to them and their personal or social significance. As a result, studies which concentrate on estimations of the frequency of everyday events tend to obscure the fundamental processes involved in frequency estimation, on which these heuristics and biases operate (see Howell, 1973). Towards the end of this section, the estimates we make of everyday events will be returned to, but first let us consider evidence on frequency estimation which comes from more constrained tasks.

Frequency judgements of constituent and superordinate events

It seems clear, from a variety of studies, that people are capable of discriminating between events that occur once and those which occur more often, even where the repeated event occurs just twice. Thus, for example, Greene (1984, 1990) has shown that situational frequency discriminations of words occurring once or twice were above chance, when subjects were not expecting to have to make frequency-related judgements. However, it is also clear that performance is improved where subjects are required to develop associations to items, or otherwise meaningfully encode those items they encounter (Fisk and Schneider, 1984; Greene, 1986, 1990). This advantage for more effortful or meaningful encoding may also reflect the findings of Woodley and Ellis (1989) that frequency estimates for the occurrence of pictorial information appear more accurate than for verbal information, and also that accuracy of frequency information and types of retrieval cue (i.e. visual or oral) interact (Fig 6.5).

Fig 6.5 Actual and estimated frequency of events as a function of event-type and retrieval cue (after Woodley and Ellis, 1989).

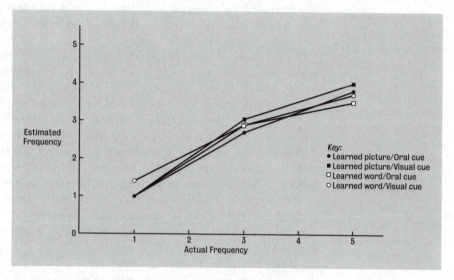

Effortful encoding and frequency judgements

It also seems likely, on the basis of a number of studies, that people are not only sensitive to the frequency of events, but also to the frequency of constituent and superordinate elements. Alba, Chromiak, Hasher and Attig (1980) demonstrated that adults could estimate the frequency of implicitly referenced events (category names) when they were presented with individual events (category instances). Hock, Malcus and Hasher (1986) show across a series of studies, in which the frequencies of occurrence of different strings and of the letters composing the strings were varied orthogonally, that people are able to discriminate the frequency of occurrence for both strings and their constituent letters. This was so at relatively long exposure durations, but accurate judgement of letter frequency was much reduced with briefer presentations. However, in results which appear at variance with these, Whitlow and Skaar (1979) report that the frequencies of constituent elements and superordinate elements were found to be only weakly related to each other.

Hintzman, Curran and Oppy (1992) report a series of studies in which subjects are asked to determine the frequency with which items, such as holiday slides or singular nouns, were presented. Hintzman and colleagues found that while subjects were more likely to estimate the frequency of 'old' items reasonably accurately, they also tended to think that items which had not actually been presented (i.e. mirror images of the slides, or plurals of the singular nouns) had occurred in proportion to the incidence of 'old' items. Hintzman and colleagues describe this as 'registration without learning', such that 'repetition has registered in some manner, even though the subjects appear not to have learned more about the internal structure of the repeated stimulus' (1992, p. 671). This is in spite of the fact that the orienting tasks during presentation ranged from preparing for an unspecified 'memory test' to decisions about whether the presented item was animate, and even though subjects were alerted to the singular–plural variations in test items and told to reject plurals. These results suggest that the relationships between judgements about categorical and constituent frequency may be illusory.

On the basis of findings reported by Barsalou and Ross (1986), it would appear that strategic processing is not necessary for sensitivity to the frequency of non-presented information, but that sensitivity is reduced when strategic processing conflicts with well-established representations and becomes possible in the absence of well-established representations when appropriate strategic processing is used. It is also clear from the studies by Hock, Malcus and Hasher (1986) that the encoding of frequency information takes some time, and that while intentional processing of frequency information is not necessary for frequency discriminations to be made, performance is much improved if this is so. Furthermore, although frequency information relating to both verbal and pictorial information can be encoded with intentions to do so, the information encoded is retrieved inaccurately, such that people mistakenly treat items which were not presented as relatively frequent, if they are related to events which did occur (see Hintzman, Curran and Oppy, 1992). These findings raise some doubts about the adequacy of those accounts which suggest that where events occur often frequency information is acquired 'automatically'.

Explaining encoding of frequency information

Since the mid-1980s contradictory explanations have emerged with regard to the encoding and retrieval of fundamental information. Some (e.g. Hasher and Zacks, 1984) have proposed that judgements of frequency of occurrence reflect the 'direct' or 'automatic' coding of frequency information. Others challenge this view (e.g. Naveh-Benjamin and Jonides, 1986; Greene, 1989), and suggest the event frequency derives from estimation of frequency from characteristics of memory traces that are not direct frequency codes. Instead, estimates are based on the numbers of events retrieved, or the ease with which they are retrieved. Greene (1989) has shown that three factors which influence recall (i.e. generation, organisation of category constituents, provision of extra list cues), also affect category frequency estimation. Other recall-enhancing strategies (i.e. repeated estimation/recall and specific event priming rather than generic priming of event classes – Thompson and Mingay, 1991) also influence the estimates produced. Some have also argued, perhaps simplistically, that by increasing the time available for retrieval more events should be recalled, and thus estimates of frequency should increase. However, a variety of studies do not show the anticipated effects of increased retrieval time (e.g. Alba et al. 1980; Thompson and Mingay, 1991).

The Hasher and Zacks view (Hasher and Zacks, 1979, 1984) is that information about frequency of occurrence is stored in memory by an implicit or automatic encoding process. They support this claim by showing that task variables (e.g., instructions, and competing demands) and subject variables (e.g. age and cognitive ability) do not influence the encoding process. As might be expected with such a controversial hypothesis, substantial research effort has been devoted to seeking to replicate, or test more precisely, the claims made. I have already considered above some of the evidence which casts doubt on these claims, albeit concentrating on different aspects of these studies.

With regard to the effects of intentional/unintentional instructions, Greene (1990) shows clearly that effortful processing and anticipating test conditions improve frequency estimation. Research by Sanders, Gonzalez, Murphy, Liddle and Vitina (1987) shows similar effects. They also showed that frequency processing accuracy was interfered with by the additional demands imposed by a concurrent cover, although frequency processing did occur under incidental conditions (see also Shaklee and Mims, 1982). Naveh-Benjamin and Jonides (1986) show that intentional-elaborative rehearsal leads to better frequency discriminability, a higher absolute level of judged frequencies, and less dispersion of the frequency judgements than those in the incidental-maintenance condition. More importantly, perhaps, they also show that merely changing the level of difficulty of a secondary task (count in ones, or subtract 3 or subtract 11, from a large starting number) changes how well subjects perform when estimating the frequency of words they have just heard (Fig 6.6), even though they were expecting the frequency judgement task.

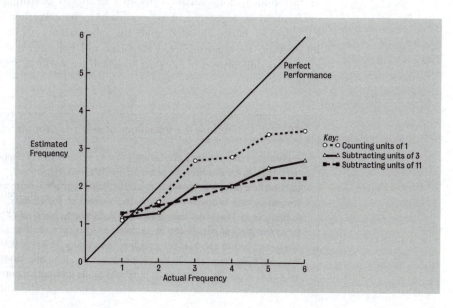

Fig 6.6 Intention encoding of frequency is disrupted by the difficulty of concurrent tasks (after Naveh-Benjamin and Jonides, 1987).

With regard to subject variables, the picture has been equally bleak for the Hasher and Zacks hypothesis. A number of studies show that age influences frequency estimation (e.g. Kausler, Lichty, and Hakami, 1984; di-Pellegrino, Nichelli, Faglioni, 1988), while several authors have also shown that intellectual ability also influences frequency discrimination (Woodley and Ellis, 1989; Tweedy and Vakil, 1988).

Hasher and Zacks' conception of automaticity has also been criticised at a theoretical level (Fisk and Schneider, 1984; Fisk, 1986; Logan, 1988). The Hasher and Zacks view that the automatic encoding of various stimulus dimensions (e.g. frequency of occurrence) is not influenced by manipulations of attention, intention, strategy or multiple task conditions, has obvious limitations, given the results reported above. These results are what would be anticipated if automaticity is seen as the result of protracted consistent attention in visual search tasks (e.g. Shiffrin and Schneider, 1977; Schneider and Shiffrin, 1977), or as the result of the obligatory encoding and retrieval of instances (Logan, 1988). In the next chapter, we will return to the issue of the role of attention and automaticity in the encoding of other fundamental information (i.e. time).

Many studies cite evidence which is contrary to the notion that frequency information is automatically encoded; in most cases these show that frequency estimation can be improved where the subject effortfully and strategically engages in the task. This does not mean that some registration of frequency information does not occur in the absence of an intention to encode, merely that it can be encoded in ways which lead to more effective retrieval where there is an intention to do so. This raises another issue, since in virtually all of the studies what is tested is the access to or retrieval of frequency information, rather than its encoding. The Hintzman, Curran and Oppy (1992) study, which may also be seen as an analysis of how event frequency processes go wrong, clearly indicates that encoding of event frequency information is both inaccurate and relatively undiscriminating. When people come to make frequency estimates on the basis of this information, whatever records or traces remain of information that is unintentionally registered, it is very likely to be corrupted by information which has already been encoded and the associations which develop from that information to superordinate categories and constituent events. This may pose enormous difficulties for the ways in which we perform a wide range of everyday tasks.

BOX 6.2: Estimating the frequency of everyday events

Estimating the frequency of everyday events is particularly important for a range of purposes. If, for example, as some believe, the risk attributed to an event depends in part on how likely we think it is to occur, then inaccurate estimates of event frequency may cause us mistakenly to believe that something is more risky than it actually is, or less risky than it actually is. Similarly, because of the ease with which large numbers of people can be sampled using questionnaires, social researchers are often tempted to ask questions such as 'how many times did you visit a doctor in the last year?'. As we will see in the next chapter, the temporal period may also be a source of error, but for present purposes let us concentrate on individuals' estimates of frequency. Thompson and Mingay (1991) carried out a study in which subjects recorded the frequency of a range of everyday events (e.g. movies attended, long-distance phone calls), visits to health providers (i.e. doctor, nurse, dentist), and so on in the preceding week. After making 13 of such weekly records, subjects were asked how many events of each type had happened in the preceding nine weeks. This was actually a date boundary, 1 October, which occurred four weeks after recording began. Thompson and Mingay group the events into different frequency categories (0–5, 6–10, 11–20, 20+ actual occurrences). The figure shows the data reported in their first study, with low-frequency events being thought to have occurred more frequently, and higher frequency events being thought to have happened less often. This is generally found to be the case for low- and high-frequency estimations. Thus the Thompson and Mingay data show that frequency estimation is non-veridical, which I feel calls into question their procedure of having subjects record the frequency of certain types of event in the preceding week. Nevertheless the findings reflect an important lesson: people do not seem to estimate the frequency of events accurately, and depending on the actual frequency of the events being estimated, the bias in the error observed alters dramatically.

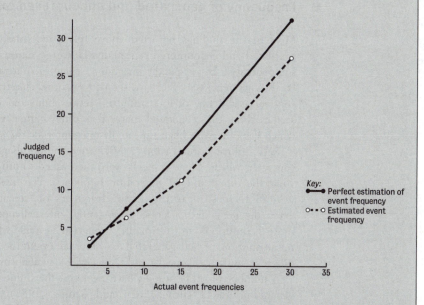

Estimating the frequency of everyday events (after Thompson and Mingay, 1991).

The Thompson and Mingay paper actually sets out to test hypotheses derived from Greene's (1989) multiple trace theory of frequency estimation (also known as the exemplar retrieval account), but their results are far from conclusive. They show that the time available for making estimates does not affect performance, and rather ungenerously interpret this as evidence against the retrieval-based account, since more time to retrieve does not enhance performance. If retrieval is in parallel, however, as many theories we have considered in previous chapters have suggested, then time allocation should make minimal difference. They show, supporting the Greene's exemplar-retrieval account, that having a second estimation reduces underestimation overall. Unfortunately, we do not know whether this leads to an increased overestimation of low-frequency events, or increased accuracy for these estimates, nor is it entirely clear that the effect of the first estimate is not merely to increase availability of information, rather than to enhance accuracy. Finally, in line with their interpretation of Greene's position, they show that being encouraged to think, in general, about the types of things which generally make up a particular event, yields greater underestimation of frequencies than being encouraged to think of a specific example of an event. Unfortunately, the effect of even these specific event instructions does not improve estimation accuracy more than no instructions at all, thus leaving us in something of an interpretative quandary. Do general instructions actually disimprove performance, or, without instructions do people actually usually think of a specific event, and then derive an estimate of frequency for that class of events on that basis? It is thus very difficult to use the Thompson and Mingay data for theoretical purposes, but the basic effect they report is nevertheless important.

■ Frequency of generated and encountered experience

Most of the findings reported above relate to situations in which an event is presented and encountered repeatedly. However, experience of events can also be self-generated: by repeatedly imagining, saying or otherwise thinking about it, that is, through rehearsal. We have seen in previous chapters that rehearsal can be a very successful way of increasing the retrievability of events. A number of other studies show that generated material is often better remembered that than that which has otherwise been repeatedly encountered (the *generation effect*).

Raye, Johnson and Taylor (1980) varied the number of times subjects saw and generated words. Some subjects were then asked to judge presentation frequency, while the others judged generation frequency. The findings showed that subjects were more sensitive to the relative frequency of internally generated, rather than externally generated, events. Importantly, internally generated events produced more confusion in estimating external event frequency. This apparent misattribution of self-generated to external events is also reported in a rather different study by Slamecka and Graf (1978), which was described earlier.

A number of other studies have explored the influences on, and limits of, the generation effect. Nairne, Pusen, and Widner (1985) showed that no generation effect was obtained where the items to be remembered were artificial or meaningless non-words. In one study subjects read or generated stimuli which they thought were words but which were actually experimenter-generated non-words. A second study showed that while experimenter-generated meanings for these words were well retrieved, the items again showed no generation effect. These findings were taken as evidence that items must be represented in some internal lexicon in order for the generation effect to occur, that is, believing that items are words, and even attributing meanings to these items, is not sufficient for the effect to occur. The third study reported in the same paper has gained rather more attention, since it appeared to show that real words which are relatively low in frequency also failed to show a generation effect, thus apparently showing that mental representation was not itself sufficient. Freund, Sanders, Bell and Jennings (1975) also showed that having subjects actively produce an association was more beneficial than having them simply read one that was provided.

More recently, Greene (1988) has confirmed this finding, but Gardiner, Gregg and Hampton (1988) and Nairne and Widner (1988) have not, finding generation effects with low-frequency items. It seems likely that these apparent contradictions can be resolved by distinguishing between word frequency, as indexed by the frequency of occurrence of a word in the language, and the extent to which the word is 'familiar' to the subject who encounters it. Low frequency words, with which the subject is unfamiliar, do not show the generation effect; low frequency words with which the subject is familiar do. Thus, contrary to Nairne's earlier findings, given sufficient experience with non-words, subjects should actually show the generation effect with stimuli which are not actually words. In the previous chapter, we encountered other studies which also demonstrated that enhancing some lexical representation cannot be the basis of the generation effect. More recently, the suggestion has been made that the generation effect actually requires recollective experience in order to occur. Thus subjects correctly recognised words they had said rather than read, but only where they claimed to be able to remember the circumstances under which the item was initially encoded (see Gregg and Gardiner, 1991). This may also reflect a difference in the subjective frequency or familiarity of these events.

■ Episodic recognition

Each of the foregoing frequency-based effects depends on the individual's capacity to determine that an event or item has occurred before, or is similar in important respects to one that has taken place before. In other words the individual must recognise that some event more or less repeats one that has occurred earlier. This linkage between frequency judgements and memory makes both subjective and theoretical sense. As Wixted (1992) points out, subjects consistently, but mistakenly, predict that memorability was directly correlated with frequency of usage. More importantly, many models of the recognition process incorporate two postulates: the detection of familiarity and the utilisation of retrieval mechanisms as additive and separate processes (Horton and Mills, 1984). Mandler (1980), for example, suggests that the phenomenal experience of familiarity is assigned to intraevent organisational integrative processes, while retrieval depends on interevent elaborative processes. A number of different sources of evidence relate to this dissociation: the mirror effect, associative influences on recognition and, more generally, difficulties with simple trace-strength accounts of recognition.

The mirror effect

The *mirror effect* refers to the common finding that hit and false alarm rates on a recognition test are inversely related. That is, the better the subject is at correctly determining that an item has been encountered previously, the less likely the subject is to mistakenly consider that the item had occurred earlier when it had not. Glanzer and Adams (1985), who first drew attention to the effect, describe it a different but related way: 'classes of stimuli that are accurately recognised as old when old are also accurately recognised as new when new; those that are poorly recognised as old when old are also poorly recognised as new when new' (p. 8). A number of studies have shown that the effect holds for stimuli which vary in word frequency, concreteness, and meaningfulness (Glanzer and Adams, 1985; Hockley, 1994), and encoding and retrieval operations (Glanzer and Adams, 1990; Hintzman 1994). The effect is reflected both in measures of accuracy and response latency. The implication of the effect, because of its generality, is that variables which influence recognition performance change responding to both 'new' and 'old' items.

Glanzer, Adams and Iverson (1991) proposed attention/likelihood theory in order to account for the mirror effect. The likelihood of an item being thought new or old is described in distributions which underlie performance. These distributions derive from parameters which reflect the 'true state' of the subject's memory and the subject's estimate of this 'true state'. Hintzman (1994) has recently suggested that these parameters actually reflect the 'learnability' of an item by a particular subject. In part, these distributions also reflect the features of an item which the subject has encoded. When the number of features sampled is reduced, for example by speed instructions or by briefer exposure of items, there will be bilateral movement of the response distributions of both new and old items towards each other and some midpoint. As a result, recognition performance should be impaired. Thus, when recognition accuracy is decreased for old stimuli, it is also decreased for new stimuli. These predictions have been confirmed by Kim and Glanzer (1993). Strength theories of memory have difficulty in accounting for such findings, although these difficulties are in part eased by Hintzman's suggestion that the parameters of the underlying memory distributions reflect item learnability.

Associative influences on recognition

Let us now turn to the role that associative influences play in recognition performance. Zechmeister and Gude (1974) found, contrary to expectations of the frequency or strength theory of recognition memory, that recognition errors were significantly fewer when subjects were instructed to think of associations to, or the dictionary meanings of, common nouns during encoding, than when instructed to simply repeat or to visualise the spelling of those words. Subjects were able retrieve the kind of encoding activity applied to the words. This indicates that subjects have available more information than frequency when making recognition decisions. Work by Underwood (1974, 1976) showed that associative context, specified in terms of the strength of the association between two words in a pair, is a contributory, but not a critical factor, in recognition performance. Results from the first of these papers also showed criterion differences in making frequency judgements as compared with recognition decisions.

Later, Proctor (1977) showed that accuracy in correctly discriminating items was greater when frequency judgements were made than when either old–new recognition judgements or recognition-confidence judgements were made. A second study revealed that frequency judgements and recognition-confidence judgements (using similar numerical scales) were assigned to test items. Thus, different information in memory is evaluated when judging frequency than when making recognition judgements, and it would seem that this information facilitates recognition accuracy.

Underwood's ascription of a greater influence of frequency information in recognition judgements is echoed in a later study by Raye (1976). She carried out a study in which undergraduates studied lists of words using a high- or low-organisation mnemonic strategy. On a subsequent recognition test, old items were blocked by study lists or randomly ordered. It was predicted that organisational information would be used in recognition decisions, the blocked test facilitating performance more for high-organisation items. The predicted effect was not found on a standard recognition test, but was found on a recognition test requiring list discrimination. The order of test items also influenced clustering in later recall. Raye interprets these findings as indicating that occurrence information may be the basis for recognition decisions, even though organisational information is available. Hintzman and Stern (1984) investigated the proposition that recognition decisions display slower forgetting than do discriminations among frequencies greater than zero. On the frequency-discrimination test, subjects were presented with pairs of the pictures and had to decide which member had occurred more often in the presentation list by choosing one of four frequency combinations. Since the findings show no evidence of differential forgetting, the results were taken by Hintzman and Stern to support the view that the information underlying recognition memory and memory for frequency is qualitatively the same.

Although several of the studies reported above take issue with the proposed differences between frequency-based and associatively based processes involved in recognition, recent research appears to confirm that recognition decisions are based on contextual retrieval of specific trace information, in addition to an assessment of item strength. Three studies by Horton, Pavlick and Moulin-Julian (1993) address these issues. The first two experiments showed that as associative relatedness between items increased, correct recognition responses that were accompanied by successful cued recall of the same target items also increased. When correct recognition responses were not accompanied by successful cued recall, they increased in frequency as associative relatedness declined. The third study involved both a type of processing manipulation and levels of processing manipulation. A semantic emphasis led to more correct recognition responses accompanied by successful recall, while a non-semantic emphasis at study led to more correct recognition responses that were not recalled. These results provide clear support for the suggestion that retrieval-based and familiarity-based processes in recognition are separable.

There is also evidence that the two processes are physiologically differentiable. Smith and Halgren (1989) report that unilateral anterior temporal lobectomy in the language-dominant (left) hemisphere impairs initial recognition accuracy without affecting the rate at which repetition improves performance. The implication that the temporal lobe contributes to retrieval rather than strength during recognition is supported by simultaneous event related potential (ERP) recordings. In normal subjects, the large ERP difference between repeated and non-repeated words does not increase with increasing study, and is associated with contextual integration in other tasks. Thus, the lack of a repetition-induced ERP difference after left anterior temporal lobectomy provides converging evidence for a critical role of the temporal lobe in contextual retrieval during recognition, and also, of course, for differences between the two components of recognition.

Summary: Frequency and its implications

This chapter began by showing that repeatedly processing items during learning allows us to process those items more accurately and quickly later during learning. However, it is clear that more benefit accrues, at least with respect to the speed of learning, where only similar items are encountered during learning. With respect to retention, however, the picture changes, and the durability of what is learned is clearly enhanced where the learning experience is more heterogeneous. These learning and retention effects fit reasonably well with the findings on the effects of spacing and repetition. Immediate repetition appears to lead to less attention being devoted to the repeated item, and, as a result, less durability. With greater spacing, that is, with conditions which approximate distributed rather than massed practice, remembering is more durable. This way of understanding how practice and repetition relate to each other is strengthened by findings which indicate that spacing effects emerge more strongly from circumstances in which subjects are intentionally processing events, with a view to having to remember them later. In later chapters we will return to this issue, but it is also striking that where repetitions are made more distinctive, through, for example, interruption, this relatively artificial boundary imposed on the events appears to ensure that they are more likely to be remembered.

Taken together, the findings described above cast doubt on the notion that event frequency is automatically encoded, other than, perhaps, at the most trivial level. The fact that people are apparently insensitive to whether a word was previously encountered in its singular or plural form, or what the orientation of a picture was, convinces me, at least, that frequency registration of more complex stimulus attributes, and especially combinations of stimulus attributes are not learned without some effort, and probably not without conscious registration. While separate episodic traces may be laid down, even of closely repeated similar events, our access to the detailed contents of these records would appear to be limited. The implications of how frequency influences memory and decision making are therefore very profound. At the same time that learning is strengthened and made more durable, our ability to make fine discriminations between how often something has happened in the past is limited. In the next chapter, we will encounter another problem with event memory, that is, remembering when something happened.

■ Further reading

Hintzman, D. L. (1990). Human learning and memory: Connections and dissociations. *Annual Review of Psychology, 41,* 109–39.

Hintzman, D. L., Curran, T. and Oppy, B. (1992). Effects of similarity and repetition on memory: Registration without learning? *Journal of Experimental Psychology: Learning, Memory and Cognition, 18,* 667–80.

Kahana, M. J. and Greene, R. L. (1993). Effects of spacing on memory for homogenous lists. *Journal of Experimental Psychology: Learning, Memory and Cognition, 19,* 159–62.

Morrison, J. (ed.) (1991). Training for performance: Principles of applied human learning. Chichester: Wiley.

Naveh-Benjamin, M. and Jonides, J. (1986). On the automaticity of frequency coding: Effects of competing task load, encoding strategy, and intention. *Journal of Experimental Psychology: Learning, Memory and Cognition, 12,* 378–86.

Park, J. and Kanwisher, N. (1994). Determinants of the repetition blindness effect. *Journal of Experimental Psychology: Human Perception and Performance, 20,* 500–15.

Patrick, J. (1992). *Training: Research and practice.* London: Academic Press.

Discussion points

- Think about learning an everyday task like driving. Which elements might reflect massed practice, and which distributed practice?
- Compare and contrast the spacing effect and repetition blindness.
- Do we misjudge frequency? Why?
- How does repetition influence recognition?

Chapter 7

Time and duration

> **Chapter outline:** This chapter discusses different ways of thinking about time and how we make different types of temporal judgement. The focus is primarily on the relationship between event memory and judgements of temporal order, duration judgements and the dating of memories. Each of these are discussed in the wider context of event memory, and, in particular, in terms of our access to and use of temporal information.

Key topics | • The notion of time
| • Event duration
| • Knowing when events took place
| • Summary: Relationships between time and memory
| • Further reading

■ The notion of time

There is a strong sense throughout writings on time that it relates to change (Fraisse, 1963; Gibson, 1975; Block, 1990). Within this view, *linear time* encourages us to believe that there is a time which is past and a time which will be future. There is also a 'time' in which minimal change appears to occur. It is this we call the present. This notion that there is a past, present and future gives rise to the *chronological illusion* – that is the linearity of time is something we impose, rather than its being an inherent property of time itself. While the illusion is strong, thinking about our lives also reveals that there is also a repetitive or periodical quality about time. This is what is referred to as *cyclic time* (see Friedman, 1993).

Block (1990) distinguishes three different ways in which time has been considered. *Temporal succession* relates to the sequential order of events. Thus, for example, in order to change gear in a manual vehicle, we must first depress the clutch, shift the gear lever into neutral and then to the target gear, then release the clutch. In any successful gear-change with this fixed order, any element within it predicts what will happen next, and also what has happened immediately beforehand. However, it is worth bearing in mind that even this familiar example is not without its complications. The 'first' event, clutch depression, does not specify which gear will be selected, or even whether a higher or lower gear will be selected. Similarly, the 'last' event in the sequence, clutch release, does not uniquely determine which action will be performed next, for example, pressure might be applied to (or increased on) either the brake or accelerator. These events might actually be determined by events preceding clutch depression (e.g. slowing, using brake or accelerator), or clutch release (e.g. selection of higher gear predicts more acceleration, selection of lower gear predicts further slowing). We can also think about the intervals between the elements of this sequence, the total time taken to change gear, or indeed the time which has elapsed since we changed gear. These all relate to what is called *temporal duration*. Finally, *temporal perspective* refers to our experience of, as well as our attitudes to and beliefs about, time. We might, for example, believe that our ability to change gear is quicker in some cars than in others, that we wish to 'save' time, or that our school days were the best days of our lives. Temporal perspective is very strongly influenced by the chronological illusion, but many temporal judgements involve some interplay between temporal succession, duration and perspective. In this chapter, three issues will be addressed: determining the order of events, knowing how long events have lasted and knowing when an event took place.

The order of events

In previous chapters we noted how people might make use of onset and offset asynchronies to detect the presence of more than one event. Allen and Kautz (1985) identify 13 different temporal relationships between two events. One event may be before, or after, another. It may meet or be met by another. It may overlap or be overlapped by another event. An event can start or be started by another, finish or be finished by another event, or may equal, occur during or contain a second event. In the simplest case, with two items, classification into one of these relationships helps to identify the temporal relationships between the events. Hintzman and Block (1971) showed, in a study in which subjects were required to judge the serial position of words in a list, that judged versus actual positions were very accurate. The slope of the function relating judged and actual position is steeper for items occurring in the first 35–50 seconds, and more gradual but still positive for the remainder of the list. This differential sensitivity to relative spacing depending on when events occur is also found in other types of study. For example, relative primacy or recency has been shown to be greater for pairs of events that occurred in the initial positions in a series (Marshall, Chen and Jeter, 1989). Together, these results and those of Tzeng (1973) and colleagues suggests that some time-related information about events, and about relationships between events, is encoded as part of the memory of an event. This occurs with or without forewarning that serial order judgements might be required (Auday, Sullivan and Cross, 1988).

BOX 7.1: Assessing sequential order

Tzeng (1973) describes a number of studies in which subjects were presented with long lists of words, which they were told they would have to recall later. In fact, when the list had been presented, subjects were given a sheet of paper on which all the words encountered earlier were typed in a random order. Subjects had to judge where on the list (i.e. in which tenth rather than its actual position) each item had been presented. In the first study, for some subjects the words encountered were 50 randomly selected high frequency words, while others read the five most frequently occurring exemplars in 10 different categories. The hit rates, that is, number of words correctly placed in the 10 deciles were highly similar for both related and random lists. The fact that spontaneous organisation of related items does not disrupt this encoding of temporal order suggests that at least this form of encoding does not require intentional resources. That the effect does not rely on overt or covert rehearsal is clearly demonstrated in the second study reported in Tzeng's paper. Here, subjects in one of three groups either engaged in free rehearsal, repeated rehearsal (i.e. rehearsed the presented word until the next word was presented), or were not allowed to rehearse (i.e. subjects engaged in a backward counting task between presentations of words). Once again the hit-rates were equivalent across each of the groups.

While these results demonstrate that subjects know more or less where in a list particular items occurred, it is also very clear from the other data presented by Tzeng, that this judgement is far from error free. For a start, it is clear that blocking items into deciles serves to obscure some of the inaccuracy in judged serial position; items which were adjacent to each other at presentation were sometimes remembered as having occurred perhaps 10 or 20 items away from each other. The data replotted from Tzeng's first experiment shows that, with the exception of the initial and final items in a list, which might in any case be expected to be remembered best, subjects have a tendency to believe earlier items were presented later than they actually were, while later items are generally thought to have occurred earlier. Thus, while people are clearly sensitive to ordinal position, and this sensitivity

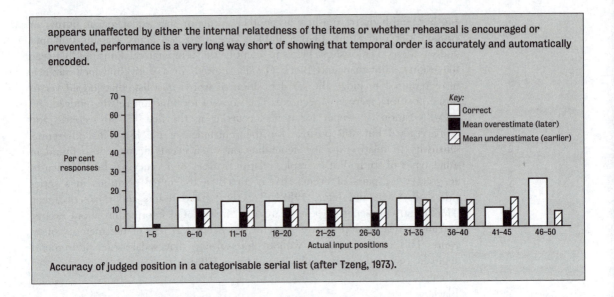

appears unaffected by either the internal relatedness of the items or whether rehearsal is encouraged or prevented, performance is a very long way short of showing that temporal order is accurately and automatically encoded.

Accuracy of judged position in a categorisable serial list (after Tzeng, 1973).

Temporal order and event schemata

With regard to more complex events, as discussed in Chapters 3 and 4, many theories of comprehension and memory postulate the existence of prototypical event-based schemata (e.g. Bower, Black and Turner, 1979; Schank and Abelson, 1977; Graesser and Nakamura, 1982). Most conceptions of schemata suggest that schemata are 'temporally ordered event concepts' (Trafimow and Wyer, 1993, p. 366). Broadly speaking, each schema is comprised of *schema-identifying* events or concepts – a generic label which can be used to describe a collection of interrelated activities, such as using a car-wash, going to a restaurant or getting ready for work in the morning. Each of these includes other *schema-instantiating* events or concepts, such as driving to the service station, buying a ticket, manoeuvring the vehicle to the water source, waiting for the washing procedure to proceed, and moving off again.

We may not all share schema-identifying or, especially schema-instantiating events, but very substantial overlaps would be expected between individuals who share the same culture or practices. While schema-like representations do not need to be formed through repeated or direct experience of the events which comprise a schema, it seems reasonable to assume that most are. Economical representations of common elements of routine events afford many benefits. For the most part, they provide us with reliable guidance as to what is likely to occur in a given situation, what may be expected to happen next, and even for remembering what may have happened. As such, schemata might be thought to provide us with a dependable basis for determining the temporal order of events. While this may well suffice in many situations, such a self-contained schema-based event memory would provide only a way of representing events which occur very frequently or are typical of certain events or situations. This would not allow schemata to develop or change, and might even mitigate their being learned through exposure. It would also prevent events which are unrelated to schemata being remembered in connection with a particular situation, for example, an occasion when I was slow to close my window in a car wash with rather wet and sudsy consequences! Sometimes, it may be very important to learn from experiences which are very unlikely to be schema-instantiated. These problems also make schemata less reliable as indicators of temporal order. Robert Wyer and colleagues have proposed a theory of how schema theory might be revised in order to address these issues (see Wyer and Srull, 1989).

Let us first consider how the events which are usually experienced in given situations might be represented. When people encounter events that instantiate concepts which define a particular schema, they may encode these events in terms of the schema-instantiated concepts. They also spontaneously infer that other schema-instantiated events, of which they were unaware, also took place. Thus every schema-instantiated event is represented as having occurred in each situation, and is thus referred to by Trafimow and Wyer as the 'complete-representation model'. This leads to false positives in recall and recognition of schema-related events and reinforces the coherence and consistency of the schema. This is a rather extreme version of the theory considered by Bower, Black and Turner (1979) and Graesser and Nakamura (1982). An alternative view, also considered by Graesser and Nakamura (1982), is that only those schema-instantiated events actually encountered are represented for any particular situation. Because only some of the schema-instantiated events which define a particular schema may be represented, this 'partial-representation' model also incorporated a 'tag' or pointer which refers to the actual schema used to process the events. A third possibility, the 'no-representation model', for which there has been some empirical support (e.g. Wyer and Srull, 1989), is that schema-instantiated events are not represented or stored at all, since they can easily be reconstructed from prior knowledge. Instead, what is represented is a pointer or tag which identifies the schema used, and a set of equivalence statements which identify the values of schema variables for a particular episode (e.g. car-wash = located at Shell station at Hills Road, Cambridge).

Thus, the three alternatives vary in the extent to which particular qualities of the events encountered in a schema-defined episode are actually represented, and in the referential role fulfilled by tags or pointers. What none cope with comfortably are the issues raised above – how is schema-unrelated information incorporated into the representation formed? Trafimow and Wyer (1993) have proposed an alternative which can do so. They assume that in order to avoid redundancy, schema-instantiating events are not usually represented. An exception to this is where there is a need to localise a schema-unrelated event within a schema-defined sequence. This is done by linking the schema-unrelated event to some contiguous schema-instantiated event which did occur, although Trafimow and Wyer (1993) also consider that a particular schema-unrelated event may be associated with other contiguous schema-unrelated events. Thus, as a result of such linking, 'the schema-instantiating event as well as the unrelated event becomes part of the representation that is retained in memory. Other instantiating events, however, do not have this localising function, and so they are not included' (1993, p. 366). In cases where it is sufficient to remember some general context in which a schema-unrelated event takes place (e.g. that getting wet while in a car occurred in a car-wash rather than somewhere else), the theory allows for the possibility that the schema-unrelated event might become associated with the schema-identifying event (e.g. car-washes in general), rather than with specific schema-instantiating events such as rolling up the window having initiated the wash. This has the advantage that a schema-unrelated event which occurred in a particular context may be associated with a more general structure, thus facilitating transfer of what is learned across situations.

Another issue also addressed by Trafimow and Wyer is that sometimes schema instantiations incorporate features which are situation-specific (e.g. the colour of the car in front when waiting in traffic), and that these cannot be reconstructed on the basis of the schema-defining concept used. According to the 'selective-representation' theory they propose, unless some schema-unrelated event occurred, such details would stand little chance of being remembered. In such situations, they propose that subjects construct and store a set of equivalence statements which permit features to be instantiated. These are stored with the pointer used to refer to the schema-identifying concept. These equivalence statements are later used to reconstruct the sequence of events that occurred, even though representations of the events themselves were not stored. Because such features are stored with the pointer, which presumably only includes details of some occasions on which the schema has been used (e.g. the first time, see Robinson, 1982; or the most recent occasion, see Morton, Hammersley and Bekerian, 1985), this allows them to become unbound. This would allow the migration of event features which, as we noted earlier, occurs in some retrieval situations (see also Treisman and Schmidt, 1982; Park and Kanwisher, 1994).

The selective representation model of event memory

Trafimow and Wyer (1993) report findings from three studies which support their 'selective-representation model' of event memory, but which cannot easily be accounted for within the other three models briefly considered above. Subjects read four prose passages, each describing a different sequence of events (e.g. photocopying). Some of the events in each passage instantiated concepts that defined a particular schema (e.g. 'Joe put in the coin and pushed the button', p. 368), some were schema-unrelated (e.g. 'He realised he had developed a headache', p. 368). The passages differed in terms of (a) whether the schema-identifying event (e.g. 'Thus Joe had copied the piece of paper') occurred at the end of the sequence, or at its beginning, and (b) whether the number of schema-instantiating events mentioned varied, while the number of schema-unrelated events was held constant (Experiment 1), or whether the number of instantiating events was held constant, but the number of schema-unrelated events varied (Experiment 2). In both cases, the subject's task was to recall the passage, with the incidence of recall of events and the order in which they were encountered and remembered being assessed. The third study they report is similar, but focuses explicitly on the incidence of intrusions as a function of the inclusion or exclusion of schema-unrelated events.

Trafimow and Wyer's (1993) results showed that increasing the number of schema-unrelated events in a passage increased the likelihood of recalling schema-instantiating events that were mentioned, but increasing the number of instantiating events which were mentioned had little influence on the recall of schema-unrelated events. They also showed that the probability of recalling an instantiating event was substantially higher if an unrelated event had been recalled, than if an instantiating event had been recalled, with instantiating events adjacent to recalled schema-unrelated events being the most likely to be retrieved. Finally, Trafimow and Wyer also report that increasing the number of unrelated events presented actually increased the number of schema-instantiated items being recalled, but it decreased the likelihood of schema-instantiating events which were not mentioned in the passage being falsely remembered (i.e. intrusions).

Two implications of this theory are particularly noteworthy in the present context. The first is that this 'selective-representation model' of event memory explicitly links the temporal order of events which might be inferred from a schema, to, at least, an ordinal representation of when instantiated and uninstantiated events occurred. Secondly, although it is not explicitly addressed in their paper, the model proposed by Wyer and colleagues also allows that where a schema-unrelated event repeatedly occurs in a particular situation, especially where it is continually linked to the same schema-instantiated event, it too can become schema-instantiated. With respect to the encoding and retrieval of temporal order, however, both the results from relatively simple situations, as well as those which are more complex, support models in which time-related information about events and relationships between events is encoded as part of the memory for an event. They also support the notion that this information, which is commonly referred to as a time-tag, is contextual or episodic in nature. At the end of this chapter we will return to this *time-tagging hypothesis*.

Event duration

The selective-representation model considered above offers a useful and well-supported way of thinking about how temporal order for events might be determined, but it gives no insight into how long an event may have lasted. It has generally been found that durations from seconds to minutes are accurately perceived (Allan, 1979; Michon, 1985), so are minutes to hours, when marked by the usual events which indicate the passage of time (e.g. day, night, meals, fatigue, etc.). Without such markers, experienced duration is somewhat shortened, and more variable. Aschoff (1985) investigated the temporal performance of people who lived in prolonged temporal isolation, for periods ranging from seven to thirty days. Aschoff had people make relatively long (i.e. one hour) or short (10 to 120 seconds) time judgements. He found considerable variability across produced times, but average attempts to produce a period of 10 seconds were slightly longer (11.7 seconds), while attempts to produce relatively longer time periods (120 seconds) averaged 116.8 seconds. These results are consistent with many frequency judgement studies, as discussed in the previous chapter, in which people tend to overestimate small quantities and underestimate large quantities. For the longer judgements, Aschoff required subjects to signal spontaneously every subjective hour when awake. These produced times averaging slightly longer than an hour, but perhaps more importantly, and unlike the shorter estimates, they correlated positively with how long each individual had been awake, as well as with the length of their sleep–wake cycle (i.e. circadian rhythm). Although temporally isolated, Aschoff's subjects were allowed to exercise, listen to music and read. However, very similar results emerged from studies in which subjects were not allowed to carry out such activities. The findings of Campbell (1986) and Lavie and Webb (1975) both show that individuals' subjective view of one hour is actually in the region of 67 minutes. Thus far I have intentionally blurred what is a very significant distinction with respect to event duration – that between judging how long a completed event lasted (*retrospective duration judgement*), and how long an ongoing experience must continue before reaching some criterion (*prospective duration judgement*).

There are many puzzling, but nevertheless robust, findings with regard to duration estimation. Two will be concentrated on here. The first is known as the *filled duration illusion*. Vroon (1970) asked subjects to estimate how long an interval of 60 seconds had lasted. If 60 tones were presented during the interval, it was thought to have lasted longer than when 30 tones were encountered in the one-minute period (Fig 7.1). It has also been shown that duration estimates increase where subjects have to classify the tones into high and low categories. Arguably, this offers another explanation for why the proverbial watched kettle never boils, other than impatience on the part of the tea-maker!

Fig 7.1 Judged length of 60 seconds filled with 30 or 60 tones (after Vroon, 1970).

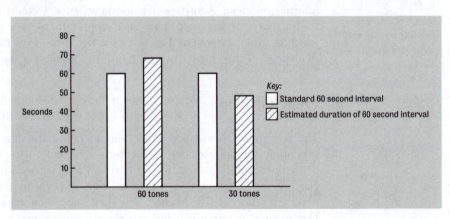

The second intriguing set of results might be termed the *duration estimation paradox*. When subjects are asked to make a prospective duration estimate, that is, to signal when a prespecified period has elapsed Brown (1985; Brown and Stubbs, 1989) has shown that the verbal estimates they give are longer and more accurate than when subjects are asked to make a retrospective duration estimate, that is, to say for how long a completed event lasted. Earlier, Hicks, Miller and Kinsbourne (1976) found that prospective judgements are shortened if subjects engage in a more demanding task whilst also making prospective time estimates. Similarly, although in a more rigorous study, Zakay (1993) has shown that if people are asked to say when a particular period (e.g. 12 seconds) has elapsed, where the interval is empty people give larger estimates than if the interval is filled (Fig 7.2). In contrast, Zakay showed in the same paper that when subjects are asked to indicate how long a completed interval had lasted, they gave larger estimates when the interval was filled, rather than empty. Thus, within an ongoing experience, time is shortened by increases in complexity or processing load, while the same experience, once completed, will be remembered as having taken longer. Two accounts of this phenomenon, one centred on attention, and one centred on memory, emerge from the literature. These deal, respectively, with prospective and retrospective estimation. Fraisse (1963) anticipated the spirit of this difference between the two accounts by suggesting that 'direct time judgements (are) founded immediately in the changes we experience and later on the changes we remember' (p. 234).

Fig 7.2 Estimated duration of 12-second interval as a function of estimation method and concurrent tasks (after Zakay, 1993).

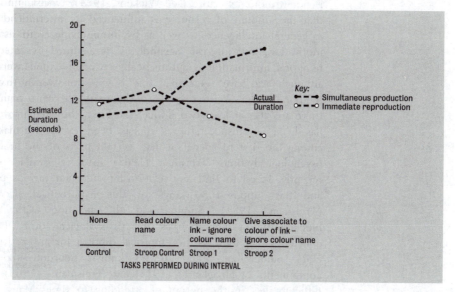

Attentional metaphors and prospective duration estimation

The attentional model suggests that while engaged in a task (i.e. main task), but also being aware that they must interrupt or end their performance after a prespecified interval has elapsed (i.e. supplementary task), subjects devote attention both to the main task and 'to time itself' (see Underwood, 1975). Because the available resources are limited, and must be shared between the two tasks (see Kahneman, 1973), devoting more attention to the main task reduces the attention paid to time itself (see Thomas and Brown, 1974; Thomas and Weaver, 1975). The presumption is not that estimates of elapsed time become more variable, which is what might be expected where less control is exercised over a process. Instead, because their attention is taken up with the main task, in effect, people do not notice time passing. As a result, when the attention resource devoted to the main task increases, people believe that less time has passed, with the result that when asked to indicate when a specified period has elapsed, they respond later in time. The theory suggests that putative event markers, which indicate the completion of smaller units of time, are missed by some putative counting process. According to this view, prospective estimations require the subject to determine at some point how many 'subjective time units' would be required to fill the pre-specified period. These are then counted down as, so to speak, time passes. This would clearly account for the widely observed tendency for prospective time estimates to increase with the level of demand imposed by simultaneous activities. However, the account has many inherent problems, some of which relate to the assumptions made about attention, and others which relate to the existence of a time processor.

Two difficulties arise with regard to the model's assumptions about attention. In the first place, the assumption that processing resources are fixed is not without its critics (see Wickens, 1984). One might expect, for example, that the amount of resource is influenced by interindividual differences, such as general intelligence, as well as by intraindividual differences, such as fatigue, motivation, and interest. Secondly, it is assumed by at least one theory that temporal information is automatically encoded (e.g. Hasher and Zacks, 1984), although we have seen that this is questionable, at least with respect to temporal order. With respect to the existence of a putative time processor, there are also at least two difficulties. First, the search for some internal clock has been as unsuccessful as it has been exhaustive. Hoagland (1933) was among the first to speculate that 'certain parts of the brain' (p. 283) underlie psychological time. Treisman (1963) made a similar proposal, but, more recently, failed to find any relationship between various physiological rhythms and the supposed workings of this hypothetical pacemaking mechanism (Treisman, 1984). Summarising the position with regard to possible biochemical or neural basis for psychological time, Block (1990, p. 15) concludes that there is 'no empirical support for any relatively simple internal-clock model, and there is no known neurophysiological basis for the components of Hoagland's (1933) and Treisman's (1963) model'. The second difficulty lies in the notion of attending to time. Many (e.g. Gibson, 1975) suggest that there is no such thing as time, merely an awareness of change. That is not to say that we cannot attend to the types of change from which we normally infer that something has ended or something different has occurred. It is just that what we are attending to in these circumstances, or failing to attend to because of some demanding simultaneous task, is not time, but change. Furthermore, the limits of what is known as the psychological present, that is the feeling of being in or part of time, have been suggested to be from a few seconds to up to 30 seconds (Boring, 1963), but most authors bound the psychological present at some 5–7 seconds (e.g. Michon (1978) 7–8s; Fraisse (1984) 2–5s, Block (1979) 5s). This limit, which is somewhere near that usually assumed for the dynamic functioning of the short-term memory stores (see Baddeley, 1986), seems too high to allow for mechanisms such as that supposed by Underwood and Thomas to provide the levels of differentiation we can readily observe.

Turning briefly to the retrospective case, assuming no other process is involved, subjects who were asked to say, subsequently, how long an experience had lasted would remember or reconstruct the number of subjective time units noticed during the task. If the main task was demanding, people would believe it to have lasted for less time than a similar period in which the main task was not as demanding. Thus, when extrapolated to the retrospective case, the attentional theory of duration estimation predicts results which are opposite to those widely obtained.

Storage metaphors and retrospective duration estimation

James (1890) noted that duration in passing lengthens when 'we grow attentive to the passage of time itself' whereas duration in retrospect lengthens as a function of 'the multitudinousness of the memories which time affords' (p. 624). Ornstein (1969) drew attention to the relationship between remembering and duration estimation, in a view which has become known as the storage size metaphor. Ornstein suggests that time estimation is a function of storage size, which is in turn a function of the complexity of the processing required to store the information. The greater the complexity, the greater the resulting storage size and thus the longer the corresponding time estimates of the duration of those events will be. Taken simply, the more we remember of an event, the longer we believe our direct experience of it lasted. There is empirical support for such a position (e.g. Ornstein, 1969; Avant, Lyman and Antes, 1975; Michon, 1965), but it is rather indirect, and it is not difficult to be sceptical about whether adequate measures of storage size, complexity and organisation were actually available.

This view has, perhaps, been mistakenly represented as proposing a direct relationship between the amount that can be recalled from an interval, and the length of that interval. A variety of studies demonstrate that the case for such a relationship is rather weak. Loftus, Schooler, Boone and Kline (1987) studied the relationship between arousal and estimated duration, by contrasting the amount remembered from films of staged bank robberies. The findings show that in each case the length of these films of simulated bank robberies were overestimated. However, a '"low stress" version (which) depicted the bank robber entering the bank and calmly handing a note to the teller' (Loftus et al., 1987, p. 8) was thought to have taken less time than a '"high stress" version (which) depicted the robber displaying an automatic pistol, and using profane and threatening language' (Loftus et al., 1987, p. 8). No correlation was observed between the degree of reported arousal induced by the film and the estimate of its duration, nor was there any reliable relationship between the amount or accuracy of recall and the magnitude of duration estimates. It might be thought that the finding that more arousing events are recalled as having lasted longer is in line with Ornstein's account of duration estimation, but it is also in line with many other results which have shown that filled intervals are perceived as having lasted longer than similarly long unfilled intervals (Zakay, 1993).

Predebon (1984) attempted to manipulate amount recalled, and examine the effect of this manipulation on duration estimation, by capitalising on the Bransford and Johnson (1972) finding that providing a title prior to learning a prose passage reliably increased the number of ideas which could be recalled from it. Predebon argued, following Ornstein, that if more could be remembered from the passage, when preceded by its title, its presentation time should be estimated to be longer than when less could be recalled from it. However, while Predebon's study successfully replicated the Bransford and Johnson finding, the increased amount recalled did not result in different estimates of how long the passage had been presented for. Debra Bekerian and I recently replicated this study (Groeger and Bekerian, 1995), with higher levels of recall, but otherwise very similar findings.

Fig 7.3 Estimated duration as a function of mixed and separated processing tasks (after Block and Reed, 1978).

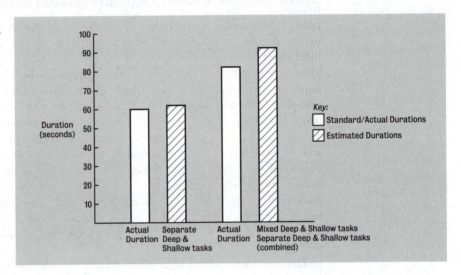

Block and Reed (1978) found that subjects remembered a duration as being longer, to the extent that changes in the processing context had occurred (Fig 7.3). They suggest that this kind of information is apparently encoded as an integral part of the memory representations of stimulus events. Block and Reed proposed what they called a contextual change model of remembered duration. According to this model, remembered duration involves a cognitive reconstruction, based on retrieving contextual information that is stored as an integral part of the memory encodings of events, rather than a reconstruction based on retrieving stimulus information per se. 'The greater are the encoded and retrievable contextual changes, the longer is the remembered duration of a time period' (Block, 1990, p. 25). Block (1982) showed that previous experience in a particular environment (a room containing an experimenter, various objects, and so on) shortened the remembered duration of a subsequent time period spent in that environment. One interpretation of this finding is that more contextual changes occur during a period spent in unfamiliar surroundings. This explanation is supported by the additional finding that if the encoding of environmental context is different in some way during a second time period, the relative duration of that time period lengthens. It seems likely that invoking a schema alters the range of intrinsic contextual changes which occur when reading a passage, in that fewer alternative interpretations are likely to be formed and discarded. If that was so, then remembered duration, while it might not be related to the enhanced level of recall, might still reflect the operation of a schema, such that presenting a schema-invoking title before the passage is heard should lead to a shorter remembered duration.

It is of course possible that neither amount recalled nor accuracy adequately reflect 'storage size' in Ornstein's terms. Instead, perhaps, Miller, Hicks and Willette, (1978, p. 178) capture more the spirit of Ornstein's view, by suggesting that 'duration judgements are based on memory for the amount of processing done', rather than on the amount remembered. In a sense this is undermined by our own failure, together with that of Predebon, to demonstrate a link between enhanced recall (through provision of thematic information) and differences in retrospective duration estimation. It is reasonable to suppose that people do rather more processing when confronted with an untitled passage which they will have to remember than when confronted with the same passage with the type of thematic information which might be expected to invoke schematic processing. This would predict, on the basis of some implicit memory of the processing done, that passages from which more can be remembered through reliance on a schema, should be judged to have had a shorter presentation time than passages which do not readily invoke a single schema.

There is another reason for expecting this pattern of results. Invoking a schema should promote recall. The earlier discussion of Wyer's work strongly suggests that in the titled passage condition, very little of the passage information should be represented, since it is virtually all consistent with the schema invoked. As a result, rather more processing resource and space (in Ornstein's terms) would be required for the untitled passage. Thus, greater recall should be associated with shorter estimates of retrospective duration, in contradiction to the pattern which might be expected from the 'amount recalled' view. Unfortunately, rather than observing a difference in the opposite direction to that predicted by the storage size hypothesis, no difference is found.

It is worth noting in respect of this, that the Groeger and Bekerian (1995) study included a further condition. Subjects were asked to indicate, while listening to the passage, that 20 seconds had passed from the first word they had heard. Preceding passages with titles had a very substantial effect. Once again, subjects remembered more passage information when thematic information was made available to them, just as we might expect on the basis of the Bransford and Johnson studies. What is rather more important, however, is that subjects who had been informed of the title of the passage they were about to hear actually signalled earlier that the 20-second period had elapsed (Fig 7.4). Thus, when subjects were, we presume, having to devote rather more attention to encoding the passage, they gave higher prospective estimates of duration – the result typically found. The amount recalled was similar in both the retrospective and prospective estimation conditions, and the estimates given were unrelated to the amount recalled. It might be suggested that the effect of preceding the passage with its title is to render much more of the information encountered schema-consistent. Without the title, the effect should be to increase the number of events tagged as having taken place, thus increasing the individual's sense of more having happened, more time having elapsed, and thus, an earlier response. The opposite to this happened. It is possible that the promise of the contextually based account might still be rescued. It is conceivable that introducing thematic information does not manipulate context. It is also possible that as the passage proceeds, subjects derive their own organisation and interpretation of the passages used, such that by the end of the passage both groups have an equivalent, schema-based, interpretation of the passage, although only the supplied schema is sufficient to influence recall. This would result in no differences in retrospective duration estimates. From a contextual point of view, the differences in prospective estimation brought about by titling the passages may reflect the state of processing before a stable interpretation of the passage has been formed.

Fig 7.4 Prose memory and duration estimation as a function of estimation method and passage labelling (after Groeger and Bekerian, 1995).

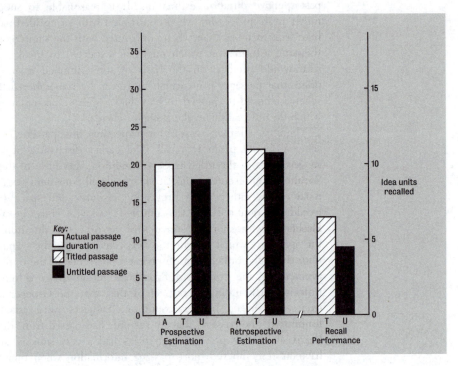

The findings considered in Figure 7.4 leave us with two accounts of duration estimation, one for prospective estimates and one for retrospective estimates, which do not account very well for findings within their own task constraints, and offer little by way of satisfactory explanation of how findings relate to the other type of estimate. The third possibility, the context-based account proposed by Block, which can explain several instances of the presence and absence of some of the predicted findings, has, however, a fundamental difficulty: as presently constituted, it 'does not propose any independent way of measuring the amount of change in cognitive context' (Block, 1990, p. 26).

■ Knowing when events took place

Knowing when events took place, or how many events of a particular kind have taken place within a specified period, is another important way in which we make use of temporal information. Three different types of theory of how we perform such tasks can be distinguished. There are those that assume that some temporal code (or code which supports later temporal processing) is laid down when an episode is encoded; those that assume that no such code is laid down at encoding, that is, episodes are encoded in a way that preserves their temporal relations with each other; and those that assume that temporal information is not directly encoded, but is derived as required from certain qualities of the retrieved memory. Friedman (1993), in a recent review of the literature on the dating of past events, refers to these as location, association and distance theories. They might as conveniently be referred to as theories that propose direct encoding, relational encoding and derivation of temporal information. In the next sections we pay particular attention to the direct encoding and derived accounts; the relational account, because it is inherently unsatisfactory, is only discussed in passing.

Direct encoding of temporal information

As mentioned above, direct encoding theories, those Friedman (1993) calls 'location theories', propose that information which supports temporal judgements is laid down at the time of encoding and later retrieved. This might be achieved in various ways, the most obvious of which is *time-tagging* (e.g. Tzeng, 1976; Hasher and Zacks, 1979, 1984). Such time-tags may be actual dates or times, but this is probably accidental and a function of the intrinsic memorability of a date (e.g. St Valentine's Day massacre) or of a time (e.g. earthquakes that occur around noon – Friedman, 1987). There is abundant evidence that dates and times are very poor retrieval cues. Wagenaar (1986), in an extensive diary study over a period of several years in which memorable events were recorded daily, found that only 2 per cent of events could be retrieved when dates were used as the sole retrieval cue (Fig 7.5). Similarly, Brewer (1988) and Barsalou (1988) have both shown in very different studies that dates were consistently worst among a large range of different retrieval cues.

Among the different date or time cues that have been investigated, month, weekday–weekend and hour have been shown to be better than day of the week or date (Friedman, 1987; Friedman and Wilkins, 1985). In what have been termed 'scale effects', a number of authors have demonstrated that certain cues are useful for dating specific lengths of time. For example, in 1986, Friedman (1987) investigated people's memory for the Ohio earthquake, which took place at 11.50 a.m., on Friday, 31 January 1986. People reliably remembered that it had taken place that year, and the time of day when it occurred, but did not remember the day of the week, day of month, or month in which it occurred. In a rather different study, Robinson (1982) showed that events which took place near the mid-points of the academic year were poorly recalled, but using semesters as boundaries appeared to improve dating accuracy. The poor performance of temporal cues as aids to retrieval, as well as the differential effectiveness of different temporal cues, strongly suggests that if events are time-tagged, these time-tags are not like some form of time-stamp. Tzeng, Lee and Wetzel (1979) suggest that many different forms of contextual time-tags are used, that is, implicit associations to an event or other events in an episode,

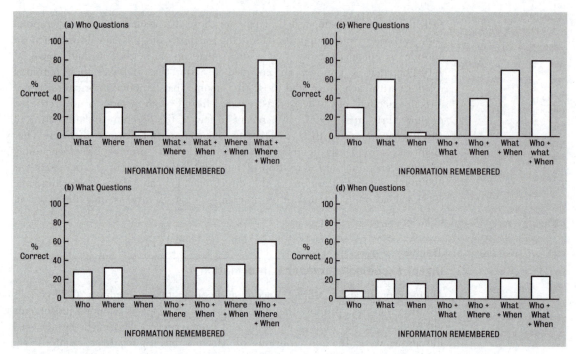

Fig 7.5   Retrieval cues and remembering who, what, where and when (after Wagenaar, 1986).

rather than time-stamping per se. That is, temporally useful information is acquired in the course of other types of cognitive processing. Although this information need not be encoded for the purpose of supporting later temporal processing, it is clear that an intention to remember the events in question enhances performance. Tzeng, Lee and Wetzel (1979), for example, show that the serial order of events that subjects are told to remember is more accurately retrieved than the serial order of items that subjects are told to forget.

One possibility that has been addressed by Estes (1972, 1985) is that when an event occurs it takes its place within an on-going episode, or establishes a new one. Events and episodes are themselves associated with control elements (e.g. beginnings, ends, etc.), at different levels in a chronologically organised hierarchy of event memories (which relate events over much longer periods of time). With an account which has become known as *encoding perturbation theory*, temporal judgements involve 'mentally searching through the sequence of memory representations until the representations of the indicated item or items are located', then responding 'on the basis of the temporal relations between these and the reference points' (Estes, 1985, p. 161). Because events are related to control elements at higher levels in the event hierarchy, they are obviously associated with different periods in time. The result of this is that, unless the order of events is rehearsed, events are 'perturbed' forwards or backwards in linear time, leading to a loss of temporal information with the encoding of new events (i.e. as processing changes occur, and hence as time 'passes'). There is good support for this perturbation idea, from dating studies (e.g. Huttenlocher, Hedges and Bradburn, 1990), and from phenomena known as *forward* and *backward telescoping*, which we will discuss below.

One of the difficulties with encoding perturbation theory is its explicit assumption that event hierarchies are chronologically organised. Evidence we will discuss later in the context of personal memories, together with our earlier discussion of the script- or grammar-like nature of memory for prose, tempts me to see event hierarchies as being less linearly organised than is implied by the term 'chronological'. There is much evidence to suggest that some, perhaps more loose, temporal order is used as a basis for encoding and retrieval. Studies show that estimates of when items were presented, or the order in which presentations occurred, are more accurate when presentations involve or support temporal organisation, such as when random rather than non-random lists are used, when items are blocked by semantic category, or different processing requirements, or are presented in different environments (see Friedman, 1993). This implies that temporal boundaries or contextual changes can serve as a basis for approximately locating events in time.

Derived temporal information

On the basis of what we have considered above, some of the information that supports temporal judgements appears almost incidental to what we might normally regard as 'time'. Theories that suggest that temporal information is derived, rather than directly encoded, rely on processes that are correlated with the passage of time. Thus, information about the age of a memory is created by processes that operate between the time of encoding and the time of retrieval.

One class of such theories relates to the strength or elaborateness of the information remembered. For example, Hinrichs (1970) suggests that each item in memory has a strength which decays with time, whether because of lack of use or interference from subsequent events. When an event occurred will be determined by the strength of the trace, where stronger traces are judged to be due to more recent events. Michon (1990) advances a similar notion. A related model is based upon the number of propositions retrieved rather than trace strength (Brown, Rips and Shevell, 1985). Both theories assume that the passage of time affects memories in a way that produces cues to their age. Quantitative temporal information is derived from some non-temporal attribute of what is remembered (e.g. strength, accessibility, or elaborateness). Thus, Block (1982) has shown that shallow-processed words were more likely to be thought to have been presented in the first of a number of lists. Pictures from a mixed set of pictures and nouns were both better recognised and judged, on average, as being more recent than nouns or judgements of distances in the past (Fozard and Weinert, 1972). While the suggestion that events for which memories are more detailed, more vivid and more readily accessed seem more recent has intuitive appeal, studies show that this is not the case. Thompson, Skowronski and Lee (1988) had subjects write down one unique event each day, and three months later date and rate their memory for the event. Well-remembered events were not judged as more recent than poorly remembered items. However, higher memorability (Thompson, 1982), clarity of memory (Thompson, Skowronski and Lee, 1988) and recognition confidence (Flexser and Bower, 1984) are all related to greater accuracy in dating events. This is one reason why people are better at making temporal judgements about more recent events; the other is that the time scales for recent events are obviously more restricted (e.g. Baddeley, Lewis and

Nimmo-Smith, 1978; Huttenlocher *et al*, 1990). In short, recent events are of course more memorable, but more memorable events are not necessarily more recent (see also Bartlett and Snelus, 1980; Fozard and Weinert, 1972; Jackson, Michon, Boonstra, de Jonge and de Veld Harsenhorst, 1986).

The so-called strength theories considered above can be represented by an archaeological metaphor, that of radio-carbon dating. An intrinsic attribute decays at an (approximately) known rate over time, allowing us to date precisely when it was created. A different archaeological metaphor can be used to summarise chronological organisation theory (Koffka, 1936; Murdock, 1974), that is, that the detritus of living forms separate layers of deposits that relate to different time periods. This theory suggests that judging the time of a target event depends on information about the age of a memory, such as the number of 'layers' or of intervening events. The effectiveness of different forms of organisation (random versus non-random lists) and gross temporal contexts (different lists or task-environments) in promoting dating accuracy support the importance of such temporal layering, but many other theories also account for such findings. Friedman (1993) also considers another theory of this sort, which he calls 'contextual overlap'. Briefly, context is associated with events as they are encoded. These contextual elements change with the passage of time: 'the degree of match between the context available at the test (the retrieval cue) and the encoding contexts ... forms an ordinal measure of recency' (Glenberg, Bradley, Kraus and Renzaglia, 1983). To extend the 'layering' analogy, if the subjective temporal distances of events in the past are derived from the amount of contextual overlap, or the shared detritus from older and more recent settlements, then such distances should be underestimated when the two contexts overlap more than would usually be the case for a given amount of elapsed time.

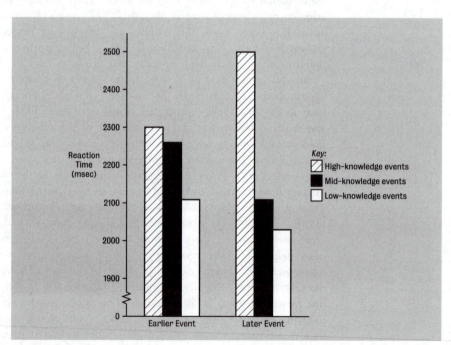

Fig 7.6 Comparison of target events with earlier or later events, as a function of event knowledge (after Brown, Rips and Shevell, 1985).

One way in which this suggestion might be explored is through the priming of temporal judgements. If the contextual overlap or layering notion is true then one might expect that encountering events from one domain might serve to improve the accuracy with which other events from that domain can be dated. Although they did not set out to test this hypothesis, results reported by Brown, Rips and Shevell (1985) suggest that this may well be so. They found that when political target events occurred was judged more accurately if they had to be related to presidential terms, but non-political events were dated more accurately when they had to be related to two life periods – high school periods and school years (Fig 7.6). Thus, as might be expected from the contextual overlap theory, temporal judgements are mediated or facilitated by judgement about other domains. Just as with those theories that are based upon the notion that information supporting temporal judgements is directly encoded, contextual information again plays a significant role in the dating of events. In the next chapter, we will explore the notion of context and its encoding more fully. Before we do so, however, there is another aspect of the Brown, Rips and Shevell study which warrants attention.

Temporal telescoping

Brown, Rips and Shevell (1985) provide evidence that dates are estimated rather than remembered. Subjects dated 50 events which had taken place in the period from 1977 to 1982. They found that the information about each event (i.e. number of propositions) that could be recalled was systematically related to the judged recency of the event. Where larger numbers of propositions could be recalled, events were dated on average as being more recent, by an average of some 0.28 years. Low-knowledge events were dated as being less recent, by an average of 0.17 years from their actual date of occurrence. The dating of events as more recent, or less recent, refer respectively to forward and backward telescoping. As Brown and colleagues show, the telescoping tendency is in part determined by the knowledge one has about events.

In general, more attention has been paid to forward telescoping, since it appears to be the more prevalent phenomenon. There are systematic biases which may underlie both its apparent prevalence and actual occurrence. Bradburn, Rips and Shevell (1987), for example, suggest that the target events that are generally used in dating studies are often more salient. As a result of this, the greater detail that can be retrieved about the events concerned, causes them to be judged as more recent. The relative salience of target and non-target events offers an explanation of why forward telescoping occurs. Following Murdock (1974), Thompson, Skowronski and Lee (1988) and Huttenlocher, Hedges and Prohaska (1988) suggest that people judge the time of occurrence on the basis of an estimate of the number of events intervening between it and the present. The more time has elapsed, the more intervening items are forgotten, thus distorting subjective time toward the present (Fig 7.7). As with other explanations regarding the salience or memorability of certain episodes, this too runs into the difficulty that memories that are rated as being especially clear are not necessarily displaced towards the present (e.g. Rubin and Baddeley, 1989). A number of studies other than that by Brown, Rips and Shevell also report backward telescoping of events (e.g. Tzeng, 1976; Rubin and Baddeley, 1989). Requiring that events are dated in relation to the present is one of the reasons why backward telescoping is less frequently observed. Obviously events that are yet to take place cannot be dated as having already taken place, thus only forward slippage in dating is possible. Where the end point is not the present, both types of error can and do apply. Baddeley, Lewis and Nimmo-Smith (1978), for instance, carried out a study in which panel subjects at the Applied Psychology Unit were asked to identify the date on which they last served as a subject. They found that there was a striking relationship between the recency of the event and the standard deviation of the estimate given. It increased by 19 days for each 100 days of elapsed time, thus showing that dating accuracy becomes more variable with increases in intervening time.

Fig 7.7 Backward and forwarding telescoping as a function of time since event (after Thompson, Skowronski and Lee, 1988).

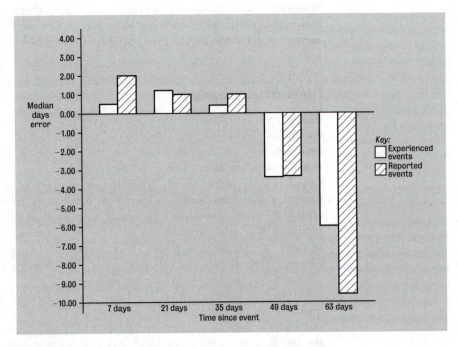

Supplied or self-generated reference points, or temporal landmarks, influence dating accuracy considerably. Loftus and Marburger (1983) showed substantial improvements when the dates of target events were judged in relation to another notable event (the eruption of Mt St Helens volcano), than when such a landmark was not supplied. Dating accuracy was also improved by using questions which emphasised particular temporal landmarks (e.g. 'since Christmas', rather than 'in the last six months'). In a result which has considerable implications for studies of individuals' self-reported exposure to risk, Loftus and Marburger also report that forward telescoping was more prevalent with very emotional events. Thus, survey questions which pose questions such as 'how many traffic accidents have you had in the last three years?' may serve to inflate the reported number of accidents in a particular period because the more traumatic incidents are likely to be imported from another period. Use of landmarks may serve to overcome this effect. For example, Means, Mingay, Nigam and Zarrow (1988) had subjects make use of links to personal landmarks (e.g. birthdays, holidays, etc.) to date events like repeated visits to hospital, and showed that such 'personal time lines' produce more accurate estimates of when subjects visited health care services in a 12-month period. The results of these studies show, just as might be expected from the contextual overlap theory described above, that use of events promotes dating accuracy in related events, but not in events of all kinds. The practical implications of this are that landmarks need to be chosen carefully in order to maximise their effectiveness, and to minimise the disruption of dating or retrieval that may result from the priming of what, to the experimenter, would seem to be irrelevant events.

These landmark studies make it unlikely that telescoping can be explained solely in terms of the ages of events, or the relative accessibility of memories for the events in question. The range of events to be considered also exerts an influence on dating accuracy (e.g. Huttenlocher, Hedges and Prohaska, 1988), while telescoping is reduced still further if analysis is restricted to events that the subject is confident of remembering (Thompson, Skowronski and Lee, 1988). Together, these findings suggest that telescoping is not caused by vividness of memory codes, or by progressive shortening or lengthening, but by imprecision in the way time is represented and the way subjects try to solve the dating tasks with which they are confronted (Huttenlocher, Hedges and Prohaska, 1988; Huttenlocher, Hedges and Bradburn, 1990; Rubin and Baddeley, 1989). Huttenlocher and colleagues suggest that temporal representations are essentially metric, but events are represented at several different levels of precision, based on calendar time (i.e. in terms of hours, days, months). If information at one level of the hierarchy is lost, the boundaries arising from the more gross temporal units systematically bias the estimate produced. There is good support for the Huttenlocher proposal. More recent studies extend the model and point to two sources of error which may also underlie forward telescoping (see Huttenlocher, Hedges and Bradburn, 1990).

One source of error is subjects' imposition of an upper boundary on reports, based on their notion of what would constitute reasonable answers to the questions asked. This boundary truncates the distribution of reports, yielding systematically biased estimates. It should be noted here that the surface form of the question may also introduce bias. Thus, temporally marked questions (e.g. 'how *long* ago was it?') systematically bias the direction of error in people's estimates (see Yarmey, 1990). The other factor is subjects' use of rounded (prototypic) values. These values, although stated in days, actually represent larger temporal categories (e.g. 14, 21, 30, 60 days ago). The distance between rounded values increases as the temporal categories become larger. Because of decreasing precision in memory and this increase in the distance between rounded values, a broader range of values is rounded down rather than up, again leading to forward bias (see Huttenlocher, Hedges and Bradburn, 1990). While the Huttenlocher model is a determined, and largely successful, attempt to model temporal estimation, its reliance on calendar-based representations seems at odds with findings which emerge from the studies of personal memories we consider in later chapters, and appears to imply a consistency in the way different levels of information are lost.

■ Summary: Relationships between time and memory

Taken together, the results discussed above in relation to temporal order, duration and dating studies point strongly to the reconstructive nature of temporal judgements. That is, people store information about the environment in which events are encountered, as well as, perhaps, their interpretations of and reactions to these events, along with specific details of some of the events encountered. When asked to judge when an event occurred, or to make some judgement about its duration, this contextual information is interpreted in the light of their rich knowledge of social, natural and personal time patterns (i.e. what Block, 1990 calls temporal perspective), and a small minority of salient events for which exact dates are known/have been learned. This reconstructive account of temporal processing can be sustained without direct time-tagging, and without assuming perturbation or chronological organisation of episodic memory. However, the work of Huttenlocher and colleagues provides a powerful framework within which the dating of events can be understood. Its advantage over earlier similar formulations (e.g. Lee and Estes, 1981) is that temporal position is defined with respect to an external framework (i.e. calendar time), and not simply to the succession of events. While this poses its own problems, the relative imprecision of serial order decisions even for adjacent items, discussed at the outset of this chapter, is perhaps a more telling weakness. Furthermore, the fact that the directionality of the errors in dating is specified, helps to account neatly for both forward and backwards telescoping.

The relative dearth of retrievable reliable temporal information, and its inherent qualitative variability mitigates against accounts of temporal processing, which suggest that temporal information is directly encoded. This being so, just as with information about event frequency, there is reason to question accounts which link the concept of automaticity and the encoding of fundamental information of this kind.

Obviously, the studies above should cause us to question very seriously the reliability of accounts where witnesses to events 'remember' information about when events occurred, or their duration. We have a somewhat more satisfactory account of how memories may be dated, or at least of sources of bias that may influence the estimates made. We are some way, however, from understanding how the durations of on-going or completed events may be assessed. The accounts which are most satisfactory are those that stress the role that selectively represented schema-inconsistent events, or shifts in processing contexts, may play. In the next chapter we will explore the effects of context and changes in context in greater detail.

■ Further reading

Block, R. A. (1990). *Cognitive models of psychological time.* Hillsdale, NJ: Erlbaum.

Brown, N. R., Rips, L. J. and Shevell, S. K. (1985). The subjective dates of natural events in very long-term memory. *Cognitive Psychology, 17,* 139–77.

Conway, M. A. (1990). *Autobiographical memory.* Buckingham: Open University Press.

Friedman, W. J. (1993). Memory for the time of past events. *Psychological Bulletin,* *113,* 44–66.

Macar, F., Pouthas, V. and Friedman, W. J. (1992). *Time, action and cognition.* Dordrecht: Klewer Academic Publishers.

Trafimow, D. and Wyer, R. S. Jr (1993). Cognitive representation of mundane social events. *Journal of Personality and Social Psychology, 64,* 365–76.

Zakay, D. (1993). Time estimation methods – do they influence prospective duration estimates? *Perception, 22,* 91–101.

Discussion points

- Think of a number of everyday tasks in which you rely upon prospective and retrospective estimates of duration. How could the circumstances in which these tasks are performed disrupt your estimates?
- How would Trafimow and Wyer's account of temporal succession explain the paradoxical findings on duration estimation?
- Why do we misremember when things happened?
- Discuss the Hasher and Zacks proposal that fundamental information, such as frequency, location and time, are automatically encoded.

Chapter 8

Context and source

Chapter outline: This book has already described many instances in which context has served as an explanation of, or at least an important variable in, many of the findings we have discussed in relation to events, frequency and temporal information processing. This chapter considers studies in which context at encoding, at retrieval, or both – were deliberately manipulated. The results from these studies are discussed in terms of different models of recall and recognition, in an attempt to understand why context effects on recognition are less reliably observed than context effects on recall. Finally, the ways in which context changes and context reinstatement may underlie difficulties in picture-based person and face recognition are described and discussed.

Key topics
- Context: Interpretation, location and state
- Encoding context and retrieval
- Context effects in recall and recognition
- Context and face recognition
- Attention and the encoding and retrieval of context
- Summary: Context and familiarity, source and resource
- Further reading

■ Context: Interpretation, location and state

Context, as we have already seen, is used in subtly different ways by different authors. Here, I deliberately wish to take a broad view of the effects that changes in, or reinstatement of, context can have on remembering and failure to retrieve. Thus, the following sections range from manipulations of the 'non-target' materials present at encoding and retrieval with the aim of altering the ways in which a 'target' is interpreted, to circumstances where the materials learned and retrieved were identical at encoding and retrieval, but where the environment or the physical state of the person performing the experiment were radically different.

Semantic context

There are many simple demonstrations of the effects of how changes in meaning can be biased by the context in which they are encountered. For example, we might read polysemous words (e.g. 'palm') along with other words which bias one towards one of its meanings, for example, 'fingers', 'thumb', 'hand', 'knuckle'. Later we might read another list, such as 'fern', 'leaf', 'branch', 'coconut', 'palm', and have to determine whether any of the words appeared on the earlier list. A variety of studies show *context-dependent* effects in such situations (e.g. Light and Carter-Sobell, 1970; Hunt and Ellis, 1974); that is, where the semantic context is altered between encoding and retrieval, we are more likely not to recognise that 'palm' was repeated in both lists. Similar results can be obtained using changes to a sentential context (e.g. Encoding: 'They were stuck in a traffic jam'; Retrieval: 'They enjoyed eating the jam') or by altering the associates with which target words are paired (e.g. Encoding: 'jam-traffic' or 'palm-tree' ; Retrieval: 'jam-fruit' or 'palm-hand').

It seems clear that the context which is operative in such situations is not just that given by the materials surrounding the item to be remembered, but also the interpretation built on the basis of this information. Barclay, Bransford, Franks, McCarrell and Nitsch (1974) tested subjects' cued recall of target words originally presented in sentences (e.g. 'The man tuned the piano' or 'The man lifted the piano'). In the subsequent cued-recall procedure subjects were presented with phrases such as 'something melodious – ?' or 'something heavy – ?'. Barclay and colleagues showed that subjects recalled the target word where the retrieval cue related to the sentential context in which the word was originally encountered (i.e. lifted, heavy; tuned, melodious).

Location and environmental context

Context effects extend well beyond mere changes in the meaning of what is to be learned or remembered. Changes in the environment between learning and test can also have quite dramatic effects. Smith (1979) reports a study in which three groups of subjects originally learned 80 common words in a particular location (a basement). Each group later attempted to recall these words. Those who recalled the words back in the same basement recalled 23 per cent of the words from the original list, while those who carried out the recall test in a very differently furnished room, several floors away from the basement, remembered significantly fewer (15 per cent). Interestingly, the third group were tested in a similar room, but were instructed to recollect as much as possible of their surroundings when in the basement. This group recalled 22 per cent of the original list, significantly more than the other subjects who remembered in the changed context, but almost as many as those who actually returned to the basement for the recall task.

Fig 8.1 Correct and false person identification as a function of context reinstatement and retention interval (after Smith and Vela, 1992).

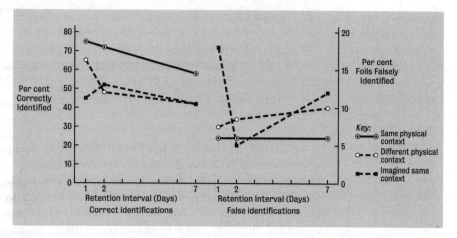

Smith and Vela (1992) report a more 'naturalistic' study, in which effortful *context reinstatement* was not successful. A psychology lecture was interrupted by someone who claimed to be looking for a female student whose birthday it was. Failing to find her in the class, he left. Later, students attending the lecture were asked to identify the individual who interrupted the lecture, either in the original setting, or in a different room. Some of the latter subjects were specifically asked to imagine the previous incident. Subjects who performed the identification task in the original environment were better able to identify the individual than subjects who were tested in a different room. Those who were asked to reinstate the context prior to making the identification did particularly badly. (The percentage of false identifications in Fig 8.1 refers to the percentage of positive identifications for any of the nine incorrect line-up faces.) At first sight, the results of these two studies by Smith appear to conflict. However, as we shall see below, there are many other parallels to these contrasting results.

Earlier, Godden and Baddeley (1975) investigated divers' ability to recall 40 common words which they had learned on land or under 15 feet of water. There was no difference in the overall level of recall on land and under water. Similarly, it mattered little in terms of overall performance whether the words had been learned on land or under water. The striking result that Godden and Baddeley report is that where the test and learning environment were the same, subjects performed about 40 per cent better on the recall task. A further study by Godden and Baddeley (1980) presents an equally striking result. Where divers were asked to recognise the words they had previously seen they performed equally well irrespective of whether or not the learning and test environments were equivalent (Fig 8.2).

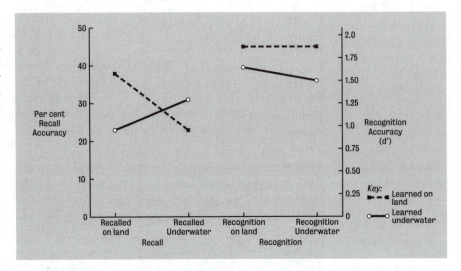

Fig 8.2 Recall and recognition of words learned on land and underwater (after Godden and Baddeley, 1975, 1980).

As we will see below, it has proved difficult to demonstrate context effects where retrieval is assessed using recognition paradigms. Nevertheless, the key message from the above studies is that at least with regard to recall, the greater the differences between the learning and test environment, the less successful recall is likely to be. This would obviously prove extremely limiting were contextual similarity alone to determine retrieval success. As we will also see below, this is far from being the case.

State dependence

One way of holding constant both the external learning and testing context, and the materials studied and retrieved, is to manipulate the state of the individual taking part in the task. There is much evidence that purports to show that subjects do better in retrieval tasks if they study and are tested when sober, or study and are tested when in some drug-induced state, than where the learning and retrieval states are different (e.g. Eich, Weringartner, Stillman and Gillin, 1975; Goodwin, Powell, Bremer, Hoine and Sterne, 1969).

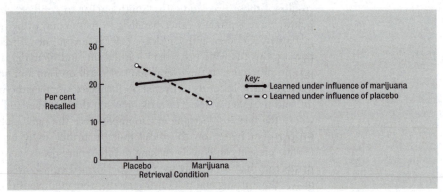

Fig 8.3 Word recall as a function of marijuana smoking at encoding and/ or retrieval (after Eich, Weingartner, Stillman and Gillin, 1975).

Eich and colleagues had subjects learn a list of words after smoking an untreated cigarette or smoking a cigarette containing marijuana. They attempted to recall these words four hours later, after smoking tobacco only or tobacco plus marijuana (Fig 8.3). Two important findings emerged from this study. First, as we might expect on the basis of the studies reviewed earlier, subjects were able to recall more when their state at recall matched their state during study. Secondly, subjects performed worse when study was undertaken while under the influence of marijuana. Goodwin and colleagues report very similar effects with sober and 'drunk' subjects. On the first day of the experiment, subjects made up eight paired associates when intoxicated or sober. The day after they had to recall these word pairs. Once again, similarity between encoding and retrieval conditions promoted recall, but overall, performance was worse when subjects were drunk than when sober. Also, in results which parallel those reported above, these *state-dependent* effects were evident when recall was used as the retrieval task, but not when recognition was used (Fig 8.4).

Fig 8.4 Relearning words and recognising pictures when intoxicated and sober (after Goodwin, Powell, Bremer, Hoine and Stern, 1969).

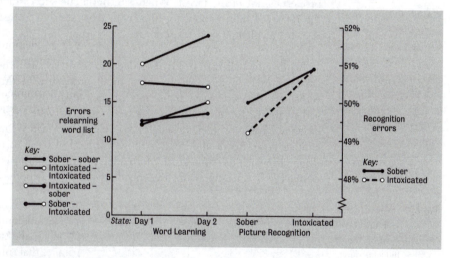

The findings reported in the studies above are at once both fascinating and frustrating. Taken together, these results raise a number of issues. What do we mean by context? Why does context influence recall, but not recognition? To what extent does context really influence remembering? After all, although I am sitting at my desk in Guildford, surrounded by the blue walls and pink carpet of my office, I can clearly recall foolishly stretching out on a Land Rover on a dusty dry veldt in Kenya to photograph lions which had just killed. As far as I can tell there is no contextual overlap, whether this be semantic, environmental or in terms of my internal state between now and that time almost 10 years ago. In the next section we examine the notion of context more closely.

■ Encoding context and retrieval

In the studies described above, what constituted context ranged from the other items encountered during learning and retrieval, to gross changes in the environment in which learning and retrieval took place, and differences in the internal state of the individual being tested. At least in recall studies, changes in context between test and retrieval reduce memory performance. This encourages the view that at least some of the circumstances in which encoding takes place form part of, or at least facilitate access to, the experience an individual stores.

Encoding specificity

Tulving (1975, 1983) presented a general principle which seeks to capture the relationship between encoding and retrieval. Tulving's *encoding-specificity principle* states that memory performance is best when the cues present at testing match those that were encoded at the study. The effectiveness with which any retrieval cue accesses a particular memory trace (what Tulving calls an *engram*) increases as it shares more properties with the item to be retrieved, and as it contains fewer properties not in the target. When a retrieval cue successfully accesses an engram, the retrieved information, together with that available from the retrieval cue, give rise to a phenomenal experience of 'certain aspects of the original event' (Tulving, 1976, p. 40) – what Tulving called *synergistic ecphory*.

Reddy and Bellezza (1983) recorded subjects' verbalisations while they studied a list of words. At test, which was a recall procedure in this case, subjects again verbalised, or were given transcripts of their own, or other subjects' study phase verbalisations. Recall condition was free, cued, or yoked (i.e. individual objects in different groups were matched for memory performance and then contrasted on another task). Reddy and Bellezza show that level of recall was directly related to the degree to which the contextual information produced during encoding was reinstated during recall, thus supporting the encoding-specificity hypothesis (Fig 8.5).

Fig 8.5 Word recall as a function of reinstatement of own or others' thoughts during learning (after Reddy and Belezza, 1983).

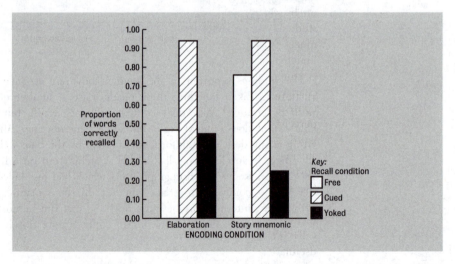

The Reddy and Bellezza study provides further evidence that increased overlap between encoding and retrieval facilitates remembering, but what is actually encoded? Although it is ultimately a circular and unfalsifiable answer to this question, Tulving (1983) proposes that if the stimulus leads to the retrieval of the target item, then elements of the retrieval cue are assumed to have been encoded. Where retrieval does not occur following the presentation of a certain cue, it is assumed not to have been encoded. Thus, what is encoded is that for which successful retrieval cues can be found. While the Tulving framework has many virtues, it does not help us to understand why context generally fails to influence remembering where recognition, rather than recall, is used as the memory index. We will return to this issue below, but first let us consider some alternative approaches to the problem of defining context.

Independent and interacting context

Hewitt (1973) distinguishes between *intrinsic context* and *extrinsic context*. The former refers to integral aspects of a target stimulus, while the latter refers to those aspects of the stimulus situation which are present when the target is encountered, but which are not themselves integral to the target. Thus, to choose examples from the studies discussed above, intrinsic context refers to the semantic, interpretative or sentential environment in which words to be learned are encountered. On land or under water, different rooms, sober and intoxicated are all examples of extrinsic contexts. Another way of thinking about this distinction is the extent to which a contextual change would alter the meaning or immediate characteristics of the target – being sober does not change the words I am hearing, but the words being spoken by someone I am with, rather than my simply hearing them coming from a radio speaker in a room in which I sit alone, would do so.

It seems clear that intrinsic and extrinsic contexts can interact. Eich (1985) had subjects learn words by forming an image for each of the nouns on a list, or by integrating each of the nouns into the context in which they were studied. Variations in context affected the performance of the latter group much more. Baddeley (1982, 1990) distinguishes between what he calls 'independent context' and 'interactive context'. In the former 'the information is stored together with the trace of the stimulus, but does not fundamentally change the trace' (Baddeley, 1990, p. 287). This is contrasted with interactive context in which 'context actually changes the way in which the stimulus is perceived' (p. 287). Thus, for example, biasing the way in which a polysemous word is interpreted (e.g. palm as hand, rather than palm as tree) involves the storing of a different memory trace, while learning the word in a wet or dry environment does not do so. Baddeley suggests that the effects which arise in the former case are due to encoding, whereas those that occur in the latter case are due to retrieval. As we shall see in later chapters, where exceptional memory and memory improvement techniques are considered, what Baddeley calls interactive context greatly facilitates remembering. The distinction is a useful one, because it makes the important point that in order to understand why context has effects in some circumstances, and not in others, we need to understand what is being encoded. Unfortunately, the Baddeley account is less helpful about how we can determine whether context will be independent or interactive.

Instances, headings and records

The Morton and Bekerian (1986) 'headed records' memory framework, and Logan's (1988) instance theory, help to identify the key elements of an 'instance' or episodic trace, and may help us to understand the effects of context a little more. According to Logan, instances include the goal the subject is trying to attain (e.g. learn this list of words), the stimuli encountered in pursuit of this goal (i.e. the words on the list, subjects' interpretation of instructions given together with any situational factors attended to), the interpretations made of the stimuli encountered in pursuit of that goal (e.g. 'these words seem related to each other', or 'why are we being tested in a basement?', or 'this isn't where we were before'), and any responses made. Thought about in this way, unless specific instructions are given by the experimenter, or unless the situation in which subjects learn is remarkable in some way, there is little reason to assume that context will be encoded, and thus no reason to believe that it will aid retrieval. To use the language of headed records, headings comprise literal representations of an event, including environmental features, and internal state registers automatically, together with some information about reflecting mood and physiological state, location (i.e. where we are, e.g. which country, city, general locale), temporal detail (e.g. what day it is, time of day, etc.), and source information (e.g. who one is talking to). Unless the retrieval description being used to guide the search for records specifies these contextual details, then facilitation or inhibition of retrieval will not be influenced by context. Even where the study environment is remarkable in some way, unless it is associated with the goals that the subject is trying to attain (either intentionally or incidentally), context should be encoded independently of the items to be remembered. That is, it may feature in the content of a record of a particular experience, but it is unlikely to be a useful way of later remembering something learned in those circumstances. As we shall see below, the notion that context is automatically registered has been severely challenged by recent empirical results.

■ Context effects in recall and recognition

Although there are exceptions, some of which will be considered below, contextual manipulations facilitate or inhibit recall but do not influence recognition. I have been arguing above that the reason context influences remembering is because it allows items to be encoded distinctively and aids retrieval. In order to understand why these two traditional measures of remembering show different effects of context, we need to know more about the differences between recall and recognition, particularly with respect to how we construe the retrieval process.

Generation–recognition models of retrieval

Watkins and Gardiner (1979) provide a detailed, if dated, overview of these *generation–recognition* models of retrieval. According to such models, the retrieval process begins by generating candidates for the target item being sought. Once generated, these items are then subjected to a recognition process, which, if successful, leads to one of the candidates being designated as the retrieved target item. Traditional accounts (e.g. Anderson and Bower, 1972; Kintsch, 1970) assume that when an item is studied, some representation of that item, based on previous exposures to it, is marked or 'tagged' as having been recently encountered. Under recall conditions, subjects generate a range of items which might have occurred during the study phase. The representations of these items are then searched for in order to determine whether they have been marked or tagged as having recently occurred. Under recognition conditions, target and distractor items are searched for, again with the purpose of determining whether they have recently occurred.

This explanation clearly accounts for the frequently observed superiority of recognition over recall performance, but largely, if not exclusively, because recall requires candidate items to be generated, with concomitant scope for error, while in recognition no generation is required. The account also serves to explain why the difficulty of recognition can be manipulated by increasing the similarity between target and distracter items. Bahrick (1970) sought to quantify the contributions of both processes. He first had a group of subjects generate words in relation to particular categories. This yielded a measure of generation likelihood for a particular item. A second group were required to learn a subset of these generated words and then identify which of them occurred again in a subsequent recognition list. This yielded a recognition likelihood for each item. A third group learned a list of these items, and subsequently attempted to recall them. The likelihood of an item being retrieved was well predicted by a joint function of its generation and recognition likelihood.

The generate–recognise account also explains other standard findings. The so-called frequency paradox involves differential effects of word frequency on recall and recognition performance. Words we often come across are better retrieved under recall than under recognition conditions, while rare words are better recognised than recalled. The generate–recognise account explains this finding by suggesting that high-frequency events are more likely to be generated effectively but, assuming distractor items have been carefully selected, high-frequency events are also more likely to have been (spuriously or irrelevantly) marked as recently encountered. Thus recognition suffers relative to recall. With low-frequency events, the generation process struggles to find appropriate candidates.

Just as high-frequency items are more likely to be generated, thus leading to an advantage for recall of high- rather than low-frequency items, events which are associated with those previously generated are more likely to be generated during retrieval. Thus, as Kintsch (1968) shows, organisation of stimulus material generally enhances recall performance more than it does recognition. Similarly, it is obvious why the generate–recognise account would lead to schema-consistent recall, and why, in recognition studies, schema-consistent information is no more accurately recognised than schema-inconsistent information, but schema-consistent information is generally more likely to be judged as 'old', even where it was not encountered during the study phase (see Locksley, Stangor, Hepburn, Grosovsky and Hochstrasser, 1984).

Recognition failure

BOX 8.1: Recognition failure

The clear implication of generate–recognise models of retrieval is, however, as Tulving and colleagues (Tulving and Osler, 1968; Tulving and Thomson, 1973) pointed out, that items which can be recalled should also be recognised. In demonstrating a phenomenon which has become known as *recognition failure*, they showed that the traditional generate and recognise framework could not be the whole story. Prior to the experiment proper, pairs of items which are strongly associated are selected (e.g. rain–umbrella; Santa–sleigh), and one element of each pair is used to produce another set of pairs. This time, however, the pairs are only weakly associated (e.g. rain–cow; Santa–fox), if at all. The experiment proper has four phases. First, subjects study the low-association pairs. Next, subjects are presented with a list of items which were the high-association items not included in the weak association pairs (i.e. umbrella, sleigh), and asked to produce four words which are associated with each. The original, highly associated items are often spontaneously produced (e.g. rain, Santa). The third phase requires subjects to identify those items which they produced as associates, which were actually included on the list originally studied (i.e. rain, Santa). As Tulving and colleagues showed, subjects often fail to recognise these 'old' items. The fourth, and final, stage of the study involves the presentation of the original low-association paired items (i.e. those underlined above), with subjects having to recall the item they had earlier associated with it (i.e. rain; Santa). This they do rather well, demonstrating that items which cannot apparently be recognised can be recalled, which is clearly counter to the generate–recognise model.

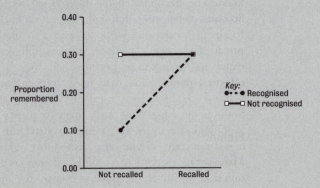

Dissociation between recallable and recognisible words (after Tulving and Wiseman, 1975).

Flexser and Tulving (1978) carried out a meta-analysis of some 89 studies that demonstrated the recognition-failure finding described in Box 8.1, showing a positive, but not substantial, relationship between recall probability and recognition probability. This Tulving–Wiseman law (Wiseman and Tulving, 1975), that is, the existence of an invariant relationship between cued recall and recognition and, thus, just one process involved in retrieval, has been challenged by a number of researchers. Santa and Lamwers (1974), for instance, have shown that if instructions are altered, making it clearer for subjects to know what is required of them, the effect reported by Tulving and colleagues is much reduced. Rabinowitz, Mandler and Barsalou (1977) addressed another aspect of the procedure, showing that the target (e.g. umbrella) learned in association with a particular cue (e.g. rain), was less effective at promoting retrieval of the cue, than was the cue at promoting retrieval of the target. When this asymmetry was explored further it became clear that the Tulving findings rely on circumstances in which recall tests produce better memory performance than recognition tests. Hintzman (1992) has suggested that the Tulving–Wiseman law is largely artifactual, although more recent analyses by Tulving and Flexser (1992) have attempted to rebut Hintzman's objections.

It should be noted that although the generate–recognise model purports to account for free recall, many of the demonstrations which show that a single process governs retrieval actually relate to cued recall, rather than free recall. Another set of findings that strengthen the view that recall and recognition rely on different processes are, of course, those that show that studies involving recall show effects of context manipulations, while those involving recognition do not. The encoding specificity principle accounts for the difference between recall and recognition findings largely in terms of the extent of overlap between the memory trace (which may or may not include encoding context information) and the retrieval context (which may or may not share encoding context information). The generate–recognise framework, on the other hand, allows for this direct relationship between the memory trace and the retrieval context, but also, through the generation process, allows information about the encoding context, as well as that available in the retrieval context, to be accessed. Within this account, recognition that only has the retrieval context to rely upon, is less likely to show effects of changes in encoding and retrieval contexts. Neither account precludes the possibility of contextual effects being observed within recognition experiments. Indeed, explorations of the recognition process suggest that such effects should indeed be observed, under certain circumstances.

Elements of recognition

Mandler (1980, 1981) suggests that there are two stages involved in recognition: one that involves *familiarity*, a sense of having encountered something in the past; and another that requires *source memory*, or a sense of where this feeling of familiarity comes from, that is, the context in which it was originally encountered. Earlier, Mandler and Boeck (1974) conducted a study in which words were spontaneously grouped into categories by subjects. Those who categorised words into relatively more categories performed better on recall and recognition tests of their recollection of these words, reflecting their differential ability to make distinctions and organise during the learning phase. A week later, subjects carried out a timed recognition task, with each subject's responses being separated into those which were relatively fast and those which were relatively slow. For slow responses, the effect of organisation during encoding was demonstrated once again, whereas faster recognition decisions showed no effect of initial organisation. They concluded, on the basis of this separation, that faster responses reflected familiarity, while slower responses came about because of a more effortful, context-dependent process operating within recognition.

Atkinson and Juola (1974) examined the time taken by subjects to decide whether words they were presented with had occurred in a study list they had encountered earlier (i.e. targets), or whether they were distractors. On the first presentation of these words, it took about 100 ms longer to determine that a word was a target than it took to determine that it was a distractor. This pattern altered radically as the test was repeated. The time taken for subjects to decide that words were targets decreased, whereas the time taken to determine that a word was a distractor increased (Fig 8.6). Atkinson and Juola argue that distractor decisions could be made more rapidly initially simply because they were less familiar. With repeated testing, however, familiarity alone is insufficient for reliable performance, and an alternative strategy must be adopted. This leads to a speeding of target decisions (targets having been studied previously), but the familiarity build-up serves to slow distractor-decisions, because it is no longer a cue which reliably discriminates between targets and distractors.

Fig 8.6 Remembering words seen before: effects of repeating targets and distractors at test (after Atkinson and Juola, 1974).

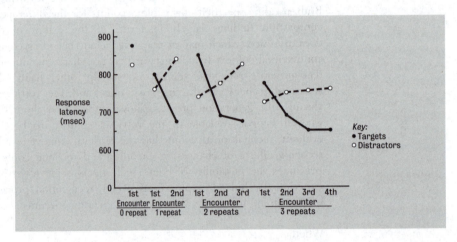

Studies by Johnston, Dark and Jacoby (1985) go some way towards clarifying how these two recognition processes operate. Source memory, or context retrieval as it is sometimes referred to, is seen as a search process, and as such is sensitive to stimulus organisation and divided attention (see below). Familiarity, on the other hand, is based upon *perceptual fluency* (i.e. the rapidity with which a previously encountered event can be identified on a subsequent presentation). Their studies required subjects to identify a word and to say whether they had encountered it in degraded presentations made prior to the test phase. They argued that identification times, which are indicative of perceptual fluency, should be shorter for items that subjects say they had encountered previously, whether or not this decision was correct. This is exactly the pattern of results they report (Fig 8.7) (Johnston, Dark and Jacoby, 1985) and that were later replicated, under more controlled circumstances, by Johnson and colleagues. This combination of a rapid, data-driven, perceptual-fluency process, together with a slower, search-based, source-memory process within recognition, has gained widespread acceptance.

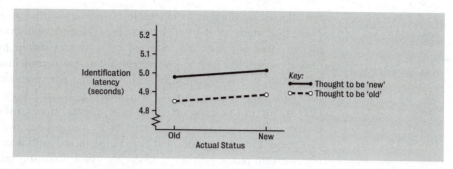

Fig 8.7 Identification latencies for degraded words thought to be old or new as a function of their actual old–new status (after Johnston, Dark and Jacoby, 1985).

Should there be context effects with recognition?

It is as if our description of recall, which relies on an effortful context-dependent generation process, followed by a less effortful decision process as to whether a particular item has occurred, is the reverse of our conception of recognition. Both recall and recognition include processes which should be influenced by context. However, because the generation phase plays a greater role in recall than does the source memory process in recognition, it is hardly surprising that context effects are more widely demonstrated in recall studies. However, recognition studies should also show effects of context, but only where the recognition decision to be made is sufficiently demanding so as to preclude the use of context-free perceptually based strategies for making the decision (or where the subject is motivated to use the more effortful process). There is some evidence that this is the case, as we shall see in the next section, when recognition accuracy is at a premium.

■ Context and face recognition

Whether or not faces can be reliably recognised in different contexts is obviously of profound importance, especially where, for example, the witness to a crime may be required to identify the perpetrators from a line-up or large number of mug-shots. The absence of widespread context effects on recognition might encourage us to think that our ability to recognise people in these circumstances might be quite reliable. Extensive studies of context effects on face recognition challenge this view.

Recognising faces in the context of other faces and descriptions

Bower and Karlin (1974), in some of the earliest studies in this area, suggested that differences between encoding and retrieval contexts have relatively little effect. Subjects made judgements about the likeableness or about the gender of a series of faces. Performance on a subsequent recognition memory test was substantially better for photographs judged for likeableness or honesty than for photographs about which gender judgements had been made. These findings were not affected by whether or not subjects were attempting to learn about the faces. Their final study is of more interest here, since it showed that face recognition memory was not materially affected by a context manipulation, which involved testing recognition for the photograph when it was presented alone, alongside an old picture it had been studied with, or with a new picture. More recent studies have obtained what appear to be conflicting results. Watkins, Ho and Tulving (1976), for instance, report three experiments which show that a face studied beside another face was more likely to be recognised when the other face was also present at recognition, and that faces studied with accompanying descriptive phrases were recognised better where the study context was again re-presented.

Kerr and Winograd (1982) report four experiments, which assess the effects of alterations in verbal encoding context on face recognition. The verbal context, which consisted of short descriptive phrases about the person shown, was manipulated by varying the number of these phrases across faces. Subjects initially studied faces either alone or accompanied by one or more descriptive phrases. Their results show that people were more likely to recognise a face when they had received information about the person than when they had not, and also that where the verbal encoding context was particularly elaborate (i.e. several descriptive statements), recognition was improved dramatically where all of this context was reinstated. Baddeley and Woodhead (1982) report similar findings, in respect of the effects of elaboration on face recognition. However, in another study reported in the same paper, they show that presentation of a previously encountered (verbal) context did not so much serve to enhance recognition accuracy for faces, but instead biased subjects towards believing that the faces had been encountered before. One can see how these results can be incorporated within a schema-like explanation. Where new faces are consistent with the schematic verbal description, it is to be expected, as we have already seen, that false positives will increase. Nevertheless, even though recognition accuracy is not being improved in this case, it is still clear that contextual information is influencing recognition.

Orientation at encoding and retrieval

While the manipulations used in these studies were largely motivated by a desire to vary the complexity of processing during encoding, with the anticipated effect of deeper processing leading to improved retrieval, they also raise other theoretical and practical issues. Given the distinctions made above between the stronger effects of contexts which interact with, or alter the encoding of, the material to be learned, it seems clear why some orienting tasks (e.g. those that require personal judgements about the photographs) lead to greater reductions in recognition performance than others. From a practical point of view, it shows that one may be more likely to recognise an individual if some interpretation or impression is formed about the person, at the time of encoding (e.g. he is acting suspiciously), than if one merely tries to encode details about that individual's appearance (e.g. the person is wearing an anorak). Where one is later encouraged to make similar evaluations (e.g. can you identify the burglar from these mug-shots?), recognition should be enhanced. If, however, you later have to make discriminations between many similar individuals on the basis of physical attributes, having formed some personal judgements at encoding may make recognition suffer. Finally, with respect to orientation at encoding, it is also worth bearing in mind the findings of Woodhead, Baddeley and Simmonds (1979), who showed that extensive training on isolated facial features did not lead to improvements in overall face recognition. Nevertheless, physical appearance is obviously important. For example, Patterson and Baddeley (1977) showed that simple changes in appearance (e.g. false beard, wig, etc.) produce profound decrements in recognition performance, as do changes in pose and expression (see below, Davies and Milne, 1982).

Familiarity, source and location

A study by Brown, Deffenbacher and Sturgill (1977) took a rather different tack, by investigating whether people were able reliably to determine where they had seen an individual. In their first study, subjects participating in an unexpected memory test reliably identified people they had previously seen, but failed reliably to determine in which of two rooms they had seen them. In two subsequent studies, where subjects were or were not expecting to have to remember the photographs they saw, both experiments provided evidence of considerable confusion in mug-shot and line-up identifications, as well as a lack of correlation between eyewitness accuracy and confidence. These results parallel the distinction made above between recognition judgements based on familiarity and source information.

A number of studies have sought to investigate the effects on recognition performance of changing the location in which an individual is seen. Beales and Parkin (1984) showed that people were better able to recognise that an individual had been seen in a previous study phase where the photograph portrayed the individual in the original, rather than in a different, context. This difference between same- and changed-context performance was greater when, during the learning phase, subjects performed a trait-processing task (i.e. subjects judged the likeability of the individual) than when subjects made facial appearance judgements during encoding (i.e. determining the most distinctive physical feature of each face).

Memon and Bruce (1983) also showed effects of encoding strategy and context change on recognition memory for faces. Their first study contrasted recognition for faces following different orientation tasks, that is, encoding faces in terms of traits or physical features. Faces were portrayed in distinctive background contexts that, at test, were either the same (e.g. the same bank), changed (e.g. church and park), or changed but of the same type (e.g. two restaurants). Recognition accuracy and latency were significantly impaired following changes in context: false alarms increased significantly following the presentation of new faces in old contexts. A subsequent study showed that trait encoding was more susceptible to manipulations of context than feature encoding. Thomson, Robertson and Vogt (1982) also report strong context effects on person recognition in a study in which the locations in which individuals were photographed, the actions they appeared to be taking, and the clothes worn, were varied systematically.

Beales and Parkin (1984) suggest, with respect to their own study, that the contextual influences they observed demonstrate that strong context effects occur even when context is irrelevant to the central task. While the location in which an individual is seen may be irrelevant, as subjects choose to construe the task they are required to perform, it seems to me that it is at least possible that the locations in which an individual is seen provide support for subjects in making some implicit personal judgements about the individual photographed. An earlier paper by Davies and Milne (1982) bears upon this issue. They report two experiments which examined the influence of context on face recognition accuracy for novel and familiar faces. Context was manipulated by varying the physical background against which the faces appeared, and also through alterations in the pose and expression of the individual's photographed. Changes in pose plus expression and context significantly reduced recognition accuracy for the target faces. In the second study reported by Davies and Milne, the faces of celebrities replaced the unknown faces used in the first study. For well-known faces, the influence of context was eliminated but the effects of pose and expression were maintained. However, when only faces that were actually identified by subjects were considered, Davies and Milne report that the effects of pose and expression, too, were eliminated.

With regard to the practical aspects of eye-witness identification, even though recognition judgements can be unreliable when the individual is portrayed in a different location, or where their physical appearance is different, these difficulties probably only apply to people who are not known to the witness. From a theoretical point of view, the findings considered in this section reinforce the argument made above with regard to when we might expect to find context effects in recognition tasks. Where the recognition judgement can be made simply on the basis of perceptual information, context effects are likely to be very limited. Where the task used requires more complex processing, especially if the source of one's sense of familiarity with a stimulus must be interrogated, then context effects are likely to be observed.

■ Attention and the encoding and retrieval of context

From the studies discussed above it would appear as if whether or not context interacts with, or is relevant to, the object of study, both recall and recognition performance can be influenced by changes in the study environment between encoding and retrieval. Certainly, where the context is relevant to the object of study, and especially where it alters the interpretation we might make about the object, the effects of context are more powerful and more widely observed. For the reasons considered above, such effects are most likely to be observed in recall than in recognition tasks. Unfortunately, studies have not yet been carried out that would allow us to assess the extent to which attention is directed to what the experimenter may consider irrelevant contextual details. This makes it very difficult to decide whether the context in which something is encountered, or the interpretation we may make of it, must be attended to in order for effects of context change or reinstatement to be subsequently observed. There are, however, a number of studies which have been carried out in relation to implicit memory which offer some useful insights (See Box 8.2).

BOX 8.2: Context and divided attention

Jacoby, Woloshyn and Kelley (1989) explored the effect on context of having subjects attend to two tasks simultaneously (i.e. *divided attention*). Subjects read lists of names under conditions of full attention or divided attention (i.e. monitored strings of random digits for runs of three odd numbers with one digit being spoken every two seconds), and were then presented with a second list, composed of names they had already read and the names of well-known people. The subject's task was to identify the famous names in the second list, and they were explicitly told that any names they remembered from the previously read list should be rejected as non-famous. The results showed that subjects who read the list of non-famous names under divided-attention conditions were less able to reject the old, non-famous items. Obviously, encountering names before the test phase is likely to add to their familiarity, while famous names will themselves be familiar for other reasons. The task for the subject is therefore to discriminate between those names which are familiar simply because they occurred in the earlier test, and those which are familiar but were not read as part of the earlier list. There are two ways in which this decision might be made. One basis for the discrimination might be the differential strength of the familiarity of the items. However, this makes unwarranted assumptions about the relative strengths of recently, and repeatedly but not recently, encountered events. An alternative basis would simply be to access the source of this familiarity. Interpreted in this way, Jacoby's results would suggest that context-based source information is less reliably encoded when learning occurs under divided attention conditions.

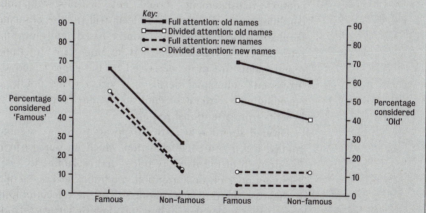

False fame and divided attention (after Jacoby, Woloshyn and Kelley, 1989).

Jacoby has also investigated the effects of divided attention on retrieval. Jacoby (1991) reports a study in which subjects engaged in a secondary task (monitoring strings of auditorially presented digits for particular sequences), while attempting to determine whether words they saw were words they had heard earlier, or had seen earlier. Prior to the learning phase subjects read a list of 15 words. They then heard another list of 15 words. During the recognition test, subjects saw all 30 words, together with 15 words not previously presented. Their task was to identify only those words they had heard earlier. Subjects made source errors (i.e. identified 'seen' words as 'heard' words) in about 40 per cent of cases, with the tendency to make source judgement errors increasing where the test was carried out with a simultaneous secondary task. These results suggest that access to what Mandler would term source memory is disrupted by dividing subjects' attention between two tasks. Since source memory, rather than familiarity, is thought to be the basis of context effects, where attentional demand is high, context will exercise less influence, and responding will instead rely on what may be misattributed familiarity. Where attention can be devoted to the recognition task itself, one would expect fewer unwanted false positives (i.e. false identification of a witness because the surrounding location is similar to one earlier encountered), and subjects may be more able to benefit from contextual similarities between learning and retrieval. Jacoby and colleagues capture part of these sentiments in the following remark: 'Rather than being a prerequisite for producing effects of the past, conscious recollection can be a means of escaping misleading effects of the past' (Jacoby, Woloshyn and Kelley, 1989, p. 115).

■ Summary: Context and familiarity, source and resource

The foregoing sections illustrate reliable, albeit relatively weak, effects of changes between the context in which information is learned, and that in which we later seek to retrieve that information. It matters considerably whether we are seeking to recall that information, or merely detect whether a particular stimulus has already been encountered. This does not mean that effects of context change and context reinstatement should not be observed under recognition-retrieval conditions, merely that such effects will not be observed where a less effortful, familiarity-based, rather than source-based, judgement is sufficient to meet the retrieval task's requirements. It is important to stress here that these task requirements are those perceived by the subject, and that sometimes effects of 'irrelevant' contextual details may occur. This points to the need to see the encoding and retrieval of context as something that is goal-directed, and which benefits from attentional resource.

Divided attention at retrieval appears to reduce a subject's ability to access the context-based source information which encourages reliance on some sense of the strength of the memory trace, that is, familiarity or perceptual fluency, while learning under divided attention conditions makes encoding of context less likely. If these results can be extrapolated to the effects of context per se, they would suggest that under demanding encoding or retrieval conditions, changes in study-test context will lead to poorer recall and recognition, and the facilitative effects of context reinstatement should not be observed. These effects of divided attention on encoding and retrieval of contextual information, once again, point to the unreliable nature of 'automatic' encoding of fundamental information, in this case of location and other source-related information.

There is a parallel here also with the account given in the previous chapter about how time estimation is affected by increased task demands. If less contextual information is indeed encoded in such circumstances, and contextual change is the basis of time estimation (e.g. as suggested by Block, 1990), then our assessment of how quickly time is passing should become unreliable. It also follows that context reinstatement should actually be less effective in circumstances where subjects were distracted or otherwise subject to increased attentional demands during encoding, or retrieval. This may be particularly important when emotional arousal is increased when people are witnessing an event, or indeed when acting as witnesses. We will return particularly to the effects of context reinstatement in a later chapter when we consider ways of enhancing retrieval.

■ Further reading

Anderson, J. R. (1995). *Learning and memory: An integrated approach*. New York: Wiley.

Jacoby, L. L. (1991). A process dissociation framework: Separating automatic from intentional uses of memory. *Journal of Memory and Language, 30,* 513–41.

Searleman, A. and Herrmann, D. (1994). *Memory from a broader perspective*. New York: McGraw-Hill.

Smith, S. M. (1994). Theoretical principles of context-dependent memory. In P. E. Morris and M. Gruneberg (eds) *Theoretical aspects of memory*. London: Routledge.

Tulving, E. (1983) *Elements of episodic memory*. Oxford: Oxford University Press.

Tulving, E. and Thomson, D. M. (1973) Encoding specificity and retrieval processes in episodic memory. *Psychological Review, 80,* 352–73.

Discussion points

- Compare and contrast state-dependent and context-dependent learning.
- Describe the relationship between context, source, familiarity and attention.
- Describe the similarities and differences between Tulving's notion of encoding specificity and episodic (i.e. instance-based) accounts of encoding and retrieval.
- How important are context effects for understanding memory and remembering?

Chapter 9

Emotional arousal

Chapter outline: This chapter describes and discusses the role that emotional states and arousal play in memory and remembering. After an initial overview of the concept of emotion, the chapter describes the key findings with respect to mood dependence and congruence; the impact that being in a heightened emotional state through fear, anxiety or depression might have on attention, encoding and retrieval; and the consequences these effects of emotional arousal might be expected to have in everyday circumstances.

Key topics
- Emotions and arousal
- Arousal, encoding and retrieval
- Spontaneous emotional reactions
- Induced and natural mood states
- Anxiety and depression
- Summary: Arousal, emotion and remembering
- Further reading

■ Emotions and arousal

There is widespread acceptance of the view that there are a relatively small number of what are referred to as *basic emotions*, which combine in various ways to yield the panoply of emotional expression with which we may be more familiar. These are: 'anger', 'disgust', 'fear', 'happiness' and 'sadness', although some would make a case for 'surprise' also being regarded in this basic universal set of emotions (see Ekman, 1973; Oatley and Johnson-Laird, 1987). Emotions have also been seen as an abstract, high-level description of the relationship between people and their environment (e.g. Lazarus and Smith, 1988); as providing a basis for determining action, in that emotions are seen as having an adaptive or functional purpose (e.g. Thayer, 1989); and as a means of facilitating social cohesion, through the coordination of mutual action in groups of individuals, by means of, for example, facial expressions and other emotional signals (e.g. Thayer, 1989).

The concept of arousal has also been subject to a range of definitions, both semantic and operational. Physiologically speaking, there is abundant evidence that a range of indices, not all of them interrelated, underlie what we would ordinarily refer to as arousal (see Venables, 1984; Hockey, 1984). Following authors like Thayer (1989), what we refer to as arousal here is perhaps best understood as the individual's phenomenological experience of feeling more or less energetic and more or less calm or tense. These sensations are underpinned by physiological changes. Thus, what we mean by arousal is primarily psychological, rather than physiological. What concerns us in this chapter is how the experience of arousal, especially where it is interpreted emotionally, influences information processing, most especially the encoding and retrieval of information. Before turning directly to the relationship between these basic emotions and memory, it is worth sketching briefly the main ways in which emotional processing has been depicted.

Theories of emotional processing

Schacter (1964) suggested that the experience of emotion requires both a subjective feeling, which reflects some level of physiological arousal, and the availability of a label for that arousal, derived from a cognitive appraisal of the source of that arousal. Within this account physiological arousal was considered to be non-specific, while cognitive appraisal was said to be determined by interpretations of proximal stimuli on the basis of the memories we have relating to those stimuli. Although there have been many attempts to test this theory, it has proved particularly difficult to do so satisfactorily, since both the level of arousal and the scope for attribution and appraisal must be independently manipulated. The fact that it has proved difficult to do so satisfactorily is itself rather damaging to the theory.

Lazarus (Lazarus, Kanner and Folkman, 1980; Lazarus and Folkman, 1984) in his *transactional account of emotional processing* suggests that 'emotion arises from how a person construes the outcome, actual or anticipated, of a transaction or bit of commerce with the environment' (Lazarus, Kanner and Folkman, 1980, p. 192). This construal depends on the appraisal of any environmental event, which continues as the event unfolds, in terms of (1) whether it is irrelevant to an individual's sense of well-being, benign or stressful, and (2) the likely success of the personal or environmental resources which might be deployed to deal with the event. Lazarus distinguishes three ways in which stressful events are evaluated: in terms of (a) their past history of harm or loss, (b) the threat of future injury or loss and (c) something which Lazarus calls 'challenge', which is related to a potential for gain given successful coping or mastery. Within this framework, emotions are regarded as a complex of cognitive appraisals, action impulses and patterned somatic reactions. There are a number of points of contrast with the Schacter view, most notably Lazarus' assumption that emotions are associated with specific physiological response profiles, and also the sense of continual appraisal, action, reaction and reappraisal which dominates the transactionalist view. While there has been a considerable amount of empirical support for the Lazarus view, it has been criticised by many for being too general, for its lack of a formal description of the appraisal processes, and for its lack of concern with the antecedents of specific emotional states (e.g. Brewin, 1988).

Weiner (1986) gives an account of the interdependence of cognition and emotion in which positive and negative affects occur because of recent positive and negative results, with the colour or differentiation of a particular emotion depending on the attributions the individual makes about the causes of these positive and negative outcomes. Thus, for example, the tendency to attribute successes or failures to one's own activities can lead to a sense of pride, shame, guilt, and so on, while the perceived controllability of outcomes is said to underlie feelings of anger (where another, in control, acts negatively) or pity (where others suffer from something outside their control). Brewin (1988) provides a thoughtful overview of this sort of attribution-based account of emotional processing.

While the next sections will not directly address the attribution issue, it is clear that attribution, interpretation, and past history of success or failure, are not only core aspects of theories of emotional processing, but all depend crucially on memorial processes.

■ Arousal, encoding and retrieval

Each of the accounts briefly considered above sees emotion as some label or explanatory construct for a perceived change in arousal. Arousal has a well-documented, but somewhat paradoxical effect on encoding and retention.

Emotionally laden materials and arousal

The standard demonstrations of this come from studies by Kleinsmith and Kaplan (1963, 1964). Kleinsmith and Kaplan (1963) selected eight words for subjects to learn. These words were made up of four which would be likely to evoke a strong reaction (e.g. vomit, rape), and four others which were thought to be emotionally neutral (e.g. dance, swim). Kleinsmith and Kaplan confirmed this by recording *galvanic skin responses* to the pairing between each number and word. Galvanic skin response, or skin conductance level as it is now more widely known, provides an electrical measure of the skin's conductance, which, because of increases in perspiration, reflects increases in level of arousal. Kleinsmith and Kaplan went on to show that fewer arousal-inducing words were retrieved than neutral words when retention was tested two minutes after learning; that is, people learned or remembered less emotional information than emotionally neutral information (Fig 9.1). When retention was tested 20 minutes after learning, retention was more or less equivalent for emotional and neutral material. Emotional material was better retained than when tested immediately after learning; neutral information was less well retained than it had been in the immediate retrieval condition. By one week later this trend was still clearer, retention of emotional material was now better than neutral material (although still not quite as retrievable as neutral material was in the immediate test) (Fig 9.1). This indicates that the emotionally charged material was indeed learned, and was retrievable, but that retrieval increased with the interval between learning and test.

Fig 9.1 Differential recall of nonsense syllable paired associates as a function of arousal level (after Kleinsmith and Kaplan, 1964).

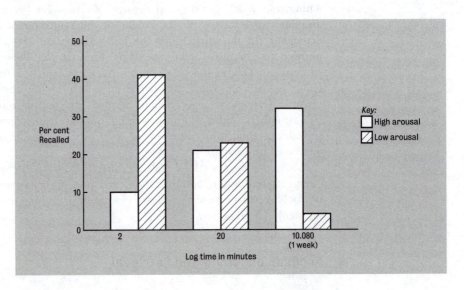

Parkin, Lewinsohn and Folkard (1982), report analogous findings from a study which contrasted retention of associates to negatively toned words (e.g. anger, fear) with retention of associations to neutral words (e.g. window, cow). More associates of neutral words were remembered when retention was tested immediately (92.0 per cent), than were associations to negative words (80.3 per cent). However, while retention tests one week later revealed that performance overall was worse, retrieval of associations to negatively toned items (70.3 per cent) was actually better than for neutral items (61.0 per cent).

One possibility with both studies is that emotionally neutral words were actually higher frequency items than those which substantially increased emotion. This would account for the initial decrement in the retention of emotionally laden terms. However, this would not explain the apparent reversal in fortunes of the two types of stimuli. For this, one might appeal to a different explanation, such as that as time proceeds higher frequency items will occur more often without the digit or other associate with which it was originally paired, while less frequent words are obviously less likely to do so. As such the retrieval cue is more likely to lead to successful retrieval as the delay between learning and retrieval increases. This explanation runs into difficulty, however, with the retention test in Kleinsmith and Kaplan's study, which occurred some 20 minutes after learning. As Kleinsmith and Kaplan (1964) demonstrated empirically differential frequency does not offer a satisfactory explanation of these results, since the effects also emerged when nonsense syllables rather than actual words were used as stimuli.

Time of day and arousal

Other, more mundane, influences of arousal are also apparent. Folkard, Monk, Bradbury and Rosenthal (1977) had subjects in their early teens learn a prose passage at 09.00 or at 15.00. Those who learned the story in the morning showed better immediate recall than those who learned the passage in the

Fig 9.2 Effects of delay and time of day on recall (after Folkhard, Monk, Bradbury and Rosenthal, 1977).

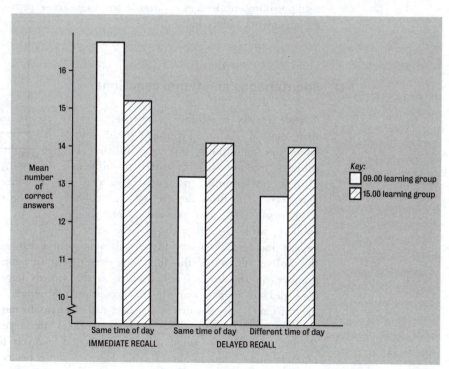

afternoon (Fig 9.2). At first sight this is puzzling, since a wide range of literature would suggest that for the average young person highest levels of arousal are reached in the afternoon. Furthermore, Eysenck (1992) suggests that learning tends to be best at times of the day associated with higher levels of arousal. This apparent paradox can be resolved by closely examining the effects reported. Those subjects tested in the morning, and thus presumably experiencing lower levels of arousal, indeed learned and retrieved the prose passage better than those who were presumably experiencing higher levels of arousal at study and test (i.e. the afternoon group). When tested a week later, however, the retention of students in the morning-learning group was worse than that of students who learned the story one week earlier in the afternoon group (Fig 9.2). Thus, learning, as indexed by an individual's ability to retain information over longer periods of time, seems be enhanced by higher levels of arousal, although it is worth repeating that, once again, immediate retrieval of information was worse for the high-arousal than for the low-arousal group.

While there are other explanations of these findings, it is tempting to see them as parallel to those of Kleinsmith and Kaplan. If learning is assessed immediately, high-arousal information, and neutral information learned when arousal is relatively high, is less well retained than low-arousal information, or neutral information learned in low-arousal circumstances. However, when tested after a substantial delay, this pattern is reversed. This encouraged the view that increased arousal somehow masks the actual level to which emotional material is learned, where retention is assessed a short time after learning, but serves to reduce the rate at which forgetting occurs over time. Revelle and Loftus (1990) provide a detailed review of a wide range of studies in which different manipulations and indices of arousal are used. These provide general support for the arguments adduced above.

■ Spontaneous emotional reactions

A wide variety of studies show that negative events are less well encoded than neutral events. Typically, these studies have been conducted under laboratory conditions, but rely on the affective qualities of the materials subjects interact with in order to influence processing. Loftus and Burns (1982), for example, presented two very similar films to groups of bank employees. The films depicted a bank robbery and the subsequent escape of a gunman. One film showed a boy being shot in the face during the robbery, while the other showed the same events other than this particularly violent incident. Memory for details was poorer for subjects who watched the violent version of the film (e.g. 4 per cent of subjects remembered the number on the boy's baseball shirt in the violent condition, while 28 per cent did so in the non-violent condition). Similarly, patients were more likely to recognise a nurse's assistant rather than the nurse who had actually injected them, when these hospital workers took part in later line-ups (Peters, 1988). A range of work carried out under more controlled circumstances helps to shed further light on these issues.

Central and peripheral information in traumatic settings

Box 9.1: The fate of details in traumatic experience

Subjects watched one of two sets of 15 slides (neutral and traumatic). In fact, the two sets of slides differed only in respect of the middle five slides. The first five slides (Phase 1) in both sets showed identical slides of 'a mother and her 7-year-old son leaving a house. They walked through a park, across a bridge, and then through a downtown area' (Christianson and Loftus, 1987, p. 228). The last five slides (Phase 3) in each case showed 'the mother making a phone call and eventually returning to her neighbourhood and her house'. The crucial difference between the two sets was that while in the neutral set the middle five slides (Phase 2) showed 'the mother and son looking for a taxi, going to school in the taxi and finally ... leaving her son at school', the traumatic version showed 'the boy being hit by a car, lying on the bonnet bleeding heavily from an eye injury. Next the boy is transported by an ambulance to a hospital, and in the last slide the mother leaves her son at the hospital' (Christianson and Loftus, 1987, p. 228). All slides in the middle phases, across both neutral and traumatic conditions, had earlier been rated as equally complex and distinctive. Each slide was seen for three seconds, and followed by the next slide seven seconds later. While watching the slides all subjects were encouraged to write down the most distinguishing feature of each slide. Subjects were tested either 20 minutes or two weeks after the slides had been watched. Subjects were first required to write down all of the distinguishing features of the slides they had earlier noted (recall). After this they were presented with four versions of each of the original slides, and had to indicate which they had seen earlier. The findings appeared quite clear-cut. Recall of distinctive details was better for those taken from traumatic slides than from neutral slides, and this effect became more noticeable as the interval between watching the slides and being tested increased. Recognition of which slides had earlier been presented, on the other hand, appeared to have been impaired by the presence of traumatic material.

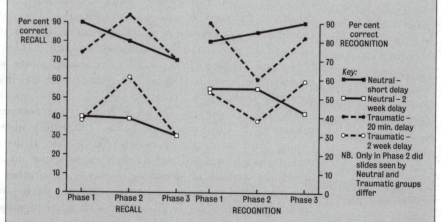

Recall and recognition of traumatic and neutral slides as a function of retention interval (after Christianson and Loftus, 1987).

A study by Heuer and Reisberg (1990) shows what happens to such effects over time. Different groups of subjects saw slide sequences that were equivalent in terms of complexity and structure, but which differed in the level of emotion they were designed to evoke. Two weeks later subjects' ability to retrieve (recall and recognise) the story's plot and memory for small details shown in the slide sequence (e.g. the colour of the door behind characters in the sequence) was tested in a 'surprise' memory test. Subjects who watched the emotional version were able to retrieve both more plot and detailed information from the slide sequences than subjects who watched the neutral version. Subjects who watched the neutral version, but who had been given explicit instructions to remember as much as they could, performed as well as those who merely watched the emotional version, when tested on their ability to retrieve plot-related information. However, they did not remember details as well as those subjects who saw the slide sequence containing emotional slides.

Note that there is a contradiction here between the results reported by Heuer and Reisberg (1990), who show enhanced recall, and especially recognition, for both peripheral and central details in arousal conditions, and those of Christianson and Loftus (1987), who show improved recall in the arousal condition, but poorer recognition in the arousal condition. There are a number of crucial methodological differences between the studies. First, Heuer and Reisberg's (1990) descriptions of what constitutes central and peripheral detail, and those of Christianson and Loftus (1987) are very different. Heuer and Reisberg (1990) make their central–peripheral distinction on the basis of Eleanor Rosch's notion of what constitutes basic information (i.e. 'that level of abstraction that is appropriate for using, thinking about or naming an object in most situations in which the object occurs', Rosch, 1978, p. 43). Any aspects of an object which were not as invariant across situations as this definition requires were classified as peripheral details. Importantly, the central–peripheral distinction is made with respect to the information in the slide without special reference to the source of the arousal. Christianson and Loftus (1987), on the other hand, had subjects write down the most distinctive feature of each slide, which provided a basis for determining what constitutes central information. These two ways of looking at what are central and peripheral scene details can therefore be orthogonal to each other. Latterly, work in this area has converged on a description of central information, which is that which relates to the source of the arousal and the details associated with it (Christianson, 1992). Burke, Heuer and Reisberg (1992, p. 287), for example, have shown that memory is enhanced for lower level detail 'when that detail information was spatially and temporally linked to the arousal event'.

The other important difference between the two studies was that, while subjects in the Christianson and Loftus (1987) study were busy during encoding writing down the distinctive aspects of each slide, Heuer and Reisberg's (1990) subjects merely watched and passively encoded the information. Arguably, the attentional demands of identifying distinctive information, and the rehearsal this involved, served to distract subjects away from those peripheral aspects of the scene which would have facilitated better recognition performance. This would be expected to be especially the case in arousal conditions, where still more demands are made upon a limited attentional capacity. There is some support for this proposal from work reported below, and from research that Peter Chapman and I recently reported.

In these studies, subjects received a surprise recognition test about 30 minutes after watching and rating films of relatively mundane driving scenarios (see

Chapman and Groeger, 1995). As an orientation task, subjects rated the films on various dimensions (e.g. the riskiness, complexity and business of the scenes depicted). It turned out that the results that emerged were independent of the orientation task. What did matter was how risky the driving scenes depicted on the videos were. Those which earlier had been judged, by a different group of subjects, to be intrinsically more risky, were better recognised than those which were less risky. The relationship between recognition and riskiness was reliably positive for those films which were relatively more risky, but reliably negative for those which were less risky. We interpreted these results as indicating that where risk is encountered during encoding, it is well encoded and supports later retrieval. Where risk is not encountered during encoding, but during retrieval, it serves to distract attention away from those cues which might otherwise facilitate recognition. Threat attracts attention to the details about the source of that threat. Sometimes the details which are attended to will serve as cues which allow an 'old' film to be recognised as such. However, where an original film was not risky, but its matched distractor films were, attention was less likely to be devoted to those non-risky aspects of the 'safe' scene which would allow a correct identification to be made. In these circumstances, the overall similarity of the films used serves to allow these risky distracters to be incorrectly identified as previously seen scenes.

Attention focusing: The Easterbrook hypothesis

As long as we agree that 'central' information should be defined with respect to the source of arousal, rather than in terms of its complexity or invariance, all of these results can be interpreted in a wider framework known as the *Easterbrook hypothesis* (Easterbrook, 1959). This predicted that in circumstances of extreme arousal people attend to a narrower range of aspects of the situation in which they find themselves, rather than the whole situation. At relatively low levels of arousal, according to Easterbrook, a wide range of information is attended to and encoded. As arousal increases, attention focuses and less information is encoded. With still higher increases in arousal, attention narrows still further and some of the information necessary for successful performance is not encoded. This has lead to the phrase *weapon focus* to describe the impact of extreme emotion on memory. These notions were originally derived from research on animals, but have gained substantial support from studies of the effects of extreme arousal on human memory (see Deffenbacher, 1983, 1991; Eysenck, 1992 for extensive review of earlier research on this topic).

But do these studies really mean that attention narrows or is focused upon certain aspects of an episode? There is evidence, for example, that central, arousing or distressing details (e.g. a bleeding head), are more frequently looked at, although are fixated for shorter periods of time (see Christianson, Loftus, Hoffman and Loftus, 1991). This does not necessarily mean that attention 'narrows'. Another possibility is that it is not the distribution of attention which 'narrows' but what we have referred to previously as our attention span. More generally, threat or anxiety-provoking situations are associated with a reduction in digit span (i.e. a test of immediate memory which is also thought of as a measure of available attention). Thus, Chris Idizkowski and Alan Baddeley found that just before speaking in public the average digit span of anxious subjects reduced from 8 to 7.25 (see Idizkowski and Baddeley, 1983). Novice parachutists, facing their first jump, were also reported to have digit span reductions (Idizkowski and Baddeley, 1987). Earlier, Simonov, Frolov, Evtushenko and Sviridov (1977) had shown that, immediately before they jumped, even experienced parachutists were worse at performing a task which required them to recognise digits presented against a confusing background. These, together with other studies also showing attentional decrements in threatening situations, suggest that less is likely to be attended to when arousal increases. What is attended to, however, seems to be well-remembered.

There is an obvious parallel here between the discussion above about central and peripheral information, attention focusing and other forms of environmental or task-related context. This is especially so in the case of the research of Jacoby, Woloshyn and Kelley (1989), discussed in the previous chapter. There, dividing attention during the learning phase reduced the subjects' ability to encode contextual cues. These would have allowed the sorts of source-related judgements required when recognition becomes difficult. In the studies reported above, attention to wider aspects of the situation in which an event occurs is also restricted, although not, this time, by a secondary task, but by the emotional implications of the primary task itself. Despite this parallel, there are, however, a range of studies which show that effects of context and emotion are not equivalent. These studies are typified by those in which the experimenter has sought to manipulate the mood of the subject, in order to avoid some of the methodological difficulties of the work described above, for example, a range of different affective responses which might be generated (e.g. fear, excitement, etc.), not all of which might be expected to have the same impact on attention or memory.

Induced and natural mood states

It was initially thought, on the basis of studies by Lloyd and Lishman (1975) and Gordon Bower, that just as similarity between encoding context and retrieval context would enhance remembering, so too would overlap between affective states at study and test (i.e. *mood-dependent memory*). Before assessing the findings in support of this position it is worthwhile briefly outlining Gordon Bower's network theory of emotional processing, since it neatly summarises the influential background beliefs and predictions of many in this area of research.

Bower (1981) suggested that emotions can be thought of as nodes within an interconnected network, in the same way that propositions might be represented within a semantic network. Emotion nodes are activated by external events, or through activation of network nodes associated with that emotion. Because activated nodes influence or prime each other, through a process known as 'spreading activation', one can begin to see how emotions can be externally or internally generated, and how feelings and interpretations about an unfolding event can change. Bower describes three types of influence which might be expected from this formulation: mood state-dependent memory, mood-congruent memory and mood-congruent judgement or interpretation. We discuss the first two of these below in some detail.

Mood dependence and congruence

Mood-dependent memory as indicated above, is analogous to the idea of state-dependent memory, that is, the degree of overlap between study and test conditions predicts the success with which information will be retrieved. A number of studies of mood-related materials appear to provide support for this position. A variety of different methods have been used. Some, such as Lloyd and Lishman (1975), for example, have made use of screening measures to find subjects with appropriate levels of the relevant trait emotional states. They showed that the higher patients scored on the Beck Depression Inventory, the faster they were able to recall unpleasant experiences. Bower (1981), on the other hand, used hypnosis with normal subjects in order to induce the state desired (by the experimenter). Subjects hypnotised to be happy or sad read a passage about two individuals, Jack and André, who respectively had relatively sad or happy lives. Subjects claimed to have identified with the character whose life was consistent with their induced hypnotic state. Later, unhypnotised, they recalled what they could from the passage. 'Happy' subjects recalled about equal amounts of happy and sad facts, but 'sad' subjects remembered 80 per cent of the sad facts from the passage, but only 20 per cent of the more positive facts. In the more typical mood-induction paradigm, Teasdale and Fogarty (1979) used the Velten (1968) mood-induction procedure, which requires subjects to read and contemplate a range of emotionally toned statements. They found that subjects in a sad and anxious mood were slower at evoking positive thoughts. Similarly, Teasdale and Russell (1983) showed that mood at retrieval substantially influences the statements subjects remember about themselves (Fig 9.3, p. 198).

It will be noted from the studies mentioned above that, while demonstrations of the fact that mood influences memory are widespread, there are very few that show the clear effects observed in the state-dependent literature (i.e. that reinstatement of the original encoding conditions enhances recall). In fact, most of the reliable effects observed can be equally well interpreted in terms of *mood-congruent memory*, where the state in which the person remembers the information, rather than the match between test and study state, influences what is retrieved. Thus we tend to remember information which is consistent with how we currently feel. One key test of the difference between the two proposals is of what happens with material which is emotionally neutral. If the effects we observe are simply due to mood-congruent retrieval, then neutral material should be remembered equally well (or rather equally badly) by people irrespective of whether the mood induced at study and test are positive or negative and irrespective of whether they match each other. Mood-dependent recall, on the other hand, should show that where mood at encoding and retrieval match there should be greater remembering of neutral material than when the study and test moods do not match. Studies by Bower, Monteiro and Gilligan (1978) and Teasdale and Russell (1983) which include mood manipulations and neutral words show no evidence of state-dependent memory.

Fig 9.3 Recall of positive, negative and neutral trait words in elated and depressed mood states (after Teasdale and Russell, 1983).

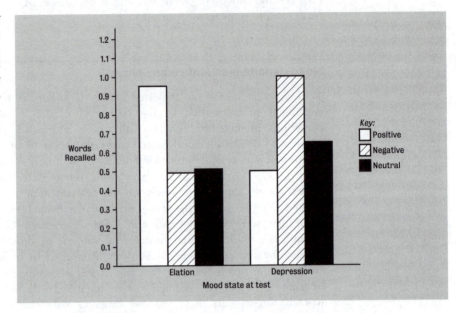

Difficulties with dependence and congruence

In a very widely cited review, Blaney (1986) concludes that while there is very substantial evidence in favour of mood-congruent effects on retrieval, that which relates to mood-dependent effects is much less convincing and equivocal. This seems a reasonable conclusion to draw on the basis of the available evidence. However, and understandably, virtually all of the studies in this area have used emotionally valenced materials; procedures to select people with relatively stable emotional-processing characteristics; or procedures which have sought to induce what might, uncritically, be regarded as similar states. Most of the studies which have reported context effects, as reviewed in the previous chapter, have tended to use neutral materials, rather than materials biased towards one context or another, and subjects who were comparatively unbiased with respect to the context in which they found themselves. It is far from clear that if the standards which are required in order to demonstrate influences of mood on memory were extended to the emotionally neutral study of contextual influences, context dependencies between study and test would still be obtained. There are many more powerful influences available in the experimental situations which have been used. Were ways to be found of amplifying the relatively subtle context-like effects of mood dependence, without also escalating the other influences, then I believe they would still be observed. There is some evidence for this, although it is not unequivocal.

Fig 9.4 Mean
proportion of generate
and read items recalled
as a function of encoding
and retrieval moods
(after Eich and Metcalfe,
1989).

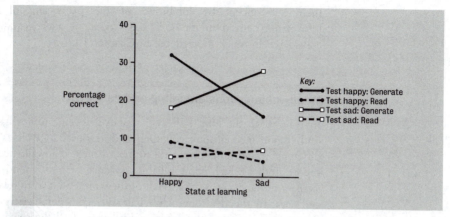

Eich and Metcalfe (1989) took advantage of the fact that recall is substantially enhanced where subjects are required to generate words rather than simply read them (as reported by Slamecka and Graf, 1978). Subjects read items to be remembered (e.g. vanilla) or generated them in response to cues that were very likely to evoke the target word (e.g. milkshake flavours: chocolate, ????). Subjects studied or recalled while in happy or sad moods, which were induced by having them listen to happy or sad music. Eich and Metcalfe showed small, but mood-dependent, effects when the orienting task used simply required subjects to read the words. However, when subjects were required to generate the target items, a far more pronounced mood-dependent effect was observed (Fig 9.4). It seems likely that the read–generate procedure engages subjects in more active encoding of materials. Arguably, this more active encoding is similar to what Baddeley (1990), in discussing the basis of context effects, refers to as interactive encoding of context, that is, cases where the context is incorporated into the trace of what is learned, thus serving as a powerful cue in later retrieval. Thus, as we might have anticipated, the strategies used during encoding are likely to exert considerable influence on the results observed. The effectiveness of mood induction procedures, and the extent of the emotional valance implicated by the materials used, add further complexity to results in this area.

It should be noted that it is typically found that positive and negative materials are not equally sensitive to manipulation, that is, they show *mood asymmetry*. Thus, for example, it has been shown by Isen, Shalker, Clark and Carp (1978) that feedback on task success enhanced recall of previously endorsed adjectives which refer to positive personality traits. Feedback on task failure did not influence recall of negative personality traits. It is possible that differences in subjects' preparedness to attribute success and failure to themselves underlie these sorts of effects. Power and Brewin (1990), for instance, carried out a study in which subjects read phrases that represented positive and negative esteem-related or survival-threatening events, and then judged whether positive and negative trait adjectives applied to them. Subjects took significantly longer to endorse negative adjectives if the preceding esteem-related priming stimulus was negatively valenced than if it was positively valenced. Power and Brewin (1990) suggest that in the face of a potential challenge to self-esteem, normal individuals may protect their self-concept by inhibition of the processing of negative self-related information stored in memory. *Self-relevance* is addressed further below, and is considered in much more detail in Chapter 10.

Mood-incongruous encoding and retrieval

In contrast to the effects described above, recent studies have also demonstrated both mood-incongruous encoding and retrieval as well as differences between different mood-induction procedures. Rinck, Glowalla and Schneider (1992) report studies which show reliable evidence of both mood-congruous and *mood-incongruous encoding* (Fig 9.5). Half of the words used were relatively mild in positive and negative affective tone, while half were considerably stronger in affective tone. Before subjects rated the emotional valence of all these words, they underwent a 'happy' or 'sad' mood induction procedure. Subjects subsequently recalled the words in a 'normal' mood state. In both of the studies they report, mood-congruent recall was observed for the strongly valenced emotional items. However, in both cases also, the more weakly valenced items actually showed significant mood-incongruent recall. That is, weakly positive words were better recalled when they had been learned in a negative mood state. Rinck and colleagues showed that mildly toned words are more difficult to evaluate when they are incongruous with the current mood state. They suggest that the difficulty, as reflected by the extra time taken to make these judgements, allows greater elaboration in the encoding of these materials than is carried out with consistent mildly toned or strongly valenced items. As we might expect, greater elaboration results in more durable encoding and, hence, enhanced remembering.

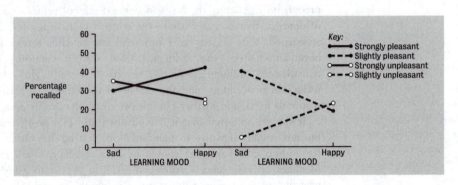

Fig 9.5 Recall of slightly and strongly pleasant and unpleasant words as a function of mood at learning (after Rinck, Glowalla and Schneider, 1992).

Mood incongruous retrieval has also been demonstrated recently. Parrott and Sabini (1990) explored subjects' ability to retrieve personal (i.e. autobiographical) memories under different mood-induction procedures. In some of the studies, naturally arising circumstances were used to increase 'happy' or 'sad' states (i.e. people receiving better or worse than expected results from an examination, sunny versus cloudy weather, background music). Under these circumstances, subjects were actually significantly more effective at retrieving personal memories which were incongruous with the prevailing mood. When a more typical, and thus artificial, mood-induction procedure was used (i.e. suitable music together with instructions to work actively at experiencing a particular mood), mood-congruous retrieval of autobiographical memories was observed. It may be that under more naturalistic mood-change circumstances, dependable personal memories become more available and retrievable so as to facilitate the restoration of affective balance. Although the studies by Rinck and colleagues deal with encoding rather than retrieval, it is tempting to see their results and those of Parrott and Sabini, as reflecting differential effects in the absence of particularly strongly valenced situations or materials. Nevertheless, the key point for present circumstances is that mood effects are asymmetric, and that both mood-congruity and mood-incongruity effects have been observed on encoding and retrieval.

It should be noted that this range of task-determined effects of affect require considerable revision of the network models of affect and cognition proposed by Bower. Unfortunately, it is beyond the scope of this chapter to consider alternative models, but the reader is referred to excellent recent books by Wells and Matthews (1994) and especially to Teasdale and Barnard (1993).

■ Anxiety and depression

Baddeley (1990) summarises the similarities and differences in emotional processing in anxious and depressed subjects. Paraphrasing their account, depression impairs overall performance by reducing processing at input, and by biasing both learning and recall through the mood-congruency effect. This results in a consistent bias, for the depressed patient, towards perceiving and recalling items that are consistent with the depressed mood, and a preoccupation with, and rehearsal of, the negative events of the past. In contrast, the anxious patient is preoccupied with the threat implied by future events, such that there is a readiness to perceive threat-related stimuli, although probably not a tendency to analyse these in detail. Both groups will tend to overestimate the likelihood of negative events, although for different reasons. Depressive patients are more likely to have negative past events more readily available on which to base their decision, while anxious patients are more likely to encounter a broader range of stimuli which they find suggestive of the threat. While this may be a useful way of conceiving of how anxiety and depression differ from each other, the empirical findings available offer a much less clear differentiation between the two. (For contrasting views on this issue see Teasdale and Barnard, 1993; Williams, Watts, MacLeod and Matthews, 1988; Wells and Matthews, 1994). One of the reasons why there is much less differentiation is that anxiety and depression frequently co-exist, and as such, without careful prescreening of subjects, those in apparently different groups may actually be more similar than is intended. However, even when such precautions are taken, similarities in findings still emerge.

Butler and Matthews (1983) asked anxious, depressed and normal people to rate the likelihood of occurrence of pleasant and unpleasant events to themselves and to others. Groups rated the likelihood of pleasant events similarly, but both the anxious and depressed think unpleasant things are more likely to happen to them than to others. In a later study, Butler and Matthews (1987) showed that, as an examination approached, anxious subjects believed that unpleasant events were increasingly more likely to happen to them, but they did not change their estimate of likelihood of unpleasant events occurring to others.

Attentional biases in anxiety and depression

Various effects have been ascribed to attentional differences in anxious subjects. Eysenck, MacLeod and Matthews (1987) had subjects listen to, and later recall carefully chosen homophones (e.g. dye/die; pane/pain, etc.), showing that anxious subjects were more likely to write down the more threatening word. Since there is some evidence for bias in recall by anxious subjects the effects reported by Eysenck and colleagues cannot be attributed unequivocally to attentional or encoding effects. Fraser Watts and colleagues capitalised on the standard *Stroop effect*, namely that when asked to name the colour of ink in which a word is written, if that word is itself a different colour word, ink-colour naming is slowed. Watts, McKenna, Sharrock and Tresize (1986) developed an *emotional Stroop* procedure, in which spider-phobic patients were required to name the colours in which different words were written (Fig 9.6). When the words to be colour-named were spider-related (e.g. crawly, hairy, etc.) colour naming slowed substantially. After subjects had undergone a treatment programme to reduce the impact of their phobia, the interference from spider-related words on colour naming was much reduced. This seems to provide clear evidence of an attentional, or preattentional, influence in anxious patients, which is what we might expect on the basis of the caricature of anxiety and depression differences provided above.

However, it should be noted that Williams and Broadbent (1986) using a similar procedure showed that people who had recently tried unsuccessfully to commit suicide, were more affected by words such as 'overdose' than by generally negative words. Of course, it may be that this interference arises because of the self-referential nature of the words used, and that this, rather than attentional similarities in anxious and depressed patients leads to the observed slowing in responding.

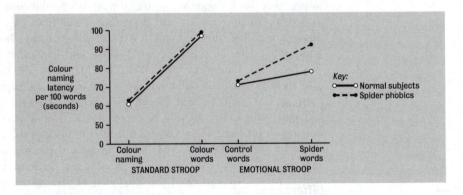

Fig 9.6 Standard and emotional Stroop test performance as a function of phobic status (after Watts, McKenna, Sharrock and Tresize, 1986).

One of the difficulties with this work is that these early versions of the emotional Stroop technique used large cards on which what would be expected to be interfering and non-interfering emotional words were printed in different colours. While this greatly enhanced the ease with which it could be used in clinical settings, having to rely on a time per card, rather than a time per word, may obscure effects on the naming latencies on individual words which would discriminate between the two groups (e.g. a general slowing on all words on a list containing interfering and non-interfering items rather than much greater but more selective slowing of naming for interfering items only). Thus, it seems evident that attentional disturbances are widely observed in these groups. However, without more careful studies attributing attentional biases towards or away from the threat-producing stimulus, it is very difficult to draw conclusions about the precise nature of the attentional disturbance, and its likely impact on encoding.

Availability of congruent information

The congruence effects noted above may actually serve to obscure a consistent finding which may be important both from a clinical and from a theoretical point of view. That is, it is not the case that depressive people have only negative information available to them.

A variety of studies show that this negative information is largely restricted to themselves, and is not extended to all others. In a study by Bradley and Matthews (1983) depressed patients recalled more negative words in relation to self, but actually recalled more positive information in relation to others. Analogously, Teasdale and others (cited in Teasdale and Barnard, 1993, pp. 189–90) report a rather clever study in which Weissman and Beck's (1978) Dysfunctional Attitude Scale was adapted. Rather than requiring subjects to endorse attitude statements such as 'If a person I love does not love me it means that I am unlovable', John Teasdale and colleagues had subjects complete sentences such as 'Always to put others' interests before your own is a recipe for _____'. Their reasoning was that the original result obtained by Weissman and Beck, that subjects' tendency to endorse negative statements declines as depression eases, would suggest that, when depressed, subjects should actually complete their sentences with positive words (e.g. 'Always to put others' interests before your own is a recipe for success or happiness'), whereas in remission subjects should gravitate towards more negative, but more functional, completion (e.g. 'Always to put others' interests before your own is a recipe for disaster or unhappiness').

Taken together, these results suggest that congruence must be searched for very carefully and interpreted cautiously. It seems likely to be limited in scope to judgements about the patients themselves, and appears to relate to the interpretation made, or sentiments expressed, rather than to the surface meaning or actual words used.

Differences in remembering in anxious and depressed patients

There has been some controversy with respect to the extent to which depression and anxiety have different influences on remembering. It seems to be generally the case that self-referent information is better recalled (e.g. Breck and Smith, 1983; Claeys, 1990; Claeys, Deboeck and Viaene, 1976). In a study in which subjects were carefully prescreened in order to identify two groups of subjects – non-anxious depressed and test-anxious non-depressed, Ingram, Kendall, Smith, Donnell and Ronan (1987) showed that there is considerable cognitive specificity in emotional distress. Subjects were asked to determine the self-relevance or otherwise of self-referent depressive and self-referent anxious trait adjectives. Depressed subjects endorsed fewer statements than anxious subjects, but even when this was statistically corrected for, anxious subjects remembered more anxiety-related adjectives, while depressed subjects remembered more depression-related adjectives.

Other studies provide a less clear picture. Mogg, Mathews and Weinman (1987) did not find that recall of threat-related words is worse among patients with general anxiety state, while in a later study Matthews, Mogg, May and Eysenck (1989) found no evidence of better cued recall of threat-related words in trait-anxious subjects, although they did find that anxious subjects were more likely to complete word-stems (e.g. fe- ??) with anxiety-related words rather than neutral words they had previously encountered (e.g. 'fear' rather than 'feet') (Fig 9.7). This points to a possible role for what in previous chapters we identified as an implicit, familiarity-based aspect of remembering (especially in aspects of the recognition task). Research by Watts, Trezise and Sharrock (1986) with spider-phobic patients supports this interpretation. Spider phobics were significantly less likely to recall phobia-related words, but more likely to recognise them. In a further study in that paper, they found poorer recognition of larger, presumably more anxiety-provoking spiders, than for smaller ones. In other words, as we observed much earlier, in threatening situations subjects may tend to encode less, specifically fewer 'source'-related details, which may be crucial to the success of later attempts to remember in demanding memory tasks.

Fig 9.7 Cued recall and word completion of threatening and neutral words as a function of anxiety (after Matthews, Mogg, May and Eysenck, 1989).

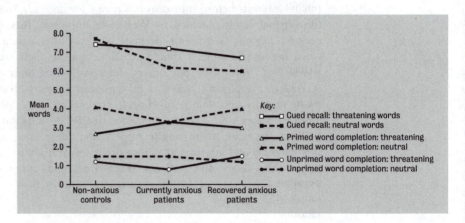

Depressive patients are also said to have encoding deficits, being said to rely on less elaborate encoding strategies (e.g. Weingartner, Miller and Murphy, 1977; Johnson and Magaro, 1987). Along such lines, attempts have been made to demonstrate that the relatively poorer memory of depressed subjects is due to encoding deficiencies rather than to retrieval problems (e.g. lack of effort in the recall task). Watts and Sharrock (1987) carried out a study of depressives' prose recall in which recall demands were manipulated and minimised. They showed that even when only single word answers were required, greater recall decrements were observed in a depressed group. While this study demonstrates that differential remembering effects among depressive patients may not lie in less effort being devoted to recall, it does not demonstrate that the effects unequivocally lie at encoding. In this regard, it would be interesting if the study by Rinck and colleagues, which was discussed above in relation to mood-incongruous encoding, was repeated with depressed patients. If the encoding deficit account is true, then it would be expected that the mood-incongruity effect with mildly toned affective words, which is said to be due to more elaborative encoding of mild words, should disappear, and only the mood-congruity effect with more emotional materials should be observed.

Finally, in anticipation of some material we will encounter later, one other effect of depression on remembering is worthy of note. Williams and Broadbent (1986) showed that people who had recently attempted suicide, when asked to retrieve particular types of personal memory, were able to do it, albeit slowly, but that the memories lacked specific episodic details. In a later study, Moore, Watts and Williams (1988) also demonstrated that the recollections of depressed patients appear excessively general, being more generic, that is, less specific and less episodic, than those of control subjects. It is possible that this, once again, is due to some restriction on the encoding of specific episodic, source, and information. However, it is also possible that the rumination on previous life events, which served to maintain depressive states, may actually give rise to a phenomenon known as *re-episodic blurring*, in which repeated retrieval of particular episodic memories leads them to become amalgamated with similar memories, causing them to become more general, to lose specific details, and to alter even the physical perspective from which they are recalled. We will discuss this phenomenon more in the next chapter, in which we discuss many other aspects of personal autobiographical memories.

Summary: Arousal, emotion and remembering

At the outset of this chapter I summarised a view of emotions and arousal which suggested that these reflected an abstract high-level description of the relationship between a person and his or her environment, and that individual's phenomenological experience of feelings. The environment, or context, in which individuals perform tasks, if we include in it the nature of the task they are also performing, clearly has a substantial influence on how well events which provoke emotion, or events which take place when the individuals are experiencing emotion, are remembered. Thus, the material used, or stimuli processed, the time of day and energy levels of the individual, together with his or her attributions about the causes of the emotional arousal, all conspire to influence what is remembered.

Where the emotion experienced is unpleasant, and especially where it is self-relevant (whether concerning one's self, or threatening to it), details about the causal agent of the emotional change seem to be briefly unavailable, but it is probable that its gist is remembered. As the interval between experiencing the event and remembering it increases, perhaps even over the course of minutes, more detail about the events which are central to the emotional experience are also recovered. In time, of course, these will be lost, although there is good empirical evidence to suggest that such gist and detail may be available for longer than similar, but non-emotionally toned, information. It would seem that information about aspects of the event which did not provoke the increase in emotional arousal are unlikely to be attended to, and are much less likely to be remembered. As we also saw in earlier chapters, it would seem that only very rudimentary aspects of unattended situations are remembered.

There are similarities between the effects of context, as described in the previous chapter, and some of the issues addressed above. However, at least given the current state of research, context and emotion seem not invariably to influence remembering in the same way. They differ, for example, in respect of the notion of dependence, which is typically observed in the way remembering is benefited through reinstatement of context. Congruence, rather than dependence, seems characteristic of the relationship between emotion and remembering. However, given the range of relationships which have been demonstrated, especially in the last five or so years (e.g. dependence, independence, congruence and incongruence), a reappraisal of what is considered the typical relationship will soon be timely. Another difference lies in the different types of effects which seem to be observed with recall and recognition. As pointed out earlier, context effects may be less apparent with recognition because the remembering required is sufficiently easy not to require a reliance on source information. With emotion, it may be that attentional allocation does indeed change, making certain types of information less likely to be encoded in a way which allows them to be directly accessed later. Recall procedures may simply be insufficiently precise to observe these restrictions on the registration of information in emotional circumstances. It may be such differences in the sensitivity of different indices of remembering which underlie the different effects of recall and recognition with phobic materials, and the bias in remembering certain types of phobia-related information (e.g. smaller spiders seem to be better recognised than larger spiders).

■ Further reading

Blaney, P. H. (1986). Affect and memory: A review. *Psychological Bulletin.* 99, 229–46.

Burke, A., Heuer, F. and Reisberg, D. (1992). Remembering emotional events. *Memory & Cognition, 20,* 277–90.

Christianson, S. A. (1992). *The handbook of emotion and memory: Research and theory.* Hillsdale, NJ: Lawrence Erlbaum.

Eich, J. E. (1989). Theoretical issues in state-dependent memory. In H. L. Roediger III and F. I. M. Craik (Eds) *Varieties of memory and consciousness: Essays in Honor of Endel Tulving.* Hillsdale, N.J: Erlbaum.

Eysenck, M. W. (1992). *Anxiety: The cognitive perspective.* London: Lawrence Erlbaum.

Revelle, W. A. and Loftus, D. A. (1990). Individual differences and arousal: Implications for the study of mood and memory. *Cognition and Emotion, 4,* 209–37.

Teasdale, J. D. and Barnard, P. J. (1993). *Affect, cognition and change: Re-modelling depressive thought.* London: Lawrence Erlbaum.

Wells, A. and Matthews, G. (1994). *Attention and emotion: A clinical perspective.* London: Lawrence Erlbaum.

Discussion points	

- What effect does delayed retrieval have on our memory for traumatic events?
- Compare and contrast the effects of context change and emotional arousal on remembering and forgetting.
- Does attention really focus? Comment with respect to effects of increased attentional demand reported on context processing and emotional arousal.
- How similar are the effects of transitory and more enduring emotional states on remembering?

Chapter 10

Remembering one's self

Chapter outline: In the chapters up to this point we have concentrated on what were, for the most part, laboratory explorations of memory phenomena and factors influencing remembering. In this chapter we take a rather broader focus, considering in greater detail memories which have a greater personal or autobiographical significance. In particular, this chapter focuses on why memories of our own past are important, our ability to retrieve our earliest memories, retrieval of widely experienced events (i.e. flashbulb memories), and the controversial area of memories of childhood abuse (i.e. the false memory debate).

Key topics

- The self and personal information processing
- Earliest memories of self
- Flashbulb memories
- Experimental and field studies of personal memories
- Case studies of personal memories
- Lost and recovered Memories
- Summary: Personal memories
- Further reading

■ The self and personal information processing

At first sight, the notion of a self seems some distance from the sorts of ideas and evidence we have encountered thus far. However, a variety of very different types of result show that self-relevant information is especially well remembered. Thus, for example, even in experimental studies of memory, where the encoding or orienting task is systematically varied, it is generally found that when information is encoded in terms of its personal significance, it is better remembered than the same information encoded in terms of its surface or even semantic attributes (see Baddeley, 1990). We have also seen in previous chapters how contextual changes which actively involve the experiencer are most likely to aid or inhibit retrieval. Similarly, words which are self-relevant are read more quickly than neutral words which have been matched in terms of length, frequency, and part of speech (Geller and Shaver, 1976). Finally, Cohen, Peterson and Mantini (1987) have shown, in a series of experiments, that actions that are performed by the rememberer are retrieved more effectively than those that the rememberer has demonstrated to them by another, or which are read about. A number of authors have attempted to describe how memory and one's notion of self might interact.

The notion of 'self'

Markus and Nurius (1986) defined what they call 'possible selves', that is, cognitive-affective knowledge structures which are used in processing of self-relevant events. Together, these define what we consider ourselves to be, what we might aspire to being and what we fear we may become. Groeger and Grande (1996) invoke similar ideas in describing what they term 'task-related selves', which reflect the consistent views we form of ourselves as competent performers of everyday tasks. Thus, for example, as we show in our study, drivers' assessments of their driving competence are quite stable across time. This stability increases with the amount of driving experience drivers have, but is weakened by the number of accidents in which they have been involved. Work is currently under way to explore the relationship between these stable views of our own ability and the ways in which we remember events which might serve to strengthen or challenge this view of ourselves as competent performers.

Brewer (1986) has also attempted to identify what the self is in information processing terms, claiming that the self is composed of an 'experiencing ego', a self-schema, and an associated set of personal memories and autobiographical facts. Brewer (1986) defines this experiencing ego as the conscious experiencing entity which is the subject of autobiographical memories, and the *self-schema* as a generic cognitive structure containing information about the individual's goals, attitudes and references.

The self-system delineated by Neisser (1988) is rather more thorough, embracing five different sources of self-relevant information. These include the *ecological self*, which gives us our unique self-centred physical perspective on the world and the *interpersonal self*, which comprises the species-specific behaviour which people communicate to each other. These two together form a perceiving self, which allows us to be aware of our immediate situation, of where we are and what we are doing, and which also allows us to be aware of our social interactions, of who we are with and what is going on. It is because of the combination of these sources of information that I know that I am sitting in a room, talking to an attractive woman about relatively mundane events. This perceiving self is the subject of an excellent book edited by Neisser (1993).

Neisser also describes the *private self*, which is uniquely personal and affords us our sense of identity, and the *conceptual self*, which gives us culture-specific knowledge of the nature and workings of our own minds. It is because of this information that I know that the triviality of the conversation I am having with someone very dear to me, indicates that the relationship between us is ending. Neisser (1994) describes development of the private and conceptual selves, which together support what is properly termed 'self-knowledge'.

The fifth form of self-relevant information was originally termed the temporally extended self (see Neisser, 1988). Neisser (1994) provides a fascinating series of papers devoted to what he now terms the *remembering self*, which is involved in extending and developing personal relations, through the maintenance, revision and presentation of our own personal narrative. Neisser points out that there is not just one 'remembered self', which is permanently established by some fixed set of memory traces. Instead 'different occasions must, should, and do' elicit different accounts of the past' (Neisser, 1994, p. vii). It is this self which tells both of the sorrow of the relationship which has ended, and later, of the sense of value which has emerged from it.

In the following sections we will examine many different ways in which the peculiar qualities of personal information processing, if not actually these notions of self, can be observed.

Earliest memories of self

What is the earliest memory you can recall from your childhood? The earliest real memory I have, that I know is not a reconstruction from others' tales, or from family photographs, or some reconstruction from events which actually occurred later, is near to, rather than directly of, a traumatic incident. The overall quality of that memory is still very vivid. In the most vivid part of the memory, I am standing in the hallway of my family home in Cork, dripping wet. I had fallen into, and had been dragged out of, a pond in the University grounds opposite, but some way from home. Madge, a woman who helped my mother with housework around the time of my sister's infancy, is on her knees scrubbing the stone-tiled hallway, and because of that the front door is open. I seem to recall my mother coming out of the kitchen, but not much else. A less vivid part of the memory relates to playing with reeds or bamboo canes at the edge of the frozen pond. It was obviously winter, although this is an inference. I know it was Friday, because it was, ironically, bath day. I surmise it was late afternoon, but I have no actual memory of the time of day or what the year was, although I cannot have been much more than four years old at the time. I have absolutely no memory of going to the pond, where I was forbidden to play, falling in, being in or being dragged out of the water, by 'Adie Blanc' (to this day I do not know if that was his real name or correct spelling), a playmate at the time. This story is much-rehearsed, but first-hand details of it are known only to three or four people. There are no other external records of it, except perhaps that to this day I have both a fascination with and no small fear of swimming, the edges of pools, and water in anything larger than a glass!

Although the story recounted above serves primarily to illustrate my earliest memory, aspects of it serve to highlight other issues we will address in the sections below: the vividness of some personal recollections, the ways in which they appear to influence the beliefs and expectations we have about our selves, the extent to which they are shared by others at the time, and the loss of detailed information in traumatic circumstances.

Infantile amnesia

The phenomenon of *infantile amnesia*, or the inaccessibility of early childhood memories, has been a concern of psychologists since the 1940s (e.g. Dudycha and Dudycha, 1941; Schachtel, 1947; Waldfogel, 1948; White and Pillemer, 1979; Nelson, 1988; Howe and Courage, 1993). There is some agreement that the availability of early memories decreases with age with very little being retrieved from before three or four years of age (Dudycha and Dudycha, 1941; Waldfogel, 1948 (see Fig 10.1)).

Fig 10.1   Frequency of memories prior to eighth birthday (after Waldfogel, 1948).

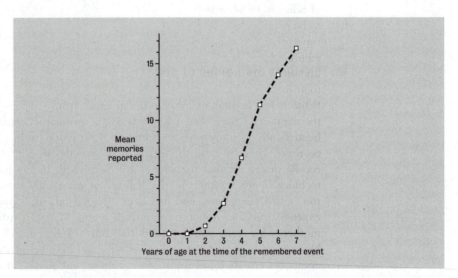

Box 10.1: Remembering the births of siblings

In a cleverly designed study, Sheingold and Tenny (1982) focused on children's memory for a specific datable event (i.e. the birth of a sibling when they themselves were four years of age), rather than using a free recall task as others had done. Groups of 4-, 8- and 12-year-old children were asked 20 questions about the circumstances of the birth (e.g. what time of day their mother left for the hospital; who took care of them when she had gone; what day of the week the mother and the baby came home from hospital; what presents the baby got; whether they themselves received any presents). The answers given were subsequently verified in consultation with the child's mother. Sheingold and Tenny (1982) found that 4-, 8- and 12-year-old children remembered similar amounts, about 10–12 items, even though the event was obviously more recent for the youngest children. A second study studied what teenage students remembered of the birth of a sibling. They found that those students who were three years of age or more at the time when this sibling was born remembered as much of the event as did those who were nine or more years of age, thus confirming the earlier result. However, this study also showed that where the birth of the sibling occurred when the respondent was younger than three years of age, very few details about the event could be retrieved.

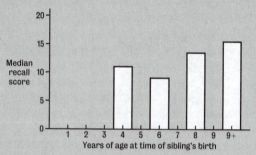

Median recall scores as a function of age for sibling births reported by college students (after Skeingold and Tenny, 1982).

Some of the details of my first near-drowning (yes, there have been others!) are to be expected from the research described above: my earliest memory dates from a time when I was three to four years of age, and it is associated with particularly emotional content (see Waldfogel, 1948; Crovitz and Harvey, 1979). This partly undermines the explanation of infantile amnesia attributed to Freud (1901). That is, following the rejection of infant sexual desires for my mother, said to have occurred before the resolution of my oedipal stage, about three to five years of age, I repress the earliest periods of my life. Instead I 'retrieve' *screen memories*, or fabricated neutral recollective experience, which shares superficial similarities with the repressed memory, used to block emotional experience. It is possible that my recollection of dripping with water in the hallway is a screen memory, which serves to block the more traumatic aspects of the experience, that is, actually falling into the pool. Certainly, I can remember no traumatic details, and my phenomenal experience of remembering those events now is relief at being safe and of my mother, having established that I was in no danger, scolding my adventurousness. However, as we will see later, psychogenic amnesia, or loss of details of traumatic events, sometimes accompanies particularly highly arousing experiences.

Explanations of infantile amnesia

A number of more plausible explanations have been made as to the basis of infantile amnesia. One rather obvious attempt at 'explanation' is to suggest that there is no phenomenon to be explained. That is, interference or decay through the passage of time are separately or jointly sufficient to explain the dearth of early memories. This would suggest that rates of forgetting should be identical, irrespective of the age of the individual at encoding and at retrieval. Wetzler and Sweeney (1986), in a meta-analysis of several studies show clearly that there is disproportionate loss of early memories, and clear discontinuities relating to one's first years in the functions which ordinarily describe forgetting (Fig 10.2). This effectively disposes of the decay and interference explanation.

Fig 10.2 Hypothetical distribution of recallable autobiographical memories (after Wetzler and Sweeney, 1986).

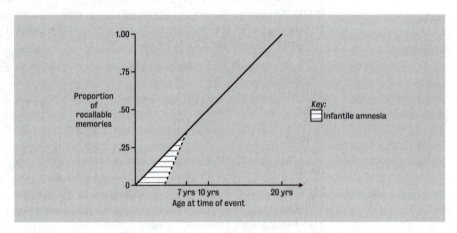

A second type of explanation is that there are fundamental changes between individuals who are doing the encoding, their brain, state of world knowledge or ability to process information and individuals who seek to retrieve whatever might have been stored. Schachtel (1947) suggests that children lack sufficient linguistic ability to encode their memories verbally, and lack the schemata which facilitate the organisation of event memories. Although worded differently, similar accounts have been offered by Neisser (1976), Winograd and Killinger (1983) and Nelson (1988). These have tended to emphasise the differences between, and efficacy of, the encoding strategies used, and the relative lack of prior experience (and, hence, reduced availability of schematic organisational structures which are likely to endure and support learning and retrieval). Moscovitch's (1985) explanation is similar, but rather more anatomical, suggesting that crucial brain structures have not yet developed at the time of encoding; they later do develop, rendering knowledge previously encoded inaccessible, although for reasons related more to hardware than software compared with those identified by others. Each of these explanations contain obvious grains of truth, but also some rather large assumptions about the plasticity or otherwise of brain function as well as the relationship of localisation, brain function and information processing in infants. The assumptions about differential abilities intentionally to use more elaborate encoding strategies are probably true (in the light of work later described in this book), but those about the role played by language in the sophistication of event memory and availability of schemata have been challenged by fascinating recent work by Nelson (1991), Howe and Courage (1993) and Fivush (1994).

Nelson (1991), for example, has shown that children as young as two years of age have available, and use, detailed narrative structures, and that both general and specific event knowledge is well established by three years of age. Nelson presents monologues of a two-year-old girl which show that parental talk about past and future events was available as a model for the child to use to formulate and verbalise her own memories and anticipation. The little girl produced coherent accounts of past happenings and future activities based on, and going beyond, these models. By three years of age, she could tell a good story about her own life events, but did not recount a fictional story that had been read to her in the same coherent narrative mode. Fivush (1994) is replete with similar examples, showing on the basis of structured parent–child conversations, that four-year-olds possessed detailed knowledge of trips they made to Disneyland when they were no more than two years of age. Whatever encoding strategies are being used by these very young children they are clearly sufficient to support quite detailed remembering of much earlier events. This raises the question, of course, of what other changes in processing occur beyond those already mentioned.

Recent work on the development of children's *theory of mind* (see Perner, 1992), that is, the knowledge that people have independent or separate ways of thinking and construing, offers what appears to be a very strong possible explanation. The conclusion reached by Howe and Courage (1993, p. 305), following a thorough and insightful review, is that 'infantile amnesia is a chimera of a previously unexplored relationship between the development of a cognitive sense of self and the personalisation of event memory'. Later in this chapter we explore how similar notions of what we are influence the things we remember.

■ Flashbulb memories

Although they acquired this particular name only after the work of Brown and Kulik (1977), *flashbulb memories*, that is, individuals' recollections of widely experienced events and the circumstances in which these were encoded, have been studied for almost a century. As such, they are amongst the oldest of formally studied naturalistic memory phenomena. While interest has waned from time to time, memories of events from the assassination of Abraham Lincoln (Colegrove, 1899), and assassinations of John F. Kennedy and Martin Luther King (Brown and Kulik, 1977), to the Challenger disaster (Neisser and Harsch, 1992) and the resignation of Margaret Thatcher (Conway, 1994) have received close scrutiny. The reason for this attention owes as much to the pragmatics of memory researchers as it does to the theoretical significance of what were, at one point, believed to be a special class of memories.

Early studies of flashbulb memories

Brown and Kulik (1977) studied the memories people had for their hearing about 10 events of considerable importance (e.g. assassinations of John F. Kennedy and Martin Luther King). They found that almost everyone tested could remember, with what they suggested was almost perceptual clarity, where they were when they heard the news, what they were doing, how (i.e. from whom) they heard the news, the aftermath of the newsworthy events, and how they felt on hearing the news. This closely parallels the findings reported by Colegrove (1899) in which of the 179 people tested, almost 80 per cent seemed to have detailed memories of where they were and what they were doing when they heard that Lincoln had been shot. What Brown and Kulik (1977) also showed, however, is that a range of other personal memories which, at encoding, evoked a high level of surprise, high level of consequentiality, and emotional arousal, resulted in what they considered to be a permanent memory for incidental concomitants of surprising and consequential events. This did not occur, they suggested, for encoding situations in which these variables did not attain sufficiently high levels. Where surprise, consequentiality and emotional arousal do attain high levels, these encoding variables influence the frequency of rehearsal, covert and overt, which, in turn, affects the degree of elaboration in the memory that can be elicited experimentally. Brown and Kulik (1977) draw a parallel between what they term a 'Now Print!' mechanism and Livingston's (1967) neurophysiological theory in which both postulate a special neural mechanism which, triggered by dramatic events, causes the whole scene to be printed in memory. There are a variety of reasons for doubting this speculation: veridicality, the role of rehearsal and the attribution of consequentiality to the events remembered.

Vividness, veridicality and consequentiality: Memories or reconstructions?

One prediction that arises directly from the speculations of Brown and Kulik (1977) is that flashbulb memories are necessarily correct. There are a number of demonstrations that this is not so, but three are particularly noteworthy. The first relates to Ulrich Neisser's own flashbulb memory of the bombing of Pearl Harbour in December 1941. Neisser (1982) recounts that he was listening to a baseball commentary on the radio when the programme was interrupted by a news flash. As Thompson and Cowan (1986) subsequently clarified, the radio commentary in question was actually of a grid-iron football game, rather than a baseball game. McCloskey, Wible and Cohen (1988) report a study in which subjects completed a questionnaire three days after the Challenger space shuttle disaster (January 1986), and some nine months later. While many of their subjects reported the vividness of recall which is a hallmark of flashbulb memories, many of the details they reported about how, where and when they heard the news differed between the two occasions.

Fig 10.3 Loss of detail from original memories of the Challenger disaster (January 1986) as a function of retention interval (after Neisser and Harsch, 1992).

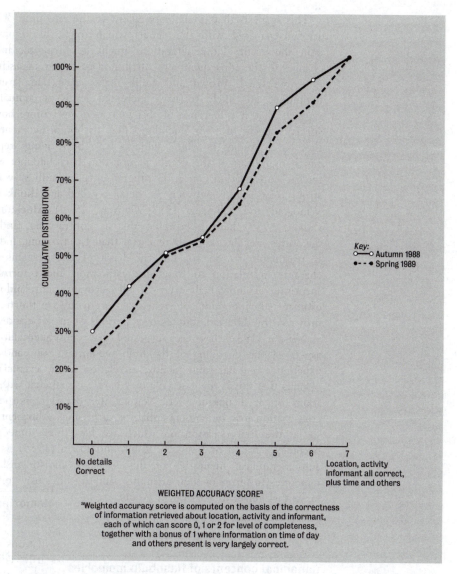

Key:
○—○ Autumn 1988
●--● Spring 1989

WEIGHTED ACCURACY SCORE[a]

[a]Weighted accuracy score is computed on the basis of the correctness of information retrieved about location, activity and informant, each of which can score 0, 1 or 2 for level of completeness, together with a bonus of 1 where information on time of day and others present is very largely correct.

Neisser and Harsch (1992) report a similar study, in which memory for the circumstances of hearing about the space shuttle disaster was tested. Figure 10.3 shows how little detail of original accounts was maintained after several months. Interest in this study also centres on the stability of particular attributes of the memory. Neisser and Harsch (1992) report that less than a third (30 per cent) of the information remembered was correct from occasion to occasion, while a further 22 per cent of the attributes remembered were partially correct, leaving nearly half of the details 'remembered' being quite incorrect. Together these studies make clear that the vividness of a memory should not be taken to indicate that it is accurate. Presumably, were it actually the case that the circumstances pertaining during the encoding of consequential information were directly encoded, such inaccuracies would not arise.

This suggests that events subsequent to the encoding of information alter or are amalgamated with the details which might be remembered immediately after the event. These alterations might be brought about by, for instance, changes in the consequentiality attributed to the event and the extent to which it is rehearsed. Brown and Kulik make clear that flashbulb memories, by definition, are likely to have increased levels of rehearsal. Neisser (1986) suggests that it is because of this increased level of rehearsal, rather than any special aspects of their encoding, that flashbulb memories have the qualities they have. Studies in which subjects have been asked to assess the extent to which memories of the events in question have been re-experienced (through media, conversation, etc.) or otherwise rehearsed, have not typically shown strong relationships between the detail recalled and the extent of rehearsal (see Winograd and Killinger, 1983; Conway, 1994). However, while some (e.g. Cohen, 1989) have interpreted this as contrary to the view that flashbulb memories are due more to rehearsal than to encoding, I do not believe that it is reasonable to do so. On the basis of the research reviewed in earlier chapters in relation to frequency estimation and remembering, it would be surprising if individuals were at all accurate or reliable in their ability to estimate the amount of rehearsal occurring in very different situations, provoked by different sources over periods of many years.

Neisser (1982) has also suggested that consequentiality is not a necessary aspect of the encoding of flashbulb memories, but can also derive from the experience one has subsequently, in relation to the events in question. It seems obvious that this is the case. We may have a casual chat with someone in a coffee room or at a photocopier. Neither the occasion nor the contents of the conversation may be consequential, or surprising, although meeting may turn out to be the first occasion on which we have met someone who, years later, becomes a friend or lover. As Rubin and Kozin (1984) have pointed out, vivid autobiographical memories of this sort are indistinguishable from flashbulb memories in terms of their attributes, and are obviously consequential only in so far as they relate to subsequent events.

Canonical contents of flashbulb memories

One further aspect of flashbulb memory is worthy of mention. Brown and Kulik's original proposal, that such memories were the result of some special mechanism, was based upon the fact that they appeared to have a canonical structure, minimally including information about: the location in which the news broke, the ongoing event interrupted, the source of the information, the affect evoked and the aftermath of the event in question. Neisser (1982) criticises this view, suggesting that these attributes together comprise the basis of conventional narratives. The coherent structure may merely reflect the schematic structure which allows us to exchange our personal experience of the events, which may be the occasion of much conversation and story telling. This point has considerable force, for two different types of reason.

The first is based on the empirical evidence reported by Winograd and Killinger (1983), namely that the elements of this canonical structure are certainly not inevitably recalled, nor are they recalled equally often. Thus, for example, studies of adults' recollection of the circumstances in which they heard about the assassination of Kennedy included details about the location (90 per cent), on-going activity (77 per cent), information source (70 per cent) and aftermath of the events (43 per cent). It seems reasonable to suppose that if all these elements were canonically related, it should not be the case that some are be retrieved with twice the frequency of others.

Secondly, Morley (1993) describes a study in which recollection of everyday pain among 137 medical students was contrasted with non-pain events. The data show that the former give rise to flashbulb-like memories, being rated as having been more surprising, having induced more negative emotional change, and having provoked greater change in on-going activity than their non-pain event counterparts. Morley also investigated the relationship between remembering the pain event, experiencing the pain, and reexperiencing the sensory aspects of the pain. Each of these would be expected to be a canonical aspect of a flashbulb memory. None of the subjects reported sensory reexperiencing of the pain, and 41 per cent of the subjects were unable to recall the sensory quality of the pain-event. The extent to which subjects reported distress in relation to the pain was associated with the reported frequency with which the pain event was rehearsed, and with ratings of emotional and activity change induced by the pain event. In contrast, ratings of the intensity and sensory quality of the pain were associated with the reported vividness of the pain event memory. Thus, what would be expected to be canonical aspects of the flashbulb memory of a pain event are actually separable, and are systematically related to different external metamemorial qualities (i.e. capacity to induce rehearsal, and reported vividness). In a previous chapter, it was found that many sensory aspects of experience are encoded independently of each other, rather than conjointly (see Chapters 1 and 5). These studies show that even in very emotionally arousing circumstances, what might reasonably be regarded as canonical aspects of a memory record are not encoded in an all-or-none fashion.

Status of flashbulb memories

In summary, although flashbulb memories have been a fruitful area of exploitation of naturalistic memory, there is very little reason to believe that they constitute special types of memory. It does not seem surprising that events that may be regarded as watersheds in particular phases of life and are comparatively rare, give rise to the segmentation experience. By virtue of being at the beginning or culmination of a sequence of events, they might also be expected to be intrinsically more memorable. Where the events in question also serve to change our lives, even by temporarily changing our outlook or the values we place on events, such as removing the leader of the political party we support, or give rise to thoughts about the justifiability of the money spent on space research, it would be surprising if there was not some qualitative shift in the attention we devote to the events concerned, and if there was not some coherence and consistency about their retrieval. The apparent similarities between the canonical attributes of flashbulb memories and general narrative structures facilitates the telling and retelling of both. However, flashbulb memories may serve another function, in allowing one's own personal narratives to be more easily related to, and interleaved with, external historical events, which others might also be expected to remember in similar ways. This issue will be returned to below, where the organisation of personal memories is discussed.

Experimental and field studies of personal memories

The foregoing sections discuss studies in which individuals' memories for a particular but unspecified event, namely, their earliest memory, and individuals' memories for a specific event which is not peculiar to them, were extensively studied. These offer certain insights into certain aspects of personal memories. However, they do not address others: What information do selves contain? How is this information organised? Does it change?

What do we remember of our lives?

One way of addressing this first issue is simply to ask people what they can remember. Variants of this very simple procedure have yielded important results. Cohen and Faulkner (1988) asked people to describe their most vivid memories, and having done so to rate these memories on various dimensions. They found that vividness correlated reliably with emotion and consequentiality or importance, and with the amount of rehearsal the memory had received. The relative importance of these factors in determining vividness of memory varied with the age of subjects making the report; for older subjects the amount of thought about the events in question was the most influential factor, while for younger subjects it was the emotionality and importance of the event remembered. About three-quarters of the memories described could be categorised into various types: those dealing with: births, marriages and deaths, (22 per cent); holidays (12 per cent); family (8 per cent); illness/injury (8 per cent); education (8 per cent); war (6 per cent); love (5 per cent); recreation/ sports (5 per cent) and trivia of various sorts (8 per cent). As might be expected, these vary with age, as Rubin and Kozin (1984), using a more homogenous, younger sample, showed. When subjects were asked to describe their three clearest memories, the most commonly reported events were accidents and injuries, sports, and those involving the opposite sex. These studies help to identify the more 'outstanding' memories we probably all have. Brewer's classic studies (see below) suggest that we can recall quite a lot of our everyday lives, as long as appropriate cues are available, and the interval between an event's occurrence and being asked about it is not very long.

Box 10.2: Remembering everyday events

Brewer (1988) reports two very detailed studies of what students remember from their everyday lives. It is the second of these studies, particularly the cued recall results, which concern us here. The 10 participants were asked to record their thoughts and actions at random intervals over about a two-week period, together with the time (day of week, date and time of day), emotion, location, the frequency of the events, any relationships between thoughts and actions, as well as a range of other ratings. In order to ensure that such recordings were made, the subjects carried devices which 'bleeped' whenever a record was to be made (about once every two hours). These could be switched off when the subjects did not wish to record their thoughts (e.g. when asleep or when writing would have been difficult). In all some 654 autobiographical events were collected. Subjects were given a cued recall test (i.e. were shown one cue, e.g. location, and asked to recall the rest of the information on the card) 7, 30 or 53 days after they had recorded the event.

  Cued recall was scored such that an event was regarded as correctly recalled where responses included 'some correct information, even if this was possibly inferred information' (Brewer, 1988, p. 50). Overall, locations were best remembered, followed by actions and then thoughts, but access to particular types of information was better with some cues than with others. Thus, actions are better recalled with thought cues (34 per cent correct overall), and thoughts with action cues (37 per cent). Cues for where events took place are less effective (actions cued with locations: 18 per cent; thoughts cued with locations: 7 per cent), while the time when an event occurred proved a particularly ineffective cue (actions: 9 per cent; thoughts: 5 per cent). Cueing with time of occurrence frequently led to the retrieval of the wrong action (33 per cent) or wrong thought (18 per cent), as did cueing with location (wrong action retrieved: 16 per cent; wrong thought retrieved: 13 per cent). Even the best performing cues for each type of information frequently led to the wrong event being remembered (wrong action, when cued with correct thought: 17 per cent; wrong thought, when cued with correct action: 22 per cent).

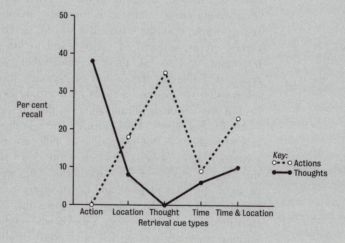

Correct recall of thoughts and actions given various cues (after Brewer, 1988)

Similar results emerged from studies we considered earlier in respect of how well the dates of events are remembered. Huttenlocher, Hedges and Prohaska (1988) show that across a wide range of everyday events (e.g. going to the movies, eating at restaurants, etc.) recently performed activities, that is, within the last week or so, are accurately dated and relatively well remembered, but beyond this, dating inaccuracy increases and events may not be retrieved at all. Pause for a moment and think about all that you did yesterday, in the order in which it happened, and then do the same for the day before. Now do the same thing for those same days last year. You are, I suspect, much less sure of what you did when, and you have also remembered less about last year's events than about yesterday's. Now try to do the same exercise with your last birthday, and with the birthday before that. Even though your memory of it is probably not as vivid as is your memory of yesterday, it is probably much better remembered than other events a year ago, and your memories of your birthday before last are also more confidently held. It is not the passage of time, but the consequentiality, self-relevance and distinctiveness which underlie these differences.

Personal relationships and personal strivings

As well as asking people what they remember, there is much to be gained from using less direct methods. For example, work by Bower and Gilligan (1979) provides evidence of incidental memory for trait adjectives where the decision made was directly about one's self, or one's mother. On the other hand, memory for trait words was worse when the trait adjectives were judged in reference to a less familiar person. It is tempting to believe that it would be possible to map out a graded structure of personal relationships using incidental memory of trait words to identify the closeness felt to different individuals.

Even using indirect methods, it does not seem reasonable to expect that memory for all aspects of everyday life might be detected. As we have seen from previous chapters, schema-like structures are used to interpret and remember much of what we encounter in our everyday lives. However, the powerful nature of schemata ensure that much mundane activity does not need to give rise to lasting, single, episodic traces. But we do, nevertheless, spontaneously remember certain events, and indeed, when asked to list those that are most vivid, most important, and so on, there is remarkable consistency across those that are reported. Following the notion of Neisser's interpersonal self, the self-relevant information we possess includes information about what we believe ourselves to be, but also about significant others in our lives.

Moffitt and Singer (1994) identify one role these personally important memories may play, showing that personal goals influence the affective responses we have to memories, and vice versa. Subjects wrote down self-defining memories and judged the affective quality of these memories. One week later they generated a list of personal objectives or goals, and (a) attempted to repeat the self-defining memories exercise, (b) rated them along 10 dimensions, and (c) indicated the relevance of their memories to the strivings. Subjects who recalled more memories relevant to the attainment of their strivings felt more positively about their memories. Subjects who listed greater percentages of things they wished to avoid in the future, that is, avoidance strivings, also recalled more memories related to the non-attainment of their strivings. Subjects with higher percentages of avoidance strivings also recalled memories which were less positive. Moffit and Singer also show that how their subjects felt about their personal goals was heavily influenced by the self-defining memories they had recorded a week earlier.

If the strivings, objectives and goals we have relate to our memories, then we might expect that over the period of our lives, there would be more change in the reliability with which we remember goal- or striving-related information than in the extent to which personal factual information is retained. Field (1981) reports data derived from interviews, carried out on people at 30, at 47 and at 70 years of age, which contained questions about family, education, occupation, and relationships with spouses and children. The average correlation for factual questions over this period was 0.88, but for questions about emotions and attitudes it was 0.43. The studies of Cohen and Faulkner and Rubin and Kozin, cited above, show that many of what we consider to be the memories most important to ourselves relate to emotion, evaluations and relationships. The Field data show that the 'self' of which these memories is comprised changes over the course of one's life.

Discontinuities in remembering personal memories

A number of studies, as well as that of Field (1981) show that even in adulthood, all of our life is not equally well remembered. These have been very usefully summarised by Rubin, Wetzler and Nebes (1986). Many of the studies on which their meta-analysis is based have made use of a procedure developed by Galton (1883), in which a cue word (e.g. pond) is given to a subject, who is then generally asked to describe and date some personally experienced event associated with the cue word. The recollection is then generally rated for certain qualities, such as vividness and detail (e.g. Crovitz and Schiffman, 1974), or the time taken to recollect the event is measured (e.g. Robinson, 1976). Rubin and colleagues plotted the dates of each of the memories retrieved across a range of different studies showing a remarkably linear relationship between the logarithm of number of memories produced per hour and the logarithm of the reported time which had elapsed since encoding (Fig 10.4). This linear log–log plot is also known as a *power law*. We will encounter these again in our discussions of skill development (Chapter 12).

Fig 10.4 Differential rates of retrieval from phases of one's life as a function of age (after Rubin, Wetzler and Nebes, 1986).

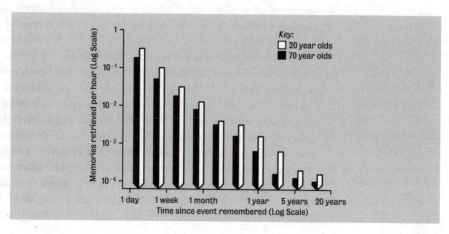

A number of aspects of this plot are worthy of note: one relating to the general shape of the function, the others to the discontinuities that are evident. The first is that memories are more retrievable from our recent past than from some time ago. Because this is plotted logarithmically, it obscures the standard scalloped shape of a power function. It also means, by virtue of being a power function, that ease of retrieval which is plotted here decreases at a constant, rather than an accelerating or decelerating rate. If this pattern were true both for individuals and groups, then, if we knew that an individual was likely to retrieve an event from yesterday, and from last week, we should be able to predict quite well how likely it would be that the individual could retrieve a memory from a year ago, or from 10 years ago. This would be of considerable importance for studies that rely on dating of memories and might even provide a basis for determining the likelihood that a spontaneously retrieved memory is confabulated or real. Thus far, such properties of power laws have not been taken advantage of as much as they merit.

A second aspect of the plot worthy of comment is the *reminiscence peak*, noted by Rubin and colleagues, which relates to the apparent overrepresentation of memories of events dating from when the rememberer would have been between 10 and 30 years of age. This over-representation was also found by Cohen and Faulkner (1988), who suggest that this occurs because many highly significant life events are naturally clustered in these years. As demographic and other social changes occur, for example, as people marry later, have children later in life, and so on, it will be interesting to see whether this reminiscence peak shifts across the age spectrum.

Although not evident from the function plotted in Figure 10.4, two other points should be made. First, data from a study of college students by Rubin (1982) shows a strong deviation from the standard power law when the memories recollected were in the region of 12 to 18 years old. Given our discussion above of the relative dearth of memories from early childhood, this deviation is precisely what we would expect. This portion of the general function does not have the same constant rate of deceleration that is evident for the rest of the function. Fitzgerald and Lawrence (1984) point to another discontinuity in this general pattern. They found that for older subjects the rate of decline in the numbers of memories elicited slowed sharply, in that the incidence of memories of events from more than 20 years ago was about the same as the incidence of memories which were reported to be some 60 years old (see also Cohen and Faulkner, 1988).

The studies just discussed show that the age of the rememberer can clearly exert a considerable influence on the slope of the function we find when data are plotted in this way. This partly reflects the age effect noted by Fitzgerald and Lawrence, but also the relative recency of memories making up the reminiscence peak. Some studies, such as that reported by Rubin, Wetzler and Nebes (1986), show a pronounced recency effect in the age of the memories retrieved, while others, such as Holding, Noonan, Pfau and Holding (1986), show a pronounced primacy effect. This can largely be explained by differences in the procedures used. In the study of Rubin and colleagues, subjects work through all the cue words used to elicit memories, and then, on a second pass, date the memories which have been described. In the study by Holding and colleagues, subjects retrieve a memory in response to a cue word, date this memory and then pass to the next cue word. Findings reported by Rabbitt and Winthrope (1988) show why these procedural differences yield these different patterns of results. Rabbitt and Winthrope (1988) found that when subjects retrieved a memory from one period of their life they were much more likely to follow this with other memories from that period than to switch to another period. Thus, if subjects retrieve a memory in relation to a cue word, and date it as an early memory, the memories subsequently retrieved are also likely to be early, because they will be searched for in terms of both association to the cue word and the temporal cues derived from the previously retrieved memory, which has, of course, been explicitly dated. The Rubin procedure is more likely to produce memories that are retrieved more evenly from across the subject's lifetime (see also Conway, 1990).

Personalisation of time

The differences in the relative retrievability of older memories, noted above, are borne out by a number of studies which have measured reaction times in performing various memory-related tasks. Poon and Fozard (1978), for example, studied the time three groups of subjects (young adults, middle-aged and elderly males) needed to name pictures of objects commonly used now, but not half a century ago, objects used then but not now, and contemporary and dated objects in common use in both periods. Older subjects named the dated unique objects that were relatively more familiar to them more rapidly than did younger adults, while the reverse was true for contemporary unique objects. No age difference in the speed of naming common contemporary objects was found.

Halpern (1988) has shown that individuals do not store and remember songs in isolation, but instead within a rich system of relationships which, at least for those without some musical sophistication, are based on non-musical aspects of the songs. Halpern (1988) showed that if candidate songs were selected from among songs previously categorised into those that were similar and dissimilar, those chosen from within the same categories were more readily confused during a speeded verification task. One basis on which this organisation might occur is in terms of the importance of the tunes at various periods in our past.

Knowledge of popular songs, dating from 1921 to 1974, among middle-aged and elderly subjects was studied by Bartlett and Snelus (1980). Subjects judged how familiar each song was to them, and when it was popular. When a song was recognised, they were encouraged to try to recall its lyrics and estimated when they had last heard the song. Middle-aged subjects made relatively few recognition responses to songs from the 1920s and 1930s, when they would not have been very old, if alive at all, while older subjects did recognise these. The last-heard judgements of all subjects were highly correlated with actual year-of-popularity. Melodies, rather than titles, were better able to cue recall of lyrics, but the type of cue used did not alter subjects' judgements of when the song had been popular. However, temporal judgements were substantially more accurate for songs that were recognised than for those that were not recognised, even when the lyrics of these songs could not be recalled. These studies, because they all relate to the age of the memory that the subject retrieves, might suggest that the personal memory is chronologically organised. There is abundant evidence, reviewed in Chapter 7, that subjects do not retrieve traditional temporal units very accurately, nor do they do so in an all-or-none fashion.

It has been suggested by Conway and Bekerian (1987), that rather than these canonical time units (e.g. minutes, days, etc.) personal histories are instead organised in terms of lifetime periods (e.g. schooldays, university, etc.). Their study clearly shows that retrieval was considerably facilitated by lifetime period cues. Robinson (1976) has shown, in a study of subjects' retrieval times for memories to action, emotion and object cues, that the organisation of personal memories is almost certainly not affectively based. In addition to these findings, and given the relative instability of the affective components of personal memories pointed out by Field (1981), affect is unlikely to afford an effective, stable basis for organising personal memories.

More recently, Burt, Mitchell, Raggatt and Jones (1995) found differences in cueing effectiveness, as indexed by memory for context retrieval times, between target and distracter autobiographical photographs. They suggest that these results indicate that autobiographical event memory structures are formed around the most unique event attribute. Burt and colleagues also report that rehearsal of an event and occurrence of an experience within an extended event (e.g., a holiday) also predicted memory retrieval time. Thus, like those of Conway and Bekerian (1987), these results suggest that extended periods of time that relate to specific activities or concerns, may be the basis on which personal memories are organised, albeit around what might be termed focal memories for that time of one's life.

■ Case studies of personal memories

There are a small number of highly influential case studies of one individual's memories. Neisser (1981) reports a detailed analysis of the memory of John Dean, a Nixon aide during the Watergate crisis. The testimony, running to several hundreds of pages, conveys an amazing level of detailed recollection. However, as Neisser makes very clear, while the gist of these recollections was substantially accurate, much of the detail was inaccurate or misplaced. A further point worthy of note was that Dean tended to remember himself as more central to events that he had actually been. Two other case studies have contributed rather more to our knowledge of personal memories.

Marigold Linton

Linton (1975, 1982, 1986) recorded two events in her diary every day, writing the details on separate index cards, which she later used to test her retention. Over a period of six years she continued with this recording procedure, testing herself every month on two randomly chosen cards. This impressive diligence in recording and testing is matched by a similarly high level of retention. Even after three to four years, some 65 per cent of the incidents she recorded were remembered, albeit not always in great detail. An aspect of the testing procedure used provided a serendipitous, but important finding. Cards were drawn at random, but some were, by chance, drawn more frequently than others. Analysis of her performance on these repeated incidents was systematically better than for those which had not previously been tested (Fig 10.5). It is easy to see why this might be so: since the retrieval of these items was more practised, they were reexperienced more recently than others, and of course, relearning was also possible.

Fig 10.5 Forgetting as a function of number of retrieval attempts (after Linton, 1978).

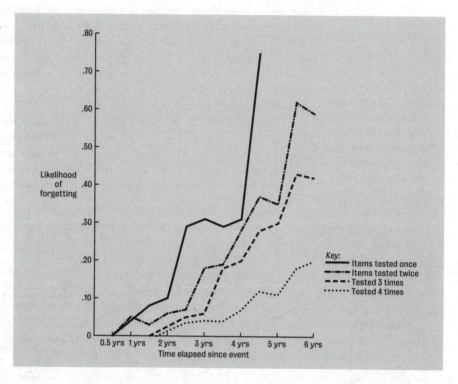

Linton also judged the importance and emotionality of events both when the original recording was made, and also at retrieval. Linton notes her tendency to forget less pleasant incidents more rapidly. Interestingly, in the light of our discussions above with regard to the desirability of an emotional organisation of personal memories, she found that the rated importance and emotionality at encoding and retrieval showed rather poor agreement. Another aspect of the findings Linton reports is also worthy of comment, namely, that repeated events appeared to lose their particular episodic qualities, leaving the memory of the type of event readily accessible, but only its generic aspects. Neisser (1986), in describing a phenomenon he calls re-episodic blurring, also notes that frequently encountered events lose episodic information, leading to abstraction and generalisation of what is retrieved. Nigro and Neisser (1983) suggest that in such cases, when the events are remembered they seem to shift from a person- (i.e. self) centred to an observer-centred viewpoint on the memory. It is perhaps worth noting that in remembering my earliest memory, it feels as if I am seeing the scene from a different perspective than if I was merely looking through the eyes of a not quite three foot tall four-year-old.

Willem Wagenaar

Wagenaar (1986, 1994) carried out a similar exercise to that of Linton, albeit using a rather more sound procedure. He recorded one or two of the most remarkable incidents per day, over a four-year period, taking care to report who else was involved in the incident, what actually happened, where the incident had occurred, and when it occurred. Each event was rated in terms of what he termed its 'salience', that is, how often the event might be expected to recur (i.e. once per day, once per week, once per month, once per year, etc.), the degree of emotional involvement evoked by the incident (i.e. none, little, moderate, considerable, extreme), and the valence of these emotions (extremely unpleasant to extremely pleasant). In the main part of the study, these detailed records of 1,605 incidents allowed him systematically to investigate the relative cueing power of the 'who', 'what', 'where', 'when' cues in isolation and in combination with each other. Overall, memory for the recorded events declined from about 70 per cent after one year to about 45 per cent after five years (Fig 10.6).

Fig 10.6 Recalling autobiographical events is a function of salience, pleasantness and emotional involvement (after Wagenaar, 1986).

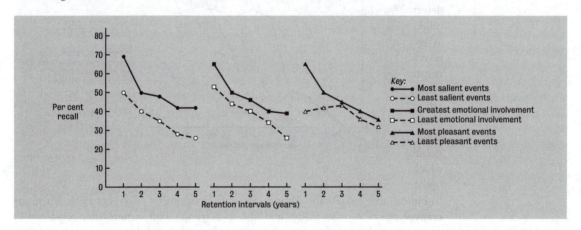

Wagenaar shows that 'who', 'what' and 'where' cues were almost equally effective when used in isolation, but cueing himself with when an event occurred was almost always associated with poorer memory. Not surprisingly, when cues were combined, retrieval improved substantially, even some five years after the original event. Moderate and high levels of salience and emotional involvement were associated with substantially higher rates of recall than events that were likely to recur on a daily or weekly basis, or that were associated with little or no emotional involvement. The shapes of the functions are remarkably similar, remaining more or less parallel across the five-year period (Fig 10.6). Interestingly, very unpleasant incidents are less likely to be recalled than pleasant or very pleasant incidents for up to two years after the incidents occurred, but by the third year pleasant and unpleasant events seem to be equally memorable (Fig 10.6). It is possible that this differential remembering of positive and negative events is actually motivated rather than merely an accident of encoding, vividness, distinctiveness and so forth, that is, perhaps what we remember and forget fulfils a role in our individual psychological make-up. This is the next issue we address.

Is memory self-serving?

At the outset of this part of the chapter, I briefly mentioned Neisser's (1981) study of the memory of John Dean, pointing out that Dean's recollections appeared to place him more at the centre of events than he was shown to have been. Both Linton and Wagenaar, in their early accounts of their data, show clearly that emotionally negative information is less well retained than positive information, thus raising the possibility that memory is self-serving (i.e. that memory helps to maintain self-esteem, or a positive view of self).

Wagenaar (1994) has recently presented a detailed analysis of 120 very pleasant and very unpleasant memories drawn from his corpus of recordings. By contrasting memories for events in which he played the major positive or negative role with those in which these roles were played by others, he sought to determine whether memory is self-serving. Wagenaar shows that while very unpleasant incidents where he himself was the active agent were more than twice as well recalled as where others were the agent, this pattern almost completely reversed for very pleasant incidents; that is, incidents in which he took the negative part were more memorable than those in which he took the positive part. In his painstaking way, Wagenaar rules out explanations due to differences in retention periods, different cueing orders, differences in salience and other memory distortions. Wagenaar postulates that the self is updated through relatively slow, rather than relatively fast, processes in personal memory, thus preserving stability of self, but resulting in gradual change. He distinguishes three ways in which these slow updating processes may operate: through suppressing the updating episodic information; storing both the old rule plus a tag (which is used to indicate that there is exceptional episodic information to be borne in mind); or concept-driven adaptation, in which the updating episodic information is distorted so as to be more similar to the schematic information already available.

Wagenaar found no evidence of suppression of negative self-related information, or distortion of the information about self so as to render it less negative (or more negative when the actors are others, as might be predicted by self-enhancement theory, see Brown, 1986). However, he still found that negative events about self are better retained than positive ones, and concludes that the schema plus tag explanation offers the best explanation of his findings. However, Baddeley (1994), in discussing the paper, demurs from accepting the conclusions he draws, not least Wagenaar's speculations about relatively slow and relatively fast processes in personal memory updating. Baddeley is especially critical of Wagenaar's plumping for a schema plus tag explanation, which Baddeley has frequently been critical of in the past. Instead, Baddeley suggests that the differences between episodic and procedural learning are sufficient to account for the findings, since procedural learning is both slow (thus allowing for stability and gradual change), but also proceeds without leaving the subject with any explicit recollection of the experiences which produced the learning (see Richardson-Klavehn and Bjork, 1988). Baddeley then reverts to explanations in terms of perceptual, storage and retrieval biases in order to account for the evident increased retention of personally negative incidents.

I am not sure that I would wish to go the full mile with Wagenaar with regard to the explanation of his results, but Baddeley's dismissal of them seems rather peremptory. As we have seen in an earlier chapter, the schema plus tag framework offers powerful accounts of event memory and both temporal sequencing and dating (e.g. Trafimow and Wyer, 1993). Because of this I feel that Wagenaar's proposal merits closer scrutiny. What Wagenaar does not address is the possibility that he may actually have a tendency to be rather self-critical or self-effacing, a possibility raised by Neisser (1994, p. 13), and which those of us who know Willem Wagenaar a little might agree with. Given that, it may well be that memory is indeed self-serving, without the need to appeal to some special mechanism in order to accumulate and store exceptional, schema-inconsistent, information about one's self. Rather more data is required in order to resolve these issues. Recently a very troubling and vitriolic debate has rendered this issue a far from academic concern.

■ Lost and recovered memories

Although the phenomenon of remembering something we believed ourselves to have forgotten is an everyday event, the status of certain types of retrieval from memory has proved very controversial. Specifically, in recent years, the terms false memory and *recovered memory* have been used to refer to accounts of traumatic events, not hitherto reported by the client, which are produced during therapy. Unfortunately, especially with regard to child sexual abuse (CSA), the suffering of victims of abuse and false accusations, and others' abhorrence of the crimes involved, have sometimes led contributors to the debate to hold what they might otherwise regard as unreasonable or unscientific views. The extremes of opinion reflect the belief that (a) the accounts given are memories of events that actually happened to the client, or that (b) forgetting, and hence subsequent memory recovery, of material of this sort is impossible, and the accounts are therefore fictitious. Often these points of view are supported by a number of rather debatable claims. In the sections below I use the term *recovered memory* (RM), without prejudice to whether the accounts given by victims are wholly, or partly based on actual episodes of abuse. The reader is referred to excellent special issues of *Applied Cognitive Psychology* (1994) and *Consciousness and Cognition* (1995) for more detailed consideration of these issues.

Some unreasonable claims

The debate about the veridicality of recovered memories has not been helped by a range of rather absurd suggestions. These have included the following claims:

1. *Since some recovered memories are unbelievable, all must be false.* Rather more frequently than one might expect, some purported victims of child sexual abuse (CSA) have claimed that their abusers were actually Martians who abducted, and subsequently abused them. Purveyors of the view that recovered memories are false have suggested that the impossibility of these accounts being true implies the falsity of all accusations (see Lindsay and Read, 1994). It should also be noted that Dittburner and Persinger (1993) have shown that suggestibility, ease of hypnosis, and estimates of the prevalence of childhood sexual abuse or alien abduction in the general population are all positively correlated.

2. *Since some RMs can be substantiated, all must be true.* The same paucity of logic is evident among some of those who believe that RMs reflect actual events. The more unlikely accounts are simply dismissed as being due to trauma-induced delusional states provoked by the abuse (see below).

3. *There is good evidence that CSA survivors suffer from depression, eating disorders, sexual dysfunction, low self-esteem, difficulty in maintaining relationships, suicidal or self-destructive thoughts. Therefore, people who suffer from these conditions are CSA victims.* This is obviously an illogical position. Nevertheless CSA survivors are indeed more likely to be depressed than non-abused people (22 per cent vs. 6 per cent). They are also more likely to be anxious (37 per cent vs. 14 per cent). Rather surprisingly perhaps, the incidence of bulimia among CSA survivors is greater than the incidence of anorexia nervosa (Lindsay and Read, 1994). This increased incidence is suggestive, but it is rather difficult to disentangle from these relationships the effects of other contributory factors such as the severity of abuse, the quality of early and later support, or inherent biological vulnerability to such disorders. Because of this it is very difficult, if it is possible at all, to determine the causal role of CSA in the incidence or severity of these disorders. Even were this to prove possible, finding a causal role of CSA in the incidence of, say, bulimia, should obviously not encourage us to believe that all bulimics have been sexually abused in their childhood.

4. *Repression does not exist, so there is therefore no mechanism to support 'memory recovery'.* Few cognitive psychologists support the Freudian notion of repression, with all its colourful dependence on early sexual rejection, screen memories, and so on. However, the fact that sometimes we forget, or are less likely to retrieve, things that are less pleasant (e.g. see Linton, 1975), that amnesia can be remarkably selective (see Baddeley, 1990; Morton, 1991), and that what we ordinarily retrieve is self-supporting (see Salovey and Singer, 1993) seems uncontroversial. These seem to offer a number of alternative reasons for retrieval failure, which may amount to motivated forgetting of specific information.

5. *Recovered memories are impossible; people just don't forget such things.* It seems unlikely that dramatic, repeated, incidents would leave no available traces in memory. After all, in terms of much of what has been discussed in previous chapters, such conditions should lead not only to durable encoding, but also to successful retrieval, albeit not necessarily of episodic details (but see Means and Loftus, 1991 for procedures which may retrieve episodic details from repeated events). Two issues need to be borne in mind here: (a) a distinction needs to be drawn between what can be retrieved and what is reported, and

(b) numerous incidences of trauma-induced amnesia have been recounted in the literature. These are addressed in more detail below.

6. *Therapists plant such thoughts, and implantation by therapists may occur more in certain types of therapy than in others.* Given the therapist's influential position in the therapist–client dyad, there can be no doubt that a suggestible client and unscrupulous therapist can create 'false memories'. Ritualistic or satanic forms of 'therapeutic' intervention give reasonable cause for concern from this point of view. However, difficulties may also arise from more routine aspects of more mundane forms of therapy. There is ample evidence from laboratory-based studies that subjects can be misled into remembering events which never happened (see Lindsay and Read, 1994; Chapter 5 in this book), and that some individuals are susceptible to failures of reality monitoring, that is, difficulty in distinguishing between those things that were imagined and those actually done or experienced (Lindsay and Johnson, 1987; Smith, 1979). Thus, role-playing, attempts at reexperiencing events from different perspectives and other similar techniques, may serve to create 'event' memories which may later be used by client and/or therapist to derive a view of the client as a person who has been abused. If such a view becomes established, the scope for this new 'self-schema' to reinterpret former experiences in a consistent, meaningful and ultimately memorable way is obvious.

There is therefore some basis for the claims and counter-claims made by those involved in the recovered memory debate. Ultimately, however, the dearth of verifiable evidence of 'lost', 'unreported', or 'spontaneously recovered' instances undermines any attempt to resolve the issue satisfactorily. Recently, some researchers have reported data which certainly helps.

Experimental studies of unsolicited intimacies

Saywitz, Goodman, Nicholas and Moan (1991) investigated female children's memories of a physical examination involving genital touch. A total of 72 five- and seven-year-old girls received one of two standardised medical checks-up: half received a medical examination which included a genital examination, involving vaginal and anal examination, while the medical examination received by the other half included an assessment of their spinal formation (i.e. scoliosis), which required the doctor touching the child's back. Memories were later solicited through free recall, anatomically detailed doll demonstration, and direct and misleading questions. Children in both age groups massively underreported anal and vaginal touching in the free recall and doll demonstration conditions (Not reported: anal (Free: 89 per cent; Demonstration: 89 per cent); vaginal (Free: 78 per cent; Demonstration: 83 per cent). No children falsely free recalled or demonstrated touching in the non-genital condition. Only when actually asked directly about it did the majority of girls in the genital touch condition admit that it had happened (anal: 69 per cent; vaginal: 86 per cent). Under these direct questioning conditions, some (3 from 36) of those who had not been touched said that it had happened. All subjects reporting anal or genital touching were questioned further. Two of those falsely reporting being touched failed to give further details, while one said that 'it tickled' and the 'doctor used a long stick'. Although resistance to influence by misleading questions was very high, children were more likely to answer misleading questions incorrectly when tested one month, rather than a week, after the examination. Younger children were also more likely to answer abuse-related misleading questions incorrectly than their older peers. These results, considered from the point of view of recovered memories, give some pause for thought. Among children at least, free disclosure of genital contact with others is unlikely, but direct and misleading questioning may both give rise to false reporting, with increased intervals between the experience and the interview also adding to this tendency.

Work reported by Leippe, Romanczyk and Manion (1991) is in a similar vein. Adults and children were tested on their direct memory for the events and participants during a six-minute period in which a test, purportedly to assess skin sensitivity was carried out. During this test, subjects were touched on the hands, arm, ear, nose and forehead by the male experimenter – the test being interrupted towards its end for some nine seconds by a female confederate, who enquired about the room's availability. Although all subjects indicated that they had felt each touch as it was administered, subsequently, younger children (aged between 5 and 6 years of age) gave less complete free recalls and answered correctly fewer direct questions about the incidents that transpired than did older children (aged between 9 and 10 years of age) and adults. In subsequent photographic line-ups, in which well-matched foils were matched for similarity with the intruder and toucher, the children were less likely to recognise the experimenter who had touched them during the test, and were poorer still at identifying the intruder than were adults. There is no evidence that subjects were stressed during the brief interview. On the other hand, Goodman, Hirschman, Hepps and Rudy (1991) showed that three- to seven-year-old children who exhibited more stress whilst having injections were better able subsequently to freely recall details of the event and were more resistant to suggestion. This is consistent with the studies above which show attention focusing in stressful situations, and improved retrieval for those details associated with the source of the distress. Less peripheral aspects of the situation would not be expected to show the same effects. However, it also implies that events that are not considered stressful at the time of encoding will be less well remembered and may not show this central–peripheral distinction (see relative lack of intruder–toucher identification differences, i.e. 73 per cent and 77 per cent respectively, in the work reported by Leippe, Romanczyk and Manion, 1991).

Traumatic personal memories

Wagenaar and Groeneweg (1990) describe in detail the recollections of prisoners at the infamous Erika concentration camp during the Second World War. Fifteen prisoners released from the camp happen to have been questioned about their experiences in the mid- to late-1940s. Later, as part of the case against Marinus De Rijke, a suspected Nazi war criminal, they were interviewed again, some 40 years later. Although many relatively mundane aspects of camp life were consistently remembered, the statements of these individuals in respect of major traumatic incidents were dramatically inconsistent. The following examples are taken from Wagenaar and Groeneweg (1990, p. 84).

Witness L. van der M. was beaten up by De Rijke, and was unable to walk for days. In 1984 he remembered only receiving an occasional kick. He also witnessed the murdering of a Jewish fellow-prisoner, but had forgotten all about it in 1984.

Witness G.S. reported that the guards Diepgrond and Boxmeer had drowned a prisoner in a water trough. He did not remember this in 1984, and even denied having said it.

Witness P.C. reported how a man died in his crib. The next day De Rijke and Boxmeer came in to drag the body away in a most repulsive manner. In 1984 P.C. had forgotten the incident, and De Rijke as well.

Witness G.H.V. saw how a fellow-prisoner was maltreated by De Rijke and Boxmeer, till the man died. In 1984 he had forgotten both names. In 1943 he reported how another prisoner De V. was violently assaulted by Boxmeer. In 1984 he reported that De V. was the perpetrator.

(Wagenaar and Groeneweg, 1990, p. 84)

Although we all forget surnames, it seems hard to believe that people who have caused one sustained cruelty over a long period of time should be forgotten, and that whole incidents of this sort are completely lost to the experiencer. Nevertheless, when confronted with their original statements 14 of the 15 former prisoners claimed to remember the incidents concerned. The inconsistency of these accounts by adult witnesses and victims, several decades apart, serves to show the difficulty in determining how decades of denial of abuse, and the later acceptance during therapy of its occurrence, should be interpreted. Although the evidence is frequently based on studies that do not involve the same levels of emotionality or trauma, the empirical data available seem to me to indicate that all results are possible: false allegations can be evoked by normal therapeutic procedures; truthful accounts can be forgotten and never retrieved, perhaps irrespective of the procedures used to re-invoke them; and because of the skill and support of the therapist, forgotten, true accounts can be retrieved.

Summary: Personal memories

Brewer (1988) distinguishes between: (a) personal memories, that is, particular episodes from a person's past; (b) autobiographical facts, that is, non-episodic memories of a person's past; (c) generic personal memories, that is, memories which incorporate several repeated events, and (d) the self-schema, which develops through an accumulation of 'nonimaginal autobiographical knowledge' (Brewer, 1988, p. 23). From the evidence considered above, and especially that later in Chapter 13, it would seem that while the first three of these are functional from a very early age, developing a self-schema and realising that one's own thoughts and experiences are separate from those that others have, takes rather longer. It would seem that long-term retention of personal memories before such self-knowledge has been acquired is unlikely, resulting in what has been termed 'infantile amnesia'.

Flashbulb memories appear to share many characteristics with other personal memories. Despite the early enthusiasm for theories that suggested that personal memories were veridical copies of the original experience (e.g. Brown and Kulik's 'Now Print' mechanism), reconstruction theories such as that developed by Brewer (1986) offer a better framework within which to understand the evidence presented above. Summarising this view, Brewer states that 'recent personal memories retain a relatively large amount of specific information from the original experience (e.g. location, point of view) but that with time, or under strong schema-based processes, the original experience can be reconstructed to produce a new nonveridical personal memory that retains most of the phenomenal characteristics of other personal memories' (Brewer, 1986, p. 44). Actions, thoughts and locations appear to be the cornerstones of such memories, but as shown in previous chapters, studies of personal memories also suggest that temporal and emotional information, and the consequentiality originally attributed to the event, does not appear to enjoy similar status or reliability. Nevertheless, despite these limitations, given the available evidence, the suggestion that 'recent personal memories are reasonably accurate copies of the individual's original phenomenal experience' (Brewer, 1988, p. 87), offers an acceptable summary.

Repeated retrieval of personal memories, or reexperiencing of similar events, serves not only to make them more available, but also makes them more likely to become subject to reconstructive bias. Where the personal events being remembered are much less recent, and the act of remembering them is infrequent, retrieval will also be unreliable, if it is possible at all. The self-serving nature of personal memory merits rather more empirical exploration than it has had. Without this, I suspect that we may not achieve a satisfactory understanding of what appear to be paradoxical effects of traumatic experience, namely, that while self-relevance is among the most powerful influences on learning and retention, what seem like major, self-defining, painful personal events are sometimes not very easily retrieved. Perhaps in their own ways both remembering and forgetting operate in service of the self.

Further reading

Applied Cognitive Psychology (1994). Volume 8.

Brewer, W. F. (1988). Memory for randomly sampled autobiographical events. In U. Neisser and E. Winograd (eds), *Remembering reconsidered: Ecological and traditional approaches to the study of memory.* New York: Cambridge University Press.

Consciousness and Cognition (1995). Volumes 3 & 4.

Conway, M. A. (1990). *Autobiographical memory.* Buckingham: Open University Press.

Conway, M. A. (1994). *Flashbulb memories.* London: Lawrence Erlbaum.

Howe, M. L. and Courage, M. L. (1993). On resolving the enigma of infantile amnesia. *Psychological Bulletin, 113,* 305–26.

Neisser, U. (ed.) (1993). *The perceived self: Ecological and interpersonal sources of self-knowledge.* Cambridge: Cambridge University Press.

Neisser, U. and Fivush, R. (eds) (1994). *The remembering self: Construction and accuracy in the self-narrative.* Cambridge: Cambridge University Press.

Discussion points

- What is your earliest memory? Describe it in as much detail as you can, indicating where you think you are relying on sources other than your recollections in your description.
- Contrast the advantages and disadvantages of laboratory-based and diary-based studies of personal memory.
- Discuss the relationship between the 'Now Print!' hypothesis and theories of episodic (i.e. instance- or trace-based) memory.
- Why might memory for traumatic personal events change over time? Would we ever forget them?

Chapter 11

Exceptional remembering

Chapter outline: Imagine for a moment that the telephone rings. A friend is calling with the new telephone number of someone with whom you have lost contact. Assuming your friend says the number just once, how confident are you that you will remember it correctly? On average, as we saw in Chapter 2, immediate span for recalling digits in the correct order is in the region of seven numbers – uncomfortably close to the length of a telephone number. In all likelihood, you would take the trouble to write the number down, and use this rather than your recollection of the friend saying the number when you later dial it. This shows us something about our confidence limits in our ability to remember, and also our tendency to rely on memory aids when these limits are reached. By contrast, the memory abilities of someone like S.F., who was capable of remembering 80 digits in their correct order, seem freakish and perhaps irrelevant to our everyday use of memory. This chapter in part attempts to show that this is not true, and that we all have, or can have, what seem like exceptional memory abilities. We first overview the memory abilities of people said to have exceptional memory abilities (i.e. mnemonists), and consider one theoretical account of these. We then consider how we can adapt these ideas to enhance our own memory performance, and finally examine in detail one application of related ideas that is widely used in evidential settings.

Key topics
- Exceptional memory
- Skilled memory
- Mnemonics and memory aids
- The Cognitive Interview principles
- Summary: is exceptional memory all that exceptional?
- Further reading

■ Exceptional memory

Later in this section, something of the range of exceptional feats of remembering attributed to a range of individuals reported in the literature will be considered. Before discussing the general principles that emerge from these, we first consider a couple of case studies.

Rajan

Rajan Mahadevan entered the *Guinness Book of Records* after a feat performed in his home town of Mangalore, India. At 24 years of age, over a period of 3 hours and 49 minutes, he managed to recite correctly the first 31,811 digits of pi (i.e. the ratio of a circle's radius to its circumference). Some years later, when he enrolled as a graduate student in psychology at the Kansas State University, his digit span was measured at 43 when digits were spoken, and 28 digits with visual presentation. Two years, and much memory testing later, Rajan's digit span had increased to 63 for digits he had heard, and 59 for visually presented digits (see Thompson, Cowan and Frieman, 1993). This increased digit span over a period of two years, and the greater improvement in immediate memory for visually presented digits, shows clearly the malleability or plasticity of abilities.

A number of very detailed investigations of Rajan's memory skill have been carried out in order to explore the basis of his superior memorial abilities. One such study examined Rajan's ability to recall the first 10,000 digits of pi when cued by position. A total of 2,000 positions were cued in a random order. Rajan's error rate was just 4.2 per cent, and his median time taken to retrieve a digit was just 13 seconds. The majority of his errors appeared to be due to miscounting rather than to misremembering. The pattern of errors seemed closely to reflect the source from which he had originally learned the numbers (i.e. a paper by Shanks and Wrench, 1962, in which the digits of pi are grouped in columns of 10 digits, with 10 columns making up each row, each page of

Fig 11.1   Rajan's differential memory performance for high and low frequency words and categorised lists (after Vogl and Thompson, 1995).

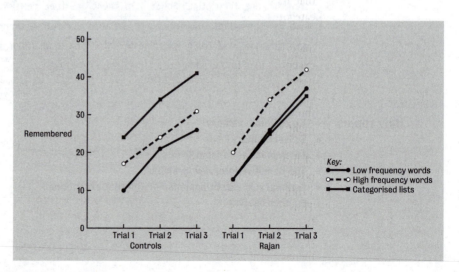

Key:
- Low frequency words
- High frequency words
- Categorised lists

paper showing 5,000 digits, made up of five blocks of 1,000 digits). According to analyses of his response times, and his own self-reports, Rajan was able to locate the correct row of 100 digits quickly, and having done so, simply counted across to the cued position. He further claimed that he encoded the digits in chunks of 10, just as in the Shanks and Wrench paper. In order to test this speculation Thompson, Cowan and Frieman (1993) contrasted his retrieval times for the next five digits when cued with a sequence of 10 digits that occupied a whole column, or that spanned two columns (i.e. last five of previous column and first five of next column), across the first 10,000 digits of pi. The difference in Rajan's response time to call out the five following digits was just 8 seconds when the 10 cue digits were a complete column, and 81 seconds where the cued digits spanned strings.

A range of other studies have been carried out to assess whether Rajan's exceptional memory performance is specific to digits. Vogl and Thompson (1995) report a study in which Rajan's memory for lists of words was contrasted with that of normal subjects. The word lists were 50 disyllabic, eight-letter, high- and low-frequency words, and a categorised list of 49 words (with seven words in seven different categories). Each list was presented and recalled three times. On average, after three trials, the control group remembered 26 low-frequency words, and 32 high-frequency words, while Rajan remembered 36 low-frequency words and 42 high-frequency words (Fig 11.1). This seemed to indicate a facility for remembering verbal materials as well as his obvious superiority with numbers. However, this supposition is undermined by exploration of the organisation inherent in Rajan's responding. This revealed a very high degree of subjective organisation (Tulving, 1962), in this case a tendency to recall the unrelated words in the same order on each recall trial. Thus, Rajan tended to use the same strategy that he used when learning numerical material; in this case he attended to the first 12 to 15 words presented which he had not yet learned successfully. Note that this does not appear to take account of the meanings of the words presented or to make use of their semantics to facilitate organisation and retrieval. This suggestion can be formally tested by contrasting Rajan's memory for the categorised lists with that of the control group. Controls remembered 41 of the 49 words from the categorised list, while Rajan remembered just 35 (Fig 11.1).

Thompson, Cowan and Frieman (1993) show that with a range of other verbal materials, Rajan's performance is no better than normal. This may be because his exceptional memory is specific to numbers, or because his favoured location-based strategy is less effective in these cases. Recently, a study by Biederman, Cooper, Fox and Mahadevan (1992) appears to have confirmed that the former is the case. The authors tested whether Rajan's spatial memory was also exceptional. Eight control subjects and Rajan were instructed to remember the position and orientation of 48 images of common objects shown either to the left or the right of fixation and facing either left or right. Rajan's accuracy for judging whether the position and orientation of these pictures had changed when they were shown in a different sequence was lower than that of control subjects for both judgements. Thus even with materials where spatial location information is at a premium, Rajan's truly exceptional ability to remember numbers using a spatial encoding strategy did not lead to superior performance, thus suggesting that his exceptional memory is restricted to digits.

S.F.

The striking feature of Rajan's memory performance is his facility with numerical materials. It seems clear that this benefited both from practice and extensive study, and there is documentary evidence of a change in his digit span over a number of years. Although his earliest measured digit span was in the region of 12 to 15 items, measured about a year before his phenomenal feat of reciting pi (see Horn, 1981), it is likely that this reflects the use of strategies which were already well developed. In contrast, S.F., when first assessed, had an average span of seven digits (Chase and Ericsson, 1981). Beginning in May 1978 S.F., an undergraduate at Carnegie-Mellon University in Pittsburgh and a committed long-distance runner, trained his memory span for an hour or so a day, several days a week over a two-year period. This training involved his reading a string of unrelated digits at a rate of one per second. Having read a digit string, he then attempted to recall it, increasing the next string by one digit if successful, and decreasing it by one where unsuccessful. The result, after some 250 hours of training and testing, was a digit span of 80 digits (Fig 11.2). Note how closely it approximates a power function of the amount of practice S.F. has had.

Fig 11.2   S.F.'s digit span as a function of practice (log-log plot) (after Ericsson and Faivre, 1988).

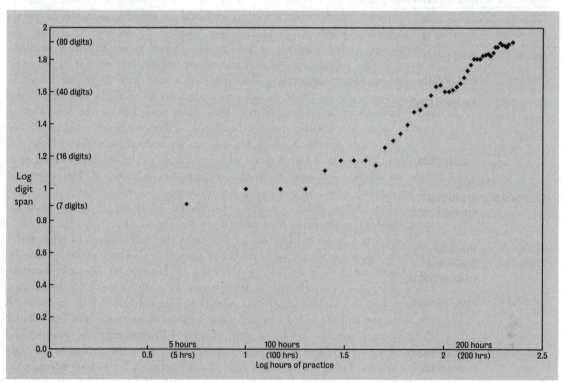

Ericsson, Chase and Faloon (1980) offer an excellent insight into the strategies S.F. used in order to develop this capacity. Initially, he grouped digit sequences in terms of his knowledge of the time taken to run various distances (e.g. 3,596 was encoded as '3 minutes and 59 point 6 seconds, just below a 4-minute time for a mile', see Ericsson and Kintsch, 1995, p. 216). This, and a similar encoding strategy based on ages and dates, was sufficient for him reliably to recall around 18 digits. However, beyond this level, he encountered difficulty in remembering the correct order in which these chunks should be retrieved, which he eventually resolved by spatially grouping the chunks. These larger units were then hierarchically organised to allow powerful and quite flexible retrieval. This was confirmed by Chase and Ericsson (1981) who showed that S.F was reliably able to report the digits located at different areas of the hierarchical retrieval structure on request. Similar techniques have been used to train other mnemonists, the most successful of whom is D.D. Despite having normal range digit span at the outset of training, D.D's last recorded digit span was 106 (Ericsson and Stasewski, 1989).

These data confirm that given very substantial motivation, and the intellectual ability to develop and adhere to appropriate strategies, average memory abilities can be highly developed. However, just as with Rajan, the exceptional abilities of S.F. and D.D. were restricted to numerical material. Both consistently show more or less average performance for letter span and words.

Box 11.1: Exceptional rememberers

Mnemonist	Reported by	Materials	Level of ability	Strategy used	Specificity
Inaudi	Binet (1894)	Digits	25 at 1 per sec.	Auditory imagery	Yes
Diamondi	Binet (1894)	Digits	Circa 20	Visual imagery	Yes
Finkelstein	Weinland (1948)	Digits	39 visual presentation 20 auditory presentation on a 'mental chalkboard'	Visualised digits in own handwriting	Yes
	Sandor (1932)	Letter span and visual forms	Average Average		
S.F. and D.D.	Chase and Ericsson (1981)	Digits Letters and words	From average to 80 with training Average	Extensive practice Encoded as running times	Yes
Rajan	Thompson, Cowan and Frieman (1993)	Digits	Unpractised digit span circa 15 after 2 years training circa 60	Learned by location, not imagery	Yes
Bubbles	Ceci, DiSimone	Digits	Forward and backward span 15–20	Location within string	Digits and playing cards only
J.C.	Ericsson and Poison (1988)	Restaurant food orders	20 detailed orders recalled	Associations between orders Worked as waiter	Limited transfer to lists
Ruckle	Muller (1911)	Digits Nonsense syllables Colours Nonsense figures	Circa 60 Exceptional	Visual imagery and semantic association	No

continued

Mnemonist	Reported by	Materials	Level of ability	Strategy used	Specificity
Shereshevskii	Luria (1968)	Word lists Digit matrices Nonsense words	Exceptional	Flexible use of stories and imagery Method of loci	No
V.P.	Hunt and Love (1972)	Prose Chess	Exceptional 7 simultaneous blindfold games	Recorded materials into verbal associations	No
T.E.	Wilding and Valentine (1985)	Digits Stories Faces	Exceptional Exceptional Exceptional	Figure-alphabet recording and many other mnemonic strategies	No
Aitken	Hunter (1977)	Digits	15 with 2 sec. visual presentation 20 with 5 sec. auditory presentation Maths professor and violinist	Meaningful patterns and rhythm	No

Specificity of exceptional memory

As we can see from Box 11.1, there are reports that other mnemonists have had exceptional memory abilities which are much less specific that those of Rajan, S.F., or D.D., such as Ruckle (Muller, 1911) and Shereshevskii (Luria, 1968). While the latter showed exceptional performance for numerical and verbal materials, it is likely that both had a facility with a much wider range of different encoding strategies which underpinned this exceptional performance. According to Luria (1968), in his wonderful description of Shereshevskii's memory abilities, graphic visual images were sometimes used to encode digit matrices, the *method of loci* to learn more complex verbal materials, as well as the integration of different sensory modality information which was greatly facilitated by his *synaesthesia*. This flexibility of encoding strategy, while leading to exceptional performance in a number of domains, does not need to imply that Shereshevskii was qualitatively different to the other mnemonists considered here, in just the same way that exceptional skill in one sports domain is unusual, but does not preclude exceptional skill in another. We will return to this issue in the next chapter, but, at least with respect to the exceptional memory abilities of the mnemonists we have considered above, there is very little evidence that exceptional abilities extend beyond the limits of the particular strategies which the mnemonist has learned to use effectively.

■ Skilled memory

Memory abilities of skilled performers

A range of studies in an increasing number of domains have demonstrated superior performance on the part of those skilled in that domain, when compared with those who are less skilled. Thus, for example, Chase and Simon (1973) showed that chess experts have available to them a vast number of specific chess patterns (or chunks), which allows them rapidly to recognise several patterns in a chess position they encounter, which in turn allows them to encode these efficiently and recall them effectively, even given the suggestion that the number of chunks which can be held in short-term memory is restricted (see Miller, 1956; Chapter 2 in this volume). One might thus expect that the chess experts' advantage in remembering where pieces were placed should extend only to those situations in which the positions of pieces were legitimate within the context of the game, and perhaps even where they were non-random. This is precisely the finding reported by Chase and Simon (1973) with respect to chess (see Fig 11.3), with similar results also reported for games such as go (Reitman, 1976) and bridge (Charness, 1979); activities such as electronics (Egan and Schwartz, 1979), computer programming (McKeithen, Reitman, Rueter and Hirtle, 1981) and medicine (Norman, Brooks and Allen, 1989); as well as sports and pastimes such as dance, basketball and hockey (Allard and Starkes, 1991) and even figure skating (Deakin and Allard, 1991).

Fig 11.3 Memory for legitimately located and randomly located chess pieces as a function of practice and enterprise (after Chase and Simon, 1973).

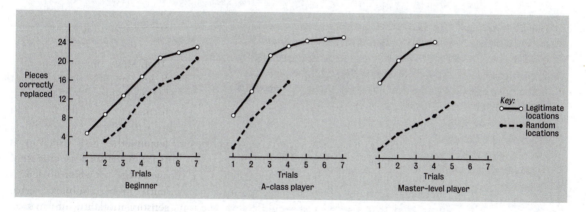

Some of these results were anticipated in the early work of de Groot (1966) on chess expertise. Expert and relatively unskilled players were contrasted in a number of ways. Experts, for example, when shown a chess board position taken from a game for just five seconds, were able to remember 90 per cent of the positions of pieces. Average club players, on the other hand, remembered only about 40 per cent of the positions of pieces in that time, taking a further four five-second glances to reach the 90 per cent level. In this work, de Groot also showed that chess experts, having selected their next move, were able to describe the positioning of pieces on the board very accurately. Later, Lane and Robertson

(1979) showed that knowing or not knowing that they would have to recall the position of pieces on the board did not affect the accuracy of recall, as long as these expert chess players had first decided upon their next move (Fig 11.4). Obviously, part of determining one's next move is a detailed consideration of the positioning of other pieces, and this allows for some degree of effective reconstruction to take place.

Fig 11.4 Expert chess players' recall of piece location as a function of orienting tasks and intention to learn (after Lane and Robertson, 1979).

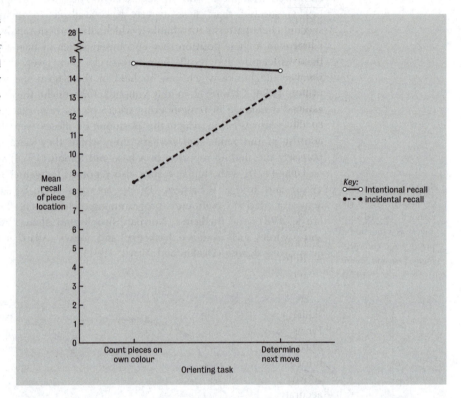

Importantly, when the experts were performing some other task which also encouraged them to look at all the pieces and their positions, such as counting the number of pieces whose colour matched the colour square on which they sat, incidental learning of chess piece position was minimal. Where subjects were instructed that a recall test would follow (i.e. an intentional learning task), but where the orienting task was the same, recall was substantially better (see Lane and Robertson, 1979). Similarly, incidental memory for data on patients after a medical review and diagnosis is far greater for medical experts than for medical students (Norman, Brooks and Allen, 1989). However, with respect to the Lane and Robertson study, for example, one might argue that the piece–square matching task does not encourage subjects to consider the interrelatedness of the pieces in the same way that deciding on the next move does. This might lead to reduced recall performance, not because of the absence and expectation that recall will be assessed, but because the orienting tasks (move selection, colour matching of pieces and squares) differ in the effectiveness of the encoding they promote. Despite this reservation, the intriguing implication of these results is that the extensive knowledge of experts only affords a real advantage where it is addressed or deployed in a way that is consistent with how it is normally used during expert performance.

Skilled memory theory

Chase and Ericsson (1982) proposed 'skilled memory theory', which has recently been extended by Ericsson and Kintsch (1995). The theory attempts to explain the exceptional memory performance of both task experts and mnemonists by claiming that such exceptional abilities reflect the use of more enduring memory rather than an expanded transient memory, but the capacity to do so is limited to specific tasks or domains. Specifically, 'individuals can acquire memory skill to accommodate expanded demands for working memory in a specific task domain' (Ericsson and Kintsch, 1995, p. 232).

The key elements of their proposal are as follows:

1. Material is encoded meaningfully, using preexisting knowledge.
2. Encoding involves attaching retrieval cues to some specified structure built on existing knowledge.
3. Doing so becomes progressively faster with increasing practice.
4. Retrieval involves the reinstatement of earlier mental states together with the retrieval cues associated with information in long-term memory.

As Ericsson and Kintsch make clear in their excellent recent paper, this skilled memory facility is attainable only under very restricted circumstances. First, 'subjects must be able to rapidly store information in LTM; this requires a large body of relevant knowledge and patterns for the particular type of information involved' (Ericsson and Kintsch, 1995, p. 215). Secondly, 'the activity must be very familiar to the experts because only then can they accurately anticipate future demands for retrieval of relevant information' (Ericsson and Kintsch, 1995, p. 215). Together these allow more enduring selective storage of information. Thirdly, 'subjects must associate the encoded information with appropriate retrieval cues. This association allows them to activate a particular retrieval cue at a later time and thus partially reinstates the conditions of encoding to retrieve the desired information from LTM' (Ericsson and Kintsch, 1995, p. 216). Sets of retrieval cues can become organised into stable structures, which are equivalent to what they term 'retrieval schemata'.

Ericsson and Kintsch's extended skilled memory theory appears to cope well with a broad range of empirical findings, and offers a useful new perspective on skilled behaviour, which we will consider in the next chapter. The restrictions placed upon this use of long term memory to support well-practised activity may also offer another way of thinking about the selective decrements which occur with various types of neurological dysfunction (e.g. the preservation of some procedural knowledge in dense amnesia), an issue which will also be addressed in a later chapter.

■ Mnemonics and memory aids

Those of us who feel that we do not have exceptional memories rely heavily on external aids to remind us of particular things or of when things should be done. These external memory aids may be rather formal electronic or paper diaries and calendars, or more informal notes, 'Post-its', or milk bottles left upside down reminding us that we need to buy more milk. Those of us raised as Roman Catholics remember well the rosary beads which were used as place markers to ensure that appropriate numbers of prayers of each type were said in the appropriate order, with numerous 'Hail Mary's, and 'Glory Be's punctuating contemplation of various Glorious, Sorrowful or Joyful Mysteries. Because of the ritualistic nature of the prayers, and especially because of their repetitiveness, rosary beads provide a ready solution to the difficulty which such repetitive tasks pose for the rememberer. I am reminded of another external memory aid which was widely employed in Ireland in the early eighteenth century. During the Penal Laws (1695, 1704, 1728), in an attempt to suppress the native Gaelic culture, children were punished for speaking Irish in school. Each 'offence' was noted by a marking a 'tally stick' placed around the child's neck, with the day's 'tally' being converted into beatings at the end of class.

External memory aids

Hunter (1977) offers a fascinating discussion of how the difficulty posed by having months of different durations is solved by different cultures. In Thailand, the names of months are adapted to reflect their length. Those with -on endings have 30 days (e.g. September: Kanyayon, November: Prusjikayon), those with -om endings have 31 (e.g. January: Magarakom, March: Minakom), while February (Kumpapan) is the only month with an -an suffix. Other cultures (e.g. Iran) actually regroup the longer and shorter months, such that all those with 31 days are in the first six months of the year, followed by five with 30 days, and the last month of the year which has 29 days. Baddeley (1982) and Searleman and Herrmann (1994) describe various methods of knuckle counting, which is traditionally used in some European (e.g. Greece, Finland), Asian (Tibet, China) and South American (e.g. Chile, Argentina) countries. Clench your fist, and count off the months of the year on knuckles and the gaps between them. January is on a knuckle, February on a gap, March on a knuckle, April on a gap, May on a knuckle, June on a gap, and July on a knuckle; continue counting the months off, returning to the first knuckle, and so on. All those months on knuckles are 31 days long, all others are shorter. There are other alternatives to these external memory aids or reminders, which we readily use under a broad range of circumstances. As defined by Searleman and Herrmann (1994, p. 353), mnemonics 'refer to the use of internal strategies or methods to make it easier to encode, store and/or retrieve information'. These range from simple rhymes to rather complex strategies for determining the day of the week on which any date falls (see below), and learning foreign language vocabulary.

A range of rhymes are taught to us as children to aid us with what seem like rather tricky problems at the time. Thus, for example, 'Thirty days hath September, April, June and November...', and 'I before E, except after C' offer us useful ways of knowing the numbers of days in the month, or simple spelling rules. These are widely used across cultures. An example I recall using extensively when learning to spell in Gaelic as a child, *'leathan le leathan, caol le caol'*, literally broad with broad, thin with thin, governs the letter order of vowels before and after consonants. First letter mnemonics are also very widely used. These come in two forms: acronyms (i.e. a word composed of the first letters of words to be remembered), such as HOMES (the Great Lakes, i.e. Huron, Ontario, Michigan, Erie, Superior), ROYGBIV (colours of the spectrum, i.e. red, orange, yellow, green, blue, indigo, violet), or OCEAN (the so-called big-five personality factors: openness, conscientiousness, extraversion, agreeableness, and neuroticism), and acrostics, in which the first letters of a series of words are used as reminders, such as 'Richard Of York Gave Battle In Vain' (colours of the spectrum) or 'On Old Olympus' Towering Top, A Finn And a German Viewed Some Hops' (the 12 cranial nerves: olfactory, optic, oculomotor, trochlear, trigeminal, abducens, facial, auditory, glossopharyngeal, vagus, spinal accessory, hypoglossal). The verse 'When Will This Silly Head Remember, Just How Easy Each Endeavour, Remains Having Had Help. Eclipsing Every Reasoning, Harassing, Hazy, Egotist's Method; Elaborately Jumbling Clear Concise Conjecture, With A Grand Gravity Giving Out Vexation', is an acrostic which gives the first letter of every English monarch from William the Conqueror to Victoria! Perhaps the sauciest acrostic is 'Lazy French Tarts Lie Naked In Anticipation', which stands for: lacrimal, frontal, trochlear, lateral, nasociliary, internal, abducens, the seven nerves in the superior orbital tissue. These types of external memory aids have also been described as 'naive' mnemonics (i.e. because they are made use of naturally, without formal training or instruction). These are contrasted with 'technical' mnemonics by Bellezza (1982).

Technical mnemonics

Technical mnemonics rely on the encoding scheme that is used to transform the information to be learned into some other type of format. For example, *peg-word* techniques are useful for learning lists where the order of things is important. The peg-word method operates on the basis that, for example, the numbers one to ten are associated with similar sounding words (i.e. so called clang associations), and the technique depends on the imageability and ease of semantic association enabled by these clang associates. Thus: one is a bun, two is a shoe, three is a tree, four is a door, five is a hive, six is sticks, seven is heaven, eight is gate, nine is line, ten is hen. To learn an ordered list, such as: beef, spider, train, ship, book, girl, radio, dog, rock, ball, images of the items to be remembered are associated with the clang associate (e.g. the tenth item might be remembered as a hen with its beak wide open carrying a ball). They can then be retrieved by simply recalling the number (e.g. ten), clang association (e.g. hen), and the image associated with it (e.g. hen with ball in mouth).

The *method of loci* can also be used for this purpose. To use this method, items to be remembered are associated with familiar locations, which are subsequently mentally visited in order to retrieve the target items. I might imagine going home, stepping over a joint of <u>beef</u> on the path, putting my key in the lock and disturbing a <u>spider</u> near the key hole, walking along the hall to the bottom of the stairs, where a toy <u>train</u> is on the bottom step, climbing the stairs to the bathroom, where there is a <u>ship</u> in the bath, which is being played with by a <u>girl</u>, and so forth. Later, by mentally retracing my steps I can easily remember the more or less random list of words I tried to learn. Story mnemonics operate in a similar way: the narrative structure of a story is analogous to the structure imposed on the materials to be remembered by associating it with various locations and mentally visiting these in turn. In *number–letter mnemonics*, the similarity between the visual characteristics of digits and consonants, for example, 1 and t, 9 and p (mirror image), 6 and b, 3 and m (3 on its side), 2 and N (2 on its side), can be used to generate words, for example, 'batman' which might help me to remember a bank account pin number (i.e. 6132).

Searleman and Herrmann (1994), following Highbee (1988), describe a technique for determining which *day of the week* any day *in a particular year* falls upon, which I find fascinating. There are a number of stages in the technique. You need to know the number of days in each month in the year, methods for which have been described above. Next you need to know the date of the first Sunday in each month, which requires learning 12 digits for each year. Thus, for 1997, the numbers which you need to remember are: January: 5, February: 2, March: 2, April: 6, May: 4, June: 1, July: 6, August: 3, September: 7, October: 5, November: 2, December: 7. All one has to do in order to determine, for example the day of the week on which 15 January 1997 falls, is to take the date of the first Sunday (i.e. 5th) and add the maximum number of sevens which can be added to this date without exceeding the target date to get the date of the nearest Sunday (i.e. 5 plus 7 = 12), and then count forwards until the target date is reached (i.e. Monday 13, Tuesday 14, Wednesday 15). Thus, my birthday in 1997 will be on a Wednesday, while Christmas day will fall on a Thursday.

In fact it is not necessary to remember the dates of the first Sunday in each month, merely the first Sunday in January. Given that date, and the following 12-word rhyme 'At Dover Dwelt George Brown Esquire, Good Christopher French, And David Fryer', it is possible to calculate the day of the month of each first Sunday (A = date of first Sunday in January, B = Monday (i.e. A + 1), C = Tuesday (A + 2), D = Wednesday (A + 3), E = Thursday (A + 4), F = Friday (A + 5), G = Saturday (A + 6)).

After a little practice, this technique can be used quite impressively, although its utility, other than as a 'piece' for a rather dull party is rather questionable.

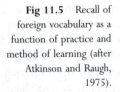

Fig 11.5 Recall of foreign vocabulary as a function of practice and method of learning (after Atkinson and Raugh, 1975).

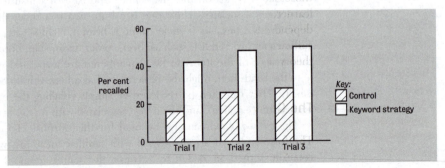

Rather more useful is the *linkword language system* (see Gruneberg, 1985, 1992). Atkinson and Raugh (1975) showed that the translations of non-English words (e.g. *zdanie*, Russian for 'building') can be easily remembered if the foreign words is first associated with an English word (e.g. dawn). This English sound-alike is then imaged (e.g. imagine the sun rising) together with the meaning of the foreign word (e.g. the sun rising and glittering off the windows of a large skyscraper). Atkinson and Raugh (1975), and in their subsequent work, demonstrated that this keyword strategy is more successful for vocabulary learning than other strategies (Fig 11.5). Its effects are certainly durable: I first learned this Russian word, together with an number of others, during a psychology laboratory class in Cork in 1980, and I remember their translations to this day.

Why are mnemonics effective?

Mnemonic techniques are both diverting and, when used effectively, can be very impressive indeed. Studies which have sought to quantify the advantage of using memory strategies of the types discussed above have generally found a substantial advantage for mnemonic techniques (see Highbee, 1988; McDaniel and Kerwin, 1987; Searleman and Herrmann, 1994). However, there are a number of caveats which must be added to this. First, as we have seen above, certain types of mnemonics are effective in rather restricted circumstances. Secondly, the successful use of mnemonics requires a substantial degree of practice, and their successful deployment is also subject to individual differences, especially in the construction, maintenance or manipulation of images (Johnson, Raye, Wang and Taylor, 1979). Furthermore, although these techniques offer substantial advantages, even those who have undergone specific memory improvement training using such strategies have frequently been shown not to continue to make use of the techniques they have learned (see Bellezza, 1983; Highbee, 1988). More generally, there is a difficulty in determining what the 'active agents' are in their success. If you have tried to use the strategies discussed above, a number of things will have happened. Mnemonics focus attention on attributes of material to be remembered. Using mnemonics may actually increase effort to learn on the part of the memoriser, and also, of course, as part of many mnemonic techniques, material is organised so as to be more meaningful, bizarre or unusual. Thus, although mnemonics appear to give people the possibility of demonstrating exceptional memory abilities, they do so largely by capitalising on those aspects of the material to be learned, the learning situation, and the learner, which ordinarily lead to effective retrieval. Similarly, their successful use depends on practice in using the technique in question, and a knowledge base sufficiently rich to support performance, just as is envisaged in skilled memory theory, as discussed above.

■ The Cognitive Interview principles

The foregoing sections have focused attention on ways in which ability to encode, retain and retrieve information can be changed by effort, domain knowledge and the successful deployment of strategies that combine properties which, it is widely agreed, enhance memorability. In many settings, especially where we unexpectedly witness an event, there is no opportunity to train extensively for an upcoming memory test, no substantial domain experience, and no possibility of carefully choosing and adapting a favoured mnemonic device before the experience begins. Few applications of the principles of retrieval enhancement have been as important as the *Cognitive Interview*, variants of which are widely used by police forces on both sides of the Atlantic.

In order to enhance retrieval in evidential situations, Geiselman, Fisher, Firstenberg, Hutton, Sullivan, Avetissan and Prosk (1984) devised a set of techniques which have come to be known as the Cognitive Interview (CI). In reviewing the cognitive basis of the CI, and its revisions (Fisher, Geiselman, and Amador, 1989; Fisher and Geiselman, 1992), Bekerian and Dennett (1993, p. 275) conclude that 'The cognitive interview technique (CI) has proven to be one of the most successful areas of applied memory research'. The principles on which the CI are based are described below.

Reinstating the encoding context

Rememberers are encouraged to reexperience as much of the situation to be remembered as possible, by attempting to recreate their feelings, thoughts and reactions to events, as well as other contextual details such as the surroundings, and so on. Obviously, as one might expect from our discussion earlier of context effects, Tulving's encoding specificity principle (Tulving and Thomson, 1973) allows a ready explanation of why this should facilitate retrieval. Context reinstatement is assumed to provide additional retrieval cues by reinstating features present at the time of the original encoding. While this can almost be accepted at face value, on the basis of earlier chapters, I think a number of caveats need to be added.

Context effects have been widely demonstrated when the circumstances of recall are close to those in which the information was first acquired. However, there is a dearth of findings that demonstrate context reinstatement effects where recognition, rather than recall is required. Although I believe that context effects will be observed where the recognition task is sufficiently difficult, that is, where the source of any sense of familiarity needs to be considered before a recognition decision is made, there is little evidence for this. For this reason, while context reinstatement might reasonably be expected to enhance a witness's recall, deciding which individuals look familiar among hundreds of mug-shot photographs should not benefit from context reinstatement.

Furthermore, as part of the context reinstatement procedure, witnesses are asked not only to recreate the physical circumstances of the original event, but also to attempt to recreate their thoughts and feelings about the event. As we have seen in Chapters 9 and 10, emotional appraisal is not only very labile, and a poor cue to other memories, but retrieval of mood-dependent, congruent and incongruent materials have all been demonstrated. Also, reinstatement of some types of detail might be expected to be more effective at retrieving particular types of information (see Brewer, 1988; Chapter 10 of this volume). Thus, reinstating location may facilitate the retrieval of both action-detail and thought-detail, although not equally effectively, whereas 'What were you doing at 10 p.m. on Monday 1st July?' may be much less effective at eliciting reliable information.

It must also be borne in mind that the benefits of context are curtailed where attentional resources at encoding, or at retrieval, are restricted. It seems reasonable to assume that attentional resource (or transitory storage) is restricted during the excitement or fear of witnessing a crime, and that the regime of a formal interview and the consequentiality of what is being undertaken may also reduce available resources at retrieval. Such restrictions may obviously serve to curtail context effects, and those of context reinstatement.

Despite these riders, it does appear that the CI increases the amount of correct information remembered without increasing the number of errors observed (see Bekerian and Dennett, 1993), but we must be cautious about how we interpret retrieval failures after the CI has been used. For example, given the limited evidence for context effects in recognition procedures, we should not be overly optimistic about the CI's chances of improving performance on identification parades.

Reporting everything, irrespective of the level of confidence in the material reported

The rationale behind this is that although confidence and accuracy are related (e.g. Loftus, 1979; Noon and Hollin, 1987), the relationship is unreliable (Kassin, Ellworth & Smith, 1989), and thus differences in subjective cut-off points may undermine performance, while externalising information may itself serve to promote retrieval of other details.

Once again, while externalising information may well promote the retrieval of other details, as Brewer (1988) points out, not all types of detail are effective cues of different types of material. Further, there is obviously a risk that erroneously produced detail may actually serve to promote the retrieval of other erroneous details and irrelevant events, or perhaps lead to the blending of different events. We also need to be cautious of encouraging soliloquies unencumbered by any need for accuracy, given that self-generated actions and speech tend to be more memorable than those that are witnessed.

Encouraging multiple recalls

This suggestion, which is part of the revised CI, is based on the supposition that repeated recall attempts leads to an increase in reminiscence relative to the level of forgetting (i.e. hypermnesia, see Payne, 1986; Shaw and Bekerian, 1991). However, hypermnesia can prove a rather elusive phenomenon, and must obviously rely on reconstruction, rather than retrieval, where the information was not encoded to begin with.

Recalling events in a different order

The rationale here is that since instance-based episodic information is stored during encoding (e.g. Logan, 1988; Norman and Bobrow, 1978; Morton, Hammersley and Bekerian, 1985), and a range of alternative retrieval descriptions may be used as part of the retrieval process, encouraging recall in a different order may increase the amount of material reported. However, as is clear from other research in the eyewitness testimony literature, the order in which retrieval is required may materially and detrimentally affect the amount and accuracy of what is retrieved (e.g. Bekerian and Bowers, 1983). Furthermore, reexperiencing the events in a different order, since it is likely to influence retrieval of the narrative coherence of the events, seems likely to undermine context reinstatement. Because of these difficulties, this particular principle is less widely adhered to by CI enthusiasts.

Encourage changes in perspectives, in order to force change in retrieval description

As Bekerian and Dennett (1993) astutely point out, the theoretical support for this proposal is derived from Anderson and Pichert's (1978) task, in which rememberers shift their conceptual perspective, or reinstate a different schema for thinking about the situation, rather than requiring a change in perceptual perspective which the CI encourages. Unfortunately, the same literature also shows quite clearly that such results rely on the instantiating of some schema-like structure, which serves to increase correct retrieval, but also increases the potential for error. Although it is the strongest claim for the CI that error rates do not increase, the confusion as to whether it is a conceptual or perceptual perspective which is being reinstated, and the strong prediction of increased error resulting from schema-influenced retrieval, should encourage us to examine this claim very closely.

Status of the Cognitive Interview

Taken together, although the principles on which the CI are based have some theoretical motivation, the implementation of this theoretical basis within the CI is not always convincing. There are a number of other issues which need to be considered in relation to the use of the CI.

For obvious reasons, evidence for the CI is largely based on staged incidents, slides or video. However, as discussed earlier in relation to the impact of emotional arousal on memory, there is good reason to believe that such staged incidents are unlikely to result in levels of arousal commensurate with those that occur in situations which are actually threatening or frightening. Because there is good evidence to believe that attention distribution and/or encoding may be dramatically affected in such situations (e.g. Burke, Heuer and Riesberg, 1992), extrapolating from staged to actual incidents is fraught with difficulty. If, as one would predict on the basis of the Easterbrook hypothesis and weapon focus, certain types of details are simply not encoded, what emerges as the result of context reinstatement must be based on inference rather than recollection. This is obviously problematical from a legal point of view. Indeed, it is suggested by Bekerian and Dennett (1993) and Memon, Wark, Bull and Koehnken (in press) that the CI particularly enhances retrieval of what might otherwise be considered to be 'peripheral' detail (see Chapter 9). If such details are not encoded, and cannot therefore be retrieved, little reliable benefit can accrue from the externalising of information, which is thought to promote retrieval of other details (Reporting everything, see above).

Another difficulty is that since the CI depends crucially on the retrieval of episodic information, it may prove less useful and reliable in circumstances in which episodic information is restricted, for example, as the result of high levels of similarity between repeated situations (what Neisser, 1988 referred to as re-episodic blurring, see Chapter 10). Thus, where a crime is repeated and quasi-ritualistic, as in some forms of child abuse, one might argue that the CI may be of reduced utility. Fisher and Geiselman (1992) suggest that the CI may be most effective in informationally dense situations (i.e. where the number of actions is high and the pace at which they occur rapid). Obviously, a scenario in which relatively little happens, as Bekerian and Dennett (1993) point out, may be easier to retrieve spontaneously simply because of a reduced memory load. They also point out that 'Causally linked actions or episodes are easier to reconstruct, primarily because the person has a macro-structure on which to rely (e.g. Bransford and Johnson, 1972). It could be argued that the CI will not be as effective on scenarios which are causally linked as the scenarios already have a (sic) extant structure through which retrieval can be guided' (Bekerian and Dennett, 1993, p. 289).

Even where the technique might prove successful, if context reinstatement were to prove effective, then it is to be anticipated that the CI may increase flashbacks (see Fisher and Geiselman, 1992), thus greatly increasing the trauma experienced by the rememberer, and should therefore be used with caution. Finally, the claim that the CI increases the amount of correct information without increasing errors has recently been challenged by Memon, Wark, Bull and Koehnken (in press), when compared with a structured interview.

■ Summary: Is exceptional memory all that exceptional?

The previous section raises more general issues about the CI and its efficacy, since in some circumstances, the CI may be effective not because of the cognitive principles on which it is based, but because of the rapport building and greater care in interviewing which the CI encourages. Nevertheless, although issue can be taken with aspects of the CI, it has unquestionably been shown to be effective in a very broad range of circumstances. However, although proponents proudly point to its theoretical foundations, there is reason to be cautious about whether the theoretical inferences are actually appropriate. Because it enjoys a special status as, perhaps, a flagship of applied memory research, I think it is all the more important that the theoretical basis of the CI is properly established.

Improving the accuracy with which information is retrieved in evidential settings is obviously of societal importance. However, the factors which influence this accuracy are also of profound theoretical importance – here at least, theory and application are intimately intertwined.

Although the CI seeks to take advantage of many well-recognised properties of human memory, the contrast in emphasis between CI research, and that of skilled memory is quite striking. Much of the latter literature emphasises the need to locate newly acquired information securely within what the individual already knows, and the need to repeatedly practise retrieving that information. For the witness to a crime, this would seem neither practicable or desirable, but there is much to be lost from having the two literatures as dissociated from each other as they appear to be.

In circumstances where people are expecting to have to remember, and where they are well-practised at doing so with the particular type of material, there is no denying the impressive memory performance of some of the individuals considered above. The faltering uncertainty with which we try to retain an unfamiliar telephone number is sobering indeed when we think that some people can comfortably deal with digit strings 10 times that length. Of course, as pointed out above, they do not do so without considerable effort, and considerable virtuosity in recoding and reorganising the material they try to retain and retrieve. There is very little convincing evidence that such highly unusual levels of performance extend much beyond specific types of materials, or the well-tried strategies mnemonists develop. Those whose performance appears less specific do also seem to have developed a broader range of strategies. Similarly, those who display exceptional memory abilities as part of their skills in some domain (e.g. chess, bridge, etc.), have exceptional ability only within that domain, and arguably only within the well-practised, legitimate uses of material from that domain. Of course the relationship between different types of strategy and different types of material is not isomorphic; certain types of strategy may be more effective at dealing with a broader range of different types of materials than others. Similarly, expertise in one domain may facilitate performance in other domains, depending on the degree of overlap in the processing requirements of the tasks within the two domains. Despite the advantages these exceptional individuals appear to enjoy, the strategies used do little more than capitalise on processing and memory characteristics which the vast majority of us share. I believe that any of us, or at least most of us, given the dedicated application of appropriate encoding and retrieval strategies, can perform as if we have exceptional memories. In fact, I believe that most of us demonstrate what in laboratory contexts might seem exceptional memory abilities in our everyday lives, as we shall see in the next chapter.

■ Further reading

Bekerian, D. A. and Dennett, J. L. (1993). The Cognitive Interview technique: Reviving the issues. *Applied Cognitive Psychology, 7*, 275–97.

Ericsson, K. A. and Kintsch, W. (1995). Long-term working. *Psychological Review, 102*, 211–45.

Fisher, R. P. and Geiselman, R. E. (1992). *Memory enhancing techniques for investigative interviewing: The Cognitive Interview.* Springfield Ill: Charles C Thomas.

Luria, A. R. (1968). *The mind of a mnemonist.* New York: Basic Books.

Memon, A., Wark, L., Bull, R. and Koehnken, G. (in press). Isolating the effects of the Cognitive Interview technique. *British Journal of Psychology.*

Vogl, R. J. and Thompson, C. P. (1995). The specificity and durability of Rajan's memory. In A. F. Healy and L. E. Bourne (eds) *Learning and memory of knowledge and skills.* Thousand Oaks, CA.: Sage.

Discussion points

- We all have the capacity to have exceptional memory abilities. Discuss.
- Skilled memory theory implies that we no longer need separate short-term memory processes and structures. Discuss.
- Choose any three mnemonic strategies you use to remember particular information. Why do they work? When do they fail?
- Critically evaluate the Cognitive Interview technique, its theoretical basis and practical application.

Chapter 12

Procedural memories and skill

Chapter outline: Earlier, in discussing different types of memory, we distinguished between three types of knowledge. First we considered semantic or declarative knowledge, that is, generic factual or categorical information which does not include the particular experiences of the rememberer during the encoding of information, which are peculiar to a specific situation. We distinguished this from procedural knowledge, generic information which supports the performance of some activity but which, once again, does not include the particular experiences of the rememberer during the encoding of particular pieces of information. Finally, we also considered the evidence which suggests that we also have a third type of knowledge, namely episodic knowledge, in which particular instances of information we have encountered are retained. In this chapter, the development and maintenance of procedural knowledge is considered in detail, but a number of the issues addressed previously will also be reconsidered. Specifically, we return to the issue of automaticity, schema theories, implicit–explicit learning and the separation between semantic and procedural knowledge.

Key topics
- Procedural knowledge, procedures and skill
- The role of practice
- Benefits and drawbacks of prior knowledge
- Generic and episodic knowledge: Theories of skill acquisition
- Summary: Episodic and generic procedural memory
- Further reading

▪ Procedural knowledge, procedures and skill

Memory theorists have had something of an on–off relationship with skill. Generally, since much early work on skill related to motor activity, while generally memory researchers concentrated on different material, the research under the memory banner and that under the skills banner has tended to remain relatively separate. As a result, what skills theorists had to say about memory went relatively unheeded by memory researchers, as did what memory researchers had to say about skill. The cognitive revolution, most particularly that wave of activity that focused attention on how performance depends upon, and reflects the externalisation of, knowledge, has brought about a considerable and overdue change. Hence, talk of procedural knowledge, how it might be acquired, stored and retrieved, is effectively a discussion about skill, its acquisition, and how it is maintained and performed.

Skilled behaviour

A skill is any repertoire of acquired purposeful behaviour at which an individual can become proficient. Skilled performance is characterised by a range of quantitative and qualitative changes in behaviour. Generally speaking, skilled performers take less time to complete tasks and commit fewer and less serious errors. The techniques that skilled performers use are often different to those of less experienced unskilled performers. They adopt less effortful and more effective working methods, and there is more evidence of close connections between actions and stimulus inputs. Finally, skilled performers are frequently said to have different attentional patterns to unskilled performers, have greater ability to cope with additional simultaneous tasks, and are better able to resist the deleterious effects of fatigue and stress (see Annett, 1991).

Skills research has continued throughout the development of psychology as a scientific discipline. Much attention has been devoted to the investigation of changes in the performance of simple laboratory tasks involving perceptual-motor skills such as tracking or cognitive tasks, for example, learning of simple verbal or pictorial materials. There are a number of exceptions to this, from the early work of Bryan and Harter (1897) to work carried out to support military or space research (see Schendel and Hagman, 1991). Whatever the task studied, or the theoretical orientation of the investigators involved, there is general agreement that skills develop as a consequence of instruction and transfer from other tasks, practice on the task itself, and feedback on performance. There is also broad agreement that skill acquisition is best viewed as a three-stage process, and on the nature of those stages, although the terminology used differs considerably.

Stages in the acquisition of skills

The ACT* theory outlined by Anderson (1983) regards the acquisition of skill as a form of knowledge compilation in which general *production rules* (i.e.

'procedures' or ways of using information) come to govern specific segments of declarative knowledge (i.e. information and beliefs about things). As learning proceeds, a core of relatively specific segments of declarative knowledge becomes directly incorporated into production rules (or 'proceduralised'). Learners are considered to proceed through a phase dominated by declarative knowledge, a phase where this knowledge is 'compiled' into productions which might, for example, support action, and finally to the level where this knowledge becomes 'proceduralised'. An earlier view of skill acquisition, that proposed by Fitts (1964; Fitts and Posner, 1967), will be used to explain the nature of the three stages as they might apply to an everyday skill such as learning to drive.

According to Fitts (1964) and Fitts and Posner (1967), skill acquisition is characterised by a shift from cognitive to non-cognitive control, moving progressively through a 'cognitive' phase, an 'associative' phase, and ultimately an 'autonomous' phase. The initial ('cognitive') phase in the learning of any skill is dominated by the learning rules (e.g. always check whether car is in gear before commencing start-up routine), procedures (e.g. mirror-signal-manoeuvre) and other items of factual knowledge (e.g. other motorists dislike hesitancy), by means of instruction or trial and error and feedback. Information gained about the traffic system whether as a pedestrian, passenger or rider, and actions which are part of other skills (e.g. motor co-ordination, judgements of speed and distance acquired through games or other forms of travel) are selected and rearranged into elements that might serve the new skill. The second ('associative') and third ('autonomous') phases are dominated by practice rather than by instruction, but feedback on errors in performance is still essential. During these phases stimuli become increasingly associated with responses (the associative phase), and responses with each other, such that chain reactions are set in train. At this stage, actions and decisions are 'corrected' or 'tuned' by feedback, perhaps as provided by an instructor. As practice continues and the performance of components of a manoeuvre become regular (or predictable), performance of the manoeuvre as a whole becomes increasingly independent of cognitive control and external feedback (the autonomous phase, or 'closed loop control').

Monitoring and control as skills develop

Monitoring or control of performance moves from (1) conscious monitoring of behaviour (on the part of the performer or an instructor) at the early stages of skilled performance, to (2) adjustment or correction of practised skill components, to (3) relative independence from 'external' sources of feedback and increased reliance on feedback from individual components of the task (i.e. task-intrinsic feedback). Such levels of skill and control are often regarded as being nested within a hierarchical structure (Underwood and Everatt, 1996). Hence, at any skill level the slowing of one component causes disruption, or a consequent slowing in the other associated components of a manoeuvre. At the highest skill level, however, the performer is not, one suspects, conscious of such slowing or distortion, and may ordinarily not even be aware of its results. This has been elegantly demonstrated under laboratory conditions by Rabbitt (see Rabbitt, 1993), in a phenomenon known as *post-error slowing*. Here, even in a highly routine, well-practised task which involves a sequence of simple actions, when an incorrect response is made, following responses are slowed, even though the subjects later report not being aware that errors have been made.

There are a number of consequences of a portion of activity becoming 'autonomous'. One consequence is that the well-practised activities become less amenable to change and disruption. Another is that they place less demand on attentional capacities (see Anderson, 1983 and Baddeley, 1986). This is partly because individual components have become more organised, and partly because there is less need to monitor external sources for feedback on current performance. As a result, the way we make use of external information also changes. Rumelhart and Norman (1978) suggest that new knowledge is accumulated ('accreted') and that processes dealing with new information can also be 'tuned', that is, selectively adjusted to take account of new information, or even restructured (Cheng, 1985). At a more mundane level, for the learner driver, concerns about acquisition of vehicle control skills are initially paramount. However, once these become more or less 'autonomous', aspects of the driving task above and beyond vehicle control skills now stand a better chance of being successfully acquired. For the experienced driver, the consequence of components becoming 'autonomous' is that driving- and non-driving-related tasks can be carried out simultaneously without a decrement in performance.

■ The role of practice

Practice is generally assumed to be essential for skill development. Precisely how much practice is required depends on a number of factors, including the difficulty of the task, the criterion to be reached, transfer from similarity to skills already possessed, the type of practice and feedback available, and the aptitudes of the person learning the skill (Ackerman, 1988). It is generally the case that extensive practice is required for proficiency in a skill, most especially where the requirement is that it should become 'automated'.

Box 12.1: Effects of long-term practice

To emphasise the points made above, let us consider the role of practice in quite simple tasks. Continued practice improves performance, but it does not necessarily lead to perfection, nor indeed to stable performance. Consider, for example, the findings reported by Crossman (1959) who studied the time taken by an experienced cigar roller to perform a highly practised task. After the first million trials (over a period of one year), the operation took on average about 10 minutes. After a further million trials the time required was around 8 minutes, a reduction of some 20 per cent. This should encourage caution when estimating how long it will take (either in time or amount of practice) to acquire a skill, and what the effects of continued practice are likely to be.

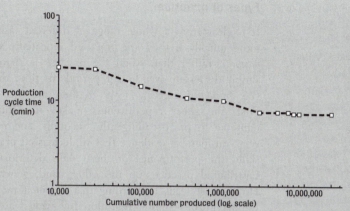

Practice and speed in cigar making (after Crossman, 1959).

Examining the figure taken from Crossman closely we see that even in a comparatively simple, yet skilled task like cigar rolling, performance had not reached an asymptote even after two years of highly frequent and extensive practice. Certainly performance settles down from time to time but while the direction of change is always consistent, performance is far from stable over the acquisition period studied. In a task like cigar rolling, where the same operation is carried out every time the task is performed, one would predict an improvement due to practice until a performance asymptote is reached. In terms used by Schneider and Shiffrin (1977), such a task involves 'consistent mapping', that is, use of an identical rule to govern performance each and every time the task is carried out. Schneider and Shiffrin distinguish tasks of this sort from those that involve 'variable mapping', that is, where the same stimulus may require different types of response under certain conditions. Performance on tasks involving 'variable mapping' does improve initially, but is otherwise unaffected by repeated practice.

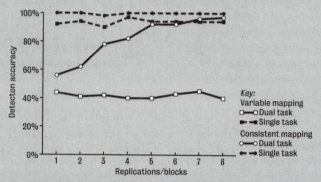

Consistently and variably mapped semantic search as a function of practice and single- or dual-task conditions (after Schneider and Fisk, 1984).

Under laboratory conditions, Schneider and Fisk (1984) have demonstrated that where 'constant mapping' and 'variable mapping' of rules is required, not only does the effect of practice differ in each case, but also combining each task with a secondary task yields differential effects. This now almost axiomatic differentiation of tasks, between those which are, or can become, 'automated' and those who will always require a substantial degree of 'controlled' supervision, is crucial to how we conceptualise the acquisition of skill.

Types of practice

It is clear from a whole range of different tasks that skills are acquired much more quickly if they are practised repeatedly without interruption (i.e. *massed practice*), rather than when the practice is shared with some other task, or is simply dispersed over longer periods of time than it takes to perform the task (i.e. *distributed practice*). However, there are two difficulties with massed practice. First, the sheer repetitiveness makes it difficult to maintain motivation to continue to practise diligently. Secondly, and much more importantly, there is very considerable evidence that while massed practice increases the acquisition of skills, the performance of these skills deteriorates more rapidly after training. Distributed practice, on the other hand, generally leads to slower acquisition. However, it leads to learning that is much more durable. Thus, as a study by Keppel (1964) shows, retention following learning by massed practice initially leads to better retention of words than learning by distributed practice. However, as the retention interval increases, the advantage of massed practice learning reduces markedly, such that for retention intervals of one day or longer, learning by distributed practice is associated with far greater retention (Fig 12.1).

Fig 12.1 Retention following learning through distributed or massed practice (after Keppel, 1964).

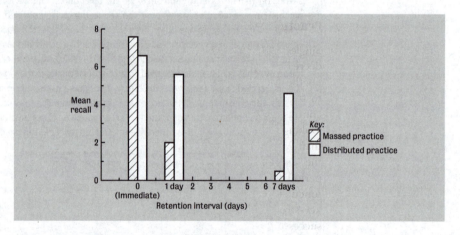

For verbal tasks, acquisition is better when the interval between task repetitions is minimised (i.e. massed training), but retention is better when the interval between repetitions is increased (i.e. spaced training, see Crowder, 1976; Glover and Corkhill, 1987; Greene, 1989). In general the retention benefits of spaced training for verbal tasks increase as the interval between repetitions increases (Crowder 1976) provided that the interval is not too long (Glenberg, 1974; Young, 1966). Presumably, when the interval is too long excessive forgetting occurs between repetitions, and learning suffers (see Atkinson and Shiffrin, 1968).

There are a variety of factors said to underlie these differences between massed and distributed practice. Massed practice strengthens response patterns. This allows the respondent simply to continue emitting the same response, from memory, and pay only minimal attention to the initiating conditions. With distributed practice, however, the learner must devote more attention to determining which stimulus goes with which response, as well as practising the response itself. This accounts for the initial differences in acquisition rates. Later, when training has ended, and the novice is required to perform the learned component, those task-components learned under distributed practice will have an advantage, since the performer will have learned more completely how to distinguish appropriate from inappropriate initiating stimuli. Learning to drive under real driving conditions has obvious advantages in this respect, since with the possible exception of driving straight ahead in the absence of other road users, the actions the driver is expected to perform do not immediately repeat each other without interruption by some other activity. It is obvious, but perhaps very important, that when it comes to learning to drive, two identical manoeuvres never follow each other. There is certainly no opportunity for the pupil to practise, say, overtaking, or turning right, without driving ahead in another lane for some period of time. This helps to divide the task up into more meaningful units (i.e. manoeuvres). Thus, simply because of the nature of the driving task, drivers learn under 'distributed' practice conditions, that is, those that result in relatively slow but more robust learning.

Practice and successful performance

Singley and Anderson (1989) have shown that the time taken to edit text decreased as a function of the number of days of practice (Fig 12.2). On average, on the first day, subjects took about eight minutes to edit a page. This reduced to two minutes by the sixth day of training. Singley and Anderson (1989) further contrasted the way in which the time was spent over the course of practice, looking at the time spent typing and thinking time (i.e. any period when longer than 2 seconds elapsed between keystrokes). As can be seen in Figure 12.2, while the execution time remained more or less constant throughout the training period, it was thinking time that was associated with the strong reduction as a function of practice. The lack of change in execution time suggests that prior key-stroking experience, acquired outside this particular task, transfers successfully to the new task. Had practice continued, we might expect the thinking time to reduce still further, until it too becomes stable.

Fig 12.2 Changes in components of text-editing skill as a function of practice (after Singley and Anderson, 1989).

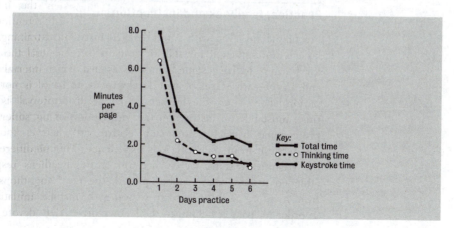

In general, learning curves, that is, plots of the level of performance during skill acquisition against task experience and practice, are negatively accelerated. A variety of such mathematical descriptions of learning are reported in the literature, but there is now general agreement that most skills develop as a power function of practice (see Newell and Rosenbloom, 1981; Anderson, 1995). This has been known for some time. Snoddy (1926), for example suggested that the log of some performance index plotted against the log of the number of trials yields a linear function, that is, there is a *power law* relationship between success and practice. The Singley and Anderson (1989) study shows that overall skill acquisition proceeds as a power function of practice, but it also shows that where there are several elements within a task, those that have not been highly learned previously will show the strongest reductions as a function of practice.

Newell and Rosenbloom (1981) demonstrate that a power law relationship holds between practice and the successful performance of a wide range of simple skills. Although many of the indices of skill depend on error rates or performance times, they suggest that a power law relationship should hold for any type of index of skill, and also for more complex skills. Anderson (1982) makes a similar point, suggesting that complex skills should show the power law relationship because complex skills are composed of more simple component skills which are themselves acquired as a power function of practice, on the basis of simple associative learning. Recently, Groeger and Clegg (1994), using the rate of instruction reduction as an index of skill acquisition, have shown that the growth of driving skill is a power function of the amount of practice the pupil has had. The study shows clearly that individual manoeuvres (e.g. turning right at a crossroads, or driving ahead on a bend) are learned as a power function of the number of times such manoeuvres have been carried out, and that the component activities of the driving task (e.g. car control, observation, etc) are also acquired as a power function of practice. Thus, these results confirm Anderson's speculations about the growth of skill in complex tasks; the components of complex tasks are governed by power laws, which in turn govern the acquisition of the task as a whole.

Practice, feedback and instruction

Practice alone, even with some detailed instructions about how to carry out the task, is not sufficient for skill to develop (see Fabiani et al., 1989). It is crucial for learners to have some standards against which to assess their performance and, in the early stages of skill development, to have consistent feedback on their performance. Thus, the learner driver, confronting a driving task for the first time, must rely on instruction (i.e. description of the task requirements) from a professional instructor, friend or relative and whatever knowledge or skills they can retrieve from their previous experience. This places substantial demands on the cognitive system, largely because of the need to identify what should be attended to and what can be ignored, the need to retrieve relevant knowledge from memory, and the need to reason with, manipulate or reorganise knowledge in order to make it helpful to the learner driver's efforts.

Thorndike (1932) noted that the reinforcing effects of *knowledge of results* (KR) in strengthening the stimulus–response bond were best served when KR was provided as close to the relevant response and on as many occasions as possible. In actual fact, it was subsequently shown that strict temporal contiguity between performance and feedback can be violated without detrimental effects on learning, provided that the interval between response and feedback is not filled with other activities (Large and Thorndike, 1935). Bilodeau and Bilodeau (1958) independently varied the interval between response and KR and post-KR delay. They demonstrated that delay of KR, as such, was of no consequence, and also that rate of learning was directly proportional to the absolute number of trials on which KR was provided. More recent research has served to qualify these general principles.

Fig 12.3 Acquisition and retention of timing skill as a function of feedback regime and retention interval (after Schmidt, Young, Swinnen and Shapiro 1989).

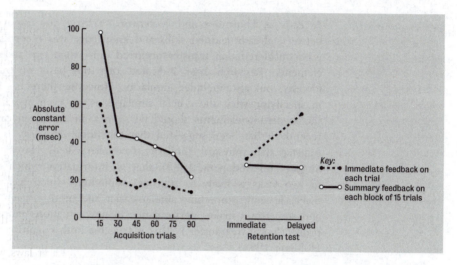

For motor skills, when performance is evaluated by a long-term retention test, individuals who receive more or better KR perform best during acquisition, but typically perform worse during retention, than individuals who receive less useful KR or have KR gradually withdrawn during practice (see Schmidt, Young, Swinnen and Shapiro, 1989, Fig 12.3 above). The explanation for this is that less detailed KR, and the gradual withdrawal of KR, encourages the performer to rely more on task-intrinsic feedback for the remainder of the training period. As observed by Schmidt et al. (1989), these results suggest that KR is essential for initial guidance, but at some point during learning it can produce a kind of dependency. Much earlier, Annett and Kay (1957) pointed out that the provision of temporary KR is only of value if the trainee can subsequently get all the information needed from cues which are intrinsic to the task. Another of the drawbacks of extensive immediate feedback is that it may mask, or distract the learner's attention away from the task-intrinsic cues which can continue to be used to guide behaviour long after formal training has ended (see Boldovici, 1987; Kinkade, 1963). Recent work suggests that it is very important to consider what we are expecting the learner to learn from the feedback we provide. Studying subjects' ability to make sinusoidal movements, Wulf, Schmidt and Deubel (1993) distinguish between how feedback influences the development of a more general understanding of a whole movement pattern, and what they refer to as parametrerisation, that is, the 'tuning' of specific aspects of performance. They showed quite conclusively that learning of the general movement was better with intermittent feedback (63 per cent of trials), but learning of the timing and force of movements was better when feedback was given after each trial.

■ Benefits and drawbacks of prior knowledge

As early as Thorndike and Woodworth (1901), the importance of the transfer between already learned skills and knowledge was recognised. At that stage, it was considered that transfer occurred only when two tasks contained identical elements. Research later indicated that the basis of transfer was not only identity, but also included similarity. However, there has been some difficulty in specifying what the crucial similarity is, or even at what level of generality the mediating elements should be sought, in any given case of transfer. More recently it has been suggested that functional similarity is more important for transfer than physical similarity (see also Allen, Hayes and Buffardi, 1986; Singley and Anderson, 1985), that is, information which is put to similar use in two tasks is likely to transfer. Something which has already been learned makes learning something similar easier and more efficient ('positive transfer'), and sometimes makes performance in new situations more difficult and error-prone ('negative transfer'). This is true for both cognitive and motor skills (see Holding, 1991).

Transfer of training

A number of studies have explored how what is learned in one circumstance transfers to another. Koh and Meyer (1991) report a study in which subjects were required to produce temporal judgements which reflected the separation of two visually presented stimuli. In all, subjects experienced 12 different separations of the visual stimuli, but only received feedback on the four smallest and the four largest separations. Nevertheless, despite not receiving information about how well they had performed these 'middle' judgements, Koh and Meyer showed that subjects learned to make appropriate temporal judgements (see Figure 12.4). Thus, even without feedback, given a range of experiences, subjects were able to extrapolate to other situations. Another notable feature of the Koh and Meyer data is that the estimates for the transfer points fell directly on the same power function as those more extreme points on which information had been given.

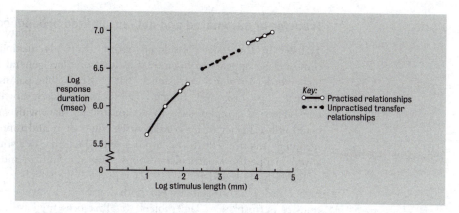

Fig 12.4 Transfer of training on a length-duration estimation task (after Koh and Meyer, 1991).

Earlier, Catalano and Kleiner (1984) had subjects watch an object moving at the equivalent of 5, 7, 9 or 11 mph. The subjects' task was to press a button when the object reached a particular point; these reaction times served as the dependent variable. Some subjects trained on just one speed (i.e. constant speed training), while another group made decisions about each of the four speeds during the learning phase (i.e. variable speed training). By the end of the learning session, the constant group were responding significantly more quickly than the variable speed group (38 msec versus 52 msec). However, when both groups were tested on a new set of speeds, not encountered during the learning phase (i.e. 1, 3, 13, 15 mph), those who encountered more speeds during training were able to respond more accurately than those who had practised on just one speed (Fig 12.5). These results suggest that what subjects learn in the constant speed training group is rather more restricted than what is learned by the variable speed group. This gives the latter group an advantage when the performance required of them lies outside the range of experiences they have had during learning. Taken together, these two studies show that transfer of training depends on the composition and variability of prior practice, as predicted in Schmidt's (1988a, 1988b) schema theory of motor control (but see van Rossum, 1990).

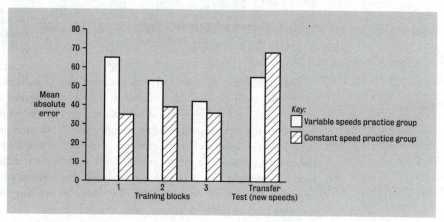

Fig 12.5 Transfer of learning to new speed conditions following training on one or more speeds (after Catalano and Kleiner, 1984).

Transfer of automated and not-automated procedures

Transfer in the tasks considered above, from practised tasks to other highly similar tasks, appears to operate at at least one level of the task. That is, there is higher order or global consistency that clearly facilitates task performance. Other studies (e.g. Fisk and Eboch, 1989) have added to the understanding of consistency in complex tasks by demonstrating that, in conditions where subjects could utilise higher order consistencies (rules or relationships), normal consistent mapping practice effects occurred even when the individual stimuli were not always mapped to a particular response (see also Shiffrin and Czerwinski, 1988).

Recently, Fisk and Jones (1992) report results which explore the influence of higher order inconsistencies on both learning of lower-level task elements and transfer performance. The subject was first presented with a category label (e.g. 'human body parts') for 20 seconds, and then with three words in a column, one of which was a member of that category. The subject's task was to indicate whether the top, middle or bottom word was a member of the target category. The other two words, the 'distractors', were also members of semantic categories used in the study, although they were not 'targets' for that trial. Typical of such studies, the training was very extensive, with 12 one-hour sessions and 9,792 trials. The study essentially asked two questions. Does whether a word appears consistently as a target (consistent mapping), or sometimes as a target and sometimes as a distractor (varied mapping), influence the time taken to make target or non-target decisions about it? How does the balance of consistent and varied mapping affect performance when people are required to make category judgements about new items from those categories on which they have trained?

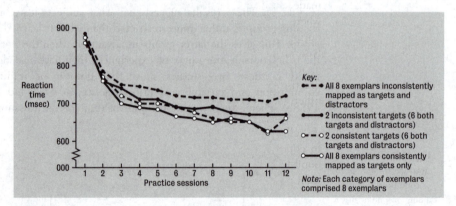

Fig 12.6 Time taken to classify targets encountered in consistent and inconsistent task environments (after Fisk and Jones, 1992).

The first thing to establish was whether this paradigm shows the traditional performance difference with consistent and varied mapping trials. As is clear from Figure 12.6, performance was substantially faster where words were always targets and never distractors, and slowest when a word's status as target or distractor was completely inconsistent (each category exemplar was a target as often as it was a distractor). When the performance with consistently mapped items (i.e. every time it is present it is a target) is examined, the number of other items from that category which are inconsistent (i.e. appear as targets and distractors) is unimportant; making the same response every time the same thing appears is unaffected by whether you sometimes make different responses to items from the same category. At a very general level, and not seeking to do injustice to the elegance of Fisk's research, when you have always previously braked at an amber signal at a particular junction, you are more likely to brake there in the future – it doesn't matter whether you have driven through some amber lights at other locations in the past. When the performance with varied mapping items is examined, the more consistent mapping there is within that category, the better performance will be, even for inconsistent items (although the error rates are similar, circa 95 per cent correct). This means that, even if you do not consistently respond in a particular way to one exemplar from a category, the more exemplars from that category that you have responded consistently to, the more similar your performance will be to this, even on items to which you have responded inconsistently. To return to our traffic light example, the more amber lights in different locations you have driven through, the more likely you are to drive through at traffic lights where previously you might or might not have stopped.

But what happens when you encounter a junction you have not encountered before? As the Fisk and Jones study shows, this may depend on how consistently you have stopped at junctions in the past. As Figure 12.7 shows, the more consistent exemplars were (i.e. always targets) during learning, the better transfer was to new members of the category. As the uncertainty during learning about whether an item was to be responded to as a target or distracter increases, so does the difficulty in responding quickly to new items from that category.

The key difference between these studies and the results of Catalano and Kleiner (1984) and Koh and Meyer (1991), is that in those studies subjects had always made consistent responses during training trials. What Fisk's results show is that where the consistency of the ways in which we respond to a particular stimulus during training is low, it is unlikely that we will cope with new stimuli of the same type effectively. Other studies by Fisk, Lee and Rogers (1991) demonstrate quite clearly that responding to something (or ignoring it) which we have already practised responding to (or ignoring) transfers positively to new contexts. On the other hand, responding to something we have learned to ignore, or ignoring something we have learned to respond to is extremely difficult. If these results really do reflect how we learn in complex situations, then when we are training someone to cope with new situations we need to be particularly careful to ensure that the pupil has responded to similar stimuli consistently in the past, anticipate where we want positive and negative transfer, and train accordingly.

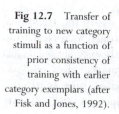

Fig 12.7 Transfer of training to new category stimuli as a function of prior consistency of training with earlier category exemplars (after Fisk and Jones, 1992).

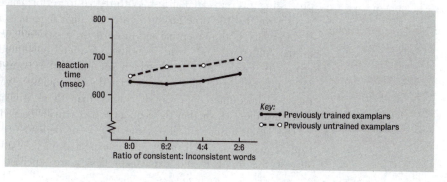

Procedural reinstatement

Fendrich, Gesi, Healy and Bourne (1995) suggest that the basis of transfer is what they term *procedural reinstatement*. That is, following earlier suggestions made by Kolers and Roediger (1984) 'retention depends on the degree to which procedures executed, and thereby exercised, at study are reinstated at test' (Fendich et al., 1995, p. 87). A range of evidence is presented to support this proposal, but one example serves to illustrate the proposal. Subjects read or typed a series of four-digit numbers during the learning phase of the study. Those who typed the sequences used either the numerical keys on the top row of a standard keyboard, or used the numerical keypad. In the test phase, one week later, all subjects typed four-digit sequences. This time, some of the subjects who had initially used the keypad typed the digits using the row of numerical keys, and vice versa. Subjects who simply read the digits at study used the keypad or row of numerical keys at test. Some of the important findings from this study are presented in Figure 12.8.

Fig 12.8 Effects of changing responses to stimuli at a study and test on recognition accuracy (after Fendrich, Gesi, Healy and Bourne, 1995).

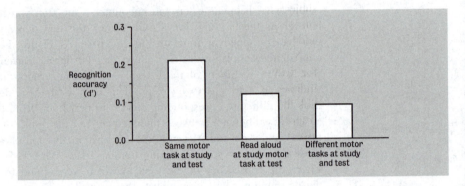

Overall the results demonstrate evidence of learning using both an implicit test (shorter typing times for sequences of digits that had been typed during the learning phase) and an explicit test (recognition of previously encountered sequences). The more specific results Fendrich and colleagues report are more important. Explicit recognition judgements were more accurate when they were entered in the same manner at study and test than when the entry methods differed. Thus, repetition of motoric procedures from study to test enhances recognition memory. Secondly, adding motoric processing to the study task only improved recognition when that processing was reinstated at test. With regard to performance on the implicit test, it was shown that the time taken to enter the digit sequences in the 'same' condition (i.e. in which both perceptual and motoric processes were repeated) was lower than in the 'different' and 'read' conditions (where only perceptual processing was repeated). Finally, in a result which parallels that reported by Jacoby and Dallas (1981), faster entry times were associated with sequences which the subject thought they had encountered previously, rather than those which they considered were new, regardless of whether the sequences had actually been previously encountered.

The latter result indicates some degree of dependence between implicit and explicit measures, which might not be expected on the basis of other findings that suggest that implicit and explicit processes are stochastically independent (e.g.

Kolers, 1976; Tulving, 1985). Such independence has also been demonstrated by Howard, Mutter and Howard (1992), in a procedural learning task inspired by the work of Nissen and Bullemer (1987). In the standard condition, subjects were merely instructed to press a key under the position where an asterisk appeared. The asterisk appeared in one of four positions. When a series of 10 trials was repeatedly presented, key press reaction times decreased relative to when the series was random, thus demonstrating that subjects had acquired procedural knowledge. What Howard and colleagues went on to show was that this learning was implicit, since with the procedure slightly changed (i.e. subjects were instructed to press the key under the position where they expected the asterisk to appear next), there was little evidence that subjects were explicitly able to predict the sequence. One possibility is that even though the tasks of Howard and colleagues and Fendrich and colleagues both demonstrate procedural learning, the data entry task largely does so for a task that Jacoby (1983) would describe as data-driven processing, with little or no conceptual processing. The sequence prediction task, on the other hand, seems to require rather more conceptually driven processing. The fact that younger subjects show a greater degree of success on the prediction task than older subjects (in whom explicit, conceptually driven processing is thought to be less effective), adds some weight to this interpretation.

Nevertheless, the procedural reinstatement hypothesis is particularly important, for two reasons. It encourages us to question how watertight the supposed independence of implicit and explicit measures is, and it demonstrates a direct link between recognition of visual stimuli and the opportunities available for responding to them. This has direct implications for how we might adequately assess individuals' ability to, for example, detect dangerous driving situations (see Groeger and Chapman, 1996).

Generic and episodic knowledge: Theories of skill acquisition

At the outset of this chapter it was stressed that there is broad agreement that as skill is acquired, the performer moves through various stages during which performance is more or less effortful, and more or less consistent. Traditionally, there have been different emphases in explanations of how this comes about, between so-called exercise theories (which suggest that each learning trial offers an opportunity to acquire new information or to strengthen associations between stimuli and responses) and selection theories (which propose that trials offer the opportunity to strengthen some aspect of behaviour while weakening others). Thus, for example, Crossman (1959) suggests that when learning perceptual-motor-based skill tasks, subjects sample methods of performing the tasks until they find the fastest one. The assumption is that there is a pool of alternative methods that are selected at random. The results of performance are compared, and if the method chosen was faster, the probability of selecting it for the next trial is increased. However, there is no provision for learning new methods or improving old ones as practice progresses; subjects must know or have available all methods when they begin. In contrast, Welford (1987) suggests that in, for example, choice reaction time tasks practice has the effect of making the connections between stimuli and responses more distinctive. Practice increases the signal-to-noise ratio of stimuli (i.e. detecting which stimuli are relevant and which are not). Since making one response rather than another is seen as depending on stimulus discriminability (i.e. the individual's ability to detect which stimuli to respond to), reaction time and errors are progressively reduced by repeated practice.

More recently, this separation between exercise and selection accounts has become rather more blurred, with the majority of views of skill acquisition suggesting that repeated practice builds or strengthens connections between stimulus and response elements. Of particular importance, given their ubiquity, are the explanations these theories offer of how learning comes to have a power law relationship with practice.

Strength theories of skill acquisition

Newell and Rosenbloom (1981; Rosenbloom and Newell, 1986), proposed a theory based on the idea of chunking. Chunking, as proposed by Newell and Rosenbloom (1981), involves the grouping of any set of mental entities, perceptual or motor, which can be dealt with as a single unit. Chunking is regarded as an automatic process which after practice, allows elementary chunks to become grouped together as larger chunks. Newell and Rosenbloom argue that subjects acquire responses to stimulus patterns or chunks, which they then execute the next time the pattern occurs. They assume that subjects learn patterns at several different levels, some encompassing single elements, some encompassing the whole stimulus. They argue that smaller patterns recur more frequently than larger patterns, so smaller components will be learned most quickly. This accounts for the power-function speed-up. As practice proceeds, subjects will have learned most of the smaller patterns and will no longer benefit from subsequent occurrences. The Newell and Rosenbloom theory also suggests that subjects will tend to benefit from larger patterns later in practice because such larger patterns recur less often, and because there are more of them to be learned. Thus, initial learning will be rapid, as the smaller patterns are acquired and utilised, and later learning will be relatively slow, as the larger patterns are gradually learned and occasionally utilised.

Mackay (1982), although critical of the assumption that chunks govern skilled behaviour, offers an analogous account of skill acquisition. For Mackay, learning occurs by strengthening connections between nodes in a network that describes the representation underlying perception and action. Performance improvement, as reflected in the speeding up of performance, occurs in two ways. First, connections are strengthened in proportion to the difference between the current strength and the maximum possible strength. This 'strengthening' proportion is constant over learning, implying that changes in strength will be greater early in learning. Secondly, representation is hierarchical, such that the higher nodes are fewer in number and less likely to be at their maximum strength than the lower nodes. Thus, early learning would be dominated by larger changes in the strength of a few higher nodes, and later learning would be dominated by small changes in the strength of all nodes. This also accounts for the power law of learning. Furthermore, it is a strength theory and assumes abstract levels of representation, across which nodes associated with each other through practice prime each other. This allows larger performance units to develop as required by task performance.

Mackay's notion of proportional strengthening of connections and gradual reduction of the difference between the current strength of a node and its maximum strength is similar to that proposed by Walter Schneider, who distinguishes between priority learning and association learning. For Schneider (Schneider, 1985; Schneider and Detwiler, 1987), *priority learning* attracts attention to display positions that are likely to contain targets, while *association learning* serves to connect stimuli and responses. According to Schneider, the mechanism underlying both kinds of learning is proportional to strengthening. After each successful trial, priority and associative strength are both increased by an amount proportional to the difference between current strength and maximum possible strength.

Although still a strength theory, Anderson's (1982, 1987) proposal includes a number of different learning mechanisms. Some are involved with translating verbal instructions into procedures for performing a task (i.e. *proceduralisation,* the formation of production rules that represent condition-action and underlie procedural knowledge), one involves simple strengthening, while a third involves generalising and differentiating existing procedures. This last learning mechanism, *composition,* involves collapsing a series of steps into one by combining adjacent procedures. The amount of practice necessary to reduce a complex procedure to a single step depends on the number of steps to be combined and on the probability of combining adjacent steps. The more steps and the lower the probability of combining, the longer it will take. Composition reduces the number of steps by a constant proportion on each iteration of the procedure, producing rapid learning early in practice and slower learning later on. *Strengthening* involves increasing the speed with which productions are excluded from consideration (as in earlier selection theories). It operates mainly on composed productions, increasing the strength in each exposure by a constant proportion. Strengthening and composition work together to produce the power-function speed-up.

Instance theories of skill acquisition

A rather different approach is adopted by Gordon Logan. According to Logan's *instance theory* (1988), each encounter with a stimulus is encoded, stored and retrieved separately. Each instance contains contextual details of the processing episode, the goal the subject is trying to attain, any stimulus encountered in pursuit of that goal, the interpretation of stimuli encountered, and the response made. When the stimulus is later reencountered in the context of the same goal, some proportion of the processing episodes in which it participated is retrieved. Instance theory assumes that encoding into memory is an obligatory, unavoidable consequence of attention, and that attention to a stimulus is sufficient to commit it to memory. Similarly, retrieval from memory is also an obligatory, unavoidable consequence of attention. Attention to a stimulus is sufficient to retrieve from memory whatever has been associated with it in the past. Retrieval itself occurs without attention, but although it is both obligatory and automatic, Logan points out that this should not be taken to imply that it is necessarily inevitably successful, nor indeed easy, in all circumstances. These assumptions offer an easy account of the results of Fendrich and colleagues discussed above with regard to procedural reinstatement.

According to instance theory, the experienced performer can choose to respond on the basis of the retrieved information, and will do so if it is coherent and consistent with the goals of the current task, or to run off the relevant algorithm and compute an interpretation and a response. Instance theory proposes that novices begin with a general algorithm that is sufficient to perform the task they are confronted with. As they gain experience, novices learn specific solutions to specific problems, which are retrieved when the same problems are encountered again. Then, they can respond with the solution retrieved from memory or the one computed by the algorithm. In essence, Logan suggests a race between memory processes and algorithmic solution, the memory process itself being a race between stored episodes – the algorithm races against the fastest instance retrieved from memory. It is bound to lose as training progresses because the finishing time of the algorithm stays the same while the finishing time for the retrieval process decreases, since many more appropriate instances are available for retrieval. At some point, the learner may have gained enough experience to respond with a solution from memory on every trial and abandon the algorithm entirely. At that point, their performance is said to be automatic, that is, 'automaticity is memory retrieval: performance is automatic when it is based on single step direct-access retrieval of past solutions from memory' (Logan, 1988, p. 493). It is important to note that according to instance theory, automaticity may emerge after relatively few encounters with a stimulus. Learning proceeds through the accumulation of separate episodic traces, which produces a gradual transition from algorithm processing to memory-based processing.

Contrasts between strength and instance theories

Instance theory, because it depends on the encoding, storage and retrieval of episodic traces has many parallels with existing theories of episodic memory (Hintzman, 1976; Jacoby and Brooks, 1984); semantic memory (Landauer, 1975); categorisation (Jacoby and Brooks, 1984; Medin and Schaffer, 1978); judgement (Kahneman and Miller, 1986) and problem solving (Ross, 1984), as well as with the headed records model of memory (Morton, Hammersley and Bekerian, 1985). In instance theory, retrieval becomes more likely as experience increases because each experience lays down a separate trace that may be recruited at the time of retrieval. The more experience a performer has, the more likely he or she is to retrieve an appropriate instance from their past experience. In strength theories, retrieval is made more likely by strengthening a connection between a generic representation of a stimulus and a generic representation of its interpretation or response. There are clear links here with categorisation performance, as described earlier, in which single exposures are combined into a single generic prototypic representation, which is compared with incoming stimuli. However, prototypes by themselves are not enough to account for categorisation performance; specific exemplars or instances are also important in categorisation (Medin and Smith, 1984).

According to the instance theory, each prior episode is represented in memory, whereas strength theories represent past history by a single strength measure, discarding details of individual episodes (practice strengthens connections between generic stimuli and generic responses). Strength theories suggest that different interpretations of a stimulus effectively cancel each other out, whereas in instance theory, each interpretation is preserved, because it suggests that a separate trace or instance is encoded on each trial. The two theories also suggest differences in the extent of transfer which will be observed with automated skills. In instance theory, automatisation involves learning specific responses to specific stimuli. The underlying processes need not change at all; subjects are still capable of using the algorithm at any point in practice, and memory retrieval may operate in the same way regardless of the amount of information to be retrieved. Thus, as a result, 'automaticity is specific to the stimuli and the situation experienced during training. Transfer to novel situations should be poor.' (Logan, 1988, p. 494). Strength theories, on the other hand, predict greater transferability, since they suggest that the underlying process becomes more efficient, reducing the amount of resources required or the number of steps to be executed (Anderson, 1982; Kolers, 1975; La Berge and Samuels, 1974). In such cases, learning should transfer just as well to novel situations with untrained stimuli as it does to familiar situations with trained stimuli (see Shiffrin and Dumais, 1981; Fisk and Jones, 1992; Logan, 1988).

Finally, instance theories and strength theories also differ in their assumptions concerning the hierarchical nature of skilled behaviour. Strength theories assume that, as task experience increases, larger skill units are formed, and that these reflect an hierarchical organisation (e.g. McKay, 1982; Newell and Rosenbloom, 1981). Instance theory, on the other hand, does not require that skilled behaviour will be hierarchically determined, since individual episodes are not thought to aggregate into larger structures. This does not mean that consistency of behaviour is less likely from an instance point of view, since the same episodic trace may be repeatedly retrieved, thus increasing the consistency which is a hallmark of skilled behaviour (e.g. McLeod, McLaughlin and Nimmo-Smith, 1985; Naveh-Benjamin and Jonides, 1984).

■ Summary: Episodic and generic procedural memory

At the outset of this chapter, the generally accepted view of how skills are acquired was outlined. In many ways the sections which succeeded have served only to show how such a transition can be facilitated and inhibited. However, they have sought to do so in such a way as to highlight the relationships between the skill and memory literatures.

Although it is an issue which surfaced a long time ago, the massed–distributed practice distinction continues to be theoretically challenging, especially where we link it to issues such as the spacing effect and our access to episodic or generic knowledge. The effects of adding to the task-intrinsic information available, through feedback and/or instruction, the fact that practice and performance are so intrinsically linked, and, especially, the almost universal finding of the power law of practice across a very wide range of tasks and measures, are also significant in this respect. Furthermore, the finding that one's past history of use of information (stimuli or responses) serves to determine how successfully such information can be reused, and can influence our handling of new information, also raises issues which are not only fundamental to skills research, but which are also core issues in memory.

Much of the foregoing sections have wrestled with what is generally regarded as a debate about attention. I think it is also a debate about memory. This is more obviously so with Logan's instance theory, making a strong case as it does for the preservation of both specific episodic information about a past stimulus interaction, and the existence of generic algorithmic procedures. Strength theories, however, in assuming some hierarchical organisation of skilled behaviour, such that increasingly lower levels of the hierarchy are more under direct stimulus control and less amenable to direct conscious access, are clearly also making assumptions about the structure of memory, and the conditions under which retrieval is successful. Both types of theory assume the existence of enduring histories of past action, which are accessed in order to allow performance in the present to be guided and overseen. In this they perhaps differ less than it might at first seem from the idea propounded by Ericsson and Kintsch (1995), which we considered in the previous chapter. I do not think we are anywhere close to having a satisfactory resolution of these issues, but I feel it may be profitable for researchers to concentrate a little more on the assumptions about memory and its operation which underlie the different theories.

■ Further reading

Ericsson, K. A. and Kintsch, W. (1995). Long-term working. *Psychological Review, 102,* 211–45.

Healy, A. F. and Bourne L. E. (eds) (1995). *Learning and memory of knowledge and skills.* Thousand Oaks, CA: Sage.

Logan, G. D. (1988). Towards and instance theory of automatisation. *Psychological Review, 95,* 492–527.

Mackay, D. G. (1982). The problem of flexibility, fluency and speed-and-accuracy trade off in skilled behaviour. *Psychological Review, 89,* 483–506.

Morrison, J. (ed.) (1991). *Training for performance: Principles of applied human learning.* Chichester: Wiley.

Patrick, J. (1992). *Training: Research and practice.* London: Academic Press.

Underwood, G. and Everatt, J. (1996). Automatic and controlled information processing: The role of attention in the processing of novelty. In O. Neumann and A. F. Sanders (eds) *Handbook of Perception and Action 3: Attention.* London: Academic Press.

Discussion points
- Discuss the relationship between memory and skill.
- There are few ubiquitious laws in psychology. Is the power law of practice one?
- How does what we know transfer to new situations? What limits this transfer?
- Compare and contrast strength and instance theories of skill acquisition.

Chapter 13

Memory and age

Chapter outline: This chapter describes studies in which very young infants appear to demonstrate both learning and retrieval abilities, and considers how these memory capacities develop in the older child, and the extent to which we have evidence for assuming that such abilities decline in old age. In particular, we focus on the extent to which implicit and explicit memory tasks show different patterns across the life span, and how aware people are of these and other changes in their own memory ability.

Key topics
- Neonate and Infant memory
- Children's memory
- Older memory
- Summary: Inferring age effects from retrieval performance: the need for caution
- Further reading

Neonate and infant memory

A number of studies of very newly born children clearly show that there is some capacity for memory in these extremely young children. Studies of older infants show what, at first sight, seems an amazingly rich store of memories, and the ability to access these effectively. Given the limited response repertoire of the subjects, infant and neonate memory has almost always been demonstrated through the use of indirect tests of memory, whether through increases or decreases in activity levels, or orientation preferences. Direct tests are rather more rare, but, as we shall see, there is considerable evidence that very young children do indeed possess quite a range of memory skills.

Neonate preferences for mother's voice

I find some of the work carried out in this area very impressive, especially the remarkably inventive way researchers have applied reasonably standard empirical methods to what seem almost intractable scientific questions. Thus, for example, as a study by DeCasper and Fifer (1980) shows, new-born infants show a distinct preference for tape recordings of their mother's voice, being prepared to modulate their sucking in order to hear it again. All of the infants tested lived in a group nursery, with their night feeding, and what DeCasper and Fifer decorously refer to as their 'general care', being handled by various nursery personnel. By the time of testing, infants were less than three days old, and had had at most 12 hours contact with their mothers.

The first of the two studies DeCasper and Fifer (1980) describe shows that neonates can be conditioned to suck on an artificial nipple more frequently, or less frequently, than a baseline established in that session, depending on which action led to the voice of the child's mother or the voice of another child's mother being heard reading the same prose passage. The second study, of 16 female neonates, confirmed and extended these results using a different paradigm. Infants first heard a four-second burst of 400-Hz tone or four seconds of silence. This was followed by a mother's voice (maternal or non-maternal). For eight of the infants, a sucking burst initiated during the tone period turned off the tone and produced the prose passage read by the infant's mother, whereas sucking bursts during a no-tone period produced the non-maternal voice. The voice continued for as long as the sucking, and after two seconds without sucking another randomly selected silence-tone trial began. The tone–mother's voice, silence–non-maternal voice relationship was reversed for the other eight infants, and in all the test lasted for 20 minutes. Summarising their results, DeCasper and Fifer report that:

During the first third of the testing session, the infants were as likely to suck during a stimulus period correlated with the maternal voice as during one correlated with the non-maternal voice. However, in the last third of the session the infants sucked during the stimulus periods associated with their mother's voice approximately 24 per cent more often than during those associated with the non-maternal voice ...

Thus, at the beginning of testing there was no indication of stimulus discrimination or voice preference. By the end of the 20 minute session, feedback from the maternal voice produced clear evidence of an auditory discrimination.

(DeCasper and Fifer, 1980, p. 1174)

Together, these studies demonstrate not only a discrimination between two human voices, but also preference for what is, presumably, the more familiar voice to them, and the ability to learn the relatively simple associative contingency between different actions and an external stimulus (see Fig 13.1).

Fig 13.1 Infants suck more actively when hearing their own mother's voice (after DeCasper and Fifer, 1980).

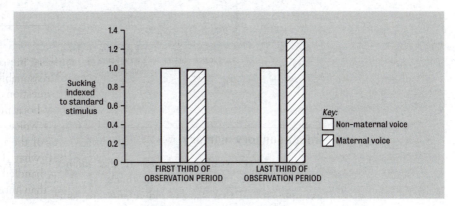

Towards the end of their paper, DeCasper and Fifer speculate that the minimal postnatal contact with the babies' mothers does not account for the differentiation between female voices that they report, and suggest that the infant's intrauterine experience provides the basis for this discrimination. This would suggest that because the father is in less direct contact with the foetus, and because the typically lower frequency sounds of the male carry less well to the child in utero (Querleu and Renard, 1981), postnatal preference for the father's voice should not be as strong. This was confirmed in a subsequent study by DeCasper and Spence (1986), showing that early postnatal experience with the father's voice does not result in a preference for the father's voice over that of another male. The importance of prenatal familiarity with the mother's voice was further stressed in a later study by DeCasper and Spence (1986). This showed that infants exhibited a preference for stories which their mother had read aloud, twice a day, during the last six weeks of her pregnancy, over those not previously read aloud by their mother (Fig 13.2).

These studies demonstrate that very young infants have some memory for the past, and the contingencies which have brought about certain events. We do not, of course, know that specific memories (i.e. episodic knowledge) are being intentionally addressed, that is, we cannot infer that infants have the capacity for explicit memory. However, the results do demonstrate that neonates, and perhaps even foetuses, possess a sophisticated capacity for implicit processing.

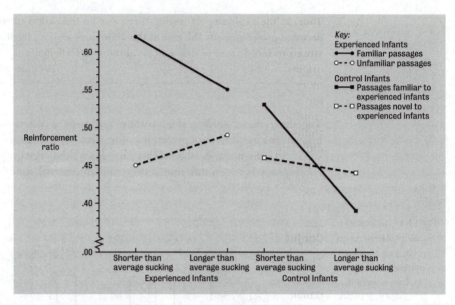

Infant sensory memory

A range of early studies demonstrate that infants less than a few weeks old are capable of recognising their mother's smell. Thus, Macfarlane (1975), for example, found that six-day-old infants are more likely to turn towards breast pads worn by their mother, rather than those which had been worn by another nursing mother. Other work, however, suggests that this olfactory discrimination only becomes reliable in children about six weeks old. Gottfried and Rose (1980) report data which suggest that at least at 12 months old, infants are capable of tactile recognition memory. It is worth noting that this tendency to orient towards a familiar stimulus, frequently observed above in the context of auditory, tactile and olfactory stimuli, is only sometimes demonstrated with visual stimuli.

Using one of two stimuli, both composed of black and white squares, Friedman (1972) showed that the percentage of time for which infants between one and four days old look at the pattern reduces as the number of one-minute presentations of the pattern increases. This indicates that even these very young children show *habituation*, (i.e. a decrease in response level to a related event). However, when the pattern presented was switched after a few trials, the infant's interest in the stimulus, as indexed by the time spent looking at it, returned almost to the original level (i.e. they demonstrate recovery from habituation, which is referred to as *dishabituation*). This habituation–dishabituation paradigm shows that visual stimuli lose their novelty, which implies that there is some residual memory for what the infant has seen. However, other researchers (e.g. Weizman, Cohen and Pratt, 1971; Wetherford and Cohen, 1973) suggest that generally young infants have a tendency to prefer the familiar, while older infants have a preference for novel stimuli. This obviously conflicts with the Friedman findings. It also underscores some of the problems with the habituation–dishabituation paradigm. Other difficulties include the difficulty of inferring that failure to attend to a new stimulus may indicate that the infant has forgotten about the original stimulus, or that the child remembers, but does not choose to devote more attention to the novel stimulus (see Sophian, 1980 for discussion). A further limitation is that the habituation–dishabituation paradigm only considers recognition for a stimulus, and typically does not test children's ability or desire to make use of the information they have learned. These difficulties have largely been overcome by a remarkably neat piece of experimentation, which resulted in the development of a new paradigm – the conjugate-reinforcement paradigm.

Conjugate-reinforcement paradigm

The *conjugate-reinforcement* paradigm has been used extensively by Carolyn Rovee-Collier in order to study the memory of infants when they are motivated to remember. The task is simple, but is sufficiently variable to allow a range of issues to be systematically addressed.

BOX 13.1: Infants' memory abilities

Typically, the conjugate-reinforcement paradigm involves the following stages. In the training condition (usually nine minutes), one end of a ribbon is attached to a mobile suspended over the child's cot, while the other end is attached to the child's ankle. The child learns that by moving one of its legs (i.e. kicking), it can cause the mobile to shake and spin. Before the procedure begins, for three minutes, the baseline activity level of the leg to which the ribbon is attached is measured. This is contrasted with the level of activity of the leg when it is attached to the mobile, and with the level of activity in a final three-minute period, during which the ribbon is again detached from the mobile. This latter phase provides an immediate retention test. In the standard procedure, these three phases are repeated again 24 hours later. The initial period in the first session provides a baseline, while the final phase in the second session reflects the infant's final level of acquisition. On subsequent testing, if a child forgets completely that moving its foot will activate the mobile, the activity for that leg in the first three-minute period should be the same as in the baseline condition. Forgetting and retention are operationally defined as follows. Forgetting is indexed by the infant's kick-rate during the long-term retention test (i.e. the first three minutes when the child is first tested after the two-session training has been completed), relative to the infant's kick-rate at the end of training (i.e. the immediate retention test). Retention, on the other hand, is indexed by the infant's kick-rate during the long-term retention test relative to the infant's kick-rate during the baseline period (i.e. before the ribbon tied to the child's ankle was ever connected to the mobile).

The figure shows the performance of two- and three-month-old children, tested at between one and fourteen days delay after the completion of the two-session training. The fact that most of the ratios are below 1 indicates that retention is affected by the extent of the delay between training and test (kick-rate in the long-term retention test is lower than that in the immediate retention test at the end of training). The conjugate-reinforcement paradigm is obviously sensitive to small age differences. Two-month-old children have forgotten completely by the second day after training (i.e. responding in the long-term retention test is no different to the initial baseline level). In contrast, this occurs with the three-month-old children only after delays of some 13 or 14 days (see Greco, Rovee-Collier, Hayne, Griesler and Earley, 1986; Rovee-Collier, 1989).

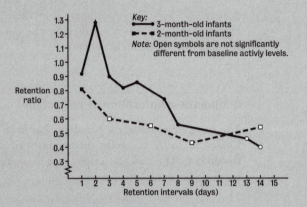

Infants retention of information about the mobile encountered during two sessions of training, as a function of retention interval (after Greco, Rovee-Collier, Hayne, Griesler and Early, 1986).

In a number of studies, Rovee-Collier and colleagues have demonstrated that even the retention of two-month-old children can be extended beyond 14 days, if training, instead of being 'massed' in two nine-minute training sessions is instead 'distributed' over three six-minute sessions (Enright, Rovee-Collier, Fagen and Caniglia, 1983; Vander Linde, Morrongiello and Rovee-Collier, 1985), while in other studies, four-month-old infants can 'remember' events from five weeks previously (Greco, Rovee-Collier, Hayne, Griesler and Earley, 1986). Furthermore, even where the kicking-rate on long-term retention is not different to that of the baseline, there is good evidence to suggest that reminding can resuscitate or reactivate the memory. Thus, when 13 days after training forgetting was complete by three-month-olds, making the mobile move served to increase performance in the next long-term retention test to levels previously observed only in the immediate retention test. In contrast, infants who were reminded some 27 days after training continued to respond at the baseline level until they too were reminded. Reminding also served to increase kick-rate substantially even for a group who received the reminder 34 days after training (see Figure 13.3), Rovee-Collier has offered an intriguing explanation of this, which will be considered below. But first let me try to overview some of the more important findings from this very rich research programme.

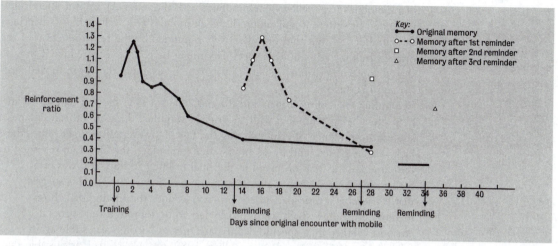

Fig 13.3 Forgetting and reminding of 3-month old infants (after Rovee-Collier, 1989).

Qualities of infant memory

The results from the conjugate-reinforcement paradigm strongly refute the suggestions of earlier authors who have claimed that infant retention during the first year of life is of the order of seconds (e.g. Werner and Perlmutter, 1979). However, they do much more than that. Variants of the paradigm have demonstrated a number of very important properties of infant memory. These include:

1. Retrieval is remarkably stimulus-specific: if different numbers of novel mobile objects are substituted for familiar ones during a retention test one day after training, infants' responding on the retention test is reduced (Fagen, Rovee and Kaplan, 1976); two-month-olds behave as if they have completely forgotten after just one day if more than one object on the mobile is changed (Hayne, Greco, Earley, Griesler and Rovee-Collier, 1986).

2. Infant memory is context dependent: if three-month-old infants are trained using the standard training method with a particular coloured cloth lining, testing seven days later reveals excellent retention where the same cot surround/lining is used, but little or no evidence of retention where the cot surround is different (Rovee-Collier, Griesler and Earley, 1985); three-month-old infants will generalise to a novel stimulus (i.e. trained on yellow-block mobiles with alphanumeric characters; tested with metal butterfly wind chime mobile) to which they would otherwise not respond, but only where the same red and blue cot surround/ lining was used during both the training and in the testing of the generalisation procedure (Rovee-Collier, 1989); generalisation can also occur on the basis of an object's functional characteristics (e.g. movement or sound).

3. Reminding is specific: just as retrieval is highly specific to the original training context, objects only act as effective reminders if they are very similar to objects encountered during training. A mobile differing in terms of just one object from that used in training is not an effective reminder (Rovee-Collier, Patterson and Hayne, 1985). Similarly, infants trained with alphanumeric

block mobiles (e.g. yellow-block mobiles with the letter A) are not effectively reminded by different alphanumeric block mobiles (e.g. yellow blocks bearing the number '2'), but they are effectively reminded by the reintroduction of the original training stimuli. This specificity might be expected to reduce if they shared some other, more general, property, for example they both moved, see (4) and (5), below.

4. Reminding takes time: Fagen and Rovee-Collier (1983) showed that up to an hour after being reminded with an original stimulus, three-month-old infants showed no evidence of remembering the task. However, after eight hours the kick-rate increased, and by 24 hours after reminding, the kick-rate returned to the same level as that observed in the final training session, and was even higher still some 72 hours after reminding (see Figure 13.3). This suggests that retrieval is a time-dependent process, as does the finding that those memory attributes which were initially last to be forgotten (e.g. general attributes rather than specific details) are first to become accessible again following reminding (see Rovee-Collier, 1989, pp. 164–65). It is possible that the characteristic shape of the retention curve, that is, peaking after the initial test, reflects an accrual of reminding brought about by the previous test session, against a background of habituation and forgetting.

5. Infants develop and use categorical knowledge: training with multiple, perceptibly different, mobile objects results in memories which are sensitive to category membership. Studies indicate that these categorical effects can result from a contextual similarity, temporal contiguity, the physical attributes of the stimulus, or its functional characteristics (i.e. whether it moves or makes noise) (see Rovee-Collier, 1989).

In addition to their obvious fascination from a memory point of view, these studies show that quite sophisticated recognition for visual objects is obviously present very early in life and develops rapidly in the six- to twelve-month period (see Kail, 1990). This memory is relatively robust over time, and seems to be predictive of later performance. Thus, for example, children aged six months at the time of encoding have been shown to remember repeated events (Myers, Clifton and Clarkson, 1987) and single events (Perris, Myers and Clifton, 1990) over a two-year period. Taken together these results strongly suggest that many of the properties of our adult memory are in place and functional in the infant, although they are obviously constrained by the limited environment and response capabilities of the child. As these restrictions ease, other similarities also emerge. Such changes appear to be facilitated by the initial levels of recognition memory of which these infants were earlier shown to be capable. Thus, studies show significant relationships between infant recognition memory and vocabulary skills at three, four, five and seven years of age (Fagan, 1984), while Rose and Wallace (1985) report relationships between recognition memory skills and intelligence scores at two, three, and six years of age.

■ Children's memory

Some of the difficulties encountered in assessing the memory abilities of infants are reduced as children get older, but explaining the task, a shared understanding of what is required, attention and the motivation to carry out the task are still substantial obstacles. As a result, and especially in the light of the work by Rovee-Collier discussed above, I think it very likely that we understate the memory abilities of younger children, and perhaps certain tasks exaggerate developmental differences. In general, children have been shown in a wide range of studies to have very good recognition for previously encountered items, but often very poor recall (see Myers and Perlmutter, 1978; Perlmutter, 1984).

Rehearsal, strategies and working memory

When recall is formally measured, traditional indices of capacity show a strong developmental trend. Thus, for example, digit span increases markedly as the child ages, being an average of two digits at two years of age, an average of five digits for five-year-olds, and increasing to the average adult rate of seven digits when children are in their early teens (see Dempster, 1981). One suggestion is that memory capacity changes as the child ages, with there being more slots available in short-term memory (e.g. see Pascual-Leone, 1970; 1987). This is, however, undermined by the fact that age effects in children's memory are substantially reduced when the stimuli used in the assessment are unfamiliar, or where rehearsal opportunities are reduced (e.g. Dempster, 1985). Similarly, if one accepts the view that short-term or working memory is heavily involved in task control, then a digit span of two items would suggest far more restricted competence than is readily observed with two-year-old children.

Related to these digit span issues are the recent findings from Gathercole and colleagues, which strongly suggest that phonological knowledge and phonological reading skills are important in vocabulary learning in younger children learning their first language, and older children learning their second. Thus, Gathercole and Baddeley (1990) have demonstrated that ability to learn and remember nonsense words (e.g. 'sommel') was a very good predictor of the child's phonological skills, while Gathercole, Willis, Emslie and Baddeley (1992) report that ability to report non-words predicts well the size of a young child's vocabulary. The issue of how these findings relate to the development of working memory is addressed in much greater detail in Gathercole and Adams (1994).

Another possibility which has been explored is that children vary in their use of strategies that can serve to enhance memory. The role of rehearsal has received most attention, following early research by Flavell, Beach and Chinsky (1966). This research showed that children, when required to remember two of seven pictures they were shown, differed strongly in their tendency to use rehearsal. Rehearsal, as indexed by the frequency of overt rehearsal or silent rehearsal detected by a skilled lip reader, increased from just 10 per cent in five-year-olds, to 60 per cent in the seven-year-olds tested and 85 per cent of the ten-year-old subjects. However, this study does not necessarily reflect an inability to rehearse, but might also reflect a lack of motivation to do so, or failure to realise the benefits of doing so. This has been explored in studies by Cuvo. In one of these studies, Cuvo (1974) had nine- and twelve-year-olds and teenage students attempt to recall words, knowing that they would receive a reward for each word they recalled. Some words were more highly rewarded than others (i.e. 1 cent for some, 10 cents for others). As might be expected the older subjects rehearsed the high incentive words more frequently than the low incentive words, the older children showed a slight bias towards rehearsing the high value words, but the nine-year-olds rehearsed the high- and low-value words to the same extent. As might be expected on the basis of what you have already read large differences in recall were demonstrated across the groups.

Fig 13.4 Children's free and cued-recall as a function of age (after Ceci and Howe 1978).

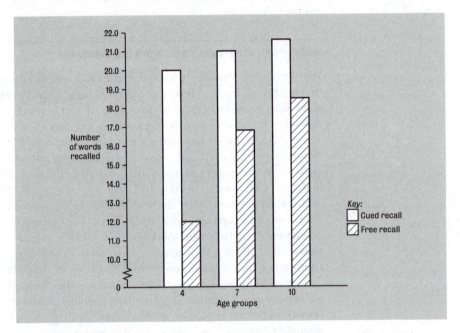

One of the many difficulties in understanding the basis of developmental differences in retention of information over time is knowing whether the materials have been sufficiently well encoded in the first place. Ceci and Howe (1978) showed that four-, seven- and ten-year-old children learned lists of words to the same extent, as indexed by an immediate cued recall test, but free-recalled very different amounts a day later (Fig 13.4). Both the amount recalled, and differences in spontaneous organisation in retrieval, reflected a strong developmental trend. Thus, even where the level of initial learning is equated, recall differences still emerge strongly. That the observed differences in retrieval strategy are important here has more recently been shown by Schneider and Pressley (1989), who have shown that younger children have inefficient search strategies during recall.

Organisation and categorisation

A number of studies have explored children's use of organisation and categorisation. Moely, Olson, Halwes and Flavell (1969) suggested that spontaneous use of organisational strategies does not develop until the age of 10 or 11, but that much younger children could be instructed to use these effectively. More recently, Melkman, Tversky and Baratz (1981) have shown developmental changes in the way in which stimuli are organised. Four-, five- and nine-year-old children could indeed organise material reliably, although the basis on which they did so varied with colour, form and category respectively reflecting the organisational basis used for the three age groups. Earlier, Denney and Ziobrowski (1972; cited by Rovee-Collier, 1989) had shown that younger children tend to use functional (i.e. what it does) rather than conceptual (i.e. things that are similar) categories. These results are analogous to the results of Rovee-Collier and colleagues which demonstrate the development and use of both perceptual and functional categorisation in infants.

More recently, Alan Parkin and colleagues (see Parkin, 1993) have explored the development of more strategic uses of memory, by examining the effect of spacing on recognition and recall at different stages of development (see Chapter 6 for discussion of spacing effects). Greene (1989) has shown that spacing effects emerge in recall tasks whether or not subjects are expecting a memory test, but found that the expectation of a memory test (i.e. intentional memory) was required for spacing effects to emerge in recognition. Later, Toppino (1991) has shown that even in these circumstances, performance of an attention-demanding concurrent task prevents the spacing effect emerging in recognition. What Parkin and colleagues showed was that while spacing effects emerge in recall tasks with five- and ten-year-old children, only older children show a spacing effect where recognition is used as the index of remembering. While it is arguable whether rehearsal underlies the spacing effect in recall, it is clear that a more strategic use of one's memory abilities is required for spacing effects to emerge in recognition. The study reported by Parkin shows that younger children demonstrably do fail to show spacing effects in recognition. This may suggest that intentional memorising, or direct measures of explicit memory may not be effective in younger children.

Indirect tests of children's memory

Although so far relatively few studies have been carried out, tasks that place greater stress on the use of implicit processes appear to be performed more effectively than those that require explicit or intentional access to, and control of, retrieval. Carroll, Byrne and Kirsner (1985) measured five-, seven- and ten-year-old children's speed in naming pictures. These pictures were then represented and renamed (providing an implicit measure), and decisions were made about whether each had or had not been seen earlier (i.e. explicit measure). Recognition performance showed an age-related improvement. Importantly, naming latency was significantly quicker for previously named pictures, and this effect was constant across age groups. The study by Carroll and colleagues also included a depth of processing manipulation, which required the children to decide whether there was a cross visible on the object in the picture (shallow processing), or how heavy the depicted object would be (deep processing). Rather unusually, both measures of explicit and implicit memory showed a depth of processing effect. Depth of processing influences are not observed in studies of adult implicit memory.

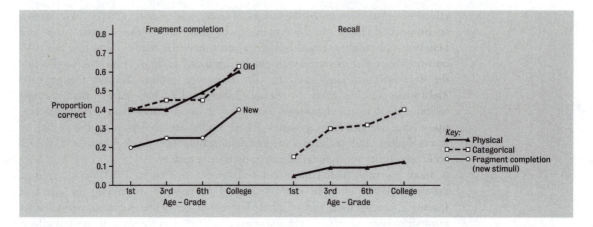

Fig 13.5 Fragment completion and free recall as a function of age and encoding condition (after Naito, 1990).

In contrast, Naito (1990) reports that repetition priming, as indexed by fragment completion performance, was consistently observed in a study of adults and six- to eleven-year-old children, and that the extent of this implicit memory effect showed neither any evidence of age-relatedness or a semantic–non-semantic depth of processing manipulation. In contrast, recall showed both age and depth of processing effects in the anticipated direction (Fig 13.5). Alan Parkin (Parkin and Streete, 1988) investigated the picture completion performance of three-, five-, and seven-year-old children and adults, finding clear evidence of perceptual learning in all groups, the level of which appeared to be unaffected by age. However, a subsequent re-analysis of these data by Parkin suggested that the level of implicit memory as indexed by baseline performance was age-related, but that this age-related trend disappeared when subjects level of explicit (i.e. old–new recognition) performance was taken into account. Given our earlier discussion about the role of both familiarity and source components in recognition, it is arguable that old–new recognition tasks do not provide a clean and unambiguous measure of explicit performance. We have already observed as much with regard to the inter-dependence of implicit and explicit measures in relation to procedural reinstatement (see Chapter 12). Furthermore, younger children typically do worse on other measures of explicit processing. Because of this, suggesting as Parkin (1993) does, that his earlier results are ambiguous with regard to an age effect on implicit processing is perhaps overly critical. Arguably, these results, those reported by Rovee-Collier and those of DeCasper and Fifer with infants, which we discussed at length above, strongly suggest that implicit processing is available for use at a very early age. The requirement to control strategically their memorial processes is clearly more problematical.

Children's metamemory: Realising one's memory is fallible

Taken together, these studies imply that where children are required to use their memory resources strategically, they often fail to do so. It is clear from the studies discussed above that when motivated to do so, they can perform satisfactorily as required. It is interesting in this regard to consider findings on children's self-reported memory prowess – preschool children believe themselves to have better memories than their peers of the same age, and about a third believe they never forget anything (Wellman, 1977). While these may have been particularly insightful children, it seems more likely that young children lack a sense of themselves, and thus of their limitations and those of others (see Howe and Courage, 1993 for an excellent review of this issue). Without a belief in the fallibility of one's own memory it is hard to see why one would ever embark upon elaborate strategies for improving it. The sense that one's memory is fallible is evident in older children, that is, those in final preteen years (see Wellman. 1977), the stage when most studies detect a use, albeit not entirely successful, of a more strategic approach to memory. Some researchers report that the relationship between metamemory and memory performance is rather weak (e.g. Cavanaugh and Perlmutter, 1982), but more recent and, arguably, better controlled studies have reported a more impressive correlation (e.g. Wellman, 1983; Schneider, 1985; Borkowski, Milstead and Hale, 1988). Later work by Wellman (1989) suggests that younger children do indeed use memory strategies, they just do so ineffectively. Whether their use is motivated by imitation of adults, or the feeling that some effort is required to remember, is not at all clear. There is evidence from a number of studies that children can develop memory competencies in restricted domains that exercise a fascination for them. Thus, Chi and Koeske (1983) report a remarkable study of a four-year-old's detailed knowledge of the dinosaur world (and that in the pre-Jurassic Park period!), while Weinert (1986) has shown that among nine- to twelve-year-old children, 'older' football novices recall less than 'younger' football experts.

I suspect that when we come to carry out studies which genuinely tap the knowledge and memory processes of younger children, in tasks that are relevant to them and that they are motivated to perform, in the same way that Rovee-Collier has done with infants, we will find that we have seriously understated childrens' memory abilities. Obviously, as with adults, practice at encoding and retrieval, together with the development of a rich knowledge base, are likely to lead to better performance in memory assessments. Perhaps in most instances, at least until the advent of more formal schooling and the exploration of a less constrained environment, children can get by with a sense of familiarity for things they have and have not already encountered, and the development of 'explicit' memory skills is at less of a premium.

■ Older memory

Much earlier in this book, we considered the view that once forgetting has slowed, that which can still be retrieved achieves the status of being permanent (see Bahrick, 1984; Bahrick and Hall, 1991; Conway, Cohen, Stanhope, 1991; see Chapter 3). Even if such memories are effectively permanent, this need not mean that they are necessarily retrievable, whether by direct or indirect means. In the following sections we will consider encoding in older people, and what is and is not retrievable by older subjects. First, however, we consider the general views which have been thought to typify memory in older people.

Decline and failing human memory?

The repeated encoding and accessing of these memories is held by some (e.g. Neisser, 1984) to ensure that they become more generic, lack episodic detail and become rather stereotypical. Such schematic effects should be characteristic of older rememberers. Others have questioned whether there are such qualitative differences in the older and more recent memories of older subjects (e.g. Rabbitt, 1993). The implication is that the knowledge base built through a near lifetime of experience is preserved, but becomes more difficult to use to perform tasks. This typifies the view of Salthouse (1988) who characterises older memory as reflecting the running of a voluminous library by an increasingly frail librarian.

This offers a rather negative view of the impact of ageing on memory. It is misleading from two points of view. First, while there is abundant evidence of decline, it is not necessarily consistent across all cognitive functioning, and secondly, attributing the decline to age per se is far from straightforward. In considering the impact of growing old on memory, it is important, but very difficult, to distinguish between the contributions of a number of different variables. Thus, we do not become old without having gained and repeatedly practised certain skills (e.g. speaking, reading, etc.), without having failed to practise some skills for long periods of time (e.g. meeting fewer new people and having to learn their names), without an accumulation of damage brought about by environmental and personal causes (e.g. alcohol, drugs, depression, stress, etc.), and without an ever-increasing likelihood of sustaining some debilitating condition. Throughout this book we have reviewed evidence which shows that such factors exert a considerable influence on memory performance. Because of this it is unsurprising to find that, as we shall see, older people often do less well on memory tasks. The interpretation of these differences is, however, rather more complicated.

The pattern of deficits

There appears to be relatively little decline in sensory memory with age; such differences that have been observed are thought to be attentional deficits (Kausler, 1991). Obviously, attentional deficits would restrict the encoding of materials in attention-demanding or more complex circumstances, and thus we might anticipate memory deficits. However, the picture is rather less clear with respect to the functioning of transitory memory in older people. Thus, for example, Parkin and Walter have suggested that older subjects show relatively normal digit span, but rather greater transitory memory deficits when these are indexed by performance on the Brown–Peterson task (Parkin and Walter, 1991, 1992). Earlier, Craik (1977) had also reported no age-group differences among older subjects on digit span, but also no differences in the performance of older subjects on the Brown–Peterson task, nor indeed was there any marked difference in the size of recency effects observed. There is thus some evidence to suggest that transitory memory deficits are more prevalent in older people. However, failure to control for attentional deficits may sometimes underlie these effects.

Tests of recognition performance also show a conflicting picture. Using the Multiple Item Recognition Memory test, Kausler and Klein (1978) demonstrated that older subjects were more distracted by irrelevant items. Rabbitt (1993), in a range of better controlled studies, has shown that recognition accuracy, as measured by d', does indeed decline with age. These differences in findings help to make a number of points. First, as in our earlier discussion of recognition processes (see Chapter 8), it is essential to draw a distinction between recognition tasks which can be performed adequately by relying only on some context-free familiarity based processing, and those more difficult recognition tasks that require access to context-dependent explicit recollection. Given the results reported earlier that appear to show that attentional demand reduces encoding context effects, and the benefits of contextual similarity during retrieval, if we accept the view that attentional resource is limited in the older subject, we can see why source-based recognition performance might be expected to decline with age. Secondly, it is obviously important to contrast tasks that measure performance on the basis of reaction times rather than accuracy. As has been very clearly shown in virtually every study that has included them as an index, reaction times and speeded responses in general have been shown to decline with age (see Salthouse, 1991; Rabbitt, 1993). A third issue which these studies raise is the extent to which recognition performance requires implicit rather than explicit memory. Where recognition tasks can proceed on the basis of implicit processes, then effects of ageing should be less likely to be observed, given the suggestion that among older subjects, performance on implicit tasks appears much less likely to be affected than performance on explicit tasks (Kausler, 1991; Light, 1991; Russo and Parkin, 1993; Chiarello and Hoyer, 1988; Hultsch, Masson and Small, 1991). Howard and Howard (1992), using a version of the Nissen and Bullemer (1987) sequence learning task, have shown that young and older adult subjects show similar levels of sequence learning when this is measured using an implicit criterion (i.e. the increase in speed with which the current target location is signalled), but that older subjects perform less well when required to predict where the target will be located next (i.e. explicit criterion). The error rates of older subjects were substantially higher in the generation phase of the study (see Figure 13.6).

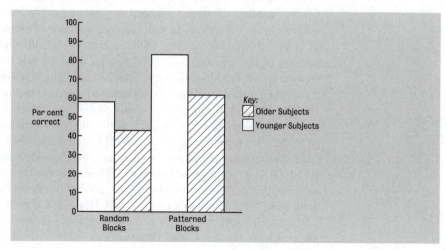

Fig 13.6 Correctly predicted next positions as a function of age in random and patterned presentations (after Howard and Howard, 1992).

What these studies indicate is that explicit tests of memory functioning, which may require intentional encoding of information or explicit retrieval of past instances or episodic knowledge, is more likely to be problematic. It follows from this that when recall, rather than recognition, is used as an index of memory processing, older people should perform substantially worse. As we shall see in the next section, this depends a great deal on what it is subjects are trying to retrieve.

Preservation of abilities

There is considerable consensus with regard to the preservation of verbal or semantic knowledge in elderly people. Thus, Salthouse (1982) shows that semantic memory is unaffected by age, while in the elegant work of Pat Rabbitt (e.g. see Rabbitt, 1993) such is the conviction that semantic performance is stable across the age range that scores on tests such as the Mill Hill vocabulary scale (where respondents have to select from six alternatives the closest synonym to a target word) are used as a basis for matching subjects across age ranges (allowing 'pre-morbid' intelligence to be equated).

In tests of semantic processing that are more demanding, however, older subjects do tend to perform less well. Botwinick and Storandt (1974) have shown that older subjects tended to give poorer definitions on the vocabulary sub-test of the Wechsler Adult Intelligence Scale (WAIS), while Bowles and Poon (1985) have shown that older subjects performed worse on a 'reverse' vocabulary test (i.e. where the subject is given a definition and has to produce that word to which the definition relates). Linking both the suggestion that implicit processes survive ageing better than explicit processes, and that semantic knowledge may be relatively robust across ages, Howard (1991) demonstrated that prior presentation of words facilitated lexical decisions, although the facilitation was at a lower level than is observed with younger subjects. These priming effects have been interpreted as showing that the semantic system remains intact, but that activation of the semantic system (e.g. during retrieval) is slower.

Rabbitt (1993) reviews a number of studies that show that even with the relative stability of simple vocabulary performance (i.e. synonym choice), age differences across a range of tasks are not constant. The scores of a large sample of older subjects on the Mill Hill vocabulary test and AH4 IQ test, cumulative learning of lists of words, subjects' free recall of 30 words and accuracy (d$'$) for recognition of line drawings were standardised. This has the effect of taking into account individual variation in performance on the Mill Hill test. Figure 13.7, after Rabbitt and Abson (1991), shows the average difference between attainment on the vocabulary test and on each of the other tests for each of the age groups. As is clear from the figure, when Mill Hill scores are taken from scores on other tasks, performance on the vocabulary test by the oldest subjects is substantially ahead of their performance on the AH4 intelligence test. For for the youngest subjects, this position is reversed. Thus, general intellectual functioning (i.e. what Spearman, 1927 referred to as 'g', and Horn and Cattell (1966) termed 'fluid intelligence') seems to decline with age, while vocabulary skills are comparatively preserved. As the graph also demonstrates, even controlling for these preserved abilities, performance on cumulative learning of word lists keeps pace with this change in general intellectual functioning (i.e. declines with age), but as age increases, performance on free recall and picture recognition decline much more sharply.

Fig 13.7 Preservation of function in different age groups, controlling for verbal ability (after Rabbitt and Abson, 1991).

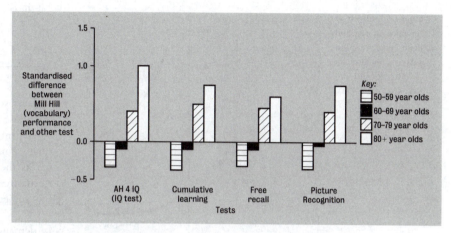

Rabbitt's results make abundantly clear the potential for dependencies between current levels of intellectual functioning, both as assessed by general measures, and those that are more specific to certain domains, and performance on standard free recall and recognition measures. It seems likely that the conflicting patterns of results noted above, with respect to attention, transitory memory and recognition performance, are due to lack of appropriate matching-ability levels across age groups. What the work of Rabbitt's Manchester group also makes clear is that only for some older people can broadly based decline in cognitive processing be anticipated with age. However, in many more older people we should expect greater preservation of function, and especially uneven preservation across function, than would be anticipated on the basis of the degradation of a single processing parameter as envisaged by Horn and Cattell (1966), and Salthouse (1991).

It is also clear that in some cases at least, prolonged practice may be of particular benefit to older people. Rabbitt (1993) discusses a study in which 94 subjects, in four age decades between 50 and 89 years of age, practised two versions of a spatial-location choice reaction task (i.e. respond with one of four fingers when a target appears in one of four locations, but do so for (a) the target currently presented, or (b) for the target presented before the current target, performing some 800 trials on each of five days. The results replicate findings reported elsewhere (e.g. Rabbitt and Goward, 1993), which show that the youngest groups are fastest, but show less improvement with practice, while the oldest are slowest, but show most improvement with practice. Practice reduces the already small differences between younger and older and higher or lower test-score groups by improving the performance of the less able, while leaving the performance of the more able relatively unchanged. Thus, one important aspect of remediation may simply be to ensure that practice is persevered with. Obviously, this may serve to limit episodic and context-based effects, but the increased practice may serve to encourage greater reliance on more implicit retrieval processes. Figure 13.8 shows the general pattern of interactions between effects of practice and task difficulty, which the foregoing results qualify.

Fig 13.8 Effects of
practice on easy and
difficult choice reaction
tests as a function IQ
(after Rabbitt and
Goward, 1993).

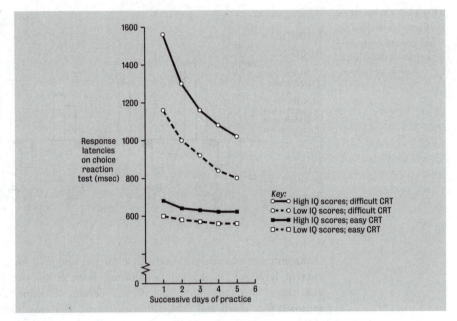

Awareness of memory difficulties

Older subjects' awareness of the declines in functioning described above varies. Some studies have shown that older subjects are more optimistic than younger subjects about how they will perform in forthcoming memory tasks (Bruce, Coyne and Botwinick, 1982; Lovelace and Marsh, 1985; but see Rabbitt and Abson, 1991, who show the interrelationship of mood, depression and age), but this optimism usually turns out to be misplaced. Hertzog, Dixon and Hultsch (1990), on the other hand, show that older subjects recall fewer words from categorised and uncategorised lists than younger subjects, although they did realise that this was the case. There is also evidence that older subjects are less strategic, make less use of mnemonic strategies (Poon, Walsh-Sweeney and Fozard, 1980), and take less advantage of cues derived from the context in which they encounter the items to be remembered (see Micco and Masson, 1992). Encouraging greater use of simple mnemonics and other memory aids is an essential feature of remediation (see Searleman and Herrmann, 1994, and below).

In general, a reasonable summary of these findings is that the older subject is less affected if the task involves meaningful, highly practised or well-learned material, regardless of whether it is short- or long-term, as long as no active manipulation or reorganisation is required, and so long as the subject is not being asked to remember peripheral or unpredictable aspects of the situation.

The extent to which such effects will be manifested will depend in part on practice within the domain, especially for difficult tasks, and especially for relatively simple tasks, on the individual's level of intellectual functioning (see Rabbitt, 1993, for discussion of this intelligence–practice–age–complexity interaction).

■ Summary: Inferring age effects from retrieval performance: the need for caution

This chapter has attempted to consider the types of memory performance typical of subjects both younger and older than those who typically comprise the subject populations in experimental psychology. Remarkable ingenuity has been demonstrated, particularly by some researchers, in attempting adequately to assess the memory competencies of these very different subject groups. Both groups appear respectively to show quite reliable performance with regard to sensory memory, and appear to show limited but increasing, and decreasing but limited, performance on traditional transitory memory tasks. Although obviously different, both much older and much younger subjects show that memories, or at least some aspects of these memories, are quite durable. Somewhat surprisingly, perhaps, infants show that they notice and retrieve quite subtle stimulus characteristics, that they can and do categorise information, and show effects of context, relearning, priming, recognition and to a lesser extent, recall.

Given the obvious sophistication of infants' memorial abilities, it seems somewhat surprising that older children and adult subjects remember their early childhood so poorly (see Chapter 10). There are two points worth making in respect of how these findings relate to what has been termed 'infantile amnesia'. First, the studies in which infants demonstrate that they possess a broad range of memory function, normally attributed solely to older children or adults, typically require indirect access to what has previously been learned. It is possible that infants are intentionally accessing episodic traces of earlier situations, but it is hard to find studies that require such access in order to be carried out successfully, and on which infants perform well. Secondly, the lack of awareness of self, as pointed out by authors such as Howe and Courage (1993), may severely limit our ability to access information about a 'self' which has not yet formed. Thus, the absence of explicit access to episodic information and the development of selfhood may render early information inaccessible by older rememberers. However, given that children have gained the ability to distinguish their thoughts from those of others, and can demonstrate the capacity to retrieve episodic information, there is every reason to believe that where sufficiently creative retrieval methodologies are employed, a child will prove to be as reliable a witness as would an older person (see Chapters 9, 10, 11; Flin and Spencer, 1995).

There is little question that performance declines with age, but there is rather more difficulty in predicting what will and will not decline and at what age it will do so. It seems clear that the effects of age alone are substantially smaller than the effects of age-related dysfunction (see next chapter), that some abilities decline sharply (e.g. reaction times) and others do so much less sharply (e.g.

vocabulary skills), and that the rate of decline may also be related to wider intellectual functioning. That said, it also seems likely that those areas in which the individual has had very substantial practice (that is, generally, although not necessarily, procedural skills), and those that allow a wider range of retrieval routes (and thus meaningful materials), are most likely to withstand the ravages of time.

There are some easy parallels to be drawn between the memory abilities of very young children and those of older people. In would seem that our ability to learn implicitly is established and functions well from early infancy, and is also very reliably present in older subjects. Similarly, it would seem that retrieval indices that depend on explicit memory, whether through the phenomenal experience of remembering, or the retrieval of specific episodic details with regard to the circumstances in which particular pieces of information were encountered, are absent or, at the very least, unreliable in both the very young and the very old. This is an easy comparison, but I believe it is a rather facile one. First, many of the studies of older people are hampered by the uncertainty of whether what is being observed simply reflects age, or whether it is a complex cocktail of a range of other variables, all of which might be expected to affect performance (e.g. substantial prior practice, recent inactivity, cognitive or emotional changes that occur in many older people, individual differences in intellectual ability, and memory tasks which are relatively alien to the requirements elderly people normally have for remembering). Secondly, as we have seen in earlier chapters, and to a lesser extent in this one, the distinction between implicit and explicit processing, and between the results of direct and indirect tests of retrieval, do not inevitably reflect a binary distinction between different types of memory. If these actually reflect a continuum of functioning, rather than discrete functions, it obviously becomes difficult to claim with any certainty that this or that function is wholly functional or wholly absent. Thirdly, when neither motivation, the required attentional capacity, nor perhaps the ability to comprehend the nature of the task's requirements can be guaranteed, one must be very cautious about what conclusions can legitimately be drawn.

■ Further reading

Flin, R. and Spencer, J. R. (1995). *Children as witnesses*. London: Academic Press.

Gathercole, S. E. and Baddeley, A. D. (1993). Phonological working memory: A critical building block for reading development and vocabulary acquisition? Special issue: Prediction of reading and spelling evidence from European longitudinal research. *European Journal of Psychology of Education, 8,* 259–72.

Howe, M. L. and Courage, M. L. (1993). On resolving the enigma of infantile amnesia. *Psychological Bulletin, 113,* 305–26.

Rabbitt, P. M. A. (1993). Crystal quest: A search for the basis of maintenance of practised skills into old age. In A. D. Baddeley and L. Weiskrantz (eds) *Attention: Selection, awareness and control: A tribute to Donald Broadbent.* Oxford: Clarendon Press.

Rovee-Collier, C. (1989). The joy of kicking: Memories, motives, and mobiles. In P. R. Solomon, G. R. Goethals, C. M. Kelley and B. R. Stephens (eds). *Memory: Interdisciplinary approaches*. New York: Springer-Verlag.

Stuart-Hamilton, I. (1994). *The psychology of ageing.* London: Jessica Kingsley Publishers.

Discussion points	

- Infants possess an extensive capacity to take account of their world, and retrieve previous experience of it. Discuss.
- The limitations observed in children's memory reflect shortcomings of the experimental procedures used rather than of the children concerned. Discuss.
- How does developing, changing and losing a sense of self influence what is remembered?
- Are there parallels between the functioning of memory in the very young and the very old? Are they illusory?

Chapter 14

Memory dysfunction

Chapter outline: This chapter examines how memory and remembering are disrupted by neurological trauma. After a brief overview of brain structure, the chapter reviews current evidence with regard to a broad range of dysfunctional states. The review covers cortical dementias, such as Alzheimer's disease, frontal lobe dementia and Pick's disease, sub-cortical dementias, such as Huntington's and Parkinson's diseases and progressive supranuclear palsy, and amnesias, including those arising from viral encephalitis, Korsakoff's psychosis and psychogenic sources. In each case, where specifiable, the risk factors and brain lesions associated with the condition, and especially the cognitive difficulties experienced by such patients, are described.

Key topics
- Brain structure and function: an overview
- Cortical dementias
- Sub-cortical dementias
- Amnesias
- Summary: Dysfunctional and everyday memory
- Further reading

◼ Brain structure and function: an overview

The human brain is, quite literally, inconceivably complex. It is thought to consist of about 10,000,000,000 nerve cells or neurones (Beaumont, 1988), although estimates range as high as one hundred times this number (see Strange, 1992). As if this wasn't enough, the nervous system is dynamic, that is, 'its activity modifies its performance, its internal relationships, and capacity to mediate stimuli from the outside' (Lezak, 1995, p. 46).

Brain composition

As far as it will concern us here, the brain is composed of nerve cell bodies, fibres (*axons*, which are generally outputs from the neurone, and *dendrites*, which generally take inputs to the neurone) that extend from the nerve cell bodies and act as lines of communication; cells that primarily provide structural support (*glia*); and an elaborate network of blood vessels that maintain a rich supply of nutrients to the extremely oxygen-dependent brain tissue (Damasio, 1983). There are several exceptions to these broad generalisations. For example, dorsal root ganglion cells have no dendrites, the cell body lies to the side of a continuous axon, and there are many brain sites where dendrites are known to act as outputs as well as inputs. Neurones are grouped in homogenous communities called nuclei, i.e. groups of similar nerve cells projecting to the same area of the nervous system, and whose afferent fibres likewise have common origins. Concentrations of neurones make up the brain areas which are typically portrayed as in Figure 14.1.

Fig 14.1a Medial view of the brain.

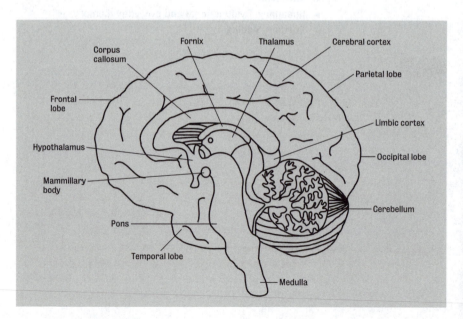

Fig 14.1b Major structures of the limbic system.

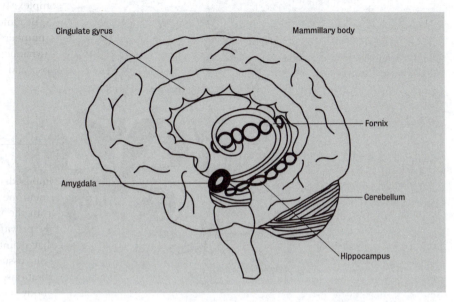

Fig 14.1c Location of the diencephalon and the basal ganglia.

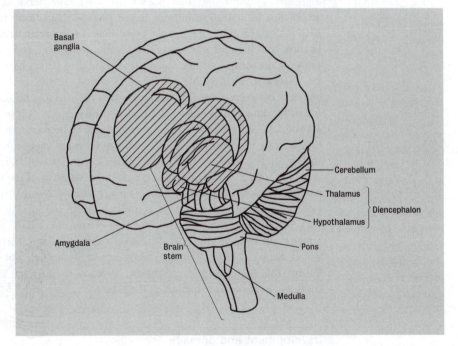

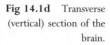

Fig 14.1d Transverse (vertical) section of the brain.

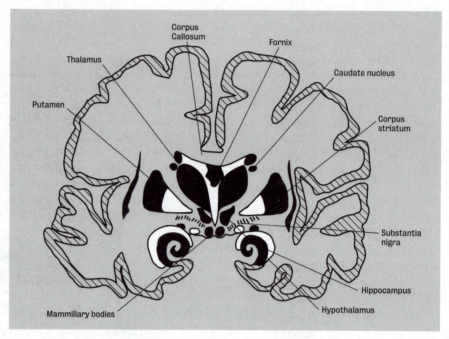

Neurones do not connect directly with each other. Instead, gaps between the ends of dendrites and cell bodies are chemically bridged by the release and acceptance of neurotransmitters, in the process that is known as a *synapse*. A single neurone can produce and release more than one neurotransmitter; these have been likened to 'chemical messengers' (Hokfelt, Johansson and Goldstein, 1984). The range of neurotransmitters, some one hundred of which have been discovered thus far (National Advisory Mental Health Council, 1988), facilitate different synaptic contacts between neurones, which in turn have widely different effects. However, for such contact to be made, the chemical messenger, as it were, must produce the appropriate chemical password for its message to be received (i.e. neurotransmitters only activate receptor sites which conform chemically). Green (1987) has estimated that a single neurone may have synaptic contact with several thousand other neurones, often widely dispersed across different areas of the brain. These potential patterns of activation across the brain are altered by age. As the organism gains experience, neuronal activation stimulates nerve cell growth and thus elaboration with corresponding synaptic proliferation (Diamond, 1990). Stimulation applied to a neural pathway heightens that pathway's sensitivity and increases the efficacy with which neuronal excitation can be transmitted through synapses (Dudai, 1989). Where this stimulation is recurrent, it leads to *long-term potentiation*, that is, a readiness to make such contact in the future.

Development and damage

Cells in the mature nervous system differ from all other cells in the body in that they do not divide, multiply or in any other way replenish themselves. Once a nerve cell dies (during normal development, due to atrophy or as the result of damage), connective tissue or surrounding neurones fill the space left by the dead neurone. When a nerve cell is injured or diseased, it may stop functioning and where it does so the circuits to which it contributes will be disrupted. Sometimes circuits may regenerate, because the damaged cell resumes functioning, or because other connections between the same locations develop or become strengthened (this is referred to as *neuroplasticity*). However, because new nerve cells cannot replace old ones, when a circuit loses a sufficiently great number of neurones, the broken circuit can neither be reactivated nor replaced, giving rise to what are commonly called *lesions* (i.e. localised abnormal tissue changes, Lezak, 1995, p. 46). One focal lesion can affect many functions when the damaged neural structure is involved with more or less different functions, thus producing a neurobehavioural *syndrome* (i.e. a cluster of deficits which tend to occur together with some regularity, Lezak, 1995, p. 46).

The efforts that have been made to localise damage, and to assess remaining function, has gained enormously from collaborations between clinical and cognitive psychologists, but especially from technological developments in the measurement of cerebral blood flow and brain imaging techniques in general (e.g. computerised tomography (CT), positron emission tomography (PET), magnetic resonance imaging (MRI)). Before we consider the damage to memory that results from a range of dysfunctions, it is worth bearing the following two points in mind. First, much of the earlier work in clinical neuropsychology has relied on far more crude assessments of damage, and is thus to be treated with some circumspection. Secondly, such is the complexity of the brain, especially its interconnectedness and the range of chemical changes of which different regions of the brain are capable, that determining whether functions are absent or not, and precisely where certain functions might be localised, is very difficult indeed. I am reminded of the story of the person who wondered whether spiders have ears, and decided to resolve the issue empirically. Placing a spider on the table, and making a loud noise, he noticed that the spider ran away. After retrieving the spider and removing its legs, he again made the same loud noise, but this time detected no movement from the spider. Obviously, because we know a great deal about the properties of legs and ears, we know that it would be foolish to conclude that the spider hears through its legs. There is an obvious moral here with which we as a scientific community need to wrestle.

Cortical dementias

Alzheimer's disease

About 7 per cent of all those aged over 65 years of age suffer from the progressive degeneration of nerve cells in the cerebral hemispheres that is now referred to as Alzheimer's disease (Gurland and Cross, 1986), its incidence doubling every five years (i.e. 14 per cent of 70-year-old people, etc.; Bachman, Wolf, Linn, et al., 1993). Alzheimer's disease is accompanied by profound changes in cognitive functioning, but considerable variation across cases and rates of deterioration in different functions is widely observed. Especially in cases where onset is before 70 years of age, there is very substantial evidence of heredity, estimated to be in the region of between 35 and 40 per cent (Amaducci, Bocca and Schoenberg, 1986) and still higher where the condition has appeared in successive generations. Recent research has localised Alzheimer's disease to chromosome 21, which is also the chromosome associated with Down's syndrome (Jarvik, 1988). Head trauma is also strongly associated with increased likelihood of Alzheimer's disease (Mortimer and Pirozzolo, 1985). Such traumas are thought to weaken the immune system through breakdown of the blood–brain barrier following concussion, thus allowing greater access of viruses and toxins to the brain. Some studies have suggested that smoking, solvents and aluminium are also associated with greater risk (U.S. Congress, 1987).

Loss of neurones, especially in the temporal lobes and brain stem nuclei (i.e. in the basal nucleus in the forebrain, raphe nucleus in the mid-brain and the locus coeruleus at the anterior pontine level; Rossor, 1987), reduced production of associated neurotransmitters (i.e. basal nucleus: cholinergic projections to cerebral cortex and hippocampus; locus coeruleus: noradrenaline; raphe nucleus: serotonin) and reduced neuronal communications (e.g. somatostatin), serve to disconnect temporal lobe structures from the remainder of the cerebral cortex and prefrontal from parietal structures. Respectively, these account for the typical memory deficits of Alzheimer patients and their reduced ability to divide and switch attention (Parasuraman and Haxby, 1993).

A depressingly broad range of deterioration in function has been reported in Alzheimer patients, although the severity and detectability of these difficulties depend in part on the age of onset of the disease. Alzheimer patients have been shown to have more difficulty than matched normals with respect to visual discrimination, spatial judgements and perceptual organisation (Cogan, 1985; Mendez, Mendez, Martin, et al., 1990). These are more severe where patients also have impaired eye-movements. Patients also experience olfactory deficits, particularly in recognition, and this is sometimes seen as an early indication of early onset of Alzheimer's disease (Doty, Reyes and Gregor, 1987). On the positive side, again with respect to sensorimotor performance, motor problems are rare (Adams, 1984; Cummings, 1988), although this may simply reflect the lack of difficulty of some of the motor tasks used. Where these tasks are more complex, difficulties are apparent (Grafman, Weingarter, Newhouse, et al., 1990), but this may obviously reflect an attentional rather than a motor deficit.

Attentional deficits are also widely reported. These include: diminished immediate memory span (Morris and Baddeley, 1988), defective focusing and shifting of attention (Nebes and Brady, 1989), defective dividing of attention (Nebes, 1992), and slowed choice reaction time (Nestor, Parasuraman and Haxby, 1991). While these deficits are characteristic of later stages of the disease, in that it has been observed that visual, verbal span and sustained attention are satisfactory in its early stages (Schacter, Kaszniak, and Kihlstrom, 1989), the emergence of such deficits are nevertheless regarded as a reliable early indicator (Parasuraman and Haxby, 1993).

These attentional difficulties are also manifested in deficits of transitory memory. Thus, reduced performance is frequently found on the Brown–Peterson task (Morris and Baddeley, 1988), with particularly rapid and steep loss where the delay involved exceeds 15 seconds (Albert, Moss and Milberg, 1989). Such transitory memory deficits are typical but not inevitable (Becker, 1988) and are sometimes very severe in the early stages of the disease. These difficulties were compounded where transitory memory tasks are paired with an additional distractor task (Morris and Kopelman, 1986). This difficulty in maintaining temporary information may reflect a difficulty with rote learning (Delis, Massman, Butters, et al., 1991), and is almost certainly reflected in the reduced primacy effect in Alzheimer patients reported by some authors (e.g. Massmann, Delis and Butters, 1993), and the relative absence of proactive inhibition (Cushman, Como, Booth and Caine, 1988).

Some of the ways in which more enduring remembering is normally facilitated do not benefit the Alzheimer patient. Thus, there appears to be no benefit derived from gist or other conceptual relationships (Nebes, 1992), no benefit of semantic categorisation (Herlitz and Viitanen, 1991) or repetition (Weingartner, Eckardt, Grafman, et al., 1993). There is poor prospective memory (Huppert and Beardsall, 1993), limited effectiveness of verbal cueing (Herlitz and Viitanen, 1991), and no benefit of imagery on retention (Ober, Koss, Friedland, and Delis, 1985). These findings do not challenge the view that in Alzheimer patients memory deficits reflect predominantly short-term impairments (Baddeley, Della Sala and Spinnler, 1991), although they do suggest that intentional or strategic limitations, which may well reflect deficits in working memory, are also evident. The picture with regard to the utility of non-intentional remembering appears to be limited to certain types of materials.

Backman and Herlitz (1990) had normal adults and age-matched demented patients, thought to have Alzheimer's disease, study photographs of well-known individuals, some contemporary and some whose fame was rather dated. Subjects had to indicate whether they thought the faces were familiar and select the correct name for each face in a four-alternative forced-choice test. All subjects thought more of the dated faces were familiar than contemporary faces and performed better for dated than for contemporary faces in the name recognition task. However, in a later recognition test, when asked to select those faces they had seen in the earlier study phase, and those which they had not, normal subjects performed better for dated than for contemporary faces, whereas the Alzheimer group performed equally well for both types. Backman and Herlitz (1990) conclude that Alzheimer's disease is associated with a deficit in the ability to use task-relevant prior knowledge to enhance episodic remembering. Later, Lipinska, Backman and Herlitz (1992) replicated these results, but showed that when subjects were required to generate unique statements about dated and contemporary faces at encoding, this procedure did serve to enhance performance on an episodic recognition test. They conclude that differences between normal old and mildly demented individuals in the ability to utilise cognitive support for remembering, may be differences in degree of ability, rather than reflecting a qualitative difference between normal elderly people and Alzheimer patients. Nevertheless, what the results do show is that monitoring the source of any sense of familiarity does indeed pose particular difficulties, as has been noted by a number of authors in recognition tasks (e.g. Eslinger and Damasio, 1986; McWalter, Montaldi, Bhutani, et al., 1991; Rapcsak, Kentros and Rubens, 1990).

The interaction between contextual cueing and prior experience with materials is neatly exemplified in two experiments by Hart, Smith and Swash (1985), that examined recognition memory for several types of stimulus material in older Alzheimer's disease patients and normal older controls. Although performance deficits were demonstrated for previously unencountered verbal and abstract stimuli (geometric shapes and histology slides), memory for faces was relatively intact in the patient group. Hart, Smith and Swash (1985) showed that patients made more false positive responses than did controls, but this could not be accounted for by a general disinhibition of responding, and seemed more likely to be due to a contextual processing deficit.

Mack, Patterson, Schnell and Whitehouse (1993) compared the test performance of Alzheimer patients and that of age-matched older subjects, on a wide range of tasks. Their analyses revealed that Alzheimer patients did significantly worse on all tests (Fig 14.2), while a factor analysis of performance on all tests showed that results clustered into a visual perceptual factor, and factors for transient memory, enduring memory and linguistic performance.

Fig 14.2 Differences between Alzheimer patients and older controls on various cognitive tests (after Mack, Patterson, Schnell and Whitehouse, 1993).

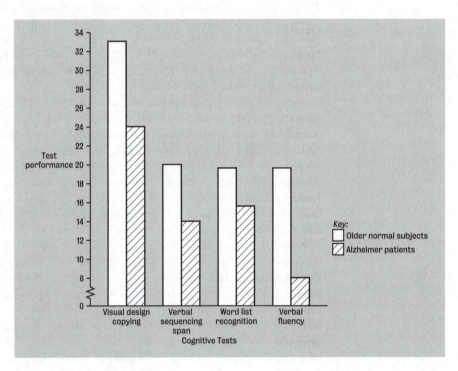

General deficits have also been reported by Gabrieli, Keane, Stanger, Kjelgaard, et al. (1994). Using the Gollin Incomplete Pictures Test (in which subjects are required to identify fragmented pictures of common objects), they showed that perceptual priming remains intact in Alzheimer's disease, but that these patients perform less well than age-matched controls on tests of recall, recognition and word-completion priming. They interpret these results as indicating that separable neural networks mediate different kinds of repetition priming. There is some support for this proposition from recent work by Bondi, Kaszniak, Rapcsak and Butters (1993), who have shown that Alzheimer patients perform relatively normally on a fragmented pictured test, but not on a stem completion task.

Needless to add, this panoply of deficits gives rise to many emotional changes. These range from reduced spontaneity, disinterest, passivity and aimless wandering to bursts of violence and destructiveness, suspiciousness and paranoia (Haley, Brown and Levine, 1987). The incidence of depression is thought to decrease as the severity of dementia increases, only to be replaced by hallucinations and delusions in some 20 to 70 per cent of cases (see Lopez, Becker, Bremner, et al., 1991). In its earlier stages some aspects of everyday life are continued with for longer than is in the interests of the sufferer's own safety and that of others. For example, although, for their age, a high proportion of Alzheimer's patients do give up driving, about 80 per cent of those who continue get lost and one in two or three become involved in car accidents (Kaszniak, Keyl and Albert, 1991)

Frontal lobe dementia and Pick's disease

Two types of frontal lobe dysfunction have been distinguished. Pick's disease, typically has its onset in the person's fifties, while frontal lobe dementia, typically has an earlier onset, but after the age of forty. Although Pick's disease has been known about for longer, the incidence of Pick's disease in the adult population is substantially lower (0.1 per cent, see Lishman, 1987) than that estimated for frontal lobe dementia (circa 2 per cent, see Neary and Sowden, 1991). Pick's disease is associated with autosomal dominant inheritance (at levels of some 20–50 per cent , Cummings, 1992), while in frontal lobe dementia the incidence of dementia in first-degree relatives is very high (some 50 per cent, Neary and Sowden, 1991), thus showing that it too is also transmitted as an autosomal dominant disease. The incidence of recent head injury appears to have a small effect if any (see Mortimer and Pirozzolo, 1985).

As might be expected, in both cases deterioration in frontal areas of the brain is very marked, but Pick's and frontal lobe patients do appear to have characteristically different patterns of damage. Thus, Pick's disease is marked by extensive atrophy in the temporal and frontal neocortex, with the amygdala suffering deterioration early in the disease's onset. In most cases, the occipital and parietal lobes are unaffected, and the temporal gyrus, hippocampus and cerebellum also largely spared (Chui, 1989). The pattern of damage with frontal lobe dementia is similar, in that the frontal and temporal lobes sustain significant atrophy, while the corpus striatum, thalamus, cerebellum and brainstem appear intact (Moss, Albert, and Kemper, 1992; Neary and Sowden, 1991) see Fig 14.1. On the other hand, it is usual to find damage to areas of parietal cortex, and although the hippocampus and amygdala remain unaffected, there is damage to surrounding regions. Thus, perhaps the key neurological difference (in addition to the presence in one case of Pick's bodies, i.e. Pick's cells containing degraded protein) is that damage to the amygdala is almost universal in Pick patients, but quite unusual in those with frontal lobe dementia. In later stages, both can be similar to Alzheimer's disease and an autopsy may be required for final diagnosis.

As with Alzheimers, although not to the same extent, the nucleus basalis is reduced in size, and thalamic and basal ganglia atrophy is common.

In both conditions, personality and behaviour problems tend to emerge earlier than cognitive deficits (Moss, Albert and Kemper, 1992). Frequently, such difficulties are reflected in social disinhibition, poor judgement and impulsivity, boorishness, apathy or impaired capacity for sustained motivation, compulsions and meaningless tactile searching (Cummings, 1992). As a result, both groups of patients tend to be uncooperative in assessment situations, thus insight into the cognitive decline that accompanies Pick's and frontal lobe dementia is relatively limited. That said, speech-disorders are prominent, hyperorality, empty speech, or slowed dysfluent speech are reasonably typical, although memory deficits are not prominent (Albert, Moss and Milberg, 1989; Neary and Sowden, 1991). However, the effects of the gross frontal damage common to both groups are evident in their disordered executive functions, limited abstraction abilities and reasoning deficits (Moss, Albert and Kemper, 1992). Such patients, even early in the disease, have great difficulty in remaining orientated and in maintaining routines.

Sub-cortical dementias

Huntington's disease

This disease was previously referred to as Huntington's chorea (chorea from the Greek meaning dance), because sufferers tend to exhibit involuntary, spasmodic movements. The early focus on the motor aspects of the disease has tended to obscure the fact that patients also endure profound personality and cognitive difficulties. Importantly, from a diagnostic point of view, these motor, cognitive and emotional changes may differ in severity and also as a function of when disease-onset occurs (Folstein, 1989). Huntington's disease affects about 0.01 per cent of the general population, but is lower in non-Caucasians. About 25 per cent of sufferers manifest the disease in their fifties, but the average age of onset is in the forties. However, this age-based onset pattern is misleading, since cases have even been detected before five and after 70 years of age (Tobin, 1990). The disease is autosomal dominant, with half of all offspring of the carrier parent eventually acquiring the disease, although onset is later and the effects less severe when passed from mother to child. The faithful transmission from parent to child allows for early and reliable diagnosis, with the possibility that the onset of the disease may be anticipated for many years before it takes effect.

The anatomical characterisation of the disease is of progressive atrophy of the caudate nucleus and the putamen, together with structures in the corpus striatum (Fig 14.1). There is controversy as to whether the atrophy extends to cortical regions, some suggest deterioration in the cerebellum, thalamic nuclei and other sub-cortical regions (Tobin, 1990). Deterioration of the corpus striatum brings about alterations in the levels of neurotransmitters in this region, especially reductions in the levels of gamma aminobutyric acid (GABA), which at normal levels has an inhibitory effect. There is an increase in excitatory neurotransmitters, and together these changes provoke increases in the

Huntington patients characteristically tortuous involuntary movement spasms. Because the caudate nucleus projects to the prefrontal cortex, atrophy in this region effects a disconnection between the two, resulting in disease characteristics that share many similarities with frontal lobe disorders, even where patients have no prefrontal lesions (Cummings and Benson, 1990).

Olfactory identification is impaired early in the course of the disease (Moberg, Pearlson, Speedy, et al., 1987), while sense of touch is also frequently diminished (Myers, 1983). Typically, eye movements are slow to be initiated, short and jerky on approach to a target, and patients have difficulty in maintaining their gaze on a target once it is located. Initiation of other movements is also slow, and motor coordination is poor, especially on the non-preferred hand (Bradshaw, Philips, Dennis, et al., 1992).

Attention span, as indexed by digit span, deteriorates from normal levels, while difficulties in maintaining and shifting attention are also observed (Folstein, 1989). Huntington patients are very vulnerable to interference effects, as shown by their poor performance on the Brown–Peterson task (Butters and Grady, 1977). Acquisition of new material is poor (Delis, Massman, Butters, et al., 1991), and these problems are compounded by retrieval difficulties. The latter is demonstrated by the fact that retrieval can be enhanced where cueing or a recognition procedure is used to assess remembering (Massman, Delis, and Butters, et al., 1990). However, as the disease progresses, recognition performance also deteriorates, such that discrimination between information that the patient has attempted to learn and new information becomes increasingly difficult (Kremer, Delis, Blusewicz, et al., 1988). Huntington patients show virtually normal priming some time after onset (Heindel, Salmon, Shults, et al., 1989), showing that learning and implicit memory still function. Similarly, studies show that Huntington patients show reliable, if reduced, primacy and recency effects (Massman, Delis, Butters, et al., 1990).

Strategic use of memory resources is greatly impaired in Huntington patients. Spontaneous use of rehearsal or imagery at encoding is very limited (Butters and Grady, 1977; Weingartner, Caine and Ebert, 1979), while capitalising on the semantics of the materials to be learned does occur, but is also unreliable (Weingartner, Caine and Ebert, 1979). Serial learning is thought to be virtually impossible for these patients (Caine, Ebert and Weingarten, 1977), and procedural learning is also impaired (Butters, Salmon, Heindel and Graham, 1988; Paulsen, Butters, Salmon, et al., 1993), as is generalisation of learned procedures (Bylsma, Brandt, and Strauss, 1990), although less so in the early stages (Saint-Cyr and Taylor, 1992). The fact that these deteriorations occur, as do deteriorations in speech production (e.g. articulation, rate and intensity of delivery), even though vocabulary, syntax, and grammatical aspects of speech do not worsen until late into the course of the disease (Bayles, 1988), show the differential impact of Huntington's disease on procedural and declarative aspects of memory.

Story recall is quite poor, especially when recall is delayed rather than immediate (Caine, Bamford, Schiffer, et al., 1986), however, emotionally toned materials are recalled better, even after a delay (Granholm, Wolfe and Butters, 1985). Whether this is because of the greater attention devoted to affective material, or because of the increased self-relevance of the material among patients who suffer considerable emotional trauma, is unclear. There is little doubt that the condition is emotionally debilitating.

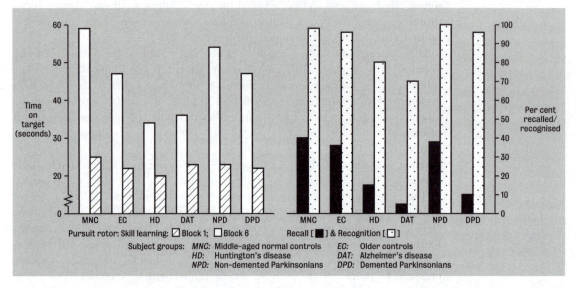

Fig 14.3 Differences between Alzheimer, Parkinson and Huntington patients and normal controls on recall, recognition and skill learning tasks (after Heindel, Salmon, Shults, Walicke and Butters, 1989).

Heindel, Salmon, Shults, Walicke and Butters (1989) report a study in which the performance of matched patients suffering from Huntington's disease, Alzheimer's disease, as well as dementing and non-dementing Parkinson's disease patients, on skill learning, recall and recognition tasks was compared with that of middle-aged and elderly controls. Figure 14.3 shows that after practice groups perform the motor skill task similarly, but initial performance on this, as well as explicit memory tasks, show wide variations.

Caine, Hunt, Weingartner and Ebert, (1978) suggest that Huntington patients are 'acutely aware of their cognitive abilities' (p. 381). About 10 per cent of patients present with mania (Folstein 1989), while it has been estimated that up to 18 per cent present with schizophrenic-like delusional symptoms, although bizarre hallucinations are rare. Irritability, suspiciousness, obsessionality, aggression and sexual promiscuity in the early stages of the disease are all widely reported (Cummings, 1986). Some 50 per cent of patients suffer from depression at some stage in the course of the disease, with one in five suffering from chronic depression (Folstein, 1989). Whether or not these emotional changes are a reaction to the commencement of what is, in most cases, a long-anticipated progressive and terminal deterioration of function, is not clear. The incidence of depression, for example, is higher than in Alzheimer patients, although the level of self-awareness is probably not as acute throughout the course of the disease, and depression precedes the onset of motor and cognitive symptoms in many cases.

Parkinson's disease

As with Huntington's disease, there are pronounced motor aspects of Parkinson's disease. Parkinsonian patients exhibit a characteristic 'resting tremor' (i.e. rapid rhythmical shaking of limbs, jaw and tongue which disappears with voluntary movement), muscular rigidity, difficulty in initiating movements (*akinesia*), and sometimes motor slowing (*bradykinesia*). Together these result in a characteristic expressionless, unblinking stare (*masked facies*), dysarthric speech, general loss of agility and fine coordination, and the typical shuffling gait with little steps. In total Parkinson's disease is thought to affect some 0.20 per cent of the general population (Granerus, 1990), but the incidence rises sharply among the over-fifties (estimated to be 1 per cent, Adams and Victor, 1981). There is little evidence that heredity is an important causal factor, but viral encephalitis and other postviral conditions, effects of neuroleptic drugs and toxins are all thought to contribute (Tanner, 1989). Repeated head trauma, such as that arising from sports like boxing, are also thought greatly to increase the likelihood of developing Parkinson's disease. The great Mohammed Ali is thought to be a sad case in point (Della Sala and Mazzini, 1989).

The anatomical characterisation of the disease is of progressive basal ganglia dysfunction (see Fig 14.1), generally resulting from degeneration of the substantia nigra impacta, and a resulting failure to synthesise dopamine (Freedman, 1990). Basal ganglia project to the neocortex, particularly to the frontal areas, via the thalamus. The dopamine depletion leads to frontal disconnections and thus to the presence and severity of motor problems. Cell loss also occurs in the locus coeruleus and basalis nucleus (Granerus, 1990), with a concomitant underproduction of non-dopaminergic neurotransmitters. Parkinsonian patients also tend to have abnormally long evoked potential latencies (Goodin, 1992). Adult patients in whom onset is before 40 years of age tend to have a slower progression with fewer cognitive disorders, and less dementia (Levin, Tomer and Rey, 1992). Older-onset patients experience a more rapid decline, cognitive impairment and 10 times the level of dementia of early-onset patients (Golbe, 1991).

There is also some evidence of sensory deficits, most Parkinsonian patients having a defective sense of smell (Doty, Deems and Stellar, 1988), and about a third of patients complaining of sensory discomfort, pain, numbness, cold or burning sensations (Bannister, 1992). Parkinsonian patients typically experience attentional deficits, although these are not always observed when attention is measured by digit span, being either within normal limits (Huber and Shuttleworth, 1990) or impaired (Sullivan and Sagar, 1988). Instead, attentional deficits emerge in complex tasks requiring switching or sustained attention (Cummings, 1986; Wright, Burns, Geffen and Geffen, 1990), and in making calculations which require mental tracking (as in the Paced Auditory Serial Addition Task, Huber and Shuttleworth, 1990).

The suggestion above that relatively passive transitory memory is intact in such patients, because there is inconsistent evidence about decrements in digit span performance, is supported by the fact that Parkinson patients appear normal on Brown–Peterson tasks, at least with delays of up to 15 seconds. Performance deteriorates rapidly where a distractor task is introduced during the delay (Sullivan, Sagar, Cooper and Jordan, 1993). However, since short-term recall of word lists or stories is impaired (Brown and Marsden, 1988), it is questionable whether transitory memory is, in fact, intact. In terms of more enduring memory, Parkinsonian patients perform relatively well in cued recall, paired associate or recognition tasks (Beatty, 1992) and they also take advantage of categorisation where the material to be learned facilitates this, but patients are unlikely to initiate these retrieval strategies themselves (Brown and Marsden, 1988).

Parkinsonian patients experience profound procedural difficulties. This would appear to be more than a motor deficit, since sequencing and ordering tasks in general pose very great problems for them (Vriezen and Moscovitch, 1990), as does the performance of procedural skills (Haarland and Harrington, 1990). Although dysfluencies in speech are widely observed in Parkinsonian patients, vocabulary, syntax and grammatical knowledge appear to be intact (Bayles, 1988). Their quality of speech, phrase length and overall output do suffer, at least partly because of the motor control deficits such patients suffer. However, it should be noted that in more discrete tasks, word-finding and retrieval difficulties are common (Beatty, 1992), while naming studies also provide equivocal results about the abilities of different patient groups (Gurd and Ward, 1989).

Bondi and Kaszniak (1991) report four experiments which examined implicit and explicit memory in Alzheimer and Parkinson disease patients and healthy older subjects. Alzheimer patients were impaired on all explicit tests and on word stem-completion priming, but were intact on pursuit-rotor tracking and the skill learning component of the fragmented pictures test (Fig 14.4). Parkinson patients were significantly better than Alzheimer patients on all explicit memory tests, but were selectively impaired on the skill learning component of the fragmented pictures test. Finally, a mirror-reading test was given to Parkinson patients and control subjects, with no significant differences found in performances between groups. Once again, because of the characteristically different damage suffered by these two groups of patients, this study suggests that different brain circuits underlie different implicit and explicit memory domains.

Fig 14.4 Perceptual memory and skill-learning in Alzheimer and Parkinsonian patients and normal controls (after Bondi and Kaszniak, 1991).

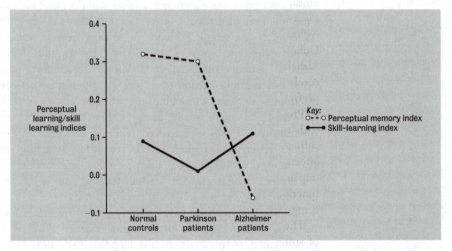

Parkinson patients consistently fail tests evaluating both conceptual and executive functions. Errors normally arise when first required to formulate a strategy, but once a solution is required, they perform at near normal levels (Saint-Cyr and Taylor, 1992). In fact, Parkinson disease patients are similar in some respects to those with frontal lobe damage (Haarland and Harrington, 1990), with characteristics of prefrontal dysfunction, such as difficulties in switching or maintaining a set, in initiating responses, in serial and temporal ordering, in generating strategies, in cognitive slowing and diminished productivity (Cronin-Golumb, 1990; Dubois, Boller, Pillon, Agid, 1991).

In recent years, it has been thought that artificially correcting the dopamine imbalance in Parkinsonian patients by supplying an artificial substitute will reduce the effects of the disease. Although this compound, L-dopa, can slow progression of the disease (Mortimer, 1988), it does not improve slowed mental speed (Dubois and Pillon, 1992) and its effects diminish substantially within two to three years of drug treatment (Granerus, 1990). Finally, it should be noted that L-dopa does produce side effects, including mild psychotic effects, hallucinations, paranoia, confusional states (Conn, 1989) and, as might be expected, dyskinesia (Strange, 1992).

Progressive supranuclear palsy

Progressive supranuclear palsy is a sub-cortical dementia which also alters cortical operations, particularly tasks dependent on prefrontal functioning, which progressively deteriorate as sub-cortical interconnections break down. It is a rare condition, affecting 0.0014 per cent of the general population, although it is possible that this is a substantial underestimate, since in some cases progressive supranuclear palsy patients are misdiagnosed as Parkinsonian. Such misdiagnoses are thought to account for in the region of over 10 per cent of Parkinsonian patients (Golbe, 1991). Onset of progressive supranuclear palsy is normally in the sixties, and is non-familial (Duvoisin, 1992). Lesion sites are typically between the upper brain stem and the basal ganglia, with damage to the thalamic and limbic structures of the temporal lobes (Jellinger and Bancher, 1992) see Fig 14.1. There is also substantial degeneration of connections between these regions and the prefrontal cortex, resulting in hypometabolism (Blin, Baron, Dubois, et al., 1990). Autopsies also reveal neurofibral tangles typical of Alzheimer's disease, although these are more commonly found in the brain stem, cerebellum and basal ganglia, and, more rarely, in the hippocampus and prefrontal cortex (as is the case in Alzheimer's disease.)

Progressive supranuclear palsy sufferers experience considerable difficulties with regard to the initiation of activity, but Lishman (1987) suggests that given sufficient time to respond, patients perform quite well. Lishman summarises the effects on memory as follows: 'Memory as such appeared not to be truly impaired, but rather the timing mechanism which enables the memory system to function at normal speed' (Lishman, 1987, p. 568). Later evidence seriously brings the accuracy of such a summary into question.

The comparative rarity of the disease means that only relatively small samples of sufferers are available for investigation. This makes comparisons across people at different stages of the disease almost impossible, with the consequent difficulty of extrapolating from small samples across a greater range. Progressive supranuclear palsy patients certainly appear to have occulomotor defects (Kimura, Barnett, and Burkhart, 1981; Troost, 1992). Their characteristic difficulty in this respect lies in their inability to control downward gaze, and hence patients experience frightful difficulties when it comes to a host of everyday tasks such as eating, walking, reading, etc. Beyond this, there is also evidence of visuo-spatial deficits, as revealed by drawing tests (Pillon, Dubois, Lhermitte and Agid, 1986). More broadly, there is also some evidence of wider decrements in procedural skill, since patients have difficulty in performing sequential hand movements, even when not engaged in copying tasks (Milberg and Albert, 1989).

Milberg and Albert (1989) suggest that attention span is more or less normal, and mental tracking is also relatively unimpaired, although deficits are more noticeable with more complex tasks (Grafman, Litvan, Gomez and Chase, 1990). Typically, in progressive supranuclear palsy patients reaction time and central processing are slowed (Pillon and Dubois, 1992). Contrary to earlier, more optimistic reports, progressive supranuclear palsy patients seem to experience memory problems in most tasks, excepting simple span (Milberg and Albert, 1989; Pillon and Dubois, 1992). These patients do exhibit implicit learning, and although significantly impaired by comparison with normal people, they are less impaired than Alzheimer patients (Milberg and Albert, 1989). Patients also experience word-finding problems (Au, Albert, Obler, 1988) and dysfluency (Pillon, Dubois, Ploska and Agid, 1991), and to a lesser extent are deficient in confrontation naming (Milberg and Albert, 1989). These problems may, however, be due to the characteristic difficulty of progressive supranuclear palsy patients in initiating activity, which is evident from their performance on other timed tasks (e.g. picture completion, Kimura, Barnett and Burkhart, 1981; picture arrangement, Grafman, Litvan, Gomez and Chase, 1990; and block design, Milberg and Albert, 1989).

As might be expected, perhaps, in such patients in whom much intact processing capability sits alongside profound deficits, emotional incontinence, depression or euphoria is much in evidence (Dubois, Pillon, Legault, et al., 1988), as are apathy and inertia (Albert, Feldman and Willis, 1974; Peretz and Cumming, 1984).

■ Amnesias

While the conditions considered above could hardly be said to be well understood, amnesia is still less so. This condition, of literally being unable to remember, arises from a number of sources, including viral infection (e.g. herpes simplex encephalitis), vitamin deficiency, psychological trauma, and insults to the brain sustained through accidental head injuries or operative treatments. This range of causes also implies damage to a range of different brain sites, and different degrees of deterioration in function. It also means that the indicative rates of involvement, and ages of onset, used above for the other dysfunctions considered in this chapter would be almost meaningless in the case of amnesia. Instead, this section focuses rather more on the functional characteristics of amnesia, including other information where available.

The functional characteristics of what is referred to as 'amnesic syndrome' (see Baddeley, 1990; Parkin, 1993) include a more or less intact working memory, difficulty in new episodic learning and intact semantic memory. Some patients appear to have substantial decrements in autobiographical memory (e.g. Wilson, 1982), while other patients, also described as amnesics, have been found to have little difficulty in recalling events from their own past, although events temporally close to the onset of amnesia may be selectively impaired (see Baddeley and Wilson, 1986). Procedural learning is thought to be more or less intact in classic amnesic patients, since a wide range of tasks (e.g. learning to use a pursuit rotor, reversed script reading and inverted mirror drawing) show normal rates of learning and performance, even though the patient may claim to have no recollection of performing the task previously, or even of the identity of the therapist with whom they previously learned the task (see Baddeley, 1990). In this section, we will look at the neurological basis of amnesia, although this will be rather less precise than for some of the conditions considered above, but especially at the different types of amnesia and their functional characteristics.

Summarising what has been written in a number of places above, more enduring storage of information involves a number of processes occurring at cellular level. These include neurochemical alterations in the neurone (nerve cell), neurochemical alterations of the synapse (the point of interaction between nerve cell endings) that may account for differences in the amount of neurotransmitter released or taken up at the synaptic juncture, elaboration of the dendritic (branching out) structures of the neurone to increase the number of contacts made with other cells (Mayes, 1988; Rosenzweig, 1984), and perhaps the pruning of some connections with disuse (Edelman, 1989; Singer, 1990). As we have seen above, given the range of damage sustained as a result of the different conditions, there does not seem to be a single site for stored memories; instead, memories involve neuronal contributions from many cortical and sub-cortical centres (Penfield, 1968; Squire, 1987; Thatcher and John, 1977).

When registration or storage processes are impaired by disease or accident, the capacity for acquisition of new information may range from minimal, to what is thought to be total, disruption (Kapur, 1988; Mayes, 1988). Temporary disruption of acquisition processes, which often follows head injury or electroconvulsive therapy for psychiatric conditions, obliterates memory for the period of impairment. Inability or impaired ability to remember events beginning with the onset of the disruption is called *anterograde amnesia*. Loss of memory for events preceding the onset of brain damage, whether by trauma or disease, is called *retrograde amnesia*. The former is thought to result from hippocampal damage (Warrington and MacCarthy, 1988), while retrieval problems of retrograde amnesia have been associated with diencephalic lesions, most specifically with nuclei in the mamilliary bodies and/or the thalamus (Mayes, 1988; Squire, 1987) and interconnecting pathways (Markowitsch, 1988) (Fig 14.1). Long-enduring retrograde amnesia over periods of several years is usually accompanied by an equally prominent anterograde amnesia. In moderate to severe head trauma, impairment of new learning is likely to be extensive, while retrograde amnesia is frequently found to be more limited. It is very unusual for dense retrograde amnesia to occur organically without a consequent diminution of ability to learn new information, or to relearn old information (Kopelman, 1987)

Viral encephalitis: Herpes simplex encephalitis

Lishman (1987) distinguishes some 24 different types of viral encephalitis, among the most interesting of which, from a memory point of view, is herpes simplex encephalitis. Those who survive the severe stages of this infectious condition affecting limbic system grey matter will have lost extensive medial temporal and orbital tissue, usually including damage to the hippocampus, and to the amygdala (thus causing a difficulty in control of basic drives, e.g. eating, sexual behaviour), as well as those aspects of the frontal lobe involved in response inhibition and goal-directed activity and appropriate social behaviour (see Damasio and van Hoesen, 1985). Sufferers typically have extensive anterograde amnesia, some retrograde amnesia and profound social problems. The hippocampal lesions appear to compromise new learning, in contrast to Korsakoff's patients, whose thalamic and mamilliary damage appears to result in retrieval difficulties (see below).

Warrington and MacCarthy (1988) investigated the memory deficits of a 54-year-old male patient with severe, selective encephalitic amnesia. They contrast his performance with a group of age-matched controls. Warrington and MacCarthy (1988) show that the patient's retrograde deficit for both personal and public events encompassed his entire adult life, yet he retained knowledge of words introduced into his vocabulary during the retrograde period. He was unable to recall, recognise, and place in temporal order the names and faces of famous people for all time periods sampled. However, his recall of either a famous face or name was significantly facilitated by the verbal cue of the person's first name or the initial letter of the famous person's surname, and his ability to select a previously seen famous face from non-famous faces was normal. Warrington and McCarthy (1988) suggest that names and faces of famous people were represented in both a vocabulary-like fact memory system that was preserved, and a cognitively mediated schemata that was functionally inoperative in this patient.

A different aspect of viral encephalic deficits was investigated to some effect by Mehta, Newcombe and deHaan (1992). They report a case study of a 21-year-old, left-handed male police cadet who was diagnosed as having herpes encephalitis. When his performance was contrasted with that of a group of matched policemen, he showed consistently more severe deficits in recognising things visually and in retrieving knowledge of living as compared with non-living items. When he was required to make judgements of visual similarity for named objects, for object-pictures, and for the factual properties of these stimuli, the same disproportionate difficulty in processing living objects was found in these tasks and in forced-choice recognition. Since no deficit was found on analogous tasks concerned with word-shape similarities, Mehta, Newcombe and deHaan (1992) suggest that the damage due to his viral infection had caused a highly selective decrement in his ability to access the visual properties of a sub-classification within his semantic or declarative knowledge. This supports the notion that visual properties and more semantic properties are separately represented and that declarative knowledge is categorically based.

Korsakoff's psychosis

In normal parlance, this condition is associated with alcoholism. However, this is both inaccurate and unhelpful. Lezak (1995) distinguishes Korsakoff's psychosis from the effects of chronic alcoholism as follows. Only Korsakoff's patients will have sustained significant lesions in structures throughout the diencephalon, along with depressed neurotransmitter levels. Unlike alcoholism, Korsakoff's syndrome has a sudden onset, often appearing as a residual condition of a massive confusional state. Korsakoff patients are also distinguished by having occulomotor and gait abnormalities, marked personality alterations, extreme passivity and emotional blandness, and considerably reduced ability to generate self-serving and goal-directed activity, together with a lack of social independence. 'These two groups are further distinguished by the absence of confabulation and, not least, by the relative mildness and scattered incidence of memory deficits in chronic alcoholics' (Lezak, 1995, p. 258).

Nevertheless, there is a very real link with alcohol abuse. Korsakoff's psychosis is frequently brought on by a particularly heavy bout of drinking, lasting several weeks, during which poor or limited eating results in a reduction of thiamine (i.e. Vitamin B) availability, while liver disease reduces thiamine metabolism (Brust, 1993). These changes result in cell death in those brain regions which are thiamine dependent (Joyce, 1987). In acute and untreated conditions, these thiamine-depleted patients may also suffer confusion and disordered eye and limb movements (Wernicke's encephalopathy, Walton, 1994). Importantly, genetic defects in thiamine metabolism, which may result in increased vulnerability to thiamine deficiency when dietary intake is insufficient, have been identified in some Korsakoff patients (Blass and Gibson, 1977). Typically, Korsakoff's patients show haemorrhagic lesions in specific thalamic nuclei and in the mamilliary bodies, usually with lesions in other structures of the limbic system (Brust, 1993). Reductions in activity in Maynert's nucleus basalis and in the basal forebrain, which in turn reduces activity in the cholinergic system, have also been reported (Butters and Stuss, 1989; Joyce, 1987), see Fig 14.1.

Performance of Korsakoff patients on the WAIS and its components is similar to that of alcoholics (Ryan and Butters, 1986), in that performance on tests where speed is crucial is relatively poor, while tests that assess competence on over-learned skills, such as vocabulary and arithmetic, are comparatively normal. Other reaction time-based tests reveal that both auditory and visually presented materials are identified more slowly and processed more slowly (see Oscar-Berman, 1980; Parkinson, 1979). Relatively simple measures of attention (e.g. span) show relatively little decrement, but more demanding tests of attentional capacity (e.g. dividing or switching attention) typically reveal more substantial deficits (Oscar-Berman, 1984). These findings are further supported by differences in the performance of Korsakoff patients on different types of memory task.

Performance on short term memory tasks is thought to be relatively normal (Butters and Grady, 1977; Kopelman, 1985, 1986, but see Leng and Parkin, 1988a, 1988b). On the other hand, a number of authors suggest that patients suffering from Korsakoff's syndrome show both anterograde and retrograde memory deficits (Butters, 1985; Butters and Stuss, 1989; Parkin, 1991). Such a pairing is only infrequently observed among alcoholic patients. While patients retain access to events that occur during the preceding minutes, using information gained since the onset of the psychosis appears to be impossible. Korsakoff patients also demonstrate poor and inconsistent retrieval of very remote events. This retrograde deficit may be the basis of the typically observed confabulation of Korsakoff patients, in which information derived from chronologically distinct periods is blended together in a rather bizarre fashion (Lezak, Howieson and McGavin, 1983, cited in Lezak 1995; Kopelman, 1987). Among Korsakoff patients, recall performance is very susceptible to proactive interference (Leng and Parkin, 1988b), although this is reduced where long periods of rehearsal have been possible (Butters, 1984), and where patients are capable of making use of visual imagery (Leng and Parkin, 1988a). The fact that recognition tests demonstrate greater retrieval than might be expected on the basis of recall performance suggests that learning does indeed take place, but that it is less successful where effortful, controlled, or conscious encoding recollection is at a premium. If this were the case, then measures of implicit memory, such as priming, might be expected to show relatively normal performance, which they do (Nissen, Willingham and Hartman, 1989; Shimamura, Salmon, Squire and Butters, 1987). It is certainly the case that strategic performance is also diminished, as exemplified by the relatively poor performance of Korsakoff patients on tests requiring hypothesis generation and problem solving (Butters, 1985).

The capacity for learning and recalling sequential information is also much reduced (Lezak, Howieson and McGavin, 1983, cited in Lezak 1995; Shimamura, Janowsky and Squire, 1990). Inability to source-monitor, and to make use of, contextual temporal cues may also underlie the Korsakoff patients tendency for intrusion errors and errors where material encountered earlier is inappropriately used (i.e. perseveration), often across different modalities (Jacobs, Troster, Butters, et al., 1990). Where learning has been successful, Korsakoff patients show relatively normal forgetting rates (Kopelman, 1985), and the capacity for relatively simple skill learning also appears to be intact (Martone, Butters, Payne, et al., 1984).

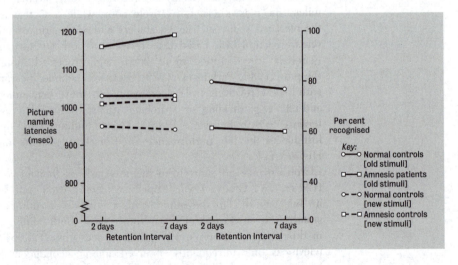

Fig 14.5 Naming latencies and word recognition in amnesic patients and normal controls (after Cave and Squire, 1992).

Cave and Squire (1992) report two experiments, in which the ability of amnesic patients to exhibit long-lasting perceptual priming after a single exposure to pictures was evaluated. Subjects named pictures as quickly as possible on a single occasion, and later named the same pictures mixed with new pictures. In the first study, amnesic patients exhibited fully intact priming effects, lasting at least seven days (Fig 14.5). In the second study, this long-lasting priming effect for both amnesic and normal subjects was shown to depend both on highly specific visual information and on less visual, more conceptual information. In contrast, recognition memory was severely impaired in the patients, as assessed by both accuracy and response time. The results show that priming effects, even on the basis of a single exposure, can be very long-lasting in amnesic patients, just as it can be in normal subjects, and suggest, once again, that recognition cannot necessarily depend on familiarity or priming alone.

Psychogenic amnesia

Schacter and Kihlstrom (1989) distinguish non-pathological amnesias (i.e. 'normal' memory loss of dreams, childhood, etc.) from pathological functional amnesias (i.e. memory loss caused by organic difficulties, or by psychogenic factors such as extreme stress and emotional trauma). Sometimes a distinction is drawn between those who are organically amnesic (i.e. have sustained damage to the neurological structures that support memory) and those who, because of psychological trauma, have become functionally amnesic (e.g. Mace and Trimble, 1991).

Kopelman (1987) reviews the cases of a number of patients who temporarily suffered amnesia. Among them is E.F., a 46-year-old man who, in addition to suffering a range of major traumas (heart surgery, major depression and treatment by electroconvulsive therapy, at least two attempted suicides, and three marriages), repeatedly suffered loss of memory over the previous five years. He would regain consciousness, with no recollection of where he had been, often miles from home. Such incidences of psychogenic amnesia are thought to arise as the result of major psychological trauma and may last from several hours to many years.

Schacter, Wang, Tulving and Freedman (1982) describe the remarkable case of the patient P.M. who presented at a Toronto hospital, complaining of back pains, with little knowledge of who he was, except that he was nicknamed 'Lumberjack', and that he had worked in the city as a courier the previous year. What might be termed his semantic memory, or factual knowledge, seemed intact, but he had lost all personal information beyond his immediate personal past (i.e. a few days). His amnesia cleared shortly afterwards, when watching the final episode of James Clavell's *Shogun* on television, in which an elaborate cremation service is depicted. P.N. reported that as he watched the scene, an image of his grandfather appeared in his mind, giving rise to the impression that he was remembering his grandfather's death and the funeral which followed. In terms we have used earlier in this book, especially with regard to 'remembering one's self', it was as if the televised scenes served to reinstate his 'old self'. Despite the evident personal impact of the death of P.N.'s grandfather, this information was not available to him during his 'Lumberjack' phase.

Although both patients may reflect psychogenic amnesia or fugue states, in view of the discussions above there is also reason to distinguish between the two. While P.N. remembered both his prior self and his 'Lumberjack' period, E.F. was unable to remember the incidents which took place during those occasions in which he 'blanked out', but when not in a fugue state was able to remember events prior to the onset of his condition. Furthermore, it seems likely that E.F., through the circulatory difficulties that provoked his heart surgery and the E.C.T. used to ameliorate his depression, had actually suffered organic damage.

More generally, the apparent separation of selves that occurs in fugue states is thoughtfully considered by Morton (1991,1994) in his discussion of the memorial basis of multiple personality disorder. One case he discusses is particularly noteworthy. Jonah, a 27-year-old patient originally reported by Brandsma and Ludwig (1974), was admitted to hospital following long periods during which he had lost his memory. During some such incidents, a violent personality emerged (which he referred to as Usoffa Abdulla, Son of Omega). In the course of his hospitalisation, three additional personalities, each with its own identity, were also observed, sometimes under hypnosis, sometimes emerging spontaneously. Remarkably, it was possible to measure the intelligence of all four personalities – all four were within the low normal range, all four responding identically to each of the same content or factual items in the tests. A variety of other studies were carried out to assess the degree of transfer of learning between personalities. These revealed that lists of paired associates learned by one personality were not completely learned by other personalities, although some degree of transfer was noted. No awareness of previously having learned the words was claimed by the 'self' being tested. Where the words used were personally significant to one of the personalities, substantial electrodermal activity was noted, but not when the same words were presented to Jonah's other personalities. Morton draws a strong parallel between the forgetting that may occur following child sexual abuse (CSA) and multiple personality disorder. Although this is highly controversial (see Beitchman, Zucker, Hood, et al. 1992), a causal link between CSA and multiple personality disorder has also been suggested by others (e.g. Bliss, 1986). Putnam, Guroff, Silberman, Barban and Post (1986), for instance, in one study of a very large number of multiple personality disorder patients, found that 83 per cent had suffered childhood sexual abuse, and a 75 per cent incidence of physical abuse during childhood.

Understanding amnesia

Baddeley (1990) discusses a number of theories that purport to explain amnesic functioning. In doing so he makes clear that amnesics encode information as normal people do (e.g. they show substantial depth of processing effects across a range of tasks, see Cermak and Reale, 1978; Meudell, Mayes and Neary, 1980), that forgetting occurs at similar rates for normal people and amnesics (Warrington and Weiskrantz, 1970; Huppert and Piercy, 1978) and that amnesics are no more susceptible to interference from previously acquired information, and from newly acquired information, than are normal subjects (e.g. Warrington and Weiskrantz, 1978, but see also Parkin and Leng, 1993). Thus although there are substantial deficits in memory performance, when their memory performance relative to normal subjects is adjusted (e.g. through using longer presentation times for amnesics, or by using longer delays before retrieval is required for normal subjects) there is little evidence of qualitative differences in memorial functioning.

There is one caveat to this, and in it lies the basis for an account of amnesic functioning for which there is increasing support; that is, amnesic subjects seem particularly disadvantaged when the context in which information was acquired is important for its retrieval. It seems likely that such information is encoded. Mayes, Downes, Shoqeirat and Hall (1993), for example, show that encoding of colours, location, size, and semantic category are all preserved, albeit briefly, in amnesic patients. However, such information is not retrieved when performance should have depended on (long-term) memory abilities at which they show impairments. In a much earlier study, Huppert and Piercy (1978) had subjects look at pictures of scenes or objects on successive days. Pictures were presented once or twice during a session, after which, on the second day, subjects were asked to judge whether the item they were presented with during a test phase had been seen on the first or second day, or whether the item had been presented once or twice – thus seeking to distinguish between familiarity based upon frequency of presentation and a sense of familiarity based on the recency of presentation. Normal subjects were correctly able to determine which repeated pictures had actually been presented on the first day, and which had been seen on the second day. Amnesics, on the other hand, tended to believe that repeated first day items had actually been seen more recently. This general pattern was subsequently replicated by Meudell, Mayes, Ostergaard and Pickering (1985), even when the memory performance of normals was equated with amnesics by extending the delay. This is particularly important, since it shows that amnesics and those with intact memory systems are differentially sensitive to certain types of contextual information.

Although some interpret these results in terms of an amnesic contextual processing deficit, somewhat akin to source amnesia (see Mayes, Meudell and Pickering, 1985; Shimamura and Squire, 1987), Baddeley does not consider that contextual cues necessarily have special status, and that instead, amnesic deficits can be accounted for by suggesting that 'one aspect of learning, that involved in episodic memory, involves storing the product of cognitive links or associations that were previously separate' (Baddeley, 1990, p. 426), and supports this argument by citing an earlier study by Weiskrantz (1982), which found that 'amnesic patients are very good at learning high association pairs where links already exist, but become progressively worse as the link becomes more and more remote, being particularly bad when previously unrelated material must be linked' (Baddeley 1990, p. 426). Learning such associative links may include associating the context in which learning takes place with what is learned, or more specific within-task linkages. Support for this type of explanation comes from a study reported by Kovner, Mattis and Pass (1985). They showed that amnesics were able to learn well over one hundred words when these were embedded in either a ridiculous or a logical story. Irrespective of the story context used, these patients demonstrated perfect free recall at intervals up to seven weeks between list exposure and recall. These results challenge the view that amnesic patients are unable freely to recall large amounts of new information within a newly acquired context, and emphasise Baddeley's point about the utility of linkages between items to be learned. The obvious strength of this explanation is that it can account, not only for the contextual effects discussed above, but also the studies in which some learning deficits have been noted, and the preserved ability to develop procedural knowledge or skill.

With respect to this latter point, this suggests that procedural knowledge may be more easily acquired by the amnesic simply because the associations between elements of a task are much less random than may be the case for tasks that require the learning of more declarative or episodically dependent knowledge. It is thus the inherent predictability of the relationships between different components of a skill that allow it to be acquired. Where the components of a skill are less predictable, that is, less constrained by the circumstances in which the task must be performed or in which the components of a task are not mutually interdependent, amnesic patient's will have just as much difficulty in acquiring procedural knowledge as they do with any other novel information. Interestingly, this may also help to explain why frequency of occurrence, rather than recency of occurrence, determines amnesic decisions in the Huppert and Piercy study described above.

Tranel and Damasio (1993) describe the case of a 63-year-old man who, following bilateral damage to the entire medial temporal lobe and interconnected cortices in the anterior temporal and medial frontal regions, developed a severe learning defect for all types and levels of factual knowledge, including faces. In five careful experiments, Tranel and Damasio show that despite this damage the patient could acquire a non-conscious bond between entirely new persons and the affective valence they displayed. They draw two very important points from these findings. First, this patient's lesions guarantee that the entorhinal and perirhinal cortices, hippocampus, amygdala, and higher-order neocortices in the anterior temporal region are not required to support this form of covert learning. Secondly, this demonstration is possible only in a patient such as this, because in individuals with normal or only partially impaired factual learning, fact memory will contaminate the performance. In a much larger study, on the effects of preoperative hippocampal damage on a range of different memory tasks, Miller, Munoz and Finmore (1993) showed results which are similar in a number of respects. When recall was required 45 minutes after the initial presentation of the material, hippocampal sclerosis was associated with a significantly poor ability to remember short prose passages, a complex geometric figure, and paired-word associates, but hippocampal damage seemed to have no effect on attention span, recognition memory, the ability to copy a figure, or the ability to recall a short story immediately after its presentation.

■ Summary: Dysfunctional and everyday memory

The disease- and trauma-induced deteriorations in cognitive functioning we have considered at some length above leave us with a relatively untidy picture of memory and remembering. At present, we are very far from agreement about the precise functional nature of the deficits associated with each condition, and there is an imprecise mapping of these functions onto brain structures. This raises a fundamental issue: what is the role of studies of dysfunction?

In part what we are trying to do is to understand disorders of memory more fully such that more effective remediation can be developed. More broadly, however, I believe that what we are trying to do is to use different sources of evidence to validate each other, in an attempt to limit the types of explanation that we use to describe memory operations in us all, however intact or damaged we may be. Baddeley (1990) draws attention to the difficulties arising from relying only on studies of disease: 'Having a group that is diagnostically pure does not mean that one can assume a pure or indeed homogenous memory deficit' (Baddeley, 1990, p. 410), while studies of damaged areas alone is limited by the fact that 'lesions are rarely clearly circumscribed and will usually affect more than one part of the brain' (p. 410). However, on their own, functional descriptions based on what people can and cannot do, unconstrained by the need to ground such accounts in neurology and anatomy, leaves us merely with deduction and empirical virtuosity as a basis for determining how memory operates. When combined however, these different sources of knowledge constrain levels of explanation in ways that are very demanding, but are ultimately more likely to bear fruit.

The evidence we have considered in this chapter and earlier in this book combines to identify characteristics of memory and remembering in which we can have some confidence. There is now substantial evidence that memory can be separated into what appear to be separate functional systems, which comprise information about our own personal past, factual or declarative information, and procedural knowledge which supports performance. These systems, in the developed brain without significant damage, cooperate to facilitate remembering. These memorial systems, to a greater or lesser extent, comprise interconnected information which is specific to the circumstances in which the information was encountered and reencountered, and knowledge of each sort which is not specific to particular instances. Attentional deficits, whether transitory or enduring, limit our ability to encode such situation specific information, and also limit our ability to benefit from the reinstatement of these cues. The amount of prior experience we have already had with such information may serve to ease or exacerbate these tendencies. The ways in which memory is addressed range from direct intentional attempts to retrieve specific information to the incidental recruitment of past experience which overlaps with the task we are currently engaged in. It seems likely that there are multiple routes to accessing past experience. Each can allow satisfactory remembering, although not always the phenomenal experience of doing so.

■ Further reading

Baddeley, A. D., Wilson, B. A. and Watts, F. N. (eds) (1995). *Handbook of memory disorders*. Chichester: John Wiley & Sons.

Bradshaw, J. L. and Mattingley, J. B. (1995). *Clinical neuropsychology: Behavioural and brain science*. San Diego, CA: Academic Press.

Campbell, R. and Conway, M. A. (1995). *Broken memories*. Oxford: Blackwell.

Carpenter, R. H. S. (1996). *Neurophysiology*. London: Arnold.

Kosslyn, S. M. and Koenig, O. (1992). *Wet mind: The new cognitive neuroscience.* New York: Free Press.

Lezak, M. D. (1995). *Neuropsychological assessment.* Oxford: Oxford University Press.

Discussion points

- What differences in memory functioning distinguish between cortical and sub-cortical dementias?
- How independent are implicit and explicit memory? Comment with respect to studies of normal and pathological states.
- How do people come to be amnesic?
- What do neuropsychological studies of memory and cognitive functioning contribute to our understanding of normal memory processes?

activation: theoretical construct that describes the readiness for use of some stored element.

agnosia: inability, arising through brain damage, to recognise sensory stimuli.

akinesia: muscular rigidity, difficulties initiating movements.

Alzheimer's disease: a fatal form of dementia, generally associated with old age, in which memory difficulties are particularly prominent.

amygdala: part of the brain in the medial temporal regions that is involved in the consolidation of generic factual information.

anoetic: Tulving's term for learning and retrieval that requires no conscious awareness similar to procedural knowledge.

anterograde amnesia: inability or impaired ability to remember events beginning with and following the onset of some disruption.

aphasia: loss of language functions following brain damage.

articulatory loop: component of Baddeley's 'working memory' that is said to refresh acoustic information and transform written language into a phonological code.

articulatory suppression: occurs when a subject, in addition to performing the immediate memory task, is prevented from using articulatory mechanisms by having to repeat sounds, whether these are meaningful or meaningless.

association learning: serves to connect stimuli and responses, often through repetition.

asymmetric confusability effect: occurs where people are presented with simple and complex pictures and have to decide in a later recognition test whether they have previously seen simple or complex forms of each. Recognition accuracy is greater for the simple than the complex picture.

asynchrony: temporal spacing between the occurrence of presentations.

attention focusing: tendency for people to concentrate on key elements of a situation, especially under conditions of increased arousal.

automaticity: the suggestion that performance can become resource free through practice or through rapid retrieval of past solutions to current problems.

autonoetic: Tulving's term for an individual's sense of self-awareness that accompanies episodic information.

autonomous stage: final stage of Fitts's three-phase model of skill acquisition, in which performance becomes automatic.

axons: fibres that serve communication neurones, usually only carrying outputs from a neurone.

backward telescoping: remembering events as less recent or more distant in time than they actually were.

basic emotions: 'anger', 'disgust', 'fear', 'happiness', 'sadness', and perhaps 'surprise'.

binaurally: where same presentation is made separately to both ears.

bradykinesia: motor slowing.

Brown–Peterson task: procedure for studying how long newly acquired information is available without rehearsal, typically involves being given a low load (e.g. three letters) closely followed by another task which prevents rehearsal, after which recall of the original material is required.

CAT (computerised axial tomography): a brain-scanning procedure in which rotating X-ray beams projected through the subject's head provide multiple brain images from different perspectives.

central executive: component of Baddeley's 'working memory' that controls strategic processing and attention allocation and supervises the operation of the phonological loop and visuospatial sketch pad.

cerebellum: part of the brain involved in balance and movement, thought to serve as a store for proceduralised knowledge.

cerebral cortex: top layer of the brain, a sheet of neural tissue about 1 square metre in which subcortical areas are wrapped.

chronological illusion: the belief that time is linear.

chunks: combinations of stimuli with some inherent organisation, probably derived through repeated exposure.

classical view of category membership: the notion that category membership can be determined on the basis of necessary and sufficient attributes, that categories have fixed boundaries, and that all the category members sharing such characteristics are equally representative of that category.

closed loop performance: used when the performance of a sequence of activities depends only on feedback from the performance of individual components of that activity.

coexistence hypothesis: the suggestion that similar experiences do not 'overwrite' each other but that both forms of information coexist in memory.

conduction aphasia: difficulty in repetition and in some cases in articulation and comprehension of speech.

Thought to be due to lesions which interrupt the nerve fibres connecting Broca's and Wernicke's areas.

coordinality assumption: the suggestion that no processing other than that required to perform the orienting task is performed on a stimulus.

cognitive economy: the notion that hierarchical structure and inheritance of attributes are determined by reduction of duplication.

Cognitive Interview: interview procedure for eliciting reliable information from witnesses, relies on re-instatement of the original context.

cognitive stage: initial stage of skill acquisition, according to Fitts, involves effortful performance and working from declarative knowledge.

composition: within skill acquisition involves collapsing a series of steps into one by combining adjacent procedures.

conceptual self: comprises culture-specific knowledge on the nature and workings of our own minds.

conceptual-masking hypothesis: occurs where a new and meaningful visual event automatically disrupts processing of a previously glimpsed picture if that visual event is new and meaningful. Standard results show that a blank field, repeating the same picture, and new nonsense picture did not disrupt memory as much as a new meaningful picture.

congruency effect:. where a positive decision about a stimulus encountered during an orienting task ensures that stimulus is generally better remembered than when a negative decision about it was made.

conjugate-reinforcement: paradigm used to explore infant memory, in which children's willingness to manipulate their environment is used as the basis for assessing their ability to remember previous experience in that environment.

constant ratio rule: states that the probability of recall of any item is the ratio of the interitem interval divided by the delay between item presentation time and the start of recall.

context-dependent: requires that the context in which encoding takes place is replicated when retrieval is required.

continuous distraction: a technique in which the learner is prevented from rehearsing items by the requirement that an additional task is performed between the presentation of each item.

controlled processing: where, because of inexperience or the varied nature of the material, subjects engage in effortful, intentional processing of events.

cyclic time: the impression that there is a repetitive or periodical quality about time.

decay: theoretical position that suggests that the strength, and thus the accessibility, of memory traces declines with time.

declarative knowledge: factual information, generally accessible to consciousness.

delayed recall: procedure in which subjects are required to retrieve items some time after the presentation of those items has ceased, generally having to perform some additional task in the interim.

dendrites: fibres that generally take inputs to the neurone from the axons of other neurones.

dichoptically: where stimuli are presented to each eye separately.

direct memory measures: those tasks in which the retrieval instructions make reference to a target event (or target events) in the personal history of the subject.

dishabituation: technique whereby subjects demonstrate recovery from habituation.

displacement: an account of forgetting which suggested that because the short-term stores were of limited capacity, when more material than the capacity of the store was to be learned, new items displaced older items from the short-term store.

distinctiveness: from a levels-of-processing viewpoint, the more distinctive the representation is of an item in memory, the deeper the level of processing it has received.

distributed practice: practice during which similar and dissimilar activities are mixed within the same episode and where learning episodes may be temporally more disparate.

divided attention: the effect of having subjects attend to more than one task simultaneously.

dorsomedial thalamic nuclei: area of the diencephalon that is thought to be involved in the consolidation of declarative knowledge.

dual-task methodology: this involves getting the subject to do two things at once; the logic is that if the two tasks are similar to each other, needing access to the same information, processes or stores, then performance on one or other task, or both tasks, will suffer.

duration estimation paradox: when subjects are asked to make a prospective duration estimate, that is, to signal when a pre-specified period has elapsed, their verbal estimates are longer and more accurate than when subjects are asked to make a retrospective duration estimate, that is, to say how for how long a completed event lasted.

Easterbrook hypothesis: during extreme arousal people attend to a narrower range of aspects of the situation in which they find themselves, rather than to the whole situation.

echoic image: the persistence of some record of an auditory experience.

ecological self: this gives us our unique self-centred physical perspective on the world.

elaborateness: the elaboration hypothesis suggests that deep processing leads to a more rich, complex encoding, which allows a broader range of retrieval routes, and consequently, less likelihood of retrieval failure.

elaborative rehearsal: where an item to be remembered is thought about from different points of view, or processes in different ways.

emotional Stroop: procedure in which subjects are required to name the colours in which different emotionally laden words are written.

encoding perturbation theory: this assumes that temporal information is hierarchically organised into larger and larger units; thus, when information is lost from some level of the hierarchy, events are 'perturbed' forwards or backwards in linear time.

encoding-specificity principle: this states that memory performance is best when the cues present when subjects are tested match those that were encoded at the study.

energy masking: where presentations which are of a similar energy (or brightness) level to the information to be remembered serve to wipe or wash out the record of the registered information, or prevent its being registered in the first place.

engram: Tulving's term for the brain-based record produced by learning something.

event related potential (ERP): electrical activity in the brain that occurs in response to a specific, known stimulus.

exemplar theory: the suggestion that in categorisation tasks we draw on knowledge about category members rather than on information which is derived from our experience with members of the category as a whole.

exercise theories/selection theories: theories of skill acquisition which postulate that through exercise (or practice), a standard way of performing will be determined which selects those elements which recur in successful performance.

exhaustive serial search: retrieval strategy in which every item in memory is searched in a serial fashion until all items have been considered, even if a target item has been detected earlier in the search process.

experiencing ego: the conscious experiencing entity that is the subject of autobiographical memories.

explicit memory: memory that requires conscious recollection of prior experiences and, according to some, even awareness of the learning episode.

extrinsic context: those aspects of the stimulus situation that are present when the target is encountered, but which are not themselves integral to the target.

familiarity: a sense of having encountered something in the past.

feature-integration theory: an account of the role of visual attention being to 'glue' together separate aspects of a stimulus, such as colour and form (e.g., 'red' and the letter T) so that it is seen as an object which conjoins both properties (e.g., a red T).

filled duration illusion: this arises where two intervals of identical durations are thought to have lasted different amounts of time as a function of the relative complexity of those events comprising the two intervals.

flashbulb memories: individuals' recollections of widely experienced events and the circumstances in which these were encoded.

fluency task: a task which requires subjects to produce as many items which conform to a particular rule within a given amount of time.

forward telescoping: remembering events as more recent or less distant in time than they actually were.

fragment completion: a task in which subjects are presented with an incomplete picture or word, and are asked to complete it as they choose.

free recall: procedure in which subjects are allowed to recall the items learned in any order they wish.

frequency attenuation effect: the result of the greater availability of 'episodic traces' of high frequency words.

frequency paradox: this refers to the differential effects of word-frequency on recall and recognition performance. Words we often come across are better retrieved under recall than under recognition conditions, while rare words are better recognised than recalled.

frontal cortex: region at the front of the cerebral cortex that includes the motor and prefrontal cortex.

fuzzy boundaries: refers to theories of categorisation that suggest that there is no fixed point at which something ceases to be a member of one category and becomes a member of another.

galvanic skin response: skin conductance level, as it is now more widely known, provides an electrical measure of the skin's conductance, which, because of increases in perspiration, reflect increases in level of arousal.

generalisation: where the response made to one stimulus is newly extended from that already learned in connection with another stimulus.

generation effect: the finding that subjects who generate their own associations for words or events perform better than subjects who learn associations provided by others that are simply listened to or read.

generation–recognition: a family of models of retrieval, according to which the retrieval process begins by generating candidates for the target item being sought, and continues to subject these to a recognition process, which if successful, leads to one of the candidates being designated as the retrieved target item.

glia: cells that primarily provide structural support.

graded structure: theory that some category members are further away from the prototype than others, or are less typical category members than others.

graphemic priming: an increased readiness to use a particular stimulus because it has been preceded by something structurally similar.

habituation: a decrease in response level to a related event.

hippocampus: sub-cortical area of the brain, in the medial temporal regions, thought to be critical to the formation of permanent memories, especially those involving declarative knowledge.

Huntington's disease: disease that results in dementia and lack of precision and timing of movement control.

hypothalamus: subcortical area involved in motivation and regulation of the expression of basic drives.

iconic memory: the persistence of some record of a visual experience.

illusory conjunctions: this suggests, according to feature-integration theory, that attributes of a previously encountered stimulus can be wrongly recombined.

implicit memory: retrieval that does not require reference to a specific episode, performed in the absence of conscious recollection.

incidental learning: the learning that results when an individual is not consciously attempting to learn.

indirect memory measures: those tasks requiring the subject to engage in some motor or cognitive activity, in which the instructions given refer only to the task at hand, do not make reference to prior events, and from which evidence of retrieval of prior knowledge is later inferred.

infantile amnesia: the inaccessibility of early childhood memories.

instance theory: theory that suggests that each encounter with a stimulus is encoded, stored and retrieved separately; before sufficient instances are available to support performance, people rely on algorithms rather than instance retrieval.

intentional learning: the learning that results following an effort to learn.

interpersonal self: this comprises the species-specific behaviour that people communicate to each other.

intrinsic context: those attributes of the stimulus situation that are integral to the way in which some target stimulus is processed.

inversion effect: this refers to the fact that recognition of other-race faces is more disrupted by inversion than is the recognition of own-race faces.

knowledge of results: feedback regarding the level of success of prior performance.

Korsakoff's syndrome: brain disorder associated with long-term alcohol abuse and nutritional deficits, although not necessarily alcoholism, characterised by anterograde amnesia and some loss of long-term autobiographical memories.

leading questions: a form of questioning that biases the rememberer towards retrieving certain aspects of an original event.

lesions: localised abnormal changes in brain tissue, sustained through injury or disease.

limited capacity parallel retrieval models: these assume that the speed with which a decision can be made (i.e. that an item within a set and the probe item are the same) depends on how much processing resource is available for the task, and that this resource is limited, and is divided equally and simultaneously among all the candidate responses to that decision.

linear time: the notion that there exist non-overlapping periods of time that are past and present and a time that will be future.

linkword language system: a system of vocabulary learning that requires the subject to blend a phonological image of the word to be learned with a visual image based on that sound, which is also relevant to the meaning of the word to be learned.

long-term potentiation: a readiness for neurones previously in contact to make such contact in the future.

long-term store: originally thought to be a unitary store of information, said to be unlimited in capacity and duration.

maintenance rehearsal: procedure in which an item might simply be repeatedly said or thought about in an identical fashion.

mamillary bodies: structures in the diencephalon associated with consolidation of declarative knowledge.

masked facies: the term used to refer to the expressionless, unblinking stare characteristic of Parkinsonian patients.

massed practice: refers to situations in which an activity or highly similar activities, and no others, are encountered repeatedly within learning episodes which are close to each other in time.

medial temporal regions: areas of the brain in which the hippocampus and the amygdala are located.

method of loci: method for learning the sequential order of more complex materials, in which each element of the information to be learned is associated with separate locations.

minimal core encoding: thought by levels-of-processing theorists to involve structural analysis and some degree of semantic analysis.

mirror effect: refers to the finding that hit and false alarm rates on a recognition test are inversely related.

misinformation effect: the provision of inaccurate information between encoding and retrieval with a view to biasing retrieval towards certain, false, aspects of the original information.

modal model: comprised the sensory information registers, a short-term and a long-term store.

mood asymmetry: the finding that cognitive processing of positive and negatively toned materials are not equally sensitive to manipulation.

mood-congruent memory: where the state in which a person retrieves information, rather than the match between test and study state, influences what is remembered.

mood-dependent memory: the suggestion that similarity between one's mood at encoding and one's mood at retrieval enhances remembering.

mood-incongruent encoding: the finding that where mildly, rather than strongly, emotionally valenced words are used as stimuli, subjects appear more likely to encode events that are inconsistent with the subject's current mood state.

mood-incongruous retrieval: the finding that, where naturalistic mood induction procedures are used, subjects are more effective at retrieving personal memories that were incongruous with the prevailing mood.

movement-time effect: the time required to physically or metaphorically perform a particular action; provides a visuo-spatial counterpart to the word-length effect.

MRI (magnetic resonance imaging): brain-scanning technique in which radio-frequency pulses bombard the head of a subject, while it is surrounded by a strong magnetic field; images of the brain are derived from the signals it emits in response.

neuroplasticity: occurs where the individual regains some function lost following brain damage; it arises because damaged cells resume functioning, or because other connections between the same locations develop or become strengthened.

noetic: Tulving's term for an individual's sense of having encountered information previously, but while being unaware of the source of this familiarity; similar to semantic or declarative knowledge.

nonsense syllable: meaningless combination of consonants or consonants and vowels, used as stimulus materials where materials relatively unbiased by prior experience is required.

nuclei: neurones grouped in homogenous communities, projecting to the same area of the nervous system and whose afferent fibres likewise have common origins.

number–letter mnemonics: method of encoding letters or words to be learned in a specific order by generating some visuo-spatial imagery link between numbers and letters.

occipital lobe: brain area at the back of the cerebral cortex that is mainly involved in vision.

open loop performance: sequence of action performed without waiting for feedback from the results of earlier actions.

orienting task: the task a subject is asked to engage in when incidental or intentional learning is taking place.

parietal lobe: brain area at the top of the cerebral cortex that is mainly involved in higher sensory functions.

partial report technique: technique developed by Sperling in which following brief exposure of a stimulus array, the subject is required to report some specified sub-set of what was presented.

pattern masking: occurs where preceding or subsequent presentations are visually similar to the information to be remembered, especially where the interval between the pattern mask and the target presentation is relatively brief.

peg-word: mnemonic technique for ordered list learning, based on finding words that sound like numbers, and then forming an image linking these numerical sound-alikes and the words to be learned.

perceptual fluency: the rapidity with which a previously encountered event can be identified on a subsequent presentation.

perseveration: difficulty in switching from one rule to another, especially frequent in patients with frontal lobe damage.

PET (positron emission tomography): brain-scanning procedure that measures metabolic activity in different areas of the brain; very mildly radioactive glucose is introduced to the blood stream, and the take-up of this by different neurones is measured by a radiation detector.

phonological priming: an increased readiness to use a particular stimulus because it has been preceded by something that sounds similar.

phonological similarity effect: shows that subjects find it more difficult to remember strings that are phonologically similar than those that are not, especially where the delay between learning and retrieving is relatively brief.

picture superiority effect: shows that recall and recognition of pictorial information is better than purely verbal information, and also that non-verbal memory storage is more stable than verbal memory storage over intervals of hours to days.

post-error slowing: effect emerging from highly routine well-practised tasks that shows that when an incorrect response is made, following responses are slowed, even though subjects may later report not being aware that errors have been made.

post-traumatic stress disorder: disruption in cognitive function, especially memory flash-backs to events associated with some precipitating traumatic experience.

power law of practice: the finding that the log of some performance index plotted against the log of the number of trials yields a linear function, that is, there

is a power law relationship between success and practice.

precedence effect: the finding that only the first sound to arrive at the ears appears to be used in its localisation.

primacy effect: the tendency for the first items in a sequence to be better remembered than items towards the middle of that sequence.

priming: prior exposure to an identical or related stimulus that serves to increase the readiness with which it or the related stimulus can be used.

priority learning: assumption that is part of strength theories of automatisation, and suggests that one effect of learning is to attract attention to display positions that are likely to contain targets.

private self: comprises the uniquely personal information that affords us our sense of identity.

proactive interference: where old information interferes with the acquisition of related new information.

proceduralisation: the formation of production rules that represent condition-action (i.e., a rule that requires that some precondition is met before a particular action is performed) and underlie procedural knowledge.

procedural knowledge: knowledge of how to perform various tasks, generally not directly accessible to conscious recollection.

procedural reinstatement: the postulate that retention depends on the degree to which procedures executed, and thereby exercised, at study are reinstated at test.

production rules: condition-action rules that govern processing.

prospective duration judgement: estimation of how much time has elapsed since the start of an activity that has not yet ended.

prototype theory: theory of categorisation that does not attempt to identify the boundary conditions for category membership, but instead uses the concept of an average category member (or prototype), which is based upon the experience one has had with category members.

psychogenic amnesia: the loss of personal information following extreme emotional trauma.

Ranschburg effect: poor recall of repeated items which are presented in short sequences.

recency effect: the tendency for the last items in a sequence to be better remembered than items towards the middle of that sequence.

recognition failure: shows that in certain circumstances items which can be recalled cannot be recognised.

recovered memory: term used to refer to the suggestion that memories of abuse or trauma can be lost but subsequently remembered as the result of some therapeutic process, without prejudice to whether the accounts given by victims are wholly, or partly, based on actual episodes of abuse.

redintegrative memory: ability to recognise degraded versions of previously encountered stimuli.

reepisodic blurring: where repeated retrieval of particular episodic memories leads them to become amalgamated with similar memories, causing them to become more general, to lose specific details and to alter in the perspective from which they are recalled.

release from proactive interference: the finding that a category shift revitalises acquisition of information that is diminished because of its similarity to already learned information.

remembering self: self that is involved in extending and developing personal relations, through the maintenance, revision and presentation of our own personal narrative.

reminiscence peak: relates to the apparent overrepresentation of memories of events dating from when the rememberer would have been between 10 and 30 years of age.

repetition blindness effect: effect in which literal repetition of an item severely diminishes the processing of the second presentation of that item.

repetition priming effect: processing of an identical item is facilitated by its having been presented previously; this is stronger for low-frequency words than for high-frequency words.

retroactive interference: reduced ability to remember previously learned information because of its similarity to newly acquired information.

retrograde amnesia: loss of memory for events preceding the onset of brain damage, whether this arises through trauma or disease.

retrospective duration judgement: estimation of how long a completed event lasted.

schema: a mental model or representation, built up through experience, about a person, object, situation, or event, and that comprises fixed and variable information.

schema-identifying: applied to events or concepts that serve to discriminate one schema from another.

schema-instantiating: applied to events or concepts that serve to activate one schema rather than another.

screen memories: fabricated neutral recollective experience, that shares superficial similarities with the repressed memory, used to block emotional experience.

self-relevance effect: deciding that material is personally relevant leads to better recall.

self-schema: a generic cognitive structure containing information about the individual's goals, attitudes and references.

semantic priming: priming where the basis of the relationship is semantic.

semantic similarity effect: shows that subjects find it more difficult to remember strings that are semantically similar than those that are not, especially where the delay between learning and retrieving is relatively long.

sensory information stores: these briefly preserve records of the sensory characteristics of the information that has been encoded, although the persistence of the perceptual record varies with the sensory modality activated.

serial position curve: curve representing the finding that items encountered towards the beginning and end of some lists are better recalled than those occupying the middle positions in the list.

serial recall: the requirement to remember items in the order in which they were encountered, serves greatly to reduce the recency effect.

short-term store: part of the modal model responsible for immediate memory and transfer of newly acquired information to long-term memory.

source amnesia: amnesia relating to the distinction between episodic memories and those lacking specific information regarding the learning episode.

source memory: a sense of where a feeling of familiarity comes from, that is, the context in which it was originally encountered.

spacing effect: the finding that events will be remembered better if they are relatively far away from each other, rather than if they follow each other immediately.

state-dependent: the suggestion that similarity between one's state or level of arousal at encoding and that at retrieval enhances remembering.

Sternberg paradigm: requires subjects to hold a number of items in memory and then to decide, as quickly as possible, whether a 'probe' item is a member of the memorised set.

storage size metaphor: one interpretation of why we believe events had a particular duration, i.e., that events which occupy more, or more complex, memory storage will be thought to have lasted longer.

story mnemonics: these reflect one way of remembering complex sequential information, by associating the elements to be remembered with parts of a story, which in its retelling can promote the remembering of the desired information.

strengthening: process within some theories of skill acquisition that involves increasing the speed with which productions are excluded from consideration.

Stroop effect: the performance decrement that occurs when subjects are asked to name the colour in which a word is written, if that word itself refers to another colour.

suffix effect: categorical similarity between the penultimate and final events in some presented list interferes with memory performance of the penultimate item.

synaesthesia: combination of imagery derived from different modalities.

synapse: chemical process whereby gaps between the ends of dendrites and cell bodies are chemically bridged by the release and acceptance of neurotransmitters.

syndrome: a cluster of deficits that tend to occur together with some regularity.

synergistic ecphory: refers to what we experience when a retrieval cue successfully accesses an engram; the retrieved information together with that available from the retrieval cue give rise to a phenomenal experience of 'certain aspects of the original event' (Tulving, 1976, p. 40).

tachistoscope: device for controlling the illumination and presentation order of visual stimuli.

temporal duration: the time an event took to complete.

temporal lobe: area at the side of the cerebral cortex that contains the main auditory areas and is also involved in object recognition.

temporal perspective: an individual's experience of, as well as attitudes and beliefs about, time.

temporal succession: order in which events occurred.

theory of mind: the knowledge that people have independent or separate ways of thinking and construing events.

time-tagging hypothesis: time-related information about events and relationships between events is encoded as part of the memory for an event.

trace decay theory: an account of forgetting suggesting that, without revitalisation through rehearsal or recoding, the record of an experience grows less accessible over time.

transactional account of emotional processing: suggests that emotion arises from how a person construes the outcome, actual or anticipated, of some transaction with the environment.

transfer-appropriate processing: term suggesting that remembering is maximised where the processing carried out during encoding matches the requirements of the retrieval task, rather than because of the depth to which an encoded item has been processed.

Tulving–Wiseman law: the suggestion that recall and recognition are at best weakly correlated, reflecting the fact that both methods of retrieval depend on different retrieval processes.

unattended speech effect: immediate recall of visually presented words or digits is impaired if the visual presentation is accompanied by irrelevant spoken material.

updating: the process whereby new information is incorporated within an existing memory record, such that old information is lost.

vacant slot hypothesis: One interpretation of why post-event information disrupts memory for events, i.e., that the new information incorporated in the memory record adds to, but does not replace, original information.

visuo-spatial sketch pad: component of Baddeley's working memory model which deals with visuo-spatial materials, spatial tasks and orientation.

von Restorff effect: increased likelihood of retrieval of items which are conceptually or perceptually distinctive from those already studied.

weapon focus: describes the impact of extreme emotion on memory, that is, through restricting the range of stimulus attributes reported to those that are the source of the emotional change.

whole report: the requirement to report all of the items presented in a memory trial rather than some sub-set of those items.

word-length effect: the time taken to read words aloud and the successful immediate recall of words are closely related.

Abelson, R.P. (1981). Psychological status of the script concept. *American Psychologist, 36,* 715–29.

Abravenel, E. (1973). Retention of shape information under haptic or visual acquisition. *Perceptual and Motor Skills, 36,* 683–90.

Ackerman, P.L. (1988). Determinants of individual differences during skill acquisition: Cognitive abilities and information processing. *Journal of Experimental Psychology: General, 117,* 288–318.

Adams, R.D. (1984). Aging and human locomotion. In M.L. Albert (Ed.), *Clinical neurology of aging.* New York: Oxford University Press.

Adams, R.D. & Victor, M. (1981). *Principles of neurology.* New York: McGraw-Hill.

Aitchison, J. (1994). *Words in the mind.* Oxford: Blackwell.

Alba, J.W., Chromiak, W., Hasher, L. & Attig, M.S. (1980). Automatic encoding of category size information. *Journal of Experimental Psychology: Human Learning and Memory, 6,* 370–78.

Alba, J.W. & Hasher, L. (1983). Is memory schematic? *Psychological Bulletin, 93,* 203–31.

Albert, M.L., Feldman, R.G. & Willis, A.L. (1974). The 'subcortical dementia' of progressive supranuclear palsy. *Journal of Neurology, Neurosurgery and Psychiatry, 37,* 121–30.

Albert, M.S., Moss, M.B., & Milberg, W. (1989). Memory testing to improve the differential diagnosis of Alzheimer's disease. In K. Igbal, H.M. Wisniewski & B. Winblad (Eds), *Alzheimer's disease and related disorders.* New York: Alan R. Liss.

Allan, L.G. (1979). The perception of time. *Perception and Psychophysics, 26,* 340–54.

Allard, F. & Starkes, J.L. (1991). Motor-skill experts in sports, dance and other domains. In K.A. Ericsson & J. Smith (Eds), *Towards a general theory of expertise: Prospects and limits,* pp. 126–52. Cambridge: Cambridge University Press.

Allen, J.A., Hays, R.T. & Buffardi, L. (1986). Maintenance training, simulator fidelity and individual differences in transfer of training. *Human Factors, 28,* 497–509.

Allen, J.F. & Kautz, H.A. (1985). A model of naive temporal reasoning. In J.R. Hobbs & R.C. Moore (Eds), *Formal theories of the commonsense world,* pp. 251–68. Norwood, NJ: Ablex.

Amaducci, L.A., Bocca, W.A., & Schoenberg, B.S. (1986). Origin of the distinction between Alzheimer's disease and senile dementia: How history can clarify nosology. *Neurology, 36,* 1497–9.

Anderson, J.R. (1982). Acquisition of cognitive skill. *Psychological Review, 89,* 369–406.

Anderson, J.R. (1983). *The architecture of cognition.* Cambridge, MA:Harvard University Press.

Anderson, J.R. (1987). Methodologies for studying human knowledge. *Behavioral and Brain Sciences, 10,* 467–505.

Anderson, J.R. (1991) Is human cognition adaptive? *Behavioral and Brain Sciences, 14(3),* 471–517.

Anderson, J.R. (1995). *Learning and memory: An integrated approach.* New York: John Wiley.

Anderson, J.R. & Bower, G.H. (1972). Recognition and retrieval processes in free recall. *Psychological Review, 79,* 97–123.

Anderson, J.R. & Milson, R. (1989). Human memory: An adaptive perspective. *Psychological Review. 96(4),* 703–19.

Anderson, J.R. & Pichert, J.W. (1978). Recall of previously unrecallable information following a shift in perspective. *Journal of Verbal Learning and Verbal Behavior, 17,* 1–12.

Anderson, J.R., Pichert, J.W. & Shirey, L.L (1983). Effects of the reader's schema at different points in time. *Journal of Educational Psychology, 75,* 271–79.

Anderson, J.R. & Reder, L.M. (1979). An elaborative processing explanation of depth of processing. In L.S. Cermak & F.I.M. Craik (Eds), *Levels of processing in human memory,* pp. 385–403. Hillsdale, NJ: Lawrence Erlbaum.

Annett, J. (1991). Skill acquisition. In J.E. Morrison (Ed.), *Training for performance: Principles of applied human learning,* pp. 13–51. Chichester: John Wiley.

Annet, J. & Kay, H. (1957). Knowledge of results and skilled performance. *Occupational Psychology, 31,* 69–79.

Antes, J.R. & Kristjanson, A.F. (1993). Effects of capacity demands on picture viewing. *Perception and Psychophysics, 54,* 808–13.

Armstrong, S.L., Gleitman, L.R. & Gleitman, H. (1983) What some concepts might not be. *Cognition, 13,* 263–308.

Aschoff, J. (1985). Circadian timing. New York Academy of Sciences conference on timing and time perception: Rhythmic patterns and music (1983, New York). *Annals of the New York Academy of Sciences, 423,* 442–68.

Atkinson, R.C. & Juolah, J.F. (1974). Search and decision processes in recognition memory. In D.H. Krantz, R.C. Atkinson, R.D. Luce & P. Suppes (Eds), *Contemporary developments in mathematical psychology*. San Francisco: W.H. Freeman.

Atkinson, R.C. & Raugh, M.R. (1975). An application of the mnemonic keyword method to the acquisition of a Russian vocabulary. *Journal of Experimental Psychology: Human Learning and Memory, 104*, 126–33.

Atkinson, R.C. & Shiffrin, R.M. (1968). Human memory: A proposed system and its control processes. In K.W. Spence & J.T. Spence (Eds), *The psychology of learning and memory, Vol. 2*. New York: Academic Press.

Au, R., Albert, M.L., & Obler, L.K. (1988). Clinical forum. The relation of aphasia to dementia. *Aphasiology, 2*, 161–73.

Auday, B.C., Sullivan, C. & Cross, H.A. (1988). The effects of constrained rehearsal on judgments of temporal order. *Bulletin of the Psychonomic Society, 26*, 548–51.

Avant, L.L, Lyman, P.J. & Antes, J.R. (1975). Effects of stimulus familiarity upon judged visual duration. *Perception and Psychophysics, 17*, 253–62.

Ayres, T.J., Jonides, J., Reitman, J.S., Egan, J.C. & Howard, D.A. (1979). Differing suffix effects for the same physical suffix. *Journal of Experimental Psychology: Human Learning and Memory, 5*, 315–21.

Bachman, D.L., Wolf, P.A., Linn, et al. (1993). Incidence of dementia and probable Alzheimer's disease in general population: The Framingham study. *Neurology, 43*, 515–19.

Backman, L., & Herlitz,. (1990). The relationship between prior knowledge and face recognition memory in normal aging and Alzheimer's disease. *Journals of Gerontology, 45*, 94–100.

Baddeley, A.D. (1966a). Short-term memory for word sequences as a function of acoustic, semantic and formal similarity. *Quarterly Journal of Experimental Psychology, 18*, 362–65.

Baddeley, A.D. (1966b). The influence of acoustic and semantic similarity on long-term memory for word sequences. *Quarterly Journal of Experimental Psychology, 18*, 302–9.

Baddeley, A.D. (1968). A three-minute reasoning test based on grammatical transformations. *Psychonomic Science, 10*, 341–2.

Baddeley, A.D. (1982). Domains of recollection. *Psychological Review, 89*, 708–29.

Baddeley, A.D. (1986). *Working Memory*. Oxford: Oxford University Press.

Baddeley, A.D. (1990). *Human Memory: Theory and Practice*. Hove: Lawrence Erlbaum.

Baddeley, A.D. (1993). Short-term phonological memory and long-term learning: A single case study. *European Journal of Cognitive Psychology, 5*, 129–48.

Baddeley, A.D. (1994). The remembered self and the enacted self. In U. Neisser, & R. Fivush (Eds), *The remembering self: Construction and accuracy in the self-narrative*. Cambridge: Cambridge University Press.

Baddeley, A.D., Della Sala, S. & Spinnler, H. (1991). The two-component hypothesis of memory deficit in Alzheimer's disease. *Journal of Clinical and Experimental Neuropsychology, 13*, 372–80.

Baddeley, A.D. & Ecob, J.R. (1973). Reaction time and short-term memory: a trace strength alternative to high speed exhaustive scanning hypothesis. *Quarterly Journal of Experimental Psychology, 25*, 229–40.

Baddeley, A.D., Grant, S., Wight, E. & Thomson, N. (1975). Imagery and visual working memory. In P.M.A. Rabbitt & S. Dornic (Eds), *Attention and performance, Vol. 5*. London: Academic Press.

Baddeley, A.D. & Hitch, G.J. (1974). Working memory. In G.H. Bower (Ed.), *The psychology of learning and motivation, Vol. 8*. London: Academic Press.

Baddeley, A.D. & Hitch, G.J. (1977). Recency re-examined. In S. Dornic (Ed.), *Attention and performance, Vol. 6*, pp. 647–67. Hillsdale, NJ: Lawrence Erlbaum.

Baddeley, A.D., Lewis, V.J. & Nimmo-Smith, I. (1978). When did you last...? In M.M. Gruneberg, P.E. Morris & R.N. Sykes (Eds), *Practical aspects of memory*, pp. 77–83. London: Academic Press.

Baddeley, A.D., Lewis, V.J. & Vallar, G. (1984). Exploring the articulatory loop. *Quarterly Journal of Experimental Psychology, 36*, 233–52.

Baddeley, A.D., Lewis, V.J., Eldridge, M. & Thomson, N. (1984). Attention and retrieval from long-term memory. *Journal of Experimental Psychology: General, 113*, 518–40.

Baddeley, A.D. & Lieberman, K. (1980). Spatial working memory. In R. Nickerson (Ed.), *Attention and performance, Vol. VIII*. Hillsdale, NJ: Lawrence Erlbaum.

Baddeley, A.D. & Longman, D.J.A. (1978). The influence of length and frequency of training sessions on the rate of learning to type. *Ergonomics, 21*, 627–35.

Baddeley, A.D., Papagno, C. & Vallar, G. (1988). When long-term learning depends on short-term storage. *Journal of Memory and Language, 27,* 586–95.

Baddeley, A.D., Thomson, N. & Buchanan, M. (1975). Word length and the structure of short-term memory. *Journal of Verbal Learning and Verbal Behavior, 14,* 575–89.

Baddeley, A.D. & Wilson, B. (1986). Amnesia, autobiographical memory and confabulation. In D.C. Rubin (Ed.), *Autobiographical memory,* pp. 225–52. Cambridge: Cambridge University Press.

Baddeley, A.D., Wilson, B.A. and Watts, F.N. (Eds) (1995). *Handbook of memory disorders.* Chichester: John Wiley & Sons.

Baddeley, A.D. & Woodhead, M. (1982). Depth of processing, context and face recognition. *Canadian Journal of Psychology, 36,* 148–64.

Baggett, P. (1975). Memory for explicit and implicit information in picture stories. *Journal of Verbal Learning and Verbal Behavior, 14,* 538–48.

Bahrick, H.P. (1970). Two-phase model for prompted recall. *Psychological Review, 77,* 215–22.

Bahrick, H.P. (1984). Semantic memory content in permastore: Fifty years of memory for Spanish learned in school. *Journal of Experimental Psychology: General, 113,* 1–24.

Bahrick, H.P., Bahrick, P.O. & Wittlinger, R.P. (1975). Fifty years of memory for names and faces: A cross-sectional approach. *Journal of Experimental Psychology: General, 104,* 54–75.

Bahrick, H.P. & Hall, L.K. (1991). Lifetime maintenance of high school mathematics content. *Journal of Experimental Psychology: General, 120,* 20–33.

Bainbridge, J.V., Lewandowsky, S. & Kirsner, K. (1993). Context effects in repetition priming are sense effects. *Memory and Cognition, 21,* 619–26.

Baker, L. (1978). Processing temporal relationships in simple stories: Effects of input sequence. *Journal of Verbal Learning and Verbal Behavior, 17(5),* 559–72.

Banaji, M.R. & Crowder, R.C. (1989). The bankruptcy of everyday memory. *American Psychologist, 44,* 1185–93.

Bannister, R. (1992). *Brain and Bannister's clinical neurology.* Oxford: Oxford University Press.

Barclay, J.R., Bransford, J.D., Franks, J.J., McCarrell, N.S. & Nitsch, K. (1974). Comprehension and semantic flexibility. *Journal of Verbal Learning and Verbal Behavior, 13,* 471–81.

Barker, L.M.& Weaver, C.A. (1983). Rapid, permanent, loss of memory for absolute intensity of taste and smell. *Bulletin of the Psychonomic Society, 21(4),* 281–4.

Barsalou, L.W. (1983). Ad hoc categories. *Memory and Cognition, 11,* 211–27.

Barsalou, L.W. (1988). The content and organization of autobiographical memories. In U. Neisser & E. Winograd (Eds), *Remembering reconsidered.* Cambridge: Cambridge University Press.

Barsalou, L.W. (1992). *Cognitive psychology: An overview for cognitive scientists.* Hillsdale, NJ: Lawrence Erlbaum.

Barsalou, L.W. & Ross, B.H. (1986). The roles of automatic and strategic processing in sensitivity to superordinate and property frequency. *Journal of Experimental Psychology: Learning, Memory and Cognition, 12,* 116–34.

Barsalou, L.W. & Sewell, D.R. (1984). *Constructing representations of categories from different points of view.* Emory Cognition Project Report No 2, Emory University, Atlanta.

Bartlett, F.C. (1932). *Remembering.* Cambridge: Cambridge University Press.

Bartlett, J.C. (1977). Remembering environmental sounds: The role of verbalization at input. *Memory and Cognition, 5,* 404–14.

Bartlett, J.C., Hurry, S. & Thorley, W. (1984). Typicality and familiarity of faces. *Memory and Cognition, 12,* 219–28.

Bartlett, J.C. & Snelus, P. (1980). Lifespan memory for popular songs. *American Journal of Psychology, 93,* 551–60.

Basso, A., Spinnler, H., Vallar, G. & Zanobio, E. (1982). Left hemisphere damage and selected impairment of auditory verbal short-term memory: A case study. *Neuropsychologia, 20,* 263–74.

Bayles, K.A. (1988). Dementia: The clinical perspective. *Archives of Neurology, 48,* 155–9.

Beales, S.A. & Parkin, A.J. (1984). Context and facial memory: The influence of different processing strategies. *Human Learning Journal of Practical Research and Applications, 3,* 257–64.

Beatty, W.W. (1992). Memory disturbances in Parkinson's disease. In S.J. Huber & J.L. Cummings (Eds), *Parkinson's disease.* New York: Oxford University Press.

Beaumont, J.G. (1988). *Understanding neuropsychology.* Oxford: Basil Blackwell.

Becker, J.T. (1988) Working memory and secondary memory defects in Alzheimer's disease. *Journal of Clinical and Experimental Neuropsychology, 10,* 739–53.

Beitchman, J.H., Zucker, K.J., Hood, J.E., DaCosta, G.A., & Cassavia, E. (1992). A review of the long-term effects of child sexual abuse. *Child Abuse and Neglect, 16(1)*, 101–18.

Bekerian, D.A. & Bowers, J.M. (1983). Eyewitness testimony: Were we misled? *Journal of Experimental Psychology: Learning, Memory and Cognition, 9*, 139–45.

Bekerian, D.A. & Dennett, J.L. (1993). The Cognitive Interview Technique: Reviving the issues. *Applied Cognitive Psychology, 7*, 275–97.

Bekerian, D.A. & Goodrich, S.J. (1995). Telling the truth in the recovered memory debate. *Consciousness and Cognition: An International Journal, 4*, 120–24.

Bellezza, F.S. (1982). Updating memory using mnemonic devices. *Cognitive Psychology, 14*, 301–27.

Bellezza, F.S. (1983). Mnemonic-device instruction with adults. In M. Pressley & J.R. Levin (Eds), *Cognitive strategy research: Psychological foundations*. New York: Springer-Verlag.

Belli, R.F. (1989). Influences of misleading postevent information: Misinformation interference and acceptance. *Journal of Experimental Psychology: General, 118*, 72–85.

Berry, D.C. & Broadbent, D.E. (1984). On the relationship between task performance and associated verbalizable knowledge. *Quarterly Journal of Experimental Psychology: Human Experimental Psychology, 36A*, 209–31.

Besson, M. & Kutas, M. (1993). The many facets of repetition: A cued-recall and event-related potential analysis of repeating words in same versus different sentence contexts. *Journal of Experimental Psychology: Learning, Memory and Cognition, 19*, 1115–33.

Biederman, I., Blickle, T.W., Teitelbaum, R.C. & Klatsky, G.J. (1988). Object search in nonsense displays. *Journal of Experimental Psychology: Learning, Memory and Cognition, 14*, 456–67.

Biederman, I., Cooper, E.E., Fox, P.W. and Mahadevan, R.S. (1992). Unexceptional spatial memory in an exceptional memorist. *Journal of Experimental Psychology: Learning, Memory and Cognition, 18*, 654–7.

Bilodeau, E.A. & Bilodeau, I.M. (1958). Variable frequency knowledge of results and the learning of simple skill. *Journal of Experimental Psychology, 55*, 379–83.

Binet, A. (1894). *Psychologie des grandes calculateurs et joueurs d'échecs*. Paris: Librane Hachette.

Bishop, D.V. & Robson, J. (1989). Unimpaired short-term memory and rhyme judgment in congenitally speechless individuals: Implications for the notion of 'articulatory coding'. *Quarterly Journal of Experimental Psychology: Human Experimental Psychology, 41*, 123–40.

Bjork, R.A. & Whitten, W.B. (1974). Recency-sensitive retrieval processes in long-term free recall. *Cognitive Psychology, 6*, 173–89.

Black, J.B. & Bower, G.H. (1979). Episodes as chunks in narrative memory. *Journal of Verbal Learning and Verbal Behavior, 18*, 309–18.

Blaney, P.H. (1986). Affect and memory: A review. *Psychological Bulletin, 99*, 229–46.

Blass, J.P., & Gibson, G.E. (1977). Abnormality of a thiamine-requiring enzyme in patients with Wernicke-Korsakoff syndrome. *New England Journal of Medicine. 297*, 1367–70.

Blin, J., Baron, J.C., Dubois, B. et al, (1990). Positron emission tomography study of progressive supranuclear palsy: Brain hypometabolic pattern and clinicometabolic correlations. *Archives of Neurology, 47*, 747–52.

Bliss, E.L. (1986). *Multiple personality, allied disorders, and hypnosis*. New York: Oxford University Press.

Block, R.A. (1979). Time and consciousness. In G. Underwood & R. Stevens (Eds), *Aspects of consciousness: Vol. 1. Psychological issues*, pp. 179–217. London: Academic Press.

Block, R.A. (1982). Temporal judgments and contextual change. *Journal of Experimental Psychology: Learning, Memory and Cognition, 8*, 530–44.

Block, R.A. (1990). *Cognitive models of psychological time*. Hillsdale, NJ: Lawrence Erlbaum.

Block, R.A. & Reed, M.A. (1978). Remembered duration: Evidence for a contextual-change hypothesis. *Journal of Experimental Psychology: Human Learning and Memory, 4*, 656–65.

Boldovici, J.A. (1987). Measuring transfer in military settings. In S.M. Cormier & J.D. Hagman (Eds), *Transfer of learning*, pp. 239–60. San Diego, CA: Academic Press.

Boltz, M.G. (1992). Temporal accent structure and the remembering of filmed narratives. *Journal of Experimental Psychology: Human Perception and Performance, 18*, 90–105.

Boltz, M.G., Schulkind, M. & Kantra, S. (1991). Effects of background music on the remembering of filmed events. *Memory and Cognition, 19*, 593–606.

Bondi, M.W. & Kaszniak, A.W. (1991). Implicit and explicit memory in Alzheimer's disease and Parkinson's disease. *Journal of Clinical and Experimental Neuropsychology, 13*, 339–58.

Bondi, M.W., Kaszniak, A.W., Rapcsak, S.Z., & Butters, M.A. (1993). Implicit and explicit memory following anterior communicating artery aneurysm rupture. *Brain and Cognition, 22*(2), 213–29.

Boring, E.G. (1963). *The physical dimensions of consciousness.* New York: Dover.

Borkowski, J.G., Milstead, M. & Hale, C. (1988). Components of children's metamemory: Implications for strategy generalization. In F.E. Weinert and M. Perlmutter (Eds), *Memory development: Universal changes and individual differences*, pp. 73–100. Hillsdale, NJ: Erlbaum.

Botwinick, J. & Storandt, M. (1974). *Memory-related functions and age.* Springfield, IL: C.C. Thomas.

Bower, G.H. (1976). Experiments on story understanding and recall. *Quarterly Journal of Experimental Psychology, 28*, 511–34.

Bower, G.H. (1981). Mood and memory. *American Psychologist, 36*, 129–48.

Bower, G.H., Black, J.B. & Turner, T.J. (1979). Scripts in memory for text. *Cognitive Psychology, 11*, 177–220.

Bower, G.H. & Gilligan, S.G. (1979). Remembering information related to one's self. *Journal of Research in Personality, 13*, 420–32.

Bower, G.H. & Holyoak, K. (1973). Encoding and recognition memory for naturalistic sounds. *Journal of Experimental Psychology, 101(2)*, 360–66.

Bower, G.H. & Karlin, M.B. (1974). Depth of processing pictures of faces and recognition memory. *Journal of Experimental Psychology, 103*, 751–7.

Bower, G.H., Monteiro, K.P. & Gilligan, S.G. (1978). Emotional mood and context for learning and recall. *Journal of Verbal Learning and Verbal Behavior, 17*, 573–87.

Bower, G.H. & Springston, F. (1970). Pauses as recoding points in letter series. *Journal of Experimental Psychology, 83*, 421–30.

Bowles, N.L. & Poon, L.W. (1985). Effects of priming in word retrieval. *Journal of Experimental Psychology: Learning, Memory and Cognition, 11*, 272–83.

Bradburn, N.M., Rips, L.J. & Shevell, S.K. (1987). Answering autobiographical questions: The impact of memory and inference on surveys. *Science, 236*, 157–61.

Bradley, B. & Matthews, A. (1983). Negative self-schemata in clinical depression. *British Journal of Clinical Psychology, 22*, 173–82.

Bradshaw, J.L. and Mattingley, J.B. (1995). *Clinical neuropsychology: Behavioural and brain science.* San Diego, CA: Academic Press.

Bradshaw, J.L., Philips, J.G., Dennis, C., et al., (1992) Initiation and execution of movements in those suffering from and at risk of developing Huntington's disease. *Journal of Clinical and Experimental Neuropsychology, 14*, 179–92.

Brandsma, J.M. & Ludwig, A.M. (1974). Encoding and recognition memory for naturalistic sounds. *International Journal of Clinical and Experimental Hypnosis, 22(3)*, 216–33.

Bransford, J.D. & Johnson, M.K. (1972). Contextual prerequisites for understanding: Some investigations of comprehension and recall. *Journal of Verbal Learning and Verbal Behaviour, 11*, 717–26.

Bray, J.F. & Robbins, D. (1976). Frequency judgments and the spacing effect: Immediate and delayed performance. *Bulletin of the Psychonomic Society, 7*, 47–9.

Breck, B.E. & Smith, S.H. (1983). Encoding and recognition memory for naturalistic sounds. *Social Behavior and Personality, 11(2)*, 71–6.

Brewer, W.F. (1986). What is autobiographical memory? In D.C. Rubin (Ed.), *Autobiographical memory.* Cambridge: Cambridge University Press.

Brewer, W.F. (1988). Memory for randomly sampled autobiographical events. In U. Neisser & E. Winograd (Eds), *Remembering reconsidered: Ecological and traditional approaches to the study of memory.* New York: Cambridge University Press.

Brewin, C.R. (1988). *Cognitive foundations of clinical psychology.* Hove: Lawrence Erlbaum.

Broadbent, D.E. (1958). *Perception and communication.* London: Pergamon Press.

Brooks, L.R. (1967). The suppression of visualization by reading. *Quarterly Journal of Experimental Psychology, 19*, 289–99.

Brooks, L.R. (1968). Spatial and verbal components of the act of recall. *Canadian Journal of Psychology, 22*, 349–68.

Brooks, L.R. (1987). Decentralized control of categorization: The role of prior processing episodes. In U. Neisser & E. Winograd (Eds), *Remembering reconsidered: Ecological and traditional approaches to the study of memory*, pp. 141–74. New York: Cambridge University Press.

Brown, E., Deffenbacher, K. & Sturgill, W. (1977). Memory for faces and the circumstances of encounter. *Journal of Applied Psychology, 62*, 311–18.

Brown, J.D. (1986). Evaluations of self and others: Self-enhancement biases in social judgements. *Social Cognition, 4*, 353–76.

Brown, N.R., Rips, L.J. & Shevell, S.K. (1985). The subjective dates of natural events in very long-term memory. *Cognitive Psychology, 17,* 139–77.

Brown, N.R., Tickner, A.H. & Simmonds, D.C.V. (1969). Interference between concurrent tasks of driving and telephoning. *Journal of Applied Psychology, 53,* 419–24.

Brown, R. & Kulik, J. (1977). Flashbulb memories. *Cognition, 5,* 73–99.

Brown, R.G. & Marsden, C.D. (1988). 'Subcortical dementia': The neuropsychological evidence. *Neuroscience,* 25, 363–87.

Brown, S.W. (1985). Time perception and attention: The effects of prospective versus retrospective paradigms and task demands on perceived duration. *Perception and Psychophysics, 38,* 115–24.

Brown, S.W. & Stubbs, A. (1989). The psychophysics of retrospective and prospective timing. *Perception, 17,* 297–310.

Bruce, P.R., Coyne, A.C. & Botwinick, J. (1982). Adult age differences in metamemory. *Journal of Gerontology, 37(3),* 354–7.

Bruce, V., Burton, A.M. & Dench, N. (1994). What's distinctive about a distinctive face? *Quarterly Journal of Experimental Psychology: Human Experimental Psychology, 47A,* 119–41.

Bruce, V., Doyle, T., Dench, N. & Burton, A.M. (1991). Remembering facial configurations. *Cognition, 38,* 109–44.

Bruce, V., Valentine, T. & Baddeley, A.D. (1987). The basis of the 3/4 view advantage in face recognition. *Applied Cognitive Psychology, 1,* 109–20.

Bruce, V. & Young, A. (1986). Understanding face recognition. *British Journal of Psychology, 77,* 305–27.

Brust, J.C.W. (1993). *Neurological aspects of substance abuse.* Boston: Butterworth-Heinemann.

Bryan, W.L. & Harter, N. (1897). Studies in the physiology and psychology of the telegraphic language. *Psychological Review, 4,* 27–53.

Burke, A., Heuer, F., & Reisberg, D. (1992). Remembering emotional events. *Memory and Cognition, 20,* 277–90.

Burt, C.D.B., Mitchell, D.A., Raggatt, P.T.F., Jones, C.A., et. al. (1995). A snapshot of autobiographical memory retrieval characteristics. *Applied Cognitive Psychology, 9(1),* 61–74.

Butler, G. & Matthews, A. (1983). Cognitive processes in anxiety. *Advances in Behaviour Therapy, 5,* 51–62.

Butler, G. & Matthews, A. (1987). Anticipatory anxiety and risk perception. *Cognitive Therapy and Research, 91,* 551–65.

Butters, N. (1984). Alcoholic Korsakoff's syndrome: An update. *Seminars in Neurology. 4,* 226–44.

Butters, N. (1985). Alcoholic Korsakoff's syndrome: Some unresolved issues concerning etiology, neuropathology, and cognitive defecits. *Journal of Clinical and Experimental Neuropsychology, 7,* 181–210.

Butters, N. & Grady, M. (1977). Effect of predistractor delays on the short-term memory performance of patients with Korsakoff's and Huntington's disease. *Neuropsychologia, 15,* 701–6.

Butters, N., Salmon, D.P., Heindel, W. & Graham, E. (1988). Episodic, semantic, and procedural memory: Some comparisons of Alzheimer's and Parkinson's patients. In R.D. Terry (Ed.), *Aging and the brain.* New York: Raven Press.

Butters, N. & Stuss, D.T. (1989). Diencephalic amnesia. In F. Boller & J. Grafman (Eds.), *Handbook of neuropsychology, Vol. 3.* Amsterdam: Elsevier.

Bylsma, F.W., Brandt, J. & Strauss, M.E. (1990). Aspects of procedural memory are differentially impaired in Huntington's disease. *Archives of Clinical Neuropsychology, 5,* 287–97.

Caccamise, D.J. & Kintsch, W. (1978). Recognition of important and unimportant statements from stories. *American Journal of Psychology, 91,* 651–7.

Caine, E.D., Bamford, K.A., Schiffer, R.B., et al. (1986). A controlled neuropsychological comparison of Huntington's disease and multiplesclerosis. *Archives of Neurology, 43,* 249–54.

Caine, E.D., Ebert, M.H. & Weingarten, H. (1977). An outline for the analysis of dementia. *Neurology, 23,* 1087–92.

Caine, E.D., Hunt, R.D., Weingartner, H. & Ebert, M.H. (1978). Huntington's dementia. *Archives of General Psychiatry, 35,* 377–84.

Campbell, R. & Conway, M.A. (1995). *Broken memories.* Oxford: Blackwell.

Campbell, S.S. (1986). Estimation of empty time. *Human Neurobiology, 5,* 205–7.

Carpenter, R.H.S. (1996). *Neurophysiology.* London: Arnold.

Carroll, M.V., Byrne, B., & Kirsner, K. (1985). Autobiographical memory and perceptual learning: A developmental study using picture recognition, naming latency, and perceptual identification. *Memory and Cognition, 13,* 273–9.

Catalano, J.F. and Kleiner, B.M. (1984). Distant transfer in coincident timing as a function of variability of practice. *Perceptual and Motor Skills, 58*, 851–6.

Cavanagh, J.P. (1972). Relation between the immediate memory span and the memory search rate. *Psychological Review, 79*, 525–30.

Cavanaugh, J.C. & Perlmutter, M. (1982) Metamemory: A critical examination. *Child Development, 53*, 11–28.

Cave, C.B. & Squire, L.R. (1992). Intact and long-lasting repetition priming in amnesia. *Journal of Experimental Psychology: Learning, Memory and Cognition, 18*, 509–20.

Ceci, S.J., Caves, R.D. & Howe, M.J. (1981). Children's long-term memory for information that is incongruous with their prior knowledge. *British Journal of Psychology, 72*, 443–50.

Ceci, S.J., DeSimone, M. & Johnson, S. (1992). Memory in context: A case study of 'Bubbles P.', a gifted but uneven memorizer. In D.J. Hermann, H. Weingartner, A. Searleman & C.L. McEvoy (Eds), *Memory improvement: Implications for memory theory*, pp. 169–89. New York: Springer-Verlag.

Ceci, S.J. & Howe, M.J. (1978). Age-related differences in recall as a function of retrieval flexibility. *Journal of Experimental Child Psychology, 26*, 432–42.

Cermak, L.S. & Reale, L. (1978). Depth of processing and retention of words by alcoholic Korsakoff patients. *Journal of Experimental Psychology: Human Learning and Memory, 4*, 165–74.

Challis, B.H. (1993). Spacing effects on cued-memory tests depend on level of processing. *Journal of Experimental Psychology: Learning, Memory and Cognition, 19*, 389–96.

Challis, B.H., & Sidhu, R. (1993). Dissociative effect of massed repetition on implicit and explicit measures of memory. *Journal of Experimental Psychology: Learning, Memory and Cognition, 19*, 115–27.

Chance, J.E. & Goldstein, A.G. (1987). Retention interval and face recognition: Response latency measures. *Bulletin of the Psychonomic Society, 25*, 415–18.

Chance, J.E., Turner, A.L. & Goldstein, A.G. (1982). Development of differential recognition for own- and other-race faces. *Journal of Psychology, 112*, 29–37.

Chapman, P.R., & Groeger, J.A. (1995) Arousal and memory for everyday events: Subjective risk and the recognition of driving situations. Manuscript submitted for publication.

Charness, N. (1979). Components of skill in bridge. *Canadian Journal of Psychology, 33*, 1–16.

Chase, W.G. & Ericsson, K.A. (1981). Skilled memory. In J.R. Anderson (Ed.), *Cognitive skills and their acquisition*, pp. 141–89. Hillsdale, NJ: Erlbaum.

Chase, W.G. & Simon, H.A. (1973). Perception in chess. *Cognitive Psychology, 4*, 5–81.

Cheng, P.W. (1985). Restructuring versus automaticity: Alternative accounts of skill acquisition. *Psychological Review, 92*, 414–23.

Chi, M.T. & Koeske, R.D. (1983). Network representation of a child's dinosaur knowledge. *Developmental Psychology, 19*, 29–39.

Chiarello, C. & Hoyer, W.J. (1988). Adult age differences in implicit and explicit memory: Time course and encoding effects. *Psychology and Aging, 3*, 358–66.

Chincotta, D. & Underwood, G. (1996). Mother tongue, language of schooling and bilingual digit span. *British Journal of Psychology, 87(2)*, 193–208.

Christianson, S.A. (1992). *The handbook of emotion and memory: Research and theory.* Hillsdale, NJ: Lawrence Erlbaum.

Christianson, S.A. & Loftus, E.F. (1987). Memory for traumatic events. *Applied Cognitive Psychology, 1*, 225–39.

Christianson, S.A., Loftus, E.F., Hoffman, H. and Loftus, G. (1991). Eye fixations and memory for emotional events. *Journal of Experimental Psychology: Learning, Memory and Cognition, 17*, 693–701.

Chui, H.C. (1989). Dementia: A review emphasising the clinicopathologic correlation and brain-behaviour relationships. *Archives of Neurology, 46*, 806–14.

Churchland, P.S. and Sejnowski, T.J. (1992). *The computational brain.* Cambridge, MA: MIT Press.

Claeys, W. (1990). On the spontaneity of behaviour categorization and its implications for personality measurement. *European Journal of Personality, 4(3)*, 173–86.

Claeys, W., Deboeck, P. & Viaene, N. (1976). Field-dependence and stability of self-view. *Perceptual and Motor Skills, 43(2)*, 563–66.

Cofer, C.N. (1967). Conditions for the use of verbal associations. *Psychological Bulletin, 68*, 1–12.

Cogan, D.G. (1985). Visual disturbances with focal progressive dementing disease. *Americal Journal of Opthamology. 100*, 68–72.

Cohen, G. (1989). *Memory in the real world.* Hove: Erlbaum.

Cohen, G. & Faulkner, D. (1988). Life span changes in autobiographical memory. In M.M. Gruneberg, P.E.

Morris, & R.N. Sykes (Eds), *Practical aspects of memory: Current research and issues.* Chichester: John Wiley.

Cohen, R.L., Peterson, M. & Mantini, A.T. (1987). Interevent differences in event memory: Why are some events more recallable than others? *Memory and Cognition, 15(2)*, 109–18.

Colegrove, F.W. (1899). Individual memories. *American Journal of Psychology, 10,* 228–55.

Colle, H.A. & Welsh, A. (1976). Acoustic masking in primary memory. *Journal of Verbal Learning And Verbal Behavior, 15,* 17–31.

Collins, A.M. & Loftus, E.F. (1975). A reading-activation theory of semantic processing. *Psychological Review, 82,* 407–28.

Collins, A.M. & Quillian, M.R. (1969). Retrieval time from semantic memory. *Journal of Verbal Learning and Verbal Behavior, 8,* 240–47.

Coltheart, M. (1983). Ecological necessity of iconic memory. *Behavioural and Brain Sciences, 6,* 17–18.

Conn, D.K. (1989). Neuropsychiatric syndromes in the elderly: An overview. In D.K. Conn, A. Grek & J. Sadavoy (Eds), *Psychiatric consequences of brain disease in the elderly: A focus on management.* New York: Plenum Press.

Conrad, R. (1964). Acoustic confusion in immediate memory. *British Journal of Psychology, 55,* 75–84.

Conrad, R. (1972). Short-term memory in the deaf: A test for speech coding. *British Journal of Psychology, 63,* 173–80.

Conrad, R. & Hull, A.J. (1964). Information, acoustic confusion and memory span. *British Journal of Psychology, 55,* 429–32.

Conway, M.A. (1990). *Autobiographical memory.* Buckingham: Open University Press.

Conway, M.A., (1994). *Flashbulb memories.* London: Lawrence Erlbaum.

Conway, M.A. & Bekerian, D.A. (1987). Organization in autobiographical memory. *Memory and Cognition, 15(2),* 119–32.

Conway, M.A., Cohen, G., & Stanhope, N. (1991). On the very long-term retention of knowledge acquired through formal education: Twelve years of cognitive psychology. *Journal of Experimental Psychology: General, 120(4),* 395–409.

Corman, C.N. and Wickens, D.D. (1968). Retroactive inhibition in short-term memory. *Journal of Verbal Behaior, 7,* 16–19.

Courtois, M.R. & Mueller, J.H. (1981). Target and distractor typicality in facial recognition. *Journal of Applied Psychology, 66,* 639–45.

Cowan, N., Lichti, W., & Grove, T. (1988). Memory for unattended speech during silent reading. In M.M. Gruneberg, P.E. Morris, & R.N. Sykes (Eds), *Practical aspects of memory: Current research and issues, Vol. 2: Clinical and educational implications,* pp. 327–32. Chichester: John Wiley.

Craik, F.I.M. (1977). 'A level of analysis' view of memory. In P. Pliner, L. Krames & T.M. Allaway (Eds), *Communication and affect, Vol.2: Language and thought.* New York: Academic Press.

Craik, F.I.M. & Lockhart, R.S. (1972). Levels of processing: A framework for memory research. *Journal of Verbal Learning and Verbal Behavior, 11,* 671–84.

Craik, F.I.M. & Lockhart, R.S. (1986). CHARM is not enough: Comments on Eich's model of cued recall. *Psychological Review, 93,* 360–64.

Craik, F.I.M. & Tulving, E. (1975). Depth of processing and the retention of words in episodic memory. *Journal of Experimental Psychology: General, 104,* 268–94.

Craik, F.I.M. & Watkins, M.J. (1973). The role of rehearsal in short-term memory. *Journal of Verbal Learning and Verbal Behavior, 12,* 599–607.

Cronin-Golumb, A. (1990). Abstract thought in aging and age-related neurological disease. In F. Boller & J. Grafman (Eds), *Handbook of neuropsychology, Vol. 3.* Amsterdam: Elsevier.

Crook, T.H., Youngjohn, J.R., & Larrabee, G.J. (1990). The Misplaced Objects Test: A measure of everyday visual memory. *Journal of Clinical and Experimental Neuropsychology, 12(6),* 819–33.

Crossman, E.R.F.W. (1959). A theory of the acquisition of speed skill. *Ergonomics, 2,* 153–66.

Crovitz, H.F. & Harvey, M.T. (1979). Visual imagery vs semantic category as encoding conditions. *Bulletin of the Psychonomic Society, 13(5),* 291–2.

Crovitz, H.F. & Schiffman, H. (1974). Frequency of episodic memories as a function of age. *Bulletin of the Psychonomic Society, 4,* 517–18.

Crowder, R.G. (1971). The sound of vowels and consonants in immediate memory. *Journal of Verbal Learning and Verbal Behavior, 10,* 587–96.

Crowder, R.G. (1976). *Principles of learning and memory.* Hillsdale, NJ: Lawrence Erlbaum.

Crowder, R.G. & Morton, J. (1969). Precategorical acoustic storage (PAS). *Perception and Psychophysics, 5,* 365–73.

Cuddy, L.J. & Jacoby, L.L. (1982). When forgetting helps memory: An analysis of repetition effects. *Journal of Verbal Learning and Verbal Behavior, 21*, 451–67.

Cummings, J.L. (1986). Subcortical dementia: Neuropsychology, neuropsychiatry and pathophysiology. *British Journal of Psychiatry, 149*, 682–97.

Cummings, J.L. (1988). Dementia of the Alzheimer type: Challenges of definition and clinical diagnosis. In H.A. Whitaker (Ed.), *Neurological studies of nonfocal brain damage: Dementia and trauma.* New York: Springer-Verlag.

Cummings, J.L. (1992). Neuropsychiatric aspects of Alzheimer's disease and other dementing illnesses. In S.C. Yudofsky and R.E. Hales (Eds), *American Psychiatric Press textbook of neuropsychiatry.* Washington, D.C: American Psychiatric Press.

Cummings, J.L. & Benson, D.F. (1990). Subcortical mechanisms and human thought. In J.L. Cummings (Ed.), *Subcortical dementia.* New York: Oxford University Press.

Cushman, L.A., Como, P.G., Booth, H. & Caine, E.D. (1988). Cued recall and release from proactive interference in Alzheimer's disease. *Journal of Clinical and Experimental Neuropsychology, 10*, 685–92.

Cuvo, A.J. (1974). Incentive level influence on overt rehearsal and free recall as a function of age. *Journal of Experimental Child Psychology, 18*, 167–81.

Damasio, A.R. & van Hoesen, G.W. (1985). Emotional disturbances associated with focal lesions of the limbic frontal lobe. In K. Heilman & P. Satz (Eds), *Neuropsychology of human emotion.* New York : Guildford Press.

Damasio, H. (1983). A computerised tomographic guide to the identification of cerebral vascular territories. *Archives of Neurology, 40*, 138–42.

Darwin, C.J., Turvey, M.T. & Crowder, R.G. (1972). An auditory analogue of the Sperling partial report procedure: Evidence for brief auditory storage. *Cognitive Psychology, 3*, 255–67.

Davidson, D. & Hoe, S. (1993). Children's recall and recognition memory for typical and atypical actions in script-based stories. *Journal of Experimental Child Psychology, 55*, 104–26.

Davidson, P.W., Cambardella, P., Stenerson, S., Carney, G. (1974). Influences of age and tasks memory demand on matching shapes within and across vision and touch. *Perceptual and Motor Skills, 39(1)*, 187–92.

Davies, G. & Milne, A. (1982). Recognising faces in and out of context. *Current Psychological Research, 2*, 235–46.

Deakin, J.M. & Allard, F. (1991). Skilled memory in expert figure skaters. *Memory and Cognition, 19*, 79–86.

Deatherage, B.H. & Evans, T.R. (1969). Binaural masking: Backward, forward and simultaneous effects. *Journal of the Acoustical Society of America, 46*, 362–71.

deBoeck, P. & Claeys, W. (1978). Field independence and recognition of trait names in an incidental learning paradigm. *Perceptual and Motor Skills, 47(1)*, 307–11.

DeCasper, A.J. & Fifer, W.P. (1980). Of human bonding: Newborns prefer their mothers' voices, *Science, 208*, 1174–6.

DeCasper, A.J. & Spence, M.J. (1986). Prenatal maternal speech influences newborns' perception of speech sounds. *Infant Behavior and Development, 9*, 133–50.

Deffenbacher, K.A. (1983). The influence of arousal on reliability of testimony. In S.M.A. Lloyd-Bostock & B.R. Clifford (Eds.), *Evaluating witness evidence.* Chichester: John Wiley.

Deffenbacher, K.A. (1991). A maturing of research on the behaviour of eyewitnesses. *Applied Cognitive Psychology, 5(5)*, 377–402.

de Groot, A.D. (1966). Perception and memory versus thought: Some old ideas and recent findings. In B. Kleinmuntz (Ed.), *Problem solving.* New York: Wiley.

de Haan, E.H., Young, A.W. & Newcombe, F. (1991). A dissociation between the sense of familiarity and access to semantic information concerning familiar people. Special issue: Face recognition. *European Journal of Cognitive Psychology, 3*, 51–67.

Delis, D.C., Massman, P.J., Butters, N. et al. (1991). Profiles of demented and amnesic patients on the California Verbal Learning Test: Implications for the assessment of memory disorders. *Psychological Assessment, 3*, 19–26.

Della Sala, S. & Mazzini, L. (1989). Posttraumatic extrapyramidal syndrome: Case report. *Italian Journal of Neurosciences, 11*, 65–9.

Dempster, F.N. (1981). Memory span: Sources of individual and developmental differences. *Psychological Bulletin, 89*, 63–100.

Dempster, F.N. (1985). Proactive interference in sentence recall: Topic-similarity effects and individual differences. *Memory and Cognition, 13*, 81–89.

Denney, N. and Ziobrowski, M. (1972). Developmental

changes in clustering behavior. *Journal of Experimental Child Psychology, 13,* 275–82.

Dewhurst, S.A. & Conway, M.A. (1994). Pictures, images and recollective experience. *Journal of Experimental Psychology: Learning, Memory and Cognition, 20,* 1088–98.

Diamond, M.C. (1990). How the brain grows in response to experience. In R.E. Ornstein (Ed.), *The healing brain: A scientific reader.* New York: Guildford Press.

Diamond, R. & Carey, S. (1986). Why faces are and are not special: An effect of expertise. *Journal of Experimental Psychology: General, 115,* 107–17.

di Pellegrino, G., Nichelli, P. and Faglioni, P. (1988). Frequency and recognition judgments by young and elderly adults. *Neuropsychologia, 26,* 765–8.

Dittburner, T.L., & Persinger, M.A. (1993). Intensity of amnesia during hypnosis is positively correlated with estimated prevalence of sexual abuse and alien abductions: Implications for the False Memory Syndrome. *Perceptual and Motor Skills, 77,* 895–8.

Dodson, C. & Reisberg, D. (1991). Indirect testing of eyewitness memory: The (non) effect of misinformation. *Bulletin of the Psychonomic Society, 29,* 333–6.

Doty, R.L., Deems, D.A., & Stellar, S. (1988). Olfactory dysfunction in Parkinsonianism: A general deficit unrelated to neurologic signs, disease stage, or disease duration. *Neurology, 38,* 1237–44.

Doty, R.L., Reyes, P.F., & Gregor, T. (1987). Presence of both odor identification and detection deficits in Alzheimer's disease. *Brain Research Bulletin, 18,* 597–600.

Dubois, B., Boller, F., Pillon, B. & Agid, Y (1991). Cognitive deficits in Parkinson's disease. In F. Boller & J. Grafman (Eds), *Handbook of neuropsychology, Vol. 5.* Amsterdam: Elsevier.

Dubois, B. & Pillon, B. (1992). Biochemical correlates of cognitive changes and dementia in Parkinson's disease. In S.J. Huber & J.L. Cummings (Eds), *Parkinson's disease: Neurobehavioral aspects.* New York: Oxford University Press.

Dubois, B., Pillon, B., Legault, F. et al. (1988). Slowing of cognitive processing in progressive supranuclear palsy. *Archives of Neurology, 45,* 1194–9.

Dudai, Y. (1989). *The neurobiology of memory: Concepts, findings and trends.* New York: Oxford University Press.

Dudycha, G.J. and Dudycha, M.M. (1941). Childhood memories: A review of the literature. *Psychological Bulletin, 38,* 668–82.

Duncan, J., Williams, P. & Brown, I. (1991). Components of driving skill: Experience does not mean expertise. *Ergonomics, 34,* 919–37.

Duvoisin, R.C. (1992). Clinical diagnosis. In I. Litvan & Y. Agid (Eds), *Progressive supranuclear palsy: Clinical and research approaches.* New York: Oxford University Press.

Easterbrook, J. (1959). The effect of emotion on cue utilization and the organization of behaviour. *Psychological Review, 66,* 183–201.

Ebbinghaus, H. (1964). *Memory: A contribution to experimental psychology.* New York: Dover Publications (Trans. from original German (1885) *Über das Gedächtnis.* Leipzig: Dunker).

Edelman, G.M. (1989). *The remembered present: A biological theory of consciousness.* New York: Basic Books.

Efron, R. (1970a). The relationship between the duration of a stimulus and the duration of a perception. *Neuropsychologia, 8,* 37–55.

Efron, R. (1970b). The minimum duration of a perception. *Neuropsychologia, 8,* 57–63.

Efron, R. (1970c). Effect of stimulus duration on perceptual onset and offset latencies. *Perception and Psychophysics, 8,* 231–4.

Egan, D.E. & Schwartz, B.J. (1979). Chunking in recall of symbolic drawings. *Memory and Cognition, 7,* 149–58.

Eich, J.E. (1985). Context, memory, and integrated item/context imagery. *Journal of Experimental Psychology: Learning, Memory and Cognition, 11,* 764–70.

Eich, J.E. & Metcalfe, J. (1989) Mood dependent memory for internal versus external events. *Journal of Experimental Psychology: Learning, Memory and Cognition. 15,* 443–55.

Eich, J.E., Weingartner, H., Stillman, R.C. & Gillin, J.C. (1975). State-dependent accessibility of retrieval cues in the retention of a categorized list. *Journal of Verbal Learning and Verbal Behavior, 14,* 408–17.

Ekman, P. (1973). Cross-cultural studies of facial expression. In P. Ekman (Ed.), *Darwin and facial expression: A century of research in review.* New York: Academic Press.

Ellis, N.C. & Hennelly, R.A. (1980). A bilingual word-length effect: Implications for intelligence testing and the relative ease of mental calculation in Welsh and English. *British Journal of Psychology, 71,* 43–51.

Engen, T. (1987). Remembering odors and their names. *American Scientist, 75,* 497–503.

Enright, M.K., Rovee-Collier, C.K., Fagen, J.W. & Caniglia, K. (1983). The effects of distributed training on retention of operant conditioning in human infants. *Journal of Experimental Child Psychology, 36,* 209–25.

Ericsson, K.A., Chase, W.G. & Faloon, S. (1980). Acquisition of a memory skill. *Science, 208,* 1181–2.

Ericsson, K.A. & Faivre, I.A. (1988). What's exceptional about exceptional abilities? In L.K. Obler and D. Fein (Eds), *The exceptional brain: Neuropsychology of talent and special abilities,* pp. 436–73. New York: Guilford Press.

Ericsson, K.A. & Kintsch, W. (1995). Long-term working memory. *Psychological Review, 102,* 211–45.

Ericsson, K.A. & Polson, P.G. (1988). A cognitive analysis of exceptional memory for restaurant orders. In M.T.H. Chi, R. Glaser & M.J. Farr (Eds), *The nature of expertise,* pp. 23–70. Hillsdale, NJ: Erlbaum.

Ericsson, K.A. & Staszewski, J. (1989). Skilled memory and expertise: Mechanisms of exceptional performance. In D. Klahr and K. Kotovsky (Eds), *Complex information processing: The impact of Herbert A. Simon,* pp. 235–67. Hillsdale, NJ: Erlbaum.

Eslinger, P.J. & Damasio, A.R (1986). Preserved motor learning in Alzheimer's disease: Implications for anatomy and behavior. *Journal of Neuroscience, 6,* 3006–9.

Estes, W.K. (1972). An associative basis for coding and organization in memory. In A.W. Melton & E. Martin (Eds), *Coding processes in human memory.* Washington, DC: Winston.

Estes, W.K. (1985). Levels of association theory. *Journal of Experimental Psychology: Learning, Memory and Cognition, 11,* 450–4.

Eysenck, M. W. (1992). *Anxiety: The cognitive perspective.* London: Lawrence Erlbaum.

Eysenck, M.W., MacLeod, C. & Mathews, A. (1987). Cognitive functioning in anxiety. *Psychological Research, 49,* 189–95.

Fabiani, M., Buckley, J., Gratton, G., Coles, M.G.H., Donchin, E. & Logie, R. (1989). The training of complex task performance. *Acta Psychologica, 71,* 259–99.

Fagen, J.F. (1984). The relationship of novelty preferences during infancy to later intelligence and later recognition memory. *Intelligence, 5,* 121–30.

Fagen, J.F., Rovee, C.K., & Kaplan, M.G. (1976). Psychophysical scaling of stimulus similarity in 3-month-old infants and adults. *Journal of Experimental Child Psychology, 22,* 272–81.

Fagen, J.W. & Rovee-Collier, C.K. (1983). Memory

retrieval: A time-locked process in infancy. *Science, 222,* 1349–51.

Farah, M.J. (1988). Is visual imagery really visual? Overlooked evidence from neuropsychology. *Psychological Review, 95,* 307–17.

Farah, M.J, Rochlin, R. & Klein, K.L. (1994). Orientation invariance and geometric primitives in shape recognition. *Cognitive Science, 18,* 325–44.

Fehm, W. G., Reutter, K., Zenz, H., Born, J. et.al. (1993). Are circadian variations in taste thresholds cortisol dependent? *Journal of Psychophysiology, 7,* 65–72.

Fendrich, D.W., Gesi, A.T., Healy, A.F. & Bourne, L.E. (1995). The contribution of procedural re-instatement to implicit and explicit memory effects in a motor task. In A.F. Healy & L.E. Bourne (Eds.) *Learning and memory of knowledge and skills.* Thousand Oaks, CA: Sage.

Field, D. (1981). Retrospective reports by healthy intelligent elderly people of personal events of their adult lives. *International Journal of Behavioural Development, 4,* 77–97.

Fisher, R.P. & Geiselman, R.E (1992). *Memory-enhancing techniques for investigative interviewing: The Cognitive Interview.* Springfield IL: Charles C. Thomas.

Fisher, R.P., Geiselman, R.E., & Amador, M. (1989). Field test of the cognitive interview: Enhancing the recollection of actual victims and witnesses of crime. *Journal of Applied Psychology, 74,* 722–7.

Fisk, A.D. (1986). Frequency encoding is not inevitable and is not automatic: A reply to Hasher and Zacks. Special issue: Psychotherapy research. *American Psychologist, 41,* 215–16.

Fisk, A.D. & Eboch, M. (1989). An automatic/controlled processing theory application to training component map reading skills. *Applied Ergonomics, 20,* 2–8.

Fisk, A.D. & Jones, C.D. (1992). Global versus local consistency: Effects of degree of within-category consistency on performance and learning. *Human Factors, 34,* 693–705.

Fisk, A.D., Lee, M.D. & Rogers, W.A. (1991). Recombination of automatic processing components: The effects of transfer, reversal, and conflict situations. Special issue: Training theory, methods and technology. *Human Factors, 33,* 267–80.

Fisk, A.D. & Schneider, W. (1984). Memory as a function of attention, level of processing, and automatization. *Journal of Experimental Psychology: Learning, Memory and Cognition, 10,* 181–97.

Fitts, P.M. (1964). Perceptual-motor skill learning. In A.W. Melton (Ed.), *Categories of human learning*. New York: Academic Press.

Fitts, P.M. & Posner, M.I. (1967). *Human performance*. Belmont, CA: Brooks-Cole Publishing Co.

Fitzgerald, J.M. & Lawrence, R. (1984). Autobiographical memory across the life-span. *Journal of Gerontology, 39*, 692–8.

Fivush, R. (1994). Constructing narrative, emotion, and self in parent–child conversations about the past. In U. Neisser & R. Fivush (Eds.), *The remembering self: Construction and accuracy in the self-narrative*. Cambridge: Cambridge University Press.

Flavell, J.H., Beach, D.H. & Chinsky, J.M. (1966). Spontaneous verbal rehearsal in a memory task as a function of age. *Child Development, 37*, 283–99.

Flexser, A.J. & Bower, G.H. (1974). How frequency affects recency judgments: A model for recency discrimination. *Journal of Experimental Psychology, 103*, 706–16.

Flexser, A.J. and Tulving, E. (1978). Retrieval independence in recognition and recall. *Psychological Review, 85*, 153–71.

Flin, R., & Spencer, J.R. (1995). Children as witnesses: Legal and psychological perspectives. *Journal of Child Psychology and Psychiatry and Allied Disciplines, 36(2)*, 171–89.

Folkard, S., Monk, T.H., Bradbury, R. and Rosenthall, J. (1977). Time of day effects in school children's immediate and delayed recall of meaningful material. *British Journal of Psychology, 68*, 45–50.

Folstein, S.E. (1989). *Huntington's disease*. Baltimore, MD: The Johns Hopkins University Press.

Forster, K.I. & Davis, C. (1984). Repetition priming and frequency attenuation in lexical access. *Journal of Experimental Psychology: Learning, Memory and Cognition, 10*, 680–98.

Fozard, J.L. & Weinert, J.R. (1972). Absolute judgments of recency for pictures and nouns after various numbers of intervening items. *Journal of Experimental Psychology, 95*, 472–4.

Fraisse, P. (1963). *The psychology of time*. (J. Leith, Trans.). New York: Harper and Row.

Fraisse, P. (1984). Perception and estimation of time. *Annual Review of Psychology, 35*, 1–36.

Freedman, M. (1990) Parkinson's disease. In J.L. Cummings (Ed.), *Subcortical dementia*. New York: Oxford University Press.

Freud, S. (1901). *The psychopathology of everyday life*. (A. Tyson, Trans.) New York: W.W. Norton.

Freund, J.S., Sanders, K., Bell, R.J. & Jennings, B. (1975). Associations as cues in recognition memory. *Bulletin of the Psychonomic Society, 6*, 364–6.

Friedman, S. (1972). Habituation and recovery of visual response in the alert human newborn. *Journal of Experimental Child Psychology, 13*, 339–49.

Friedman, W.J. (1987). A follow-up to 'Scale effects in memory for the time of events': The earthquake study. *Memory and Cognition, 15*, 518–20.

Friedman, W.J. (1993). Memory for the time of past events. *Psychological Bulletin, 113*, 44–66.

Friedman, W.J. & Wilkins, A.J. (1985). Scale effects in memory for the time of events. *Memory and Cognition, 13*, 168–75.

Frieske, D.A. & Park, D.C. (1993). Effects of organization and working memory on age differences in memory for scene information. *Experimental Aging Research, 19*, 321–32.

Fritzen, J. (1975). Intralist repetition effects in free recall. *Journal of Experimental Psychology: Human Learning and Memory, 104*, 756–63.

Gabrieli, J.D.E., Keane, M.M., Stanger, B.Z., Kjelgaard, M.M., et al. (1994). Dissociations among structural-perceptual, lexical-semantic, and event-fact memory systems in Alzheimer, amnesic, and normal subjects. *Cortex, 30*, 1, 75–103.

Galambos, J.A. & Rips, L.J. (1982). Memory for routines. *Journal of Verbal Learning and Verbal Behavior, 21*, 260–81.

Galton, F. (1883). Inquiries into human faculty and its development. London: Dent (Everyman Edition).

Gardiner, J.M. (1988). Functional aspects of recollective experience. *Memory and Cognition, 16*, 309–13.

Gardiner, J.M., Craik, F.I.M. & Birtwistle, J. (1972). Retrieval cues and release from proactive inhibition. *Journal of Verbal Learning and Verbal Behavior, 11*, 778–83.

Gardiner, J.M., Gregg, V.H. & Hampton, J.A. (1988). Word frequency and generation effects. *Journal of Experimental Psychology: Learning, Memory and Cognition, 14*, 687–93.

Gathercole, S.E., & Adams, A.M. (1994). Children's phonological working memory: Contributions of long-term knowledge and rehearsal. *Journal of Memory and Language, 33(5)*, 672–88.

Gathercole, S.E. & Baddeley, A.D. (1990). The role of phonological memory in vocabulary acquisition – a study of young children learning new names. *British Journal of Psychology, 81,* 439–54.

Gathercole, S.E. & Baddeley, A.D. (1993). Phonological working memory: A critical building block for reading development and vocabulary acquisition? Special issue: Prediction of reading and spelling evidence from European longitudinal research. *European Journal of Psychology of Education, 8,* 259–72.

Gathercole, S.E., Willis, C., Emslie, H. & Baddeley, A.D. (1992). Phonological memory and vocabulary development during the early school years: A longitudinal study. *Developmental Psychology, 28,* 887–98.

Gee, J.P & Grosjean, F. (1984). Empirical evidence for narrative structure. *Cognitive Science, 8,* 59–85.

Geiselman, R.E., Fisher, R.P., Firstenberg, I., Hutton, L.A., Sullivan, S., Avetissan, I., & Prosk, A. (1984). Enhancement of eyewitness memory: An empirical evaluation of the cognitive interview. *Journal of Police Science and Administration, 12,* 74–80.

Geller, V. & Shaver, P. (1976). Cognitive consequences of self-awareness. *Journal of Experimental Social Psychology, 12(1),* 99–108.

Gernsbacher, M.A. (1985). Surface information loss in comprehension. *Cognitive Psychology, 17,* 324–63.

Gibbs, R.W. & Tenney, Y.J. (1980). The concept of scripts in understanding stories. *Journal of Psycholinguistic Research, 9,* 275–84.

Gibson, J.J. (1975). Events are perceivable but time is not. In J.T. Fraser & N. Lawrence (Eds), *The study of time II.* New York: Springer-Verlag.

Gillund, G. & Shiffrin, R.M. (1981). Free recall of complex pictures and abstract words. *Journal of Verbal Learning and Verbal Behavior, 20,* 575–92.

Gillund, G. & Shiffrin, R.M. (1984). A retrieval model for both recognition and recall. *Psychological Review, 91,* 1–67.

Glanzer, M. (1972). Storage mechanisms in recall. In G.H. Bower (Ed.), *The psychology of learning and motivation: Advances in research and theory, Vol. V.* New York: Academic Press.

Glanzer, M. & Adams, J.K. (1985). The mirror effect in recognition memory. *Memory and Cognition, 13,* 8–20.

Glanzer, M. & Adams, J.K. (1990). The mirror effect in recognition memory: Data and theory. *Journal of Experimental Psychology: Learning, Memory and Cognition, 16,* 5–16.

Glanzer, M., Adams, J.K. & Iverson, G. (1991). Forgetting and the mirror effect in recognition memory: Concentering of underlying distributions. *Journal of Experimental Psychology: Learning, Memory and Cognition, 17,* 81–93.

Glanzer, M. & Cunitz, A.R. (1966). Two storage mechanisms in free recall. *Journal of Verbal Learning and Verbal Behavior, 5,* 351–60.

Glanzer, M. & Razell, M. (1974). The size of the unit in short-term storage. *Journal of Verbal Learning and Verbal Behavior, 13,* 114–31.

Glass, A.L. (1984). Effect of memory set on reaction time. In J.R. Anderson & S.M. Kosslyn (Eds), *Tutorials in learning and memory,* pp. 119–36. New York: W.H. Freeman.

Glenberg, A.M. (1974). Retrieval factors and the lag effect (Tech. Rep. No. 49). Ann Arbor, MI: Human Performance Center, The University of Michigan.

Glenberg, A.M., Bradley, M.M., Kraus, T.A. & Renzaglia, G.J. (1983). Studies of the long-term recency effect: Support for a contextually guided retrieval hypothesis. *Journal of Experimental Psychology: Learning, Memory and Cognition, 9,* 231–55.

Glenberg, A.M, Bradley, M.M. & Stevenson, J.A. et al. (1980). A two-process account of long-term serial position effects. *Journal of Experimental Psychology: Human Learning and Memory, 6,* 355–69.

Glenberg, A.M., Smith, S.M. & Green, C. (1977). Type I rehearsal: Maintenance and more. *Journal of Verbal Learning and Verbal Behavior, 16,* 339–52.

Glenn, C.G. (1978). The role of episodic structure and of story length in children's recall of simple stories. *Journal of Verbal Learning and Verbal Behavior, 17,* 229–47.

Glover, J.A. & Corkhill, A.J. (1987). Influence of paraphrased repetitions on the spacing effect. *Journal of Educational Psychology, 79,* 198–9.

Glucksberg, S. & Cowan, G.N. Jr. (1970). Memory for nonattended auditory material. *Cognitive Psychology, 1,* 149–56.

Godden, D.R. & Baddeley, A.D. (1975). Context-dependent memory in two natural environments: On land and underwater. *British Journal of Psychology, 66,* 325–31.

Godden, D. & Baddeley, A.D. (1980). When does context influence recognition memory? *British Journal of Psychology, 71,* 99–104.

Golbe, L.I. (1991). Young-onset Parkinson's disease: A clinical review. *Neurology, 41,* 168–73.

Goldstein, A.G. & Chance, J.E. (1980). Memory for faces and schema theory. *Journal of Psychology, 105,* 47–59.

Goldstein, A.G. & Chance, J.E. (1985). Effects of training on Japanese face recognition: Reduction of the other-race effect. *Bulletin of the Psychonomic Society, 23,* 211–14.

Goldstein, A.G., Chance, J.E., Hoisington, M. & Buescher, K. (1982). Recognition memory for pictures: Dynamic versus static stimuli. *Bulletin of the Psychonomic Society, 20,* 37–40.

Goodin, D.S. (1992). Electrophysiological correlates of dementia in Parkinson's disease. In S.J Huber & J.L. Cummings (Eds), *Parkinson's disease: Neurobehavioral aspects.* New York: Oxford University Press.

Goodman, G.S., Hirschman, J.E., Hepps, D., & Rudy, L. (1991). Children's memory for stressful events. *Merrill Palmer Quarterly, 37,* 1, 109–57.

Goodwin, D.W., Powell, B., Bremer, D., Hoine, H. & Sterne, J. (1969). Alcohol and recall: State-dependent effects in man. *Science, 163,* 1358–60.

Gottfried, A.W., Rose, S.A. (1980) Tactile recognition memory in infants. *Child Development, 51(1),* 69–74.

Graesser, A.C. & Nakamura, G.V. (1982). The impact of a schema on comprehension and memory. In G.H. Bower (Ed.), *The psychology of learning and motivation: Advances in research and theory.* San Diego, CA: Academic Press.

Graf, P. & Schacter, D.L. (1985). Implicit and explicit memory for new associations in normal and amnesic subjects. *Journal of Experimental Psychology: Learning, Memory and Cognition, 13,* 45–53.

Grafman, J., Litvan, I., Gomez, C. and Chase, T.N. (1990). Frontal lobe function in progressive supranuclear palsy. *Archives of Neurology, 47,* 553–61.

Grafman, J., Weingarter, H., Newhouse, P.A.. et al. (1990). Implicit learning in patients with Alzheimer's disease. *Psychopharmacology, 23,* 94–101.

Granerus, A.K. (1990). Update on Parkinson's disease: Current considerations and geriatric aspects. In M. Beringer & S.I. Finkel, (Eds), *Clinical and scientific psychogeriatrics, Vol. 2: The interface between psychiatry and neurology.* New York: Springer.

Granholm, E., Wolfe, J., & Butters, N. (1985). Affective-arousal factors in the recall of thematic stories by amnesic and demented patients. *Developmental Neuropsychology, 1,* 317–33.

Greco, C., Rovee-Collier, C.K., Hayne, H., Griesler, P., & Earley, L. (1986). Ontogeny of early event memory: 1. Forgetting and retrieval by 2- and 3- month-olds. *Infant Behavior and Development, 9,* 441–60.

Green, S. (1987). *Physiological psychology.* New York: Routledge and Kegan Paul.

Greene, R.L. (1984). Incidental learning of event frequency. *Memory and Cognition, 12,* 90–95.

Greene, R.L. (1986). Effects of intentionality and strategy on memory for frequency. *Journal of Experimental Psychology: Learning, Memory and Cognition, 12,* 489–95.

Greene, R.L. (1988). Generation effects in frequency judgment. *Journal of Experimental Psychology: Learning, Memory and Cognition, 14,* 298–304.

Greene, R.L. (1989). Spacing effects in memory: Evidence for a two-process account. *Journal of Experimental Psychology: Learning, Memory and Cognition, 15,* 371–7.

Greene, R.L. (1990). Memory for pair frequency. *Journal of Experimental Psychology: Learning, Memory and Cognition, 16,* 110–16.

Gregg, V.H. & Gardiner, J.M. (1991). Components of conscious awareness in a long-term modality effect. *British Journal of Psychology, 82,* 153–62.

Groeger, J.A. (1986). Predominant and non-predominant analysis: Effects of level of presentation. *British Journal of Psychology, 77,* 109–16.

Groeger, J.A. (1988). Qualitatively different effects of undetected and unidentified auditory primes. *Quarterly Journal of Experimental Psychology: Human Experimental Psychology, 40A,* 323–39.

Groeger, J.A. & Bekerian, D.A. (1995). Why time flies when you're thinking about washing and kite building: A reappraisal of the relationship between memory and time. Paper presented at the Annual Conference of the Cognitive Section of the British Psychological Society, Bristol, U.K.

Groeger, J.A. & Chapman, P.R. (1996). Judgement of traffic scenes: The role of danger and difficulty. *Applied Cognitive Psychology, 10,* 349–64.

Groeger, J.A. & Clegg, B.A. (1994). Reduction in the rate of driving instruction: An index of pupils' learning. Proceedings of the 23rd International Congress of Applied Psychology, Madrid, July 17th–22nd, 1994.

Groeger, J.A. & Grande, G.E. (1996). Self-preserving assessments of skill? *British Journal of Psychology, 87,* 61–79.

Gruneberg, M.M. (1985). *Computer Linkword: French, German, Spanish, Italian, Greek, Russian, Dutch, Portuguese, Hebrew.* Penfield, NY: Artworx.

Gruneberg, M.M. (1992). The practical application of memory aids: Knowing how, knowing when, and knowing when not. In M.M. Gruneberg and P.E. Morris (Eds), *Aspects of memory*, 2nd edn., pp. 168–95. London: Routledge.

Gurd, J.M. & Ward, D.D. (1989). Retrieval from semantic and letter-initial categories in patients with Parkinson's disease. *Neuropsychologia, 27*, 743–6.

Gurland, B.J. & Cross, P.S. (1986). Public health perspectives on clinical memory testing of Alzheimer's disease and related disorders. In L.W. Poon (Ed.) *Clinical memory assessment of older adults.* Washington, D.C: American Psychological Association.

Haarland, K.Y. & Harrington, D.L. (1990). Complex movement behaviour: Towards understanding cortical and subcortical interactions in regulating control processes. In G.R. Hammond (Ed.), *Advances in psychology: Cerebral control of speech and limb movements.* Amsterdam: Elsevier.

Haber, R.N. & Myers, B.L. (1982). Memory for pictograms, pictures, and words separately and all mixed up. *Perception, 11*, 57–64.

Hagman, J.D. (1983). Presentation- and test-trial effects on acquisition and retention of distance and location. *Journal of Experimental Psychology: Learning, Memory and Cognition, 9*, 334–45.

Haig, N.D. (1986). High-resolution facial feature saliency mapping. *Perception, 15*, 373–86.

Haley, W.E., Brown, S.L., & Levine, E.G. (1987). Family caregiver appraisals of patient behavioural disturbance in senile dementia. *International Journal of Aging and Human Development, 25*, 25–34.

Halpern, A.R. (1988). Mental scanning in auditory imagery for songs. *Journal of Experimental Psychology: Learning, Memory and Cognition, 14*, 434–43.

Hanley, J.R. & Broadbent, C. (1987). The effect of unattended speech on serial recall following auditory presentation. *British Journal of Psychology, 78*, 287–97.

Hanna, A. & Loftus, G. (1992). The effect of expectation and available processing time on recognition of sequences of naturalistic scenes. *Bulletin of the Psychonomic Society, 30*, 251–4.

Hart, R.P. & O'Shanick, G.J. (1993). Forgetting rates for verbal, pictorial, and figural stimuli. *Journal of Clinical and Experimental Neuropsychology, 15*, 245–65.

Hart, S.A., Smith, C.M. & Swash, M. (1985). Recognition memory in Alzheimer's disease. *Neurobiology of Aging, 6*, 287–92.

Hasher, L. & Zacks, R.T. (1979). Automatic and effortful processes in memory. *Journal of Experimental Psychology: General, 108*, 356–88.

Hasher, L. & Zacks, R.T. (1984). Automatic processing of fundamental information: The case of frequency of occurrence. *American Psychologist, 39*, 1372–88.

Hastie, R. (1975). Intralist repetition in free recall: Effects of frequency attribute recall instructions. *Journal of Experimental Psychology: Human Learning and Memory, 104*, 3–12.

Hayne, H., Greco, C., Earley, L., Griesler, P. & Rovee-Collier, C. (1986). Ontogeny of early event memory: 2. Forgetting and retrieval by 2- and 3-month-olds. *Infant Behavior and Development, 9*, 461–72.

Head, H. (1920). *Studies in Neurology.* Oxford: Oxford Press.

Healy, A.F. & Bourne L.E. (Eds.) (1995). *Learning and memory of knowledge and skills.* Thousand Oaks, CA: Sage.

Heindel, W.C., Salmon, D.P. & Butters, N. (1991). The biasing of weight judgments in Alzheimer's and Huntington's disease: A priming or programming phenomenon? *Journal of Clinical and Experimental Neuropsychology, 13*, 189–203.

Heindel, W.C. Salmon, D.P., Shults, C.W. et al. (1989). Neuropsychological evidence for multiple implicit memory systems: A comparison of Alzheimer's, Huntington's and Parkinson's disease patients. *Journal of Neuroscience, 9*, 582–7.

Herlitz, A. & Viitanen, M. (1991). Semantic organisation and verbal episodic memory in patients with mild and moderate Alzheimer's disease. *Journal of Clinical and Experimental Neuropsychology, 7*, 305–13.

Hertzog, C., Dixon, R.A., & Hultsch, D.F. (1990). Relationships between metamemory, memory predictions, and memory task performance in adults. *Psychology and Aging, 5*, 215–27.

Heuer, F. & Reisberg, D. (1990). Vivid memories of emotional events: The accuracy of remembered minutiae. *Memory and Cognition, 18*, 496–506.

Hewitt, K. (1973). Context effects in memory: A review. Cambridge University Psychological Laboratory.

Hicks, R.E., Miller, G.W. & Kinsbourne, M. (1976). Prospective and retrospective judgments of time as a function of amount of information processed. *American Journal of Psychology, 89*, 719–30.

Higbee, K.L. (1988). *Your memory*, 2nd edn. New York: Prentice-Hall.

Hinrichs, J.V. (1970). A two-process memory-strength

theory for judgment of recency. *Psychological Review, 77,* 223–33.

Hintzman, D.L. (1976). Repetition and memory. In G.H. Bower (Ed.), *The psychology of learning and motivation: Advances in research and theory, Vol. 10.* New York: Academic Press.

Hintzman, D.L. (1986). 'Schema abstraction' in a multiple-trace memory model. *Psychological Review, 93,* 411–28.

Hintzman, D.L. (1990). Human learning and memory: Connections and dissociations. *Annual Review of Psychology, 41,* 109–39.

Hintzman, D.L. (1992). Mathematical constraints and the Tulving–Wiseman law. *Psychological Review, 99,* 536–42.

Hintzman, D.L. (1994). On explaining the mirror effect. *Journal of Experimental Psychology: Learning, Memory and Cognition, 20,* 201–5.

Hintzman, D.L. & Block, R.A. (1971). Repetition and memory: Evidence for a multiple-trace hypothesis. *Journal of Experimental Psychology, 88,* 297–306.

Hintzman, D.L. & Block, R.A. (1973). Memory for the spacing of repetitions. *Journal of Experimental Psychology, 99,* 70–4.

Hintzman, D.L., Block, R.A. & Summers, J.J. (1973). Contextual associations and memory for serial positions. *Journal of Experimental Psychology, 97,* 220–29.

Hintzman, D.L., Curran, T. & Oppy, B. (1992). Effects of similarity and repetition on memory: Registration without learning? *Journal of Experimental Psychology: Learning, Memory and Cognition, 18,* 667–80.

Hintzman, D.L. & Rogers, M.K. (1973). Spacing effects in picture memory. *Memory and Cognition, 1,* 430–4.

Hintzman, D.L. & Stern, L.D. (1984). A comparison of forgetting rates in frequency discrimination and recognition. *Bulletin of the Psychonomic Society, 22,* 409–12.

Hintzman, D.L., Summers, J.J. & Block, R.A. (1975). What causes the spacing effect? Some effects of repetition, duration, and spacing on memory for pictures. *Memory and Cognition, 3,* 287–94.

Hirsh, I.J., & Sherrick, C.E. (1961). Perceived order in different sense modalities. *Journal of Experimental Psychology, 97,* 220–306.

Hirshman, E. & Bjork, R.A. (1988). The generation effect: Support for a two-factor theory. *Journal of Experimental Psychology: Learning, Memory and Cognition, 14,* 484–94.

Hirtle, S.C. and Kallman, H.J. (1988). Memory for the locations of pictures: Evidence for hierarchical clustering. *American Journal of Psychology, 101,* 159–70.

Hiscock, M., Kinsbourne, M., Samuels, M. & Krause, A.E. (1987). Dual task performance in children: Generalized and lateralized effects of memory encoding upon the rate and variability of concurrent finger tapping. *Brain and Cognition, 6,* 24–40.

Hitch, G., Rejman, M.J. & Turner, N.C. (1980). A new perspective on the recency effect. Paper presented at the July Experimental Psychology Society meeting in Cambridge.

Hoagland, H. (1933). The physiologic control of judgments of duration: Evidence for a chemical clock. *Journal of General Psychology, 9,* 267–87.

Hock, H.S., Malcus, L. & Hasher, L. (1986). Frequency discrimination: Assessing global-level and element-level units in memory. *Journal of Experimental Psychology: Learning, Memory and Cognition, 12,* 232–40.

Hockey, G.R.J. (1984). Varieties of attentional state: The effects of the environment. In R. Parasuraman & D.R. Davies (Eds), *Varieties of attention.* New York: Academic Press.

Hockey, G.R.J., Davies, S. & Gray, M.M. (1972). Forgetting as a function of sleep at different times of day. *Experimental Psychology, 24,* 386–93.

Hockley, W.E. (1994). Reflections of the mirror effect for item and associative recognition. *Memory and Cognition, 22,* 713–22.

Hokfelt, T., Johansson, O., & Goldstein, M. (1984). Chemical anatomy of the brain. *Science, 225,* 1326–34.

Holding, D. (1991). Transfer of training. In J.E. Morrison (Ed.), *Training for performance: Principles of applied human learning,* pp. 93–125. Chichester: John Wiley.

Holding, D.H., Noonan, T.K., Pfau, H.D., Holding, C.S. (1986). Date attribution, age, and the distribution of lifetime memories. *Journal of Gerontology, 41(4),* 481–5.

Homa, D. & Viera, C. (1988). Long-term memory for pictures under conditions of thematically related foils. *Memory and Cognition, 16,* 411–21.

Hoosain, R. & Salili, F. (1987). Language differences in pronunciation speed for numbers, digit span, and mathematical ability. *Psychologia: An International Journal of Psychology in the Orient, 30,* 34–8.

Horn, J.C. (1981). Memory II. *Psychology Today, 21,* 80–81.

Horn, J.L. & Cattell, R.B. (1966). Age effects primary mental ability factors. *Journal of Gerontology, 21,* 210–20.

Horton, D.L. & Mills, C.B. (1984). Human learning and memory. *Annual Review of Psychology, 35,* 361–94.

Horton, D.L., Pavlick, T.J. & Moulin-Julian, M.W. (1993). Retrieval-based and familiarity-based recognition and the quality of information in episodic memory. *Journal of Memory and Language, 32,* 39–55.

Howard, D.V. (1991). Implicit memory: an expanding picture of cognitive aging. In K.W. Schaie and M.P. Lawton (Eds), *Annual Review of Gerontology and Geriatrics, 11,* 1–22.

Howard, D.V. & Howard, J.H. (1992). Adult age differences in the rate of learning serial patterns: Evidence from direct and indirect tests. *Psychology and Aging, 7,* 232–41.

Howard, J.H., Mutter, S.A. & Howard, D.V. (1992). Serial pattern learning by event observation. *Journal of Experimental Psychology: Learning, Memory and Cognition, 18,* 1029–39.

Howe, M.L. & Courage, M.L. (1993). On resolving the enigma of infantile amnesia. *Psychological Bulletin, 113,* 305–26.

Howell, P. & Darwin, C.J. (1977). Some properties of auditory memory for rapid formant transitions. *Memory and Cognition, 5,* 700–8.

Howell, W.C. (1973). Representation of frequency in memory. *Psychological Bulletin, 80,* 44–53.

Huber, S.J. & Shuttleworth, E.C. (1990). Neuropsychological assessment of subcortical dementia. In J.L. Cummings (Ed.), *Subcortical dementia.* New York: Oxford University Press.

Hudson, J.A. (1988). Children's memory for atypical actions in script-based stories: Evidence for a disruption effect. *Journal of Experimental Child Psychology, 46,* 159–73.

Hulme, C. & MacKenzie, S. (1992). *Working memory and severe learning difficulties.* Hove: Lawrence Erlbaum.

Hultsch, D.F., Masson, M.E. & Small, B.J. (1991). Adult age differences in direct and indirect tests of memory. *Journal of Gerontology: Psychological Sciences, 46,* 22–30.

Hunt, E. & Love, T. (1972). How good can memory be? In A.W. Melton & E. Martin (Eds), *Coding processes in human memory,* pp. 237–60. Washington, DC: Winston & Sons.

Hunt, R.R. & Ellis, H.C. (1974). Recognition memory and degree of semantic contextual change. *Journal of Experimental Psychology, 103,* 1153–9.

Hunter, I.M.L. (1977). An exceptional memory. *British Journal of Psychology, 68,* 155–64.

Huppert, F.A. & Beardsall, L. (1993). Prospective memory impairment as an early indicator of dementia. *Journal of Clinical and Experimental Neuropsychology, 15,* 805–21.

Huppert, F.A. & Piercy, M. (1978). Recognition memory in amnesic patients: Effect of temporal center and familiarity of material. *Cortex, 76(12),* 3–20.

Huttenlocher, J., Hedges, L.V. & Bradburn, N.M. (1990). Reports of elapsed time: Bounding and rounding processes in estimation. *Journal of Experimental Psychology: Learning, Memory and Cognition, 16,* 196–213.

Huttenlocher, J., Hedges, L. & Prohaska, V. (1988). Hierarchical organization in ordered domains: Estimating the dates of events. *Psychological Review, 95,* 471–84.

Hyde, T.S. & Jenkins, J.J. (1973). Recall for words as a function of semantic, graphic and syntactic orienting tasks. *Journal of Verbal Learning and Verbal Behavior, 12,* 471–80.

Idizkowski, C. & Baddeley, A.D. (1983). Fear and dangerous environments. In G.R.J. Hockey (Ed.), *Stress and fatigue in human performance.* Chichester: John Wiley.

Idizkowski, C. & Baddeley, A.D. (1987). Fear and performance of novice parachutists. *Ergonomics, 30,* 1463–74.

Ingram, R.E, Kendall, P.C., Smith, T.W., Donnell, C. and Ronan, K. (1987). Cognitive specificity in emotional distress. *Journal of Personality and Social Psychology, 53,* 734–42.

Intraub, H. (1981). Rapid conceptual identification of sequentially presented pictures. *Journal of Experimental Psychology: Human Perception and Performance, 7,* 604–10.

Intraub, H. (1984). Conceptual masking: The effects of subsequent visual events on memory for pictures. *Journal of Experimental Psychology: Learning, Memory and Cognition, 10,* 115–25.

Intraub, H., Bender, R.S. & Mangels, J.A. (1992). Looking at pictures but remembering scenes. *Journal of Experimental Psychology: Learning, Memory and Cognition, 18,* 180–91.

Intraub, H. & Hoffman, J.E. (1992). Reading and visual memory: Remembering scenes that were never seen. *American Journal of Psychology, 105,* 101–14.

Intraub, H. & Nicklos, S. (1985). Levels of processing and picture memory: The physical superiority effect. *Journal of Experimental Psychology: Learning, Memory and Cognition, 11,* 284–98.

Intraub, H. & Richardson, M. (1989). Wide-angle memories of close-up scenes. *Journal of Experimental Psychology: Learning, Memory and Cognition, 15,* 179–87.

Iran-Nejad, A. (1986). Understanding surprise-ending stories: Long-term memory schemas versus schema-independent context elements. *Journal of Mind and Behavior, 7,* 37–62.

Isen, A.M., Shalker, T.E, Clark, M., & Carp, L. (1978). Affect, accessibility of material in memory and behavior: A cognitive loop. *Journal of Personality and Social Psychology, 36,* 1–12.

Jackson, J.L., Michon, J.A., Boonstra, H., de Jonge, D. & de Veld Harsenhorst, (1986). The effect of depth of processing on experimental judgment tasks. *Acta Psychologica, 62,* 199–210.

Jacobs, D., Troster, A.I., Butters, N. et al., (1990). Intrusion errors on the Visual Reproduction Test of the Wechsler Memory Scale and the Wechsler Memory Scale-Revised: An analysis of amnesic and demented patients. *The Clinical Neuropsychologist, 4,* 177–91.

Jacoby, L.L. (1983). Remembering the data: Analyzing interactive processes in reading. *Journal of Verbal Learning and Verbal Behavior, 22,* 485–508.

Jacoby, L.L. (1991). A process dissociation framework: Separating automatic from intentional uses of memory. *Journal of Memory and Language, 30,* 513–41.

Jacoby, L.L. and Brooks, L.R. (1984). Nonanalytic cognition: Memory, perception, and concept learning. In G.H. Bower (Ed.), *The psychology of learning and motivation: Advances in research and theory Vol. 18.* New York: Academic Press.

Jacoby, L.L. & Dallas, M. (1981). On the relationship between autobiographical memory and perceptual learning. *Journal of Experimental Psychology: General, 110,* 306–40.

Jacoby, L.L., Woloshyn, V. & Kelley, C. (1989). Becoming famous without being recognized: Unconscious influences of memory produced by dividing attention. *Journal of Experimental Psychology: General, 118,* 115–25.

James, W. (1890). *Principles of psychology, Vol.1.* New York: Holt.

Jarvik, L.F. (1988). Aging of the brain: How can we prevent it? *The Gerontologist, 28,* 739–47.

Jellinger, K.A. & Bancher, C. (1992). Neuropathology. In I. Litvan & Y. Agid (Eds), *Progressive supranuclear palsy: Clinical and research approaches.* New York: Oxford University Press.

Jenkins, J.G. & Dallenbach, K.M. (1924). Obliviscence during sleep and waking. *American Journal of Psychology, 35,* 605–12.

Johnson, M.K. & Magaro, P.A. (1987). Effects of mood and severity on memory processes in depression and mania. *Psychological Bulletin, 101,* 28–40.

Johnson, M.K., Raye, C.L., Wang, A.Y. & Taylor, T.H. (1979). Fact and fantasy: The roles of accuracy and variability in confusing imaginations with perceptual experiences. *Journal of Experimental Psychology: Human Learning and Memory, 5,* 229–40.

Johnson-Laird, P.N., Herrmann, D.J. & Chaffin, R. (1984). Only connections: A critique of semantic networks. *Psychological Bulletin, 96,* 292–315.

Johnston, W.A., Dark, V.J. & Jacoby, L.L. (1985). Perceptual fluency and recognition judgments. *Journal of Experimental Psychology: Learning, Memory and Cognition, 11,* 3–11.

Jolicoeur, P. (1987). A size-congruency effect in memory for visual shape. *Memory and Cognition, 15,* 531–43.

Jones, W.P. & Anderson, J.R. (1987). Short- and long-term memory retrieval: A comparison of the effects of information load and relatedness. *Journal of Experimental Psychology: General, 116,* 137–53.

Joyce, E.M. (1987). The neurochemistry of Korsakoff's syndrome. In S.M. Stahl, S.D. Iversen & E.C. Goodman (Eds), *Cognitive neurochemistry.* Oxford: Oxford University Press.

Juurmaa, J., Lehtinen, R.S. (1988). Cross-modal transfer of forms between vision and touch. *Scandinavian Journal of Psychology, 29(2),* 95–110.

Kahana, M.J. & Greene, R.L. (1993). Effects of spacing on memory for homogenous lists. *Journal of Experimental Psychology: Learning, Memory and Cognition, 19,* 159–62.

Kahneman, D. (1973). *Attention and effort.* Englewood Cliffs, NJ: Prentice Hall.

Kahneman, D. & Miller, D.T. (1986). Norm theory: Comparing reality to its alternatives. *Psychological Review, 93,* 136–53.

Kail, R.V. (1990). *The development of memory in children.* New York: Freeman.

Kant, I. (1963). *Critique of pure reason.* London: MacMillan.

Kapur, N. (1988). *Memory disorders in clinical practice*. London: Butterworth.

Kassin, S.M., Ellsworth, P.C. & Smith, V.L. (1989). The 'general acceptance' of psychological research on eyewitness testimony: A survey of the experts. *American Psychologist, 44*, 1089–98.

Kaszniak, A.W., Keyl, P.M. & Albert, M.S. (1991). Dementia and the older driver. Special issue: Safety and mobility of elderly drivers: Part 1. *Human Factors, 33*, 527–37.

Kausler, D.H. (1991). *Experimental psychology, cognition, and human aging*. New York: Springer Verlag.

Kausler, D.H. & Klein, D.M. (1978). Age differences in processing relevant versus irrelevant stimuli in multiple item recognition memory. *Journal of Gerontology, 33*, 87–93.

Kausler, D.H., Lichty, W. & Hakami, M.K. (1984). Frequency judgments for distractor items in a short-term memory task: Instructional variation and adult age differences. *Journal of Verbal Learning and Verbal Behavior, 23*, 660–68.

Keppel, G. (1964). Facilitation in short- and long-term retention of paired associates following distributed practice in learning. *Journal of Verbal Learning and Verbal Behavior, 3*, 91–111.

Keppel, G. & Underwood, B.J. (1962). Proactive incidental tasks that differentially affect associative clustering in recall. *Journal of Experimental Psychology, 89*, 92–5.

Kerr, N.H. (1983). The role of vision in 'visual imagery' experiments: Evidence from the congenitally blind. *Journal of Experimental Psychology: General, 112*, 265–77.

Kerr, N.H. & Winograd, E. (1982). Effects of contextual elaboration on face recognition. *Memory and Cognition, 10*, 603–9.

Kesslak, J.P., Cotman, C.W., Chui, H.C., VandenNoort, S., et.al. (1988). Olfactory tests as possible probes for detecting and monitoring Alzheimer's disease. *Neurobiology of Aging, 9(4)*, 399–403.

Kim, K. & Glanzer, M. (1993). Speed versus accuracy instructions, study time, and the mirror effect. *Journal of Experimental Psychology: Learning, Memory and Cognition, 19*, 638–52.

Kimura, D., Barnett, H.J., Burkhart, G. (1981). The psychological test pattern in progressive supranuclear palsy. *Neuropsychologia, 19*, 301–6.

Kinkade, R.G.A. (1963). A differential influence of augmented feedback on learning and on performance (WADC Air Force Systems Command Tech. Rep. AMRL-TDR-63-12). Dayton, OH: US Air Force, Wright Air Development Center.

Kintsch, W. (1968). Recognition and free recall of organized lists. *Journal of Experimental Psychology, 78*, 481–7.

Kintsch, W. (1970). *Learning, memory and conceptual processes*. New York: Wiley.

Kintsch, W. & Buschke, H. (1969). Homophones and synonyms in short-term memory. *Journal of Experimental Psychology, 80*, 403–7.

Kintsch, W. & Kintsch, E.H. (1978). The role of schemata in text comprehension. *International Journal of Psycholinguistics, 5*, 17–29.

Kiphart, M.J., Auday, B.C., Cross, H.A. (1988). Short-term haptic memory for three-dimensional objects. *Perceptual and Motor Skills, 66(1)*, 79–91.

Kirkland, J. & Flanagan, D. (1979). Long-term memory and the value-size hypothesis. *Perceptual and Motor Skills, 48*, 1149–50.

Klatzky, R.L. & Forrest, F.H. (1984). Recognising familiar and unfamiliar faces. *Memory and Cognition, 12*, 60–70.

Klatzky, R.L., Lederman, S.J., & Matula, D.E. (1993). Haptic exploration in the presence of vision. *Journal of Experimental Psychology: Human Perception and Performance, 19(4)*, 726–43.

Klatzky, R.L., Martin, G.L. & Kane, R.A. (1982). Semantic interpretation effects on memory for faces. *Memory and Cognition, 10*, 195–206.

Klein, S.B. & Kihlstrom, J.F. (1986). Elaboration, organization, and the self-reference effect in memory. *Journal of Experimental Psychology: General, 115*, 26–38.

Klein, S.B., Loftus, J. & Burton, H.A. (1989). Two self-reference effects: The importance of distinguishing between self-descriptiveness judgments and autobiographical retrieval in self-referent encoding. *Journal of Personality and Social Psychology, 56*, 853–65.

Kleinsmith, L.J. & Kaplan, S. (1963). Paired associated learning as a function of arousal and interpolated interval. *Journal of Experimental Psychology, 65*, 190–93.

Kleinsmith, L.J. & Kaplan, S. (1964). Interaction of arousal and recall interval in nonsense syllable paired associate learning. *Journal of Experimental Psychology, 67*, 124–6.

Koffka, K. (1935). *Principles of Gestalt psychology*. New York: Harcourt Brace p. 285.

Koh, K. & Meyer, D.E. (1991). Function learning: Induction of continuous stimulus–response relations.

Journal of Experimental Psychology: Learning, Memory and Cognition, 17, 811–36.

Kolers, P. (1975). Memorial consequences of automatized encoding. *Journal of Experimental Psychology: Human Learning and Memory, 104,* 689–701.

Kolers, P. (1976). Reading a year later. *Journal of Experimental Psychology: Human Learning and Memory, 2,* 554–65.

Kolers, P.A. & Roediger, H.L. (1984). Procedures of mind. *Journal of Verbal Learning and Verbal Behavior, 23,* 425–49.

Kopelman, M.D. (1985). Rates of forgetting in Alzheimer-type dementia and Korsakoff's syndrome. *Neuropsychologia, 23,* 623–38.

Kopelman, M.D. (1986). Recall of anomalous sentences in dementia and amnesia. *Brain and Language, 29,* 154–70.

Kopelman, M.D. (1987). Amnesia: Organic and psychogenic. *British Journal of Psychiatry, 150,* 428–42.

Kosslyn, S.M. (1975). Information representation in visual images. *Cognitive Psychology, 7,* 341–70.

Kosslyn, S.M. (1991). A cognitive neuroscience of visual cognition: Further developments. In R.H. Logie and M. Denis (Eds), *Mental images in human cognition,* pp. 352–81. Amsterdam: Elsevier.

Kosslyn, S.M. (1994). *Image and brain: The resolution of the imagery debate.* Cambridge, MA: MIT Press.

Kosslyn, S.M., & Alper, S.N. (1977). On the pictorial properties of visual images: Effects of image size on memory for words. *Canadian Journal of Psychology, 31(1),* 32–40.

Kovner, R., Mattis, S., & Pass, R. (1985). Some amnesic patients can freely recall large amounts of information in new contexts. *Journal of Clinical and Experimental Neuropsychology, 7(4),* 395–411.

Kraft, R.N., Cantor, P. & Gottdiener, C. (1991). The coherence of visual narratives. Special issue: Cognitive processing of media. *Communication Research, 18,* 601–16.

Kramer, J.H., Delis, D.C., Blusewicz, M.J. et al. (1988). Verbal memory errors in Alzheimer's and Huntington's dementias. *Developmental Neuropsychology, 4,* 1–15.

LaBerge, D. & Samuels, S.J. (1974). Toward a theory of automatic information processing in reading. *Cognitive Psychology, 6,* 293–323.

Landauer, T.K. (1975). Memory without organization: Properties of a model with random storage and undirected retrieval. *Cognitive Psychology, 7,* 495–531.

Lane, D.M. & Robertson, L. (1979). The generality of the levels of processing hypothesis: An application to memory for chess positions. *Memory and Cognition, 7,* 253–6.

Large, I. & Thorndike, E.L. (1935). The influence of delay in the after-effect of a connection. *Journal of Experimental Psychology, 18,* 186–94.

Lavie, P. & Webb, W.B. (1975). Time estimates in a long-term time-free environment. *American Journal of Psychology, 88,* 177–86.

Lawrence, D.M., Cobb, N.J., Beard, J.I. (1978). Influence of active encoding on tactile recognition memory for common objects. *Perceptual and Motor Skills, 47(2),* 596–8.

Lazarus, R.S. & Folkman, S. (1984). *Stress, coping and appraisal.* New York: Springer.

Lazarus, R.S. & Smith, C.A. (1988). Knowledge and appraisal in the cognition–emotion relationship. *Cognition and Emotion, 2,* 281–300.

Lazarus, R.S., Kanner, A.D., & Folkman, S., (1980). Emotions: A cognitive phenomenal analysis. In R. Plutchik & H. Kellerman (Eds), *Emotion: Theory, research and experience.* New York: Academic Press.

Lee, C.L. & Estes, W.K. (1981). Item and order information in short-term memory: Evidence for multilevel perturbation processes. *Journal of Experimental Psychology: Human Learning and Memory, 7,* 149–69.

Legault, E., & Standing, L. (1992). Memory for size of drawings and of photographs. *Perceptual and Motor Skills, 75(1),* 121.

Leippe, M.R., Romanczyk, A., & Manion, A.P. (1991). Eye-witness memory for a touching experience: Accuracy differences between child and adult witnesses. *Journal of Applied Psychology, 76(3),* 367–79.

Leng, N.R., & Parkin, A.J. (1988a). Amnesic patients can benefit from instructions to use imagery: Evidence against cognitive mediation hypothesis. *Cortex, 24(1),* 33–9.

Leng, N.R., & Parkin, A.J. (1988b). Double dissociation of frontal dysfunction in organic amnesia. *British Journal of Clinical Psychology, 27(4),* 359–62.

Levin, B.E., Tomer, R., & Rey, G.J. (1992). Clinical correlates of cognitive impairment in Parkinson's disease. In S.J Huber & J.L. Cummings (Eds), *Parkinson's disease: Neurobehavioural aspects.* New York: Oxford University Press.

Lezak, M.D. (1995). *Neuropsychological assessment.* New York: Oxford University Press.

Lhermitte, F. (1983). 'Utilisation behaviour' and its relation to lesions of the frontal lobe. *Brain, 106,* 237–55.

Light, L.L. (1991). Memory and aging: Four hypotheses in search of data. *Annual Review of Psychology, 42,* 333–76.

Light, L.L. & Carter-Sobell, L. (1970). Effects of changed semantic context on recognition memory. *Journal of Verbal Learning and Verbal Behavior, 9,* 1–11.

Lindsay, D.S. & Johnson, M.K. (1987). The eyewitness suggestibility effect and memory for source. *Memory and Cognition, 16,* 1077–83.

Lindsay, D.S. & Read, J.D. (1994). Psychotherapy and memories of childhood sexual abuse: A cognitive perspective. *Applied Cognitive Psychology, 8,* 281–338.

Linton, M. (1975). Memory for real world events. In D.A. Norman & D.E. Rumelhart (Eds), *Explorations in cognition.* San Francisco: Freeman.

Linton, M. (1978). Real world memory after six years: An in vivo study of very long-term memory. In M.M. Gruneberg, P.E. Morris & R.N. Sykes (Eds), *Practical aspects of memory.* London: Academic Press.

Linton, M. (1982). Transformations of memory in everyday life. In U. Neisser (Ed.), *Memory observed: Remembering in natural contexts.* San Francisco: W.H. Freeman.

Linton, M. (1986). Ways of searching and the components of memory. In D.C. Rubin (Ed.) *Autobiographical memory.* Cambridge: Cambridge University Press.

Lipinska, B, Backman, L., & Herlitz, A. (1992). When Greta Garbo is easier to remember than Stefan Edberg: Influences of prior knowledge on recognition memory in Alzheimer's disease. *Psychology and Aging, 7(2),* 214–20.

Lishman, W.A. (1987). *Organic psychiatry.* Oxford: Blackwell.

Livingston, R.B. (1967). Brain circuitry relating to complex behavior. In G.C. Quarton, T. Melnechuck & F.O. Schmitt (Eds), *The neurosciences: A study program.* New York: Rockefeller University Press.

Lloyd, G.G. & Lishman, W.A. (1975). Effect of depression on the speed of recall of pleasant and unpleasant experiences. *Psychological medicine, 5,* 173–80.

Locksley, A., Stangor, C., Hepburn, C., Grosovsky, E., & Hochstrasser, M. (1984). The ambiguity of recognition memory tests of schema theories. *Cognitive Psychology, 16,* 421–48.

Loess, H. (1968). Short-term memory and item similarity. *Journal of Verbal Learning and Verbal Behavior, 7,* 87–92.

Loftus, E. (1974). Reconstructing memory: The incredible eyewitness. *Psychology Today, 8,* 116–19.

Loftus, E.F. (1979a). *Eyewitness testimony.* Cambridge, MA: Harvard University Press.

Loftus, E.F. (1979b). The malleability of human memory. *American Scientist, 67,* 312–20.

Loftus, E.F. (1979c). Reactions to blatantly contradictory information. *Memory and Cognition, 7,* 368–74.

Loftus, E.F. (1992). When a lie becomes memory's truth: Memory distortion after exposure to misinformation. *Current Directions in Psychological Science, 1,* 121–3.

Loftus, E.F. & Burns, T.E. (1982). Mental shock can produce retrograde amnesia. *Memory and Cognition, 10,* 318–23.

Loftus, E.F. & Greene, E. (1980). Warning: Even memory for faces may be contagious. *Law and Human Behavior, 4,* 323–34.

Loftus, E.F. & Loftus, G.R. (1980). On the permanence of stored information in the human brain. *American Psychologist, 35,* 409–20.

Loftus, E.F. & Marburger, W. (1983). Since the eruption of Mt St Helens, has anyone beaten you up? Improving the accuracy of retrospective reports with landmark events. *Memory and Cognition, 11,* 114–20.

Loftus, E.F., Miller, D.G. & Burns, H.J. (1978). Semantic integration of verbal information into a visual memory. *Journal of Experimental Psychology: Human Learning and Memory, 4,* 19–31.

Loftus, E.F. & Palmer, J.C. (1974). Reconstruction of automobile destruction: An example of the interaction between language and memory. *Journal of Verbal Learning and Verbal Behaviour, 13,* 585–9.

Loftus, E.F., Schooler, J.W., Boone, S.M. & Kline, D. (1987). Time went by so slowly: Overestimation of event duration by males and females. *Applied Cognitive Psychology, 1,* 3–13.

Loftus, G.R. & Ginn, M. (1984) Perceptual and conceptual masking of pictures. *Journal of Experimental Psychology: Learning, Memory and Cognition, 10,* 435–41.

Logan, G.D. (1988). Toward an instance theory of automatization. *Psychological Review, 95,* 492–527.

Logie, R.H. (1986). Visuo-spatial processing in working memory. *Quarterly Journal of Experimental Psychology: Human Experimental Psychology, 38A,* 229–47.

Logie, R.H. (1995). *Visuo-spatial working memory*. Hove: Lawrence Erlbaum.

Lopez, O.L., Becker, J.T., Bremner, R.P. et al. (1991). Alzheimer's disease with delusions and hallucinations: Neuropsychological and electroencephalographic correlates. *Neurology, 41*, 906–11.

Lovelace, E.A. & Marsh, G.R. (1985). Prediction and evaluation of memory performance by young and old adults. *Journal of Gerontology, 37*, 432–7.

Luria, A.R. (1968). *The mind of a mnemonist*. New York: Basic Books.

McAndrews, M.P., Glisky, E.L. & Schacter, D.L. (1987). When priming persists: Long-lasting implicit memory for a single episode in amnesic patients. *Neuropsychologia, 25*, 497–506.

McCloskey, M. & Zaragoza, M. (1985). Misleading postevent information and memory for events: Arguments and evidence against memory impairment hypotheses. *Journal of Experimental Psychology: General, 114*, 1–16.

McCloskey, M., Wible, C.G. and Cohen, N.J. (1988). Is there a special flashbulb-memory mechanism? *Journal of Experimental Psychology: General, 117*, 171–81.

McDaniel, M.A. (1984). The role of elaborative and schema processes in story memory. *Memory and Cognition, 12*, 46–51.

McDaniel, M.A. & Kerwin, M.L. (1987). Long-term prose retention: Is an organizational schema sufficient? *Discourse Processes, 10*, 237–52.

Mace, C.J. & Trimble, M.R. (1991). Psychogenic amnesias. In T. Yanagihara & R.C. Petersen (Eds), *Memory disorders: Research and clinical practice*. New York: Marcel Dekker.

Macey, W.H. & Zechmeister, E.B. (1975). Test of the multiple-trace hypothesis: The effects of temporal separation and presentation modality. *Journal of Experimental Psychology: Human Learning and Memory, 104*, 459–65.

Macfarlane, A. (1975). Olfaction in the development of social preferences of the human neonate. *Ciba Foundation Symposium, 33*, 103–17.

McGeogh, J.A. & McDonald, W.T. (1931). Meaningful relation and retroactive inhibition. *American Journal of Psychology, 43*, 579–88.

Mack, J.L., Patterson, M.B., Schnell, A.H. & Whitehouse, D.J. (1993). Performance of subjects with probable Alzheimer's disease and normal elderly controls on the Gollin Incomplete Pictures test. *Perceptual and Motor Skills, 77*, 951–69.

Mackay, D.G. (1982). The problems of flexibility, fluency, and speed-accuracy trade-off in skilled behavior. *Psychological Review, 89*, 483–506.

McKeithen, K.B., Reitman, J.S., Rueter, H.H. & Hirtle, S.C. (1981). Knowledge organization and skill differences in computer programs. *Cognitive Psychology, 13*, 307–25.

McKelvie, S.J. (1976). The role of eyes and mouth in the memory of a face. *American Journal of Psychology, 89*, 311–23.

McKelvie, S.J. (1985). Effect of depth of processing on recognition memory for normal and inverted photographs of faces. *Perceptual and Motor Skills, 60*, 503–8.

McKelvie, S.J., Standing, L., St-Jean, D. & Law, J. (1993). Gender differences in recognition memory for faces and cars: Evidence for the interest hypothesis. *Bulletin of the Psychonomic Society, 31*, 447–8.

MacLeod, C.M. (1988). Forgotten but not gone: Savings for pictures and words in long-term memory. *Journal of Experimental Psychology: Learning, Memory and Cognition, 14*, 195–212.

McLeod, P., McLaughlin, C. & Nimmo-Smith, I. (1985). Information encapsulation and automaticity: Evidence from the visual control of finely timed action. In M.I. Posner and O.S. Marin (Eds), *Attention and Performance, Vol 11*. Hillsdale, NJ: Erlbaum.

McWalter, G.J., Montaldi, D., Bhutani, G.E., et al., (1991). Paired associate learning in dementia of the Alzheimer's type. *Neuropsychology, 5*, 205–11.

McWeeny, K.H., Young, A.W., Hay, D.C. & Ellis, A.W. (1987). Putting names to faces. *British Journal of Psychology, 78*, 143–9.

Malaspina, D., Wray, A.D., Friedman, J.H., Amador, X., et al. (1994). Odor discrimination deficits in schizophrenia: Association with eye movement dysfunction. *Journal of Neuropsychiatry and Clinical Neurosciences, 6(3)*, 273–8.

Malt, B.C. & Smith, E.E. (1984). Correlated properties in natural categories. *Journal of Verbal Learning and Verbal Behavior, 23*, 250–69.

Mandler, G. (1967). Organization in memory. In K.W. Spence and J.T. Spence (Eds), *The psychology of learning and motivation, Vol. 1*, pp. 327–72. New York: Academic Press.

Mandler, G. (1980). Recognizing: The judgment of previous occurrence. *Psychological Review, 87*, 252–71.

Mandler, G. (1981). The recognition of previous encounters. *American Scientist, 69,* 211–18.

Mandler, J.M. (1984). *Stories, scripts and scenes: Aspects of schema theory.* Hillsdale, N.J: Lawrence Erlbaum.

Mandler, G. & Boeck, W. (1974). Retrieval processes in recognition. *Memory and Cognition, 2,* 613–5.

Mandler, G. & Ritchey, G.H. (1977). Long-term memory for pictures. *Journal of Experimental Psychology: Human Learning and Memory, 3,* 386–96.

Mandler, J.M., & Parker, R.E. (1976). Memory for descriptive and spatial information in complex pictures. *Journal of Experimental Psychology: Human Learning and Memory, 2(1),* 38–48.

Markowitsch, H.J. (1988). Diencephalic amnesia: A reorientation towards tracts? *Brain Research Reviews, 13,* 351–70.

Marks, W. (1991). Effects of encoding the perceptual features of pictures on memory. *Journal of Experimental Psychology: Learning, Memory and Cognition, 17,* 566–77.

Markus, H.& Nurius, P. (1986). Possible selves. *American Psychologist, 41,* 954–69.

Marohn, K.M. & Hochhaus, L. (1988a). Semantic priming increases and repetition priming decreases apparent stimulus duration. *Journal of General Psychology, 115,* 51–61.

Marohn, K.M. & Hochhaus, L. (1988b). Different-case repetition still leads to perceptual blindness. *Bulletin of the Psychonomic Society, 26,* 29–31.

Marshall, P.H., Chen, C.Y. & Jeter, B.S. (1989). Retrieval influences on tests for the automaticity of the encoding of temporal order information. *American Journal of Psychology, 102,* 39–52.

Martone, M., Butters, N., Payne, M. et al., (1984). Dissociations between skill learning and verbal recognition in amnesia and dementia. *Archives of Neurology, 41,* 965–70.

Massman, P.J., Delis, D.C., Butters, N. et al. (1990). Are all subcortical dementias alike? Verbal learning and memory in Parkinson's and Huntington's disease patients. *Journal of Clinical and Experimental Neuropsychology, 12,* 729–44.

Massman, P.J., Delis, D.C., & Butters, N. (1993). Does impaired primacy recall equal impaired long-term storage? Serial position effects in Huntington's Diesease and Alzheimer's Disease. *Developmental Neuropsychology, 9,* 1–15.

Mathews, A., Mogg, K., May, J. and Eysenck, M. (1989). Implicit and explicit memory bias in anxiety. *Journal of Abnormal Psychology, 98,* 236–40.

Matlin, M.W. (1989). *Cognition,* 2nd edn. New York: Holt, Rinehart, and Winston.

Mauro, R. & Kubovy, M. (1992). Caricature and face recognition. Special issue: Memory and cognition applied. *Memory and Cognition, 20,* 433–40.

Mayes, A.R. (1988). *Human organic memory disorders.* New York: Cambridge University Press.

Mayes, A.R., Downes, J.J., Shoqeirat, M., Hall, C., et al. (1993). Encoding ability is preserved in amnesia: Evidence from a direct test of encoding. *Neuropsychologia, 31(8),* 745–59.

Mayes, A.R., Meudell, P.R. & Pickering, A. (1985).Is organic amnesia caused by a selective deficit in remembering contextual information? *Cortex, 21,* 167–202.

Means, B. and Loftus, E.F. (1991). When personal history repeats itself: Decomposing memories for recurring events. *Applied Cognitive Psychology, 5,* 297–318.

Means, B., Mingay, D.J., Nigam, A. & Zarrow, M. (1988). A cognitive approach to enhancing health survey reports of medical visits. In M.M. Gruneberg, P.E. Morris, & R.N. Sykes (Eds), *Practical aspects of memory: Current research and issues, Vol. 1: Memory in everyday life,* pp. 536–42. Chichester: John Wiley.

Medin, D.L. & Schaffer, M.M. (1978). Context theory of classification learning. *Psychological Review, 85,* 207–38.

Medin, D.L. & Smith, E.E. (1984). Concepts and concept formation. *Annual Review of Psychology, 35,* 113–38.

Mehta, Z., Newcombe, F., & deHaan, E. (1992). Selective loss of imagery in a case of visual agnosia. *Neuropsychologia, 30(7),* 645–55.

Melkman, R., Tversky, B., Baratz, D. (1981). Developmental trends in the use of perceptual and conceptual attributes in grouping, clustering, and retrieval. *Journal of Experimental Child Psychology, 31(3),* 470–86.

Melton, A.W. & Irwin, J.M. (1940). The influence of degree of interpolated learning on retroactive inhibition and the overt transfer of specific responses. *American Journal of Psychology, 53,* 173–203.

Memon, A. & Bruce, V. (1983). The effects of encoding strategy and context change on face recognition. *Human Learning Journal of Practical Research and Applications, 2,* 313–26.

Memon, A., Wark, L., Bull, R. & Koehnken, G. (in

press). Isolating the effects of the Cognitive Interview techniques. *British Journal of Psychology*.

Mendez, M.F., Mendez, M.A, Martin, R. et al., (1990). Complex visual disturbances in Alzheimer's disease. *Neurology, 40,* 439–43.

Meudell, P.R., Mayes, A. & Neary, D. (1980). Orienting task effects on the recognition of humorous material in amnesia and normal subjects. *Journal of Clinical Neuropsychology, 2,* 1–14.

Meudell, P.R., Mayes, A.R., Ostergaard, A. & Pickering, A. (1985). Recency and frequency judgements in alcoholic amnesics and normal people with poor memory. *Cortex, 21,* 487–511.

Mewaldt, S.P. & Hinrichs, J.V. (1977). Repetition and inference in short-term memory. *Journal of Experimental Psychology: Human Learning and Memory, 3,* 572–81.

Meyer, D.E. & Schvaneveldt, R.W. (1971). Facilitation in recognizing pairs of words: Evidence of a dependence between retrieval operations. *Journal of Experimental Psychology, 90,* 227–34.

Micco, A. & Masson, M.E. (1992). Age-related differences in the specificity of verbal encoding. *Memory and Cognition, 20(3),* 244–53.

Michon, J.A. (1965). Studies on subjective duration: II. Subjective time measurement during tasks with different information content. *Acta Psychologica, 24,* 205–19.

Michon, J.A. (1978). The making of the present: A tutorial review. In J. Requin (Ed.), *Attention and performance, Vol. VII,* pp. 89–111. Hillsdale, NJ: Lawrence Erlbaum.

Michon, J.A. (1985). The complete time experiencer. In J.A. Michon & J.L. Jackson (Eds), *Time, mind and behaviour,* pp. 20–52. Berlin: Springer-Verlag.

Michon, J.A. (1990). Models of psychological time. In R.A. Block, (Ed.), *Cognitive models of psychological time.* Hillsdale, NJ: Lawrence Erlbaum.

Milberg, W. & Albert, M. (1989). Cognitive differences between patients with progressive supranuclear palsy and Alzheimer's disease. *Journal of Clinical and Experimental Neuropsychology, 11,* 605–14.

Miller, G.A. (1956). The magical number seven, plus or minus two: Some limits on our capacity for processing information. *Psychological Review, 63,* 81–97.

Miller, G.W., Hicks, R.E. & Willette, M. (1978). Effects of concurrent verbal rehearsal and temporal set upon judgments of temporal duration. *Acta Psychologica, 42,* 173–9.

Miller, L.A., Munoz, D.G., & Finmore, M. (1993). Hippocampal sclerosis and human memory. *Archives of Neurology, 50(4),* 391–4.

Milliken, B., & Jolicoeur, P. (1992). Size effects in visual recognition memory are determined by perceived size. *Memory and Cognition, 20,* 1, 83–95.

Milner, B. (1966). Amnesia following operation on the temporal lobes. In C.W.M. Whitty & O.L. Zangwill (Eds), *Amnesia,* pp. 109–33. London: Butterworths.

Mitchell, D.B. & Brown, A.S. (1988). Persistent repetition priming in picture naming and its dissociation from recognition memory. *Journal of Experimental Psychology: Learning, Memory and Cognition, 14,* 213–22.

Moberg, P.J., Pearlson, G.D., Speedy, L.J. et al. , (1987). Olfactory recognition: Differential impairments in early and late Huntington's and Alzheimer's diseases. *Journal of Clinical and Experimental Neuropsychology, 9,* 650–64.

Moely, B.E., Olson, F.A., Halwes, T.G. and Flavell, J.H. (1969). Production deficiency in young children's clustered recall. *Developmental Psychology, 1,* 26–34.

Moffitt, K.H. & Singer, J.A. (1994). Continuity in the life story: Self-defining memories, affect, and approach/avoidance personal strivings. *Journal of Personality, 62,* 21–43.

Mogg, K., Mathews, A. & Weinman, J. (1987). Memory bias in clinical anxiety. *Journal of Abnormal Psychology, 96,* 94–98.

Moore, R.G., Watts, F.N. & Williams, M.J. (1988). The specificity of personal memories in depression. *British Journal of Clinical Psychology, 27,* 275–6.

Moore, T.E., Richards, B. & Hood, J. (1984). Aging and the coding of spatial information. *Journal of Gerontology, 39,* 210–12.

Morley, S. (1993). Vivid memory for 'everyday' pains. *Pain, 55,* 55–62.

Morris, C.D., Bransford, J.D. & Franks, J.J. (1977). Levels of processing versus transfer appropriate processing. *Journal of Verbal Learning and Verbal Behaviour, 16,* 519–33.

Morris, R.D. & Baddeley, A.D. (1988). Primary and working memory functioning in Alzheimer-type dementia. *Journal of Clinical and Experimental Neuropsychology, 10,* 279–96.

Morris, R.G. & Kopelman, M.D. (1986). The memory deficits in Alzheimer-type dementia: A review. *The Quarterly Journal of Experimental Psychology, 38A,* 575–602.

Mortimer, J.A. & Pirozzolo, F.J. (1985). Remote effects of head trauma. *Developmental Neuropsychology, 1,* 215–29.

Mortimer, J.A. (1988). The dementia of Parkinson's disease. *Clinics in Geriatric Medicine, 4,* 785–97.

Morton, J. & Bekerian, D.A. (1986). Three ways of looking at memory. In N.E. Sharkey (Ed.), *Advances in cognitive science 1,* pp.43–71. Chichester: Ellis Horwood.

Morton, J. (1991). Cognitive pathologies of memory: A headed records analysis. In W. Kessen, A. Ortony, and F. Craik (Eds), *Memories, .thoughts and emotions: Essays in honor of George Mandler.* Hillsdale, NJ: Erlbaum.

Morton, J. (1994). Cognitive perspectives on memory recovery. *Applied Cognitive Psychology, 8,* 389–98.

Morton, J., Hammersley, R.H. & Bekerian, D.A. (1985). Headed records: A model for memory and its failures. *Cognition, 20,* 1–23.

Moscovitch, M. & Bentin, S. (1993). The fate of repetition effects when recognition approaches chance. *Journal of Experimental Psychology: Learning, Memory and Cognition, 19,* 148–58.

Moscovitch, M. (1985). Memory from infancy to old age: Implications for theories of normal and pathological memory. *Annals of New York Academy of Science, 444,* 78–96.

Moss, M.B., Albert, M.S., & Kemper, T.L. (1992). Neuropsychology of frontal lobe dementia. In R.F. White (Ed.), *Clinical syndromes in adult neuropsychology: The practitioner's handbook.* Amsterdam: Elsevier.

Muller, G. (1911). Zue Analyse der Gedächtnistätigkeit unter der Vorstellungsverlaufes, 1. *Zeitschrift fur Psychologie, Erganzungsband, 5,* 1–567.

Murdock, B.B., Jr. (1974). *Human memory: Theory and data.* Potomac, MD: Erlbaum.

Myers, D.C. (1983). The psychological and perceptual-motor aspects of Huntington's disease. *Rehabilitation Psychology, 28,* 13–34.

Myers, N.A., Clifton, R.K. & Clarkson, M.G. (1987). When they were very young: Almost-threes remember two years ago. *Infant Behaviour and Development, 10,* 123–32.

Myers, N.A. & Perlmutter, M. (1978). Memory in the years from two to five. In P.A. Ornstein (Ed.), *Memory development in children,* pp. 191–218. Hillsdale, NJ: Erlbaum.

Myles-Worsley, M., Johnston, W.A. & Simons, M.A. (1988). The influence of expertise on x-ray image processing. *Journal of Experimental Psychology: Learning, Memory and Cognition, 14,* 553–7.

Nagae, S. (1980). Nature of discriminating and categorizing functions of verbal labels on recognition memory for shape. *Journal of Experimental Psychology Human Learning and Memory, 6(4),* 421–9.

Nairne, J.S., Pusen, C. & Widner, R.L. (1985). Representation in the mental lexicon: Implications for theories of the generation effect. *Memory and Cognition, 13,* 183–91.

Nairne, J.S. & Widner, R.L. (1988). Familiarity and lexicality as determinants of the generation effect. *Journal of Experimental Psychology: Learning, Memory and Cognition, 14,* 694–9.

Naito, L. (1990). Repetition priming in children and adults: Age-related dissociation between implicit and explicit memory. *Journal of Experimental Child Psychology, 50,* 462–84.

National Advisory Mental Health Council (1989) *Approaching the 21st century: Opportunities for NIMH neuroscience research.* Report to Congress on the decade of the brain. Rockville, MD: National Institute of Mental Health.

Naveh-Benjamin, M. & Ayres, T.J. (1986). Digit span, reading rate and linguistic relativity. Special issue: Human memory. *Quarterly Journal of Experimental Psychology, 38,* 739–51.

Naveh-Benjamin, M. & Jonides, J. (1984). Maintenance rehearsal: A two-component analysis. *Journal of Experimental Psychology: Learning, Memory and Cognition, 10,* 369–85.

Naveh-Benjamin, M. & Jonides, J. (1986). On the automaticity of frequency coding: Effects of competing task load, encoding strategy, and intention. *Journal of Experimental Psychology: Learning, Memory and Cognition, 12,* 378–86.

Neary, D. & Sowden, J.S. (1991). Dementia of the frontal lobe type. In H.S. Levin, H.M. Eisenberg, & A.L. Benton, (Eds), *Frontal lobe function and dysfunction.* New York: Oxford University Press.

Nebes, R.D. (1992). Cognitive dysfunction in Alzheimer's disease. In F.I.M. Craik & T.A. Salthouse (Eds), *The Handbook of aging.* Hillsdale, N.J: Laurence Erlbaum.

Nebes, R.D. & Brady, C.B. (1989). Focused and divided attention in Alzheimer's disease. *Cortex, 25,* 305–15.

Neisser, U. (1967). *Cognitive psychology.* New York: Appleton-Century-Crofts.

Neisser, U. (1976). *Cognition and reality.* San Francisco: Freeman.

Neisser, U. (1978). Memory: What are the important questions? In M.M. Gruneberg, P.E. Morris, & R.N. Sykes (Eds), *Practical aspects of memory*. London: Academic Press.

Neisser, U. (1981). John Dean's memory: A case study. *Cognition, 9,* 1–22.

Neisser, U. (1982). Memorists. In U. Neisser (Ed.), *Memory observed: Remembering in natural contexts*, pp. 377–81. San Francisco: Freeman.

Neisser, U. (1984). Interpreting Harry Bahrick's discovery: What confers immunity against forgetting? *Journal of Experimental Psychology: General, 113,* 32–5.

Neisser, U. (1986). Remembering Pearl Harbor: Reply to Thompson and Cowan. *Cognition, 23,* 285–6.

Neisser, U. (1988). Time present and time past. In M.M. Gruneberg, P.E. Morris and R.N. Sykes (Eds), *Practical aspects of memory: Current research and issues, Vol. 2,* pp. 545–60. Chichester: John Wiley.

Neisser, U. (1994). Self-narratives: true and false. In U. Neisser, & R. Fivush (Eds), *The remembering self: Construction and accuracy in the self-narrative*. Cambridge: Cambridge University Press.

Neisser, U. (Ed.) (1993). *The perceived self: Ecological and interpersonal sources of self-knowledge*. Cambridge: Cambridge University Press.

Neisser, U. and Harsch, N. (1992). Phantom flashbulbs: False recollections of hearing the news about Challenger. In E. Winograd and U. Neisser (Eds), *Affect and accuracy in recall: Studies of 'flashbulb' memories*, pp. 9–31. New York: Cambridge University Press.

Nelson, K. (1986). *Event knowledge: Structure and function in development*. Hillsdale, NJ: Lawrence Erlbaum.

Nelson, K. (1988). The ontogeny of memory for real events. In U. Neisser and E. Winograd (Eds), *Remembering reconsidered: Ecological and traditional approaches to the study of memory*. Cambridge: Cambridge University Press.

Nelson, K. (1991). Remembering and telling: A developmental story. *Journal of Narrative and Life History, 1,* 109–27.

Nelson, K. & Gruendel, J. (1986). Children's scripts. In K. Nelson (Ed.), *Event knowledge: Structure and function in development*, pp. 21–46. Hillsdale, NJ: Lawrence Erlbaum.

Nelson, T.O. (1976). Reinforcement and human memory. In W.K. Estes (Ed.), *Handbook of learning and cognitive processes, Vol. 3*. Hillsdale, NJ: Lawrence Erlbaum.

Nestor, P.G., Parasuraman, R. & Haxby, J.V. (1991). Speed of information processing and attention in early Alzheimer's dementia. *Developmental Neuropsychology, 7,* 242–56.

Newell, A. & Rosenbloom, P.S. (1981). Mechanisms of skill acquisition and the law of practice. In J.R. Anderson (Ed.), *Cognitive skills and their acquisition*. Hillsdale, NJ: Erlbaum.

Newnham, C., & McKenzie, B.E. (1993). Crossmodal transfer of sequential visual and haptic shape information by clumsy children. *Perception, 22(9),* 1061–73.

Nigro, G., & Neisser, U. (1983). Point of view in personal memories. *Cognitive Psychology, 15,* 467–82.

Nissen, M.J. & Bullemer, P. (1987). Attentional requirements of learning: Evidence from performance measures. *Cognitive Psychology, 19,* 1–32.

Nissen, M.J., Willingham, D. & Hartman, M. (1989). Explicit and implicit remembering: When is learning preserved in amnesia? *Neuropsychologia, 27,* 341–52.

Noon, E. & Hollin, C. (1987). Lay knowledge of eyewitness behaviour: A British survey. *Applied Cognitive Psychology, 1,* 143–55.

Norman, D.A. and Bobrow, D.G. (1978). Descriptions: An intermediate stage in memory retrieval. *Cognitive Psychology, 11,* 107–23.

Norman, D.A. & Shallice, T. (1980). *Attention to action: Willed and automatic control of behavior*. CHIP Document No. 99, Center for Human Information Processing, University of California, San Diego, La Jolla.

Norman, D.A. & Shallice, T. (1986). Attention to action: Willed and automatic control of behavior. In R.J. Davidson, G.E. Schwartz and D. Shapiro (Eds), *Consciousness and self-regulation: Advances in research and theory, 4,* New York: Plenum Press.

Norman, G.R., Brooks, L.R. & Allen, S.W. (1989). Recall by expert medical practitioners and novices as a record of processing attention. *Journal of Experimental Psychology: Learning, Memory and Cognition, 15,* 1166–74.

Oatley, K. & Johnson-Laird, P.N. (1987). Towards a cognitive theory of emotions. *Cognition and Emotion, 1,* 29–50.

Ober, B.A., Koss, E., Friedland, R.P., & Delis, D.C. (1985). Processes of verbal memory failure in Alzheimer-type dementia. *Brain and Cognition, 4,* 90–103.

Ogden, J.A. & Corkin, S. (1991). Memories of H.M. In W.C. Abraham, M.C. Corballis and K.G. White (Eds), *Memory mechanisms: A tribute to G.V. Goddard*, pp. 195–215. Hillsdale, NJ: Erlbaum.

Ornstein, R.E. (1969). *On the experience of time.* Harmondsworth: Penguin.

Oscar-Berman, M. (1980). Neuropsychological consequences of long-term chronic alcoholism. *American Scientist, 68,* 410–19.

Oscar-Berman, M. (1984). Comparative neuropsychology and alcoholic Korsakoff's disease. In L.R. Squire & N. Butters (Eds), *Neuropsychology of memory.* New York: Guildford Press.

O'Sullivan, C.S. & Durso, F.T. (1984). Effect of schema-incongruent information on memory for stereotypical attributes. *Journal of Personality and Social Psychology, 47,* 55–70.

O'Toole, A.J., Deffenbacher, K.A., Valentin, D. & Abdi, H. (1994). Structural aspects of face recognition and the other-race effect. *Memory and Cognition, 22,* 208–24.

Owens, J., Bower, G.H. & Black, J.B. (1979). The 'soap opera' effect in story recall. *Memory and Cognition, 7,* 185–91.

Parasuraman, R. & Haxby, J.V. (1993). Attention and brain function in Alzheimer's disease: A review. *Neuropsychology, 7,* 242–72.

Park, D.C., Puglisi, J.T. (1985). Older adults' memory for the color of pictures and words. *Journal of Gerontology, 40(2),* 198–204.

Park, J. & Kanwisher, N. (1994). Determinants of the repetition blindness effect. *Journal of Experimental Psychology: Human Perception and Performance, 20,* 500–15.

Parkin, A.J. (1991). The relationship between anterograde and retrograde amnesia in alcoholic Wernicke–Korsakoff Syndrome. *Psychological Medicine, 21,* 11–14.

Parkin, A.J. (1993). *Memory: Phenomena, experiment and theory.* Oxford: Blackwell.

Parkin, A.J. & Leng, N.R.C. (1993). *Neuropsychology of amnesic syndromes.* Hove: Erlbaum.

Parkin, A.J. & Walter, B.M. (1991). Aging, short-term memory and frontal dysfunction. *Psychobiology, 19,* 175–9.

Parkin, A.J., Lewinsohn, J. & Folkard, S. (1982). The influence of emotion on immediate and delayed retention: Levinger and Clark reconsidered. *British Journal of Psychology, 73,* 389–93.

Parkin, A.J. & Streete, S. (1988). Implicit and explicit memory in young children and adults. *British Journal of Psychology, 79,* 362–9.

Parkin, A.J. & Walter, B.M. (1992). Recollective experience, normal aging, and frontal dysfunction. *Psychology and Aging, 7,* 290–98.

Parkinson, S.R. (1979). The amnesic Korsakoff syndrome: A study of selective and divided attention. *Neuropsychologia, 17,* 67–75.

Parrott, W.G. & Sabini, J. (1990). Mood and memory under natural conditions: Evidence for mood incongruent recall. *Journal of Personality and Social Psychology, 59(2),* 321–36.

Pascual-Leone, J. (1970). A mathematical model for the transition rule in Piaget's developmental stages. *Acta Psychologica, 63,* 301–45.

Pascual-Leone, J. (1987). Organismic processes for neo-Piagetian theories: A dialectical causal account of cognitive development. *International Journal of Psychology, 22,* 531–70.

Patterson, K.E. & Baddeley, A.D. (1977). When face recognition fails. *Journal of Experimental Psychology: Human Learning and Memory, 3,* 406–17.

Paulsen, J.S., Butters, N., Salmon, D.P., et al. (1993). Prism adaptation in Alzheimer's and Huntington's disease. *Neuropsychology, 14,* 1–9.

Payne, D.G. (1986). Hypermnesia for pictures and words: Testing the recall level hypothesis. *Journal of Experimental Psychology: Learning, Memory and Cognition, 12,* 16–29.

Payne, D.G., Neely, J.H. & Burns, D.J. (1986). The generation effect: Further tests of the lexical activation hypothesis. *Memory and Cognition, 14,* 246–52.

Penfield, W. (1968). Engrams in the human brain. *Proceedings of the Royal Society of Medicine. 61,* 831–40.

Peretz, J.A. & Cumming, J.L. (1984). Subcortical dementia. In Una Holden (Ed.), *Neuropsychology and aging.* New York: New York University Press.

Perlmutter, M. (1984). Continuities and discontinuities in early human memory paradigms, processes, and performance. In R. Kail and N.E. Spear (Eds.), *Comparative perspectives on the development of memory,* pp. 253–84. Hillsdale, NJ: Erlbaum.

Perner, J. (1992). Grasping the concept of representation: Its impact on 4-year-olds' theory of mind and beyond. *Human Development, 35(3),* 146–55.

Perris, E.E., Myers, N.A. & Clifton, R.K. (1990). Long-term memory for a single infancy experience. *Child Development, 61,* 1796–807.

Perruchet, P. (1989). The effect of spaced practice on explicit and implicit memory. *British Journal of Psychology, 80,* 113–30.

Peters, D.P. (1988). Eyewitness memory and arousal in a natural setting. In M.M. Gruneberg, P.E. Morris and R.N. Sykes (Eds), *Practical aspects of memory: Current research and issues*, pp. 89–94. Chichester: John Wiley & Sons.

Peterson, L.R. & Peterson, M.J. (1959). Short-term retention of individual verbal items. *Journal of Experimental Psychology, 58*, 193–8.

Peynircioglu, Z.F. (1989). The generation effect with pictures and nonsense figures. *Acta Psychologica, 70(2)*, 153–60.

Pezdek, K. (1987). Memory for pictures: A life-span study of the role of visual detail. *Child Development, 58*, 807–15.

Pezdek, K. & Chen, H.C. (1982). Developmental differences in the role of detail in picture recognition memory. *Journal of Experimental Child Psychology, 33*, 207–15.

Pezdek, K., Maki, R., Valencia-Laver, D. & Whetstone, T. (1988). Picture memory: Recognizing added and deleted details. *Journal of Experimental Psychology: Learning, Memory and Cognition, 14*, 468–76.

Pillon, B. & Dubois, B. (1992). Cognitive and behavioral impairments. In I. Litvan & Y. Agid (Eds), *Progressive supranuclear palsy: Clinical and research approaches*. New York: Oxford University Press.

Pillon, B., Dubois, B., Lhermitte, F., & Agid, Y. (1986). Heterogeneity of cognitive impairment in progressive supranuclear palsy, Parkinson's disease, and Alzheimer's disease. *Neurology, 36*, 1179–85.

Pillon, B., Dubois, B., Ploska, A., & Agid, Y. (1991). Severity and specificity cognitive impairment in progressive supranuclear palsy, Parkinson's disease, and Alzheimer's disease. *Neurology, 41*, 634–43.

Pliner, P. & Steverango, C. (1994). Effect of induced mood on memory for flavors. *Appetite, 22*, 135–48.

Plomp, R. (1964). Rate of decay of auditory sensation. *Journal of the Acoustical Society of America, 36*, 277–82.

Poon, L.W. & Fozard, J.L. (1978). Speed of retrieval from long-term memory in relation to age, familiarity, and datedness of information. *Journal of Gerontology, 33*, 711–17.

Poon, L.W., Walsh-Sweeney, L. & Fozard, J.L. (1980). Memory skill training for the elderly: Salient issues on the use of imagery mnemonics. In L.W. Poon, J.L. Fozard, L.S. Cermak, D. Arenberg & L.W. Thompson (Eds), *New directions in memory and aging*, pp. 461–84. Hillsdale, NJ: Erlbaum.

Postman, L. & Phillips, L. (1965). Short-term temporal changes in free recall. *Quarterly Journal of Experimental Psychology, 17*, 132–8.

Potter, M.C. (1976). Short-term conceptual memory for pictures. *Journal of Experimental Psychology: Human Learning and Memory, 2*, 509–22.

Potter, M.C. & Lombardi, L. (1990). Regeneration in the short-term recall of sentences. *Journal of Memory and Language, 29*, 633–54.

Poulsen, D., Kintsch, E., Kintsch, W. & Premack, D. (1979). Children's comprehension and memory for stories. *Journal of Experimental Child Psychology, 28*, 379–403.

Power, M.J. & Brewin, C.R. (1990). Self-esteem regulation in an emotional priming task. Special issue: Evaluative conditioning. *Cognition and Emotion, 4*, 39–51.

Predebon, J. (1984). Organization of stimulus events and remembered apparent duration. *Australian Journal of Psychology, 36*, 161–9.

Proctor, R.W. (1977). The relationship of frequency judgments to recognition: Facilitation of recognition and comparison to recognition-confidence judgments. *Journal of Experimental Psychology: Human Learning and Memory, 3*, 679–89.

Purdy, J.E. & Luepnitz, R.R. (1982). Immediate and long-term retention for pictorial and verbal stimuli. *Perceptual and Motor Skills, 55*, 1079–82.

Putnam, F.W., Guroff, J.J., Silberman, E.K., Barban, L. & Post, R.M. (1986). The clinical phenomenology of multiple personality disorder: 100 recent cases. *Journal of Clinical Psychiatry, 47*, 285–93.

Querleu, D. & Renard, K. (1981). Les perceptions auditives du foetus humain [Auditory perception of the human fetus]. *Medecine et Hygiene, 39*, 2101–10.

Quinn, J.G. & McConnell, J. (1994). The irrelevant picture effect in the visuo-spatial sketch pad. Paper presented at the International Conference on Working Memory, Cambridge, U.K.

Rabbitt, P.M.A. (1993). Crystal quest: A search for the basis of maintenance of practised skills into old age. In A. Baddeley and L. Weiskrantz (Eds), *Attention: Selection, awareness and control: A tribute to Donald Broadbent*, Oxford: Clarendon Press.

Rabbitt, P.M.A. & Abson, V. (1991). Do older people know how good they are? *British Journal of Psychology, 82*, 137–51.

Rabbitt, P.M.A. & Goward, L.M. (1993). Age, IQ, test score, practice, and individual differences in reaction times. *Quarterly Journal of Experimental Psychology, 46A,* 193–204.

Rabbitt, P. & Winthrope, C. (1988). What do old people remember? The Galton paradigm reconsidered. In M.M. Gruneberg, P.E. Morris & R.N. Sykes (Eds), *Practical aspects of memory: Current research and issues, Vol. 1,* pp. 301–7. Chichester: John Wiley.

Rabinowitz, J.C., Mandler, G. & Barsalou, L.W. (1977). Recognition failure: Another case of retrieval failure. *Journal of Verbal Learning and Verbal Behavior, 16,* 639–63.

Rapcsak, S.Z., Kentros, S.A. & Rubens, A.B. (1990). Impaired recognition of meaningful sounds in Alzheimer's disease. *Journal of Clinical and Experimental Neuropsychology, 14,* 801–21.

Ratner, C. & McCarthy, J. (1990). Ecologically relevant stimuli and color memory. *Journal of General Psychology, 117,* 369–77.

Raye, C.L. (1976). Recognition: Frequency or organization? *American Journal of Psychology, 89,* 645–58.

Raye, C.L., Johnson, M.K. & Taylor, T.H. (1980). Is there something special about memory for internally generated information? *Memory and Cognition, 8,* 141–8.

Reddy, B.G. & Bellezza, F.S. (1983). Encoding specificity in free recall. *Journal of Experimental Psychology: Learning, Memory and Cognition, 9,* 167–74.

Reinitz, M.T., Wright, E. & Loftus, G.R. (1989). Effects of semantic priming on visual encoding of pictures. *Journal of Experimental Psychology: General, 118,* 280–97.

Reiser, B.J., Black, J.B. & Lehnert, W.G. (1985). Thematic knowledge structures in the understanding and generation of narratives. *Discourse Processes, 8,* 357–89.

Reitman, J.S. (1976). Skilled perception in Go: Deducing memory structures from inter-response times. *Cognitive Psychology, 8,* 336–56.

Revelle, W.A. & Loftus, D.A. (1990). Individual differences and arousal: Implications for the study of mood and memory. *Cognition and Emotion, 4,* 209–37.

Reynolds, J.K. & Pezdek, K. (1992). Face recognition memory: The effects of exposure duration and encoding instruction. *Applied Cognitive Psychology, 6,* 279–92.

Rhodes, G. (1985). Lateralized processes in face recognition. *British Journal of Psychology, 76,* 249–71.

Rhodes, G. (1987). Auditory attention and the representation of spatial information. *Perception and Psychophysics, 42,* 1–14.

Rhodes, G. & Moody, J. (1990). Memory representations of unfamiliar faces: Coding of distinctive information. *New Zealand Journal of Psychology, 19,* 70–78.

Richardson-Klavehn, A. & Bjork, R.A. (1988). Measures of memory. *Annual Review of Psychology, 39,* 475–543.

Rinck, M., Glowalla, U., & Schneider, K. (1992). Mood-congruent and mood-incongruent learning. *Memory and Cognition, 20,* 1, 29–39.

Rips, L.J. (1975). Inductive judgments about natural categories. *Journal of Verbal Learning and Verbal Behavior, 14,* 665–81.

Rips, L.J., Shoben, E.J. & Smith, E.E. (1973). Semantic distance and the verification of semantic relations. *Journal of Verbal Learning and Verbal Behavior, 12,* 1–20.

Robinson, J.A. (1976). Sampling autobiographical memory. *Cognitive Psychology, 8,* 5578–95.

Robinson, J.A. (1992). First experience memories: Contexts and functions in personal histories. In M.A. Conway, D.C. Rubin, H. Spinnler & W.A. Wagenaar (Eds), *Theoretical perspectives on autobiographical memory.* Amsterdam: Kluwer Academic Publishers.

Robinson, K.M. & Standing, L. (1990). Effects of size changes on memory for words and pictures. *Perceptual and Motor Skills, 71,* 919–22.

Roediger, H.L. & Blaxton, T.A. (1987). Retrieval modes produce dissociations in memory for surface information. In D.S. Gorfein & R.S. Hoffman (Eds), *Memory and Learning: The Ebbinghaus centennial conference.* Hillsdale, NJ: Erlbaum.

Roediger, H.L. & Crowder, R.G. (1976). A serial position effect in recall of United States presidents. *Bulletin of the Psychonomic Society, 8,* 275–8.

Rogers, T.B., Kuiper, N.A. & Kirker, W.S. (1977). Self-reference and the encoding of personal information. *Journal of Personality and Social Psychology, 35,* 677–88.

Rosch, E. (1973). Natural categories. *Cognitive Psychology, 4,* 328–49.

Rosch, E.H. (1978). Principles of categorization. In E. Rosch & B. Lloyd (Eds), *Cognition and categorization,* pp. 27–48. Hillsdale, NJ: Erlbaum.

Rosch, E.H. and Mervis, C.B. (1975). Family resemblances: Studies in the internal structure of categories. *Cognitive Psychology, 7,* 573–605.

Rosch, E.H., Mervis, C.B., Gray, W., Johnson, D. & Boyes-Braem, P. (1976). Basic objects in natural categories. *Cognitive Psychology, 3,* 382–439.

Rose, S.A. (1984). Developmental changes in hemispheric specialization for tactual processing in very young children: Evidence from cross-modal transfer. *Developmental Psychology, 20,* 568–74.

Rose, S.A. & Wallace, I.F. (1985). Visual recognition memory: A predictor of later cognitive functioning in preterms. *Child Development, 56,* 843–52.

Rosenbloom & Newell, A. (1986). The chunking of goal hierarchies: A general model of practice. In R.S. Michalski, J.G. Carbonell & T.M. Mitchell (Eds), *Machine learning: An artificial intelligence approach.* Los Altos, CA: Morgan Kaufmann.

Rosenzweig, M.R. (1984). Experience, memory and the brain. *American Psychologist, 39,* 365–76.

Ross, B.H. (1984). Remindings and their effects in learning a cognitive skill. *Cognitive Psychology, 16,* 371–416.

Rossor, M. (1987). The neurochemistry of cortical dementias. In S.M. Stahl, S.D. Iversen & E.C. Goodman (Eds), *Cognitive neurochemistry.* Oxford: Oxford University Press.

Rovee-Collier, C. (1989). The joy of kicking: Memories, motives and mobiles. In P.R. Solomon, G.R. Goethals, C.M. Kelley & B.R. Stephens (Eds), *Memory: Interdisciplinary approaches.* New York: Springer Verlag.

Rovee-Collier, C., Griesler, P.C. & Earley, L.A. (1985). Contextual determinants of retention in 3-month-old infants. *Learning and Motivation, 16,* 139–57.

Rovee-Collier, C.K., Patterson, J. & Hayne, H. (1985). Specificity in the reactivation of infant memory. *Developmental Psychobiology, 18,* 559–74.

Rubin, D.C. (1982). On the retention function for autobiographical memory. *Journal of Verbal Learning and Verbal Behavior, 21,* 21–38.

Rubin, D.C. & Baddeley, A.D. (1989). Telescoping is not time compression: A model of the dating of autobiographical events. *Memory and Cognition, 17,* 653–61.

Rubin, D.C. & Kozin, M. (1984). Vivid memories. *Cognition, 16,* 81–95.

Rubin, D.C., Wetzler, S.E. & Nebes, R.D. (1986). Autobiographical memory across the lifespan. In D.C. Rubin (Ed.), *Autobiographical memory,* pp. 202–21. Cambridge: Cambridge University Press.

Rumelhart, D.E. & Norman, D.A. (1978). Accretion, tuning and restructuring: Three modes of learning. In J.W. Cotton & R.L. Klatzky (Eds), *Semantic factors in cognition,* pp. 37–53, Hillsdale, NJ: Lawrence Erlbaum.

Rundus, D. (1971). Analysis of rehearsal processes in free recall. *Journal of Experimental Psychology, 89,* 63–77.

Russo, R. & Parkin, A.J. (1993). Age differences in implicit memory: More apparent than real. *Memory and Cognition, 21,* 73–80.

Ryan, C. & Butters, N. (1986). Neuropsychology of alcoholism. In D. Wedding, A.M. Horton, Jr., & J.S. Webster (Eds), *The neuropsychology handbook.* New York: Springer.

Ryle, G. (1949). *The concept of mind.* London: Hutchinson.

Sachs, J.S. (1967). Recognition memory for syntactic and semantic aspects of connected discourse. *Perception and Psychophysics, 2,* 437–42.

Saint-Cyr, J.A. & Taylor, A.E. (1992). The mobilization of procedural learning: The 'key signature' of the basal ganglia. In L.R. Squire & N.Butters (Eds), *Neuropsychology of Memory.* New York: Guildford Press.

Salame, P. & Baddeley, A.D. (1982). Disruption of short-term memory by unattended speech: Implications for the structure of working memory. *Journal of Verbal Learning and Verbal Behavior, 21,* 150–64.

Salame, P., & Baddeley, A.D. (1987). Noise unattended speech and short-term memory. *Ergonomics, 30,* 1185–93.

Salame, P., & Baddeley, A.D. (1989). Effects of background music on phonological short-term store. *Quarterly Journal of Experimental Psychology, 41,* 107–22.

Salovey, P. & Singer, J.A. (1993). Mood-congruency effects in recall of childhood versus recent memories. Special issue: Mood and memory: Theory, research and applications. *Journal of Social Behavior and Personality, 4,* 99–120.

Salthouse, T.A. (1982). Duration estimates of two information-processing components. *Acta Psychologica, 52,* 213–26.

Salthouse, T.A. (1988). Effects of age on verbal abilities: An examination of the psychometric literature. In L.L. Light & D.M. Burke (Eds), *Language and memory in old age,* pp. 17–35. New York: Cambridge University Press.

Salthouse, T.A. (1991). *Theoretical perspectives on cognitive aging.* Hillsdale, NJ: Erlbaum.

Sanders, R.E., Gonzalez, E.O., Murphy, M.D., Liddle, C.L. and Vitina, J.R. (1987). Frequency of occurrence and the criteria for automatic processing. *Journal of Experimental Psychology: Learning, Memory and Cognition, 13,* 241–50.

Sandor, B. (1932). Die Gedächtnistätigkeit und Ardeitsweise von Rechenkünstlern. *Charakter, 1,* 47–50.

Santa, J.L. (1975). Verbal coding and reintegrative memory for shapes. *Journal of Experimental Psychology: Learning, Memory and Cognition, 104*, 286–94.

Santa, J.L. & Lamwers, L.A. (1974). Encoding specificity: Fact or artifact? *Journal of Verbal Learning and Verbal Behavior, 13*, 412–23.

Saywitz, K.J., Goodman, G.S., Nicholas, E. & Moan, S.F. (1991). Children's memories of a physical examination involving genital touch: Implications for reports of child sexual abuse. *Journal of Consulting and Clinical Psychology, 59*, 682–91.

Schachtel, E.G. (1947). On memory and childhood amnesia. *Psychiatry, 10*, 1–26.

Schacter, D.L., Chiu, C.Y.P. & Ochsner, K.N. (1993). Implicit memory: A selective review. *Annual Review of Neuroscience, 16*, 159–82.

Schacter, D.L., Harbluk, J.L., & McLachlan, D.R. (1984). Retrieval without recollection: An experimental analysis of source amnesia. *Journal of Verbal Learning and Verbal Behavior, 23*, 591–611.

Schacter, D.L., Kaszniak, A.W. & Kihlstrom, J.F. (1989). Models of memory and the understanding of memory disorders. In T. Yanagihara & R.C. Petersen (Eds), *Memory disorders: Research and clinical practice*. New York: Marcel Dekker.

Schacter, D.L. & Kihlstrom, J.F. (1989) Functional amnesia. In F. Boller & J. Grafman (Eds), *Handbook of neuropsychology, Vol. 3*. Amsterdam: Elsevier.

Schacter, D.L., Wang, P.L., Tulving, E. & Freedman, M. (1982). Functional retrograde amnesia: A quantitative case study. *Neuropsychologia, 20*, 523–32.

Schacter, S. (1964). The interaction of cognitive and physiological determinants of emotional state. In L. Berkowitz (Ed.), *Advances in experimental social psychology, Vol.1*. New York: Academic Press.

Schank, R.C. (1980). Language and memory. *Cognitive Science, 4*, 243–84.

Schank, R.C. & Abelson, R. (1977). *Scripts, plans, goals and understanding*. Hillsdale, NJ: Lawrence Erlbaum.

Schendel, J.D. & Hagman, J.D. (1991). Long-term retention of motor skills. In J.E. Morrison (Ed.), *Training for performance: Principles of applied human learning*, pp. 53-92. Chichester: John Wiley.

Schmidt, C.R. & Schmidt, S.R. (1986). The use of themes as retrieval cues in children's memory for stories. *Journal of Experimental Child Psychology, 42*, 237–55.

Schmidt, C.R., Schmidt, S.R. & Tomalis, S.M. (1984). Children's constructive processing and monitoring of stories containing anomalous information. *Child Development, 5*, 2056–71.

Schmidt, R.A. (1988a). Motor and action perspectives on motor behavior. In O.G. Meijer & K. Rother (Eds), *Complex movement behavior: The motor-action controversy*, pp. 3–44. Amsterdam: Elsevier.

Schmidt, R.A. (1988b). *Motor control and learning: A behavioral emphasis*. Champaign, IL: Human Kinetics Publishers.

Schmidt, R.A., Young, D.E., Swinnen, S. & Shapiro, D.C. (1989). Summary knowledge of results for skill acquisition: Support for the guidance hypothesis. *Journal of Experimental Psychology: Learning, Memory and Cognition, 15*, 352–59.

Schneider, W. (1985). Developmental trends in the metamemory–memory behavior relationship: An integrative review. In D.L. Forrest-Pressley, G.E. MacKinnon & T.G. Waller (Eds), *Cognition, metacognition and human performance, Vol. 1*, pp. 57–109. New York: Academic Press.

Schneider, W. & Detweiler, M. (1987). A connectionist control architecture for working memory. In G.H. Bower (Ed.), *The psychology of learning and motivation, Vol. 21*, pp. 54–119. New York: Academic Press.

Schneider, W. & Fisk, A.D. (1984). Automatic category search and its transfer. *Journal of Experimental Psychology: Learning, Memory and Cognition, 10*, 1–15.

Schneider, W. & Pressley, M. (1989). *Memory development between 2 and 20*. New York: Springer Verlag.

Schneider, W. & Shiffrin, R.M. (1977). Controlled and automatic information processing I: Detection, search and attention. *Psychological Review, 84*, 1–66.

Schwartz, B. & Reisberg, D. (1991). *Learning and memory*. New York: W.W. Norton and Company.

Searleman, A. & Herrmann, D. (1994). *Memory from a broader perspective*. New York: McGraw-Hill.

Seifert, C.M., McKoon, G., Abelson, R.P. & Ratcliff, R. (1986). Memory connections between thematically similar episodes. *Journal of Experimental Psychology: Learning, Memory and Cognition, 12*, 220–31.

Shaklee, H. & Mims, M. (1982). Sources of error in judging event covariations: Effects of memory demands. *Journal of Experimental Psychology: Learning, Memory and Cognition, 8*, 208–24.

Shallice, T. (1982). Specific impairments of planning. *Philosophical Transactions of the Royal Society of London, 298*, 199–209.

Shallice, T. & Warrington, E.K. (1970). Independent functioning of verbal memory stores: A neuropsychological study. *Quarterly Journal of Experimental Psychology, 22,* 261–73.

Shanks, D. & Wrench, J.W. Jr. (1962). Computation of pi to 100,000 decimals. *Mathematics of Computation, 16,* 76–99.

Shaughnessy, J.J. (1977). Long-term retention and the spacing effect in free-recall and frequency judgments. *American Journal of Psychology, 90,* 587–98.

Shaw, G.A. & Bekerian, D.A. (1991). Hypermnesia for high-imagery words: The effects of interpolated tasks. *Memory and Cognition, 19,* 87–94.

Shea, J.B. & Morgan, R.L. (1979). Contextual interference effects on the acquisition, retention and transfer of a motor skill. *Journal of Experimental Psychology: Human Learning and Memory, 5,* 179–87.

Sheingold, K. & Tenny, Y.J. (1982). Memory for a salient childhood event. In U. Neisser (Ed.), *Memory observed: Remembering in natural contexts.* San Francisco: W.H. Freeman and Company.

Shelton, B.R. & Searle, C.L. (1980). The influence of vision on the absolute identification of sound-source position. *Perception and Psychophysics, 28,* 589–96.

Shepard, R.N. & Metzler, J. (1971). Mental rotation of three-dimensional objects. *Science, 171,* 701–3.

Shepherd, J.W., Deregowski, J.B. & Ellis, H.D. (1974). A cross-cultural study of recognition memory for faces. *International Journal of Psychology, 9,* 205–11.

Shiffrin, R.A. (1970). Memory search. In D.A. Norman (Ed.), *Models of human memory,* pp. 375–447. New York: Academic Press.

Shiffrin, R.M. & Czerwinski, M.P. (1988). A model of automatic attention attraction when mapping is partially consistent. *Journal of Experimental Psychology: Learning, Memory and Cognition, 14,* 562–9.

Shiffrin, R.M. & Dumais, S.T. (1981). The development of automatism. In J.R. Anderson (Ed.), *Cognitive skills and their acquisition.* Hillsdale, NJ: Erlbaum.

Shiffrin, R.M. & Schneider, W. (1977). Controlled and automatic human information processing: II. Perceptual learning, automatic attending, and a general theory. *Psychological Review, 84,* 127–90.

Shimamura, A.P., Janowsky, J.S., & Squire, L.R. (1990). Memory for the temporal order of events in patients with frontal lobe lesions and amnesic patients. *Neuropsychologia, 28,* 803–13.

Shimamura, A.P., Salmon, D.P., Squire, L.R. & Butters, N. (1987). Memory dysfunction and word priming in dementia and amnesia. *Behavioral Neuroscience, 101,* 347–51.

Shimamura, A.P & Squire, L.R. (1987). A neurological study of fact memory and source amnesia. *Journal of Experimental Psychology: Learning, Memory and Cognition, 13,* 464–73.

Simonov, P.V., Frolov, M.V., Evtushenko, V.F. & Sviridov, E. (1977). Effect of emotional stress on recognition of visual patterns. *Aviation, Space and Environmental Medicine,* 856–8.

Singer, J.A. (1990). Affective responses to autobiographical memories and their relationship to long-term goals. *Journal of Personality, 58,* 535–63.

Singley, M.K. & Anderson, J.R. (1985). The transfer of text-editing skill. *Journal of Man–Machine Studies, 22,* 403–23.

Singley, M.K. & Anderson, J.R. (1989). *The transfer of cognitive skill.* Cambridge, MA: Harvard University Press.

Sinson, J. & Wetherick, N.E. (1973). Short-term retention of colour and shape information in mongol and other severely subnormal children. *Journal of Mental Deficiency Research, 17,* 177–82.

Sinson, J.C. & Wetherick, N.E. (1976). Evidence for increased mental capacity with age in Down's syndrome. *Journal of Mental Deficiency Research, 20,* 31–4.

Slamecka, N.J. & Graf, P. (1978). The generation effect: Delineation of a phenomenon. *Journal of Experimental Psychology: Human Learning and Memory, 14,* 592–604.

Sloman, S.A., Hayman, C.A.G., Ohta, N., Law, J. & Tulving, E. (1988). Forgetting in primed fragment completion. *Journal of Experimental Psychology: Learning, Memory and Cognition, 14,* 223–39.

Smith, A. (1979). Practices and principles of neuropsychology. *International Journal of Neuroscience, 9,* 233–8.

Smith, E.E., Balzano, G.J. & Walker, J.H. (1978). Nominal, perceptual, and semantic codes in picture categorization. In J.W. Cotton & R.L. Klatzky (Eds), *Semantic factors in cognition.* Hillsdale, NJ: Erlbaum.

Smith, E.E. & Medin, D.L. (1981). *Categories and concepts.* Cambridge, MA: Harvard University Press.

Smith, M.E. & Halgren, E. (1989). Dissociation of recognition memory components following temporal lobe lesions. *Journal of Experimental Psychology: Learning, Memory and Cognition, 15,* 50–60.

Smith, S.M. (1994). Theoretical principles of context-dependent memory. In P.E. Morris & M. Gruneberg (Eds), *Theoretical aspects of memory*. London: Routledge.

Smith, S.M. & Vela, E. (1992). Environmental context-dependent eyewitness recognition. *Applied Cognitive Psychology, 6,* 125–39.

Smyth, M.M. & Scholey, K.A. (1994). Characteristics of spatial memory span: Is there an analogy to the word length effect, based on movement time? *Quarterly Journal of Experimental Psychology, 47A,* 91–117.

Snoddy, G.S. (1926). Learning and stability. *Journal of Applied Psychology, 10,* 1–36.

Snodgrass, J.G. & Asiaghi, A. (1977). The pictorial superiority effect in recognition memory. *Bulletin of the Psychonomic Society, 10,* 1–4.

Sophian, C. (1980). Habituation is not enough: Novelty preferences, search, and memory in infancy. *Merrill-Palmer Quarterly, 25,* 239–57.

Spearman, C. (1927). *The abilities of man*. London: MacMillan.

Sperling, G. (1960). The information available in brief visual presentations. *Psychological Monographs: General and Applied, 74,* 1–29.

Squire, L.R. (1987). *Memory and brain*. New York: Oxford University Press.

Squire, L.R., Knowlton, B. & Musen, G. (1993). The structure and organisation of memory. *Annual Review of Psychology, 44,* 453–95.

Stefurak, D.L. & Boynton, R.M. (1986). Independence of memory for categorically different colors and shapes. *Perception and Psychophysics, 39,* 164–74.

Sternberg, S. (1966). High-speed scanning in human memory. *Science, 153,* 652–4.

Sternberg, S. (1969). The discovery of processing stages: Extensions of Donder's method. *Acta Psychologica, 30,* 276–315.

Sternberg, S. (1975). Memory scanning: New findings and current controversies. *Quarterly Journal of Experimental Psychology, 27,* 1–32.

Stevenson, R.J. & Prescott, J. (1994). The effects of prior experience with capsaicin on rating of its burn. *Chemical Senses, 19,* 651–6.

Strange, P.G. (1992). *Brain biochemistry and brain disorders*. Oxford: Oxford University Press.

Stroop, J.R. (1935). Studies of interference in serial verbal reactions. *Journal of Experimental Psychology, 18,* 643–62.

Stuart-Hamilton, I. (1994). *The psychology of ageing*. London: Jessica Kingsley Publishers.

Styles, E.A. & Allport, D.A. (1986). Perceptual integration of identity, location and colour. Symposium on visual attention and action. (1985, Bielefeld, Federal Republic of Germany). *Psychological Research, 48,* 189–200.

Sullivan, E.V. & Sagar, H.J. (1988). Nonverbal short-term impairment in Parkinson's disease. *Journal of Clinical and Experimental Neuropsychology, 10,* 34.

Sullivan, E.V., Sagar, H.J., Cooper, J.A., & Jordan, N. (1993). Verbal and nonverbal short-term memory impairment in non-treated Parkinson's disease. *Neuropsychology, 7,* 396–405.

Surber, C.F. (1982). Separable effects of motives, consequences, and presentation order on children's moral judgments. *Developmental Psychology, 18,* 257–66.

Tanner, C.M. (1989). The role of environmental toxins in the etiology of Parkinson's disease. A critical review. *Neurology, 40,* 17–31.

Teasdale, J.D. & Barnard, P. J. (1993). *Affect, cognition and change: Re-modelling depressive thought*. London: Lawrence Erlbaum.

Teasdale, J.D. & Fogarty, S.J. (1979). Differential effects of induced mood on retrieval of pleasant and unpleasant events from episodic memory. *Journal of Abnormal Psychology, 88,* 248–57.

Teasdale, J.D. & Russell, M.L. (1983). Differential effects of induced mood on the recall of positive, negative, and neutral words. *British Journal of Clinical Psychology, 22,* 163–72.

Thatcher, R.W. & John, E.R. (1977). *Foundations of the cognitive processes*. Hillsdale, N.J: Lawrence Erlbaum.

Thayer, R.E. (1989). *The biopsychology of mood and arousal*. New York: Oxford.

Thomas, E.A. & Brown, I. (1974). Time perception and the filled-duration illusion. *Perception and Psychophysics, 16,* 449–58.

Thomas, E.A. and Weaver, W.B. (1975). Cognitive processing and time perception. *Perception and Psychophysics, 17,* 363–7.

Thompson, C.P. (1982). Memory for unique personal events: The roommate study. *Memory and Cognition, 10,* 324–32.

Thompson, C.P. & Cowan, T. (1986). Flashbulb memories: A nicer interpretation of a Neisser recollection. *Cognition, 22,* 199–200.

Thompson, C.P., Cowan, T.M. & Frieman, J. (1993). *Memory search by a memorist*. Hillsdale, NJ: Erlbaum Associates.

Thompson, C.P. & Mingay, D. (1991). Estimating the frequency of everyday events. *Applied Cognitive Psychology, 5*, 497–510.

Thompson, C.P., Skowronski, J.J. & Lee, D.J. (1988). Telescoping in dating naturally occurring events. *Memory and Cognition, 16*, 461–8.

Thompson, V.A. & Paivio, A. (1994). Memory for pictures and sounds: Independence of auditory and visual codes. *Canadian Journal of Experimental Psychology, 48*, 380–98.

Thomson, D.M., Robertson, S.L. & Vogt, R. (1982). Person recognition: The effect of context. *Human Learning, 1*, 137–54.

Thorndike, E.L. (1932). *The fundamentals of learning*. New York: Teacher's College, Columbia University.

Thorndike, E.L. & Woodworth, R.S. (1901). The influence of improvement in one mental function upon the efficiency of other functions. *Psychological Review, 8*, 247–62.

Thorndyke, P.W. (1977). Cognitive structures in comprehension and memory of narrative discourse. *Cognitive Psychology, 9*, 77–110.

Tobin, A.J. (1990). Genetic disorders: Huntington's disease. In A.L. Pearlman & R.C. Collins (Eds), *Neurobiology of disease*. New York: Oxford University Press.

Toppino, T.C. (1991). The spacing effect in young children's free recall: Support for automatic-process explanations. *Memory and Cognition, 19*, 159–67.

Townsend, J.T. (1990). Serial and parallel processing: Sometimes they look like Tweedledum and Tweedledee but they can (and should) be distinguished. *Psychological Science, 1*, 46–54.

Trabasso, T. & Van-den-Broek, P. (1985). Causal thinking and the representation of narrative events. *Journal of Memory and Language, 24*, 612–30.

Trafimow, D. & Wyer, R.S. Jr. (1993). Cognitive representation of mundane social events. *Journal of Personality and Social Psychology, 64*, 365–76.

Tranel, D. & Damasio, A.R. (1993). The covert learning of affective valence does not require structures in hippocampal system or amygdala. *Journal of Cognitive Neuroscience, 5*, 79–88.

Treisman, A. & Schmidt, H. (1982). Illusory conjunctions in the perception of objects. *Cognitive Psychology, 14*, 107–41.

Treisman, M. (1963). Temporal discrimination and the indifference interval: Implications for a model of the 'internal clock'. *Psychological Monographs, 77*.

Treisman, M. (1984). Temporal rhythms and cerebral rhythms. In J. Gibbon, & L. Allen (Eds), *Timing and time perception*. New York: New York Academy of Sciences.

Troost, B.T. (1992). Neuro-opthalmological aspects. In I. Litvan & Y. Agid (Eds), *Progressive supranuclear palsy: Clinical and research approaches*. New York: Oxford University Press.

Tulving, E. (1962). Subjective organization in the free recall of 'unrelated' words. *Psychological Review, 69*, 344–54.

Tulving, E. (1972). Episodic and semantic memory. In E. Tulving and W. Donaldson (Eds), *The organization of memory*, pp. 382–404. New York: Academic Press.

Tulving, E. (1975). Ecphoric processing in recall and recognition. In J. Brown (Ed.), *Recall and recognition*. London: Wiley.

Tulving, E. (1976). Role of semantic memory in the storage and retrieval of episodic information. *Bulletin de Psychologie, 31*, 19–25.

Tulving, E. (1983). *Elements of episodic memory*. Oxford: Oxford University Press.

Tulving, E. (1985). Memory and consciousness. *Canadian Psychology, 26*, 1–12.

Tulving, E. (1989). Memory: Performance, knowledge, and experience. *European Journal of Cognitive Psychology, 1*, 3–26.

Tulving, E. & Arbuckle, T.Y. (1963). Sources of intratrial interference in immediate recall of paired associates. *Journal of Verbal Learning and Verbal Behavior, 1*, 321–34.

Tulving, E. & Flexser, A.J. (1992). On the nature of the Tulving–Wiseman function. *Psychological Review, 99*, 543–6.

Tulving, E., Hayman, C.A.G. & MacDonald, C.A. (1991). Long-lasting perceptual priming and semantic learning in amnesia: A case experiment. *Journal of Experimental Psychology: Learning, Memory and Cognition, 17*, 595–617.

Tulving, E. & Osler, S. (1968). Effectiveness of retrieval cues in memory for words. *Journal of Experimental Psychology, 77*, 593–601.

Tulving, E. & Psotka, J. (1971). Retroactive inhibition in free recall: Inaccessibility of information available in the memory store. *Journal of Experimental Psychology, 87*, 1–8.

Tulving, E., Schacter, D.L. & Stark, H.A. (1982). Priming effects in word-fragment completion are independent of recognition memory. *Journal of Experimental Psychology: Learning, Memory and Cognition, 8,* 336–42.

Tulving, E. & Thomson, D.M. (1973). Encoding specificity and retrieval processes in episodic memory. *Psychological Review, 80,* 353–73.

Tulving, E. & Wiseman, S. (1975). Relation between recognition and recognition failure of recallable words. *Bulletin of the Psychonomic Society, 6,* 79–82.

Turvey, M.T. (1973). On peripheral and central processes in vision: Inferences from an information-processing analysis of masking with patterned stimuli. *Psychological Review, 80,* 1–52.

Turvey, M.T. & Kravetz, S. (1970). Retrieval from iconic memory with shape as the selection criterion. *Perception and Psychophysics, 9,* 89–91.

Tversky, B. & Baratz, D. (1985). Memory for faces: Are caricatures better than photographs? *Memory and Cognition, 13,* 45–9.

Tversky, A. & Kahneman, D. (1973). Availability. A heuristic for judging frequency and probability. *Cognitive Psychology, 5,* 207–32.

Tweedy, J.R. & Vakil, E. (1988). Evaluating evidence for automaticity in frequency of occurrence judgments: A bias for bias? *Journal of Clinical and Experimental Neuropsychology, 10,* 664–74.

Tzeng, O.J.L. (1973). Positive recency effects in delayed free recall. *Journal of Verbal Learning and Verbal Behavior, 12,* 436–9.

Tzeng, O.J.L. (1976). A precedence effect in the processing of verbal information. *American Journal of Psychology, 89,* 577–99.

Tzeng, O.J.L., Lee, A.T. & Wetzel, C.D. (1979). Temporal coding in verbal information processing. *Journal of Experimental Psychology: Human Learning and Memory, 5,* 52–64.

Underwood, B.J. (1957). Interference and forgetting. *Psychological Review, 64,* 49–60.

Underwood, B.J. (1974). The role of association in recognition memory. *Journal of Experimental Psychology, 102,* 917–39.

Underwood, B.J. (1976). Recognition memory for pairs of words as a function of associative context. *Journal of Experimental Psychology: Learning, Memory and Cognition, 2,* 404–12.

Underwood, G. (1975). Attention and the perception of duration during encoding and retrieval. *Perception, 4,* 291–6.

Underwood, G. & Everatt, J (1996). Automatic and controlled information processing: The role of attention in the processing of novelty. In O. Neumann & A.F. Sanders (Eds), *Handbook of Perception and Action, Vol 3: Attention.* London: Academic Press.

U.S. Congress, Office of Technology Assessment (1987). *Losing a million minds: Confronting the tragedy of Alzheimer's disease and other dementias* (OTA-BA–323). Washington, DC: U.S. Government Printing Office.

Valentine, T. (1988). Upside-down faces: A review of the effect of inversion upon face recognition. *British Journal of Psychology, 79,* 471–91.

Valentine, T. (1991). A unified account of the effects of distinctiveness, inversion, and race in face recognition. *Quarterly Journal of Experimental Psychology, 43A,* 161–204.

Valentine, T. (1995). *The cognitive and computational aspects of face recognition.* London: Routledge.

Valentine, T., Bredart, S., Lawson, R. & Ward, G. (1991). What's in a name? Access to information from people's names. *European Journal of Cognitive Psychology, 3,* 147–76.

Van-den-Broek, P. & Lorch, R.F. (1993). Network representations of causal relations in memory for narrative texts: Evidence from primed recognition. Special issue: Inference generation during text comprehension. *Discourse Processes, 16,* 75–98.

Vander Linde, E., Morrongiello, B.A. & Rovee-Collier, C.K. (1985). Determinants of retention in 8-week-old infants. *Developmental Psychology, 21,* 601–13.

van Rossum, J.H. (1990). Schmidt's scheme theory: The empirical base of the variability of practice hypothesis: A critical analysis. Special issue: The learning, memory and perception of perceptual-motor skills. *Human Movement Science, 9,* 387–435.

Venables, P.H. (1984). Arousal: An examination of its status as a concept. In M.G.H. Coles, J.R. Jennings & J.P. Stern (Eds), *Psychophysiological perspectives: Festschrift for Beatrice and John Lacey.* New York: Van Nostrand.

Verfaellie, M., Bauer, R.M. & Bowers, D. (1991). Autonomic and behavioural evidence of implicit memory in amnesia. *Brain and Cognition, 15,* 10–25.

Vogl, R.J. & Thompson, C.P (1995). The specificity and durability of Rajan's memory. In A.F. Healy & L.E. Bourne (Eds), *Learning and memory of knowledge and skills.* Thousand Oaks, CA: Sage.

Vriezen, E.R. & Moscovitch, M. (1990). Memory for temporal order and conditional associative-learning in patients with Parkinson's Disease. *Neuropsychologia, 28,* 1283–93.

Vroon, P.A. (1970). Effects of presented and processed information on duration experience. *Acta Psychologica, 34,* 115–21.

von Wright, J.M. (1968). Selection in immediate visual memory. *Quarterly Journal of Experimental Psychology, 20,* 62–8.

von Wright, J.M. (1970). On selection in immediate visual memory. *Quarterly Journal of Experimental Psychology, 33,* 280–92.

Wagenaar, W.A. (1986). My memory: A study of autobiographical memory over six years. *Cognitive Psychology, 18,* 225–52.

Wagenaar, W.A. (1994). Is memory self-serving? In U. Neisser, & R. Fivush (Eds), *The remembering self: Construction and accuracy in the self-narrative.* Cambridge: Cambridge University Press.

Wagenaar, W.A. & Groeneweg, J. (1990). The memory of concentration camp survivors. *Applied Cognitive Psychology, 4,* 77–87.

Waldfogel, S. (1948). The frequency and affective character of childhood memories. *Psychological Monograph, 62,* no. 291.

Walker-Smith, G.J. (1980). Memorizing facial identity, expression and orientation. *British Journal of Psychology, 71,* 415–24.

Walton, J.N. (1994). *Brain diseases of the nervous system.* Oxford: Oxford University Press.

Warrington, E.K. & McCarthy, R.A. (1988). The fractionation of retrograde amnesia. *Brain and Cognition, 7,* 184–200.

Warrington, E.K. & Shallice, T. (1969). The selective impairment of auditory verbal short-term memory. *Brain, 92,* 885–96.

Warrington, E.K. & Weiskrantz, L. (1970). Amnesia: Consolidation or retrieval? *Nature, 228,* 628–30.

Warrington, E.K. & Weiskrantz, L. (1974). The effect of prior learning on subsequent retention in amnesic patients. *Neuropsychologia, 12,* 419–28.

Warrington, E.K. & Weiskrantz, L. (1978). Further analysis of the prior learning effect in amnesic patients. *Neuropsychologia, 16,* 169–76.

Watkins, M.J. & Gardiner, J.M. (1979). An appreciation of generate-recognize theory of recall. *Journal of Verbal Learning and Verbal Behavior, 18,* 687–704.

Watkins, M.J., Ho, E. & Tulving, E. (1976). Context effects in recognition memory for faces. *Journal of Verbal Learning and Verbal Behavior, 15,* 505–17.

Watts, F.N., McKenna, F.P., Sharrock, R. & Tresize, L. (1986). Colour naming of phobia-related words. *British Journal of Psychology, 77,* 97–108.

Watts, F.N. & Sharrock, R. (1987). Cued recall in depression. *British Journal of Clinical Psychology, 26,* 149–50.

Watts, F.N., Tresize, L. & Sharrock, R. (1986). Processing of phobic stimuli. *British Journal of Clinical Psychology, 25,* 253–9.

Waugh, N.C. & Norman, D.A. (1965). Primary memory. *Psychological Review, 72,* 89–104.

Wechsler, D. (1987) *WAIS-R manual.* New York: The Psychological Corporation.

Weiner, B. (1986). *An attributional theory of motivation and emotion.* New York: Springer Verlag.

Weinert, F.E. (1986). Developmental variations of memory performance and memory-related knowledge across the life span. In A. Sorensen, F.E. Weinert & L.R. Sherrod (Eds), *Human development: Multidisciplinary perspectives,* pp. 535–54. Hillsdale, NJ: Erlbaum.

Weingartner, H., Caine, E.D. & Ebert, M.H. (1979). Imagery, encoding and retrieval of information from memory: Some specific encoding changes in Huntington's disease. *Journal of Abnormal Psychology, 88,* 52–8.

Weingartner, H., Eckardt, M., Grafman, J. et al., (1993). The effects of repetition on memory performance in cognitively impaired patients. *Neuropsychology, 7,* 385–95.

Weingartner, H., Miller, H. & Murphy, D.L. (1977). Mood-state-dependent retrieval of verbal associations. *Journal of Abnormal Psychology, 86,* 276–84.

Weinland, J. (1948). The memory of Salo Finkelstein. *Journal of General Psychology, 39,* 243–57.

Weiskrantz, L. (1982). Comparative aspects of studies of amnesia. *Philosophical Transactions of the Royal Society, London, B, 298,* 97–109.

Weissman, A. & Beck, A.T. (1978). The dysfunctional attitudes scale. Paper presented at the meeting of the Association for the Advancement of Behavior Therapy, Chicago.

Weizmann, F., Cohen, L.B. & Pratt, J. (1971). Novelty, familiarity and the development of infant attention. *Developmental Psychology, 4,* 149–54.

Weldon, M.S. & Roediger, H.L. (1987). Altering retrieval

demands reverses the picture superiority effect. *Memory and Cognition, 15,* 269–80.

Weldon, M.S., Roediger, H.L. & Challis, B.H. (1989). The properties of retrieval cues constrain the picture superiority effect. *Memory and Cognition, 17,* 95–105.

Welford, A.T. (1987). On rates of improvement with practice. *Journal of Motor Behavior, 19,* 401–15.

Wellman, H.M. (1977). Preschoolers' understanding of memory-relevant variables. *Child Development, 48,* 1720–3.

Wellman, H.M. (1983). Metamemory revisited. In M.T.H. Chi (Ed.), *Trends in memory development research,* pp. 31–51. Basel, Switzerland: Karger.

Wellman, H.M. (1989). The early development of memory strategies. In F.E. Weinert and M. Perlmutter (Eds.), *Memory development: Universal changes and individual differences,* pp. 3–29. Hillsdale, NJ: Erlbaum.

Wells, A. & Matthews, G. (1994). *Attention and emotion: A clinical perspective.* London: Lawrence Erlbaum.

Wenger, S.K. (1979). The within-list distributed practice effect: More evidence for the inattention hypothesis. *American Journal of Psychology, 92,* 105–13.

Werner, J.S. & Perlmutter, M. (1979). Development of visual memory in infants. In H.W. Reese and L.P. Lipsitt (Eds), *Advances in child development and behavior, Vol. 1,* pp. 1–56. New York: Academic Press.

Westheimer, G. & McKee, S.P. (1977). Perception of temporal order in adjacent visual stimuli. *Vision Research, 17,* 887–92.

Wetherford, M.J. & Cohen, L.B. (1973). Developmental changes in infant visual preferences for novelty and familiarity. *Child Development, 44,* 416–24.

Wetzler, S.E. & Sweeney, D.B. (1986). Childhood amnesia: An empirical demonstration. In D.C. Rubin (Ed.), *Autobiographical memory,* pp. 191–202. Cambridge: Cambridge University Press.

White, S.H. & Pillemer, D.B. (1979). Childhood amnesia and the development of a socially accessible memory system. In J.F. Kihlstrom and F.J. Evans (Eds), *Functional disorders of memory,* pp. 29–73. Hillsdale, NJ: Erlbaum.

Whitlow, J.W. & Skaar, E. (1979). The role of numerosity in judgments of overall frequency. *Journal of Experimental Psychology: Human Learning and Memory, 5,* 409–21.

Whitten, W.B. & Bjork, R.A. (1977). Learning from tests: Effects of spacing. *Journal of Verbal Learning and Verbal Behavior, 16,* 465–78.

Wickelgren, W.A. (1965). Acoustic similarity and intrusion errors in short-term memory. *Journal of Experimental Psychology, 70,* 102–8.

Wickens, C.D. (1984). *Engineering psychology and human performance.* Columbus, OH: Charles Merrill.

Wickens, D.D. (1970). Encoding categories of words: An empirical approach to meaning. *Psychological Review, 77,* 1–15.

Wickens, D.D. (1972). Characteristics of word encoding. In A.W. Melton and E. Martin (Eds), *Coding processes in human memory,* pp. 191–215. Washington, DC: Winston.

Wickens, D.D., Born, D.G. & Allen, C.K. (1963). Proactive inhibition and item similarity in short-term memory. *Journal of Verbal Learning and Verbal Behavior, 2,* 440–45.

Wilding, J.M. & Valentine, E. (1985). One man's memory for prose, faces and names. *British Journal of Psychology, 76,* 215–19.

Williams, J.M.G. & Broadbent, D.E. (1986). Autobiographical memory in suicide attempters. *Journal of Abnormal Psychology, 95,* 145–9.

Williams, J.M.G., Watts, F.N., MacLeod, C. & Mathews, A. (1988). *Cognitive psychology and emotional disorders.* Chichester: Wiley.

Williams, M.D. & Hollan, J.D. (1981). The process of retrieval from very long-term memory. *Cognitive Science, 5,* 87–119.

Wilson, B.A. (1982). Success and failure in memory training following a cerebral vascular accident. *Cortex, 18,* 581–94.

Winograd, E. & Killinger, W.A. (1983). Relating age at encoding in early childhood to adult recall: Development of flashbulb memories. *Journal of Experimental Psychology: General, 112,* 413–22.

Wiseman, S. & Tulving, E. (1975). A test of confusion theory of encoding specificity. *Journal of Verbal Learning and Verbal Behavior, 14,* 370–81.

Wittgenstein, L. (1953). *Philosophical investigations.* New York: Macmillan.

Wixted, J.T. (1992). Subjective memorability and the mirror effect. *Journal of Experimental Psychology: Learning, Memory and Cognition, 18,* 681–90.

Woodhead, M.M., Baddeley, A.D. & Simmonds, D.C.V. (1979). On training people to recognise faces. *Ergonomics, 22,* 333–43.

Woodley, P.Z. & Ellis, N.R. (1989). Memory for frequency of occurrence: Intelligence level and retrieval cues. *Intelligence, 13,* 53–61.

Wright, M.J., Burns, R.J., Geffen, G.M. & Geffen, L.B. (1990). Covert orientation of visual attention in Parkinson's disease: An impairment in the maintenance of attention. *Neuropsychologia, 28,* 151–9.

Wu, J., Buchsbaum, M.S., Moy, K. & Denlea, N. (1993). Olfactory memory in unmedicated schizophrenics. *Schizophrenia Research, 9,* 41–47.

Wulf, G., Schmidt, R.A. & Deubel, H. (1993). Reduced feedback frequency enhances generalized motor program learning but not parameterization learning. *Journal of Experimental Psychology: Learning, Memory and Cognition, 19,* 1134–50.

Wyer, R.S. & Srull, T.K. (1989). *Memory and cognition in its social context.* Hillsdale, NJ: Erlbaum.

Yarmey, A.D. (1990). Accuracy and confidence of duration estimates following questions containing marked and unmarked modifiers. *Journal of Applied Social Psychology, 20,* 1139–49.

Young, J.L. (1966). Effects of intervals between reinforcements and test trials in paired-associate learning. (Tech. Rep. 101). Institute for mathematical studies in the social sciences, Stanford University.

Yussen, S., Huang, S.T., Mathews, S. & Evans, R. (1988). The robustness and temporal course of the story schema's influence on recall. *Journal of Experimental Psychology: Learning, Memory and Cognition, 14,* 173–9.

Zakay, D. (1993). Time estimation methods – do they influence prospective duration estimates? *Perception, 22,* 91–101.

Zaragoza, M.S. & McCloskey, M. (1989). Misleading postevent information and the memory impairment hypothesis: Comment on Belli and reply to Tversky and Tuchin. *Journal of Experimental Psychology: General, 118,* 92–9.

Zechmeister, E.B. & Gude, C. (1974). Instruction effects in recognition memory. *Bulletin of the Psychonomic Society, 3,* 13–15.

Zimler, J. & Keenan, J.M. (1983). Imagery in the congenitally blind: How visual are visual images? *Journal of Experimental Psychology: Learning, Memory and Cogntion, 9,* 269–82.

Zola-Morgan, S.M. & Squire, L.R. (1993). Neuroanatomy of memory. *Annual Review of Neuroscience, 16,* 547–63.

Index